Real Estate Review's
Guide to Real Estate Licensing Examinations

For Salespersons & Brokers

William B. French
Attorney, Realtor®, and Real Estate Consultant,
South Bend, Indiana

Stephen J. Martin
Director, Real Estate Certification Program,
Indiana University

Thomas E. Battle, III
Coordinator, Statewide Prelicensing Courses for
Salespersons and Brokers, Indiana University

WARREN, GORHAM & LAMONT
BOSTON

FOREWORD

The successful real estate professional—real estate broker or salesperson—is the supreme generalist. From the time that a seller first submits a property listing or a prospective buyer becomes a client, until title passes and the commission is paid, the professional may be called upon to demonstrate know-how or exercise talents in such diverse areas as real estate appraisal and valuation; the law of contracts; real estate finance; loan negotiations; mathematics; the law of title; and the landlord-tenant relationship.

In addition, in the professional's own relationship with the client (as well as with the other party to the transaction), he or she must be fully aware of obligations as an agent both under the general law of agency and under the real estate regulations of the particular state. Finally, in bringing to fruition a transaction that often is one of the most important in the lives of buyer and seller, the professional must develop a high level of negotiating skills as well as a sound understanding of human psychology.

The purpose of this book is to provide the student and the beginning salesperson with substantially all that he or she needs to know about the law and practice of real estate. It is more, however, than merely a compendium of useful information. It has been carefully organized to assist the reader in achieving one specific goal: successfully passing the uniform real estate licensing examination now required in more than half the United States. To that end, a number of special features are included with each chapter—a glossary of key terms; illustrations and examples; and review questions similar to those that have appeared on the uniform examination in the past. And, of course, the book will be useful for those taking a licensing examination in those states that do not utilize the uniform examination, since the basic subject matter covered is substantially the same. Finally, and far from least, it is admirably fitted to serve as a handy desk manual for those now in the real estate business, enabling them to instantly put their finger on a point of law, a mathematical procedure, or a financial technique.

Real Estate Review is proud to sponsor this book, written by three outstanding authors who among them can claim the titles of attorney, Realtor®, educator, consultant, and specialist in testing procedures. Heretofore, publications sponsored by the *Real Estate Review* have been on a more advanced level and for the experienced practitioner. Now, on the premise that the beginner in real estate, even more than the experienced practitioner, deserves a publication of the highest quality, we have sought one out. We believe the book meets the highest standards of accuracy, completeness, organization, and clarity.

Alvin L. Arnold, Editor
Real Estate Review

PREFACE

This book is intended for prospective salespersons and brokers who are preparing for real estate examinations—in particular for the Real Estate Licensing Examination (RELE) administered by the Educational Testing Service (ETS) of Princeton, New Jersey. It can be used as a classroom textbook as well as by individuals for independent study.

Based on material developed for the Real Estate Certification Program at Indiana University where it has been tested and refined over a period of several years, the book presents the fundamental aspects of real estate with detailed coverage of the legal, economic, mathematical, and ethical considerations of the subject in a manner that is easily understood.

The combined text and workbook format has proved to be extremely helpful in preparing students for the licensing examinations. Each chapter contains a series of review questions designed to test the student's knowledge of basic principles. In addition, a special section of the book contains examinations similar in content and format to those used by RELE. The appendix includes answers to all examinations appearing in the text as well as a complete working of all mathematical problems.

The book covers all the topics required by students studying for the licensing examinations. Information about a particular state's licensing laws may be obtained by contacting the appropriate state agency for its bulletin.

It would have been impossible to have completed the task of writing and organizing this book had it not been for the most capable assistance of Suzann M. Owen whose skills in editing are sincerely appreciated. Grateful thanks also go to Jody Cross, our most patient typist.

William B. French
Stephen J. Martin
Thomas E. Battle, III

Table of Contents

Part I
Preparing To Use the Text

Chapter 1
Use of the Guide

THIS book covers all major areas of the field of real estate in a format designed to be used in preparation for the uniform Real Estate License Examination (RELE).

The chapters covering real estate topics contain a vocabulary list, text discussion, suggested readings, and review questions. You should pay particular attention to the vocabulary sections. The authors have selected for inclusion those words that play a key role in understanding real estate. Real estate has its own vocabulary, as does any other discipline, and success or failure in the business and on the licensing examination depends on your ability to apply the proper terms to the situation presented. The vocabulary lists provide an excellent source of review material. A complete listing of words and their definitions appears in the glossary (Appendix G).

The text discussion in each chapter provides an in-depth explanation of the topics presented. These sections are the key to understanding each major area, and contain the source material for preparation for the uniform licensing examination.

The review questions for the chapters covering real estate topics are designed to give you feedback as to your understanding of the materials just studied. They should help each student identify his or her own strengths and weaknesses. The answers are in Appendix B.

This guide includes a chapter (Chapter 15) on real estate mathematics which contains problems and instructions as to how the math functions should be performed. It also presents, in Appendix E, a series of listing, offer, and settlement practice problems for use in checking individual mathematical skills called for in the real estate business. The

solutions to the problems appear in Appendices C and F for purposes of checking your work.

The listing, offer, and settlement practice problems should be of major concern to all students, since such problems constitute a significant portion of the uniform examination for both salespersons and brokers. There are six problems depicting different listing, offer, and settlement situations. The first problem has been worked out, in Chapter 16, as a guide for you to follow in completing the other five. Each problem should be done in its entirety. This is good preparation for both brokers and salespersons.

The two practice examinations in Chapters 18 and 19 follow the format of the uniform RELE the student will be taking. The questions on the two practice examinations are of similar difficulty and are structured like those that appear on the RELE, though they are not actual questions from examinations administered by the Educational Testing Service (ETS). The answers, forms, and math solutions to the test questions are in Appendix D. These tests should not be taken until you have completed study of all the topics presented in the text. They are the final preparation for the uniform RELE.

You will note that no sample State Test has been provided. Since each licensing agency is responsible for developing its own State Test, it is not possible to create a uniform sample. However, the subject areas normally covered on the state examinations are outlined in detail in Chapter 4. Also, the authors have provided, in the same chapter, a list of addresses of licensing agencies so that you can contact them for specific information about a State Test. This will also serve as a reference source for the future.

Chapter 2
The Real Estate Licensing Examinations

To establish a program to provide examinations for salespersons and brokers that are professionally prepared and of a consistent high quality, four jurisdictions—the District of Columbia, Maryland, North Carolina, and Virginia—sponsored development of the Real Estate Licensing Examinations (RELE) program in 1970. The representatives of the jurisdictions worked with examination specialists from the Educational Testing Service (ETS) in Princeton, N.J. to construct examinations that could be used in all four jurisdictions for real estate licensing.

As a result of the similarity of many facets of real estate nationally, the *Uniform Test* of the RELE evolved. This test measures the general knowledge and skills required uniformly among the various jurisdictions that participate in the examination program. There are two different versions of the Uniform Test: one for salesperson license candidates and one for broker license candidates. At present these examinations are used by over half of the licensing jurisdictions in the United States:

Alaska	Nebraska
Arkansas	Nevada
Delaware	New Hampshire
District of Columbia	New Jersey
Hawaii	North Carolina
Indiana	North Dakota
Iowa	Oregon
Kansas	Pennsylvania
Kentucky	South Dakota
Louisiana	Tennessee
Maryland	Vermont
Massachusetts	Virgin Islands
Minnesota	Virginia
Missouri	Wisconsin
Montana	Wyoming

Since the first examinations were given in January 1971, more than 750,000 people have taken the Real Estate Licensing Examinations (RELE) nationally.

Those who desire licenses as brokers or salespersons must also be examined on the laws, rules, regulations, and practices unique to their own jurisdictions. This portion of the RELE is known as the *State Test*. It differs in content from jurisdiction to jurisdiction, according to practice and procedure.

The State Test of the RELE is prepared by representatives of the participating jurisdictions under the guidance and with the assistance of the staff of ETS and other educators in the field of real estate. Both the Uniform Test and the State Test use objective, multiple-choice questions, and they are constantly revised to keep them current with changes in real estate law and practice. Several forms of the Uniform Test are now in use throughout the country, but all are of the same level of difficulty.

EXAMINATION APPLICATION

The jurisdiction's licensing agency determines an individual's eligibility for licensing. You should contact your particular licensing agency (see Chapter 4 for a list) for the specific requirements, since they vary from jurisdiction to jurisdiction. In some instances prelicensing education is required for an extended period prior to examination. This information may be obtained through your agency, real estate education program, or jurisdiction's licensing agency or commission.

LOCATIONS OF EXAMINATIONS

Some jurisdictions have several examination locations. If this is the case in your jurisdiction, you will be allowed to state your preference. If you are not placed at the location of your choice, then you will be placed at the location nearest to the one you prefer.

EXAMINATION DATES

Not all jurisdictions give the examinations on the same date. You should check with your jurisdiction's licensing agency for the dates on which it offers the examination. Most states schedule examinations three to four times a year. In such states as Maryland, Massachusetts, Missouri, New Jersey, and Virginia, the examination is given on the fourth Saturday of each month except December, when no examinations are given.

ADMISSION TO THE EXAMINATION

If you have registered to take the RELE administered by ETS, you should receive an admission ticket no later than 1 week prior to the examination. (The admission ticket for salesperson applicants may be sent to their sponsoring broker if that is required in a particular jurisdiction.) If you are taking some other form of test being administered by the state licensing agency itself or an agency other than ETS, you should check with your licensing agency as to the admission requirements.

Your ETS admission ticket will list the name of the examination (salesperson or broker) for which you have registered, the name and address of the assigned test center, and the time at which you should appear for your examination.

Also on the ticket is an examination number which is very important. It is the number you will use on the examination answer sheet and in any correspondence you might have with the licensing agency or ETS regarding the examination. If you should fail the examination and wish to retake it, you will be assigned another number.

You must have your admission ticket with you at the test center. If you do not receive an admission ticket 1 week prior to the examination, or if you lose your ticket, you should contact your licensing agency or ETS, which will handle the problem according to predetermined policy.

EXAMINATION CENTER ADMISSION

Report to the examination center to which you have been assigned as indicated on the admission ticket. You must have the proper admission ticket or authorization, or your name must appear on the attendance roster for the center before you will be admitted to the examination.

In addition to the admission ticket, you should bring at least three No. 2 pencils and an eraser. You also *must* have at least two pieces of identification such as a driver's license and an employment or student identification card.

INSTRUCTIONS

Instructions will be read by an examination supervisor from the manual prepared by ETS. These instructions are to guide you and ensure that the proper information is placed on the answer sheet. This also allows uniform testing conditions to prevail from center to center.

CALCULATORS AND SLIDE RULES

Not all jurisdictions permit the use of a slide rule or calculator. If they are permitted in your jurisdic-

tion, then it will be so indicated on your admission ticket. If there is doubt about this prior to receiving the admission ticket, contact your licensing agency for clarification.

The rules concerning the use and types of instruments permitted are:

1. The candidate may use only hand-held, silent, battery-operated instruments that *do not* have a paper tape printing capacity. If the instrument does not meet the above requirements, this will be grounds for immediate dismissal from the examination. If the testing supervisor determines prior to admission to the examination that the instrument does not meet the described standards, the candidate will be permitted to take the examination upon surrender of the instrument to the supervisor for the duration of the examination.
2. If the candidate's instrument should not function during the examination, this will not be grounds for challenging examination results or demanding extended time for completion of the examination.

Note: It is the opinion of ETS that calculators or slide rules are not necessary to complete the calculations needed for the examination questions. Any figuring can be done by pencil and paper in the time allotted.

EXAMINATION CENTER REGULATIONS

Each examination center adheres to the same set of examination guidelines and rules so as to ensure equality in the examination process. The basic rules are as follows:

1. No books, dictionaries, or papers of any kind (including scratch paper) will be permitted in the examination room. Any candidate found with any of these items will not be allowed to continue the examination.
2. The candidate will *not* be permitted to work beyond the prescribed time under any circumstances.
3. Any scratch work must be done in the margins of the examination booklet and not on the answer sheet. The answer sheet should contain only the candidate's identifying information and his or her responses to the questions.
4. If a candidate desires to leave the room for any purpose, permission must be obtained from the test supervisor.
5. Any candidate engaging in any form of miscon-

duct will be reported to the licensing agency. Disciplinary action will be the responsibility of the licensing agency.

TAKING THE EXAMINATION

The examinations for both salespersons and brokers consist entirely of multiple-choice questions. Upon receipt of the examination booklet the candidate should read the directions carefully so as not to miss anything which might be of importance to the examination and would cause loss of credit.

The candidate should use the allotted time carefully and economically by not wasting time in any one area. Take the questions in order and return to difficult ones later.

As indicated earlier, the answers to the questions are to be recorded on a separate answer sheet. No credit is given for answers recorded in the question booklet. The answer sheets are numbered and lettered to correspond to the questions and possible responses in the booklet. The candidate will choose the one best response from the four listed and darken the appropriate circle on the answer sheet. If the candidate marks more than one response to a single question, the question will be scored as incorrect. If an answer is changed, be sure the erasure is complete.

The score is based upon the percentage of questions the candidate answers correctly. Do not be overly concerned if there are a few questions you cannot answer. If you feel reasonably certain, do not be afraid to guess.

A more detailed discussion of examination-taking procedures is presented in Chapter 17.

EXAMINATION SCORES AND SCORE REPORTS

Each examination consists of two tests: the Uniform Test and the State Test. The examinee must pass both tests to pass the entire examination. The individual licensing agencies will determine the passing or failing percentage for each test.

If the candidate passes the examination, a report will be sent indicating PASS only. The actual numerical score will not be included, to avoid the possibility of misuse. The report may also contain certain important information from the licensing agency.

If the candidate fails the examination, separate scores will be reported for the individual parts of the examination. The scores reported are percentages of correct answers in a particular subject area. This will enable the candidate to see which areas gave him or her difficulty.

The candidate's scores are reported to the licensing agency, and an individual report is sent to the candidate. In some jurisdictions, the sponsoring broker may receive the salesperson's score report.

REVIEWING THE EXAMINATION

No provisions are made for either passing or failing candidates to review the examination results with the licensing agency or with the staff of ETS. This is necessary in order to maintain test security.

SALESPERSON'S EXAMINATION

The salesperson's examination contains 130 questions, and the examinee is permitted up to 4½ hours to complete it. The examination is divided into two separate examinations, the Uniform Test and the State Test.

The Uniform Test

The Uniform Test contains 100 multiple-choice questions in the subject areas described below. Approximately 27 questions deal with arithmetic functions. These questions are found throughout the examination and not in a separate arithmetic section.

1. *Real estate contracts (26 questions).* This section examines the general definition of essential elements of a contract and specific contracts utilized in real estate transactions, including leases, listing agreements, offer to purchase agreements, and options. Candidates are expected to interpret a completed listing contract and a completed sales contract (offer to purchase agreement). They are expected to answer questions dealing with the listing and sales contracts solely on the basis of the completed sample instruments. These questions appear at the beginning of the examination. Samples of these forms appear in Chapter 16.

2. *Financing (20 questions).* The questions in this section deal with (a) financing instruments (10 questions) and (b) means of financing (10 questions). The topics covered include sources of financing, the Federal Housing Authority (FHA), the Veterans' Administration (VA), truth in lending, basic definitions of major types of financing instruments, mortgages and their breakdown (including types, loan fees, placement procedures, terms for a loan, etc.), secondary financing, default, and foreclosure.

3. *Real estate ownership (19 questions).* (a) Deeds (6 questions), including definitions, necessary elements, recording, and acknowledgment. (b) Interests in real property (8 questions), including estates in land, ownership, public power over private property, special interests in land. (c) Condominiums (2 questions), including general information about condominiums, rights, duties, and responsibilities of ownership. (d) Federal Fair Housing Act (3 questions), including general knowledge pertaining to the act, policies, and procedures.

4. *Real estate brokerage (20 questions).* (a) Law of agency (10 questions), including types, rights, and functions of the principal agent. (b) Property management (2 questions), including general scope of the function of the property manager. (c) Settlement Procedures (8 questions), including validity of title, settlement charges, proration, credit.

5. *Real estate valuation (15 questions).* (a) Appraisal (6 questions), including general knowledge concerning the definition and approaches to value, and the process and terminology of appraisal. (b) Planning and zoning (3 questions), including public control of land use, public planning and zoning, private subdivision, and land development. (c) Property description (3 questions), including types of property descriptions, reading a plat map, and other terms and concepts. (d) Taxes and assessments (3 questions), including real property taxation, special assessments, liens, etc.

The State Test

This test contains 30 questions and requires a knowledge of the specific rules, regulations, and practices unique to each jurisdiction. The examinee should contact the licensing agency to obtain a listing of specific areas covered in this section.

BROKER'S EXAMINATION

This test contains 130 questions, and the examinee is permitted up to 4½ hours to complete it. This examination is divided into two separate tests, the Uniform Test and the State Test.

The Uniform Test

The Uniform Test contains 100 questions. The areas examined are:

1. *Real estate instruments (30 questions).* In this section the examinee must interpret a listing contract and an offer to purchase, and complete a settlement worksheet using the other two documents. Samples of this document are found in Chapter 16.

2. *Basic elements of real estate values, deeds, and contracts (20 questions).* In this section the examinee is questioned about the approaches to value, the appraisal process, the valuation of partial interests, and knowledge and application of appraisal terminology. Also tested are aspects of deeds and contracts, including the elements of a deed, types of deeds, passing title, essentials of a contract, and types and uses of contracts.

3. *Leases, property management, and real estate financing (20 questions).* In this section the examinee is questioned concerning tenancies, leases, landlord-tenant relations, and property management. The financing questions deal with types of mortgages (deeds of trust), the FHA, VA loans, and other governmental agencies and acts concerned with real estate financing.

4. *Legal and governmental aspects of real estate (10 questions).* The examinee is questioned concerning the Federal Fair Housing Act, the Truth in Lending Act including Regulation Z, interests in real property, the law of agency, the statute of frauds, planning, zoning, assessment, and taxation.

5. *Arithmetic functions (20 questions).* In this section the examinee is questioned about arithmetic problems related to real estate.

The State Test

The broker examinee should follow the same information presented to the salesperson examinee.

SUGGESTED READINGS

Real Estate Licensing Examinations: Bulletin of Information for Applicants. Educational Testing Service, most recent edition.

Part II

Understanding Real Estate Concepts

Chapter 3
The Real Estate Business

VOCABULARY

You will find it important to have a complete working knowledge of the following words and concepts found in the text or the glossary.

allodial	REALTOR®	GRI
appraising	rectangular survey	IREF
brokerage	speculative (spec) house	IREM
building and construction	topography	MAI
capital	Abbreviations:	NAR
development	AFLM	NAHB
feudal	AMO	NARELLO
financing	ARM	RESSI
land grant	ASA	RM
personal property	ASREC	RNMI
private sector	CCIM	SIR
public sector	CPM	SRA
real estate	CRB	SREA
real estate operators	CRE	SRPA
real property	FLI	WCR

REAL estate could easily be considered the most important factor in today's world. No everyday activity goes unaffected by real estate. It allows the production of food and provides the natural resources for domestic and commercial shelters. The study of real estate therefore involves all the aspects of land and structures which might be built on it.

The marketing of land and its improvement must be handled in a responsible manner, because land cannot be replenished. Also, much of it cannot be considered fit for human habitation because of its location, topography, or quality. Although some specialists have emerged, the real estate professional must have a broad understanding of all aspects of the real estate business beyond brokerage—land development, construction, sale of property, property management, and finance—if he or she is to act responsibly in dealing with this precious resource.

REAL ESTATE RESOURCES

Individuals interested in the real estate business must start by learning about the basic resources of the business itself. Obviously, the most important resource is raw land. The primary utilization of land has always been for the cultivation of crops or the pasturage of livestock. Because it is so important in producing food, great care must be exercised when introducing a new use, such as the development of residential, commercial, or industrial buildings, or recreational facilities.

Second only to its use for food production is the use of land for shelter, more commonly called housing. Housing can take all forms: from luxury single-family homes to the most modest low-income housing. Other types of improvements involve such commercial enterprises as retail stores, shopping centers, industrial concerns, warehouses, and office buildings. Our everyday lives also involve the use of real estate for schools, churches, hospitals, and recreational facilities.

The basic definition of real estate is simple but must be mastered by all who enter the business:

Real estate is defined as land and all things permanently attached to it as improvements.

The term *real property* is often used interchangeably with *real estate,* although it has a slightly expanded meaning to include the legal rights to land and its improvements. This important difference is discussed at length in Chapter 6.

REAL ESTATE RESOURCES
AND THEIR CHARACTERISTICS

Characteristics of Land

Each plot of land is unique; that is, it has its own special physical characteristics: (1) Its location is fixed; (2) no two plots are identical; (3) it is indestructible.

These three points must be considered for all plots of land. In addition, land also has other characteristics which are primarily economic in nature: (1) Usable land is relatively scarce; (2) all usable land can be improved or have its value increased when structures are built on it; (3) its location to a great extent determines its value.

Characteristics of Improvements

Over one-half of the national wealth is represented by real estate resources—that is, land and improvements. The real estate business consists primarily of individuals utilizing such resources to meet the demands of the marketplace. Perhaps the greatest demand for real estate resources lies in housing. Residential property goes beyond the single-family residence to include duplexes, triplexes, quadriplexes, apartment buildings, cooperatives, condominiums, and mobile homes. The existing supply of residential structures is great, but the demand for more housing keeps the residential construction business expanding at a rapid pace. It is the residential market where most individuals enter the real estate industry today. But this industry was not always so active. It might be helpful for you to have a basic historical perspective of what has made the industry what it is today.

ORIGINS OF REAL ESTATE
AS WE KNOW IT TODAY

Ever since human beings developed a desire to own and control the use of real estate, the laws which protect rights of ownership and restrictions on power to exercise these rights have been in the process of evolution.

The history of real estate in this country developed through a combination of two different systems, *feudal* and *allodial*. The feudal system recognizes the sovereign power of the king or the designated feudal lord as the legal owner of the property, while the allodial system recognizes that property interests are vested in the person possessing the title to the land. Obviously, the allodial system had the greater effect on our nation's development of real estate resources.

Our nation was the first to be built on the precept of private ownership of land and the right to transfer such land. Because of this, a method was required by which the transfer could be accomplished with as few problems as possible. Those who saw the need to facilitate transfers from those owning land to those who wanted to own land created colonization companies, became land agents, speculators, or auctioneers, and proceeded to form the beginning of the American real estate business.

In recognition of the increasing trade in land, the federal government passed the *Ordinance of 1785* which contained as its primary contributions to our land system:

1. The rectangular survey of land
2. Allowance for the transfer of public land to private ownership
3. Provisions for private ownership of land
4. Establishment of the process of transfer of property by deed or government patent.

While the federal government tried to have a major impact on creating a new real estate system, it could not ignore the influence other nations had on our nation's early settlers, including the method by which they took title to property. Robert Kevin Brown, in *Essentials of Real Estate,* states:

For the purpose of establishing the source of title to a parcel of land anywhere in the United States, the country as a whole may be divided into two categories:

1. Titles to land in Maine, Vermont, New Hampshire, Massachusetts, Rhode Island, Connecticut, New York, New Jersey, Pennsylvania, Delaware, Maryland, Virginia, North Carolina, South Carolina, and Georgia are found in the following sources: (a) grants made to individuals and corporations by the local proprietary owners who had ownership by virtue of charters or patents issued by the English and Dutch governments; (b) grants by the state that succeeded to that ownership; or (c) grants by the respective states of any land not so granted or conveyed and which the states acquired as successors to these governments at the close of the American Revolution.

2. Titles to land in all other states are found in the grants and patents made to individuals, corpora-

tions, states, and municipalities by the federal government, which obtained ownership of the land by virtue of concession, purchase, or discovery; or by grants and patents from any state in the United States now the owner of any ungranted or unpatented land.

From such beginnings, the real estate business experienced hampered growth for many years because of the limited number of transactions and their simplicity. Eventually the number of transactions taking place grew, and they became increasingly more complicated; such factors led to the growth of today's real estate market.

THE MODERN REAL ESTATE MARKET

The real estate market is influenced by many factors, but *supply* and *demand* are responsible for its existence. This market is somewhat different from the markets for other goods. Since real estate is immovable, its market must be a local one. If houses are selling well in California, the demand may exceed the supply, and yet a small midwestern town may have an oversupply of housing. However, housing cannot be moved across the country to an area where a greater demand exists.

It must also be noted that building new structures to meet demand takes time; thus supply cannot respond quickly to increased demand for real estate. Furthermore, large sums of money are needed; such funds invested in real estate are called *capital*. The availability or lack of such capital also limits the market for real estate by controlling the effective demand.

The sophistication of the modern real estate market causes a number of specialists to become involved in the marketplace. Perhaps one of the most difficult choices the newcomer to real estate must make involves deciding which area of the business is the most interesting.

Human Resources

Because of the high cost of purchasing real estate and the complexity involved in transferring ownership from one party to another, the most commonly found expert in real estate is the broker or salesperson who markets residential or commercial real estate. The real estate *broker* or *salesperson* is the individual who brings the parties together and negotiates the transaction, whether it be buying, selling, renting, or exchanging real estate. This is done for a fee known as a *commission*. The brokerage relationship is governed by the law of agency and involves two parties, the *agent* (broker) and the *principal* (buyer or owner).

In most states the real estate business operates with a two-tier system of licensing. The broker is the individual responsible for the transaction which takes place. On the second tier is the salesperson who must be affiliated with a particular broker who holds his or her license. Also found on this tier are brokers who are not principals in real estate firms but who perform the same sales role as salespersons. Such a broker is usually called a broker associate. These topics will be discussed at length in later chapters, and the concept of agency will also be discussed in detail.

Many areas of expertise exist within the framework of the real estate business. The following material should aid you in understanding the different areas of opportunity within this business.

1. *Brokerage (a service function)*
   a. Function: The primary function of brokers and salespersons is the same as that of any agent, namely, bringing the buyer and the seller together. The most common agency function is listing a seller's residence for sale, but this function need not be limited to residential property since commercial and industrial brokers also provide this service.
   b. Compensation: Compensation is in the form of a commission based on the *gross selling price* of the property.
   c. Opportunities: Since compensation is in direct proportion to results, it can be virtually unlimited. Commission rates vary greatly from community to community, as does division of the commission earned per sale between the broker and salesperson.

2. *Property management (a service function)*
   a. Function: Again, through an agency relationship, the property manager attempts to utilize the owner's real estate resources in such a way as to obtain the principal's desired objectives. The manager handles the day-to-day management of the real property, arranges for repairs, pays bills, supervises custodial help, rents vacancies, renders a periodic accounting to the owner, plans space, and conserves the property and surroundings.
   b. Compensation: The manager is compensated in two ways: a fee for management services, and a fee for leasing or renting. For example, a manager might earn a set percentage on each new lease signed, as well as a fee for management services.

c. Opportunities: Opportunities in this field are expanding as a result of the increase in absentee ownership and the need for specialists in operating complex properties.

3. *Financing (a service function)*
   a. Function: This service function brings together the lender and the potential user of money. The individual involved in this area is concerned with the policies of the lender as they apply to the applicant in determining his or her qualifications for the loan. Considerations involve the borrower's credit worthiness, use of the property as security for the loan, and economic trends affecting the property.
   b. Compensation: Usually this is a salaried position, with the individual working for a lending institution such as a bank, savings and loan association, or insurance company. A *mortgage broker,* however, may receive a fee for placing a loan if he or she acts in an agency capacity between the lender and borrower. The mortgage broker may also receive a fee for servicing the loan. Most mortgage brokers are independent and place loans with financial institutions as the representative of one of the parties.
   c. Opportunities: With financial arrangements becoming more and more complex, opportunities for skilled specialists are growing. In many respects, financing today is the determining factor in planning a new development, marketing existing property, or determining the future use of real property.

4. *Appraising (a service function)*
   a. Function: This is generally regarded as the most professional area in the real estate field. An appraiser is employed by a client to render an opinion of value. In this way the appraiser aids owners and users of real estate in making business decisions.
   b. Compensation: The appraiser is paid on the basis of time, knowledge, and skill and usually receives a predetermined fee agreed upon by the appraiser and the client. In no event is the fee based on a percentage of the appraised value.
   c. Opportunities: Most appraisers are independent fee appraisers and are limited only by their development of a professional standing in the community. Other appraisers are staff appraisers employed by financial institutions,

insurance companies, and industry, and work on a salary basis.

5. *Development (a productive function)*
   a. Function: This productive function adds new units to the community. Whether the developer is building an industrial park or creating a subdivision or an apartment complex, he or she is helping to mold the future character of the community.
   b. Compensation: The developer can be a firm or an individual entrepreneur who takes raw land, adds services such as streets and utilities, and, in effect, creates a development. The developer's ability to market the completed package at a profit over and above acquisition and developing costs determines the amount of compensation earned.
   c. Opportunities: In a dynamic economy where the need for housing, shopping, etc., is accelerated by an expanding population, the opportunities are good, based primarily upon the developer's resourcefulness and ability to finance within the current market.

6. *Building and construction (a productive function)*
   a. Function: Again this productive function creates new units and rehabilitates old structures, adding to the character of the community.
   b. Compensation: Profit may be on a fixed-fee basis or a percentage of a contract for a custom-built house, or may be the difference between the builder's cost and selling price on a *speculative* or *spec* house.
   c. Opportunities: Opportunities are good for the builder who can plan and organize the operation within the framework of the particular market in which he or she is operating, depending of course on ability to finance the venture.

7. *Real estate operators (service and productive functions)*
   a. Function: The function of real estate operators is to act for themselves, in contrast to acting as agents for others. They buy, sell, rent, and renovate their own real estate holdings.
   b. Compensation: Their remuneration is based on their ability to develop a profit through the operation of their own business.
   c. Opportunities: Fortunes have been built in real estate through the operation of a busi-

ness in which an individual's own energy and initiative can create a very great profit.

8. *Special services (serve in an advisory capacity to the industry)*

   a. Other experts involved in the *private sector* of the real estate business include:

      (1) Consultants—Trained persons who can advise individuals, industry, business, and governmental units on real estate matters.

      (2) Land use planners—Specialists involved in planning for the use of real estate resources, such as metropolitan or city planners.

      (3) Engineers—Specialists in the field of engineering who concentrate in an area of real estate, e.g., engineers who design structural features of buildings and civil engineers responsible for utility design and layout of subdivisions and other major projects.

      (4) Lawyers—Just as there are legal specialists in criminal or corporate law, some lawyers specialize in real estate law.

      (5) Abstract and title companies—Companies involved in bringing abstracts up to date and issuing title insurance. The title insurance field is becoming increasingly more important.

      (6) Architects—Individuals trained in the design and plan of new structures; they may also provide inspection and supervision for new buildings and serve as consultants on special projects.

      (7) Tax and accounting experts—Individuals knowledgeable about the impact and growing importance of taxes on real property.

   b. The *public* (governmental) *sector* also has experts involved in real estate:

      (1) Federal government—The federal government is directly involved in the real estate business through such agencies as the VA, Department of Housing and Urban Development (HUD), and the General Services Administration (GSA).

      (2) State government—The state's responsibility for the health, safety, and welfare of its citizens is important to the maintenance of stable values of real property. The state also participates in the planning of real estate resources and governs the real estate industry through each state's real estate commission.

      (3) Local government—Local government is involved in the use of real estate resources through the administration of zoning ordinances, building codes, metropolitan planning, and ownership of community real estate resources such as streets, parks, playgrounds, and municipal buildings.

Real Estate as a Profession

The general public views real estate practitioners as businesspeople rather than professionals, because they do not meet the established criteria for professionals. Even though a real estate practitioner does not have the same standing as a doctor or lawyer he or she must still conduct the client's business in a responsible, professional manner. Obviously each broker competes with other brokers in the community for new properties to list and sell, but at the same time the brokers work together to establish and maintain ethical standards for dealings with clients, fellow brokers, and the general public. Therefore, it is important for brokers to conduct themselves in the most *professional* manner possible.

High standards of ethical conduct are more important in the real estate business than in some other businesses where clients are familiar with the services performed. A typical real estate transaction combines a number of services which are unfamiliar to the general public. The client relies on the broker to guide him or her through the complicated maze involved in buying or selling a home. Buying a home is usually the largest single purchase an individual ever makes. It is most important therefore that the client be able to have the utmost confidence in the individual performing this critical service.

Real Estate Organizations

The real estate industry has organized several associations which operate on national, state, and local levels to promote the high standards of ethical conduct desired by those in the industry, as well as to protect the interests of the public.

By far the largest of the real estate trade associations is the *National Association of REALTORS®* *(NAR)*. NAR functions at local, state, and national levels. To be eligible to use the designation *REALTOR®*, a broker must be a member of NAR. This is accomplished by joining a local board which in turn is affiliated with a state association and the national association. Only members of NAR can use the REALTOR® designation; it is not a term to be used by just anyone in the real estate business. According to publications of NAR:

> A *REALTOR®* is defined as a professional in real estate who subscribes to a strict code of ethics as a member of the local and state boards and of NAR.

Two important aspects of NAR are its code of ethics and its special institutes which promote professionalism in real estate activities through educational programs and the publication of information regarding their areas of specialization.

A code of ethics was first adopted by the *National Association of Real Estate Boards* (NAREB) in 1913 only 5 years after it was organized. All members of NAR, the successor to NAREB, subscribe to the code which appears on pages 18-21.

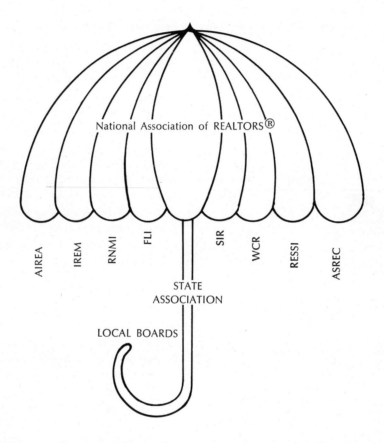

Affiliates of NAR play an important role in the development of REALTOR® members. Such affiliates are:

American Institute of Real Estate Appraisers (AIREA)

Purpose: Conducts educational programs, publishes materials, and promotes research on real estate appraisal.

Designations conferred: MAI (Member, Appraisal Institute), RM (Residential Member).

Requirements: MAI requires a combination of experience and education, as well as written and oral examinations on course work and performance on demonstration appraisals. RM requirements follow along the same line but are less strenuous.

American Society of Real Estate Counselors (ASREC)

Purpose: Conducts educational programs for counselors and advisors on real estate problems.

Designation conferred: CRE (Counselor of Real Estate).

Requirements: Strict requirements as to experience, education, and professionalism. A minimum of 10 years experience prior to application is required.

Farm and Land Institute (FLI)

Purpose: To bring together specialists in the sale, development, planning, management, and syndication of land and to establish professional standards through educational programs for members.

Designation conferred: AFLM (Accredited Farm and Land Member). This designation was formerly known as Accredited Farm and Land Broker but was changed in 1975.

Requirements: AFLM requires a set number of points to be earned according to a scale established by the institute based on experience, education, and completion of written and oral examinations.

International Real Estate Federation (IREF), American Chapter

Purpose: To promote understanding of real estate among those involved in the real estate business throughout the world.

Designation conferred: None.

Requirements: Invitation to join based on membership in a local board of REALTORS® and a demonstrated interest in real estate on an international level.

Institute of Real Estate Management (IREM)

Purpose: To professionalize members involved in all elements of property management through standards of practice, ethical considerations, and educational programs.

Designations conferred: CPM (Certified Property Manager), AMO (Accredited Management Organization), ARM (Accredited Resident Manager).

Requirements: All designations are awarded by the institute according to a point system based on experience, education, and examinations.

Realtors National Marketing Institute (RNMI)

Purpose: To provide educational programs for REALTORS® in the area of commercial and investment properties, residential sales, and real estate office administration.

Designations conferred: CRB (Certified Residential Broker), CCIM (Certified Commercial and Investment Member).

Requirements: Designation awards based on requirements of experience, education, and completion of a GRI program.

Society of Industrial Realtors (SIR)

Purpose: To provide educational opportunities for REALTORS® working with industrial property transactions.

Designation conferred: SIR (Society of Industrial Realtors).

Requirements: Ethical, educational, and experience requirements must be met prior to receiving the designation.

Real Estate Securities and Syndication Institute (RESSI)

Purpose: To provide educational opportunities in the field of marketing securities and syndication of real estate.

Designation conferred: None.

Requirements: Membership open to REALTORS® with an interest in the area of syndication or real estate securities.

Women's Council of Realtors

Purpose: To provide educational programs, training, and publications for women REALTORS® whose primary interest is in residential brokerage.

Designation conferred: None.

Requirements: An interest in furthering the role of women in real estate brokerage.

There is one other important designation which is awarded by state associations of REALTORS® throughout the nation. The GRI (Graduate Realtors Institute) is a program designed to help the REALTOR® to gain more insight and expertise in the real estate business. It involves a lengthy series of courses and examinations prior to award of the designation. While the designation itself is awarded by the state association, the program was established and is monitored by NAR to insure continuity from state to state.

Other organizations which are active in the real estate industry but are not part of NAR include the National Association of Real Estate License Law Officials (NARELLO), the Society of Real Estate Appraisers (SREA), the American Society of Appraisers (ASA), and the National Association of Home Builders (NAHB). This is not intended to be an all-inclusive listing of the associations in the real estate business but does include most of the major trade associations.

SUMMARY

While real estate is not a true profession, its members conduct themselves in a professional manner. It is necessary that they do so because of the large amounts of capital involved in real estate transactions. The importance of real estate in our everyday lives causes it to be an area demanding great knowledge. Therefore specialists are found in the many different areas of the real estate business. The complicated process of transferring real property can be eased by the use of a REALTOR,® that is, a member of NAR. The immobility of real estate and the fact that each parcel is unique causes the real estate market to be a local and therefore highly specialized one.

REALTOR®

CODE OF ETHICS
NATIONAL ASSOCIATION OF REALTORS®

Preamble . . .

Under all is the land. Upon its wise utilization and widely allocated ownership depend the survival and growth of free institutions and of our civilization. The REALTOR® should recognize that the interests of the nation and its citizens require the highest and best use of the land and the widest distribution of land ownership. They require the creation of adequate housing, the building of functioning cities, the development of productive industries and farms, and the preservation of a healthful environment.

Such interests impose obligations beyond those of ordinary commerce. They impose grave social responsibility and a patriotic duty to which the REALTOR® should dedicate himself, and for which he should be diligent in preparing himself. The REALTOR®, therefore, is zealous to maintain and improve the standards of his calling and shares with his fellow-REALTORS® a common responsibility for its integrity and honor. The term REALTOR® has come to connote competency, fairness, and high integrity resulting from adherence to a lofty ideal of moral conduct in business relations. No inducement of profit and no instruction from clients ever can justify departure from this ideal.

In the interpretation of his obligation, a REALTOR® can take no safer guide than that which has been handed down through the centuries, embodied in the Golden Rule, "Whatsoever ye would that men should do to you, do ye even so to them."

Accepting this standard as his own, every REALTOR® pledges himself to observe its spirit in all of his activities and to conduct his business in accordance with the tenets set forth below.

ARTICLE 1

The REALTOR® should keep himself informed on matters affecting real estate in his community, the state, and nation so that he may be able to contribute responsibly to public thinking on such matters.

ARTICLE 2

In justice to those who place their interests in his care, the REALTOR® should endeavor always to be informed regarding laws, proposed legislation, governmental regulations, public policies, and current market conditions in order to be in a position to advise his clients properly.

ARTICLE 3

It is the duty of the REALTOR® to protect the public against fraud, misrepresentation, and unethical practices in real estate transactions. He should endeavor to eliminate in his community any practices which could be damaging to the public or bring discredit to the real estate profession. The REALTOR® should assist the governmental agency charged with regulating the practices of brokers and salesmen in his state.

ARTICLE 4

The REALTOR® should seek no unfair advantage over other REALTORS® and should conduct his business so as to avoid controversies with other REALTORS®.

ARTICLE 5

In the best interests of society, of his associates, and his own business, the REALTOR® should willingly share with other REALTORS® the lessons of his experience and study for the benefit of the public, and should be loyal to the Board of REALTORS® of his community and active in its work.

ARTICLE 6

To prevent dissension and misunderstanding and to assure better service to the owner, the REALTOR® should urge the exclusive listing of property unless contrary to the best interest of the owner.

ARTICLE 7

In accepting employment as an agent, the REALTOR® pledges himself to protect and promote the interests of the client. This obligation of absolute fidelity to the client's interests is primary, but it does not relieve the REALTOR® of the obligation to treat fairly all parties to the transaction.

ARTICLE 8

The REALTOR® shall not accept compensation from more than one party, even if permitted by law, without the full knowledge of all parties to the transaction.

ARTICLE 9

The REALTOR® shall avoid exaggeration, misrepresentation, or concealment of pertinent facts. He has an affirmative obligation to discover adverse factors that a reasonably competent and diligent investigation would disclose.

ARTICLE 10

The REALTOR® shall not deny equal professional services to any person for reasons of race, creed, sex, or country of national origin. The REALTOR® shall not be a party to any plan or agreement to discriminate against a person or persons on the basis of race, creed, sex, or country of national origin.

ARTICLE 11

A REALTOR® is expected to provide a level of competent service in keeping with the Standards of Practice in those fields in which the REALTOR® customarily engages.

The REALTOR® shall not undertake to provide specialized professional services concerning a type of property or service that is outside his field of competence unless he engages the assistance of one who is competent on such types of property or service, or unless the facts are fully disclosed to the client. Any person engaged to provide such assistance shall be so identified to the client and his contribution to the assignment should be set forth.

The REALTOR® shall refer to the Standards of Practice of the National Association as to the degree of competence that a client has a right to expect the REALTOR® to possess, taking into consideration the complexity of the problem, the availability of expert assistance, and the opportunities for experience available to the REALTOR®.

ARTICLE 12

The REALTOR® shall not undertake to provide professional services concerning a property or its value where he has a present or contemplated interest unless such interest is specifically disclosed to all affected parties.

ARTICLE 13

The REALTOR® shall not acquire an interest in or buy for himself, any member of his immediate family, his firm or any member thereof, or any entity in which he has a substantial ownership interest, property listed with him, without making the true position known to the listing owner. In selling property owned by himself, or in which he has any interest, the REALTOR® shall reveal the facts of his ownership or interest to the purchaser.

ARTICLE 14

In the event of a controversy between REALTORS® associated with different firms, arising out of their relationship as REALTORS®, the REALTORS® shall submit the dispute to arbitration in accordance with the regulations of their board or boards rather than litigate the matter.

ARTICLE 15

If a REALTOR® is charged with unethical practice or is asked to present evidence in any disciplinary proceeding or investigation, he shall place all pertinent facts before the proper tribunal of the member board or affiliated institute, society, or council of which he is a member.

ARTICLE 16

When acting as agent, the REALTOR® shall not accept any commission, rebate, or profit on expenditures made for his principal-owner, without the principal's knowledge and consent.

ARTICLE 17

The REALTOR® shall not engage in activities that constitute the unauthorized practice of law and shall recommend that legal counsel be obtained when the interest of any party to the transaction requires it.

ARTICLE 18

The REALTOR® shall keep in a special account in an appropriate financial institution, separated from his own funds, monies coming into his possession in trust for other persons, such as escrows, trust funds, clients' monies, and other like items.

ARTICLE 19

The REALTOR® shall be careful at all times to present a true picture in his advertising and representations to the public. He shall neither advertise without disclosing his name nor permit any person associated with him to use individual names or telephone numbers, unless such person's connection with the REALTOR® is obvious in the advertisement.

ARTICLE 20

The REALTOR®, for the protection of all parties, shall see that financial obligations and commitments regarding real estate transactions are in writing, expressing the exact agreement of the parties. A copy of each agreement shall be furnished to each party upon his signing such agreement.

ARTICLE 21

The REALTOR® shall not engage in any practice or take any action inconsistent with the agency of another REALTOR®.

ARTICLE 22

In the sale of property which is exclusively listed with a REALTOR®, the REALTOR® shall utilize the services of other brokers upon mutually agreed upon terms when it is in the best interests of the client.

Negotiations concerning property which is listed exclusively shall be carried on with the listing broker, not with the owner, except with the consent of the listing broker.

ARTICLE 23

The REALTOR® shall not publicly disparage the business practice of a competitor nor volunteer an opinion of a competitor's transaction. If his opinion is sought and if the REALTOR® deems it appropriate to respond, such opinion shall be rendered with strict professional integrity and courtesy.

ARTICLE 24

The REALTOR® shall not directly or indirectly solicit the services or affiliation of an employee or independent contractor in the organization of another REALTOR® without prior notice to said REALTOR®.

NOTE: Where the word REALTOR® is used in this Code and Preamble, it shall be deemed to include REALTOR®-ASSOCIATE. Pronouns shall be considered to include REALTORS® and REALTOR®-ASSOCIATES of both genders.

The Code of Ethics was adopted in 1913. Amended at the Annual Convention in 1924, 1928, 1950, 1951, 1952, 1955, 1956, 1961, 1962, and 1974.

SUGGESTED READINGS

(See appropriate chapter in the following books.)

Brown, Robert Kevin. *Essentials of Real Estate.* Englewood Cliffs, N.J.: Prentice-Hall, Inc., 1970.

Dasso, Jerome, Alfred A. Ring, and Douglas McFall. *Fundamentals of Real Estate.* Englewood Cliffs, N.J.: Prentice Hall, Inc., 1977.

Ficek, Edmund F., Thomas P. Henderson, and Ross H. Johnson. *Real Estate Principles and Practices.* Columbus, Ohio: Charles E. Merrill Publishing Company, 1976.

Hines, Mary Alice. *Principles and Practices of Real Estate.* Homewood, Ill.: Richard D. Irwin, Inc., 1976.

O'Donnell, Paul T. and Eugene L. Maleady. *Principles of Real Estate.* Philadelphia, Pa.: W.B. Saunders Company, 1975.

Ring, Alfred A. and Jerome Dasso. *Real Estate Principles and Practices,* 8th ed. Englewood Cliffs, N.J.: Prentice-Hall, Inc., 1977.

Shenkel, William M. *The Real Estate Professional.* Homewood, Ill.: Dow Jones-Irwin, Inc., 1976.

Weimer, Arthur M., Homer Hoyt, and George F. Bloom. *Real Estate,* 7th ed. New York: The Ronald Press Company, 1978.

REVIEW QUESTIONS

See Chapter 17 for discussion of question structures.

1. The real estate business can best be described as

   I. local in nature
   II. disorganized

   (A) I only   (C) both I and II
   (B) II only   (D) neither I nor II

2. A characteristic which causes real estate to be different from other commodities is

   I. standardization
   II. long life

   (A) I only   (C) both I and II
   (B) II only   (D) neither I nor II

3. The average real estate broker earns the majority of commissions from the sale of

   (A) commercial properties
   (B) investment properties
   (C) residential properties
   (D) industrial properties

4. Real estate brokerage is governed by

   (A) the law of agency
   (B) the statute of frauds
   (C) abstracting title
   (D) commercial transactions

5. The public sector includes

   I. federal, state, and local levels of government
   II. General Services Administration (GSA)

   (A) I only   (C) both I and II
   (B) II only   (D) neither I nor II

6. Real estate can be defined as

   I. land only
   II. land plus permanently attached improvements

   (A) I only   (C) both I and II
   (B) II only   (D) neither I nor II

7. The Ordinance of 1785 has as its most important impact

   (A) total governmental control of real estate
   (B) the rectangular survey of land
   (C) transfer of all state real property to federal control
   (D) a revocation of all private rights to land

8. The term used to describe funds invested in real estate is

   (A) accrued depreciation
   (B) illiquidity
   (C) liquidity
   (D) capital

9. According to NAR, a REALTOR® is a

   I. professional who adheres to a code of ethics
   II. real estate licensee

   (A) I only   (C) both I and II
   (B) II only   (D) neither I nor II

10. The MAI designation is awarded by

    (A) SIR   (C) ASREC
    (B) RNMI   (D) AIREA

11. The REALTORS® code of ethics has articles of interest to

    (A) REALTORS® only
    (B) the consuming public
    (C) REALTORS® dealing with other REALTORS®
    (D) all of the above

12. In regard to exclusive listings,

    I. the REALTOR® should always encourage the practice
    II. the practice should not be recommended

    (A) I only   (C) both I and II
    (B) II only   (D) neither I nor II

13. The practice of combining personal funds with those of a client is

 (A) standard practice
 (B) a form of escrow account
 (C) unethical
 (D) two of the above

14. Residential real estate brokerage commissions are usually calculated on the basis of

 (A) gross sales price
 (B) net sales price
 (C) a set percentage of the net sales price
 (D) none of the above

15. In dealing with legal questions arising from real estate transactions, a broker should

 I. provide legal advice on all questions
 II. provide legal advice only after giving the client the name of an attorney

 (A) I only
 (B) II only
 (C) both I and II
 (D) neither I nor II

16. Classification of residential real property includes

 (A) triplexes
 (B) cooperatives
 (C) condominiums
 (D) all of the above

17. The real estate market is controlled through the forces of

 I. supply
 II. demand

 (A) I only
 (B) II only
 (C) both I and II
 (D) neither I nor II

18. NAR functions on which level(s)?

 (A) local
 (B) state
 (C) national
 (D) all of the above

19. The NAR code of ethics

 I. was first adopted in 1908 at the conception of NAREB
 II. was not adopted by all states until 1928

 (A) I only
 (B) II only
 (C) both I and II
 (D) neither I nor II

20. A broker acting as the agent for an owner

 I. must account for the owner's funds
 II. can accept funds from any party in any transaction

 (A) I only
 (B) II only
 (C) both I and II
 (D) neither I nor II

Chapter 4

Regulation of the Real Estate Business

VOCABULARY

You will find it important to have a complete working knowledge of the following words and concepts found in the text or the glossary.

blockbusting
Civil Rights Act of 1866
commingling of funds
Consumer Protection Act of 1968
discriminatory practices
Federal Fair Housing Law (Title VIII,
   Civil Rights Act of 1968)

misrepresentation
panic selling
police powers
racial steering
reciprocity
Regulation Z
truth in lending

undisclosed principal
Abbreviations:
FHA
HUD
NARELLO
RESPA

BECAUSE of its importance and because of the large amounts of capital involved, real estate is highly regulated. All levels of government have laws concerning real estate. Federal regulations are extensive but have the greatest impact in two areas —finance and civil rights. State regulations primarily affect the licensing of real estate practitioners and the establishment of codes protecting the public in many areas of construction and development. Real estate controls by local governments are discussed in Chapter 5.

FEDERAL INFLUENCES

The federal government's influence on real estate extends into federal subsidies through governmental housing programs, civil rights, and fair housing, and into consumer protection through the Truth-in-Lending Act, the Consumer Protection Act of 1968, and, most recently, the Real Estate Settlement Procedures Act (RESPA).

Formation of the Public Housing Administration in 1937 was the first major step in increasing the federal government's role in real estate. This control continued to grow, until now the head of the major regulatory body, the Department of Housing and Urban Development (HUD), occupies a presidential cabinet position in the federal government.

HUD was created in 1965 by combining the Public Housing Administration, Federal Housing Administration (FHA), Federal National Mortgage Association (Fannie Mae), and Urban Renewal. HUD's primary purpose is to coordinate, with state and local governments, the use of federal government resources to solve housing problems facing the nation.

One thrust of HUD is in the area of fair housing. The basis of fair housing in the United States is not new but stems from the Civil Rights Act of 1866 and has since been strengthened considerably.

Fair Housing Laws
Civil Rights Act of 1866

After the Civil War, Congress passed a Civil Rights Act prohibiting racial discrimination in housing as well as in ownership of land. It allowed the complainant to go directly to a federal court in a case involving racial discrimination.

Federal Fair Housing Law (Title VIII, Civil Rights Act of 1968)

By 1968, Congress recognized a need to build upon the Civil Rights Act of 1866. The Civil Rights Act of 1968 made it illegal to discriminate not only on the basis of race but also on the basis of color, religion, or national origin. In 1974, the 1968 act was amended to include discrimination on the basis of sex. Specifically, Title VIII of the act means that no one may refuse to rent, lease, or sell to another because of reasons of race, color, national origin, religion, or sex.

To comply with the act, a licensee must refuse to accept any listing with discriminatory restrictions. Furthermore, after a property is listed, the owner may not refuse to sell to a member of a minority group. It is important that clients realize the importance of this act.

Specifically, Title VIII of the Civil Rights Act of 1968 prohibits the following discriminatory practices (where the action is based upon race, color, religion, national origin, or sex):

1. Refusal to rent, lease, sell, or negotiate with any individual
2. The offering of different terms or conditions for the purchase or rental of a property to different individuals
3. Advertising that a property is available only to certain types of individuals
4. Denying loans or providing different financial conditions to different individuals (This is directed primarily at commercial lending institutions such as banks, savings and loan institutions, and insurance companies.)
5. Making false statements regarding the availability of housing for sale or rent.

In addition to the list given here, one other very important violation of the act is to call attention to the possibility that any minority group may move into an area in an attempt to persuade an owner to rent or sell. This practice, known as *panic selling*, is illegal. The term *blockbusting* is also used to connote a similar illegal practice of introducing a nonconforming user into a neighborhood to benefit financially by representing that a change in a neighborhood is taking place with respect to race, national origin, color, or sex. Such activity can affect the stability of a neighborhood and can cause panic selling.

Complaint Procedures

One of HUD's most important roles is administration of the Federal Fair Housing Law. HUD has instituted services aimed at clarifying and explaining the law so as to prevent misunderstandings. More important is the right of the complainant to go directly to the federal courts without even filing a complaint with HUD; however, individuals who feel they have a legitimate complaint should file such a

complaint with the owner or manager of the property or the local Board of REALTORS®, if a REALTOR® is involved. If they are not satisfied after taking such action, they may proceed to a local or state civil rights commission. Going to the federal courts should probably be the last alternative.

Racial Steering

It is important that a licensee not "steer" a client toward a property for discriminatory reasons. The prospect, not the licensee, must pick the location. To steer the client away from property in a particular neighborhood or to limit the choice of housing based on any of the reasons listed in Title VIII is prohibited. Clients must choose from the properties listed the ones they wish to visit and consider for purchase.

Fair Housing Practices Today and Tomorrow

The real estate business is continuing its efforts to make Title VIII work. Such steps include equal opportunity in hiring policies, added training regarding discriminatory practices, utilization of nonracist advertising, and the clearly established policy regarding the nonacceptance of listings which are discriminatory in nature and are therefore illegal.

NAR is gaining support for its affirmative marketing plan in housing. The plan, which has been developed in conjunction with HUD to assure all minority groups equal access to housing, has helped local boards to clarify their position on open housing. The NAR Code for Equal Opportunity is given on page 27 and stresses the REALTOR® role.

The equal housing opportunity logo on page 29 signifies the compliance of newspapers which carry advertisements for housing for rent, lease, or sale. It must be displayed in every edition carrying real estate advertisements.

Consumer Protection Laws

Consumer concern about underlying terms and conditions in mortgages spurred the federal government to pass the *Consumer Credit Protection Act of 1969*. Included as part of this act was the *Truth-in-Lending Act*, which empowered the Federal Reserve Board to implement Regulation Z. Its objective is to let the purchaser of real property know exactly what credit charges are being paid to the lender and the exact terms of the loan. The regulation also covers advertising. A complete statement on the Truth-in-Lending Act can be found in Chapter 11.

NATIONAL ASSOCIATION OF REALTORS®

Code for Equal Opportunity

(Local Board Name Goes Here)

subscribes to the policy that equal opportunity in the acquisition of housing can best be accomplished through leadership, example, education, and the mutual co-operation of the real estate industry and the public. In the spirit of this endeavor, this board proclaims the following provisions of its Code for Equal Opportunity to which each member is obligated to adhere:

1. In the sale, purchase, exchange, rental, or lease of real property, REALTORS' and their REALTOR ASSOCIATES have the responsibility to offer equal service to all clients and prospects without regard to race, color, religion, or national origin. This encompasses:

   A. Standing ready to enter broker-client relationships or to show property equally to members of all racial, creedal, or ethnic groups.

   B. Receiving all formal written offers and communicating them to the owner.

   C. Exerting their best efforts to conclude all transactions.

   D. Maintaining equal opportunity employment practices.

2. Members, individually and collectively, in performing their agency functions have no right or responsibility to volunteer information regarding the racial, creedal, or ethnic composition of any neighborhood or any part thereof.

3. Members shall not engage in any activity which has the purpose of inducing panic selling.

4. Members shall not print, display, or circulate any statement or advertisement with respect to the sale or rental of a dwelling that indicates any preference, limitations, or discrimination based on race, color, religion, or ethnic background.

5. Members who violate the spirit or any provision of this Code for Equal Opportunity shall be subject to disciplinary action.

Those who feel they have been discriminated against
may contact the management of this office
or the Board of REALTORS®

FIG. 4-1—NAR Code for Equal Opportunity. Outline of the obligations of a REALTOR® under the 1968 law.

U.S. DEPARTMENT OF HOUSING AND URBAN DEVELOPMENT

Federal Fair Housing Law

(Title VIII of the Civil Rights Act of 1968)

It is Illegal To Discriminate Against Any Person
Because Of Race, Color, Religion,
Or National Origin

- In the sale or rental of housing or residential lots

- In advertising the sale or rental of housing

- In the financing of housing

- In the provision of real estate brokerage services

  Blockbusting is also illegal

*Those who feel they have been discriminated against
should send complaint to*

**U.S. Department of Housing and Urban Development,
Assistant Secretary for Equal Opportunity,
Washington, D.C. 20410**

FIG. 4-2—Federal Fair Housing Law. *A topical outline of what is illegal under the
Federal Fair Housing Law (Title VIII of the Civil Rights Act of 1968).*

**EQUAL HOUSING
OPPORTUNITY**

**EQUAL HOUSING
OPPORTUNITY**

All real estate advertised in this newspaper is subject to the Federal Fair Housing Act of 1968, which makes it illegal to advertise "any preference, limitations, or discrimination based on race, color, religion, or national origin, or an intention to make any such preference, limitations, or discrimination."

This newspaper will not knowingly accept any advertising for real estate which is in violation of the law. Our readers are hereby informed that all dwellings advertised in the newspaper are required to be available on an equal opportunity basis.

FIG. 4-3—Federal Fair Housing symbol and explanation.

RESPA

A more recent act, the Real Estate Settlement Procedures Act (RESPA), was passed in 1975. It requires lending institutions to inform loan applicants of approximate settlement costs for the closing of the prospective loan. By informing the applicant in advance, it is possible for the purchaser to compare costs of different avenues of finance. More material can be found on this topic in Chapter 11.

The Magnuson-Moss Warranty/Federal Trade Commission Act

This new federal warranty legislation appears to be aimed at controlling certain abuses in connection with the warranties extended to buyers of automobiles and appliances. It is administered by the Fed-

eral Trade Commission, which has published rules under this act which became effective December 31, 1976. The act clearly has an impact upon both builders and sellers of new homes which include built-in items which would clearly be covered by the act if they were sold separately to the consumer. The act does not require that any warranty at all be given; however, if a warranty of any kind is given (and this is the normal case rather than the exception today in the new home building field), it must meet the highly technical terms of the act.

The act and its legislative history provide little assistance in applying it to the building and selling of new houses. In addition, the act tends to blur the traditional distinction between real and personal property as affected by the common law of fixtures. It will undoubtedly take some time for the practical meaning of the act to the real estate industry to be developed through test cases in the courts. Until that time, however, anyone active in either building or selling new housing must be aware that federal warranty provisions are in effect. The need for legal counsel should be apparent.

REAL ESTATE LICENSE LAW

All the states and the District of Columbia have license laws regulating real estate practitioners. The purpose of such laws is twofold: first, to protect the public by setting up specific requirements regarding standards of practice by real estate practitioners and, second, to protect the licensee from improper business practices. The laws and any rules or regulations passed by the regulatory body itself control entry into the real estate business through license and establish controls for suspension and revocation when violations occur.

The state license law must be created through an act or statute passed by the state's legislature. Once passed, it becomes an extension of the state's constitution, as do all laws. It creates a commission or licensing board and then authorizes the commission to interpret, administer, and enforce the laws. It also authorizes the commission to establish the rules and regulations used to clarify and interpret the laws passed by the legislature which relate to real estate licenses.

The power to establish such license laws stems from the *police powers* of the state—the right of the state to protect the general public in areas of public interest, such as real estate. More information about police powers appears in Chapter 5.

A real estate license, then, is a privilege, not a right, since it informs the public that the individual holding such a license is knowledgeable and has acquired the skills to act in the capacity of a real estate salesperson or broker. A real estate broker is authorized to operate his or her own real estate brokerage concern. The individual who holds a salesperson's license is held responsible by a broker who has indicated to the real estate commission his or her willingness to be responsible for the salesperson's actions.

Most state license laws fit the pattern established by the model license law written by the National Association of Real Estate License Law Officials (NARELLO). Obviously, each state has specific portions of its license law which differ from those of other states. At the end of this chapter is an outline of the material contained in your state's license law, rules, and regulations.

It is *essential* for a prospective licensee to know the laws of his or her state. You should study in detail the license law guide for your jurisdiction and any additional material your licensing agency provides to obtain a full understanding of the applicable information.

Acquiring State Materials

If you have not already obtained a copy of the license laws for the state in which you are applying for licensure, write immediately to the state licensing agency at the address listed at the end of this chapter. Application forms for licensing examinations and other materials should be available from the same address.

Your License Examination

Each state has an examination which is required prior to becoming licensed. More than half of all states use the Real Estate License Examination (RELE), prepared by the Educational Testing Service (ETS), which is an examination on all real estate topical material and specific questions concerning a particular state's real estate practices as well as that state's license law and rules and regulations. The time you spend reviewing the license law materials at the end of this chapter will be well spent.

TYPICAL LICENSING REQUIREMENTS

Even though requirements for obtaining a real estate license vary from state to state, a number of similarities do exist. As previously indicated, it is essential that a prospective licensee obtain a copy of the license laws and rules and regulations for the state in which he or she is applying for an examination. The following list is meant only to aid in understanding the broad spectrum of real estate licensing regulations. In the outline at the end of this chapter, write the requirements pertaining to your state. Take these directly from the materials obtained from the real estate commission in your jurisdiction.

1. *License.* An individual must be licensed before the transaction is initiated and, in almost all cases, prior to receiving a commission for the sale of property.
2. *Education.* State requirements vary from none at all to an academic college or university degree for a broker. Most states require a high school diploma and/or a number of required hours of classroom real estate education.
3. *Experience.* The most common requirement for a broker is 2 years' experience in real estate prior to application for licensure and/or classes at an accredited college or university in real estate subjects.
4. *Examination.* All states require sales and broker candidates to pass examinations which differ depending on the individual license.
5. *Sponsorship.* Some state laws require that sales candidates be sponsored by a licensed broker who will be the holder of the individual's license when it is issued.
6. *Minimum age.* Usually the age of majority in the state in which you are applying. The most common age is 18. Some states have different requirements for brokers and salespersons.
7. *Citizenship.* Some states still require United States citizenship, although the legality of this requirement has been challenged.
8. *Fair housing.* All states have some requirement in their license law dealing with discrimination and the licensee.
9. *Application.* Applicants for licensure must apply on the specific form provided by the state. This application must be filled out completely and delivered to the real estate commission, usually 30 to 60 days prior to the examination date. A common requirement for the application is listing references attesting to personal character. Such references are usually given by either landowners or licensed real estate brokers in the particular state.
10. *Convictions.* Almost all states have some re-

striction for licensure if the applicant has been convicted of a felony. Many states have a statute of limitations requirement as to the length of time a license can be denied on this basis.

11. *Fees.* Two categories of fees exist: first, for the original licensing of the individual; second, for periodic renewals which are required. The license law also usually includes a statement regarding the disbursement of fees collected.

12. *Reciprocity.* Many states have reciprocal licensing agreements which allow for experience or for licensure in another state.

13. *Administration of the law.* All license laws indicate how the commission is appointed or elected, what paid employees are allowed, and what their duties are.

14. *Advertising.* In all states, advertising must include the broker's name.

15. *Display of license.* All licenses must be displayed in the broker's place of business. In many states, pocket cards indicating that the individual is a licensee must also be carried.

16. *Placement of license.* When employment or affiliation is terminated by a salesperson, his or her license must be returned to the real estate commission until it is requested by a new broker.

17. *Suspension and revocation of license.* All states have license laws regulating fraudulent activities which can result in suspension or revocation of licenses. Other penalties may include fines.

18. *Real estate definition.* All states include a definition of what constitutes real estate and what types of transactions require licensing.

TYPICAL EXEMPTIONS FROM LICENSING REQUIREMENTS

It is not uncommon for states to exempt certain categories of individuals from licensure. Those most commonly exempted are:

1. Any individual selling or offering real estate for himself

2. Attorneys acting on behalf of clients as part of their law practice

3. Court-appointed administrators, executors, or trustees

4. Public officials, when involved as part of their official duties

5. Officials of regulated utilities or their employees whose real estate activities are directly related to the firm's business

6. In some states, resident managers of apartments who show vacant units.

TYPES OF VIOLATIONS RESULTING IN LICENSE SUSPENSION OR REVOCATION

1. *Discriminatory practices.* Refusal to show, sell, or lease real estate to any individual because of race, color, national origin, or sex can result in suspension or revocation of a license.

2. *Misrepresentation.* Any substantial misstatement of fact may be considered misrepresentation and may also be grounds for suspension or revocation.

3. *Commingling of funds.* All states require the keeping of clients' and brokers' funds in separate accounts, usually called escrow or trust accounts.

4. *Advertising.* Advertising which misrepresents a property is a violation in all states. Certain methods of advertising can also result in license suspension or revocation. In many states, the placement of a "For Sale" or "For Rent" sign on a property without prior written consent of the owner is a violation.

5. *Notification as a license holder.* It is essential that the licensee serve notice to any individual with whom he or she is dealing that he or she holds a real estate license. This is especially important in personal transactions, so as to provide the other party with notice that a knowledgeable real estate person is participating in the transaction.

6. *Guaranteeing future profits.* The licensee may not guarantee profits from the future sale of a property being considered for purchase.

7. *Personal benefits from expenditures made for a principal.* No licensee is allowed to receive a commission, rebate, or profit from any such expenditures.

8. *Sharing commissions with an unlicensed individual.* Only licensees may share in real estate sales fees (commissions).

9. *Conviction.* Conviction for a felony is usually grounds for revocation or suspension of a license.

10. *Failure to deliver copies of required documents.* All states have requirements regarding the delivery of listing and purchase agreements as well as closing statements.

11. *Undisclosed principal.* It is a violation for a licensee to represent more than one party or

himself in a transaction without the full knowledge of all the parties involved.

12. *Bonds.* Many states require the posting and constant renewal of a bond.

13. *Failure to submit all offers.* A licensee would commit a violation if he or she does not submit all bona fide written offers to an owner for consideration. This includes all offers received prior to written acceptance of a previous offer. All written offers must be submitted to the owner regardless of the licensee's opinion of the offer.

14. *Unethical conduct.* This category can be found in all state license laws and covers such areas as unworthy or incompetent acts, inducing parties to break a contract to enter into another, and conducting real estate transactions which demonstrate dishonesty.

Since license law varies from state to state, it is essential that you now review your state's requirements and place your understanding of the rules and regulations as well as the license law in the appropriate places in the outline which follows.

LICENSING REQUIREMENTS OUTLINE

Using the license law and licensing examination information you obtain from your own state real estate regulatory body, complete the following outline and use it as a study guide for the state portion of the RELE. (See the general descriptions of these requirements earlier in the chapter.)

1. License

_____

_____

_____

_____

2. Education

_____

_____

_____

_____

3. Experience

_____

_____

_____

_____

4. Examination

_____

_____

_____

_____

5. Sponsorship

_____

_____

6. Minimum age

_____

7. Citizenship

_____

8. Fair housing

_____

_____

_____

_____

9. Application

_____

_____

_____

10. Convictions

_____

_____

11. Fees

_____

_____

_____

12. Reciprocity

_____

_____

_____

_____

13. Administration of the law

_____

_____

_____

_____

14. Advertising

_____

_____

15. Display of license

_____

_____

16. Placement of license

_____

_____

_____

17. Suspension and revocation of license

_____

_____

_____

_____

_____

18. Real estate definition

_____

_____

_____

_____

_____

_____

STATE COMMISSIONS AND THEIR PUBLICATIONS

Alabama. Real Estate Commission, 562 State Office Building, Montgomery 36104. *Alabama Real Estate Law.*

Alaska. Division of Occupational Licensing, Department of Commerce, Pouch D, Juneau 99811. *State of Alaska, Real Estate Commission.*

Arizona. State Real Estate Department, 1645 W. Jefferson, Phoenix 85007. *Real Estate License Law.*

Arkansas. Real Estate Commission, Wallace Building, P.O. Box 3173, 101 Main St., Little Rock 72201. *Real Estate License Law and Regulations.*

California. Department of Real Estate, 714 P St., Sacramento 95814. *Instructions to License Applicants, Plan for Professional Development of the Real Estate Industry in California, Real Estate Education in California.* (For publication requests, address to the attention of Chief Deputy, Qualifications and Publications.)

Colorado. Real Estate Commission, 110 State Services Building, Denver 80203. *Colorado Real Estate Commission.*

Connecticut. Real Estate Commission, 90 West Washington St., Hartford 06115. *Real Estate Licensing, Law and Regulations Concerning the Conduct of Real Estate Brokers and Salesmen.*

Delaware. Real Estate Commission, Department of Administrative Services, Division of Business and Occupational Regulation, State House Annex, Dover 19901. *General Information, Salesmen and Brokers.*

District of Columbia. Real Estate Commission, 614 H St., NW, Washington 20001. *Real Estate and Business Chance Manual.*

Florida. Real Estate Commission, State Office Building, West Morse Boulevard, Winter Park 32789. *Florida Real Estate License Law.*

Georgia. Real Estate Commission, 166 Pryor St., SW, Atlanta 30303. *Georgia Real Estate Brokers and Salesmen Licensing Act.*

Hawaii. Real Estate Commission, Hawaii Department of Regulatory Agencies, P.O. Box 3469, Honolulu 96801. *Hawaii Real Estate License Law.*

Idaho. Real Estate Commission, State Capitol Building, Boise 83720. *Idaho Real Estate Brokers Law and Amended Rules and Regulations.*

Illinois. Department of Registration and Education, 628 E. Adams St., Springfield 62786. *Real Estate Brokers and Salesmen Act, Rules and Regulations.*

Indiana. Real Estate Commission, State Office Building, Room 1022, 100 N. Senate Ave., Indianapolis 46204. *Real Estate License Laws, Indiana Real Estate Law and Practice Manual.*

Iowa. Real Estate Commission, State Capitol, Des Moines 50319. *Real Estate License Law, Rules and Regulations.*

Kansas. Real Estate Commission, 535 Kansas Ave., Room 1212, Topeka 66603. *Kansas Real Estate Broker's License Law, Kansas Real Estate Recovery Fund Act, Kansas Statutes Annotated and Rules and Regulations.*

Kentucky. State Real Estate Commission, 100 E. Liberty St., Suite 204, Louisville 40202. *Law Governing Real Estate Brokers and Salesmen.*

Louisiana. Real Estate Commission, Department of Occupational Standards, P.O. Box 44095, Capitol Station, Baton Rouge 70804. *Louisiana Real Estate Commission Licensing Law, Louisiana Real Estate Commission Rules and Regulations.*

Maine. Real Estate Commission, State Office Building, 4th Floor, Augusta 04333. *License Law, Rules and Regulations, Real Estate Commission Reference Book.*

Maryland. Real Estate Commission, 1 S. Calvert St., Baltimore 21202. *Real Estate Law, State of Maryland.*

Massachusetts. Board of Registration of Real Estate Brokers and Salesmen, Leverett Saltonstall Building, 100 Cambridge St., Boston 02202. *Division of Registration, Rules and Regulations.*

Michigan. Real Estate Division, Department of Licensing and Regulation, 1033 S. Washington Ave., Lansing 48926. *Real Estate Red Book, Real Estate Brokers and Salesmen.*

Minnesota. Real Estate Section, State of Minnesota, 500 Metro Square Building, St. Paul 55102. *Minnesota Law, Real Estate Regulations.*

Mississippi. Real Estate Commission, Woodland Hills Building, Room 505, Old Canton Rd., Jackson 39216. *Real Estate Brokers License Act, Rules and Regulations, Code of Ethics.*

Missouri. Real Estate Commission, 3523 N. Ten Mile Dr., P.O. Box 1339, Jefferson City 65101. *Missouri Real Estate Commission, Rules and Regulations.*

Montana. Board of Real Estate, LaLonde Building, Helena 59601. *Real Estate, Professional and Occupational Licensing.*

Nebraska. Real Estate Commission, 600 S. 11th St., Suite 200, Box 94667, Lincoln 68509. *Nebraska Real Estate License Laws and Rules and Regulations, Nebraska Real Estate Appraiser License Act.*

Nevada. Real Estate Division, Department of Commerce, 201 S. Fall St., Carson City 89710. *Nevada Real Estate Licensing.*

New Hampshire. Real Estate Commission, 3 Capitol St., Concord 03301. *Real Estate Law.*

New Jersey. Real Estate Commission, Department of Insurance, P.O. Box 1510, 201 E. State St., Trenton 08625. *The New Jersey Real Estate License Act and Rules and Regulations.*

New Mexico. Real Estate Commission, 505 Marquette Ave., NW, Albuquerque 87401. *State of New Mexico Real Estate Law and Rules and Regulations.*

New York. Division of Licensing Services, Department of State, 270 Broadway, New York 10007. *Real Estate Salesmen, Real Estate Brokers.*

North Carolina. Real Estate Licensing Board, 813 BB and T Building, P.O. Box 266, Raleigh 27602. *North Carolina Real Estate Licensing Law, North Carolina Real Estate Licensing Board.*

North Dakota. Real Estate Commission, 410 E. Thayer Ave., Box 727, Bismarck 58501. *Real Estate License Law and Commission Rules and Regulations.*

Ohio. Real Estate Commission, Ohio Department of Commerce, 180 E. Broad St., 14th Floor, Columbus 43215.

Oklahoma. Real Estate Commission, Suite 100, 4040 Lincoln Blvd., Oklahoma City 73105. *Oklahoma Real Estate License Code and Rules and Regulations.*

Oregon. Real Estate Division, Department of Commerce, Commerce Building, 158 12th St., NE, Salem 97310. *Real Estate and Business Brokers and Escrow Agents.*

Pennsylvania. Commission of Professional and Occupational Affairs, Real Estate Commission, Box 2649, Harrisburg 17120. *Rules and Regulations of the State Real Estate Commission, Real Estate Brokers License Act.*

Rhode Island. Deputy Administrator, Real Estate Division, Department of Business Regulation, 109 N. Main St., Providence 02903. *Real Estate Licensing Laws and Rules and Regulations.*

South Carolina. Real Estate Commission, 900 Elmwood Ave., Columbia 29201. *License Laws and Regulations.*

South Dakota. Real Estate Commission, P.O. Box 638, Pierre 57501. *South Dakota Compiled Laws Chapter 36-21.*

Tennessee. Real Estate Commission, 556 Capitol Hill Building, Nashville 37219. *The Tennessee Real Estate Broker License Act, Rules and Regulations and Code of Ethics.*

Texas. Real Estate Commission, P.O. Box 12188, Capitol Station, Austin 78711. *Provisions of the Real Estate License Act.*

Utah. Real Estate Division, Department of Business Regulation, 330 E. Fourth St., Salt Lake City 84111. *Real Estate License Law.*

Vermont. Real Estate Commission, Montpelier 05602. *Vermont Statutes Annotated, Chapter 33 Real Estate Brokers and Salesmen, Rules of the Vermont Real Estate Commission.*

Virginia. Real Estate Commission, Department of Professional and Occupational Regulations, P.O. Box 1-x, Richmond 23202. *Virginia Real Estate Commission Manual, License Law, Fair Housing Law, and Rules and Regulations.*

Washington. Administrator, Real Estate Division, P.O. Box 247, Olympia 98504. *Law Governing Licensing of Real Estate Brokers and Salesmen.*

West Virginia. Real Estate Commission, 402 State Office Building No. 3, 1800 E. Washington St., Charleston 25305. *West Virginia Real Estate License Law and Administrative Regulations.*

Wisconsin. Real Estate Examining Board, 1400 E. Washington Ave., Madison 53702. *Wisconsin Real Estate Licensing.*

Wyoming. Real Estate Commission, 2219 Carey Ave., Cheyenne 82002. *Wyoming Real Estate Laws.*

SUGGESTED READINGS

(See appropriate chapter in the following books.)

Ficek, Edmund F., Thomas P. Henderson, and Ross H. Johnson. *Real Estate Principles and Practices.* Columbus, Ohio: Charles E. Merrill Publishing Company, 1976.

Gross, Jerome S. *Concise Desk Guide to Real Estate Practice and Procedure.* Englewood Cliffs, N.J.: Prentice-Hall, Inc., 1976.

National Association of REALTORS®. *Real Estate License Law—Suggested Pattern,* 4th ed. Chicago, 1975.

O'Donnell, Paul T. and Eugene L. Maleady. *Principles of Real Estate.* Philadelphia, Pa.: W. B. Saunders Company, 1975.

Ring, Alfred A. and Jerome Dasso. *Real Estate Principles and Practices,* 8th ed. Englewood Cliffs, N.J.: Prentice-Hall, Inc., 1977.

Weimer, Arthur M., Homer Hoyt, and George F. Bloom. *Real Estate,* 7th ed. New York: The Ronald Press Company, 1978.

REVIEW QUESTIONS

1. Real estate license laws are an example of

   (A) escheat   (C) police powers
   (B) eminent domain   (D) all of the above

2. An associate broker is defined as

   (A) a member of an association
   (B) a licensed broker who is self-employed
   (C) a licensed broker who works for a principal broker
   (D) none of the above

3. A salesperson who violates a state license law or regulation could

   I. be fined
   II. have his or her license suspended

   (A) I only   (C) both I and II
   (B) II only   (D) neither I nor II

4. Real estate license laws originate with

   (A) state legislatures
   (B) state real estate commissions
   (C) a state's governor
   (D) NAR

5. The agency of the federal government which administers fair housing laws is

   (A) VA   (C) NARELLO
   (B) HUD   (D) AIREA

6. To receive a commission, a real estate salesperson must

   I. be a REALTOR®

II. be licensed in the particular jurisdiction

   (A) I only   (C) both I and II
   (B) II only   (D) neither I nor II

7. The main purpose of the license law is to

   (A) protect the public
   (B) protect the licensee from unethical brokers
   (C) restrict competition
   (D) restrict entry of new salespersons

8. The collection of a real estate sales commission by anyone not licensed is considered

   (A) an act of duress
   (B) an unethical act
   (C) a negligent act
   (D) a license law violation

9. A real estate salesperson is responsible for his or her actions to the

   (A) mortgagor   (C) employing broker
   (B) mortgagee   (D) seller

10. Under federal law, a salesperson or broker must

   I. show listed real estate to any interested party
   II. not discriminate in the rental, sale, or lease of property

   (A) I only   (C) both I and II
   (B) II only   (D) neither I nor II

11. Which of the following are usually permitted to sell real property without a license?

    I. owners, executors, close friends
    II. attorneys, trustees, resident managers

    (A) I only
    (B) II only
    (C) both I and II
    (D) neither I nor II

12. A real estate licensee must

    I. display his or her license in the broker's place of business
    II. agree to refrain from discriminatory practices

    (A) I only
    (B) II only
    (C) both I and II
    (D) neither I nor II

13. Reciprocity means that

    I. a state accepts and recognizes the licensing requirements of another state
    II. a state trades its rules and regulations for those of another state

    (A) I only
    (B) II only
    (C) both I and II
    (D) neither I nor II

14. Real estate license laws are an example of

    (A) eminent domain
    (B) governmental interference
    (C) federal controls on real property
    (D) police powers of the state

15. To become a licensed broker, one must usually

    (A) pass an examination
    (B) be sponsored
    (C) have a specific place of business
    (D) both (A) and (C)

16. Title VIII of the Civil Rights Act allows

    (A) racial steering
    (B) direct complaint procedures
    (C) panic selling
    (D) both (A) and (C)

17. Under Title VIII, discrimination in housing takes place when individuals are denied housing on the basis of

    I. race, creed, age
    II. religion, sex, national origin

    (A) I only
    (B) II only
    (C) both I and II
    (D) neither I nor II

18. A broker is guilty of racial steering if

    I. he or she steers clients into a particular neighborhood
    II. he or she steers prospective clients to a broker of their national origin or color

    (A) I only
    (B) II only
    (C) both I and II
    (D) neither I nor II

19. Under the 1968 Federal Fair Housing Law, it is possible to

    (A) complain about discriminatory practices to HUD
    (B) take complaints directly to court
    (C) require immediate repayment of expenses caused by discriminatory practices
    (D) two of the above

20. The practice of blockbusting is acceptable

    (A) when the purchaser and seller agree to it
    (B) when the broker explains to his client that it is being practiced
    (C) when approved by HUD
    (D) never

Chapter 5
Legal Aspects of Real Estate

VOCABULARY

You will find it important to have a complete working knowledge of the following words and concepts found in the text or the glossary.

ad valorem taxes	encroachment	nonconforming use
affirmative easement	escheat	nuisance
allodial ownership	estate in land	police powers
assessment	fee simple absolute	probate homesteads
bundle of rights	fee simple determinable	profit
commercial easements in gross	feudal tenure	profit a pendre
condemnation	freehold estates	remainder
conditional fee	homestead exemption	reversion
determinable fee	leasehold estate	rezoning
dominant tenement	license	seisin
easement	life estate	servient tenement
easement appurtenant	mechanic's lien	taxation of real estate
easement in gross	municipal improvements	trespass
eminent domain	negative easement	variance
		zoning

ORIGINS AND PRESENT STATUS OF REAL ESTATE OWNERSHIP

WHILE many feel that law pertaining to the ownership of real estate changes so slowly that it is almost static, quite the contrary is true. Basic rights of ownership and interests in real estate do indeed change slowly, and in the United States today true and absolute ownership of land is recognized. Upon careful analysis, however, there are strong reasons to question this conclusion. In the discussion which follows we compare the origin of real estate ownership with the concept of ownership which exists today. The reader may then reach an independent conclusion as to the completeness of ownership recognized today.

Feudal System of Land Tenure

This system had its origins in the law of England as it developed after the Norman conquest in 1066 A.D. Under this system no one except the ruling monarch, the king, really owned real estate as we think of ownership today. Instead of granting outright ownership, the king created *feuds* which were the equivalent of today's leases of real estate. That is, the owner of the feud held it so long as he enjoyed the king's favor *and* performed the duties imposed by the king—the furnishing and support of military personnel and money to support the king (the government) being among the most important. This system of ownership is commonly referred to as *feudal tenure*, because continued ownership depended upon continuous performance of the duties imposed. Even though this form of ownership was ultimately recognized as inheritable, even inheritance was surrounded with so many restrictions that *absolute* ownership could not be achieved; it was always conditional in nature. Although this system of ownership was changed dramatically prior to the American Revolution, it was nevertheless an important cause of the revolution. The dream of Americans was absolute ownership of land. The extent to which this goal has been achieved is discussed below.

Allodial System of Land Tenure

Under the *allodial* system of land ownership, which prevails today in the United States, we feel that we own real estate absolutely, without being dependent upon the whims of a ruling monarch and without the burdensome duties which existed under the feudal system. It is true that we do own land allodially today and that our system of government clearly recognizes that fact. To have this right of ownership and to have it protected, however, some concessions must necessarily be made. The more important concessions we must make in order to have absolute ownership are outlined below.

Eminent Domain

The power of eminent domain is an inherent right reserved by the government. It is the power of governmental units literally to *take* private property when it is concluded that such action is in the best interests of the general public. The method by which this power is exercised is called *condemnation*. Privately owned property may be taken by condemning it to a public use. Several general rules apply in this area:

1. The taking or condemning of private property must be done in accordance with specific legislative authority and within the limitations of the owner's constitutional rights, both federal and state.
2. Generally, payment must be made to the landowner based upon the fair value of the property taken, and he or she may also collect payments for damages (in terms of loss of value) to the property remaining. The question of damages to the property *not* taken depends upon state law. Consider the taking of land for a new highway:

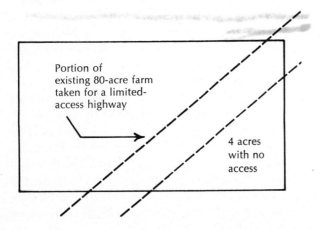

Portion of existing 80-acre farm taken for a limited-access highway

4 acres with no access

Clearly, the property owner is entitled to be paid for the strip taken; but what is the impact on the 4 acres which are "landlocked," having no access? It seems that this acreage has been substantially diminished in value and so has the farmland. State law will determine whether or not the property owner can recover the amount of this damage.

3. The power of eminent domain can be delegated to others, such as power companies, water companies, and other public utilities, so that they can condemn property to the extent that it is needed to make their services available. Generally, these are *easements* (discussed later in the chapter), as opposed to outright taking. Nevertheless, such an easement (for power lines, for example) also carries with it the right to enter upon the property and maintain the utility. Extensive damage to a crop of corn may be caused when heavy equipment is brought through a field to repair a power or gas line. The point being made here is that the power of eminent domain may be delegated even to private companies such as public utilities.
4. Once there has been a legitimate determination that private property is needed for a public purpose (i.e., the taking is not arbitrary or capricious), the landowner has no choice except to argue about the value of the property being taken. Such litigation may take years to resolve, but the taking may be as immediate as is necessary for the public purpose to be served.

Police Powers

The inherent power of government to police the conduct of its citizens is so well established that it does not merit full discussion in this book. To the extent that it affects the use of privately owned real estate it is discussed here to illustrate the limitations which may be imposed upon the concept of allodial ownership of real estate.

Perhaps the most important application of the police power occurs in the area of zoning. Zoning, whether exercised by a zoning board or commission or an area planning board or commission, determines the uses to which real estate may be put in a particular area. Obviously, the decisions of such boards and commissions have a dramatic impact upon the value of a given piece of real estate.

For example, a 5-acre tract limited to a single-family residence may have a value of $40,000, whereas, if it were zoned for heavy industrial use, it might be worth $200,000. Clearly, the zoning powers of government are very important to anyone involved in the real estate field. Three specific points merit discussion:

1. *The preexisting nonconforming use.* Suppose that a legally constituted zoning board decides that in a particular area only single-family residences with a maximum height of 40 feet will be allowed. Assume further that in the middle of this zone there is already a six-story hotel. Must the hotel be demolished or cease operation? Normally, the answer is no, because it was already in existence and presumably did not violate earlier laws or zoning ordinances. If the zoning ordinance were to require the hotel's demolition, it would be considered an act of condemnation and the owner would be entitled to be paid for the economic loss suffered. Vacant lots in the area, however, would be subject to the ordinance and would not be entitled to compensation for any loss suffered.

2. *The variance.* Even though a large area of a city is zoned for only single-family residential purposes, this fact alone might make it desirable that a convenience shopping center be established which would be a benefit to the residents rather than a detriment. To accomplish that, it is necessary to apply to the appropriate zoning body and request permission to vary the use from the existing zoning ordinance. Normally, this is the result of a public hearing, after proper notice to all nearby property owners whose property values might be affected by the outcome, and a decision by the board or commission to permit or deny the proposed variance.

3. *Rezoning.* It frequently happens that so many violations of existing zoning rules have been permitted to occur (either because residents do not object or governmental agencies are not responsive) that, for all practical purposes, the general usage of the property in the neighborhoods has in fact changed. Typically, this is seen in older neighborhoods which have been zoned for single-family residential usage but have become either multifamily, commercial, or even light industrial in terms of actual usage. When this occurs, it is possible to seek rezoning of the entire area so that remaining single-family residential properties can be sold or used for a purpose which actually is more appropriate.

Real Estate Taxation

It is obviously necessary to generate funds to pay for our governmental system which makes it pos-

sible to have absolute ownership of real estate. We are all familiar with the concept of income taxes, both federal and state. In addition, most states and local governmental units impose a tax upon real estate, including the houses or other improvements located upon the land. These taxes pay for a wide variety of local services: police protection, fire departments, schools, libraries, etc.

Since the purposes of this form of taxation are to provide benefits to the property owner, they are usually based upon the value of the property *(ad valorem)* as appraised or assessed. While this system has some built-in inequities, some arbitrary, easy-to-administer system is necessary to avoid high costs of administration. Under this system all property in a given tax unit is periodically revalued, and the necessary tax rate is applied equally to all properties. Of course, failure to pay such taxes may result in a forced sale (a *tax sale*) to pay the delinquent taxes and to assure that each property pays its fair share of such taxes.

Escheat

The doctrine of escheat has remained part of real property law for centuries. Its basic concept has not changed, but its application has been modified.

Under early English common law, even after the right to inherit real estate was recognized, only close family members could acquire real estate by inheritance. Today, even though individuals leave no legal heirs who have a statutory right to inherit property, they may leave it to others simply by executing a valid will. As a result, the doctrine of escheat is seldom seen in action; however, it does still exist.

Under modern real estate law, the rule that has developed is: If the owner of real estate dies without a valid will *(intestate)* by which he or she disposes of his or her real estate *and* there are no legal heirs entitled to inherit the property under state law, then the real estate escheats to the state in which it is located. That is, the state is a potential "heir" of all owners of real estate and takes their property unless someone else succeeds to its ownership either by virtue of disposition by a valid will or by the state rules of inheritance.

Assessments for Municipal Improvements

Very often improvements are made by municipalities which benefit all property owners in the area and presumably increase the value of their property. Paved streets, sewers, water, sidewalks, and streetlights are among the most common.

The cost of making these improvements is generally charged to the benefited property owners on some sort of pro rata basis: feet of frontage, amount of acreage, etc. As a general rule, the affected property owners are first notified of the proposed improvement, its anticipated cost, and the method of prorating this expense. They then have the opportunity, by majority vote, to decide whether or not they want the improvement. This is not, however, universally true; in more cases than not the improvement is forced upon the property owners because it is essential to the health or safety of all of them—in effect, the police power of government is exercised.

For example, the population density and the soil conditions in a particular subdivision may make it mandatory that city water and sewage disposal facilities be installed because of a threatened water pollution problem. In such a case the property owners may have no choice whatsoever in deciding whether they need or want the proposed improvements. They may nevertheless be compelled to pay for them.

Urban Planning

In recent years, in addition to the well-recognized power to zone areas for particular uses, urban or area planning programs have evolved which also have an important impact on land values. Still another exercise of the police power is exhibited in such planning which may be completely at odds with the planning of the owners of property in the affected areas.

Other Limitations

If all the above limitations on the uses to which individually owned real estate may be put appear to cast some doubt on the concept of absolute or allodial ownership today, then the point has been made. Even without the foregoing restrictions on the use and ownership of one's own property, however, there still remain the classic common-law doctrines of *trespass* and *nuisance* which provide private remedies for adjoining property owners as well as individual property owners.

No detailed discussion of this area of real property law appears necessary in this book; however, it should be known that any owner of real estate is entitled to protect his or her own property from and is restricted from the commission of trespass or nuisance. These two concepts are discussed briefly below.

Trespass

Any property owner is entitled to maintain a civil suit against a neighbor or stranger who enters upon his property without permission. This is true whether the trespass is occasional or continuous, and the law presumes that some damage, which can be measured in dollars, always occurs when there has been a trespass. For example, if a neighbor occasionally trespasses by driving across one's property or does it as a matter of habit, he may be sued for money damages or enjoined (ordered) to refrain from doing so again.

Nuisance

Regardless of what the zoning laws do *not* prohibit, an owner of real estate is entitled to insist that her neighbor refrain from using his property in such a way that it is injurious to her.

For example, even though no law prohibits it, an owner of a residential lot can be sued for damages or prohibited from using the lot as an open trash dump. This concept is so well established in the law that we have evidence of its existence as early as the year 200 B.C. While the doctrine protects the rights of individual property owners, it obviously also restricts their own property rights in the same manner.

In summing up this review of absolute ownership as we recognize it today, it might very well be asked whether or not the concept of ownership of real estate has really changed as we might have first thought when contrasting feudal versus allodial tenure. It is true that the basic character of ownership of real estate has changed, but it is also true that the cost of achieving allodial ownership has required the surrender of many rights which we may have thought of as inherent in the definition of *"ownership."* In the next chapter we consider the *bundle of rights* concept of ownership. In doing so, however, we should keep in mind the foregoing limitations on the rights of ownership.

INTERESTS IN LAND

Estates in Land

An *estate*, as distinguished from a lesser (temporary or limited) interest in land, is defined as ownership. Estates are further divided into freeholds and leaseholds. The essential characteristic in each case is the fact that the owner of a freehold estate or the lessee of a leasehold estate has an estate which gives to him or her the rights of ownership (whether unlimited or limited) as opposed to the simple right to use the property of another for a specific purpose. The important estates in land are listed below and illustrated in Fig. 5-1.

Freehold Estates (Estates for an Indefinite Period of Time)

1. *Fee simple absolute.* The highest and most complete form of ownership known under our law. It includes all rights recognized by law, including the right to create lesser estates or interests; these rights may, however, be subordinated to the rights of other members of society protected by the same law as the property owner, i.e., the owner may not maintain a nuisance, may have property taken for a public purpose, and may be restricted in his or her use for the public benefit, even though he or she owns it absolutely.

2. *Fee tail.* A fee simple absolute estate which is restricted to inheritance by direct descendants of the holder. Used in England at one time, but held to be an unreasonable restraint in almost all states today, it is in fact outlawed by statutes which convert it to a fee simple absolute.

3. *Fee simple determinable.* Sometimes referred to as a *conditional fee,* contains all the elements of the fee simple absolute except that the interest is subject to possible termination in the event that a specified condition is broken. Since the condition may never be broken or the time at which it will be broken cannot be determined at the time the interest is created, it is potentially absolute. When (and if) the condition is broken, the fee simple absolute reverts to its creator, his or her heirs, or whoever else might be named in the deed which created it. An example is:

> I hereby convey (certain property) to the Izaac Walton League of America for so long as the property is used as a conservation club. In the event such use shall cease the property is to go to the State of Michigan for use as a public park.

In this example, since there is no limitation expressed on the scope of the interest being conveyed, it is presumed to be a fee simple absolute; however, the transfer is clearly conditional upon its continued use for a specific purpose. When that condition is broken, the fee simple interest is *determined,* hence the name "fee simple determinable." In practice, the clarity with which such interests are created frequently leaves something to be desired, so that caution should be exercised in dealing with them.

4. *Life estate.* An estate in land which is limited to the lifetime of the holder (or, occasionally, the lifetime of another):

Conventional life estates: A life tenant has legal title and an estate, but rights are limited to the holder's lifetime and are basically the rights to income as opposed to principal while the remainderman or reversioner holds the balance of all rights to the fee. Duties of the life tenant consist basically of the duty to refrain from encroaching upon rights of remainder interests by wasting the principal of the real estate asset but do not involve the duty to insure the property for the remainderman, or to pay taxes beyond income produced by the property, or to pay more than the interest on existing mortgages and liens.

Legal life estates: Created by statute and dependent on the law of the state where the real estate is located. Historically, the most important legal life estates recognized by our law have been *dower* and *curtesy.* Dower is the interest that a wife has in real estate owned by her husband at his death and which was owned by him during the marriage. Curtesy is the interest of the husband in real estate owned by his wife during the marriage. For most of the history of this country this interest has been a life estate in all or part of such real estate (depending upon what other legal heirs survived the deceased owner) but normally not less than one-third. The limitations on the life estate of the surviving spouse were the same as those outlined above for conventional life estates. Coupled with the frequency of such an interest in a fractional share of real estate, the technical rules surrounding the legal life estates of dower and curtesy created inordinate complexity in land titles. In addition, modern probate codes, the homestead exemption, and the popularity of some form of joint ownership between husbands and wives seem to provide adequate protection of each spouse against the irresponsible or unfair dispositions of real estate by the other. As a result many states have completely eliminated dower and curtesy; in other states a statutory substitute has been created which makes the interest of the spouse a fee interest rather than a life estate. Almost all states have modified the interest in some way. Where the traditional legal life estates of dower and curtesy are still recognized, however, the holder of the life estate has the limited rights discussed above under conventional life estates.

Homestead Exemption

The motivation for the interests of dower and curtesy was the protection against disposition of real estate by one spouse without the concurrence of the other. In addition to this protection, there has developed in the United States the protection of the family, at least to the extent of the home, from the rights of creditors of the head of the household acting alone.

The *homestead exemption*, as the name implies, is designed to make the home exempt from creditors' claims incurred solely by the head of the household—traditionally, the husband—without the concurrence of the wife. In the absence of such concurrence, under a typical homestead exemption the homestead may not be reached by creditors, with one generally well-recognized exception—the debt incurred for purchase of the homestead in the first place.

The rules in the many states which recognize the homestead exemption are not uniform, and in many some formal declaration of the claim of the homestead exemption may be necessary to obtain its benefits. In states which recognize the homestead, it does not generally have the status of a true estate in land, but it is rather an exception of the particular property from creditors' claims. There are exceptions to this generalization, and local laws must be consulted.

The extent of property which may be claimed to be exempt as a homestead may vary widely depending on whether the home is a house on a residential lot or whether it is a farm, in which case substantial acreage and the home on it can still qualify for the homestead exemption.

In many states the right is limited by some dollar amount of value which may be claimed under the exemption. Various definitions are also found as to what constitutes a family or household from state to state. Some states have abolished the homestead exemption during a person's lifetime and recognize only a very limited homestead right for the surviving family members. These are frequently referred to as *probate homesteads*.

In view of the widespread recognition of some form of homestead (even though it is very limited in some jurisdictions), the practice of requiring the execution by both spouses of all documents transferring or creating interests in real estate is fortified.

This is true even in states which have liberalized or expanded the rights of married individuals to own real estate individually.

Leasehold Estates

Rights to the possession of real estate granted by its owner for a specified period or periods of time are called leasehold estates. They are discussed in greater detail in Chapter 9, but briefly, the types of leases include:

1. Estates for years which create rights in the tenant in the estate for a definite period of time.
2. Estates from year to year (or period to period) which are distinguished from estates for years in that they continue for successive periods until one of the parties gives notice of termination.
3. Estates at will which give the tenant the right to possession with the consent of the landlord, but the term of the estate is indefinite and either party may terminate it by giving of proper notice.
4. Estates at sufferance which arise when the tenant comes into possession of the real property lawfully and then, after his or her rights have expired, holds possession of the premises without the consent of the person entitled to possession.

OTHER INTERESTS, LESS THAN ESTATES

Easements

The fact that estates in land, as discussed above, are recognized creates the power in the holder of an estate to create lesser interests in the land. The important interests which can be created are easements, licenses, and profits. An easement is a nonpossessory interest in land owned by another, i.e., a right in the land of another which is less than the right of possession. It is an intangible right and creates no right of ownership of the land itself. Easements are categorized, and the categories must be understood because they are a benefit to the holder and represent a restriction on the rights of the owner of the property subject to the easement and therefore affect the value of each property either upward or downward. The major categories recognized today are discussed below and illustrated in Fig. 5-2.

Easements Appurtenant

The owner of one piece of land has the right to certain uses of or restrictions on the use of the land owned by another under an easement appurtenant. When such an easement exists, the two pieces of land are called:

Dominant tenement: The land benefited by the easement.

Servient tenement: The land encumbered by the easement or subject to the easement.

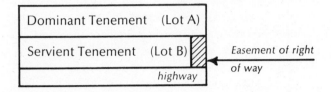

Most important is the fact that an easement appurtenant is not a mere personal right but is a right which attaches to the dominant tenement and passes with it to a new owner, *and* the servient tenement is encumbered or restricted by the easement when it is transferred to a new owner. Such an easement is said to "run with the land." This has the effect of enhancing the value of the dominant tenement and of decreasing the value of the servient tenement.

An easement appurtenant may be either affirmative or negative. That is, the servient tenement may be subject to the use of some of it by the owner of the dominant tenement (such as a right of way), or the owner of the servient tenement may be required to refrain from making certain uses of land for the benefit of the owner of the dominant tenement (such as restrictions on building structures which cut off light and air to the dominant tenement).

Easements in Gross

The right of the holder of an easement to use the property of another is created by an easement in gross. It is not related to the ownership of any adjoining property. An important easement of this type is the *commercial* easement in gross which is assignable and can be both conveyed and inherited. It is important for people active in the real estate business to be aware of this type of easement which in the past has been typically used for railroad rights of way, pipelines, and electrical and telephone lines. Such easements often pose serious title problems, because of the scope of the easement which may have been granted by an earlier owner of the property. Two common problems as discussed below illustrate the importance of the commercial easement in gross.

Electrical power line easements in the early days of the expansion of the power industry were often broadly written. It is not unusual to find in an abstract a grant of a commercial easement in gross in such terms as "the right to install electrical power lines over, under, or through any and all property which I presently own in Any County, This State." At the time that such easements were taken, much of the land to which they applied was farmland, but with the growth of the cities, this same land today may be either residential, industrial, or commercial. The existence of such broad easements is frequently a problem, simply because holders of the easement have the legal right to place power lines wherever they choose. Obviously, the owner of the property cannot build under such conditions, because he or she may incur a loss if the easement is later used. The practical solution to this problem is to obtain from the utility involved a deed which releases from the easement land which is not actually needed and limits what may be used.

Railroad rights of way which have been abandoned by companies which have long since gone out of business pose a similar problem. Generally, case law provides that upon abandonment of such a commercial easement in gross, the easement is terminated and the owner of the fee simple then owns the property free of the encumbrance of the easement. Unfortunately, the creation of such easements was often done by deeds which are ambiguous to the point that it is sometimes difficult to tell whether they were intended to convey a fee interest or an easement. Occasionally, the owner of such an easement has made a conveyance of it under the false notion that he or she owns the fee. Clearing the title to such a piece of property and proving ownership can be difficult and costly.

PROFITS

A profit in land is the right to take part of the soil or produce of land owned by someone else. The term includes the right to take soil, gravel, minerals, oil, gas, and the like, from the land of another. It is not an important interest in land today but, like the overly broad commercial easement in gross, its existence in the chain of title to a piece of real estate can be very troublesome. The legal term used to express this concept is *profit a pendre.*

LICENSES

A license is the privilege to go upon land owned by another for a specific purpose. It does not create in the holder of the license any interest in the land of the owner. It may be revoked at any time by the land owner without rendering him liable for damages to the holder of the license *unless* it was created by contract and the license was paid for by the licensee. Two simple examples illustrate the difference:

1. A permits B to hunt upon A's property without receiving payment from B. A may revoke this license at any time.
2. A stadium sells a ticket to a ballgame to a fan which grants him a license to be present for a sports event. The stadium arbitrarily ejects the fan before the event is complete. The fan has paid for the license and is entitled to be paid for this breach of contract.

ENCROACHMENTS

It frequently occurs that the buildings on one piece of real estate extend beyond the property line between two adjoining owners. In most cases this is the result of an honest error as opposed to deliberate action. Regardless of the intent of the encroaching party, however, the resulting problem can be quite troublesome. In some cases the encroaching party may acquire title to part of the adjoining property under the doctrine of adverse possession (discussed later), but in other cases he or she may be compelled to remove the encroaching structure. In either situation it may take expensive litigation to resolve the matter.

SECURITY INTERESTS

While discussed more fully in Chapter 11, it should be noted here that the use of mortgages or deeds of trust as financing devices creates potentially possessory interests in real estate in both the lender and the borrower.

A mortgagee's rights to the property are dependent upon a default by the mortgagor (the borrower) and are governed by local law. In general, when there is a default by the borrower, the mortgagee (lender) has the right to bring legal proceedings to compel the sale of the property in order to satisfy the debt.

By the same token, in most states there is a limited period of time within which the defaulting borrower may redeem the property, the *equity of redemption*, which usually permits him or her to remain in possession of the property for a limited period of time in order to pay the debt and thus redeem the property from the possibility of foreclosure.

Mechanic's Liens

While there is no uniformity among the various states and no such interest existed under common law, by statutes throughout the country some protection is afforded to the contractor who improves the property of another. He or she is generally entitled to file a lien upon the property for the value of the work materials furnished if unpaid at the end of the time period specified by local statute, and the lien may be enforced by an action quite similar to a mortgage foreclosure. Ultimately the property may even be sold to pay such claims.

The charts which immediately follow summarize the interests discussed above.

LEGAL RIGHTS IN LAND

INTERESTS WHICH ARE ESTATES IN LAND

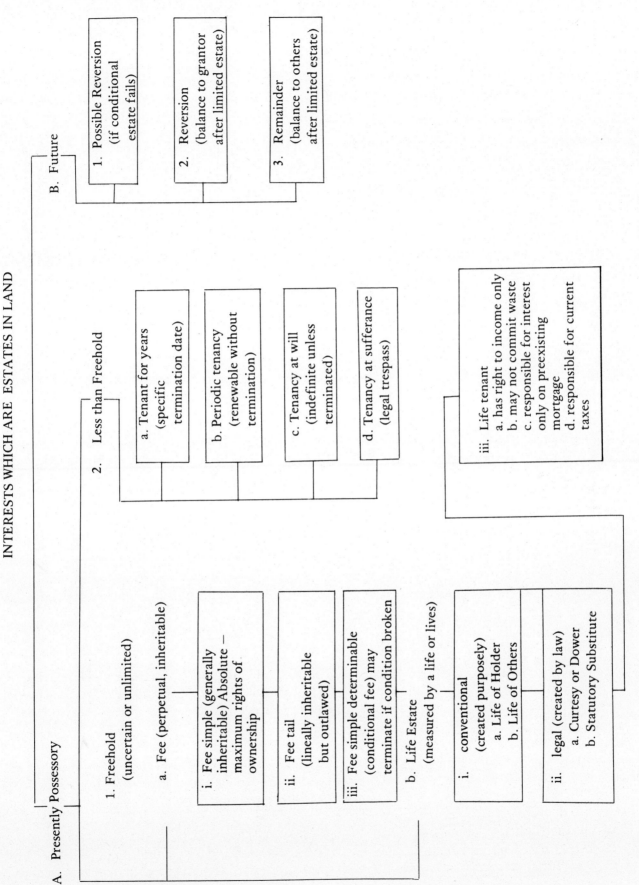

A. Presently Possessory

1. Freehold (uncertain or unlimited)

a. Fee (perpetual, inheritable)

i. Fee simple (generally inheritable) Absolute — maximum rights of ownership

ii. Fee tail (lineally inheritable but outlawed)

iii. Fee simple determinable (conditional fee) may terminate if condition broken

b. Life Estate (measured by a life or lives)

i. conventional (created purposely)
   a. Life of Holder
   b. Life of Others

ii. legal (created by law)
   a. Curtesy or Dower
   b. Statutory Substitute

2. Less than Freehold

a. Tenant for years (specific termination date)

b. Periodic tenancy (renewable without termination)

c. Tenancy at will (indefinite unless terminated)

d. Tenancy at sufferance (legal trespass)

iii. Life tenant
   a. has right to income only
   b. may not commit waste
   c. responsible for interest only on preexisting mortgage
   d. responsible for current taxes

B. Future

1. Possible Reversion (if conditional estate fails)

2. Reversion (balance to grantor after limited estate)

3. Remainder (balance to others after limited estate)

FIG. 5-1—Legal rights in land. A topical breakdown of the various interests which are estates in land.

INTERESTS WHICH ARE LESS THAN ESTATES

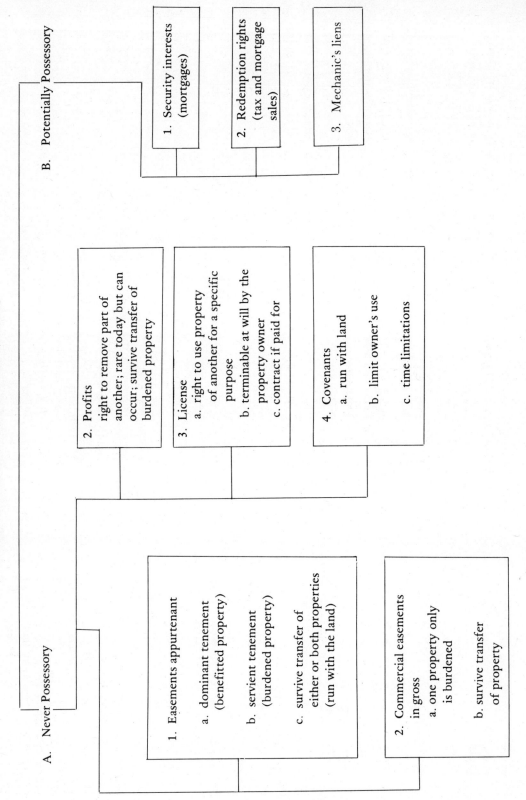

A. Never Possessory

1. Easements appurtenant

   a. dominant tenement (benefitted property)

   b. servient tenement (burdened property)

   c. survive transfer of either or both properties (run with the land)

2. Commercial easements in gross

   a. one property only is burdened

   b. survive transfer of property

2. Profits

   right to remove part of another; rare today but can occur; survive transfer of burdened property

3. License

   a. right to use property of another for a specific purpose

   b. terminable at will by the property owner

   c. contract if paid for

4. Covenants

   a. run with land

   b. limit owner's use

   c. time limitations

B. Potentially Possessory

1. Security interests (mortgages)

2. Redemption rights (tax and mortgage sales)

3. Mechanic's liens

FIG. 5-2—Interests which are less than estates. A topical breakdown of interests in land which are less than estates.

Ownership interests

	Total
Fee simple	50
Fee simple determinable	48
Life estate	51
Dower	23
Curtesy	12
Homestead	42

Forms of ownership

	Total
Individual	50
Joint tenancy	47
Tenancy in common	50
Community property	8
Tenancy by the entirety	27
Trust	51
Condominium	51

FIG. 5-3—Summary of interests recognized.

SUGGESTED READINGS

(See the appropriate chapter in the following books.)

Basye, Paul E. *Patton on Land Titles*, 2nd ed. St. Paul, Minn.: West Publishing Company, 1957.

Cartwright, John M. *Handbook of Real Estate*. Englewood Cliffs, N.J.: Prentice-Hall, Inc., 1969.

Kratovil, Robert. *Real Estate Law*, 6th ed. Englewood Cliffs, N.J.: Prentice-Hall, Inc., 1974.

Lusk, Harold and William B. French. *Law of the Real Estate Business*, 3rd ed. Homewood, Ill.: Richard D. Irwin, Inc., 1975.

MacDonald, James B. *Abstract and Title Practice*, 2nd ed. St. Paul, Minn.: West Publishing Company, 1958.

REVIEW QUESTIONS

1. The most complete form of ownership our law recognizes today is the

   (A) easement
   (B) fee simple conditional
   (C) life estate
   (D) fee simple absolute

2. The holder of a life estate measured by his or her own life

   I. has a duty to refrain from committing waste to the property
   II. is entitled to the net income the property produces

   (A) I only   (C) both I and II
   (B) II only   (D) neither I nor II

3. The owner of a fee simple absolute interest in real estate can

   I. create a life estate in A with the remainder in fee to B
   II. sell the property on a land contract to A and mortgage it to B

   (A) I only   (C) both I and II
   (B) II only   (D) neither I nor II

4. To protect against an encroachment, the purchaser should obtain

   (A) an abstract   (C) a survey
   (B) an appraisal   (D) none of the above

5. Fee simple ownership for the individual is held under

   (A) the feudal system of tenure
   (B) the allodial system of tenure
   (C) both A and B
   (D) neither A nor B

6. If a person dies intestate with no heirs with the capacity to inherit his or her real property, the property will

   (A) be foreclosed and sold at public auction
   (B) be condemned and sold under eminent domain
   (C) escheat to the state
   (D) none of the above

7. A deed to "A for life, to B for life, then to C in fee" creates in C the following interest:

   (A) a determinable fee   (C) a reversion
   (B) a remainder   (D) a fee tail

8. A legal life estate

   I. is created by statute
   II. can be a dower interest

   (A) I only   (C) both I and II
   (B) II only   (D) neither I nor II

9. A license is

   (A) less than an estate in land
   (B) assignable
   (C) inheritable
   (D) none of the above

10. The duration of a life estate is

    (A) 20 years
    (B) any fixed period
    (C) 99 years at a maximum
    (D) the life of a person

11. The power of government to absolutely take private property for a public purpose is called

I. eminent domain
II. escheat

(A) I only   (C) both I and II
(B) II only   (D) neither I nor II

12. Even though an area is zoned for single-family dwelling units only, some commercial use may be permitted if

    I. the commercial use was a preexisting non-conforming use
    II. a variance is authorized by the zoning board for a new nonconforming use

    (A) I only   (C) both I and II
    (B) II only   (D) neither I nor II

13. When the owner of real estate erects improvements on his or her property which extend over onto adjoining property, there exists a(an)

    (A) license   (C) nuisance
    (B) profit   (D) encroachment

14. In order to protect the family from the financial irresponsibility of the head of the household most states provide some form of relief from creditors called

    (A) credit insurance
    (B) homestead exemption
    (C) moratorium on all debt repayment
    (D) low interest rate debt consolidation loans

15. The right to enter upon the property of another and to take from it sand, gravel, or the like, is called a

    (A) trespass   (C) license
    (B) nuisance   (D) profit a pendre

16. An easement of light and air which restricts the building of structures on one lot in favor of another lot is

    I. a negative easement
    II. an easement appurtenant

    (A) I only   (C) both I and II
    (B) II only   (D) neither I nor II

17. A mortgagee's interest in the mortgaged property is

    (A) presently possessory
    (B) a freehold estate
    (C) potentially possessory
    (D) none of the above

18. The key element in recognizing an estate in land is

    I. the right to the exclusive possession of it
    II. the mere fact of possession

    (A) I only   (C) both I and II
    (B) II only   (D) neither I nor II

19. Freehold estates in land include

    (A) fee simple absolute
    (B) determinable fee
    (C) life estate
    (D) all of the above

20. A true easement appurtenant

    I. involves two pieces of property, one of which is benefited and the other burdened by it
    II. is extinguished when either piece of property is sold to a third party

    (A) I only   (C) both I and II
    (B) II only   (D) neither I nor II

Chapter 6
Ownership of Real Property

VOCABULARY

You will find it important to have a complete working knowledge of the following words and concepts found in the text or the glossary.

accretion
alluvion
bundle of rights
community property
condominium
cooperatives
fixtures

Horizontal Property Act
joint tenancy with right of
    survivorship
real estate
real property
regime
severalty

subdivision
survivorship
tenancy in common
tenancy by the entireties
trade fixtures
undivided interest
unities of time, title, possession,
    and interest

OWNERSHIP

BROADLY defined, ownership of real property is the holding of rights or interests in real estate. But certain clear-cut limitations exist which are briefly reviewed here. As mentioned previously, exercise of the exclusive right of ownership of private property is subject to at least four reservations placed on it by the state, and ownership is therefore never complete in the absolute sense of the word. Additionally, certain other reservations may be placed on property from both the public and private sectors. Salespersons must be aware of these reservations, since they significantly affect the use, marketability, and value of real property. These reservations in review are:

1. *Public control through the use of*
   a. Eminent domain: The right of government to take private property for public use
   b. Property taxation: Taxes imposed on owners of property (nonpayment of which can affect the ownership thereof)
   c. Zoning and building codes which limit the use of property
   d. Escheat: The reversion of private property to the state at the death of an owner without heirs.

2. *Nonpublic (private) controls*
   a. Deed restriction: Limitations placed upon the use of real property in the deed by which ownership is transferred
   b. Easement: The right to make limited use of real property owned by another without taking actual possession of it
   c. Profit: The right to take part of the soil or produce of land owned by someone else
   d. License: The privilege of going upon the land of another for some specific purpose.

Real Property

We have earlier alluded to the fact that there is a technical difference between the terms "real estate" and "real property." At this point it is important to reemphasize and amplify upon this difference. As noted earlier, the term *real estate* includes land and all things permanently attached to it. It is in this connection that the law of *fixtures* comes into play. Simply stated, items of personal property which would otherwise be governed by the laws relating to personal property ownership undergo a change when they are permanently attached to land. From that point on they are governed by the laws of real estate ownership and are no longer considered personal property. The obvious example is the construction of a residence upon a plot of land. Because it is intended that the various components are to be permanently attached to the land they become, legally, a part of the land. In short, they become what are known in the law as *fixtures* in order to distinguish them from the land itself. This transformation in character is important to recognize because from the time of permanent attachment to the land, ownership of the land includes ownership of the fixtures. Once permanently attached they may not be removed without following the laws relating to ownership of the underlying real estate. The lumber, nails, windows, furnace, etc., which were personal property before they became essential elements of a house become real estate by virtue of the permanent attachment intended. One clear-cut exception to the law of fixtures exists in the area of *trade fixtures* used in commercial or industrial real estate. When trade fixtures such as commercial refrigerators necessary to the business purposes for which the real estate is used are attached, they do not become part of the real estate and ownership of them does not pass with the transfer of ownership of the underlying real estate. Such trade fixtures can generally be severed and removed provided their removal does no structural damage to the building.

The term "real property" is more comprehensive than the term "real estate" because it includes the legal rights which flow from the ownership of real estate or land and attachments. These ownership rights may be all-inclusive in the fee simple absolute or may be very limited in, for example, a short-term lease. In an effort to sort out the various elements of "real property" or ownership of real estate, the law has come to recognize the bundle of rights concept of ownership discussed below.

Bundle of Rights

The concept of ownership of real estate as the ownership or control of a *bundle of rights* has already been suggested. Now that we have seen the wide variety of interests or rights which can exist in the same piece of real estate the concept may be clearer. For example, if an individual holds the fee simple absolute title to a piece of real estate and there are no outstanding mortgages, life estates, leases, licenses, or any of the other lesser interests we have discussed, it should be clear that the individual owns all the possible rights our law recognizes. He or she owns the whole "bundle," and as a result has the power to "unbundle" this package of rights as desired (within the limitations imposed by our legal system). To illustrate, the owner

of the fee simple can create any or all of the following interests in the same property:

1. Mortgage the property to secure a debt
2. Grant an easement of right of way to a neighbor
3. Give a license to another to hunt upon the property
4. Convey a life estate in the property to A and retain the reversionary interest or convey the remainder to B
5. Lease the property to a tenant for a period of years.

By so doing the owner "unbundles" the bundle of rights which constituted the fee simple absolute originally held. Of course, the order in which these transfers are made makes a great deal of difference, since the owner can never transfer more than he or she owns. For example, should he mortgage the property and then convey a life estate to A with the remainder to B, the interests of A and B would be subject to the rights of the mortgagee. By the same token, if the property were leased prior to conveyance, the rights of the tenant would not be cut off and the conveyance would be subject to the tenant's rights.

Ownership in Severalty

Even though the term "severalty" seems to indicate that some form of ownership is shared by two or more persons, such is not the case. The term "severalty" is a technical term meaning *sole* ownership. Therefore when we say that A owns an estate in land "in severalty" we mean that he owns it outright and in his own name alone without a co-owner.

Ownership by Co-ownership

Joint tenancies, tenancies by the entirety, and tenancies in common are common forms of co-ownership of real estate. Co-ownership of personal property, such as joint bank accounts, joint ownership of stocks, etc., is familiar to most people. Co-ownership of real estate, however, is much more sophisticated in that several different forms are recognized, and the rights of the co-owners and their creditors vary depending upon the type of co-ownership which exists. Co-ownership of real estate may be chosen by purchasers for a wide variety of reasons: to control the transfer from one owner to the other upon the death of one, to permit the pooling of resources by several individuals to buy real estate as a unit that no one of them could afford individually, etc. It must also be recognized, however, that co-ownership can result even without the co-owners intending it to happen. Frequently, this occurs as the result of inheriting real estate from a person who dies intestate. Also, the form of co-ownership may change by law, as it does when the tenancy by the entireties of a husband and wife is converted upon divorce to a tenancy in common. The owner of real estate may not really be aware of the types or consequences of co-ownership with another; however, one active in the real estate business must be aware of the differences between the forms of co-ownership and the rights of a co-owner of real estate.

The three common forms of co-ownership widely recognized are: (1) tenancy in common, (2) joint tenancy with right of survivorship, and (3) tenancy by the entirety. Each of these is discussed in detail in this section, but first certain basic differences and characteristics should be pointed out.

1. *Joint tenancy/joint tenancies.* Because of the preference of our law for tenancy in common, joint tenancies must be specifically created; that is, a deed must clearly express the intent to create a joint tenancy; the co-owners in a joint tenancy each own an undivided interest in the whole parcel which is *necessarily* equal; when one joint tenant dies, his or her interest terminates and passes automatically to the surviving tenant or tenants.

2. *Tenancy in common* is preferred generally by statute; tenants in common each own an undivided fractional interest in the real estate which is *not necessarily* equal; there is no survivorship feature.

3. *Tenancy by the entireties* is created *automatically* by a conveyance to a husband and wife; to avoid this tenancy the deed must express a contrary intent; the marriage owns the property and neither the husband nor the wife can convey any part of it individually, nor can either one individually encumber the property; by law, the survivor succeeds to the entire title upon the death of either one.

The important characteristics of these tenancies are considered below.

Joint Tenancy

1. The creation of a joint tenancy never happens by accident. The four unities of time, title, possession, and interest must exist *plus* the clearly expressed intent to create it before a joint tenancy with right of survivorship can arise. By the four *unities* we mean that each joint tenant must have acquired an equal *interest,* at the same *time,* with the same degree of ownership or *title,* as well as the same right to *possession* of the whole property in question. It is only then, along with the intent to create it, that the true joint tenancy with the right of survivorship can arise. The highly technical common-law rules for its creation are met in a deceptively simple fashion by a deed which simply recites that the real estate is "hereby conveyed to A,B,&C, equally, as joint tenants with right of survivorship and not as tenants in common." From such a conveyance the four unities, because they are not limited in any fashion, will necessarily follow.

2. The right of survivorship which exists under a true joint tenancy is one of its most important features. Upon the death of one joint tenant, the entire interest passes to the surviving tenant(s). The deceased tenant has no estate to survive him or her, and the property does not go to his or her heirs. However, when one tenant severs the joint tenancy by sale of his or her interest to another, the buyer takes the seller's share as a tenant in common. The buyer does not purchase the right of survivorship.

Tenancy in Common

1. The creation of a tenancy in common frequently happens by accident, the "accident" of dying without a will and leaving several descendants. It also happens by the "accident" of a divorce in which no definite arrangements are made in connection with real estate held by the husband and wife during the marriage as tenants by the entirety.

2. The tenants in such a tenancy each own an undivided interest in the real estate, which can be sold, mortgaged, or left to heirs without affecting the tenancy or the rights of other tenants.

3. The tenant in common has an interest which can be legally terminated individually by partition. This is an absolute right of such a tenant and in an appropriate action the court will divide the property physically or sell it and divide the proceeds. The partition of real estate held as tenants in common results when one or more of them desires to have the undivided interest of each tenant specifically segregated and set off in severalty. Where the property can be easily divided on a fair and equitable basis the court will order such division, and the tenants will thereafter own their shares (which are now *divided* as opposed to *undivided*) individually and free of

the rights of the other tenants to possession and use of the whole property. It frequently happens, however, that an equitable physical segregation of shares is not practicable; in such cases the court will order a sale of the whole property and will then order a division of the net proceeds of sale among the tenants in accordance with the fractional interests owned by each of them prior to the sale.

Tenancy by the Entireties

1. In states which recognize it, this tenancy arises from any conveyance to a man and woman who are husband and wife at the time of conveyance. It is generally not necessary that the deed express an intent to create it (as is necessary for a joint tenancy).

2. The tenancy by the entireties, while it has some of the characteristics of a joint tenancy, is not a joint tenancy in all respects. The most important difference is that neither the husband nor the wife may sell his or her interest, encumber it, or sever the tenancy (except, of course, by divorce), nor can either alone enter into a binding contract to sell or mortgage the property. The rules of tenancy by the entirety are so strict and unyielding that property cannot even be reached by creditors of either the husband or wife alone.

3. Termination: (a) By sale: Termination of tenancy by the entireties can be achieved via sale if (and only if) both husband and wife consent to the sale. (b) By death: Upon the death of either the husband or the wife, the survivor succeeds to the entire interest held by the entirety. To this extent, this tenancy is similar to the joint tenancy. (c) By divorce: In the event of the divorce of tenants by the entirety, the real estate is subsequently held by them as tenants in common. This frequently poses serious problems for the real estate broker or salesperson dealing with the property subsequent to the divorce, because all the rules applicable to tenancy in common apply. That is, each divorced spouse owns an undivided half of the property without a legal partition proceeding. The problem is particularly acute in connection with residential property. (The chart summarizes these three forms of co-ownership.)

CONDOMINIUMS

Creation of a Condominium

A true condominium is foreign to common law. The estate interests in land which we recognize and the varieties of co-ownership discussed are simply not flexible enough to permit the creation of a true condominium. Consequently it was necessary to create one by statute as a recognized form of tenancy in real estate. This was done by passage of Horizontal Property Acts. The basic steps are spelled out in detail in the statute which describes the creation of a condominium as a declaration of "horizontal property regime" on the property.

The declaration of a horizontal property regime on certain real estate must be made by all the owners who have an interest in the property. The declaration must include a detailed description of the land, a complete description of the proposed building, and a set of floor plans indicating the dimensions of each "apartment." In addition the declaration must describe the common areas which may be used by all the apartment owners, as well as other limited common areas. It must list the percentage of common area ownership belonging to each apartment owner. This percentage of ownership is the basis upon which each owner will be entitled to vote on matters relating to the whole property. By-laws must accompany the declaration to specify the procedure for election of officers and property management. The declaration and related plans, by-laws, and other documents must then be recorded with the recorder of the county in which the land is situated. The declaration is not valid unless it has been properly recorded. That is, the steps described below must be taken to impose a different set of rules for ownership of the property. This new set of rules is called *regime*.

The establishment of a condominium is similar in many respects to the formation of a corporation. It requires the establishment of by-laws and voting rights for each apartment owner in proportion to the percentage or his or her ownership. The establishment of a condominium is not absolutely irrevocable, and the property on which a horizontal property regime has been declared may be removed from the regime. The statute specifically provides for such removal; however, such removal requires that all the apartment owners (and their creditors) consent to it. When the property is removed from the regime, the apartment owners become tenants in common and their share is determined by the percentage of the common areas and facilities of the condominium they previously owned.

Rights of the Apartment Owners

Each apartment owner in the condominium has the fee simple title to his or her property and the

CO-OWNERSHIP

	Joint Tenancy With Rights of Survivorship	Tenancy In Common	Tenancy By The Entireties
Characteristics	Always equal interests a. all have right to possession of the whole property b. passes by contract of all tenants only c. will have no effect on share of decedent; it passes to surviving tenants automatically	Not necessarily equal a. exception: possession of the whole is equal b. each interest inheritable c. will may pass title to share owned by decedent	One combined ownership a. marriage owns property b. death does not change ownership c. divorce converts to T/C
Creation	Must be created on purpose a. one deed b. equal interests c. survivorship must be specified d. four unities of time, title, possession, and interest must exist	May happen accidentally a. inheritance by more than one heir b. purchase in shares which may or may not be equal c. failure to specify JTWRS	Deed to H & W creates a. fact of marriage critical b. description as H & W not necessary c. other tenancy to avoid entireties must be specified
Rights	Survivorship is key characteristic	Each tenant has an undivided share in the whole property	Only marriage has rights
Termination	Terminated by sale of one a. unities destroyed b. new owner is T/C	Sale by one does not terminate a. buyer succeeds to interest b. substitution is result	One member can't sell a. can't be dealt with by one b. H not W's agent or vice versa c. Both H & W must sign deed, mortgages, leases, etc.
Creditors	Creditor's rights a. debtor's rights limited b. creditor can become T/C	Creditor's rights a. debtor's rights survive him b. creditor can become T/C	Creditor's rights a. must be joint debt of H & W b. creditor cannot levy against H or W singly

FIG. 6–1—Co-ownership. The characteristics, creation, rights, and termination of the most common forms of co-ownership.

right to exclusive ownership and possession of the apartment. The owner also has an undivided interest in common areas and facilities. Since the owner has, by statute, an estate in land, the Horizontal Property Act gives him or her the right to deal with it as with any other estate. It can be sold, mortgaged, given away, or left to heirs. In addition, the act specifically provides that any form of co-ownership of land recognized by state law may be applied to the apartment. Therefore the ownership of the apartment may be held in tenancy by the entirety, joint tenancy with right of survivorship, or tenancy in common.

The rights and duties of each apartment owner concerning property operation and maintenance are in the by-laws of the condominium. They may be tailored as desired; however, the act specifies that certain minimums must be covered. These include: provisions for the election of a board of directors, a method of perpetuating the board, its duties, and compensation; meetings of apartment owners and how they are to be called; the necessary quorum for such a meeting; the election of a president, secretary, and treasurer; maintenance and repair of common areas; the method of collection of expenses paid by apartment owners; hiring of maintenance personnel; the method of adopting and amending administrative sales to govern the operation and use of the common areas and facilities; and the percentage of votes required to amend the by-laws. These constitute the essential by-laws. The rights of apartment owners in common areas and provisions for maintenance and repair of the condominium may be complex and may change from time to time in accordance with the by-laws. Therefore a buyer of such an interest should be thoroughly familiar with the by-laws before purchasing an apartment.

Rights of Creditors of the Apartment Owner

Each apartment is an estate characterized as real property. The owner therefore has a distinct interest which may be used as security for a loan, and has the power to mortgage this interest to secure a creditor. In the event that foreclosure of a mortgage is made necessary by a default on the part of the apartment owner, the purchaser at the foreclosure sale does not become liable for any common expenses or assessments against the apartment which occurred prior to his or her acquisition. Of course, the purchaser is liable for expenses arising after acquisition. If the defaulting owner is in arrears in paying his or her share of expenses and

assessments, this unpaid share becomes the liability of all of the apartment owners in common. The new purchaser will be liable also, but only for his or her proportionate share. Consider the following example:

A, who is one of 40 apartment owners, defaults on his mortgage which is foreclosed, and his apartment is sold. At the time of the sale he also owed $400 in expenses and assessments. The purchaser at the foreclosure sale does not become liable for the entire $400 but only for his share which is $10. Each of the other 39 owners also becomes liable for $10.

Real estate taxes and assessments by local government units are assessed against each apartment individually. That is, each apartment is taxed as though it were a separate parcel of real estate and is carried separately on the tax rolls. In the event of delinquency, the lien of taxes and assessments can only be enforced against the apartment to which it applies.

Any charges or assessments levied against an apartment by the association of apartment owners becomes a lien against the apartment. This lien is given priority over all other liens except those for taxes and any unpaid first mortgages on record. It is enforceable as though it were a mechanic's lien, and by the same procedure any purchaser of the apartment takes title subject to any liens which exist, including the lien for unpaid charges or assessments by the apartment owners' association. Such a purchaser is entitled to a statement from the association which specifies the amounts due at the time he or she takes title, and cannot be held liable for an amount in excess of the amount on that statement. This statement must be obtained separately, because it is not a matter of public record, as is the case with real estate taxes and the existence of a mortgage. By accepting a conveyance the purchaser becomes jointly liable with the sellers for all unpaid charges. As a practical matter, the new owner will have to pay them in order to remove the lien against the apartment. The purchaser is of course entitled to a contribution from the seller, but it is far better to have the statement in advance of the closing and handle the matter at the closing as a deduction from the purchase price.

COOPERATIVES

Creation of the Cooperative

Cooperative apartment projects are difficult to define in specific terms because they can be created in a variety of ways with substantially different rights and duties created in the apartment owners. The characteristic which distinguishes a cooperative apartment building is the fact that the owner-builders usually construct the building for the purpose of occupancy by themselves rather than for the purpose of investment seeking a profit. Even this generalization is subject to frequent exceptions when portions of the building are rented out to commercial users. While the typical vehicle used for construction and operation is usually a corporation, it is not essential to use this form of ownership. The various forms of co-ownership discussed above could be used, as could a partnership or trust. Even when a corporation is used, the obligations of the stockholders may differ quite drastically from those of stockholders in a normal corporation. Typically, the owner of a share of corporate stock has limited his or her risk to the purchase price. Usually, the stock certificate is freely transferable and can be bought or sold readily, assuming there is an active market for it. Stock in a corporation formed for the purpose of building and owning a cooperative may provide for the possibility of further assessment and may have severe restrictions upon its transferability.

Regardless of the vehicle used to build, own, and operate the building, there is another step in the acquisition of an apartment in a cooperative building: a long-term lease on an apartment from the building corporation to its shareholder. Ownership of the stock certificate does not normally carry with it the right to occupy a particular apartment in the building. The right to possession of an apartment and the conditions which surround it are covered by the lease agreement (called a *proprietary lease*) which usually has terms that would otherwise appear extraordinary. The lease is generally for a relatively long term (and may have to be in order to satisfy the lender who is financing the construction of the building) and usually has severe restrictions on its assignability and on subletting. Typically the sale (or, more accurately, the assignment) of the tenant's rights under the lease is subject to the prior approval of the corporation-landlord. This degree of control protects the other owner-tenants. It requires tenants to be financially responsible, because there is a definite risk that all tenants may be assessed to help pay the share of expenses left by a defaulting tenant.

Rights of Owners

The rights of the owner of a co-op apartment are found in the stock certificate (which defines the extent to which the owner can affect the management of the property) and his or her lease (which describes in detail what rights the owner has acquired and what obligations he or she has assumed). These rights and duties vary from one project to another. The typical terms of the lease can perhaps be best illustrated by considering the advantages and disadvantages the apartment owner will have. (The individual is of course an owner of stock and a tenant under a lease, which gives a limited estate in land; but he or she is not, legally at least, an owner of the real estate itself.) Some of the advantages offered by the cooperative apartment are:

1. The lease is typically long-term, because the tenant has actually paid for the cost of the apartment he or she is occupying. This feature assures the tenants of continuous occupancy.

2. The long-term nature of the lease permits the tenant a wide degree of latitude with regard to modifications made to the apartment. The tenant is allowed to customize the apartment, a practical matter since he or she will have use of it for an extended period.

3. The apartment owner pays no rent as such. Instead, a monthly assessment is paid, representing costs of maintenance, real estate taxes, and debt service on the mortgage (unless there is none). No landlord profit is involved. This cost may be offset by any rental income earned from whatever commercial space is included in the building.

4. The tenancy in a cooperative apartment tends to be stable. Not only is this dictated by the investment of each apartment owner but it can also be controlled at least to a limited extent by the tenants. This is true because they are also shareholders of the corporation which owns and manages the building. The tenants can, by exercising their rights as shareholders, control the policies established with regard to the acceptability of new tenants.

To have the advantages outlined above sacrifices must be made by the tenants in the cooperative project. Some of the more important of these are:

1. The apartment owner does not in fact own real estate, and even though the lease creates an estate under state law, he or she does not have an interest acceptable to lenders as loan security. The result is that the tenant must pay cash

for his interest or must borrow on personal credit or by using the cooperative stock as security, with the interest being higher as a result.

2. The degree of control exercised by the operating corporation which benefits the tenants, as noted earlier, creates serious problems of marketability of an individual tenant's interest. The tenant may have difficulty in finding an acceptable replacement and may not be able to sublet his or her apartment.

3. Occupancy expense is unpredictable from year to year. Since it is not rent but a sharing of common maintenance costs as well as the cost of maintenance of the individual apartment, this expense varies from year to year and tends to increase from year to year.

4. There is always the danger that some tenants will default in their obligations to maintain the building. The other tenants will then be called upon to bear proportionate shares of this unpaid expense. While they may ultimately recover it upon a sale of the defaulting tenant's interest or by suing that person, during the interim the other tenants will have this burden.

It should be clear that both the advantages and disadvantages of cooperative ownership depend upon the degree of success of the project. The overall management of the building, its reputation for quality in the community, and its ability to retain its value in the marketplace all have an impact upon the value of the interest of the individual apartment tenant-owner. Because of the complexity of the arrangement, careful investigation is required before undertaking such a project or buying into one that is already in existence.

Rights of Creditors

The typical cooperative apartment venture includes a corporation which owns and operates the building. The shareholders are the tenants not by virtue of their stock ownership but by virtue of their leases of individual apartments. As a result the creditor relationships to be considered here are twofold: creditors of the corporation itself and creditors of the individual tenants.

Creditors of the corporation have the normal rights they would have against other corporations. Typically, the major creditor of the corporation is the mortgage lender who has financed the construction of the project and holds the long-term mortgage loan on the property. It is clear that the mortgage lender will be looking to the leases and their quality as the underlying security for the repayment of the loan. Technically, of course, the lender's security is a mortgage on the whole project, and it is for this reason that individual apartment purchasers have difficulty in obtaining additional long-term financing. The rights of the lender who finances the project are the same as those of any mortgagee and are considered in detail later.

Creditors of the individual tenant-owners have a rather unusual and awkward interest to look to for security. As a result they do not normally lend money on the strength of the individual owner-tenant's interest. This fact makes financing difficult to obtain for these individuals to purchase their ownership interests. In the event that a creditor must look to the individual's interest in the cooperative apartment, he or she must take it subject to all of its limitations and may even have to contribute to the continuing expense of ownership of the interest.

SUGGESTED READINGS

(See the appropriate chapter in the following books.)

Brown, Robert Kevin. *Essentials of Real Estate.* Englewood Cliffs, N.J.: Prentice-Hall, Inc., 1970.

Kratovil, Robert. *Real Estate Law*, 6th ed. Englewood Cliffs, N.J.: Prentice-Hall, Inc., 1974.

Lusk, Harold F. and William B. French. *Law of the Real Estate Business*, 3rd ed. Homewood, Ill.: Richard D. Irwin, Inc., 1975.

Ring, Alfred A. and Jerome Dasso. *Real Estate Principles and Practices*, 8th ed. Englewood Cliffs, N.J.: Prentice-Hall, Inc., 1977.

Weimer, Arthur M., Homer Hoyt, and George F. Bloom. *Real Estate*, 7th ed. New York: The Ronald Press Company, 1978.

REVIEW QUESTIONS

1. To transfer title to property owned in a true joint tenancy

    I. the signature of any tenant is sufficient since all true joint tenants are agents of the others
    II. all tenants must join in the transfer

    (A) I only
    (B) II only
    (C) both I and II
    (D) neither I nor II

2. If tenants in common cannot agree upon the division of their interests, they can request the court to

    (A) condemn the property
    (B) escheat the property
    (C) partition the property
    (D) none of the above

3. Under tenancy in common ownership, each owner

    I. has undivided interest in the property
    II. has unity of title

    (A) I only
    (B) II only
    (C) both I and II
    (D) neither I nor II

4. Among the limitations on absolute ownership of land as we know it today is

    I. the power of eminent domain under which private property can be taken for public use
    II. the police power, under which the use to which private property may be put is controlled by governmental agencies

    (A) I only
    (B) II only
    (C) both I and II
    (D) neither I nor II

5. To mortgage property held in a tenancy by the entireties it is necessary to have the mortgage signed by

    I. the husband only, because he is head of the household under law
    II. the husband and wife both, because neither one alone has the power to deal with the property

    (A) I only
    (B) II only
    (C) both I and II
    (D) neither I nor II

6. When two individuals own real estate as joint tenants with right of survivorship,

    I. each has the right to use of the entire property for life
    II. the share of each descends to his or her heirs at death

    (A) I only
    (B) II only
    (C) both I and II
    (D) neither I nor II

7. Tenants in common

    (A) always have identical shares in the property
    (B) all have the right to use of the whole property
    (C) lose their interest at death to the surviving tenants
    (D) have interests which may not be reached by creditors

8. Under tenancy by the entireties, the interest of the deceased spouse

    I. goes to the surviving spouse by law
    II. passes by will or intestate succession to descendants or heirs

    (A) I only
    (B) II only
    (C) both I and II
    (D) neither I nor II

9. When owners of a tenancy by the entireties are divorced, they

    (A) become tenants at sufferance
    (B) become joint tenants with right of survivorship
    (C) become tenants in common
    (D) remain tenants by the entireties

10. The owner of an apartment in a condominium may

    I. sell the interest to another
    II. mortgage the interest to secure a debt

    (A) I only
    (B) II only
    (C) both I and II
    (D) neither I nor II

11. Creditors of an owner of an undivided interest as a tenant in common

    I.   may pursue that interest and force the sale of it to apply against the debt
    II. cannot pursue that interest unless the debt is that of all the tenants

    (A) I only   (C) both I and II
    (B) II only   (D) neither I nor II

12. When an individual owns property in his or her name alone, he or she has

    (A) a sole estate
    (B) an estate in severalty
    (C) an estate in common
    (D) none of the above

13. The apartment owner-tenant in a cooperative apartment building

    I.   may not be evicted for failure to pay assessments when due
    II. pays no rent because he or she owns shares in the cooperative

    (A) I only   (C) both I and II
    (B) II only   (D) neither I nor II

14. The interests of tenants in common

    (A) are always equal   (C) may be equal
    (B) are never equal   (D) both (A) and (C)

15. When the interest of one tenant under a true joint tenancy is transferred to a third party, the new owner

    I.   succeeds to all the rights of the original tenant including the right of survivorship
    II. becomes a tenant in common with the other joint tenants

    (A) I only   (C) both I and II
    (B) II only   (D) neither I nor II

16. The establishment of a condominium

    I.   is accomplished by a series of deeds to various owners establishing fee simple interests in their respective apartments

    II. must be done in strict accordance with local statutes, because the condominium is not recognized under common law

    (A) I only   (C) both I and II
    (B) II only   (D) neither I nor II

17. To transfer ownership by deed it is necessary to obtain the signatures of all the owners when they hold title as

    (A) joint tenants with right of survivorship
    (B) tenants in common
    (C) tenants by the entireties
    (D) all of the above

18. When the owner of a condominium apartment fails to pay local real estate taxes,

    I.   the delinquent taxes become a lien on all the other apartments on a pro rata basis
    II. the tax lien applies only against the apartment of the defaulting taxpayer

    (A) I only   (C) both I and II
    (B) II only   (D) neither I nor II

19. The creation of a true joint tenancy

    I.   frequently happens by accident, such as inheritance in equal shares
    II. must be intentionally created and include the unities of time, title, possession, and interest

    (A) I only   (C) both I and II
    (B) II only   (D) neither I nor II

20. Under the bundle of rights concept, the owner of the fee simple has the power to

    I.   create a life estate in A with a remainder interest in B
    II. mortgage the property and then sell the fee simple subject to the mortgage

    (A) I only   (C) both I and II
    (B) II only   (D) neither I nor II

Chapter 7

Transfer of Real Property

VOCABULARY

You will find it important to have a complete working knowledge of the following words and concepts found in the text or the glossary.

acceptance of deed
acknowledgment
administrator
adverse possession
conveyance
corporate deeds
decedent's estate
delivery of deed
descent of real estate
devise of real estate

execution of deed
executor
fiduciary deed
general warranty deed
grantee
grantor
intestate
judicial deed
legal capacity
minors' deeds

partnership deeds
quiet title proceedings
quitclaim deed
recital of consideration
special warranty deed
testate
void deeds
voidable deeds
will

TRANSFERS OF OWNERSHIP

Now that we have studied the various interests in land recognized by modern law and the various forms of ownership by which these interests may be held, it is appropriate to discuss the various methods by which ownership can be transferred. In addition we will take up the question of the quality of each ownership interest transferred and how this quality is ascertained.

One rule must be kept in mind throughout the chapter: An owner of real estate cannot transfer more than he or she owns. If, for example, the owner of real estate has only a conditional fee, he may not transfer, by sale or otherwise, more than the conditional fee. This is true even though he may execute a deed which warrants or guarantees that he owns the fee simple absolute or that the degree of ownership is *assured* by an attorney's opinion or title insurance.

By far the most common method of transferring ownership of real estate is the deed, which is the culmination of a contract to sell the real estate; but generalizations in this area are dangerous. Title

(ownership) of real estate may be transferred in other ways as well: inheritance, right of survivorship, mortgage or trust deed foreclosure, or even by a legal form of theft—adverse possession. Even if the property is *conveyed* (transferred by deed), there are several types of deeds which are commonly used, ranging from the *general warranty deed*, which includes guarantees of ownership and the quality of the title, down to the *quitclaim deed*, which transfers only what the seller has—from the fee simple absolute down to nothing. It is therefore quite important that the real estate businessperson be aware of the wide range of "products" and their "guarantees" which he or she is selling.

TYPES OF DEEDS

The General Warranty Deed

Most propositions call for execution by the seller of a general warranty deed. As the name indicates, the deed contains several warranties and covenants on the part of the seller. In many states, a so-called short form warranty deed is used. This deed includes the word "warrant," which in effect makes it a general warranty deed. In executing such a deed, the grantor (seller) makes the following warranties:

1. The grantor possesses an indefeasible fee simple title to the real estate. (A fee simple title is the highest title under the law, involving full and complete rights of ownership to the exclusion of all others.)
2. That there are no encumbrances against the real estate other than those specifically expressed in the deed.
3. That the grantee (purchaser) shall have quiet enjoyment of the real estate *and* that the grantor (seller) will warrant and defend the title to the real estate against any and all claims, from the beginning of time to the execution of the deed of conveyance.

Where there is an unbroken chain of general warranty deeds, each grantor in the chain may be liable to all subsequent grantees for any claim arising prior to the date of conveyance by that particular grantor. When the chain is broken by the execution of a deed other than a general warranty, subsequent grantees may not look for redress to any grantors who may have executed warranty deeds prior to the date when the chain was broken.

The Special Warranty Deed

The special warranty deed is a deed of limited warranty, and the warranty contained therein is limited to any claim arising out of the period of ownership of the grantor executing the deed. Thus, if an owner held title from January 1 to October 31, the owner would be executing a special warranty deed which warrants only against any claims arising out of that particular period. The owner's warranty would not extend back to the beginning of time.

The Quitclaim Deed

The quitclaim deed is a deed of release. It conveys without warranty whatever right, claim, title, or interest the grantor may have in the real estate conveyed. If the grantor has a fee simple title, the quitclaim deed will convey the same. If the grantor has no title, nothing will be conveyed by the quitclaim deed.

Quitclaim deeds are generally used to convey lesser interests in real estate, such as life estates or minor interests, and also are widely used to correct prior conveyances which have been improperly executed.

Judicial Deeds

Many titles to real estate are conveyed by judicial deeds which, as the name implies, are deeds executed pursuant to a court order. Examples of such conveyances are deeds of executors and administrators, guardians, and trustees; sheriff's deeds executed by virtue of foreclosure proceedings; and commissioner's deeds executed in partition proceedings. Such deeds, assuming that the judicial proceedings in the particular case have been legally pursued, are effectual to convey good title to real estate, but without warranties.

BASIC REQUIREMENTS OF A VALID DEED

When there is a transfer of title to real estate by *conveyance* (by a deed from the seller to the buyer), certain minimum legal requirements must be met to make the transfer of ownership effective.

The Grantor Must Have Legal Capacity

The grantor (seller or owner) must have the legal power to make a deed or transfer of ownership. The matter of legal capacity varies with the nature of the grantor. That is, the grantor may be an individual, a partnership, a trust, a corporation, a unit of government, or any other legally recognizable entity. The requirements of legal capacity are different for each one.

1. *Individuals* must be competent in terms of age and mental capacity. Generally, the age of 18 is the rule in determining whether or not an individual is a minor. If one is under the age of majority, his or her deed will be voidable and may be set aside when the age of majority is reached. The same is true of those who are *in fact* mentally incompetent to make a deed. In both cases, there is a presumption of legal capacity which may be set aside by proof of incapacity. Nevertheless, such deeds are not *void* (meaningless) at the outset; there must be proof of incompetency and affirmative action taken to set such deeds aside. There is therefore an element of risk in dealing with young persons and those who appear to be unstable at the time of the transaction.

   A different rule applies when the grantor has been *adjudged* incompetent by a local court. In such cases, the finding of incompetency is a matter of record, and all persons are bound to know what the public records reveal even though they do not in fact have this knowledge. Once there has been a formal adjudication finding that an individual is incompetent and a *guardian* (or conservator) is appointed by the court, deeds signed by the individual become *void* and no transfer of title can result. Only the legally appointed guardian can deal with the property of the incompetent.

2. Under the Uniform Partnership Act (UPA), *partnerships* may hold title to real estate in the partnership name, and any *general* partner may bind the partnership by a deed of real estate owned by it. Proof of the fact that the person executing the deed is a general partner should be shown. An attorney's opinion should always be sought before accepting the validity of a partner's deed.

3. *Corporations* are legal entities solely by virtue of statutes which permit their formation and permit them to conduct business, including the ownership and sale of real estate. A corporation may only conduct business through its authorized officers, and evidence of the authority of particular officers to convey the corporation's real estate is of crucial importance in determining the validity of the deed. This is especially true when the deed transfers real estate which represents *all* or substantially all of the assets of the corporation. In such cases it may be necessary to show not only that the board of directors has authorized the sale but also that a majority (or more in some states) of the *shareholders* have approved the transaction. There is obviously no substitute for legal counsel in such situations.

Government units have no inherent power or capacity to sell real estate, and they must therefore follow very strictly the statutes and necessary public proceedings to permit the sale of public property. In the absence of statutory authority, exercised in accordance with very technical requirements, the deeds of government units may be absolutely void. Again, legal counsel should pass upon the question of the validity of such deeds.

5. *Fiduciaries* (trustees, administrators, executors, agents, guardians) have severe limitations upon their authority to convey title to real estate. These limitations may be imposed by the agreements under which they operate or the courts who appoint them. A safe rule to follow is: whenever *anyone* purports to convey title to real estate which the records show is not owned by him or her, then strict proof of the authority to sell it must be produced. That is, there must be positive evidence of this authority either in the form of a written and recorded agreement or a court order; there must be *actual* (as opposed to apparent) authority, and there must be recorded (or recordable) evidence of such authority. The limitations on the authority of fiduciaries can hardly be overemphasized.

The Grantee(s) Must Be Named With Reasonable Certainty

More than just good business practice dictates that the grantees (buyers) be named with accuracy. It is also very important to the effectiveness of the recording systems by which the validity of titles to land is determined. Recording systems are discussed in detail in Chapter 8; however, the accuracy of the names of the grantees is important to the indexing systems used to make public records accessible and useful.

It is also important that the grantee(s) be further described in terms of the form of ownership which will result. For example, in most states it is essential to create clearly a joint tenancy with right of survivorship. Careful attorneys do not rely upon shortcuts in this area and do not use such phrases as "to John and Mary Jones, jointly." Instead the deed would read, "to John Jones and Mary Jones, as joint tenants with right of survivorship and not as tenants in common." Of course, if the creation of a tenancy in common were desired, it would be so stated and the fractional share of each of the grantees would be indicated: "to John Jones and Mary Jones as tenants in common in the following shares: as to an undivided one-third to John Jones and as to the remaining two-thirds to Mary Jones."

Care must be exercised in this portion of the deed whenever something less than the entire fee simple absolute is being transferred. The presumption is that the entire fee is being conveyed (or whatever other interest is being transferred), unless the deed clearly states a contrary intent. If the owner of the fee simple wishes, for example, to reserve a life estate to himself, the deed must clearly say so: ". . . convey and warrant all of my right, title, and interest in and to (the property described) reserving, however, to myself a life estate in said property. . . ."

In some states a deed to two people who are husband and wife automatically creates a tenancy by the entireties even though the parties are not identified as husband and wife. Once again a careful attorney describes the relationship and may even go further and specify the tenancy intended. Such a deed might read, "to John Jones and Mary Jones, husband and wife, as tenants by the entirety."

It should be noted in connection with the naming of the grantees who are today's buyers that they may be tomorrow's sellers. At that point the certainty of their identity and their interests in the real estate becomes important in determining the quality of their title and the effectiveness of their deed to pass good title.

There Must Be Words of Conveyance

Without some clearly expressed intent to transfer the ownership of real estate a deed may be ineffective in accomplishing its purpose or may at best create ambiguity as to just what its purpose is. This portion of the deed should clearly state any limitations or reservations that are intended. The standard form deeds in use today utilize terms such as "convey and warrant" in general warranty deeds, "convey and specially warrant" when a deed of limited warranty is intended, or "release and quitclaim" when no warranties of any kind are intended.

There Must Be a Recital of Consideration

As noted in the section on general contract law, the matter of consideration is a technical requirement. Most deeds do not show the full purchase price paid, so that it will remain private and not be made a matter of public record. To meet the requirement of consideration, the deed must include a statement to the effect that there was paid "$10 and other valuable consideration, the receipt of which is hereby acknowledged by the seller." One might argue that the signing and delivery of a deed to valuable real estate would not be done by the grantor without payment and that it is unnecessary to include such a statement. Its inclusion is, however, crucial as evidence that there was payment in order to bring suit against the seller upon any warranties made in the deed. It is far easier to introduce the deed as evidence than to attempt to prove payment by other evidence.

The use of a nominal sum in the recital of consideration satisfies the technical requirement of contract law that there be *some* consideration. It is not necessary to the validity of the deed that the amount expressed be the *fair value* of the property.

The Real Estate Being Conveyed Must Be Accurately Described

To identify correctly the property being conveyed, it must be described with a reasonable degree of accuracy. Great emphasis is placed on precision in the preparation of legal descriptions, and it is usually the job of an expert, the surveyor. It is

beyond the scope of this book to provide detailed coverage of this highly technical area; however, certain fundamentals are discussed below.

Almost all of the United States has been subjected to a survey by the federal government, the so-called rectangular survey. Even though there are various ways to describe real estate, they depend in almost all cases upon the rectangular survey to establish a starting point, some specific point on the surface of the earth. Additional material on this subject can be found in Chapter 8.

The Deed Must Be Executed By the Grantor(s)

To transfer title by a deed effectively, it must be *executed* by the grantor. That is, it must be signed by the grantor with the intent that ownership of some interest in land be transferred to the grantee. Of course, in the event that there are co-owners of the property and the agreement is to transfer the interests of each of them, all the owners must sign the deed. Married couples generally hold title to their residential property in some form of joint tenancy with right of survivorship. Clearly, when dealing with such property both the husband and wife must sign the deed, so that their entire interest will be effectively conveyed. Even where it is apparent that only one of them owns the property, in many states it is still necessary that both the husband and wife sign the deed to cut off the rights of dower and curtesy or their statutory substitutes. Even in states which have in recent years eliminated the necessity of the other spouse signing deeds to property owned by only one spouse, it is still required by careful practitioners. The rule in practice should be to require the signatures of both husband and wife on any deed to property owned by only one of them, unless legal counsel is sought and a contrary opinion obtained.

The execution of a deed to property owned by a partnership can be accomplished by any general partner's signature on the deed. It is of course necessary to verify that the signer is a general partner, and an attorney's approval of the effectiveness of the execution should be obtained. Much the same is true for the execution of deeds by a corporation, and a resolution of the board of directors which authorizes certain officers to execute deeds should be obtained. Again, an attorney's opinion should be sought.

The Deed Should Be Acknowledged

The term "should," as opposed to "must," is used here because in most states acknowledgment of the deed is not required to make the deed effective between the parties. As a practical matter, however, without acknowledgment, the deed cannot be recorded so as to provide notice of the transfer to the general public. The acknowledgment of a deed is more than a mere witnessing of the signatures, and only certain publicly appointed officials (usually notaries public) can take acknowledgments. *The acknowledgment of a deed is the appearance before the notary public by the signers and their declaration to the notary that their signatures were free and willful.* The notary then countersigns and seals the deed after stating upon it the above facts. Typically, this statement reads as follows:

State of _____

County of _____

_____, 19 _____

Then and there personally appeared John Jones and Mary Jones, signers and sealers of the foregoing instrument and they acknowledge the same to be their free act and deed before me. (Notary Public) _____

When the deed has been properly acknowledged, it is then eligible for recording in the public records, which constitutes notice of its contents to all persons subsequently dealing with the property conveyed.

The Deed Must Be Delivered To and Accepted By the Grantee(s)

The final steps necessary to make the deed legally operate to transfer the title to real estate are its delivery by the grantor to the grantee and the grantee's acceptance of it. In the majority of cases these steps are easily recognized and are quite straightforward. They are accomplished by a simple exchange of the deed for payment of the purchase price. Acceptance of the deed by the grantee is presumed in all but the most unusual circumstances. It is important, however, to recognize that delivery of the deed is crucial to its legal effectiveness and that it occasionally is not clear and in still other instances is legally ineffective. A few illustrations are:

1. The intent of the grantor to transfer title by delivery of the deed is a crucial element. Therefore, when the deed is handed to the grantee (or his or her lawyer, broker, or other agent) for the purpose of inspecting it for adequacy and accuracy, this does not constitute delivery even though the grantee or his or her agent has physical possession of the deed.

2. If the deed is placed in escrow, delivered to an independent third party, to be held until all the conditions of the sale are met (the most significant condition being *payment*) there again has been no legally effective delivery because the escrowee is not the agent of either party. Even though the grantor has parted with the deed, there has been no delivery because of the missing element of intent.

3. At the same time, delivery and acceptance of the deed can be accomplished by delivery to a third party who is the agent of the grantee. Frequently, this is either the grantee's attorney, lender, or even his broker.

4. Frequently, ill-advised individuals execute deeds to real estate to various relatives and place them in a safe deposit box so that they will be found after the death of the grantor. This is usually done as a will substitute to avoid the expense of probate. It is almost universally found that these deeds are ineffective for lack of delivery because they never left the control of the grantors; and of course the grantees could hardly accept them if they did not even know of their existence.

As a general rule, the fact that a deed has been executed, acknowledged, and recorded (as discussed below) creates a *presumption* that the deed has been delivered and accepted. This presumption may be rebutted upon proof that neither delivery nor acceptance was actually intended by the party so claiming; however, legal action would be required to set the record straight.

TRANSFER BY DESCENT OR DEVISE

While real estate is most commonly transferred between owners by a deed which is the result of a negotiated contract of sale, it also frequently happens that the title to real estate is transferred as a result of the owner's death. It should be recalled that certain interests in land do not survive the owner at death (for example, the life estate measured by his or her life, the license which is personal to the holder, and, as we shall see in Chapter 9, the tenant in a tenancy at will), and there is therefore no transfer of these interests. They expire when the owner expires. We should also recall that certain other interests pass by law to survivors: joint tenancy with right of survivorship and tenancy by the entireties. In each of the above categories of interest in land, expiration of the interest or its transfer are automatic and the question of inheritance is not involved. Generally speaking, all other interests in land (along with some obligations attached to ownership) descend or survive the death of the owner.

For example, if the decedent owned the entire fee simple absolute, this interest is theoretically perpetual and survives the death of the owner. In this chapter we review the general rules which apply to interests which are inheritable, what happens to them at the owner's death, and how they may be sold during the administration of his or her estate.

Alternative Dispositions of Real Property at Death

There are two basic methods by which title to real estate may be transferred at the death of the owner: If he or she makes a valid will which disposes of the real estate, it will go to the *devisees* (those named as recipients by the will) or, if there is no will, the property will *descend* to the legal heirs in accordance with local state laws of descent and distribution. It is frequently said that, if an individual makes no will, the state makes one for him. Generally speaking, these statutes result in inheritance of real estate by immediate family members (spouse, children, grandchildren) if they survive and, if they do not survive, by other close family members (parents, brothers, sisters) and, failing their survival, by more remote relatives. In the event that a valid will is executed and proven to be valid (admitted to probate), it is important to note that the right to make a will is really a privilege and is subject to limitations imposed by state law which create some restrictions on the individual's freedom to leave his property to whomever he chooses. As a general rule, these limitations favor the surviving spouse and children to whom the decedent had a legal obligation of support. As might be expected, the decedent's creditors (including death tax collectors) occupy a favored position under the maxim: A person must be just before he or she may be generous. With this truism in mind, let us outline some of the limitations which must be kept in mind in dealing with the decedent's real estate.

Limitations on Title Transfer

Generally the title to any interest in land vests immediately in *heirs* or *devisees* under the will. At the moment of death the decedent's interest passes immediately to the legal heirs if the person dies intestate (without a will), or to the named devisees

if he or she dies testate (with a valid will). While this is legally and theoretically true, this transfer of title is not final. It is subject to limitations; the limitations on the title passed to heirs or devisees are:

1. The transfer is subject to the right of the personal representative (executor or administrator) to possession of the real estate. The personal representative not only has the right to possession of the decedent's real estate but frequently has a positive duty to take possession of the property for the benefit of the estate. This possession may be constructive rather than actual when there is a tenant in possession under a valid lease, for example. In such cases the personal representative of the estate is entitled to receive the rents. The rights of the personal representative are not personal rights but may be exercised by him or her only for the benefit of the estate of the decedent.

2. The title which passes to the heirs or devisees is also subject to any and all valid claims against the decedent. The primary purpose of estate administration is to protect creditors. That is, an individual's debts must be paid before gifts can be made after death to heirs or beneficiaries of his or her will. The benefits which may flow to the heirs or devisees are therefore subject to the possibility that creditors' claims may compel sale of the property and application of the proceeds to payment of the decedent's debts.

3. The title of the heirs or devisees is also subject to the surviving spouse's rights to take his or her statutory share of the estate. The surviving spouse is generally entitled by statute to a specified share of the deceased spouse's estate. This share depends upon who else survives the decedent but is usually at least one-third of the net estate. The surviving spouse is normally entitled to this share absolutely as a matter of right, and this right may not be defeated by the decedent's will which makes a different disposition of the estate.

4. The title of the heirs or devisees is subject to all liens and encumbrances on the real estate which exist at the time of the decedent's death. As a result any mortgages or other liens pass with the property. The decedent's will may specify that debts are to be paid from some other source, such as other assets of the estate; but if the will makes no such provision, then title passes subject to all liens and encumbrances.

5. When real estate is devised by will to named

devisees, there is always the possibility that the will may be attacked. The validity of a will may be questioned for several reasons. A claim may be made that the decedent was mentally incompetent to make a will at the time it was executed; or that he or she was subjected to fraud, duress, or undue influence at the time of its execution; or even that it was not executed and witnessed according to law. If any of these grounds can be sustained, the will will be set aside and will be ineffective to pass title to the named devisees. Finding a will invalid normally results in an intestate situation in which only the legal heirs can take any interest in the decedent's real estate and other property. Any such attack is more likely when the decedent makes a property disposition to persons outside the immediate family.

6. The title of the heirs and devisees is subject to a death tax, imposed upon the decedent's estate as a result of the transfer of ownership. This estate and inheritance tax lien attaches to all property, including real estate, owned by the decedent at the time of death. The death tax lien represents a serious defect in the title of the heirs or devisees until the tax liability is determined and discharged by the estate's personal representative.

It is apparent from the foregoing limitations during administration of the estate that the title of the heirs and devisees is tenuous at best and requires further action to make it saleable. This action is the final decree of distribution by which the court having jurisdiction over the estate enters its judgment that all debts, taxes, and expenses of administration have been paid, that the claims of all parties have been settled or the time for filing them has passed without action being taken to perfect them, and that title is confirmed in the heirs or devisees.

The quality of the decedent's title at the time of death generally is unaffected by estate administration. Certainly, it is not improved by virtue of his or her death. The title which descends to the heirs or devisees is only as good as the title the decedent had during his or her lifetime. Since the passage of title through a decedent's estate is essentially a gift, no guarantee or warranty is made by the personal representative. In the absence of directions to do so in the will, liens or encumbrances on the property are not required to be cleared by the personal representative. In the event that they are not cleared during administration of the estate the heirs or devisees take the real estate subject to them. However, typical probate codes allow the personal representative to begin a quiet title action during administration to clear defects or adverse claims to the title. It may be necessary to do this if the property is to be sold during administration, since a buyer is entitled to insist upon a merchantable title. Heirs and devisees are not entitled to a merchantable title, because they are not parting with consideration; they are receiving a gift and take it with whatever defects exist.

Purchases From Decedent's Estate

The general public frequently assumes that the personal representative of a decedent's estate has complete authority to sell any of the decedent's assets, including his or her real estate. This is frequently not the case. With regard to real estate in particular, the personal representative must find authority from one of two sources: the will itself or the court having jurisdiction over the estate. Each of these sources can be looked to when there is a valid will but, when the decedent dies without a will, only the court can be looked to for the necessary authority.

When there is clear-cut authority in the will, the legally appointed executor may proceed to sell the decedent's real estate without a court order so long as he or she stays within any limitations included in the will. Even though the executor has clear-cut authority (or even directions) in the will to sell real estate, he or she can either rely upon that authority or seek a court order to sell the property. Many lawyers do not rely upon an authority given in the will when they represent the executor. It is far safer for the executor to obtain a court order authorizing the sale of the real estate and be protected by that court order from later claims that he or she failed to follow the terms in the will.

When there is no will, the personal representative (the administrator) has no alternative but to seek a court order to authorize sale of the property. The administrator cannot merely desire to sell the property. Typical probate codes spell out certain conditions under which the sale of real estate may be approved and ordered by the court. These include: (1) to pay debts, taxes, and expenses of administration; (2) to make an equitable and fair distribution of the estate; and (3) for convenience in making ultimate distribution. Unless the administrator can show that one or more of these reasons exists for sale of the decedent's real estate, the court will not authorize the sale.

When court authority is sought for the real estate

sale, either by the administrator of an intestate estate or by the executor under a will who either has no authority to sell or elects not to rely upon it, the procedure which must be followed is cumbersome and usually time-consuming. The essential steps are:

1. Before authority is sought to sell it, the property must be appraised and inventoried. The appraisal is incorporated into a formal inventory signed by the appraisers and the personal representative and filed with the court.

2. When the personal representative's petition for authority to sell is filed, the court sets a hearing date on which to decide the question and orders notice be given to interested parties allowing them the opportunity to appear and contest the matter. In the event that all interested parties agree to the sale proposed by the personal representative, they may waive this notice and the matter can be heard immediately. The petition spells out the proposed basis for the property sale. The significance of the appraisal and inventory becomes apparent at this point. If the sale is to be a private sale, the usual negotiated transaction, the sales price may not be less than the appraised value. If, however, the sale is to be a public sale, formally advertised and in strict accordance with the statutes, the sales price must be the minimum established by law.

3. Once the personal representative has the necessary authority from the court, he or she may enter into a contract to sell, subject to the court's approval, within the limits of his or her authority. The personal representative may list the property with a broker or attempt to sell it personally. As an officer of the court the personal representative need not be a licensed broker or salesperson. When a sale has been negotiated, he or she must file a further document with the court called a *report of sale* along with the proposed deed. The report of sale states that the personal representative has successfully negotiated a sale in accordance with the court's order and requests an order approving the report of sale and also that the deed itself be approved by the judge. The report of sale also indicates the amount of commission to be paid to the broker who sold the property if one is employed, so that the court's order will clearly authorize payment of this commission. Assuming that the transaction is approved, the court will enter an order approving the report of sale and the proposed deed. At this point the personal repre-

sentative is in a position to complete the closing of the sale. It is not unusual for a careful personal representative to wait until the closing has been partially completed and "the money is on the table" before obtaining the order approving the report of sale and the approval of the deed.

The foregoing procedure can be time-consuming, particularly if it is not possible to obtain waivers of notice of the hearing on the petition for authority to sell. More importantly, if the statutes are strictly followed, there are several undesirable consequences:

1. The appraisal and inventory are a matter of public record and, in some communities, are published in local papers as a news item. The availability of this information tends to establish the best price at which the property can be sold and makes it difficult for the personal representative to obtain a more favorable price.

2. Until the court enters its order authorizing the sale, the personal representative does not have final authority even to enter into an unconditional listing contract. Since this order is entered after the appraisal and inventory, the broker is also hampered in his or her efforts to obtain a favorable sale because of the public nature of the court's records.

A solution to the above problems requires the personal representative to obtain approval to delay the filing of the appraisal and inventory from the court. At the same time the listing broker must be willing to work under a listing contract, recognizing the fact that court approval of any sale will ultimately be required before he or she can earn a commission. When these steps can be accomplished prior to any sales effort, the listing price can be established on a more business-like basis rather than be dictated by the appraisal. If, in addition, waivers of notice of the hearing on the petition to sell can be obtained, it is not impossible to accomplish all the above steps requiring court action in a very short time. This preserves the confidential nature of the price-appraisal relationship and makes it possible to obtain the most favorable price for the real estate.

Limitations on the Deed

There are certain important limitations on sales of real property by a personal representative. It is important for persons in real estate to recognize these limitations whether they represent the estate which is the seller or, more importantly, the buyer.

The form of deed given by the personal representative of an estate is usually specified by local probate law. The typical words in such a deed are:

AB, as Executor of the last will of CD (or AB as Administrator of the estate of CD), by order of the _____ Court of _____ County, State of _____, entered in order book _____, on the records of said court, on page __, for and in consideration of the sum of $_____, conveys to EF the following real estate, to wit: (insert legal description)

The important point to be noted about this form of deed is that it contains no warranties. It is in effect a quitclaim deed. Because the administration of a decedent's estate is not designed to improve the quality of title to the property, the lack of warranties is especially significant. In all purchases from estates it is important that the quality of the title be carefully examined (or insured) and the technical steps required to sell property from an estate be complied with.

Competent legal counsel should be consulted in connection with purchases of real estate from a decedent's estate. Even though an attorney may represent the personal representative of the estate, the buyer should not expect the estate's attorney to represent his or her interests. To do so would create a conflict of interest for the estate's attorney. The estate's attorney is obligated to represent the estate to the best of his or her ability and cannot be expected to represent the buyer in the same transaction. The buyer's attorney inspects the necessary papers leading up to the sale to verify that they are in proper order and that the personal representative does in fact have the necessary authority to sell the property. In view of the lack of warranties in the personal representative's deed (and the fact that they might be meaningless even if they were made), his or her authority should be clearly ascertained before giving value for the deed. It is usually unnecessary to record all the documents (other than the deed), because the estate proceedings are a permanent record and the final decree shows that the estate was ultimately settled without objections. Where the real estate is located in a county other than the county of administration, however, the personal representative must record the final decree in the county in which the real estate is located.

TRANSFER OF OWNERSHIP BY ADVERSE POSSESSION

The doctrine of adverse possession is an antique of the Middle Ages that continues even today to be very useful. In a later discussion of proof of ownership by establishing an unbroken chain of title, it will be noted that, prior to the advent of recording systems, it was essential that the owner of real estate carefully preserve each and every document that evidenced claim of ownership to land. Inevitably, an important document would be lost, such as the deed to the individual who was in possession and claimed ownership. When the time came for that owner to sell the real estate, he or she was of course unable to prove ownership because the deed was lost. To solve this problem, the common law developed the doctrine of *adverse possession.*

In its simplest terms, the doctrine provided that, if the purported owner had been in complete, absolute possession of the property, with an obvious claim of ownership, for a very lengthy period of time and could prove these essential points, the court would conclude that he or she was in *fact* the owner even though he or she lacked the necessary documentary evidence to prove it. In its earliest days this doctrine, which was much more technical than the foregoing statement indicates, resulted from the necessity for establishing legal ownership to real estate without the possibility of litigation long after the actual facts could be shown by testimony or other evidence. A typical rule was that if the owner had been in actual possession which was open and notorious (obvious), exclusive (unshared), continuous, and uninterrupted, and with the claim of right of ownership for 21 years, then this individual became the owner of the legal title. When there was no recording system, communications were slow at best, and surveys were poor or not even available. The practicality of this method of acquiring title and its need were obvious, and the doctrine continued to be important in the early years of the development of the United States.

Early Use in the United States

When the United States was first settled, the doctrine of adverse possession continued to be important in establishing titles to real estate, even though the theory of the lost deed became irrelevant because of the development of recording systems under which the deed, even though lost, was unnecessary to prove legal title. The doctrine remained viable and important because large tracts of land might be owned by an individual who did not even know the boundaries of his property. Frequently, through a mistake or otherwise, one individual might take possession of another's property, improve it, or otherwise utilize it, openly and notoriously, for many years with no objection by the true legal owner. The doctrine of adverse possession found a new use: to settle disputes regarding legal title to such land. Title could be established by adverse possession on the theory that, if the true owner did not oppose the claim for a very lengthy period, then he or she lost the right to assert a claim of ownership.

As noted earlier the typical length of time of possession required to maintain a claim of ownership by adverse possession was 21 years. The justification for this "legalized stealing" of another's real estate was (and still is) that, if the true owner chose to take no action for such a long period of time, the law would not help him or her to regain lost ownership. This is consistent with the basic policy expressed in statutes of limitations which apply in many areas other than real estate: There must be an end to the possibility of litigation. There is a very practical reason for this rule: The matter of preserving evidence for such a lengthy period, as well as the lack of memory of witnesses (or even the lack of surviving witnesses at all) and the accuracy of such old evidence, all make any legal determination highly questionable. The doctrine is still recognized and useful in establishing the ownership of real estate, although the length of time has been modified in many jurisdictions so that 10 years is more common than 21 years in view of the increased efficiency of communications and the general shortening of statutes of limitations. Whenever the doctrine is relied upon to establish title to real estate, legal counsel should be consulted.

Modern Use in the United States

Today, the lack of vacant land, the ease of communications, and the fact that property values have increased so that owners are less likely to ignore their interests in real estate, have resulted in far less reliance upon the doctrine of adverse possession to establish the right of ownership of real estate. Nevertheless, adverse possession remains an important part of real estate law in the correction of boundaries between adjoining properties. It is frequently relied upon by surveyors and title insurance examiners to resolve questions of ownership

when long-standing buildings in fact encroach upon neighboring properties.

If, for example, an existing building has been encroaching upon adjoining property for many years, the title to this property may be made marketable by relying upon the doctrine of adverse possession.

One precautionary note is necessary at this point: While the doctrine applies against other individual owners, it does *not* apply against governmental units. Therefore, if a private building encroaches upon public property, such as an alley or street, the owner of the private property cannot acquire title to the publicly owned property no matter how long the encroachment may have existed without objection. Such a problem, when it occurs, must be resolved under local law, usually by obtaining a *license to encroach*, which may be a very lengthy and expensive process. Usually these problems result from the inaccuracy of early surveying techniques as compared to modern, highly accurate surveys.

Quiet Title Proceedings

Whenever title to real estate depends upon a claim by virtue of adverse possession, it may be necessary to obtain a judicial determination that acquisition of title has in fact occurred. The common name of such a proceeding is a *quiet title* suit in a local court, in which the individual who claims title brings legal action against anyone and everyone who may have or may ever have had any claim against the property, no matter how remote, to prove the validity of his or her title. Such suits typically name everyone even remotely connected with the property and "the rest of the world" as defendants. A lengthy public notice of the hearing is generally required, and the suit is a legal determination that the claimant (the plaintiff) in the proceeding is in fact the true owner of the property. Even though expensive and time-consuming, such a suit may be the only way in which good legal title may be established so that the property can be sold.

Exception Under the Torrens System

Under title registration systems, discussed later, the fact of registration and the judicial character of the proceedings by which title is established and registered, the doctrine of adverse possession does not operate to transfer ownership. In states utilizing title registration systems, the inapplicability of the doctrine is part of the statutory law. When someone other than the registered owner is in possession at the time of sale, this fact may or may not be constructive notice of a claim to the title depending upon local law. The stranger in possession may be there under an unregistered deed or an unrecorded land contract (contract for a deed).

In summary this chapter has covered the general rules regarding the transfer of ownership. It must be emphasized that these rules are *general* and that they vary from state to state. Therefore a thorough review and understanding of local law are necessary for all persons engaged in the real estate business. Whenever there is any doubt, the services of an attorney should be utilized.

SUGGESTED READINGS

(See the appropriate chapter in the following books.)

Basye, Paul E. *Patton on Land Titles*, 2nd ed. St. Paul, Minn.: West Publishing Company, 1957.

Burby, William E. *Real Property*, 3rd ed. St. Paul, Minn.: West Publishing Company, 1965.

Cartwright, John M. *Handbook of Real Estate*. Englewood Cliffs, N.J.: Prentice-Hall, Inc., 1969.

Lusk, Harold and William B. French. *Law of the Real Estate Business*, 3rd ed. Homewood, Ill.: Richard D. Irwin, Inc., 1975.

MacDonald, James B. *Abstract and Title Practice*, 2nd ed. St. Paul, Minn.: West Publishing Company, 1958.

REVIEW QUESTIONS

1. The most protection afforded a purchaser in terms of warranty of title is that provided by a

   (A) general warranty deed
   (B) special warranty deed
   (C) quitclaim deed
   (D) executor's deed

2. A deed which is voidable because the grantor is in fact mentally incompetent

   I. may not be recorded
   II. may be set aside later by legal proceedings

   (A) I only   (C) both I and II
   (B) II only   (D) neither I nor II

3. A deed will create a joint tenancy with right of survivorship if

   I. two or more grantees are named
   II. the deed clearly expresses the intent to create it

   (A) I only   (C) both I and II
   (B) II only   (D) neither I nor II

4. A deed of property for a price of $40,000 meets the consideration tests if it states that the consideration was

   I. $10 and other good and valuable consideration, the receipt of which is acknowledged
   II. $40,000, the receipt of which is acknowledged

   (A) I only   (C) both I and II
   (B) II only   (D) neither I nor II

5. To be valid, the deed must be

   (A) executed by the grantor
   (B) accepted by the grantee
   (C) both (A) and (B)
   (D) neither (A) nor (B)

6. Generally, a deed which is not acknowledged

   I. is effective between the parties to transfer title
   II. may not be recorded

   (A) I only   (C) both I and II
   (B) II only   (D) neither I nor II

7. When a deed does not specify the estate being conveyed, it is presumed to transfer

   (A) a fee simple absolute
   (B) a life estate
   (C) a determinable fee
   (D) an estate for years

8. The deed form which may convey no rights in real property is a(n)

   (A) sheriff's deed
   (B) general warranty deed
   (C) executor's deed
   (D) quitclaim deed

9. An interest in land which can be inherited is the

   (A) fee simple absolute
   (B) decedent's life estate
   (C) decedent's personal license
   (D) decedent's interest held with another as joint tenants with right of survivorship

10. In the execution of a deed by an individual there is a presumption that

    I. he or she is of legal age
    II. he or she is mentally competent

    (A) I only   (C) both I and II
    (B) II only   (D) neither I nor II

11. When title to real estate is transferred by inheritance,

    (A) all title defects are cured by probating the will
    (B) the heirs take the title subject to all defects and liens which existed at the time of the decedent's death
    (C) the heirs or devisees are entitled to immediate possession at the time of the decedent's death
    (D) both (B) and (C)

12. In the case of a partnership

    I. any partner may sign a deed
    II. evidence of a general partnership should be provided

    (A) I only   (C) both I and II
    (B) II only   (D) neither I nor II

13. Caution must be exercised when buying property from an estate because

    I. an administrator's or executor's deed has no warranties

    II. a quitclaim deed is given

    (A) I only   (C) both I and II
    (B) II only   (D) neither I nor II

14. Acquisition of title under the doctrine of adverse possession

    I. cannot be accomplished in states using the Torrens system as to registered property
    II. can be accomplished in other states if necessary facts are shown to support it

    (A) I only   (C) both I and II
    (B) II only   (D) neither I nor II

15. A person who has real property devised to him through a will is said to have acquired title by

    (A) adverse possession   (C) reversion
    (B) escheat   (D) inheritance

16. A quiet title proceeding develops when

    (A) questions arise regarding the validity of the title
    (B) the purchaser buys a property with land tenants
    (C) family members purchase a property
    (D) none of the above

17. The maximum number of grantees which can be named in a deed is

    (A) two   (C) four
    (B) three   (D) any number

18. One who acquires property under a deed is a

    (A) vendee   (C) trustee
    (B) lessee   (D) grantee

19. Title to real property passes to the grantee at the time the deed is

    (A) delivered   (C) signed
    (B) written   (D) acknowledged

20. Full and complete ownership of land as we recognize it today exists in

    (A) an absolute
    (B) a fee simple absolute
    (C) a leasehold
    (D) an estate

Chapter 8

Evidence and Assurance of Title

RECORDING SYSTEMS

To understand recording systems and how they work, and to appreciate their value, it is helpful to consider first the *chain of title* concept. This term means simply that the various transfers of ownership of a particular piece of real estate down through the years each constitute a link between each two successive owners so that a "chain" is formed which creates a history of the title to the property. More than this is involved, however, because in determining who owns the property today, we *prove* this fact by examining the "chain" to see that it is unbroken or that there are no "missing links." Before purchasing real estate today, we expect and demand that the seller demonstrate that he or she is the owner by proving that the chain of title is unbroken from the time the first private owner received title from the government. This initial transfer from the government to the first private owner was usually by a unique form of conveyance called a *patent*, although property in many areas was transferred to the first private owner through a grant, and still other property from the states themselves because the initial transfer of title was from the federal government to new state governments as they were formed and admitted to statehood.

Since we demand proof of the chain of title back through such a lengthy period of time, it is appar-

ent that the present owners have to have literally hundreds of documents in their possession to prove a chain of title. In fact, under early common law in England (and to a large extent even today) this is exactly what was required. The seller kept all the documents which formed the chain of title so as to be able to prove his or her ownership by permitting the buyer to inspect them. Fortunately, in the United States this potential problem was anticipated and dealt with by the establishment of a system for *recording* important documents as well as maintaining public records of laws, legal proceedings, and other governmental action having an impact on property rights. Our modern recording systems were based on the need to have reliable records available to the general public.

Recording Systems and How They Work

It is important at the outset to recognize that there are really two different types of records which must be consulted in constructing the complete chain of title: those which are *governmental*, or mandatory, in nature, and those which are *private*, or voluntary, in nature. The distinction is discussed below.

1. Certain matters become *public record* whether the individuals affected by them desire it or not. All state laws and local ordinances are matters of public record. In addition, however, so are

court decisions including such matters as: formal appointments of guardians or conservators; the administration of decedents' estates including the will, if any, and all final court orders; divorce decrees; judgments in civil cases for damages which may create judgment liens on the defendant's property; assessments for municipal improvements which also create liens on the property benefited; proceedings of local zoning boards or commissions; liens for delinquent real estate taxes; liens for federal estate taxes which may exist even though unrecorded; and others. The point is that there is a whole body of public records which exists quite apart from the recording system discussed below and that these public records have an impact on the chain of title in the sense that they affect the quality of the title of the present owner.

2. In addition to the above public records, each state has established a separate system for recording documents which essentially represent private transactions between parties. While there are minor variations among the states, there is essential uniformity in the purposes and general workings of all recording systems. Under these systems properly prepared and acknowledged instruments are *entitled* to be recorded with the county recorder (or registrar) who is charged with the duty of preserving them, indexing them, and making them available to the general public. When we say that a document is *entitled* to be recorded, we mean that it *may* be recorded but need not be if the parties choose not to record it. Generally, all documents which affect the title to real estate may be recorded, such as deeds, mortgages, deeds of trust, land contracts, leases, mechanic's liens, *lis pendens* (notice that a lawsuit is pending against the present owner of the real estate), powers of attorney, declarations of trust, etc. The process of recording does not affect the rights between the parties. For example, a deed which is unrecorded is still effective to convey title in most states. What the recording process does is to make the transaction a matter of public record. The most important point to understand about this voluntary recording system is that, once the document is recorded and becomes part of the public records, all persons dealing with the property are *bound* to know of its contents. That is, whether or not they *actually* know that there has been a deed of property from A to B, they are legally *obligated* to know of it. This is called *construc-*

tive notice. It is this element of the system that is so important in establishing the "links" in the chain of title. Once the document is recorded, it becomes a permanent part of the chain of title.

Who Is Protected by the Recording System?

In addition to having constructive notice of everything that is a matter of public record, persons dealing with the property are entitled to rely upon the accuracy and completeness of these records. They are protected in dealing with the property after consulting these records. This protection, that the status of title is as shown by the records in the recording system is correct, does not extend to everyone. The protection generally is available only to a *bona fide purchaser or mortgagee for value.* By this we mean that the purchaser or mortgagee may rely upon the recording system if he or she (1) gives value (money) in reliance upon the record, and (2) acts in good faith and has no actual knowledge of any *unrecorded* instrument which affects the title.

To illustrate, assume that the *owner of record* (the one whom the records show is the true owner of the property) deeds the property to purchaser A on April 1, this year, but purchaser A fails to record the deed. On April 10, this year, the owner deeds the same property to purchaser B who records the deed on that date. Who now owns the legal title? Purchaser B was entitled to rely upon the record, and it showed that the seller had legal title; assuming that purchaser B gave *value* (and here we mean a realistic price, not just nominal consideration) for the property *and* that he did not *actually* know of the earlier deed, then purchaser B is the new owner. Purchaser A is of course entitled to sue the defrauding seller, but he has lost the right to legal title by failing to record promptly. This rule is admittedly arbitrary, but it is justified by the notion that the law helps those who help themselves.

Registered Title Systems

Several states have, in addition to maintaining recording systems, adopted the *Torrens system* of registration of titles to land. Under this system, generally, the title to real estate does not pass until the deed is registered with the registrar pursuant to the controlling statute. As with the other recording systems, registration under the Torrens system is not compulsory by law but is a practical necessity to obtain the benefits of registration.

The initial registration of property under the Torrens system is accomplished by a court proceeding similar to a quiet title action (discussed in Chapter 7) in which the individual who claims title to a piece of real estate files a claim with the court in the county in which the property is located. Notice to all possible interested parties is given either by personal direct notice or by publication in local newspapers. If no one disputes the claimant's right to ownership within the statutory period specified by state law, then the court will order the title to be registered.

After the registration, the owner receives a certificate which he or she transfers to the new owner when the property is sold. The certificate is in addition to the deed. The new owner presents these documents to the registrar, and a new certificate is then issued to the new owner of the property. There is also a limited form of title insurance under this system. When the registrar erroneously issues a new certificate, any damages suffered by the injured party are paid from the fund accumulated from the fees charged for registration. Under the Torrens system the responsibilities of the registrar are much greater than those of the county recorder under the standard recording system. The county recorder usually does not have the responsibility or duty of determining the accuracy or validity of deeds which are recorded. He or she simply checks to see that they are in recordable form and then records and indexes them. Any error made in the recording process which causes damage to anyone is borne by that person without financial relief from the recorder.

ASSURANCE OF THE QUALITY OF THE TITLE

It has become customary throughout the United States to require that the seller of real estate furnish satisfactory evidence that he or she is the true owner of the property. All standard contracts for the sale of real estate contain such a requirement. The fact is that, in the absence of such a contractual requirement, the seller has no legal obligation to furnish any evidence that he owns the property he or she is selling. In such a case the buyer must look solely to whatever warranties are in the deed and the seller's financial ability to pay for a breach of warranty. Since a typical contract provides for evidence of title, however, the discussion below covers the two most common methods of title assurance in use today: the *abstract and opinion method* and *commercial title insurance.*

Under the abstract and opinion method the abstractor prepares a digest of all the relevant documents and facts which are matters of public record from the earliest history of the property under consideration, and an attorney's opinion is given, based upon these facts, as to where title is currently vested and what defects in its quality may exist.

Under the title insurance method, the insurance company, on the basis of its own research of the records, decides that the title of the proposed seller is of sufficient quality that the company will insure that the deed will pass good title to the proposed buyer.

Both of these systems are dependent upon and limited to the facts disclosed by the recording system which permits (but seldom requires) the filing of documents which can affect the title to real estate with the recorder of the county within which the real estate is located. Other records of fact maintained which can affect title (such as the record of all judgments rendered against the owner which might constitute liens on the property) must also be consulted to be sure that all public information has been investigated. Nevertheless, the basic information upon which the quality of the title is based lies in the recording system.

The Abstract and Opinion Method

Even though the law imposes upon all those who deal with real estate an obligation to investigate public records and charges them with notice or knowledge of what such an investigation would yield, it is very seldom that an individual purchaser, mortgagee, or lessee undertakes this task. He or she usually must employ others to accomplish this task and normally first employs an abstractor to make a detailed search of the records and to compile a digest of the history of the title to the property. It is usually necessary to employ an abstractor because of the tremendous volume of records which must be checked and the complexity of the public records system.

The use of an abstractor who is a specialist in the use of this system is essential today. Nevertheless, the abstractor's function, even though critically important, is one of accumulating information accurately and exhaustively rather than that of interpreting its meaning or legal significance. This latter function is the province of the attorney. It is the attorney's function to review the abstract, the history of the title to a piece of real estate, and reach a decision as to the quality of the present owner's title. Each of these functions, its protective features, and its limitations, is discussed below.

The abstract is the basic tool needed to establish who currently owns a given piece of real estate and how good his or her title is.

The abstract itself is a digest of the history of the title to a given parcel of real estate. It is not a compilation of all the documents which are recorded. That is, the abstractor does not make a copy of each and every document found in the chain of title. To do so would result, in many cases, in a very imposing book. The abstractor is highly trained and knows what portions of each document are significant in terms of ownership. The abstractor therefore abstracts each document and records in the abstract only the essential facts. For example, rather than copy the entire deed, the abstractor simply notes in the abstract:

The location of the deed in the records (the book and page where it can be found)
The date of the deed and the date of its recording
The names of the grantor and grantee
A description of the property
The type of deed
Any conditions or restrictions included in the deed.

Wherever it is necessary to have the entire contents of the document included in the abstract to understand the transaction fully, the abstractor includes the entire document.

Extent and Limitations of Coverage

The extent of the coverage of the abstract is very broad. When it is complete, it includes the history of the title from the earliest known record. As a practical matter, however, most abstracts start with the first private ownership of the property: the patent from the United States to the first individual purchaser. From that point forward the abstract shows all recorded facts that affect the title. It should be understood that a wide variety of records is consulted in addition to the deed and mortgage records. For example, the public records of all judgments, marriages, estate proceedings, and tax records, as well as certain others, are searched by the abstractor to be sure that all recorded facts and documents which might affect the quality of title are included in the abstract. It must be emphasized that the abstractor's search is restricted to the public records and does not purport to cover matters that are not in these records.

The areas not covered by the abstract are those the purchaser is expected to investigate personally and those not required to be a matter of record.

Matters that would be revealed by an inspection of the property (but not by an inspection of the record) are not covered by the abstract. That is, the abstractor does not view or inspect the property to determine whether or not there are parties other than the seller who are in possession and claim an interest (such as under an unrecorded short-term lease) and that the physical condition and layout of the property are as represented by the seller (for example, that the buildings are in fact situated on the real estate being purchased). It may require a survey to establish these facts.

The purchaser is also required to be satisfied that no encroachments or violations of restrictive covenants exist, since the abstractor has no knowledge of these facts and will not be willing to certify that such covenants are not being violated. Again, a survey may be required to establish such facts. Whatever is required to establish the necessary facts is the purchaser's responsibility.

Mechanic's liens may have a drastic effect upon the title to real estate but may not be recorded at the time of transfer of title, creation of a mortgage, or granting of a leasehold interest. The reason for this is of course that the notice of intent to hold such a lien need not be recorded until the statutory time after completion of the work. As a result, the abstract cannot preclude the possibility that such liens may be recorded for some period after the abstract is brought up to date. The abstractor will of course not accept responsibility for such liens, since it cannot be predicted whether or not the possibility of such liens exists.

The abstractor's certificate limits his liability for the quality of his work. Typical of the wording used in such certificates is: "... hereby certifies, guarantees, and warrants to whoever relies upon this certificate, including present and all future persons in interest, and this certificate runs with the real estate described in the caption hereof that the abstract is complete." Such a certification indicates the willingness of the abstractor to be liable for any errors and omissions included in his work. There is serious question, however, whether or not he can be held liable for any loss suffered by anyone who relies upon the accuracy of this work unless that person was the one who paid for it.

Attorney's Opinion on the Abstract

An attorney's opinion rendered upon the abstract is the second important step of the abstract and opinion method of title assurance. The function of the attorney in the abstract and opinion method of title assurance is critically important. The abstract is after all simply a compilation of the documents and facts which affect the title to the real estate being investigated. The abstractor makes no determination of the quality of the title; the abstractor simply reports what the record shows and who appears to be in title at the time of the abstract continuation. It is the function of the attorney to examine the abstract and determine how good the title is on the basis of the recorded facts. The attorney renders a professional opinion as to the legal effects of the documents and facts reported by the abstractor. The attorney reviews the abstract in great detail to determine that the title has in fact passed from each party who has owned it to the next party in the chain of title, whether the transfer was by deed, death, forced sale, etc. The attorney also determines that any liens or encumbrances which ever existed against the property have been satisfied so that there are no potential interests in anyone other than the apparent record title holder.

*Extent of Protection Provided
By the Abstract and Opinion Method*

The extent of the protection obtained by use of the abstract and opinion method of title assurance and its limitations are important to understand. The entire system is based upon public records and what effect these records have upon the quality of the title of the present owner. The abstract includes only matters which are in the public records and can be found by a competent and reasonable search of such records. Anything not in the records does not go into the abstract. Since the abstract is the basic information used by the attorney in forming an opinion as to the quality of the title and where it is currently vested, it necessarily follows that the attorney's opinion pertains to the record title only. If the attorney is furnished additional information, his or her opinion can be expanded to include it. For example, if the attorney is furnished with a survey which locates the improvements on the property accurately, he or she can expand the opinion to show whether or not there is any violation of restrictive covenants which dictate the location of improvements, such as setback lines, etc.

In the absence of a survey of course the obligation of making this determination remains with the proposed buyer, mortgagee, or lessee. The general rule is that the abstract and opinion method covers only matters of record. The buyer is charged with responsibility for matters which would be revealed by an inspection of the property. The buyer is not obligated to have a survey performed if he or she can determine the facts without it, but it has been held that the buyer is bound by what the survey would have shown had it been performed. In addition to the information about the physical characteristics of the property that an inspection and survey would reveal, two major limitations on this method of title assurance make it essential for the buyer to inspect the property.

The record does not necessarily show the rights of parties other than the owner who may be in possession of the property. The fact that someone other than the record owner is in possession is a fact which can be established only by inspecting the property, and the law requires the purchaser to make such an inspection on the theory that a reasonable person would do so before parting with value. Since any purchase of the property is subject to the rights of the parties who are in actual possession, it is clearly important that an inspection be performed. If someone other than the owner is in possession, the buyer must determine what rights that person claims.

Certain matters may have a severe effect upon the title and may not be recorded at the time of the sale of the property. Particularly troublesome are mechanic's liens. It is quite possible that such liens can be filed after sale of the property if the work done by the mechanic was completed shortly before the sale. Once again inspection of the property by the buyer just before the closing of the sale may reveal that work has been recently performed. If so, the buyer may be protected from later assertion of a lien by requiring evidence that the work has been paid for. It is also quite possible of course that even the most careful inspection will not reveal any evidence of repair work. In this event the buyer must rely upon the protection afforded by the seller's warranties, either in the deed or in a separate document. The important point to be noted here is that the abstract and opinion method of title assurance does not provide any protection against the possibility of liens that may result from work done or materials supplied shortly before the time the record is checked and the abstract brought up to date.

Commercial Title Insurance

The business of insuring titles was a natural outgrowth of the abstracting business, since the abstractor is the person most capable of accumulating the necessary information most efficiently. Perhaps even more important than the ability to obtain the information available from public records is the fact that, because of the abstractor's familiarity with the system, he or she is best able to judge how good the system is in a given area. The abstractor is able to evaluate a system's inherent risks, such as misfiled documents, indexing errors, records not indexed at all, or documents which for some reason have never been recorded.

While most title insurance companies have resulted from an expansion of the abstract business, title insurance is also made available by attorneys who have formed such companies to insure titles on the basis of their opinions. The phenomenal growth in the use of title insurance, in metropolitan areas particularly, is due in no small part to institutional lenders. Many mortgage lenders universally require title insurance, at least for their own interest in the property, as a condition for making the loan. This emphasis on insurance of the mortgagee's interest in the property has also made purchasers more aware of its availability and has tended to foster the growth of the title insurance business.

It is important to understand just what title insurance is. Essentially, it is a *single premium insurance policy which insures the condition of the title to a specified piece of real estate at a single precise point in time.* It does not insure that the title will not be affected by actions which occur after the date the policy is issued. It simply insures that, as of a certain date and time, the records show that a specific piece of real estate is owned by a particular owner or owners and that the title is good, subject to any exceptions which may be spelled out in the policy. The cost of the coverage, the premium paid for the policy, is established on the same basis as other casualty insurance: the amount of the coverage in terms of money and the degree of risk being assumed by the insurer which is generally a function of experience with other policies that have been issued. Policies are available for owners of property, which insure them against loss of title or the cost of satisfying a claim or encumbrance against it. Policies are also available for the protection of mortgagees to the extent of the balance owed to them by their borrower; that is, as the loan is amortized, the amount of coverage is correspondingly reduced. Lessees' policies are also available and are quite popularly used where the tenant intends to make substantial improvements to the property.

The preparation and issuance of a title insurance policy is similar in many respects to the abstract and opinion method of title assurance, with certain important exceptions. The first step is still inspection of the records to determine the chain of title and to find any defects which may exist; however, usually no abstract is prepared. Instead, the title insurer relies upon skilled personnel to trace the title and to recognize the transactions or facts which may result in a title defect. Rather than digesting every document, the title insurer digests only those which appear to pose a problem. The personnel who perform this function then report their findings to the company's title examiner, who usually is an attorney skilled in the real estate field. The decision is then made as to whether the defects found are so significant that the title cannot be insured, that it can be insured only with certain exceptions, or that it is insurable without exception because the defects found do not represent serious risk of loss.

The insurer then issues a *preliminary binder* which indicates its willingness to insure the title when acquired by the proposed new owner from the present owner. This preliminary binder is not an abstract and does not show any of the facts upon which the insurer has relied but only any significant defects for which the proposed policy does not provide any coverage. If there are serious defects, the parties to the transaction can then take corrective action to cure the defects so that the ultimate policy will be issued without exceptions.

The final policy is issued after the transaction is completed and the documents have been recorded, so that the title insurer has the opportunity to see that the record reflects the transfer to the insured. One disadvantage of title insurance is of course the fact that the purchaser, mortgagee, or lessee does not receive an abstract and does not have the opportunity to evaluate personally the degree of risk which may exist. If the purchaser, mortgagee, or lessee wants to obtain an abstract in addition to the title insurance policy, it will involve an additional expense of preparation. When the property under consideration is very valuable or where a substantial amount will be spent in the construction of improvements, a careful purchaser may obtain both a title insurance policy and an abstract so that the purchaser's attorney can be satisfied that no unusual degree of risk is involved, even if the title insurance company is willing to insure the title.

Extent and Limitations of Coverage

The extent of coverage provided by the usual title insurance policy and the limitations on that coverage should be clearly understood by anyone active in the real estate business, so as to avoid giving any unintentionally misleading advice to both purchasers and sellers. As a basic rule, the title insurance policy covers the same matters as the abstract and opinion method. That is, the same records are investigated and the same decisions made as to the quality of the title and therefore its insurability.

One very important exception to this generalization exists, however, which provides one of the most important advantages of the system: Title insurance in effect insures the accuracy of the recording system. If, for example, a document affecting the title has been improperly indexed and cannot be found by the most diligent and competent search and there is a resulting loss to the policyholder, typical title insurance policies will cover that loss, even though an abstractor could not have been held liable for failure to find the document. To this extent title insurance provides broader protection than the abstract and opinion method.

Matters that would be revealed by a survey are not covered by typical title insurance policies. However, this coverage can be obtained if the title insurer is furnished with a survey which appears adequate. One important point to remember in connection with the survey is that title insurance companies have established certain minimum standards for surveys which they recognize and accept for purposes of insuring titles. Before recommending the procurement of a survey, the broker or salesperson should determine (or caution the client to determine) just what kind of survey will be required by the title insurer to induce it to insure such matters as compliance with restrictive covenants, etc. As with the abstract and opinion method of title assurance, the title insurance policy has certain standard exceptions for the rights of parties in possession, short-term unrecorded leases or land contracts, and mechanic's liens.

Protected Parties

The parties protected by the title insurance policy are those specified in the policy itself. This is a matter of contract between the insurance company and the purchaser of the coverage. It is important to recognize that a mortgagee's policy, for example, protects only the mortgagee's interest in the property; the owner's interest is not covered. In the event of loss covered by such a policy, the balance then due on the loan will be paid to the mortgagee and the owner will be relieved from making further payment; however, the owner will suffer the loss of the property and whatever investment was made in it. To obtain protection of the owner's interest, an owner's policy must be purchased in addition to the mortgagee's policy, if one has been issued. A very important point to be aware of in connection with the owner's policy is that it protects only that owner, and in the event the property is sold the protection of the owner's policy does not transfer to the new owner. Subsequent purchasers of insured property must obtain a separate policy to cover their interests.

One person definitely not protected by the title insurance policy is the seller of the real estate. That is, the mere fact that title insurance is purchased for the benefit of the buyer does not relieve the seller from liability for any defects in the title under the owner's warranties in the deed to the purchaser. In fact, it is not unheard of for the title insurer to bring suit against the seller upon his or her warranties when there has been a loss under a policy of title insurance, particularly where the defect in the title was known or should have been known to the seller. When the insurer is required to pay a claim under the policy, the insurer acquires the *right of subrogation*. That is, the insurer acquires whatever rights the insured party would have had against the seller under his or her warranties. For example, assume that the seller knew of an assessment for sewers and that this fact was not found by the title insurer and not mentioned by the seller at the closing. When the assessment must be paid, the purchaser is entitled to look to either the seller or the title insurer for reimbursement. The simplest procedure for the purchaser is to demand that the insurer pay the assessment under the terms of the insurance policy. The title insurer, when paying the claim, succeeds to the insured party's rights and may maintain suit against the seller upon his or her warranties. Such suits have been successfully maintained by title insurance companies.

Supplementary Protection

Supplementary protection may be required in special cases in addition to the abstract and opinion method of assurance or commercial title insurance. It is clear that not every problem will be completely covered by either method. This is particularly true in the area of mechanic's liens. Two possible problems may exist at the time of sale in connection with such liens: There may be the strong possibility of such liens being filed, or it may be that such liens have already been filed and cannot be cleared before the sale is closed. A suggested solution for each is described below.

Vendor's Affidavit

When the purchaser feels there is a possibility that mechanic's liens may be filed against the property for work recently done (such as new construction or repairs which are necessary to qualify the property for the mortgage loan, quite common with FHA-insured loans), the purchaser should insist upon evidence that all contractors have been paid, and in addition require a *vendor's affidavit* (sometimes referred to by other names locally, such as a *closing affidavit*) under which the seller makes a sworn statement under the penalties for perjury that there are no such liens and that there are no circumstances which would permit such a lien to arise.

Escrow Fund

When mechanic's liens already exist against the property, there may be good and valid reasons for proceeding with the sale without obtaining releases of the claims. The purchaser may need possession of the property but be unwilling to make payment without some assurance that the lien will be discharged by the seller. The seller, however, may be anxious to complete the sale to receive the proceeds but may be unwilling to pay the mechanic the amount claimed because there is a dispute regarding the value of the work, its quality, or the amount claimed. To be forced to pay the claim at face value would reduce the net price below that which the seller might receive if free to negotiate or litigate the merits of the claim. A solution in such case is available in the form of an escrow, under which the seller deposits with an independent escrow agent sufficient funds to satisfy the claim at its face value plus any costs which might be chargeable and collectible against the property. The escrow agent is authorized to apply the funds to the satisfaction of the claim when the claim is paid and the lien discharged. A further provision for the protection of the buyer is a clause which requires resolution of the problem within a specified period of time, so that the buyer is assured of prompt resolution of the matter. Upon failure of the seller to resolve the matter within the specified time limit, the agreement should provide that the escrowee be required to apply the funds to satisfy the lien.

RESTRICTIONS ON THE TITLE
WHICH ARE ACCEPTABLE

There may be a variety of restrictions on the use of real estate being sold which are in fact benefi-

cial to the use and enjoyment of the property by the grantee and are therefore quite acceptable and do not constitute defects in the title so as to make it unmarketable. Typical of these are subdivision restrictions such as those discussed later in the chapter.

In other cases it is also possible that an existing encumbrance is an asset to the buyer. For example, there may be an existing mortgage on the property at a more favorable rate than that currently available at the time of sale. If this mortgage can be assumed by the buyer, it will be made a condition in the deed itself. The acceptance of the deed which states this condition will not breach the seller's warranty against encumbrances. This matter is more fully discussed in Chapter 10.

It is appropriate at this point to note that even though we require evidence of the quality of the seller's title prior to completion of the sale, we are generally not entitled to demand a *perfect* title because it is quite unlikely that there is such a title in existence today. What we are entitled to insist on, however, is a title which is *marketable*. That is, certain limitations on the title are acceptable under modern land title practice, and the buyer must accept the deed to such property. Easements for power lines, sewers, and other utilities which serve the property are examples of technical defects which do not make the title unmarketable.

Every state today has some form of marketable title legislation designed to cure defects in title which are very old. While there are many variations from state to state, particularly as to the length of time they cover, the basic purpose of this legislation is to invalidate any outstanding claim or to correct any error which is so old that it is unlikely to affect the marketability of the title. These statutes generally require very clear evidence of an unbroken chain of title for some lengthy period of time. Forty years is typical; however, there is no universal standard. Early statutes were of doubtful constitutionality; however, more recently such statutes have been updated and have withstood attacks on their constitutionality. In spite of this, careful title examiners always look beyond this statutory period, because such statutes frequently do not protect against governmental claims or against people who are incompetent.

LEGAL DESCRIPTIONS

Because of the dependency of the recording system on an accurate way of identifying and indexing property, it is important to understand the ways in which real estate may be legally described.

The government or rectangular survey refers to a grid of north and south lines known as meridians and east and west lines known as parallels. The vertical rows of the grid are known as *checks* and the horizontal rows are called *tiers*. The distance between principal meridians and guide meridians is 24 miles, the same as between the base line and standard parallels. A single square in the grid, known as a *tract*, is then 24 miles square and is composed of 16 townships. A township is 6 miles square (36 square miles) and is made up of 36 sections. Each section is 1 mile square (also 1 square mile) and can be divided easily for platting purposes as shown below:

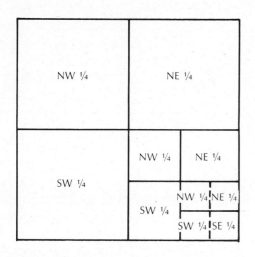

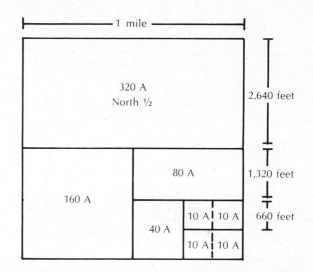

A section contains 640 acres and is 1 mile square—5,280 feet per side.

A half section contains 320 acres and is a rectangle 5,280 feet by 2,640 feet.

A quarter section contains 160 acres and is a square 2,640 feet per side.

A quarter-quarter section contains 40 acres and is a square 1,320 feet per side.

A quarter-quarter-quarter section contains 10 acres and is a square 660 feet per side.

LEGAL DESCRIPTIONS UTILIZING THE RECORD PLAT

Many residential properties are situated in subdivisions which are legally described by means of a *record plat* (sometimes called a description by *lot and block*). It is important therefore that the real estate salesperson become familiar with this type of legal description. An example of a portion of a record plat is shown in Exhibit A.

The record plat typically utilizes several means of describing real estate. First of all, the record plat employs the rectangular system (also called the government system) as a base system of reference. Section corners and section lines are sometimes referred to in the record plat. Second, the record plat typically utilizes the *metes and bounds* (measures and direction) technique to describe the outer boundary of the land included in the record plat. Finally, the record plat includes a pictorial representation of the several lots (parcels of land intended to be conveyed), streets, easements, rectangular system references, metes and bounds calls, and other information. Once the detailed surveying, calculation, and drafting have been done, it is by virtue of the pictorial illustration, which is a major part of the record plat, that subsequent description of a parcel of real property can be made relatively simple.

It should be kept in mind that, while the technical work associated with preparation of a record plat is indeed important, it is equally significant that the record plat be recorded and thus made part of the land records in the county in which the land is situated. It is with this recorded information and the representations made in the record plat that a legal description for a particular lot can be generated. For example, Lot 8, as shown in Exhibit A, would be described as follows:

Lot 8, in Block 2, of "Brandywine Section One," the plat of which was recorded Novem-

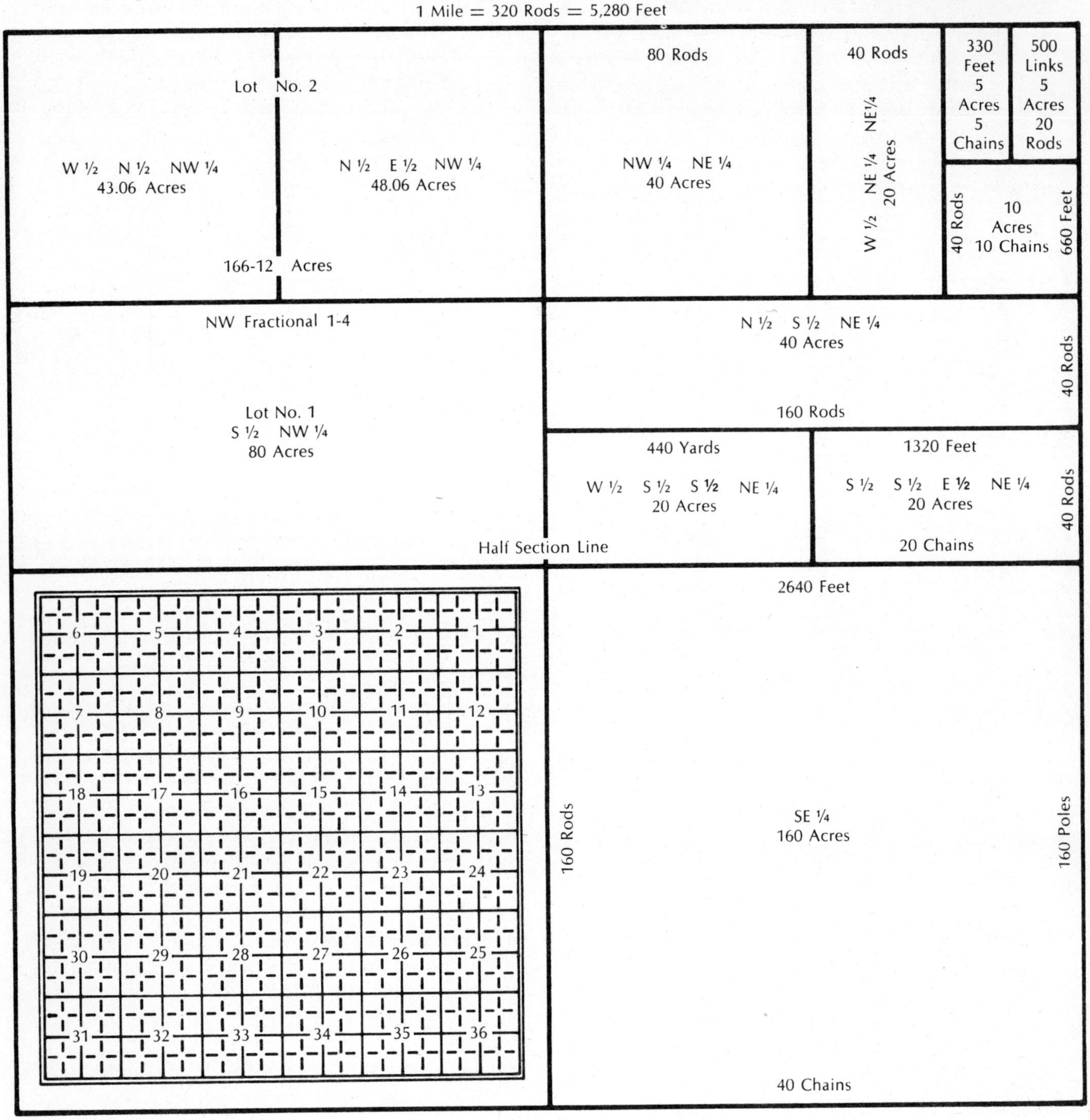
1 Mile = 320 Rods = 5,280 Feet
Lot No. 2
W ½ N ½ NW ¼
43.06 Acres
N ½ E ½ NW ¼
48.06 Acres
166-12 Acres
80 Rods
NW ¼ NE ¼
40 Acres
40 Rods
W ½ NE ¼ NE¼
20 Acres
330 Feet
5 Acres
5 Chains
500 Links
5 Acres
20 Rods
40 Rods
10 Acres
10 Chains
660 Feet
NW Fractional 1-4
Lot No. 1
S ½ NW ¼
80 Acres
N ½ S ½ NE ¼
40 Acres
160 Rods
40 Rods
440 Yards
W ½ S ½ S ½ NE ¼
20 Acres
1320 Feet
S ½ S ½ E ½ NE ¼
20 Acres
20 Chains
40 Rods
Half Section Line
6 5 4 3 2 1
7 8 9 10 11 12
18 17 16 15 14 13
19 20 21 22 23 24
30 29 28 27 26 25
31 32 33 34 35 36
2640 Feet
160 Rods
SE ¼
160 Acres
160 Poles
40 Chains

ber 12, this year, as Instrument 4653 in Book 6, pages 52 through 56, in the Office of the Recorder, Your County, Your State.

As can be surmised, a metes and bounds description of this same Lot 8 would be a difficult, time-consuming effort.

Information typically shown on a record plat, as illustrated in Exhibit A, includes:

1. Name of the subdivision
2. Lot lines (including directions and distances)
3. Lot numbers
4. Block numbers (a block usually is defined as

contiguous lots bounded by streets)

5. Building lines illustrating required setback of all structures from the street right-of-way
6. Area of the lot
7. Easements, such as utility, sewer, and drainage easements
8. Street names, width and longitudinal dimensions of right-of-way
9. North arrow and scale of drawing
10. Location and description of monuments and markers
11. Beginning point and rectangular survey references
12. Adjoining property references
13. Recording information, including time and date of recording, instrument number, book and page number, where recorded, and name of recorder
14. Curve data to be utilized by surveyors in staking particular lots.

Other information which is often included as part of the record plat but not shown in Exhibit A is:

1. Legal description of the perimeter boundary of the record plat
2. Land surveyor's certification of plat accuracy
3. Land owner's dedication of the platted ground as shown on the plat for lots, right-of-way, easements, etc.
4. Definitions of lots, easements, etc., as shown on the plat
5. Private restrictions attached to use of land

6. Enforcement provisions for restrictions on use of land
7. Reference to other pertinent recorded instruments made of part of the plat
8. Execution of the record plat by the owners of lands to be platted
9. Acknowledgment of record plat (required for recording)
10. Statements and signatures of approval from government agencies having jurisdiction over the platting process
11. Name of person preparing plat and date of preparation.

It should be remembered that, while the record plat is a highly detailed, technical representation of a particular parcel of real property, it does not replace the importance of a thorough search and opinion of title or a title policy. For example, an easement may exist on the real property which does not appear on the record plat. To cite another example, an owner may convey a portion of a lot to another person, and thus the ownership of a particular lot may be different from what is represented on the record plat.

It can be concluded, however, that while the record plat does not solve all the problems associated with transfer of title, it can make the job of transfer much simpler for the salesperson, lender, attorney, abstractor, title insurance company, land surveyor, owner, prospective purchaser, and other persons involved with the transfer of real property.

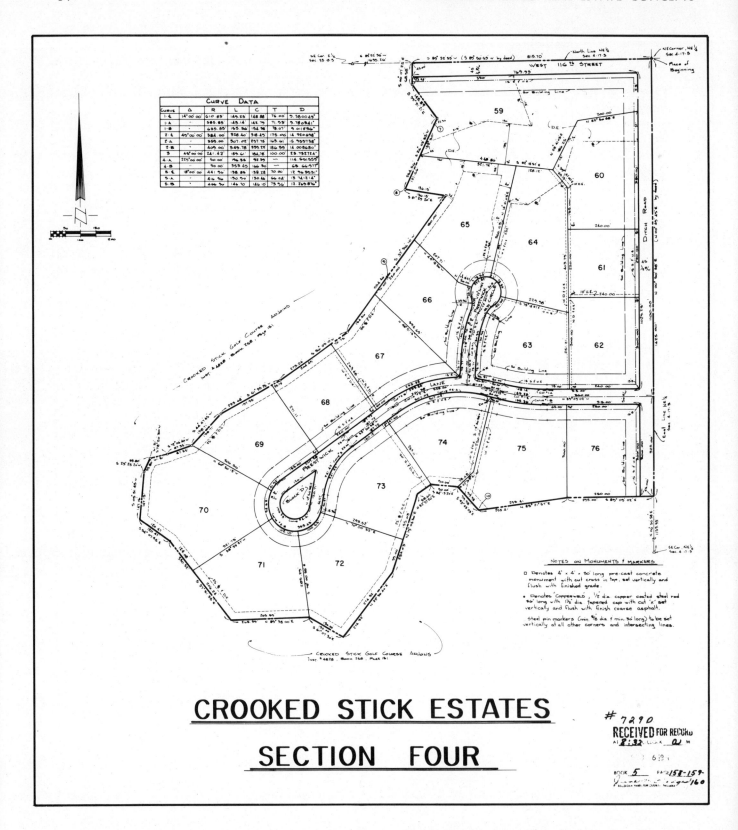

CROOKED STICK ESTATES

SECTION FOUR

FIGS. 8-1, 8-2, 8-3—Record plat. A portion of a complete record plat including lot sizes, street layouts, various power and sewer easements, building lines, land surveyor's certificate, statement of covenants of the development, signature of seller and purchaser, along with the acknowledgments necessary for recording. Courtesy of Paul I. Cripe, Inc., Indianapolis, Indiana.

I, the undersigned, hereby certify that the above plat is true and correct and represents a survey made by me of real estate described as follows:

A part of the Northeast Quarter of Section 4, Township 17 North, Range 3 East in Hamilton County, Indiana, more particularly described as follows: Beginning at the said Northeast corner of the said Northeast Quarter; thence South 89 degrees 52 minutes 35 seconds West (assumed bearing) on and along the North line of the said Northeast Quarter 801.50 feet; thence South 8 seconds East 68.98 feet; thence South 34 degrees 55 minutes 45 seconds East 137.02 feet; thence South 26 degrees 02 minutes 35 seconds West 254.56 feet; thence South 8 seconds East 136.15 feet; thence South 37 degrees 36 minutes 10 seconds West 554.46 feet; thence South 56 degrees 59 minutes 10 seconds West 275.24 feet; thence South 46 degrees 35 minutes 20 seconds West 61.31 feet; thence minutes 45 seconds West 138.71 feet; thence South 72 degrees 06 minutes 40 seconds West 40 seconds West 233.68 feet; thence South 44 degrees 47 South 23 degrees 25 minutes 20 seconds West 55.80 feet; thence South 05 degrees 51 minutes 45 seconds West 147.15 feet; thence South 54 degrees 20 seconds West 120.47 feet; thence South 37 degrees 51 minutes 55 seconds East 330.32 feet; thence North 89 degrees 38 minutes 00 seconds South 63 degrees 30 minutes East North 52 degrees 57 minutes 20 seconds East 58.60 feet; thence North 39 degrees 36 minutes 40 seconds East 374.32 feet; thence North 19 degrees 05 minutes 50 seconds East 254.03 feet; thence 99.98 feet; thence North 83 degrees 21 minutes 57 seconds East 295.00 feet to the East line of the said Northeast Quarter; thence North 00 degrees 50 seconds East or and along the said East line 1425.00 feet to the Place of Beginning, containing 38.798 acres, more or less.

Between points 7 and 8 and between points 9 and 10 as shown on the plat for "Crooked Stick Estates-Section Four", the boundary herein described is coincident with a corresponding portion of the boundary description of a certain tract set out and recorded as Instrument #4484, Book 267, pages 309-314, in the Office of the Recorder of Hamilton County, Indiana.

This subdivision consists of 18 lots, numbered 59 to 76, inclusively and . The size of the lots and widths of the streets are shown in figures denoting feet and decimal parts thereof.

This survey was made by me during the month of *March*, 1975.

Witness my signature this ___ day of ____, 1975.

Registered Land Surveyor #4028

The undersigned, **Guernsey VanRiper, Jr.**, Owner of the real ____ described herein, being a part of the land described, conveyed and recorded as Instrument #15004, Plat Book 281, pages 632 to 636, inclusively, in the Office of the Recorder of Hamilton County, Indiana, May 30, 1975 do hereby certify that we have laid off, platted and subdivided and do hereby lay off, plat and subdivide said real estate in accordance with the within plat.

This subdivision shall be known and designated as **CROOKED STICK ESTATES-SECTION FOUR**, an addition to Hamilton County, Indiana.

In order to afford adequate protection to all present and future owners of lots in this subdivision, the undersigned owners hereby adopt and establish the following protective covenants, each and all enuring to the benefit of each and every owner of any lot or lots in said subdivision, their heirs and/or assigns, binding all the same each grantor and their heirs and/or assigns.

1. All streets shown on this plat and not heretofore dedicated are hereby dedicated to the public.

2. All lots in this subdivision shall be known and described as residential lots and no lots will be resubdivided into two or more building lots.

3. No residence, dwelling house, garage, shall be erected, altered, placed or permitted to remain on any residential lot other than one single-family dwelling, a private garage, and such other outbuildings usual and incidental to the use of such residential lot.

4. No residence, dwelling house, garage, servants quarters or other structure of any nature, composition or description shall be constructed or erected on any lot until the building plans, including plot plans, specifications, plans for landscaping and property set-back lines are in conformity. In the event that the building committee may be requested shall be submitted to the building committee for its approval, said approval to be evidenced by a written instrument and stamped approval executed by the committee and delivered to the person or persons requesting such approval.

5. The building committee shall consist of three members and shall be composed of the following individuals: Guernsey VanRiper, Jr., Eugene Friedmann and Willis Adams. A majority of the said members shall constitute a quorum for approval or disapproval of any plans submitted and the decision of the majority shall control without exception and their decision shall be final. The committee shall determine whether the proposed structures, plans and specifications are in harmony of external design with existing structures and whether the building and property set-back lines are in conformity. In the event that the building committee does not plans. No charge shall be made to any purchaser of plans for examination of plans or giving approval as provided. In writing, its approval or disapproval of plans submitted within a period of 15 days after submission, the committee shall be deemed to have approved such of any of the above named members, the remaining member or members shall select the successor or successors to fill the vacancy or vacancies created. In the event of death, disability or resignation

6. No residence of dwelling shall be constructed on any lot or part thereof, unless such residence, exclusive of open porches, attached garages and basements shall have a ground floor area of 2,500 square feet if a one-story structure, or 1,500 square feet if a higher structure, provided also that in case of a building higher than one-story there shall be at least 1,000 square feet in addition to the ground floor area.

7. No trailer, shack, tent, basement, garage or other outbuilding shall be used at any time as a residence, temporary or permanent, nor shall any structure of a temporary character be used as a residence.

8. Easements: There are strips of ground as shown on the within plat marked "Drainage Easements" (D.E.), "Sewer Easements" (S.E.) and "Utility Easements" (U.E.) either separately or in any combination of the three, which are reserved for the use of the public utility companies and governmental agencies as follows: "Drainage Easements" (D.E.) are created to provide paths and courses for area and local storm drainage, either overland or in adequate underground conduit, to serve the needs of this and adjoining ground and/or public drainage system, to keep such areas or structure, including fences, shall be built upon said easement, which will obstruct flow from the area being served. "Sewer Easements" (S.E.) are created for the use of the local government agency having jurisdiction over the storm and sanitary waste disposal system of said city and/or county for the purpose of installation and maintenance of sewers, including mains, interceptor mains, ducts, poles, lines and wires; and also all rights and uses specified for sewer easements above designated. All such easements shall include the right of reasonable ingress to and egress from said strip or for the exercise of the other rights reserved.

9. No residence, dwelling house or any other structure whatsoever shall be used for the purpose of carrying on a business, trade, profession or any other calling.

10. "Building lines" (B.L.) are established as shown on this plat between which line no building shall be erected, placed, altered or permitted to remain. No structure or any part thereof shall be built or erected nearer than 20 feet to any side yard line or nearer than 25 feet to any rear lot line.

11. No fence, wall, hedge or shrub planting which obstructs sight lines at elevations between 2 and 6 feet above the street, shall be placed or permitted to remain on any corner lot within the triangular area formed by the street property lines and a line connecting points 25 feet from the intersection of said street lines, or in the case of a rounded property corner, from the intersection of the street lines extended. The same sight line limitations shall apply to any lot within 10 feet from the intersection of a street line with the edge of a driveway pavement. No trees shall be permitted to remain within such distances of such intersection unless the foliage line is maintained at sufficient height to prevent obstruction of such sight lines.

12. The owners of Lots 59, 60, 61 shall provide driveway "turn arounds" on their respective lots such that exiting vehicles need not back onto the access road. The owners of lots 62 and 76 shall also apply to the owners of lots 62 and 76 shall elect driveway access directly onto Ditch Road.

13. Block "D" as shown on the plat shall be owned in common by the owners of Lots 69, 70, 71, 72, and 73 as equi tenants in common. The whole of Block "D" will be responsible for maintaining the property. Maintenance work will include, but not be limited to cutting the grass, clean-up at reasonable intervals and general landscaping as required.

14. The private sewage disposal system shall be installed in strict compliance with the approval procedure outlined in "The Sewage System Review Procedure", recorded as Instrument # 7489, Deed Record /48, page . Each owner also covenants and agrees to connect with the public sanitary sewer within one year after such sewer is made available to his particular lot.

15. No poultry or farm animals shall be kept on any lot. This restriction shall not prohibit a resident from keeping a usual pet animal or bird properly confined to his particular lot.

16. No camper, motor home, truck, trailer or boat shall be stored in the open in public view.

17. Each homeowner shall provide and maintain on his lot a front yard light, which shall operate from dusk to dawn. Location, size and type of light are subject to the approval of the building committee.

18. The right to enforce the within provisions, restrictions and covenants by injunction, together with the right to cause the removal by due process of law of structures erected or maintained in violation thereof, is hereby dedicated and reserved to the owners of the several lots in this subdivision, their heirs or assigns and the Carmel Plan Commission, their successors or assigns, who shall be entitled to such relief without being required to show any damage of any kind to any such owner or owners by or through any such violation or attempted violation, said provisions (as they may be amended under Covenant 19) shall be in full force and effect until March 1, 2000, at which time said covenants shall be automatically extended for successive periods of ten years, unless by a vote of the majority of the then owners it is agreed that the covenants shall terminate in whole or in part.

19. Invalidation of any one of these restrictions or part thereof by judgment or court order shall not affect or render the remainder of said restrictions invalid or inoperative.

20. Any limitations or restrictions herein contained may be amended from time to time if the owners of at least two-thirds of the lots agree thereto. Each such amendment shall be evidenced by written instrument signed and acknowledged by the owner or owners concurring therein, setting forth the facts sufficient to indicate compliance with this instrument and recorded in the Office of the Recorder of Hamilton County, Indiana.

Witness our hands and seals this 20th day of October , 1975.

STATE OF INDIANA)SS
COUNTY OF MARION)

Appeared before me, the undersigned, a Notary Public, in and for said County and State, Guernsey VanRiper, Jr. and Crooked Stick Development Corporation by Guernsey VanRiper, Jr., President & John M. Kitchen, Secretary, and acknowledged the execution of the above and foregoing certificate as their voluntary act and deed for the uses and purposes therein expressed.

_____
Notary Public

My commission expires March 6, 1979.

Under authority provided by Chapter 47, Acts of 1951, of the General Assembly, State of Indiana, this plat was given approval by the Board of County Commissioners of Hamilton County, Indiana, at a meeting held on the _____ day of _____, 1975.

President
Harold W Fanta
Roy A Dean

CROOKED STICK DEVELOPMENT CORPORATION Buyer under land contract dated July 1, 1975 and recorded July 15, 1975.

By: Guernsey VanRiper, Jr.

Attest: John M. Kitchen, Secy
John M. Kitchen, Secretary

GUERNSEY VANRIPER, JR. Seller under land contract dated July 1, 1975 and recorded July 15, 1975.

Guernsey VanRiper, Jr.

Under authority provided by Chapter 174—Acts of 1947, enacted by the General Assembly of the State of Indiana, and all acts amendatory thereto and an ordinance adopted by the Town Board of Trustees of the Town of Carmel, Indiana, this plat was given approval by the Town of Carmel as follows:

Adopted by the Town Plan Commission at a meeting held March 21, 1975.

CARMEL TOWN PLAN COMMISSION

James Lofgren
President

Secretary

This instrument prepared by Paul I. Cripe, Inc, by James E. Dankert, Secretary, this 31st day of MARCH , 1975.

BRANDYWINE SECTION ONE RECORD PLAT

-LEGEND-
U.E. = UTILITY EASEMENT
S.E. = SEWER EASEMENT
D.E. = DRAINAGE EASEMENT
B.L. = BUILDING LINE

RECEIVED FOR RECORD
AT 11:50 O'CLOCK A M
NOV 12 1976
BOOK 6   PAGE 52-56
June M. Hodges
RECORDER HAMILTON COUNTY, INDIANA
INSTR.# 4653

NOTES ON MONUMENTS & MARKERS

□ DENOTES 4"x 4"x 30" LONG PRE-CAST CONCRETE MONUMENT WITH CUT CROSS IN TOP, SET VERTICALLY AND FLUSH WITH FINISHED GRADE.

• DENOTES "COPPERWELD", ½" DIA. COPPER COATED STEEL ROD 36" LONG WITH 1½" DIA. TAPERED CAP WITH CUT "X" SET VERTICALLY AND FLUSH WITH FINISH COARSE ASPHALT.

STEEL PIN MARKERS (MIN ⅝" DIA. & MIN. 30' LONG) TO BE SET VERTICALLY AT ALL OTHER CORNERS AND INTERSECTING LINES.

000.0 MINIMUM FINISH FLOOR ELEVATION FIRST FLOOR USGS 1929 DATUM

CURVE DATA

CURVE	Δ	R	L	C	T	D
1-₵	13°01'16"	1314.39'	298.71'	298.07'	150.00'	4.359106°
1-A	"	1289.39'	293.03'	292.40'	147.15'	4.443624°
1-B	"	1339.39'	304.39'	303.74'	152.85'	4.277742°
2-₵	34°00'00"	654.17'	388.19'	382.52'	200.00'	8.758552°
2-A	"	629.17'	373.36'	367.90'	192.36'	9.106551°
2-B	"	679.17'	403.03'	397.14'	207.64'	8.436135°
3-₵	29°47'03"	305.05'	158.67'	156.80'	81.12'	18.782361°
3-A	"	280.05'	145.68'	144.99'	74.47'	20.459068°
3-B	"	330.05'	171.67'	169.65'	87.77'	17.359675°

Exhibit A : A portion of a Record Plat

FIG. 8-4—Exhibit A. This record plat shows a portion of a complete record plat including lot sizes, street layouts, various power and sewer easements, building lines, etc. Courtesy of Paul I. Cripe, Inc., Indianapolis, Indiana.

SUGGESTED READINGS

(See the appropriate chapter in the following books.)

Brown, Robert Kevin. *Essentials of Real Estate.* Englewood Cliffs, N.J.: Prentice-Hall, Inc., 1970.

Burby, William E. *Real Property,* 3rd ed. St. Paul, Minn.: West Publishing Company, 1965.

Kratovil, Robert. *Real Estate Law,* 6th ed. Englewood Cliffs, N.J.: Prentice-Hall, Inc., 1974.

Ring, Alfred A. and Jerome Dasso. *Real Estate Principles and Practices,* 8th ed. Englewood Cliffs, N.J.: Prentice-Hall, Inc., 1977.

Weimer, Arthur M., Homer Hoyt, and George F. Bloom. *Real Estate,* 7th ed. New York: The Ronald Press Company, 1978.

REVIEW QUESTIONS

1. A legal description which conveys the NW ¼ of the NW ¼ of Section 24 of a specified township includes

    (A) 160 acres
    (B) 10 acres
    (C) 40 acres
    (D) 80 acres

2. Both the abstract and opinion method of assuring title and title insurance

    (A) protect the buyer against encroachments by adjoining property owners
    (B) protect the buyer against the claim of a buyer under an unrecorded land contract
    (C) protect the buyer against defects of record
    (D) protect the buyer against unrecorded mechanic's liens

3. "Lot 452 of Rolling Hills subdivision of the City of Anytown" would be part of what type of legal description?

    (A) governmental survey
    (B) metes and bounds
    (C) platted subdivision
    (D) none of the above

4. A township contains

    (A) 6 miles
    (B) 24 square miles
    (C) 36 sections
    (D) two of the above

5. Which items would appear on a subdivision plat?

    (A) sanitary sewer easement
    (B) storm sewer easement
    (C) electrical service lines
    (D) all of the above

6. Title insurance

    (A) protects the seller
    (B) protects the grantor
    (C) insures the holder against financial loss
    (D) all of the above

7. The premiums on a title insurance policy are paid

    (A) at the time of the listing
    (B) annually with the taxes
    (C) once, upon issue of the policy
    (D) none of the above

8. The mortgagee's title insurance policy protects the

    (A) seller from financial loss
    (B) purchaser from financial loss
    (C) lending institution from financial loss
    (D) none of the above

9. Under a Torrens system

    I. the registrar carefully determines that the deed presented is from the registered owner
    II. a fund is available to pay claims arising from the registrar's errors

    (A) I only
    (B) II only
    (C) both I and II
    (D) neither I nor II

10. The recording process provides the public with

    (A) title insurance
    (B) constructive notice
    (C) building permits
    (D) none of the above

11. In investigating the history of the title to a given piece of real estate, the abstractor checks

    I. public records relating to judgments, zoning ordinances, and the like

    II. records maintained by the county recorder of deeds, mortgages, mechanic's liens, and the like

    (A) I only   (C) both I and II

    (B) II only   (D) neither I nor II

12. The recording system protects a bona fide purchaser or mortgagee for value if he or she

    I. gives value in reliance upon the record

    II. is acting in good faith and has no actual knowledge of unrecorded documents which affect the title

    (A) I only   (C) both I and II

    (B) II only   (D) neither I nor II

13. To qualify for recordation a deed must be

    (A) in writing

    (B) signed by the grantor

    (C) acknowledged

    (D) all of the above

14. The county recorder's duty with regard to documents submitted for recordation includes

    I. a careful examination to verify that the document correctly describes the parties, the property, and the interest being created or transferred

    II. checking the document to see that it meets the eligibility requirements including the fact of acknowledgment

    (A) I only   (C) both I and II

    (B) II only   (D) neither I nor II

15. Under the general rules of law a purchaser of real estate is entitled as a matter of right to

    I. satisfactory evidence that the seller is the true owner of the property

    II. a general warranty deed, unless some lesser quality is agreed upon

    (A) I only   (C) both I and II

    (B) II only   (D) neither I nor II

16. The general warranty given by an abstractor is

    I. that the abstract is complete and that all properly recorded instruments are digested correctly

    II. that the current owner of record has clear and marketable title

    (A) I only   (C) both I and II

    (B) II only   (D) neither I nor II

17. The purchaser of real estate today is entitled to receive

    I. a perfect title with no defects except those included in the contract of sale

    II. a merchantable title as determined by local standards

    (A) I only   (C) both I and II

    (B) II only   (D) neither I nor II

18. When a valid claim is paid by a title insurance company, it is entitled to recoup the loss by

    I. charging it back to the insured

    II. exercising its right of subrogation and suing the seller on his warranties

    (A) I only   (C) both I and II

    (B) II only   (D) neither I nor II

19. When property which has existing title insurance is sold to a later buyer

    (A) the insurance is assigned to the new buyer so that he is covered

    (B) the title insurance company is relieved from any loss suffered by the seller when a defect is found that existed when the policy was issued

    (C) the insurance does not protect the new buyer unless the title is reexamined and a new policy issued

    (D) none of the above

20. The governmental survey refers to a grid of

    I. north and south lines called meridians

    II. east and west lines called parallels

    (A) I only   (C) both I and II

    (B) II only   (D) neither I nor II

Chapter 9

Landlord and Tenant Relationships

VOCABULARY

You will find it important to have a complete working knowledge of the following words and concepts found in the text or the glossary.

assignment of lease
burden-shifting clauses
condemnation of leased
  premises
constructive eviction
destruction of subject matter
economic waste
estate at sufferance
estate at will

estate from year to year
estate for years
eviction
forcible entry and detainer
illegality of purpose
implied warranty of fitness
indexed rent adjustments
insurable interest
invitees
leasehold estate

net, net lease
obligation to pay rent
percentage leases
periodic tenancy
recording leases
self-help
subleases
triple net lease
vacation of premises
valid lease

CURRENT STATUS OF THE LAW

DURING much of the history of the United States, the legal rights and duties of both landlords and tenants were relatively static. The common law of leases developed by the courts and supplemented by sparse statutory rules of definition of terms, rights, and obligations were vague. The result was development of the standard form lease which spelled out in considerable detail the rights and obligations of both landlord and tenant. Since the landlord historically held the better bargaining position (particularly in the area of residential leasing) the standard forms tended to be "landlord's leases." That is, they were heavily weighted in favor of the landlord and frequently were almost oppressive so far as the tenant was concerned.

Today we are witnessing a dramatic change in the law to the opposite extreme. The age of consumerism has had a great impact on traditional common law rules already. The courts are now "reading into" leases implied warranties of habitability and "reading out" exculpatory clauses which traditionally relieved the landlord from any and all liability to the tenant for defects in the leased property.

The Model Residential Landlord-Tenant Code, which has not yet received wide acceptance by state legislatures, represents a dramatic reversal of the traditional rules favoring the landlord and appears destined to be widely adopted in one form or another. Tenant rent strikes and the payment of rent to an escrow agent instead of the landlord when the condition of rented property does not meet health and safety standards have become widespread and have been granted judicial approval even where there was no legal precedent for doing so.

In short, the law governing the rights and duties of landlords and tenants alike is in a state of almost constant change, but the trend is toward an increase in the rights of the tenant with a corresponding increase in the obligations of the landlord. In the discussion which follows, the traditional common law rules are discussed, with notations added to those which have already experienced significant change.

DEFINING LEASEHOLD INTERESTS

A *leasehold* is an estate in land created by a contract called a lease. Considerable inconsistency exists in the law of leases and the landlord-tenant

91

relationship. This has resulted from the fact that the courts have sometimes applied strict property law principles and at other times have applied contract law principles in ruling on the various issues presented. Many problems are generated by characterization of the tenant's interest as an estate in land and the strict application of real property rules, but the application of contract rules in a dispute concerning an estate in land introduces its own problems. Therefore our basic definition is adequate only to the extent that it at least suggests that both contract law and real property law principles are applicable in this area.

LEASEHOLD ESTATES GENERALLY RECOGNIZED

Various types of leasehold estates have developed over a period of several hundred years in England and the United States. A wide variety of limited leasehold interests once existed in early English common law. Most of these have long ago fallen into disuse, and it is unlikely that they would be recognized by any modern court. At the same time the few leasehold interests clearly recognized today do not always provide a sufficient range of choices for all situations. No one leasehold estate that we recognize is ideal, and as a result many leases in common use today have been so drafted that they do not fit neatly into any of the categories set out below. The parties to the lease of course have the right to include almost any modification upon which they can agree. The rules governing the leasehold estates recognized by law, however, apply to the extent that the parties do not change them by contract.

Estate From Year to Year

While *estate from year to year* is the correct technical name for this leasehold estate, it is misleading in that it implies a relatively long-term lease measured in yearly increments. It is more commonly referred to as an *estate from period to period* or as a *periodic tenancy*. This tenancy is an estate which will continue for successive periods of a year, or successive periods of a fraction of a year, unless it is terminated. As suggested by this definition, the period of tenancy may be much shorter than a year. It may be from quarter to quarter, month to month, week to week or, conceivably, day to day.

While the term of the lease is specified as a year or a fraction of a year, the important characteristic of the periodic tenancy is that it renews itself or is automatically extended for another period without any affirmative action by either the landlord or the tenant. In fact, it renews itself whether they want it to or not. One or the other must take some affirmative action to terminate it.

The termination of the periodic tenancy must be accomplished by a formal notice of termination from either the landlord or the tenant. In addition, the timing of this notice is critical. That is, the party against whom the lease is being terminated is entitled to some advance notice. Unless the parties agree to some other time of notice, our statutes impose a highly technical notice provision. Notice of termination must usually be given 3 months or one whole period (whichever is less) prior to the termination date. If, for example, the tenancy is from month to month, then the amount of notice must be at least 1 month. If it is a year-to-year tenancy then, generally, notice must be given at least 3 months in advance of the termination date. The notice of termination is critical to the right to terminate the tenancy, and this technical rule is strictly enforceable.

Certain precautions in the use of the periodic tenancy are apparent from its characteristics, particularly the requirement of notice of termination. The longer the period of the lease, the more severe the consequences of failure to give timely notice of intent to terminate the lease. For example, failure on the part of the landlord to give timely notice of intent to terminate a year-to-year lease gives the tenant the absolute right to remain for another whole year. While it is true that the parties may still negotiate termination of the lease at the end of the year or at some later point, the bargaining position of the parties has drastically changed. That is, 2 months and 29 days prior to the end of the period the landlord may have to buy possession that 1 day earlier he or she could have had for nothing (where three months' notice is required). Where there are sufficient administrative controls to ensure that notice dates will not be overlooked, this tenancy may have a stabilizing effect upon occupancy without the necessity of negotiating a new lease at the end of the period. Where these controls are lacking or the lease is an occasional transaction, there is more danger that the notice date will be overlooked. For relatively short periods of course the damage which results from failure to give timely notice is minimized.

Estate for Years

An estate for years is an estate having a duration fixed in units of a year or multiples or divisions thereof. This definition, like the one for periodic tenancy, is of little help and is again misleading. The key element of the estate for years is that it *must have a definite date of expiration.* It makes no difference if the estate is for a period of time measured in terms of days, months, or years; if it has a definite expiration date, then it is an estate for years. The book, *Restatement of the Law of Property,* goes so far as to say that, if the duration of the estate cannot be precisely computed at the outset, then it is not an estate for years. This definite, *determinable date of expiration* is the key to recognizing the estate for years and is the most important feature of the leasehold estate it creates. That is, the duration of the lease is precisely stated, and there is no possibility of automatic or accidental renewal of the lease for another term. It terminates upon its expiration date without any action on the part of either the landlord or the tenant. In fact, it takes affirmative action on the part of *both* of them to continue the relationship beyond the expiration date.

The termination of the estate for years requires no specific action by either the landlord or the tenant. As noted above, when the termination date arrives, the leasehold interest of the tenant expires. The tenant is obligated to vacate the property on that date, and the landlord is entitled to retake possession. This type of lease has the advantage of certainty as to the availability of the property upon that date (assuming of course that the tenant does not wrongfully hold over), but it also creates a lack of certainty as to the continuity of occupancy. That is, unless the parties agree otherwise in the terms of the lease, the estate ends on the appointed date. The landlord is not entitled to notice from the tenant as to intentions to vacate or not and may be hesitant to bear the cost of seeking a new tenant when he or she may be able to retain an existing satisfactory tenant. However, the tenant has no degree of assurance that the leasehold estate will be available for continued occupancy or the terms which may be imposed by the landlord. To this extent then the estate for years may introduce a degree of uncertainty unacceptable to both the landlord and the tenant.

As a practical matter the estate for years may be undesirable to both the landlord and the tenant because of its definite expiration date. Because of prevailing and anticipated market conditions (or other reasons) it may be unattractive to one party or the other. If the market conditions are unsettled or the landlord anticipates that the market price for the interest being leased is likely to increase, he or she may desire an estate for years because it will provide an opportunity to renegotiate the terms of the lease at its expiration date with either the existing tenant or a new one. The landlord may not want to be "locked in" to the same terms he or she might have been willing to accept at the onset of the lease. The tenant, for precisely the same reasons, may not be willing to be exposed to a renegotiation of the terms of occupancy at the end of the term of the lease.

At this point the relative bargaining strength of the parties becomes a key factor. While the landlord may wish to be in a position to renegotiate the terms of the lease a year hence, he or she may not be able or willing to let the property sit vacant until the market price rises and, in addition, the anticipated rise may not occur. The tenant, however, may not desire exposure to renegotiation of the lease but, assuming the property is attractive to or needed by that person, he or she may not be in a position to pass up the opportunity to have its possession now even though the cost to do so may be more than the current market seems to dictate. It is at this point that the definite expiration date of the estate for years may become a thorn in the side of both parties. Frequently, the solution to the problem is a combination of two things:

1. A longer term than was initially contemplated by the tenant which will assure the landlord of a longer period of "guaranteed" occupancy and perhaps a higher rent than might otherwise be commanded by the property in the current market, plus

2. An option permitting the tenant to renew the lease for one or more additional periods of time, usually at an increased rental which provides some protection to the landlord in the form of increased return if the tenant exercises the option, and provides protection to the tenant by assuring him or her of continued availability (at a higher price) without being obligated to extend occupancy.

The above arrangement provides some measure of protection to both parties but does not of course rule out the possibility of negotiations leading to a different lease on completely different terms. It does, however, give the tenant an advantage in negotiations, and this advantage usually has to be paid for in the form of higher rent for the initial term.

Estate at Will

The term of the estate at will is unknown at its outset. That is, no termination date is specified, and neither is a period specified. It is an estate which is terminable at the will of either party and will continue indefinitely if no action is taken to terminate it by one party or the other. This feature of the tenancy at will introduces an even greater degree of uncertainty as to continued occupancy by the tenant, since he or she is free to vacate at any time after giving notice of termination, and the landlord has the same right to terminate the lease at his or her pleasure upon providing proper notice. It should be noted that the lease terminates at the death of either party.

The notice required to terminate the tenancy at will is therefore critical, since neither party has any assurance of the continuation of the estate. It is only the length of the notice that gives either party any period of time upon which to rely. Local statutes dictate the length of notice, but it may be as short as 30 days. Such notice is referred to as a "notice to quit."

Fortunately, in view of the short period of time provided for the notice to terminate the tenancy at will, this tenancy normally cannot arise by implication or by accident. It usually must be clearly and specifically created by the parties. In addition to this rule, there is also a presumption that a tenancy which is vaguely defined is treated as a month-to-month periodic tenancy. In any event, for property of real continuing value to the tenant, this tenancy should be used only with care and deliberation and with full knowledge of its consequences.

For property of lesser value of course it seems that a tenancy at will does not present a serious problem for either party. At worst (from the landlord's standpoint), it will be a month-to-month tenancy, and it may eliminate the need for a formal written lease, the expense of which is not justified.

Estate at Sufferance

The so-called estate at sufferance is not an estate in land at all. It is simply a way to distinguish between one who has been rightfully in possession of the land of another under a valid lease and then wrongfully holds over, and one who was wrongfully in possession at the outset. The *Restatement of the Law of Property* defines the tenancy at sufferance as *an interest in land which exists when a person who had a possessory interest in land by virtue of an effective conveyance wrongfully continues in possession of the land after the termination of such*

interest but without asserting a claim to a superior title. Since it is not a true estate in land, it has no termination date nor are any mechanics required to work an effective termination of the lease.

The termination of the estate at sufferance does not require notice, because it is not a true estate; however, this is not meant to imply that physical removal of the tenant is a simple matter. Even though the landlord is entitled to immediate possession, the taking of it can be quite hazardous in terms of liability for forcible entry and detainer. The problems created by self-help in this area are discussed in detail in connection with the subject of eviction later in the chapter.

CHARACTERISTICS OF A SIMPLE LEASE

A *simple lease*, as the term is used here, is intended to mean the simplest kind of agreement between the landlord and tenant under which the tenant takes possession of the landlord's property and the parties intend to create the relationship of landlord and tenant. It may be written, but it frequently is not. It is an unwritten lease or a written lease which is oversimplified that calls into play the common law and statutory law which exist today. Just as a person who dies without making a will has a will written for him or her by the statutes of intestate succession, so too do the landlord and tenant have their lease written for them by law to the extent that they fail to write it themselves. Knowledge of the rules of law which will be read into the relationship and imposed upon the parties is quite important, not only to be aware of their impact but to be forewarned as to what items ought to be agreed upon. The common law and even statutory law are in many respects outmoded and do not agree with the general rules as conceived by the average landlord and tenant.

Rights and Obligations of the Parties

It is not practical to consider the simple lease an abstract estate in land. Any study of this estate must be in terms of the rights of the parties, because these are the manifestation of the leasehold estate. This is typically the way in which attorneys approach property law. Ownership is equated to a collection or bundle of rights to hold and use the property. So it is with the simple lease; the ownership of the leasehold interest is made up of a group of rights which accrue to the tenant.

The tenant is entitled to be put into possession of the property by the landlord. Surprisingly, this rule is not universal and has not always been the common-law rule. Because the landlord is conveying to the tenant an estate in land with the exclusive right to possession, it was at one time the law that, since the tenant had an estate, he or she had sufficient interest to remove parties in possession in his or her own name. It is clear, however, that, if the landlord is to receive rent for granting possession to the tenant, the landlord ought to have the burden of removing anyone who is wrongfully (or still more important, rightfully) in possession. In short, he or she ought to be compelled to deliver that for which he or she is accepting payment. Fortunately, this rule of law is clearly established; the landlord has a positive duty to put the tenant into possession.

The landlord's right to enter upon the property for purposes of inspection is not clearly established even today. According to the pure estate theory of leases, it is clear that the landlord has no such right because he or she has conveyed an estate to the tenant whose consequent right to possession is exclusive as against everyone else, including the landlord. The normal practice is to reserve this right specifically to the landlord in the standard form leases in common use. The inclusion of such a clause has been common for so long that a strong argument could be made to the effect that this custom is so common that it has achieved the status of law. Unfortunately, the only way to prove this is to try the issue in a local court and obtain a favorable ruling. To obtain such a ruling may require an appeal to a court having appellate jurisdiction. The expense of this process far outweighs the expense of using a reliable form lease.

The right of the tenant to enjoy his or her estate in land includes the right to "sell" it by *assigning* his or her rights under the lease. Since the relationship between the landlord and the tenant is not a personal one, there is no contract law principle prohibiting assignment of the tenant's rights. It is therefore clearly established that the tenant under a valid lease has the right to sell his or her estate. It is just as clear, however, that the tenant cannot sell any more than he or she owns, and the assignee therefore takes the leasehold subject to all restrictions and limitations included in the lease. It is also firmly established that the original tenant cannot escape his or her obligations under the lease by assigning his or her interests under it to another. The tenant remains liable unless and until the landlord agrees to accept the new tenant as a substitute for the initial tenant. This requires a new agreement, however, and the landlord is under no compulsion to enter into one.

The tenant, unless specifically prohibited by the lease from doing so, has a clearly established right to create lesser estates or interests in the property. That is, the tenant may even become a landlord for the term of the leasehold estate and *sublease* the property to others. He or she can create any interest which does not exceed his or her estate in land. If the tenant has, for example, a lease for years which runs for a 3-year period, a sublease can be created for any period which is shorter, such as 2 years, 11 months, and 29 days. As with the assignment of any leasehold, the tenant cannot create broader rights to the use of the property than he or she has, and the original tenant remains primarily liable for the performance of all duties imposed upon him or her by the lease.

The obligation of the tenant to pay rent is absolute. This rule follows from the fact that the tenant has, under law, an estate in land.

Some relief from the obligation to pay rent has come to be recognized today under the contract doctrine of *absolute destruction* of the subject matter of the contract, which relieves both parties from the obligation to perform the contract. Under this doctrine, if the entire subject matter of the contract is accidentally destroyed, neither party is further obligated to perform. The application of this doctrine to the leasehold estate area typically arises when the lease covers office space on an upper floor of an office building which is completely destroyed. By giving recognition to the business reality of the situation, it is clear that the use of the land itself was not contemplated by the parties and that the parties actually dealt for something which no longer exists. In the absence of an undertaking on the part of the landlord to replace that which was bargained for, it would be grossly unfair to require the tenant to continue the payment of rent.

A tenant under a valid lease may use the property for any lawful purpose. It is clearly a matter of some importance to the landlord to know the purpose for which the leased premises will be used. This is particularly true if the lease covers one portion of a shopping center in which the landlord has given to another tenant the exclusive right to conduct a particular business. A tenant under an unrestricted lease might conduct the same business, which would result in a breach of the right of the tenant under the exclusive lease and would permit that tenant to vacate at a serious loss to the landlord. The important point is that under a lease which has no restrictions as to use, the tenant may use the property for any purpose which is legal, and the landlord is unable to compel the tenant to use the property for any restricted purpose, no matter how disastrous this might be to other tenants or to the landlord.

The right of the tenant to use the leased premises for any legal purpose may, as outlined above, work to the disadvantage of the landlord. By the same token, this right may become a real burden upon the tenant. This occurs when the tenant leases with a particular purpose in mind, which is not specified in the lease. The tenant may not avoid his or her obligations under the lease if his or her intended purpose becomes illegal. The tenant still has an estate in land which may be utilized for any *legal* purpose. The risk that the tenant's intended usage may later become illegal is the tenant's risk, not the landlord's. While this may appear to be a harsh rule to be applied against the tenant, it must be remembered that inclusion of a specific clause can be negotiated into the lease if the tenant desires this protection. Some additional consideration may of course have to be paid to the landlord to obtain this protection.

While it is true that a tenant who has specified a *particular purpose* or use for the property may be relieved of his or her obligations under the lease, this rule is very technical and its application is difficult. The illegality of the purpose of the lease must be general rather than specific as to the tenant. For example, assume that the tenant has leased space for the specific purpose of operating a tavern. If, because of a change in the laws it becomes illegal to operate a tavern on the premises the tenant has rented, then the tenant will be relieved of obligations under the lease. If, however, the tenant is unable to operate a tavern on the premises because he or she cannot qualify for a license, that person is not released from his or her obligations. The distinction between the two cases is legally significant. The risk that the tenant may not be able to qualify for a liquor license is a risk that he or she must take, but the law does not compel the tenant to take the risk of general illegality of a particular purpose. While the above example may be extreme, the same result can arise from the occurrence of a change in zoning regulations which makes illegal a use which was legal at the time the lease was consummated.

Condemnation

In the event of a condemnation of the leased premises, the tenant, since he or she has an estate in land, is entitled to be compensated for his or her interest. Under the rules which apply to a taking by eminent domain, any interest in land may be taken, but the owner is entitled to be paid for his or her interest. An important point to be considered in this connection is that the award is not usually made separately; it is made to the owner of the fee. At this point the division of the proceeds between the landlord and the tenant is the next order of business. The tenant is entitled to be paid the value of his or her leasehold interest. This is true even though the tenant may take the bulk of the award because of the value of the leasehold estate. The question of the division of the award is a highly complex legal question and requires representation of the parties by competent counsel.

The leasehold estate of the tenant represents an important encumbrance upon the fee interest of the landlord. Once the leasehold estate is effectively created, it can be extinguished only by termination in accordance with its terms or a default by the tenant. It is not extinguished or in any way affected by a conveyance of the underlying fee interest. There is merely a change in landlords, and the tenant's rights are unaffected by the conveyance. In fact, the purchase may be motivated by the desirability of the tenant and the favorable terms (to the landlord) of the lease.

Constructive Eviction

A contract doctrine that has been established under the law of landlord and tenant is the doctrine of *constructive eviction*. Under a pure estate theory of leases, there is no such thing as constructive eviction. Either the tenant is in possession or has been ousted from possession by the landlord. If the tenant is evicted, he or she is clearly under no further obligation to pay rent. Modern law has tended to place more emphasis on the *quality* of possession—whether or not the tenant has received all that was bargained for. A typical case arises in the leasing of apartments in which there is a failure on the part of the landlord to provide housing fit for human habitation. The extent to which the tenant is permitted to treat the lease as being at an end and vacate and discontinue rental payments is far from clear at the present state of development of the law. Each situation must be analyzed on the basis of its own peculiar facts, and the determination then made as to whether constructive eviction has occurred. Whether or not the tenant must actually vacate the premises to have the benefit of the doctrine is also unclear. What is clear is the need for legal counsel before acting in reliance upon this doctrine.

Risk of Destruction or Damage

The risk of destruction of the leased property is assumed to some extent by both the landlord and the tenant. Each has an insurable interest in the property, but neither has any obligation to insure the other's interest unless this burden is imposed by the terms of the lease. Since the tenant may have a continuing obligation to pay rent even if some or all of the improvements are destroyed during the terms of the lease, he or she clearly needs the protection of casualty insurance.

However, the tenant has no duty to replace the improvements which have been destroyed, and as a result the landlord who will receive the property back at the end of the lease term without the improvements which have been destroyed clearly has a need for insurance. At the same time, unless the landlord has agreed to do so in the lease, he or she has no duty to replace the improvements which have been destroyed. (The same rules apply for partial destruction or damage to the leased premises.) The solution to the problem is a well-drafted clause which spells out the duty of the landlord to repair or rebuild and the adjustment which will be made in the tenant's obligation to pay rent while repair or replacement is in process. Such a clause is difficult to draw up and should be written with great care.

Liability for Personal Injury

The landlord has no liability for personal injuries which may occur to the tenant so long as the defect which causes the injury is obvious. Nor is the landlord liable even if the defect is not obvious and would not be found by reasonable inspection, provided that the landlord warns the tenant of the defect. The landlord's liability to anyone invited upon the premises by the tenant is subject to the same limitations. That is, if the defect is obvious or a warning is given to all who can foreseeably use the premises, the landlord will not be liable for personal injuries which occur on the leased premises. Disputes frequently arise in this area and, as a result, the landlord usually insists upon a very broad exculpatory clause which frees him or her from liability for almost every conceivable injury to anyone. While such clauses may be effective as to the tenant, they are of doubtful value so far as the tenant's invitees are concerned. They can hardly have their rights foreclosed by a private agreement between the landlord and tenant of which they are unaware. Recent case law developments throughout the country suggest that, regardless of the precautions taken by the landlord to avoid liability, there appears to be almost no way to avoid the doctrine of *the implied warranty of fitness for habitability*, regardless of the nature of the defect. Several states already ignore the exculpatory clause in reading and interpreting a residential lease, and other courts have strongly hinted that they are ready to take the same position when the question is presented.

The tenant, since he or she has an estate in land over which he or she has exclusive dominion, assumes certain obligations to invitees for any personal injury they may suffer. The degree of care the tenant must exercise varies depending on his or her relationship to the invitee. That is, the tenant obviously owes a higher degree of care to one whom he or she has invited onto the premises than to one who is a trespasser. The tenant owes an even higher degree of care and responsibility to one whom he or she has invited onto the premises for the purpose of profit. That is, the *business* invitee is entitled to a greater degree of protection than the gratuitous or social invitee.

The ramifications of this area of responsibility are beyond the scope of this book, since they are highly complex. The important point is that the tenant has an obligation of reasonable care to invitees and that this obligation may not be able to be passed along to the landlord. The need for adequate insurance is obvious.

Extent of Tenant's Right To Use Property

Just as self-help on the part of the landlord is looked upon with disfavor, so is self-help by the tenant subject to sanction. Clearly, when the tenant uses more property than was included in his or her leasehold estate, the tenant is to that extent a trespasser and is treated as such by the law. A more difficult question is raised by a wrongful holding over by the tenant after the lease has been terminated either by its terms or by the breach of a condition imposed by the lease. In such a case, the tenant's original entry onto the property was not wrongful and he or she is therefore not a trespasser. However, the tenant's possession is clearly wrongful and he or she will not be permitted to maintain it against the landlord. The tenant is characterized under the law as a *tenant at sufferance*. He or she may not be forcefully evicted by the landlord, but the tenant's continued possession is at the landlord's sufferance until the landlord can take effective action to evict. The landlord is entitled to be reimbursed by the tenant at sufferance for damages, such as the loss of rental income during the period of the wrongful holding over.

Eviction of Tenant by Landlord

"Eviction," as used in this section, is intended to mean *complete and absolute dispossession of the tenant from the premises rented.* Therefore constructive eviction, considered above, is not considered here. Also, eviction as used here is restricted to the situation in which it is the landlord who causes dispossession of the tenant. Dispossession as a result of governmental action, such as eminent domain, is not included.

Grounds in Lease

The grounds on which the landlord may legally evict a tenant and retake possession of the premises must be found in the terms of the lease itself. The terms of the lease include those specifically included by the parties themselves, plus the rights and duties imposed by the statutory and common-law rules already discussed, at least to the extent that they are not in conflict with the agreement of the parties. As noted earlier, the lease represents a contract between the landlord and the tenant. Since a basic policy of our contract law is that competent parties are free to enter into any legal contract they choose, the parties have wide latitude in establishing the terms of their lease. Generally, these terms are strictly enforced. Two points of information, however, are in order.

The relative strength of the bargaining position of the parties is not ignored by the courts in considering particularly harsh conditions. This is especially true where the enforcement would work a forfeiture. Therefore, if the landlord is for some reason obviously in a position to dictate the terms of the lease, the terms must be fair. If not, they may be found to be unenforceable even though the tenant agreed to them.

When a form lease is used, if there is any uncertainty in its terms, these terms will be construed against the party who furnished the form. This rule is most important from the residential landlord's point of view. The landlord usually much prefers that a standard form of lease be used for all tenants. The uniformity which results promotes efficiency in the management of properties. While it seldom happens that a residential tenant supplies the form, this is not true in the leasing of commercial space. Frequently the tenant of commercial space insists upon the use of his or her own form and is in a strong enough bargaining position to impose its use

on the landlord. The basic rule referred to above, however, is the same in either case: The form will be construed against the party who supplied it. Again, essential fairness of the terms, clearly expressed, will make it unnecessary to resort to a legal interpretation in a court of law.

Both of the above problems have a tendency to occur together. That is, frequently the fact that one party or the other is in a stronger bargaining position permits that party to impose a form of lease on the other. Such a situation would give a court two good reasons for finding unduly harsh terms to be unenforceable.

Typical Grounds for Eviction

While the basic ground for eviction of the tenant is nonpayment of rent (which is discussed at length below), it is not unusual for the landlord to provide for other grounds which will terminate the tenant's right to remain in possession and give rise to the landlord's right to evict. Some of these are the following which are typical:

1. Noncompliance by the tenant with local ordinances which relate to health and safety
2. Bankruptcy or other insolvency of the tenant which results in the right to possession being legally transferred to a receiver or creditor
3. Failure to comply with the exclusive purpose included in the use clause
4. Indulging in immoral or unlawful practices which are prohibited on the premises.

The foregoing list is intended to be illustrative only and is far from being exhaustive. The study of any well-drafted, long-form lease will reveal other conditions and the circumstances existing at the time the lease is negotiated; its purpose and the length of its term will suggest others that are desirable to include. The important element is the clause which makes the breach of any condition grounds for terminating the tenant's right to possession and giving rise to the landlord's right to evict him or her and retake possession.

Nonpayment of rent is the typical and basic ground for eviction of the tenant by the landlord. Payment of the rent agreed upon is the basic consideration provided by the tenant in return for the continued granting of a leasehold estate in the property by the landlord. In terms of statistics, this breach of the tenant's obligation to pay rent is by far the most frequent ground for eviction. It is therefore important to understand the terms under which nonpayment of rent results in the right to evict the tenant and the conditions under which the right to evict must be carried out.

In the absence of an agreement in the lease itself to the contrary, the obligation to pay rent does not arise until the end of the term of the lease. The importance of this feature of the law should not be overlooked from either the practical or legal standpoint.

With a short-term lease (as in the case of a month-to-month tenancy), the landlord's exposure to loss is minimized, since he or she is entitled to rent at the end of the first month and is in a position to take action quickly if it is not received. The situation is otherwise, however, if the lease is for a longer term (such as a year-to-year lease or an estate for years which may terminate a year or more after its inception date), since the landlord cannot demand rent until the end of the term. The landlord's exposure to loss is substantially increased in such a situation. It is of course the usual practice to require the payment of rent on a monthly basis when the term of the lease is a year or more. The practice of providing for rent on some periodic basis throughout the term of the lease is so common that many persons feel it is the legal obligation of the tenant to pay rent in monthly installments. This is not the case, and failure to provide in the lease for such periodic payments can have serious consequences. A typical clause used in a lease which is an estate for years is: ". . . at the rental of $1,200, which the lessee agrees to pay at the rate of $100 each month during the term of this lease." Such a provision permits the landlord to treat the nonpayment of any one installment as a breach of the tenant's obligation to pay rent and to proceed to evict the tenant in accordance with the procedures outlined below.

Notice is required to terminate the lease for nonpayment of rent. This is usually statutory, and no eviction proceeding can begin until appropriate notice has been given to the tenant that the lease has been terminated and that he or she must vacate the premises for failure to pay the agreed upon rent. It must be noted that the expiration of this period is critical to the landlord's right to have possession of the property delivered up by the tenant. This period of time must of course be added to the period of time for which the rent was due, since it is not due until the end of the term (unless the parties agree otherwise). It is therefore clear that the exposure of the landlord to risk is measured by the term of the lease plus the period of notice plus the time it takes to have the tenant physically removed.

The importance of the notice which must be given to terminate the lease for nonpayment of rent lies in the fact that, at the end of the period, the landlord has no assurance that the tenant will in fact vacate and surrender possession. At the end of the term of the lease the landlord has the legal *right* to possession. Whether the landlord has the *fact* of possession is another matter entirely. If the tenant moves out and vacates the premises during this period, the landlord may enter and retake possession of the property. If, however, the tenant fails to vacate the property, the landlord must take further action (a formal eviction proceeding) to remove the tenant and regain possession. This fact further delays the retaking of possession and increases the landlord's risk of loss of rent. A partial solution to this problem is described below.

Failure to pay rent due in *advance* usually terminates the lease, and no notice of termination is required. While the general rule is, as stated earlier, that rent is due at the end of the term, the parties are free to agree to any rental arrangement they desire. If they in fact agree that the rent is payable in advance, the agreement is enforceable and local law comes into play. The significance of this rule should be apparent; it minimizes the landlord's risk of loss of rent when the tenant defaults, because the landlord knows of the default at the beginning of the term rather than at the end. In addition, the landlord's risk is still further reduced by the fact that he or she need not give notice to terminate; the tenant's right to possession is automatically terminated by failure to pay the rent when it is due. As a result, the landlord is entitled to demand possession immediately and, if it is not immediately surrendered, he or she may begin the formal eviction process at once.

The payment of rent in advance has two advantages from the landlord's standpoint. The landlord knows at the beginning of the term if there will be a default and can take action to retake possession immediately because no notice to terminate is required. It is nevertheless apparent that the landlord is still exposed to the risk of loss of rent for the period of time it takes to remove the tenant from possession effectively either by a voluntary act of the tenant or by a formal eviction proceeding. To protect against even this risk many landlords require at the outset of the lease that 2 months' rent be paid in advance, one being earmarked for the first month of the tenant's lease and the second for the last month's rent. This provides, as a practical matter, protection against loss of rent during the period it takes to remove the defaulting tenant, provided of course that this does not extend beyond one period of the lease, usually 1 month.

An advance payment should not be confused with the *damage deposit* frequently required by landlords, since the damage deposit is earmaked for extraordinary repairs made necessary by damage caused to the premises by the tenant which are in addition to *normal wear*. The landlord may be entitled to the damage deposit even if the tenant does not default in payment of rent but commits waste or unreasonable damage to the property during the tenancy. In practice the damage deposit and the last month's rent collected at the beginning of the term of the lease are frequently confused by both the landlord and the tenant. It is not at all uncommon for the tenant to forfeit the damage deposit as a penalty for breaking the lease by leaving before the end of its term. Landlords frequently accept the damage deposit in lieu of exercising the right to sue the tenant for the rent due for the balance of the term.

It should be noted in this connection that eviction is not the exclusive remedy of the landlord for a breach of the lease by the tenant. The landlord is entitled to pursue remedies for any damages he or she may suffer as a result of the tenant's breach. That is, the landlord is entitled to sue for all anticipated rents for the entire term, even though the tenant has vacated and surrendered possession prior to the end of the term. Of course, the landlord may not sit idly by and let the damages accumulate. The landlord has a duty to mitigate his or her damages. That is, the landlord must make a reasonable effort to rent the premises to another tenant for the unexpired portion of the term and deduct the *net* proceeds of such rental, after deducting expenses involved in obtaining a new tenant, from the amount owed to him or her by the defaulting tenant.

Limitations on Self-Help

Limitations on self-help by the landlord in retaking possession of the leased premises after a default by the tenant are imposed by law and are enforced by rather stern consequences for violation of the law. Self-help is generally frowned upon by the law on the theory that there is available a legal system designed to provide a peaceful means for settling all disputes. This policy is particularly forcefully administered when there is the distinct possibility of a breach of the peace because of the personal confrontation of the parties which is necessary to regain possession of property wrongfully held by an-

other. In short, forcible entry by the landlord to regain possession of the property simply is not tolerated by the law. Neither may the landlord forcefully retain the property no matter how the landlord obtains possession, unless it is done through the legal machinery of a formal eviction proceeding.

Forcible entry into the premises for which the landlord has granted a leasehold estate to the tenant is the single act most likely to provoke a drastic reaction from our legal system. When such action is indulged in by the landlord, he or she may be faced with a serious lawsuit with equally serious financial consequences. The suit by the dispossessed tenant in such a case does not proceed solely upon the *actual* damages he or she has suffered. In addition, punitive or exemplary damages are awarded by the court far in excess of any actual provable damages. These damages are, as their names suggest, designed to punish the landlord for taking the law into his or her own hands and to make an example of the landlord for others in the community. It is a rather serious matter when the landlord is charged with forcible entry.

The term "forcible entry" might mislead one into believing that the use of physical force must be involved. Case law in this area has, however, expanded the definition of the term to include fraud or trickery on the part of the landlord to obtain possession of the property and his or her subsequent forcible retention of it.

The foregoing rules clearly indicate that precautions should be taken whenever the landlord retakes possession of leased premises after a default by the tenant. Only two situations appear to permit retaking without legal proceedings: (1) when the premises have been abandoned by the defaulting tenant, and (2) when, upon being asked to vacate, the defaulting tenant does so. In all other situations, there is serious risk that the landlord will be in violation of the forcible entry and detainer law with possibly drastic consequences.

Vacation of the Premises by the Tenant

Just as there are situations in which the landlord may be justified in removing the tenant for a breach of a condition of the lease, such as nonpayment of rent, so can the tenant be sometimes justified in vacating the premises under certain conditions. That is, when the tenant is not receiving the benefit of his or her bargain, there should be an opportunity for the tenant to vacate and discontinue payment of rent. In the event of a failure of consideration (furnishing of the estate under the conditions agreed upon), it is clearly unfair to require the tenant to continue possession and the obligations imposed upon him or her by the lease.

Rights in Lease

As in the case of the landlord, the tenant's rights must be generally found in the lease itself. That is, just as the tenant may be obligated under the lease to do more than just pay rent, so may the landlord be obligated to perform more than just the bare furnishing of possession of the premises. If the landlord is to be obligated beyond the furnishing of mere possession, then this obligation must be found in the lease itself. The same rules regarding the rights and duties of the parties under their contract and the interpretation of the form lease which were discussed in regard to eviction by the landlord apply with equal force and effect to the tenant who desires to vacate and avoid obligations before the end of the term of the lease. In addition to the general rights to exclusive possession for the term of the lease without actual or constructive eviction by the landlord, typical provisions frequently negotiated for the tenant's benefit include:

1. The right to use the property for any lawful purpose
2. The right to have an exclusive right to use leased premises for a certain purpose, as in a shopping center
3. Maintenance and repair of the property by the landlord
4. The right to extend the lease for an additional term at its expiration upon predetermined conditions and rent.

Again, the above list does not purport to be conclusive. Many conditions may be imposed by the tenant, even including the option to purchase the property during the term of the lease. The nature and extent of the tenant's rights (in addition to possession) depend on the circumstances and bargaining positions of the parties at the time the lease is negotiated.

Eviction

Eviction by the landlord, a physical ouster from possession, is the basic ground which relieves the tenant of his or her obligations under the lease. Even under a pure estate theory of leases, it would be manifestly unfair to require the tenant to perform his or her part of the bargain when the landlord, by his or her own actions, makes it impossible for the tenant to have possession of the leased premises. Considered earlier were those situations in which something less than a complete ouster is involved, such as constructive eviction in which there is substantial failure of the landlord to provide the estate agreed upon. In these cases there is, in the eyes of the law, a failure of the tenant's estate which relieves the tenant of the obligation to pay for it. Of course, when governmental intervention either takes the leased premises or makes the sole purpose of the lease illegal, both parties are relieved from further performance of their duties under the lease.

Breach of a Specific Condition

Additional grounds or conditions may, by the agreement of the parties, be made conditions precedent to the tenant's obligations under the lease. Just as the landlord may restrict the tenant's use of the property to a single purpose, so is it possible that a tenant may obtain the exclusive right to use the premises for a particular purpose within a prescribed area. Such a condition of exclusivity may or may not be one which the landlord can control, but whether the landlord has control or not, the parties can agree upon such a continuing state of affairs.

When the condition of exclusivity within a particular area ceases to exist, the tenant is free to vacate and cease payment of rent or have whatever other relief the lease may provide. Where the parties have clearly established in their lease the conditions under which the tenant is obligated to continue performance of his or her obligations, at least the consequences are predictable. That is, upon a breach of the condition, the tenant may vacate the premises, stop paying rent, and be relieved of other obligations imposed by the lease. However, the lease may require the tenant to accept the breach of the condition for some period of time without being relieved of the lease's obligations. Such provisions are quite common. Also common are provisions which permit modification of the tenant's obligations on a predetermined basis when the landlord is unable to perform his or her obligations completely. Such clauses permit the parties to retain the benefits of their bargain when the breach is not material.

Requirements of a Valid Lease

In view of the complexity of the rules relating to leasehold estates and the possibility of misunderstandings between the landlord and the tenant, it seems that the lease should be carefully thought out and should be in writing so that the parties clearly understand their rights and obligations. Such a practice is strongly recommended; however, the bare legal requirements are satisfied by a great deal less in most cases. Considered below are the questions of the necessity for formality in establishing the leasehold estate, and the relationship of the landlord and the tenant.

Requirement of a Written Lease

Since a lease is, in legal effect, a conveyance of an estate in land and is also frequently a contract which cannot be performed within 1 year, it appears logical to require that it be in writing. Under the statute of frauds, as a general rule, each of the above two characteristics requires a written contract in order to make the parties' agreement enforceable. The short-term lease of real estate, however, represents a major exception to the general rule. That is, leases for short terms need not be in writing. They may be oral and are nevertheless enforceable by both the landlord and the tenant. If the lease is for an extended period, it must be in writing to comply with the statute. Two major problems must be considered in deciding whether or not the lease in a given case should be in writing: enforceability of the lease between the landlord and the tenant, and notice of its existence to third persons.

A lease between the landlord and the tenant may be enforceable even though not in writing if it is for a short period of time. The terms of the lease, to the extent that the oral agreement of the parties does not change them, are those of a simple common-law lease, which have already been discussed in detail in this chapter. It is apparent that, except for relatively short-term leases (as in the case of a month-to-month tenancy), the practice of relying upon an oral lease is hazardous and invites disputes. Seldom do the parties reach specific agreement on all the points which should be considered.

So far as third persons are concerned, the oral lease poses a serious problem. A purchaser of real estate must take it subject to the rights of tenants in possession under a valid lease. It has already been noted that sale of the fee does not cut off the rights of the seller's tenants. Since the short-term lease need not be in writing, neither must it be recorded, since there is nothing to record. Therefore a prospective purchaser, even if he or she carefully checks the records maintained by the county recorder, will not be aware of the existence of the oral lease unless he or she also inspects the property and determines what rights are claimed by whoever is in possession. While it is true that the seller normally makes certain warranties in the deed which are for the protection of the buyer, these warranties generally provide only for the payment of damages where the true facts are not as represented. Therefore, even though the buyer may have the right to sue the seller for damages resulting from the fact that the fee is encumbered by a short-term lease, this does not affect the tenant's rights to the benefits of the lease. The prudent purchaser of real estate has no choice, if he or she is to be a bona fide purchaser, but to inspect the property immediately prior to closing the sale. If the purchaser finds someone other than the seller in possession, he or she must make inquiry to determine what rights the party in possession claims. If he or she fails to do so, the purchaser may be saddled with a tenant for a relatively long term rather than having the right to the immediate possession anticipated.

Parties to the Lease Must Be Competent

Since the lease of real estate is an important agreement which has characteristics of both a conveyance and a contract, the law requires that the landlord and the tenant be competent to enter into a binding lease. There is a certain degree of risk in dealing with anyone in a business matter, and it is a practical impossibility to be certain of anyone's legal competence. This is a risk that is inherent in all business, and the real estate business is no exception. The problem may be even more acute in the real estate business, because of the fact that transactions, including leasing, are not usually entered into out of hand. That is, there is normally some discussion and negotiation involved, because of the importance of the transaction. As a result, there is more opportunity to make a judgment as to the competency of the parties and therefore less excuse for *not* making that judgment. Fortunately, there is a general presumption that all persons are competent, and to avoid contracts the incompetent person generally has the burden of proving that he or she is incompetent.

Requirement of Consideration

Since the lease is, in legal effect, a contract between the landlord and the tenant, it must meet the technical rule that consideration is essential to make it enforceable. Simply stated, the requirement of consideration means that to make a promise enforceable it must be paid for. In the lease of real estate, the basic consideration provided by the landlord is continued provision of an estate in land; for the tenant the consideration is payment of the agreed upon rent. This is of course an oversimplification, because the typical lease imposes additional duties upon both the landlord and the tenant. In each instance the lease itself shows what consideration each party must provide to support the obligations of the other party. The important point to be noted in connection with the lease of real estate is that there must be some consideration provided by each party to make the lease enforceable. It is also important to note that neither party is entitled to more than the agreed upon consideration. Consider the following situation.

Example: Landlord and tenant enter into a valid lease of an apartment for 1 year at a rent of $100 per month. After 6 months the landlord increases the rent to $125 per month, advising the tenant that the increase is dictated by increased maintenance expenses. The tenant agrees to pay the increased rent but fails to do so. The landlord sues the tenant for the increase. The tenant will prevail.

Explanation: In the above example it is clear that the parties had agreed upon the rent for the entire term of 1 year. Even though the tenant promised to pay the increased rent, he or she cannot be compelled to do so. The legal reason why the tenant does not have to keep the promise is that the landlord did not provide any consideration to make the promise binding. That is, the landlord was already legally obligated to provide space to the tenant at $100 per month. The landlord has not undertaken or promised to do anything that he or she was not already obligated to do under the lease agreement. The landlord is therefore not entitled to the increased rent but only to the rent agreed upon at the outset.

Legality of the Purpose of the Lease

As a general matter of contract law, a contract for an illegal purpose is not enforceable. So far as the lease of real estate is concerned this rule makes it impossible for either party to enforce the terms of the lease. A lease entered into for the purpose of conducting a gambling house is clearly illegal today in most states, and either party could avoid the obligations of the lease. A more serious question is raised when the lease is entered into for a purpose which is legal at the time it is negotiated but which later becomes illegal. This matter is covered earlier in the chapter.

Requirement of Recording

As noted earlier, the statute of frauds does not even require that a short-term lease be in writing. Clearly, for such leases neither is there any requirement to record the lease, because there is no writing which can be recorded. If, however, the lease is for a lengthy period, it must be in writing to be enforceable between the parties. In order to provide notice to third parties such a lease must also be recorded with the recorder of the county in which the real estate is located. Failure to do so may result in a loss by the tenant of his or her rights under the lease if the property is purchased by a bona fide purchaser from the landlord. It is not usually necessary that the entire lease be recorded, since many statutes provide for the filing of a memorandum of lease which is sufficient to protect the rights of the tenant, without requiring that a public record be made of the entire contents of the lease. The landlord may have little or no interest in seeing that the lease is recorded, since the recording of the lease primarily protects the tenant and in fact creates an encumbrance on the landlord's title. As a result it is quite common for a detailed lease to require that the landlord agree to execute a short form or memorandum of lease in recordable form so that the tenant can protect his or her interest.

A written lease, even though it is not required to be recorded because it is for a short term, may nevertheless be recorded if it is in recordable form. Short-term leases are not, as a matter of practice, recorded. This is partly because they tend to clutter up the record and, more importantly, are encumbrances on the owner's title. Once they are recorded, they continue to be defects of record and, unless they expire by their terms, evidence must later be provided that they have expired or been terminated. For example, if a lease from year to year is recorded and the tenant defaults after 6 months, the record will continue to show that he or she has an interest in the property, and in the event of sale by the landlord this defect will have to be cleared. In the event that the tenant is not cooperative, this will require litigation by the landlord (such as a quiet title action) to establish as a matter of record that the tenant has no further interest in the property. There are, however, certain situations in which the recording of a short-term lease may be important to the tenant. Assume, for example, that the tenant for some reason is not in actual possession of the property, so that his or her claim of some interest in the property is not apparent to third persons who inspect the property. In such an unusual case the tenant may desire a recordable lease so that the record will protect his or her interest as against third parties.

To be recordable the lease must of course be in writing. In addition there are other formal requirements which must be met so that the lease will be accepted by the recorder. It is essential that the lease be acknowledged. If it is not, the county recorder will not accept it for recording. (This requirement of acknowledgment is the same as that for deeds and other documents.) It goes without saying that the legal description must be accurate and sufficient to identify the property clearly. Again, this description should be as detailed as would be in a deed, and for the same reason: If it is not correct, it will not be properly indexed and may not be effective to provide notice to third persons.

Rent Adjustment Provisions

While it is true that the landlord may not arbitrarily increase the rent being charged under agreement with the tenant and that the tenant is similarly bound to pay the full rent agreed upon, it is frequently in the best interests of both parties to provide for some degree of flexibility, particularly where the term of the lease is very lengthy. With significant changes in economic conditions—real estate taxes, casualty insurance costs, and maintenance expenses—the party with the obligation to pay them may suffer serious economic loss. At the same time, the location of the leased property may by itself be an important factor in determining the fair rental value. Clauses which provide some measure of protection to both parties can be included in the lease at the outset. Several examples are:

1. *Indexed adjustment of rent.* A commonly used clause in long-term leases is one based upon some standard economic indicator maintained by an independent third party. For residential properties it is quite common to provide that the rent will be adjusted annually upon the basis of the cost-of-living statistics maintained and published by the federal government. Since this measure includes a wide variety of items which are unrelated to rents for apartments (such as the cost of food), this clause is frequently tied to only that portion of the cost of living that relates to housing. In this way, even though the trend has been upward for the most part in recent years, theoretically both the landlord and the tenant are protected from dramatic swings in the value of housing. Since the lease terms are a matter of private contract between the landlord and the

tenant, there is no reason why this provision could not also include an escalation clause to cover the increasing costs of insurance and rising real estate taxes. Such clauses need to be drafted with considerable care, the primary emphasis being on the certainty of measurement of the indicator and its application to the originally agreed upon rent.

2. *Percentage leases.* In the commercial area it is quite common to utilize a percentage lease. Such a lease includes a relatively low annual rent (but at least sufficient to cover debt service, taxes, and insurance), with a provision that the rent will be increased by a specified percentage of sales volume experienced by the tenant. Such leases are frequently encountered in shopping centers on the theory that the location in the center and its promotion by the landlord and other tenants have a direct impact upon the volume of sales generated by a particular tenant. This theory is easier to recognize when it is applied to a franchise type of operation located within a major store. For example, the shoe repair department of a large retail store is frequently operated by someone other than the store itself. In such a case it is far clearer that the traffic generated by the store's general advertising has a direct impact upon the volume of traffic and the volume of business done by the independent shoe repair department operator. Once again, considerable care must be used in drafting such a provision and several difficult questions must be negotiated:

a. What is the percentage that will be applied? That is, just how much benefit is there to the tenant in terms of increased business?

b. To what will that percentage be applied? To the gross business done or the net profit earned?

c. How will determination of the volume of sales be made to the satisfaction of both parties to the lease? An independent audit by a certified public accountant is one method; however, in the case of a relatively small operation, its expense may be prohibitive, and some less precise method may have to be accepted to make the arrangement beneficial to both parties.

3. *Burden-shifting clauses.* It is not at all uncommon to find leases which require the tenant to pay any increase in insurance costs which results from the use to which he or she is putting the property; however, the lease can go even further and provide that the tenant pay *all* insurance, real estate taxes, and maintenance expenses in addition to the agreed upon rent. In such a case we have a true *net-net-net lease.* That is, the rent received by the landlord

is net of all three expenses which are assumed by the tenant. Such leases are often used where the tenant will make substantial and expensive improvements upon the property and use it for a lengthy period of time. The price paid by the landlord to obtain such a lease is frequently the surrender of all rights to increase the rent during the term of the lease. The rate of return he receives in such cases is static and may effectively decline during inflationary periods.

4. *Combinations of all the variations discussed above* are of course quite possible, but once again it should be stressed that any combination of these provisions, each of which is complex in itself, is the job of the expert attorney. The professional property manager, however, must have a working knowledge of these variations and the ability to recognize which combination is most appropriate in a given situation, as well as the negotiating skills to structure the lease properly.

SUGGESTED READINGS

(See the appropriate chapter in the following books.)

Dasso, Jerome, Alfred A. Ring, and Douglas McFall. *Fundamentals of Real Estate.* Englewood Cliffs, N.J.: Prentice-Hall, Inc., 1977.

Downs, James C., Jr. *Principles of Real Estate Management,* 11th ed. Chicago: Institute of Real Estate Management, 1975.

Gross, Jerome S. *Concise Desk Guide to Real Estate Practice and Procedure.* Englewood Cliffs, N.J.: Prentice-Hall, Inc., 1976.

Kratovil, Robert. *Real Estate Law,* 6th ed. Engle- wood Cliffs, N.J.: Prentice-Hall, Inc., 1974.

Lusk, Harold and William B. French. *Law of the Real Estate Business,* 3rd ed. Homewood, Ill.: Richard D. Irwin, Inc., 1975.

Ring, Alfred A. and Jerome Dasso. *Real Estate Principles and Practices,* 8th ed. Englewood Cliffs, N.J.: Prentice-Hall, Inc., 1977.

Weimer, Arthur M., Homer Hoyt, and George F. Bloom. *Real Estate,* 7th ed. New York: The Ronald Press Company, 1978.

REVIEW QUESTIONS

1. Under a valid lease, the tenant

   (A) may assign his or her entire interest under the lease to another without the landlord's approval
   (B) may sublet the premises to third parties without the landlord's permission
   (C) is responsible personally to the landlord for the performance of all tenant's obligations under the lease
   (D) all of the above

2. When the leased premises are taken by the state under the power of eminent domain,

   I. the landlord and the tenant share the payment received equally
   II. the tenant is not entitled to any portion of the award

   (A) I only   (C) both I and II
   (B) II only   (D) neither I nor II

3. When a lease has a definite termination date which can be clearly established at the begin-

ning of the lease, it is called

   (A) an estate for years
   (B) an estate at sufferance
   (C) a determinable lease
   (D) a periodic tenancy

4. When the tenant under a valid lease holds over after it terminates

   I. the landlord may physically remove the tenant and his or her belongings
   II. the tenant is considered by the law to be purely a trespasser

   (A) I only   (C) both I and II
   (B) II only   (D) neither I nor II

5. A tenant under a valid lease, as a general rule,

   I. may use the property for any lawful purpose
   II. must pay the rent at the end of the term

   (A) I only   (C) both I and II
   (B) II only   (D) neither I nor II

6. A lease which automatically renews itself in the absence of notice of intent to terminate by one party or the other is called

   (A) a tenancy at sufferance
   (B) an estate from year to year
   (C) a tenancy at will
   (D) an estate for years

7. A lease which provides for a base rental plus a percentage of the gross sales of the tenant is called

   (A) an indexed lease
   (B) a sublease
   (C) a net-net-net lease
   (D) a percentage lease

8. To negotiate a valid lease

   I.   both the landlord and the tenant must be competent
   II. the lease must be for a legal purpose

   (A) I only   (C) both I and II
   (B) II only   (D) neither I nor II

9. When the leased premises consist of an office in a building completely destroyed by fire

   I.   the lease terminates under the theory that there has been a complete destruction of the subject matter of the contract
   II. the tenant must continue to pay rent under the theory that he has an estate in land and the land was not destroyed

   (A) I only   (C) both I and II
   (B) II only   (D) neither I nor II

10. Under the common law of leases the tenant has an estate in land; therefore

    I.   the tenant has the right of exclusive possession of the premises
    II. the landlord, because he owns the underlying fee, has the right to enter the leased premises at all reasonable times to inspect the property

    (A) I only   (C) both I and II
    (B) II only   (D) neither I nor II

11. An estate from year to year (periodic tenancy)
    I.   can be terminated by giving notice of intent to terminate of one full period or the statutory period, whichever is less
    II. terminates automatically at the end of the term

    (A) I only   (C) both I and II
    (B) II only   (D) neither I nor II

12. In a net-net-net lease the tenant pays for

    (A) the real estate taxes
    (B) the casualty and liability insurance
    (C) the maintenance expenses
    (D) all of the above

13. When a visitor is invited onto the leased premises by the tenant, the tenant

    I.   must warn the visitor of any dangerous condition that is not apparent
    II. has no duty to the visitor unless the visitor was invited for business purposes

    (A) I only   (C) both I and II
    (B) II only   (D) neither I nor II

14. When a tenant remains in possession after the term of the lease has expired he or she becomes

    (A) a trespasser
    (B) a tenant at will
    (C) a tenant at sufferance
    (D) none of the above

15. The tenant under a simple common-law lease

    (A) has an estate in land
    (B) is entitled to be put into possession by the landlord
    (C) may use the property for any lawful use
    (D) all of the above

16. If the sole purpose or use as stated in the lease becomes illegal

    I.   the tenant may vacate and cease paying rent
    II. the rent is automatically adjusted to 50% of the agreed upon rent

    (A) I only   (C) both I and II
    (B) II only   (D) neither I nor II

17. Under modern case law it is clear that

    I.   there is an implied warranty of fitness for habitability in residential leases

    II. there is a warranty of fitness for habitability only if it is in writing

  (A) I only   (C) both I and II

  (B) II only   (D) neither I nor II

18. When the terms of a form lease are ambiguous and harsh and are questioned in court,

    I.   the court will interpret the ambiguous term against the one who provided it

    II. the court will give consideration to the relative bargaining position of the parties at the time the lease was negotiated

  (A) I only   (C) both I and II

  (B) II only   (D) neither I nor II

19. When the tenant defaults by failing to pay the rent, the landlord may evict him or her

    I.   by physically removing the tenant, using force if necessary

    II. by filing suit for cancellation of the lease and eviction under local law

  (A) I only   (C) both I and II

  (B) II only   (D) neither I nor II

20. In the absence of a contrary agreement, rent is due

  (A) for the full term in advance

  (B) in monthly installments on the first day of each month

  (C) monthly on the last day of the month

  (D) at the end of the term of the lease

Chapter 10

Mortgages, Deeds of Trust, and Land Contracts

VOCABULARY

You will find it important to have a complete working knowledge of the following words and concepts found in the text or the glossary.

assumption of mortgage	forfeiture	priorities of mortgages
contract for a deed	grace period	promissory note
covenants	junior mortgage	purchase money mortgage
deed of trust	land contract	rescission
default	liquidated damages clause	second mortgage
deficiency judgment	mortgage	security device
encumbrance	mortgagee	senior mortgage
equitable title	mortgagor	specific performance
equity	nonrecourse	subject to a mortgage
equity of redemption	novation	trust deed
foreclosure	penalty clause	trustee
	personal liability	

THE legal aspects of financing the purchase of real estate are of obvious importance to real estate salespersons and brokers. Because of the highly technical nature of this area of the law, it is not covered in great depth in this chapter. It would be impractical to do so in any event, because of the many minor variations in this area of law from state to state. The reader should, however, be aware of the limitations upon the scope of the following discussion and be able to recognize the point at which the need for local legal counsel arises.

MORTGAGES

A mortgage is, in legal effect, a pledge of the owner's interest in real estate and the improvements on it to secure the repayment of a loan. While different states follow either the *lien* or *title* theory of mortgage law, the difference in practical effect is minimal, and the distinction is ignored in this discussion. The points made below in connection with mortgages are true regardless of the legal theory being applied to determine the rights of the parties.

A mortgage creates a lien on real estate in favor of the lender, and it is important for the reader to recognize that the owner of the real estate retains the usual rights of ownership. All the mortgagee has is the right to pursue the mortgagor's real estate to satisfy the debt which runs from mortgagor to the mortgagee. Since the mortgagor has title, he or she can sell the property, give it away, mortgage it again, or lease it. The mortgagor retains all rights of ownership (plus duties, such as payment of taxes) subject to the right of the mortgagee to foreclose against and sell the property if the mortgagor fails to pay the debt. Not until there is a default in payment of the debt (or in some other obligation set forth in the mortgage) does the mortgagee have any right to proceed against the mortgagor's real estate.

The mortgage secures repayment of a promissory note. The basic transaction which gives rise to a mortgage is a loan from the mortgagee (lender) to the mortgagor (borrower), which is evidenced by a promissory note (secured by a mortgage of real estate). Therefore a mortgage is simply a security device which creates a lien on real estate to secure the repayment of a debt. A mortgage agreement sets out the contractual aspects of the loan; such a contract is ineffective without the existence of debt.

The validity of the lien depends on existence of debt. The life of the mortgage is the debt. Without the existence of debt, there is no purpose for the mortgage, and the mortgagee can have no interest in the property.

The mortgagor may or may not be *personally* liable for the debt. In the case of a home mortgage, the borrower is personally liable for repayment of the money he or she has borrowed. The borrower executes a promissory note which personally binds him or her to repay the amount borrowed, separate and distinct from the mortgage. Therefore, if the mortgagor fails to repay the debt, the mortgagee is entitled to foreclose against the realty, have the property sold, and apply the proceeds to the debt. However, as is frequently the case, if this is insufficient to pay the debt, the mortgagor-borrower remains personally liable for the balance, the so-called *deficiency*. This point is frequently misunderstood, but it is crucial to consideration of the subject of sales of mortgaged property considered later in the chapter. However, loans on commercial property are frequently made on a *nonrecourse* basis; that is, the lender agrees to look solely to the property in the event of a default, with no personal liability on the part of the borrower.

Requirements To Create a Mortgage

The formal requirements for the execution of a mortgage are the same as those for a deed, including the requirement of acknowledgment if the mortgage is to be recorded so as to obtain the protection of the recording system.

In addition, the typical form of mortgage used today imposes certain additional duties upon the mortgagor, such as the duties to keep the property in good repair, to insure it for the benefit of both the borrower and the lender, to pay all taxes and assessments, etc. Failure to keep these *covenants* (promises) which are contractually made is a breach of the mortgage. These conditions are in addition to the underlying basic promise to pay the debt.

Sales of Mortgaged Property

Because of the theory of mortgages which gen-

erally prevails, under which the mortgagor (owner) of real estate has title to the property and the mortgagee has only a security interest which can only be exercised upon default, it is clear that the owner of mortgaged property may sell it. It is also clear, however, that the rights of the mortgagee cannot be defeated by such a conveyance, and that the mortgagor is still personally liable for the debt. There are three ways in which the mortgagor may sell his or her property, and the results of each are discussed here.

Free and Clear

In a sale free and clear of the existing mortgage, the following occurs:

1. The old mortgage is satisfied at the sale. The buyer provides sufficient cash to permit the seller to pay the debt. The seller pays the debt, and the mortgage which secures it is released by the mortgagee. Since the seller has paid the debt and the mortgage has been released, he or she has no further liability, and the property is free and clear of the encumbrance of the mortgage.

2. A new mortgage may be executed by the buyer. In many cases, the buyer simultaneously borrows money and executes a new mortgage of his or her own so that the property is actually free and clear for only an instant, and it is difficult to recognize legally what has occurred. From a practical standpoint, the property remains subject to a mortgage, but there is a new debt, a new mortgage, and a new mortgagor-owner.

3. The seller has no further liability for debt by virtue of the release by his or her mortgagor.

Subject to the Mortgage

When the existing mortgage is not satisfied at the time of sale (so that the sale will be free and clear), then there are the following results:

1. The seller remains personally liable for the debt. The original mortgagor's note is unpaid and the mortgagor's obligation to pay it remains; i.e., he or she remains personally liable for the whole debt.

2. The buyer is not liable for the debt. The buyer has no personal obligation to pay the seller's debt, because he has not contracted to do so. As a practical matter, to protect his investment, he must pay the debt; but if he fails to do so, he cannot be compelled to pay it.

3. The mortgagee's rights against the property are unchanged. Since the mortgage was an existing

encumbrance, the property is still the security for the original borrower's debt. If the debt is unpaid, the mortgagee can foreclose against the property no matter who owns it. The mortgagee may then sue the original mortgagor for any balance still due, but has no rights against the subsequent purchaser personally for any deficiency. Neither does the original mortgagor have any rights against the purchaser who bought "subject to" the mortgage.

4. In the event of a default sale and a deficiency, the seller is personally liable and the buyer has no liability to either the seller or the mortgagee. It is very important that the reader understand that the seller remains personally liable in such a sale and that the buyer does not become liable for the debt personally. The maximum risk assumed by the buyer is the loss of whatever payments he or she has made to the seller or against the mortgage debt.

Subject to the Mortgage with the Buyer Assuming and Agreeing To Pay the Mortgage Debt

When the existing mortgage is not satisfied at the time of sale, but there is an affirmative assumption of the debt by the buyer (as opposed to merely buying "subject to" the mortgage), then there are the following results:

1. The seller remains personally liable for the debt. The seller still remains personally liable on his or her note (debt) to the mortgagee. It is important to recognize that the underlying obligation of the seller to pay his or her personal debt is not affected by the fact that the buyer has assumed the obligation to pay this debt. The seller's note to the lender is unchanged, and he or she is not relieved of the obligation.

2. The buyer also becomes liable for the debt. The grantee in this situation also becomes personally liable to pay the original debt, because he has obligated himself to do so.

3. The mortgagee may collect from either or both parties to the extent of the debt and costs only. The original mortgagee now has two debtors against whom he can proceed: He may collect from either or both of them for the amount of the debt and costs of collection to the extent that the proceeds of sale are insufficient upon foreclosure. The lender is entitled to satisfaction only once, no matter how many assuming grantees there are. Each buyer who assumes the mortgage debt (no matter how many there are) becomes liable for the debt. When there is fore-

closure and collection of a deficiency judgment by the mortgagee, the last assuming buyer (who can pay it) is liable for the deficiency. The important point is that, even though a buyer assumes the mortgage debt from the original mortgagor, the original mortgagor remains liable. It is, after all, his personal debt and he cannot avoid liability by entering into a contract with another who agrees to pay it. If the assuming buyer is unable to pay the debt, the creditor (mortgagee) is still entitled to enforce the obligation against the original borrower. It is quite important therefore, in selling property which is subject to a mortgage, to determine whether or not the buyer is financially responsible.

Foreclosure Upon Default

1. Default is defined as failure to pay the debt plus other items specified in the mortgage (e.g., payment of taxes, insuring the property).

2. Foreclosure must be by a legal process. The following are the basic steps in foreclosure:
   a. A suit is filed in the county where the property is located.
   b. A judgment is obtained on the note in favor of the lender.
   c. Execution is obtained—an order to the sheriff to take possession of the property and sell it at public sale.
   d. The property is then sold at a public sale at which the lender is generally entitled to bid.
   e. The proceeds of the sale are applied to the mortgage debt, court costs, and attorney's fees.
   f. The excess goes to the mortgagor; if the proceeds are insufficient, the mortgagor remains liable for the balance.
   g. Other property of the mortgagor may be attached by the sheriff and sold to satisfy the deficiency.

3. The mortgagor has an equity of redemption. The mortgagor has the right to redeem the property after default, but this right is limited as follows:
   a. Execution of a judgment cannot be issued earlier than the statutory period provided by local law; i.e., the property cannot be sold even though a judgment has been obtained.
   b. To redeem the property, the mortgagor must pay the entire debt plus the mortgagee's costs; i.e., the mortgagor cannot just bring the payments up to date but must also pay the whole amount of the loan balance.

PRIORITIES OF MORTGAGES

It is possible for the owner of real estate to incur more than one debt, each secured by a mortgage of his or her property to different creditors. A second mortgage on real estate is commonly used. From the second mortgagee's standpoint, it is essential to recognize that his or her security interest is "junior" to that of the first mortgagee. As a result, in the event that neither secured creditor is paid, the second mortgagee must recognize that he or she must be satisfied with whatever is left from the proceeds of the foreclosure sale after the first mortgagee is completely satisfied (including the expenses of sale and collection), again on the theory that the owner-mortgagor can only pledge what he or she has, the net value of the property.

Second mortgages can be important security devices even though they are junior to the first mortgagee's lien on the property. They are frequently used to secure property improvement loans or as additional security for other loans unrelated to the property itself. This is possible because the second mortgagee can sue on the note and second mortgage and make the first mortgagee a party. Indeed, the second creditor must do so to force a foreclosure sale. Since under the typical form mortgage in use today such action may permit the first mortgagee to "deem himself insecure," the first mortgagor also forecloses on the mortgage. This permits the second mortgagee to exert great pressure upon the debtor for repayment of the second loan. Nevertheless, if the net proceeds of the sale are insufficient to pay the junior lien holder, the second mortgagee will be compelled to look to other assets of the borrower for repayment.

PURCHASE MONEY MORTGAGES

In some cases the seller is also the mortgage lender. This may result from the fact that the buyer cannot obtain favorable financing through normal sources, that the seller may view the mortgage as a good investment, or for other reasons such as income tax consequences of the sale. The seller then holds a *purchase money mortgage* which has priorities over certain other claims against the buyer-mortgagor such as other liens against the property created by the mortgagor, particularly preexisting judgments against the buyer which become a lien against all property owned or acquired by such buyer.

Technically, of course, any mortgage loan made to finance the purchase of real estate is a purchase money mortgage; however, for the commercial mortgage lender to obtain the degree of protection which would be afforded to the seller-lender, great care is taken to see that the proceeds of the loan are disbursed directly to the seller rather than to the purchaser-mortgagor and *then* to the seller. Caution must nevertheless be exercised by the mortgage lender, even if it is the seller, to be sure that the mortgage is promptly recorded since it has no priority over other mortgages or liens recorded in the interim between execution and recording.

DEEDS OF TRUST

In states which utilize the *deed of trust* in addition to or in lieu of the mortgage for purposes of securing loans on real estate, the differences, from a practical standpoint, are more apparent than real. Under the deed of trust for security purposes, the basic underlying transaction is still the same; that is, there is a loan which is evidenced by a promissory note. To this extent there is no recognizable difference from the mortgage loan transaction already discussed. The technical difference is the manner in which the loan is secured by a deed of trust. There is a deed to the real estate, which transfers legal title to the property to an independent third party *trustee*. This is done under a formal agreement which obligates the trustee to do one of two things: (1) When the loan is paid, the trustee must deed the property to the borrower (buyer), or (2) if the borrower defaults, the trustee must sell the property and pay the proceeds to the lender to the extent necessary to repay the loan; any overage then goes to the borrower.

Rights of the Parties

To understand the rights of the parties when the legal title is held by the trustee, it is first necessary to understand a few of the fundamentals of trust law. It is beyond the scope of this book to examine trust law in detail; however, two basic points must be considered:

1. Under the deed of trust (trust deed) there is a split of the title between the trustee and the beneficiaries of the trust. The trustee takes the *legal* title, and the beneficiaries retain the *equitable* title to the property. That is, the beneficiaries have the power to compel the trustee to carry out the terms of the trust: in this case the positive duty to deed the property back to the

borrower when the debt has been paid, and the negative duty to refrain from deeding it to the borrower until full payment has been made to the lender. The term "equitable title" is based on the fact that a court of equity or one having equity powers will, if petitioned by the beneficiaries, compel the trustee to carry out the duties imposed by the trust agreement.

2. It is fundamental to the law of trusts that the trustee take only so much of the legal title as is necessary to carry out the terms of the trust. Any action taken by the trustee which exceeds this built-in limitation constitutes a breach of trust and renders the trustee liable to the damaged beneficiary.

Rights of the Buyer

Because of the development of the law with regard to deeds of trust, either by statute or by case law, the buyer who is not in default has generally the same power to deal with real estate covered by a deed of trust that a mortgagor has with respect to mortgaged property. That is, the property may be sold subject to the deed of trust, with the new buyer assuming the obligations to the lender. The primary obligation to retire the debt of course remains that of the original borrower. As a practical matter, the rights of the buyer who gives a deed of trust to secure a loan are the same as those of a buyer who uses a mortgage to secure the debt.

Rights of the Lender

There is a split of authority in the area of lenders' rights under the deed of trust. In many states, either as a result of statute or case law, the theory is that any conveyance of real estate intended to secure the payment of a debt is in effect a mortgage, and local foreclosure procedures must be followed just as though it were in fact a mortgage. In these states a deed of trust is seldom used except in connection with major bond issues. In states which recognize the deed of trust which includes a power of sale upon default by the buyer as something other than a mortgage, foreclosure proceedings are not required and the buyer has no equity of redemption. In these states deeds of trust are very commonly used, and mortgages are seldom seen. A note of caution is in order here, because in states which recognize deeds of trust there is no uniform law and local law should be investigated to determine the precise rights of the parties.

LAND CONTRACTS

The basic transaction involved in a conditional sales contract or *land contract* or *contract for deed* is simply this: The seller retains title to the real estate until it is paid for, which is really no different from the usual agreement to purchase for cash. The distinguishing feature of a land contract, however, is that payment is not immediately made in full, but instead is made over a lengthy period of time, usually a number of years. The length of time involved makes it essential to specify in detail the rights and duties of the parties to the contract.

A particular form of contract has evolved for such sales, which in essence transfers the rights and burdens of ownership to the buyer during the term of the contract, subject to certain rights retained by the seller so as to provide the seller with a well-developed security interest in the property and empowering the seller to enforce the terms of the contract against the buyer. Of course, the seller retains legal title to the property, which gives him or her an inherently strong security interest. Nevertheless, the buyer has, during the term of the contract, a significant interest called *equitable title,* which gives him or her broad latitude in dealing with the property, plus the absolute right to have the legal title conveyed to him or her upon full payment. This is a significant and substantial legal right, protected by law. Still, the buyer's rights are limited by whatever terms and conditions are agreed upon by the parties, subject always to the basic rules of law governing contracts.

While land contracts are most frequently used in the sale of relatively inexpensive properties, particularly when conventional methods of financing are unavailable because of the age and condition of the property or the financial strength of the buyer is questionable, it should be kept in mind that this method of sale can be used to obtain important income tax advantages by spreading a significant capital gain over several tax years. A detailed discussion of the installment sales provisions of the Internal Revenue Code is beyond the scope of this book; however, the possibilities for tax saving should be considered whenever a significant capital gain will be incurred by the seller of real estate. The basic features of land contract sales are as follows.

General Contract Law Rules Apply

While local forms of contracts may vary, it remains true that general principles of contract law must be observed in conditional sales contracts for real estate. These are reviewed briefly below, since they are discussed in detail in Chapter 13.

Essentially these basic rules are:

1. The parties must be legally competent to enter into a contract.
2. The three fundamental elements of all contracts must be present: *offer, acceptance, and consideration.*
3. The contract must be in writing in order to comply with the statute of frauds, which requires that all contracts relating to the sale of real estate must be in writing in order to be legally enforceable.
4. All the rights and duties of the parties must be included in the contract.
5. If the parties intend that the contract be recorded, then it must be acknowledged (and, in some states, the name of the preparer must also be shown).

The Seller Retains Legal Title as Security

While the normal rules of contract law apply to land contracts, they are nevertheless security devices. It is frequently said that the seller under a land contract has the best security device available: legal title to the property being sold. Under a typical land contract no deed is given to the buyer until the last payment has been made. Only then is the seller obligated to transfer full legal ownership to the buyer. The following points should be emphasized:

1. The land contract is generally not treated as a mortgage. That is, the buyer does not have legal title and therefore cannot sell the fee interest. The buyer may, however, in the absence of any prohibition in the contract, *assign* his or her rights to a third party. This does not relieve the original purchaser of the obligations assumed in the initial contract. (Most forms of land contract include a clause prohibiting assignment of the buyer's rights without the seller's approval. When the assignment to a new buyer is approved by the seller, there is a *novation,* a new contract, between the seller and the new buyer. In this event the original buyer is relieved of the obligations under the original contract.)
2. There is generally no equity of redemption available to the defaulting buyer as there is under a typical mortgage. There is, instead, a *grace period* specified in the contract during which the buyer may "catch up" past-due payments and

cure the default. This is purely a matter of negotiation between the buyer and the seller at the time the contract is entered into, and it may be very short (even 1 day) or very liberal (6 months or more), depending upon the negotiating positions of the parties. (The remedies of the parties upon default by either one of them are considered later; however, it should be noted that some courts have begun to conclude that an unreasonably short grace period is inherently unfair and have treated such contracts as though they were mortgages, thus requiring foreclosure proceedings and providing an equity of redemption.) The general rule that the parties are free to make their own contracts is, however, still the fundamental law in the area of land contracts.

3. During the term of the land contract the buyer has *equitable title* only. This means that when the buyer has completed his or her side of the bargain (made all payments, etc.), he or she is entitled to a deed to the property, and a court of equity orders conveyance of the property to the buyer. Since the seller has the legal title during the term of the contract, he or she retains the power to sell the property, subject of course to the rights of the land contract buyer. The new owner of the property becomes entitled to receive payments from the contract buyer and is legally bound to convey the property to the buyer when the buyer's side of the contract is completed.
4. Along with the equitable title and the right to possession of the property during the term of the land contract the buyer generally has all the burdens and obligations which go along with home ownership. Once again, it should be noted that all duties and rights must be found in the land contract itself. The standard contract in use today shifts the burdens of ownership to the buyer, such as the duty to pay all real estate taxes and assessments, the duty to insure the property for the benefit of both seller and buyer, and the duty to repair and to refrain from "waste" of the property. Other duties may be included by specific contract provision. One point is clear: If the contract buyer improves the property (by building a house on it, for example) and then defaults, the buyer may not remove these improvements because, under the law of fixtures, they have become part of the real estate.

Rights of the Parties Upon Default

The basic defaults considered here are failure of

the purchaser to make payments under the land contract as agreed and failure of the seller to convey merchantable legal title after receiving payment of all money due from the purchaser. While a variety of other technical defaults can occur during the term of a land contract sale, these two go to the heart of the matter and represent the two types of default that are significant and common.

Default by the *seller*, by virtue of inability or unwillingness to convey title to the property to the buyer after all payments have been made, gives rise to several alternative remedies on the part of the buyer. Since the buyer is entitled to a deed after completing all his or her obligations under the contract, particularly full payment, and since real estate is unique in the eyes of the law, the buyer is entitled to the remedy of *specific performance*. That is, he or she is entitled to bring action in a court of equity which will *compel* the seller to make conveyance of the property to the buyer. The court order to do so is an absolute directive, and a failure to comply with it may result in imprisonment for contempt of court until the seller "purges" himself of the contempt by doing what he was ordered to do. This remedy is extreme and is available in only a very few cases; however, the conveyance of real estate is one of these cases.

Suppose, however, that the seller has no power to convey the property because it has been sold to another. No court can compel a defendant to do that which is impossible. When this occurs, the buyer may *rescind* the contract and obtain recovery of all payments made under the contract. Recovery based on this theory is reduced by the fair rental value of the property for the period during which the buyer was in possession; however, as a practical matter, the values judicially determined are likely to be prejudicial to the defaulting seller, since failure or inability to perform is presumably the result of his or her own fraud or mistake. If the property has been improved by the buyer in reliance upon the expectation that the seller would perform his or her obligations, the cost of these improvements is also recoverable.

The purchaser may also elect to pursue the normal remedy for breach of contract: the additional cost of purchasing comparable property. In periods of rising values of real estate and buildings, this remedy may be the most appealing to the buyer. This is particularly true where the value of the property contracted for has actually gone *down* while the value of comparable properties has gone *up*. The purchaser may be quite content to abandon the right

to the extraordinary remedy of specific performance in favor of a suit for money damages.

Default by the *purchaser,* such as the basic failure to make payments when due, gives rise to a variety of remedies for the seller. It is very important to recognize, however, that under a typical land contract sale the seller is entitled to be paid for the property sold. As a result, the damages suffered by the seller when the buyer defaults can be measured by a court in terms of *money,* which is not unique, and the remedy of specific performance, in the strict sense of the term, is not available to the seller. The seller must therefore find relief in the terms of the contract as equated to money or repossession of the property or a combination of the two:

1. When there is a default by the purchaser under a land contract, which is not cured during the grace period written into the contract, the seller typically has the right to retake possession of the property peaceably. He or she is entitled to demand possession of the property from the buyer, and the buyer is obligated to surrender it; but if he does not do so, the seller may not use force to "eject" the buyer. (The limitations are quite similar to those already discussed in the area of landlord-tenant relationships.) Legal action to "foreclose" or set aside the contract and remove the buyer is necessary.

2. In addition to the right to retake possession of the property, the seller frequently reserves in a land contract the right to retain all payments made by the buyer prior to the default as *liquidated damages.* That is, there is a forfeiture of all monies paid out by the buyer during the term of the contract prior to the default. The term "liquidated damages" represents a good-faith effort on the part of both parties to determine in advance what the damages will be in the event of a default during the term of the contract. Where this provision appears to be fair, it will be upheld by the courts. Where, however, the so-called liquidated damages clause is grossly disproportionate to the damages actually suffered by the seller when the buyer defaults, the courts will label it a *penalty clause,* an economic "club," and will not enforce the provision. Even though the defaulting buyer may commit a civil wrong which damages the seller, the courts will look closely at such a clause to determine that it is essentially fair to both parties. If it is grossly unfair to the defaulting buyer, regardless of his or her breach of contractual duties, the clause will not be enforced and the seller will have to

prove what damages have actually been sustained.

Acknowledgment and Recording of Land Contracts

Since we are presumably considering a contract of sale which is valid between the buyer and seller, the question of recording (including the technical requirements to make the contract recordable) appears to be a matter of mere technicality. This is not the case. The recordability and recording of the land contract have important consequences for both the seller and the buyer. The pros and cons of recording a land contract are discussed below.

From the buyer's standpoint, recording the land contract is of significance because it serves notice of ownership that cannot be ignored by anyone dealing with the owner of record (the seller) without recognizing the rights of the contract buyer. Even without the protection of the recording system, however, if the contract buyer is in obvious possession (that is, living in a residence which is being sold), any third party dealing with the owner of record is bound to know this fact because such a buyer is obligated to inspect the property and determine what claim the resident nonowner has to the property. The decision as to whether or not to require a contract in recordable form depends upon whether or not the contract buyer is in obvious possession of the property. Where the subject property is vacant land, the claim of ownership of the contract buyer is not obvious, and a recordable contract becomes most significant since it may be the only way that his or her claim of an interest will be effective notice to the general public. In the event that there is no notice of such a claim, either actual (by virtue of obvious possession) or constructive (by virtue of the recorded land contract), then a *bona fide purchaser for value* can cut off the buyer's equitable title by a direct purchase from the owner of record. (See the discussion in Chapter 7 with regard to the necessary qualifications of a bona fide purchaser.)

From the seller's standpoint, recording the land contract is usually considered a nuisance which "clutters up" or "clouds" the legal title to the property. This occurs when there is a default by the contract buyer. Even though there is an admission of default by the buyer and a surrender back to the seller, these facts are not generally in recordable form so that the record is cleared. (A quitclaim deed from the buyer to the seller would serve the purpose, but frequently this cannot be obtained.) In the vast majority of cases the unrecorded defaulted land contract poses no problem, simply because no one knows of it and because it has been eliminated by virtue of subsequent agreement of the parties that it is null and void. If such a contract is recorded, however, it will take some recordable action to clear the owner's record title.

As suggested above, the quitclaim deed from the defaulting buyer back to the seller will clear this defect in the title. If this is not obtainable, however, then there must be a legal proceeding which cancels the contract and clears the record title by virtue of a court decree (which is automatically part of the public records) to clear the seller's legal title. There are occasions when the resistance of the seller to entering into a recordable contract proves to be false economy. If, for example, after informal termination of the contract occurs there is a dramatic increase in the value of the property, a subsequent sale by the record owner may be hampered by unfounded claims of the defaulted land contract purchaser. While such claims may have only a nuisance value, they must be settled and they may be very costly to the owner of the property.

Land contract sales of real estate are deceptive in their apparent simplicity. Significant legal problems can arise long after the defaulted land contract has been presumed settled to the satisfaction of both parties. At the same time the impact of consumerism cannot be ignored. The trend of the law is to protect the buyer (consumer) of housing, and the impact of this movement can be expected to continue in significance and in its impact upon the rights and obligations of the parties to a sale by land contract.

SUGGESTED READINGS

(See the appropriate chapter in the following books.)

Bagby, Joseph R. *Real Estate Financing Desk Book.* Englewood Cliffs, N.J.: Institute of Business Planning, 1975.

Basye, Paul E. *Patton on Land Titles,* 2nd ed. St. Paul, Minn.: West Publishing Company, 1957.

Hoagland, Henry E., Leo D. Stone, and William B.

Brueggeman. *Real Estate Finance.* Homewood, Ill.: Richard D. Irwin, Inc., 1977.

Kratovil, Robert. *Modern Mortgage Law and Practice.* Englewood Cliffs, N.J.: Prentice-Hall, Inc., 1972.

Levine, Mark Lee. *Real Estate Transactions, Tax Planning,* 2nd ed. St. Paul, Minn.: West Publishing Company, 1976.

Lusk, Harold F. and William B. French. *Law of the*

Real Estate Business, 3rd ed. Homewood, Ill.: Richard D. Irwin, Inc., 1975.

MacDonald, James B. *Abstract and Title Practice,* 2nd ed. St. Paul, Minn.: West Publishing Company, 1958.

O'Donnell, Paul T. and Eugene L. Maleady. *Principles of Real Estate.* Philadelphia, Pa.: W. B. Saunders Company, 1975.

REVIEW QUESTIONS

1. Property encumbered by a mortgage may be sold

   I. subject to the mortgage
   II. subject to the mortgage with the buyer assuming and agreeing to pay the debt

   (A) I only
   (B) II only
   (C) both I and II
   (D) neither I nor II

2. Property subject to a deed of trust may not be

   I. sold by the owner
   II. further encumbered by a second deed of trust

   (A) I only
   (B) II only
   (C) both I and II
   (D) neither I nor II

3. A mortgage on real estate

   (A) need not be recorded to be valid
   (B) must be in writing to be valid
   (C) must be executed by the owners to be valid
   (D) all of the above

4. A deed of trust transfers legal title to

   I. the lender until the debt is paid
   II. a third party trustee until the debt is paid

   (A) I only
   (B) II only
   (C) both I and II
   (D) neither I nor II

5. When the seller takes a mortgage back from the buyer as part payment for the sale,

   (A) the seller retains legal title
   (B) the mortgage is a purchase money mortgage
   (C) the seller is entitled to possession of the property until the debt is paid

   (D) no second mortgages may be placed on the property by the buyer

6. In a sale by land contract, the buyer

   I. has equitable title to the property
   II. is entitled to a conveyance of the legal title when all payments have been made

   (A) I only
   (B) II only
   (C) both I and II
   (D) neither I nor II

7. In a sale by land contract, the seller's security is

   (A) the purchaser's written promise to pay
   (B) nonexistent
   (C) the retention of legal title to the property
   (D) the grace period in the contract

8. When the buyer under a land contract has fully performed and the seller refuses to convey the property, the buyer may

   I. sue for specific performance and compel the seller to execute a deed
   II. rescind the contract and sue for all payments made less the fair rental for the term of the contract

   (A) I only
   (B) II only
   (C) both I and II
   (D) neither I nor II

9. During the equity of redemption period in a mortgage foreclosure proceeding, the defaulting buyer

   I. may cure the default by bringing the payments up to date
   II. must pay the entire balance due plus any expenses incurred by the mortgagee

   (A) I only
   (B) II only
   (C) both I and II
   (D) neither I nor II

10. Under a deed of trust when the buyer defaults, the equity of redemption period is

    (A) 90 days   (C) 60 days
    (B) 120 days   (D) there is none

11. When property is sold subject to a mortgage or deed of trust,

    I. the seller is relieved of all liability for the debt
    II. the buyer becomes personally liable for the debt

    (A) I only   (C) both I and II
    (B) II only   (D) neither I nor II

12. Where mortgaged property is sold and the buyer assumes and agrees to pay the mortgage debt,

    I. the seller no longer has any liability for the debt
    II. the lender can recover the balance from either the seller or the buyer or both

    (A) I only   (C) both I and II
    (B) II only   (D) neither I nor II

13. In a typical land contract sale, the buyer has which of the following duties?

    (A) payment of taxes
    (B) insuring the property
    (C) maintaining the property
    (D) all of the above

14. To record a land contract

    I. it must be in writing
    II. it must be acknowledged

    (A) I only   (C) both I and II
    (B) II only   (D) neither I nor II

15. When there are two mortgages (or deeds of trust) against the same property and the borrower defaults, the proceeds of the sale of the property

    I. are divided between the lenders on a pro-rata basis
    II. are applied first to the satisfaction of the first lender even if this exhausts the proceeds

    (A) I only   (C) both I and II
    (B) II only   (D) neither I nor II

16. When the foreclosure sale of mortgaged property does not yield enough to pay off the mortgage(s), the lender(s)

    I. may pursue other assets of the borrower for the deficiency
    II. must be satisfied with the proceeds of the sale

    (A) I only   (C) both I and II
    (B) II only   (D) neither I nor II

17. When there is a foreclosure sale under a mortgage or a deed of trust and the sales price exceeds the amount of the debt, the expenses of collection are borne by the

    (A) attorney for the lender
    (B) lender
    (C) defaulting borrower
    (D) sheriff who conducted the sale

18. When the borrower has completely repaid a loan secured by a mortgage or deed of trust,

    I. the borrower is entitled to a formal release (or deed) to evidence the repayment
    II. the mortgage (or deed of trust) is no longer an enforceable lien on the property

    (A) I only   (C) both I and II
    (B) II only   (D) neither I nor II

19. When a first mortgage is unrecorded and a second mortgage lender, without actual notice of the prior mortgage, extends credit and records the second mortgage,

    I. the second mortgagee in fact becomes the first mortgagee in determining priority of repayment
    II. the borrower remains personally liable to pay both lenders

    (A) I only   (C) both I and II
    (B) II only   (D) neither I nor II

20. Sales by land contract of vacant land which will not be occupied by the buyer

    (A) are valid between the parties
    (B) should be recorded
    (C) do not provide actual notice to the third parties
    (D) all of the above

Chapter 11

Real Estate Finance

VOCABULARY

You will find it important to have a complete working knowledge of the following words and concepts found in the text or the glossary.

acceleration clause	flexible-payment mortgage	purchase money mortgage
amortization	interim financing	RESPA
balloon mortgage	junior mortgage	red-lining
blanket mortgage	loan discounts	savings and loan associations
chattel mortgage	MGIC	senior mortgage
closing statement	MIP	straight term
conditional sales contract	mortgage	swing loan
constant	mortgagee	truth in lending
conventional loan	mortgagor	VA loan
discount points	mutual savings banks	variable mortgage
FHA loan	open-end	wraparound mortgage
filtering	package mortgage	

REAL ESTATE FINANCE

A major factor contributing to the uniqueness of real estate as an economic commodity is the magnitude of the investment required in each real estate transaction. Due to this investment, the demand for credit and financing is continually growing. In most instances the prospective purchaser does not have the required funds as outlined in the sales contract and consequently must obtain funds through some source of credit. While most purchasers will have *equity* funds invested in the property through a down payment, they will also have to rely on additional funding to be obtained through *debt financing.* The most common form of debt financing is the *mortgage* loan, consisting of two separate legal instruments—a *promissory note* and a mortgage agreement.

Salespersons and brokers have found that sales are directly related to the availability of debt financing. Most of the agent's clients have had little experience in real estate buying and therefore do not realize the credit options available to them. It

is to the advantage of the salesperson to be familiar with the various forms of financing provided by lending institutions since this is the major hurdle for most purchasers. An effective salesperson needs a knowledge of lending institutions, their history, requirements, and current operations to be able to advise buyers on the alternatives available to them. As indicated earlier, the most common form of financing is the use of a mortgage loan.

THE MORTGAGE

A mortgage is an instrument by which the purchaser pledges the property being acquired to secure the debt from the lending institution. "Mortgage" is a general term and often refers to a mortgage agreement (deed of trust) or a promissory note (deed of trust note). The mortgage note sets forth the terms and conditions of repayment and makes the borrower *personally* liable for the obligation. Mortgages are considered liens and must conform to the statutes of the respective jurisdictions.

Terms, rates, and conditions of mortgages are not uniform and vary from locale to locale. Many different factors influence the mortgage, all having a great effect on the rate of interest charged. The supply of money offered by lending institutions, as well as the demand for this money, sets the basic interest rate for the mortgage. The degree of risk involved and the general condition of the economy add to the basic factors, setting the final interest rate charged on the mortgage.

The conditions found in the mortgage agreement state whether the mortgagor (owner) or the mortgagee (lender) holds the title. Varying from locale to locale, if the mortgagor has possession of the title then the mortgage acts as a lien; such states are referred to as *lien theory* states. If a trustee holds the title, then the state is considered to be a *title theory* state. Today, all states require due process of law in the event of default. Such proceedings are called foreclosures and are discussed at length in Chapter 10.

TYPES OF MORTGAGES

Mortgages can be placed into categories based on several criteria:

1. The degree of priority is determined by the time of recording. For example:
   a. Senior mortgage (first mortgage): A loan secured by a mortgage note giving the mortgagee the first claim to the property if the mortgagor fails to repay the loan.
   b. Junior mortgage: Any mortgage which is less than a first mortgage and becomes junior or subordinate to the senior claim. Junior mortgages may be listed in order of priority as second, third, fourth, etc.

2. The method of repayment varies depending on the agreement made when the loan is granted. For example:
   a. Straight term: A mortgage in which repayment of the principal is in one lump sum at the date of maturity. Interest only is paid on the principal during the term of the loan. Actual payments to principal are not made during the term.
   b. Amortized (constant): A mortgage in which a definite plan requires the repayment of certain amounts at specified times so that by the end of the term the entire debt is repaid, or amortized.
   c. Flexible payment: A mortgage which provides for terms which enable borrowers to

adjust their payments on a long-term schedule related to anticipated increases in income.
   d. Variable rate: A form of mortgage in which the interest rate fluctuates with changes in market conditions, thereby allowing the lender to better cover expenses.

Straight Term Mortgage

Straight term mortgages are seldom available to individual owners. Basically such a mortgage states that there will be no repayment of the principal until the end of the mortgage life. However, payments are made on a regular basis to cover the interest. The major drawback to this form of financing for residential purchases is that a large payment is due at the end of the mortgage term. This *balloon* payment has curtailed the use of such loans for home buyers. Its use, however, can still be found in the construction industry and in the purchase of large commercial properties. The balloon payment of principal required under a straight term mortgage has often been used in the past as a means of updating the mortgage with current interest rates. To make the final payment, the borrower obtains another mortgage at the current rate of interest. This method protects the lender from wide fluctuations in interest rates but shifts this risk back to the borrower.

Amortized Mortgage

The increased demand for mortgages has led lending institutions to offer amortized mortgages. The lender and the borrower work out the essential terms of the loan, setting the interest rate, the term (i.e., the length of the repayment period), and the principal amount to be borrowed. This type of mortgage requires that the borrower make periodic repayments reducing the balance of the loan. These payments are usually due on a monthly basis and include the interest payment as well as a part of the principal amount. This payment is called the *constant;* sample calculations of the use of constants are provided later in this chapter. The interest accrued on the unpaid portion of the debt is deducted from the repayment, and then the balance of the repayment is applied toward the outstanding principal balance. Interest due is always calculated on the remaining balance of the principal and not on the original value. These monthly payments continue until the entire amount of the mortgage is amortized. The monthly payment is determined by the amount of the loan and the interest rate. As the outstanding principal decreases, there is a corresponding drop in the amount of interest. Because of this, larger and larger portions of the equal monthly payments are applied toward the remaining balance of the loan. The drop in interest payments and the rise in principal payments allow the monthly payment to remain the same. Publications are available that list the required monthly payment for certain rates of interest, term, and loan amount. It is essential for the student to remember that the constant payment is exactly that. The principal and interest charge on a monthly basis remains the same throughout the life of the mortgage. It is simply allocated to principal and interest in a different amount each month.

Over and above the constant amount for the principal and interest payment often an additional amount is collected. These additional funds provide monies to pay property taxes and hazard insurance. Such funds are placed in accounts called *escrow accounts,* and the amount set aside is usually one-twelfth of the annual charges for taxes and also for hazard insurance. These accounts for real estate taxes and insurance can be either separate or combined into a single account.

The escrow account is set up to benefit both the mortgagor and the mortgagee. The special insurance escrow account provides a safeguard to both in the event that the property is damaged by a hazard. The property is continually protected under the insurance, and thus, no loss is incurred by either party. The mortgagor is forced to put aside money for these two purposes (taxes and insurance) on a periodic basis and consequently is not overburdened financially when payments are due. With funds available for these two purposes, no tax liens or uninsured damage can result. The monthly payment then includes payment of the *principal, interest, taxes,* and *insurance* and is often referred to as PITI payment.

These monthly payments help the borrower and the lender. The homeowner finds that he or she can manage money more easily and fit the monthly payment into his or her budget. As long as the borrower continues to pay monthly and meet his or her obligation, the lender cannot demand the full amount due or institute foreclosure proceedings on the property. Lenders see the direct reduction plan (amortization) as a benefit because, as more and more payments come in, the more security there is

behind the loan and the risk is reduced. Prepayment privileges are sometimes included in the monthly payment direct reduction plan as a means of providing a higher margin of safety for the lender than a regular monthly payment.

In some recent mortgages, however, there may be a *penalty* for prepayment. This results from the fact that recent mortgage interest rates have been at historically high levels and lenders are unwilling to permit prepayment without a penalty if the funds paid in cannot be immediately loaned out again at equivalent rates.

Sample Amortization Calculations

Following are several examples that salespersons and brokers encounter. Only partial tables are presented, and more complete tables can be found for computing constant payments for an amortized loan.

Example: What are the monthly payments for a $60,000 loan at 12% interest for 30 years?

Solution: $60,000 ÷ $1,000 equals 60. Multiply 60 by 10.29 (from Table 1) which equals $617.40 constant payment for principal and interest. Thus we find that $617.40 would be required for the monthly payment of such a loan under these terms.

A remaining balance for amortized loans is often needed, and there are tables that provide the necessary information. Table 2 is a partial loan progress table.

Example: For a 30-year loan of $40,000 at 10% interest with a remaining life of 25 years, what is the remaining balance?

Solution: The loan is 5 years old. From Table 2 a $40,000 loan after 5 years has a remaining balance of $38,640 (40 × $966).

TABLE 1

Constant Payment Table

Monthly Payments Required for a $1,000 Loan

Years	8%	9%	10%	12%
1	86.99	87.45	87.92	88.85
5	20.28	20.76	21.25	22.25
10	12.14	12.67	13.22	14.35
15	9.56	10.14	10.75	12.01
20	8.37	9.00	9.66	11.02
25	7.72	8.39	9.09	10.54
30	7.34	8.05	8.78	10.29

TABLE 2
Loan Progress Table—10%
Dollar Balance Remaining on a $1,000 Loan

Age of Loan	Original Terms in Years				
	10	15	20	25	30
1	939	970	983	991	994
2	871	936	965	980	988
3	796	899	945	969	982
4	713	858	923	956	974
5	622	813	898	942	966
10	—	506	730	846	909
15	—	—	454	688	817
20	—	—	—	428	664
25	—	—	—	—	413
30	—	—	—	—	—

OTHER TYPES OF AMORTIZED MORTGAGES

Flexible-Payment Mortgage

Advancing from straight term loans through amortized mortgages leaves one final method of loan payment to be examined. Realizing that the cost of housing was rising, the Federal Home Loan Bank on February 26, 1974, granted permission to federal savings and loan institutions to adopt a new type of repayment scheduling. These regulation changes allow borrowers to make payments based on a flexible-payment method. This schedule of repayments is determined by the borrower's present and future financial position. Realizing the housing industry needed a boost, the board allowed this repayment method to stimulate buying among home buyers who had expectations of higher future income. The repayment schedule allows for low payments in the beginning, followed by larger sums toward the middle and end of the term to satisfy the loan obligation. Two restrictions were placed on this method by the Federal Home Loan Bank Board. The interest due on the loan for each period must be fully paid by the monthly payment. Second, the loan must be on a fully amortizing basis by the end of the fifth year. With these restrictions, the lowest payment is one that merely covers the interest, and this can only occur for a period of 5 years. Provisions are allowed to cover up to 95% of the value of the property if a form of mortgage insurance covers the top portion of the loan. An example is provided by the Federal Home Loan Bank Board:

On an 8%, $30,000 mortgage, the normal monthly payment to principal and interest would be $220. Using the flexible-payment mortgage, the borrower could, instead, pay as little as $200/month (or payment as low as the interest only) for the first five years and then $230/month for the remaining term. This would enable a family with rising income expectations to purchase a home sooner than they otherwise could afford to.

Variable-Rate Mortgage

In the past few years of double-digit inflation, certain risks have developed for the mortgagee. Because of the uncertainty of the economy, variable-rate mortgages are beginning to gain some popularity. Essentially this method allows interest rates on the mortgage to fluctuate in accordance with market conditions. The rate can be raised or lowered, depending upon the supply of and demand for mortgage money. The interest rate varies with the cost of money. These fluctuations are usually only allowed at stated times throughout the term of the mortgage. This provides stability for both the mortgagor and the mortgagee and at the same time makes the return to the lender competitive with other possible investments.

At present the variable-rate mortgage is not widely used. The Federal Home Loan Bank allows some institutions to use this method; however, there must be consumer acceptance before it becomes widespread.

Blanket Mortgages

The term *blanket mortgage* indicates that more than one piece of real estate is utilized to provide the necessary security for a loan. Typically, such a mortgage is used when developing a subdivision where large expenditures are made to add the essentials to make the lots salable. These include engineering, surveying and platting, streets, utilities, and the like. The mortgage is structured so that, as each lot is sold, all or most of the proceeds from the sale of the lot is paid to the mortgage lender who then releases the mortgage only on the particular lot. The "blanket" is lifted so that one lot is released, but the mortgage continues to be effective for the remaining lots. This process continues until all the lots are sold or until the entire loan has been paid off. The term is also used when a buyer of a residence already owns a home that may be free of any mortgage. Rather than waiting to sell the first property to generate a more substantial down payment, a mortgage loan is made on both the old and new properties. The loan is then reduced by all or part of the proceeds from the sale of the old home when it is marketed; the mortgage is released as to the sold property but remains effective as to the new property.

Package Mortgages

Traditional concepts of residential mortgage lending have been changed by the trend toward the use of built-in appliances. Many of these are clearly fixtures and become part of the real estate; however, they typically have shorter life expectancies than the house itself. The emergence of the *package mortgage*, which includes such items, represents a change from traditional residential mortgage lending practices which do not include such items. While such a package mortgage is useful in many cases, particularly where the home buyer would have insufficient funds to purchase such items separately, it should be noted that many appliances will wear out long before they have been paid for, and that the long-term mortgage financial obligation may generate a great deal of interest which should be allocated to these items.

Open-End Mortgages

Under a true *open-end mortgage*, the lender agrees at the outset to advance additional funds to the borrower using the original mortgage as security for these later borrowings. Theoretically, the first lien of the mortgage lender is sufficient to protect the total advances made to the borrower, even if they exceed the amount of the original loan. The purpose of the development of this device was to avoid the expenses involved in writing a new mortgage whenever later advances are made. Legal authorities, however, are not in accord as to whether or not the lender is protected by the first mortgage if the total amount loaned exceeds the amount of the original mortgage loan. Since the record shows the original amount of the mortgage loan, subsequent bona fide lenders may assume that no additional amount is owed when this is not in fact the case. To the extent that the outstanding loan exceeds the recorded amount, the original mortgage lender may be unsecured. Because of this possibility, careful lenders usually limit later advances up to the amount of the original mortgage balance and require a new mortgage if the amount loaned exceeds the amount of the original loan.

Wraparound Mortgages

Frequently referred to as the *Canadian wraparound*, this type of mortgage is aimed at preserving the benefits of an existing mortgage on real estate which has a more favorable interest rate than is currently available. While the wraparound mortgage is generally reserved for significant commercial transactions, the concept may gain popularity in the residential area in the future.

A wraparound mortgage is a relatively new type of second mortgage under which the second mortgage lender steps into the shoes of the mortgagor and makes the payments on the first mortgage. Assume that the property justifies loans of $100,000 and that there is an existing first mortgage of $50,000 at a rate of 6%. The second mortgagee may agree to lend the owner an additional $50,000 under a wraparound mortgage at 8%, even though current rates are 9%. Under the wraparound, the mortgagor owes the second mortgagee $100,000 at 8%, and the second mortgagee (after collecting payments on the full $100,000) pays the first mortgage debt service on the $50,000 loan as it comes due and *after* the borrower has paid it to the holder of the wraparound. In effect, the wraparound lender is "assuming" the $50,000 loan at 6% but is collecting 8% on the same loan *without* laying out $50,000. The rate of return is dramatically higher for the wraparound mortgagee, even though he or she is lending $50,000 at a preferential rate. To the borrower, the combination is more attractive than borrowing the whole $100,000 at 9% as opposed to 8%. Caution is urged in the use of this device. Not only is the skilled attorney needed, but also the knowledgeable CPA with tax skills to be sure that the tax consequences do not destroy the economic advantages of the wraparound.

It should be apparent that the potential for flexibility in mortgage financing is limited only by the goals to be achieved and the ingenuity of the parties involved. For those in the real estate brokerage field, it is important to be aware of the fact that there are many ways to structure the financing of a particular transaction.

SPECIAL FORMS OF FINANCING

Second Mortgage

Prospective purchasers of real estate, particularly purchasers of homes, have always been short of capital with which to make substantial down payments. Thus it was necessary to bridge the gap, and the second mortgage became popular as a means of providing money for the down payment.

If the property is sold for $40,000 and has a $34,000 first mortgage against it, and the purchaser has $2,000 cash to make a down payment, he or she will then need a $4,000 *second* or *junior mortgage*.

Traditionally, second mortgages are short-term and carry a higher rate of interest than first mortgages. They usually consist of a series of large paybacks rather than following a form of amortization.

The second mortgage reads like the first mortgage, except that it is expected to make reference to and accept the priority of the first mortgage. Even if it does not, however, it is junior in priority to the first mortgage.

Some of the cases in which a second mortgage can be used are:

1. To make up the difference between down payment money available and the amount needed to purchase real estate.
2. Sometimes a very short-term second mortgage can be taken by the seller of real estate. This might occur in a case where the buyer has another house on which there is a sale pending but not closed, or where the buyer knows that funds are definitely coming to him or her in a short time from other sources.
3. To leverage current real estate in order to invest in other real estate or to make other investments.

Swing Loans

So-called *swing loans* generally are not secured by a mortgage. They are usually based upon the borrower's credit reputation and the "equity" he or she has in an existing house which is used to borrow money for a down payment on a new house. The same result is achieved as when the blanket mortgage (discussed above) is used for the same purpose; however, less formality is involved.

An example may help to illustrate:

The buyer owns property no. 1 which is valued at $50,000 and which has a mortgage balance of $25,000; she has an "equity" of $25,000.

The buyer needs $20,000 to make a down payment on property no. 2 to enable her to obtain favorable mortgage financing. A bank lends her $20,000 on an unsecured basis, but looking to the equity in her old house as the source of repayment.

The buyer purchases property no. 2, and when property no. 1 is sold, she repays the loan which "swings" upon the equity she had in the property.

As noted above, the borrower in this case must have a very good credit reputation to qualify for such a loan and usually must be well-known to the lender. If one or the other is lacking, the swing loan may still be made, but the lender may require an *indemnifying mortgage* which is in substance the same as a second mortgage which we have already considered.

Sale and Lease Back

This is a vehicle which has developed in recent years to permit business and industry to free capital normally tied up in real estate to apply to their own business or manufacturing operations. The user of real estate sells to an investor and then simultaneously leases back the property for a desired period of time. The user may also have an option to purchase the property again at the end of the lease.

Construction Loan

This form of "interim financing" is used during construction. It is paid out in installments during the period of construction and provides temporary financing until the house or project is ready for permanent financing. At that time, a traditional type of mortgage replaces the construction loan. This permanent mortgage is usually arranged for at the time the construction loan is negotiated.

Purchase Money Mortgage

A method of financing commonly used during periods of tight money or to purchase property which in normal circumstances could not be financed through a conventional lender is called *purchase money mortgage*. More information on the purchase money mortgage can be found in Chapter 10.

Conditional Installment Sale (Land Contract)

Another available form of financing is the *land contract* which allows the seller to retain title to the property while entering into an installment contract for its sale. The contract entered into states that the seller will deliver title to the purchaser upon completion of the installment contract. Land contracts are thoroughly discussed in Chapter 14.

The Deed of Trust

An additional finance security instrument used in many states is the *deed of trust* or the *trust deed*.

The essential features of this device are: a loan from the lender to the borrower, evidenced by a promissory note; a conveyance by the borrower of the title to an independent third party as trustee; an agreement which requires the trustee to sell the property if the borrower defaults or to deed it to the borrower when the debt is paid.

The advantage of this arrangement is the ease and speed with which the trustee can sell the property in the event of default, after which the lender may apply the proceeds of sale to satisfy the debt. No extended court proceedings are required, since the agreement of the parties gives the trustee the power to convey a good title and there is no "equity of redemption."

CONCERNS AND CONSIDERATIONS OF THE LENDER

The concerns of the lender go beyond the repayment plans mentioned earlier in this chapter. The terms and borrower's qualifications are also of great importance in determining the attractiveness of a loan. By definition the term of a mortgage is the time period extending from the original date of the mortgage to the date of its maturity. The majority of mortgages are long-term loans which range from 20 to 30 years. Terms vary from mortgage to mortgage and depend on the type and characteristics of the property and the borrower's qualifications which are contingent upon such items as the purchaser's age and income. Mortgage institutions usually have their own lending guidelines to follow as well as those state and federal regulations imposed upon them.

Upon receiving a request for a loan from a potential home buyer, the mortgagee must give some consideration to the request. Institutions usually look at the suitability of both the property (i.e., physical security) and the applicant (i.e., borrower security).

The Property As Security

When deciding on an application for a loan, the lending institution must examine the property being acquired by the applicant to determine its suitability as security for the loan. In deciding the property's value, the lender looks at the economic life of the property. This in turn is determined by its location, age, physical condition, structural soundness, and future marketability. On some types of loans the mortgagee must also look at the income-producing ability of the property. Therefore, the use of the property is one of the major considerations of the lender.

Appraisals

All lending institutions require appraisals before considering loan applications. Appraisals are estimates of the value of property. The three main methods of appraisal are the income approach, the market approach, and the cost approach. These appraisals are the source of information the various lending institutions rely on to make investment decisions. The amount of the loan is based on either the sales price or the appraised amount, whichever is lower. Buyers often find themselves paying more than the appraised price and consequently must pay the difference between the appraised price and the selling price. This usually applies to government-backed loans.

Borrower Qualifications

Having examined the quality of the property, lenders turn to the potential buyer and consider his or her ability to pay. Consequently a credit analysis follows. This is for the benefit of both the buyer and lender to lessen the chance of default. The credit analysis considers the borrower's net worth, income, job stability and the type of employment, future economic status, number of dependents, age, and other obligations and expenses. All these factors are examined to determine the applicant's financial and personal stability. Lending institutions rely heavily upon the borrower's income which can come from various sources.

Primary Income of Borrower

Primary income usually comes from a buyer's monthly net income and is an important factor. From this monthly net amount various expenses are deducted, ranging from food, clothing, and medical bills to house maintenance and automobile payments. After deducting the appropriate expense items, the lender (mortgagee) looks at the primary income remaining for the borrower to spend on housing. Lending institutions vary on the level of income that can be spent on housing, but most lenders will approve loans that require 20 to 25% of the applicant's net income being spent on housing. Due to rising construction and housing costs these figures are in a transitory state and may be higher given the economic conditions of a particular period of time. In periods of high inflation, for example, a figure of 30% might be allowed.

Secondary Income

Although primary income is of major importance to lenders, secondary income is also considered—not particularly the gross amount as much as the stability of the added income. This added income can come from several sources including stocks, other real estate, or part-time jobs. In the past lenders have not relied on the total amount of the secondary income but have used only a percentage of it, allowing for fluctuations.

Lending institutions are now paying more attention to the income added by the working woman. Consequently lenders are currently using incomes of spouses in determining loan applicant acceptability. The combined incomes have made it possible for more families to qualify for housing loans than ever before.

LENDING INSTITUTIONS

Buyers can obtain the necessary financing from various places. Mortgage arrangements are the most widely used technique of financing, and they can be obtained from the following institutions: savings and loan associations, commercial banks, mutual savings banks, life insurance companies, loan correspondents, individuals and organizations, pension funds, and real estate investment trust. (The list is arranged in order of importance.)

Most mortgages are obtained from savings and loan associations and commercial banks, as well as mutual savings banks and life insurance companies. Although the others do provide funds, they are a limited group of individuals and not readily accessible to the general public.

Savings and Loan Associations

Savings and loan associations specialize in home loans, receiving most of the required funds from local deposits in time savings accounts or certificates. Savings and loan associations are privately managed and owned financing institutions governed by state and federal regulations. They supply the greatest amount of single-family mortgage loans in the United States. In the past the associations have concentrated their efforts on this type of loan but recently have begun to diversify into home repair, construction, and multifamily housing projects. The goals of these associations are thrift and home ownership.

The basic function of the association is to provide mortgages for the community. The funds are ob-

tained from the institution's own time deposits, and interest earned on the mortgages goes to pay for the interest given on the time deposits. Statutes and federal regulations affect the level of interest, as does competition in the market. The regulations affecting federally chartered institutions are set by the Federal Home Loan Bank Board under which all savings and loans are incorporated.

Under the Federal Home Loan Bank System, the associations need not rely on local funds. The system was devised in 1932 to help solve the problems caused by dependency on local funds. The major element of the system is the ability to transfer funds from one bank to the other. The system provides for 12 regional banks assisting local savings and loans in times of tight money situations. The main idea behind federal involvement in savings and loan associations was to develop a national mortgage market. Savings and loan associations are also subject to the statutes of a particular state, and state-chartered associations come under the auspices of the state commissioner of banking.

Savings and loan associations concentrate their efforts on residential construction, usually keeping away from large commercial projects. Principally lending to single-family residences, the associations require a down payment on the mortgage. This down payment fluctuates, depending on the economic conditions and the degree of risk involved. Usually down payments range from 15 to 25% of the sales price. The maximum loan-to-value ratio is .95, thus allowing a down payment as small as 5%.

Savings and loan associations offer three major types of loans: new home construction loans, home purchase loans, and loans for other purposes, such as home improvement loans.

New Home Construction Loans

Generally, new home loans are made directly to the builder with emphasis placed on single-family housing. The associations place strict controls on the loans and pay the builder in installments. These installments correspond to the various phases of building a house, ranging from the footings to the finishing work. As builders complete the work on each step, payment is made. The associations check to see that the builder is paying the subcontractors, so that no mechanic's liens can be placed on the title. This occurs when builders fail to pay subcontractors for completed work.

Home Purchase Loans

By far, this is the association's major lending area. The institutions spend approximately 60% of available funds in this area annually. Mortgages allow people to move from their existing homes to ones that are more appropriate for their family size as well as living style. The home mortgage allows for more upward mobility in our society and thereby stimulates new housing. This trend is known as *filtering*.

Mortgage Loans for Other Purposes (Home Improvement)

As society has had to shift from an unlimited growth and resources philosophy to a more conservative growth and limited resources philosophy, there has been a similar shift in the mortgage market. As the economy began to feel the effect of the oil crisis, double-digit inflation, and energy shortages in the winter of 1977, lending institutions realized that major shifts in the demand for loans were occurring, with increasing numbers of home improvement loans being requested. Consequently savings and loan associations are increasing efforts to offer competitive rates for home improvement loans. These loans can cover any home improvement ranging from painting to roofing.

Today approximately 25 to 35% of the total loans from savings and loan associations are in this area. The associations are usually very willing to extend credit of this nature, realizing that the improvements will increase the value of the property and thereby reduce the risk of the original loan. Improvements also help maintain the neighborhood, which has a great effect on the value of the property. The loans are usually short-term in length (5 years) but can range from 3 to 20 years. If the loan is incorporated into the first mortgage, then the maturity date can be extended to 30 years.

Commercial Banks

Of major importance to the lending of mortgage money is the commercial bank. Banks often have individual departments to handle mortgages if they are interested in this type of investment. Most banks, however, concentrate on other types of loans which include short-term loans for construction. Banks are regulated by federal and/or state authorities, depending upon the nature of the charter. Regulations are placed on the ratio of the loan to the appraised value of property and/or the term of the loan. Requirements are also enforced concerning shorter mortgage terms and interest rate ceilings. Because of these federal and state restrictions, banks find it difficult to compete with other lending institutions for long-term residential loans.

Commercial banks do, however, have a significant role in real estate financing. Major financing operations of banks are concentrated in the short-term area of building operations, the builder's construction loan. Upon completion of the project the loan is transferred to a permanent mortgage which is financed by another lending institution. Banks also provide loans for home improvements.

Real estate mortgage portfolios have tended to increase in banks across the nation. They have moved from third to second place in the holding of mortgages.

Mutual Savings Banks

Like savings and loan associations, the mutual savings bank's main objective is thrift. Started in 1816 with the Philadelphia Savings Fund Society, the mutual savings banks have grown to encompass 18 states. Unlike the savings and loan associations that are spread out across the United States, the mutual savings banks are heavily concentrated in the industrialized Northeast. New York and Massachusetts possess three-fourths of the total assets of all mutual savings banks. This is due to the original intent of the savings banks to encourage factory workers to save. All mutual savings banks are state-chartered and must follow regulations established by the individual states.

They are similar to savings and loan associations in that they are operated for the benefit of the depositors and managed by a board of trustees. Their basic objective is also to pool deposits to provide mortgages and funds for potential single-family homeowners.

Life Insurance Companies

Life insurance companies offer another major source of real estate mortgage financing. In the past they have been conservative investors because of the major source of their investment dollars—policyholders. Governmental regulations have caused this conservatism in investing. Regulations state the percentage of total assets that life insurance companies can invest in mortgages because of their limited liquidity and relative risk. All insurance companies are constrained by the regulations of the state in which they are chartered. Usually they specialize in large long-term loans on major real estate projects such as shopping centers, office buildings, and large multifamily projects.

Because of the nature of the life insurance companies' funds, they usually have less fluctuation in the availability of monies to lend for real estate projects. The placement of a loan with a life insurance company is usually accomplished through a *mortgage banker* or *mortgage broker*. Very few loans are made by a life insurance company directly to a borrower.

Loan Correspondents

Many times the larger lending institutions do not have the facilities needed to make the different mortgage loans. Instead of funding loan departments in the individual institution—in an insurance company, for example—the company goes to a local agent or loan correspondent to make the mortgage loan for them. In other circumstances the company may not have a branch office in the area, in which case they utilize the loan correspondent to take advantage of his or her knowledge of the local real estate market, neighborhood and characteristics, and local economic conditions. Loan correspondents are either mortgage brokers or mortgage bankers, depending upon the type of job required.

Mortgage Brokers

The purpose of mortgage brokers is to channel mortgage funds from the large investor to real estate developers and owners. The broker serves as an intermediary between the lender and the borrower and receives a fee for the services he or she performs. Lending institutions ask the mortgage broker to find and screen property and applicants for their mortgage dollars. The closing is done in the name of the lending institution, and the mortgage broker receives a fee based on a percentage of the mortgage value.

Mortgage Bankers

Although mortgage bankers and brokers provide the same basic service of finding and matching applicants and mortgages, there is one basic distinction. Mortgage bankers use their own funds to make mortgage loans. After they originate a number of mortgages, which are closed in their name, a package of mortgages is then sold to a large financial institution and transferred to that institution. However, unlike the mortgage broker, the banker continues to service the loan for the investor. Servicing includes collecting monthly payments, paying taxes, and maintaining escrow accounts. For this servicing, the banker charges the institution a fee and also an origination fee.

METHODS OF FINANCE

Having learned about the different sources of financing available, the potential homeowner must be aware of the alternative types of financing available. One of the jobs of the broker is to familiarize the buyer with the principal types of financing. The three major areas include government-backed loans, conventional loans, and assumption of loans already in existence.

Conventional Loans

Conventional loans are loans made directly to the buyer without government guarantees or insurance. The conventional mortgage has very few regulations governing it, so the terms and conditions of the mortgage fluctuate in accordance with market conditions. As the demand for money increases, the yield on the conventional mortgage loans may be increased by increasing interest rates. During such periods, it is to the advantage of the seller to sell to a buyer acquiring a conventional loan. Nonconventional loans during these periods have high discount charges the seller would have to pay. Consequently, conventional loans play an important role in financing during times of tight money, their terms changing rapidly to reflect market conditions.

Today most loans of this nature are for 80% of the sales price, maturing in 25 or 30 years. These figures fluctuate depending upon economic conditions.

Private Mortgage Insurance

Private systems of mortgage insurance have grown in importance, and this new aspect of financing is being used in many parts of the United States. Private companies insure mortgages under conditions similar to those of the FHA. Under this system of lending, institutions have a partial guarantee of payment. The lender might loan 95% of the sales price of a property but actually insures the top 15 to 20% of the loan through a private mortgage insurance company. Such private mortgage insurance allows a high ratio of loan to value and helps stimulate the growth of the mortgage market. The concept originated with the Mortgage Guarantee Insurance Corporation (MGIC) and has grown in popularity. The insurance is paid through a one-time premium of ½ of 1% of the loan amount, collected at the time of closing, with the purchaser paying an additional premium as part of the monthly payment until that part of the loan has been amortized.

Assumption of Loans

When a purchaser takes over the payments of an existing loan, he or she is said to assume the mortgage. Under this circumstance, the purchaser pays the difference between the selling price and the loan balance to the seller. This transaction does not relieve the seller of the obligation. If the purchaser defaults, then the seller is held responsible for payments. Under an assumed mortgage, the lender has two parties who are liable for the payments. Many loans today are beginning to contain clauses that restrict assumption without prior approval of the lender.

Assumption of a loan benefits both the buyer and the seller. While relieving the seller of some of the responsibility, it also saves the buyer the cost of obtaining a new mortgage and avoids the problem of trying to obtain one in the first place. For additional discussion of this material, see Chapter 10.

Government-Backed Loans

There are two basic types of government-backed loans: the Federal Housing Administration (FHA) insures loans, and the Veterans Administration (VA) guarantees loans. Each agency places tight restrictions on the type and conditions of the mortgage involved. The federal government has had a continual interest in real estate and has been an important factor in increasing the growth of home ownership since World War II.

FHA and Its Programs

The FHA was developed under the National Housing Act of 1934. The agency's main function is to insure loans from lending institutions made for financing mortgages, thus stimulating the housing segment of the economy.

The objective of the FHA is to encourage lenders to make loans by insuring them. Lenders are then more willing to accept lower down payments, thereby increasing the opportunity for more people to obtain mortgages. The FHA insures loans; it does not lend money to individual purchasers of single-family dwellings. To finance its operation, the FHA charges a ½ of 1% mortgage insurance premium (MIP). The FHA has insured over 10 million loans since its beginning.

The FHA places restrictions upon the type of mortgage the agency will insure. These restrictions are on the terms and amount of the mortgage loan and that the physical property must meet FHA minimum property standards (MPS). To insure that such standards have been met each property must be appraised by an FHA-approved appraiser prior to the loan being made. The term of the loan under FHA insurance must be in multiples of 5 years up to a maximum of 30 years. Amounts can vary, with an upward limit of $60,000, and must be in multiples of $50. Mortgages must be paid utilizing an amortization schedule as outlined earlier, and escrow accounts must be established for collection of taxes and all insurance premiums. Interest rates charged on FHA residential loans are at a rate set by the Secretary of Housing and Urban Development. These rates are usually lower than the interest rates found on conventional loans, thus necessitating *discounts,* a topic covered later in this chapter.

The agency also requires certain guidelines pertaining to loan-to-value ratios. The guidelines for single-family residences vary depending upon the age of the property, but generally require 97% of the first $25,000 and 95% of the balance up to $60,000.

Following are examples of loan values using the FHA guidelines. The percentages are computed on the *appraisal* or *sale amount*, whichever is *lower*, and the final product is adjusted downward to be a multiple of $50.

Example: What can the amount of a loan on a property selling for $32,500 be if it is FHA-insured?

Solution:

97% of the first $25,000 = $24,250
95% of all in excess   = $ 7,125
                 total $31,375

The loan amount of $31,375 must be adjusted downward to be a multiple of $50, so the FHA-insured loan would amount to $31,350. The required down payment for this property would be $1,150 ($32,500 — $31,350).

Example: Determine the amount of an FHA-insured loan on a property selling for $45,000.

Solution:

97% of the first $25,000 = $24,250
95% of all in excess   = $19,000

The total loan would be $43,250. No adjustment is necessary. Consequently the down payment required by the loan is $1,750.

Given an example in which the loan worked out to be over $60,000, the down payment would be the difference between the sales price and the maximum loan. Under any circumstance the down payment must be provided by the assets of the purchaser. FHA requirements prevent the use of a second deed of trust or mortgage to provide the down payment.

The VA and Its Guaranteed Loans

After World War II the government recognized the need of returning veterans to obtain housing. Consequently, included in the Servicemen's Readjustment Act of 1944 was a stipulation authorizing the VA to *guarantee* veterans' loans. The act has been updated several times to include veterans of more recent American conflicts.

Under the guarantee program, lending institutions are guaranteed against loss on loans to veterans. Unlike the FHA-backed loans, the VA loans provide for the full amount of the guarantee to be refunded after reasonable efforts are made to collect upon default by a veteran. Obviously, the financial institution must attempt to satisfy its claim through foreclosure proceedings prior to applying to the VA for any deficiency.

The following groups of veterans are eligible for VA loans, and eligibility does not expire until the privilege is used.

1. Any veteran serving for 90 days or more in World War II between September 16, 1940 and July 25, 1947.
2. Veterans of the Korean conflict serving for 90 days or more, any part of which falls between June 27, 1950 and January 31, 1955.
3. Any veterans of the Vietnam era serving on active duty 90 days or more between August 5, 1964 and May 7, 1975.
4. Any veteran who has served on active duty 181 days or more after January 31, 1955.
5. Unremarried widows and wives of veterans missing in action or captured, and those meeting certain other conditions.
6. Those who qualify for restoration of previously used eligibility.

Under the current law, eligibility for VA benefits can be reestablished after an initial property mortgage under a VA loan has been paid in full and no other liabilities exist on the property. The law also allows eligibility to be restored if another veteran willingly assumes the obligations associated with that mortgage by using his eligibility.

Effective October 1, 1978, the law limits the maximum percentage of a guarantee at 60% of the loan or $25,000, whichever is less. As in the case of the FHA, a VA-approved appraiser must appraise the property prior to the loan.

Loan Discounts or Discount Points

Often lenders cannot obtain mortgage interest rates that are competitive with other types of investments on the market. In states where usury laws are used, upper limits are placed on mortgage interest rates and therefore limit the rate mortgagees can obtain on their mortgage investment. In other instances properties cannot be sold to buyers who can obtain conventional credit. They can obtain credit only if the loan is insured by the FHA or guaranteed by the VA. Under these conditions the interest rates on the loan are set by Congress, therefore not allowing the mortgagee to obtain a yield that is competitive with other investments such as mortgages made at conventional rates.

Points are a "rate adjustment factor" to increase the yield of the mortgage to a satisfactory level to allow the mortgagee to make the loan. They may be called a rate equalization factor.

Having decided the rate of interest he or she could obtain on similar loans, the lender then determines the number of points needed to make up the deficit caused by either situation given above. Using a general rule of thumb lenders have decided that each ⅛% difference between the rate for a conventional mortgage and the rate obtainable under an FHA-insured loan is equal to one discount point, and 1 point is 1% of the loan amount.

For illustrative purposes assume the lender decides he or she can obtain a yield of 8.5% on a regular mortgage not affected by FHA requirements. Then he or she will charge 8 discount points to accept the loan at 7.5%. This illustration uses the above rule of thumb.

Continuing with the previous example, upon closing the lender will disburse the face amount of the loan minus the amount charged utilizing the discount points. For example, if a mortgage is being acquired for $20,000 at 7.5% interest with 8 discount points being charged, the actual payment to the seller will be $20,000 minus 8% of the $20,000, or $18,400 total disbursement by the lender ($20,000 — $1,600). However, the lender will hold a mortgage note for the full sum of $20,000, thereby obtaining a yield of 8.5%. Under FHA and VA regulations, only the seller can pay the points. In most circumstances the purchaser must pay 1% of the loan amount to the lender as a loan origination fee. This fee is not a discount point, but a fee for placing the loan on the books of the lender, thus the term "loan origination fee."

Prepayment Penalties

Some lending institutions impose a special charge provided for in a mortgage contract which may be collected from the borrower in the event that the borrower repays all or part of the loan in advance of the maturity date. At times there is no prepayment clause and, in the event of a desire for prepayment, the mortgagor bargains with the mortgagee as to the terms of prepayment. The penalty under these circumstances could range from all to part of the unearned interest on the remaining balance of the loan.

As pointed out earlier, prepayment penalties are often built into the mortgage. These clauses vary from lender to lender but typically are a certain percentage charged if the loan is prepaid in the first 5 years and a lesser percentage if the loan is prepaid after 5 years. The clause states on what balance this percentage is to be based. Other penalties include payment of 1 to 3 months interest in exchange for the privilege to prepay. The rationale behind prepayment penalties rests on the fact that prepayment interrupts the investment plans of the mortgagee and are imposed on the mortgagor to reimburse the lending institution for the expense incurred in originating the loan.

Currently, FHA-insured and VA-guaranteed loans do not allow prepayment penalty clauses in the mortgage, and consequently no charge can be placed upon the borrower for single-family housing. Given increasing rates of interest, penalty clauses are becoming more obscure. These clauses prevent prepayment, causing mortgages to be outstanding at lower yields than the present market rate of interest. Therefore more institutions are allowing prepayment as a means to free valuable investment dollars. This allows lenders to make mortgages at higher rates that are competitive with present investment opportunities.

FEDERAL INVOLVEMENT IN REAL ESTATE FINANCE

In times of tight money and credit crunches, the federal government has felt an obligation to help the lending institutions and the public. To do this, a secondary mortgage market has been created whereby existing federal agencies buy primary mortgages from the various lending institutions, thus generating funds for further mortgage development. These agencies are the Federal National Mortgage Association, the Government National Mortgage Association, and the Federal Home Loan Mortgage Corporation. These institutions comprise the major part of the secondary market and help to balance the money policies of the Federal Reserve that might be detrimental to the well-being of the lending institutions.

Federal National Mortgage Association (FNMA)

Commonly referred to as "Fannie Mae," this association was originally a government-sponsored and is now a private corporation. Established in 1938, its main purpose is to establish a secondary mortgage market. FNMA buys existing FHA, VA, and conventional mortgages and allows the seller to continue to service the mortgage. FNMA provides a great service by attracting private capital into the housing market.

Government National Mortgage Association (GNMA)

This association purchases, services, and sells mortgages insured or guaranteed by the FHA or VA. Under Section 305 of the National Housing Act, GNMA, commonly referred to as "Ginnie Mae," is authorized to provide financing for selected types of mortgages. The association also provides assistance through the purchase of home mortgages, generally as a means of retarding or stopping a decline in mortgage lending and home-building activities which may threaten the stability of the national economy. GNMA got its start as a part of FNMA and was split off in 1968.

GNMA has specific guidelines to follow when purchasing mortgages, and these are similar to those for FHA- and/or VA-approved mortgages. When buying mortgages, GNMA stipulates that payment of the mortgage must be current. One of the primary goals of GNMA is to provide a secondary market for those loans which otherwise would not be bought because of their high risks. The activities of GNMA are conducted through the sale of securities by the U.S. Treasury.

Federal Home Loan Mortgage Corporation (FHLMC)

This corporation's goals are similar to those of FNMA and GNMA. The corporation began by buying mortgages in September 1970 and follows the general criteria of the other two. Like GNMA, the Federal Home Loan Mortgage Corporation ("Freddie Mac") is required by law to buy only mortgages that do not exceed the 80% loan-to-value ratio. One stipulation this corporation places on its purchases is that the funds the seller obtains must be circulated back into the mortgage market within 180 days after a purchase is made by the corporation. In this manner the corporation makes sure the funds it provides are available for their intended use, which is to create a market for conventional mortgage loans by buying them from savings and loan associations, pooling them, and then selling bonds, holding the mortgages as security for the bonds.

Truth in Lending

Consumer concern over underlying mortgage terms and conditions spurred passage of the Consumer Credit Protection Act in July 1969. Included in the act was the Truth-in-Lending Act which granted the Federal Reserve Board the power to implement the regulations. The board, using this power, established Regulation Z. The regulation applies to anyone who grants credit in any form. While it does not regulate interest rates, the board ensures consumers that the cost of the credit will be explicitly printed for their information. Another major purpose of Regulation Z was to standardize credit procedures, allowing consumers to shop around for the cheapest form of credit. The main emphasis of the act is on complete and full disclosure.

Effects of Regulation Z on Real Estate Transactions

The purpose of Regulation Z is not to set or regulate interest rates but to standardize the procedures involved in credit transactions. It requires that the consumer be fully aware of all the aspects of a credit transaction. It also applies to all advertising in which the seller engages.

All credit for real estate is covered under Regulation Z when it is for an individual consumer.

1. *Disclosure.* The lender must disclose what the borrower is paying for credit and what it will cost in total percentage terms. (Exception: The total finance charge in dollars paid by the parties in the transaction need not be stated.) However, the lender must still indicate the total annual percentage rate. This is done only in the sale of first mortgage on single-family dwellings. The finance charge includes interest, loan fees, inspection fees, FHA mortgage insurance fees, and discount points. Other fees should not be included. The licensee may not prepare or assist

in the preparation of such an instrument as a loan application without full disclosure.

2. *Right to rescind.* Regulation Z provides that the borrower shall have the right to rescind or cancel the transaction if it involves placing a lien against real estate which is his or her principal residence. This right must be exercised before midnight of the third business day following the transaction, allowing a 3-day "thinking" period during which the borrower can reassess the transaction. Note: The act specifically states that transactions to finance the construction of a new home or the purchase of a dwelling to be used as a home are *not* included in the right of rescission.

3. *Advertising.* Real estate advertising is greatly affected by Regulation Z. It allows general terms describing financing available to be used. But if any details are given, they must comply with the regulations. Any finance charge mentioned must be stated as an annual percentage rate. If any other credit terms are mentioned, such as the monthly payment, term of loan, or down payment required, then the following information must be given: cash price, annual percentage rate required, down payment, amount, and due date of all payments.

4. *Effect on real estate personnel.* Regulation Z does not indicate that licensees should refrain from making direct contact with lenders on behalf of prospective purchasers. Of prime importance, however, is that the lender must be the one who decides if the loan should be made. The licensee may not prepare or assist in the preparation of such an instrument as a loan application, note, mortgage, or land contract.

5. *Enforcement of Regulation Z.* A lender who fails to disclose any of the required credit information can be sued for a specified portion of the finance charge. The lender, under some circumstances, may be fined up to $5,000 or sentenced to 1 year in jail, or both.

Fig. 11-1 on page 134 illustrates a notice to the customer required by Regulation Z.

The Real Estate Settlement Procedures Act of 1974 (RESPA)

Few pieces of federal legislation in recent years have stirred as much controversy within the mortgage banking industry as RESPA. The law was intended to aid the consumer in obtaining residential mortgage financing and to minimize closing costs to the borrower by regulating the lending practices of the mortgage banking community. Even though the act was passed in 1974, to be effective June 20, 1975, it generated so much confusion and controversy that Congress made significant changes effective in January 1976 and June 1976. The comments here are related to the act as amended and effective June 30, 1976.

RESPA applies to all settlements on loans for residential properties which are "federally related." The most important aspect of this statement is that the act applies to all loans secured by a first mortgage on single- to four-family residential properties by any lender regulated by the federal government and even those whose deposits are insured by an agency of the federal government. Some other lenders are also covered by the act, but the above broad category includes the vast majority of residential mortgages made throughout the United States today. In all such mortgage settlements, the uniform settlement statement prescribed by HUD or its equivalent must be used. The form is complex by comparison with closing statements previously used and, in practice, brokers usually prepare their own closing statements to clarify the transaction for their clients.

Provisions of RESPA

1. The lender must permit the borrower to inspect the closing statement 1 day prior to the closing. This statement must disclose the anticipated closing costs to the extent that they are known at that time; the costs are precisely determined at the time of closing.
2. The lender must provide to the borrower a booklet entitled "Settlement Costs" within 3 days after taking an application for a mortgage loan which is federally related, and the lender must also provide a good faith estimate of the anticipated closing costs.

3. Limitations upon escrow account requirements by the lender are also regulated by the act. Generally, the maximum which may be required is the sum of the amount which normally would be required to maintain the account for the current month plus one-sixth of the total estimated expenses for real estate taxes and insurance for the following 12-month period.
4. Kickbacks and unearned fees are also prohibited by RESPA. Particular emphasis is placed on the relationship between the regulated lender and the title insurance companies. The lender may not, as a condition of the loan, specify the title insurer to be used.
5. The identity of the true borrower must be obtained by the lender, and the lender must make this information available to the Federal Home Loan Bank Board upon demand.
6. No fee may be charged by the lender for preparation of all of the forms required by RESPA.
7. The act requires the secretary of HUD to establish model land recording systems in selected areas of the country with the ultimate goal of establishing a uniform system which will presumably be less expensive than the systems now in operation.

While RESPA is directed at mortgage lenders, it obviously has an impact on those engaged in the real estate brokerage business, because of the industry's dependence on the easy availability of mortgage funds. Familiarity with the specified closing statement seems to be essential, if only for the purpose of being able to explain it to the buyer.

Figures 11-2 through 11-8 on pages 135-142 illustrate the basic RESPA forms necessary for a loan closing (or settlement). Pay special attention to Fig. 11-2, sections J-K for a summary of the funds to be transferred among buyer, seller, and lender. Fig. 11-5 is a summary of all settlement charges and should be studied thoroughly.

SUGGESTED READINGS

(See appropriate chapter in the following books.)

Dasso, Jerome, Alfred A. Ring, and Douglas McFall. *Fundamentals of Real Estate.* Englewood Cliffs, N.J.: Prentice-Hall, Inc., 1977.

Hoagland, Henry E., Leo D. Stone, and William B. Brueggeman. *Real Estate Finance*, 5th ed. Homewood, Ill.: Richard D. Irwin, Inc., 1977.

Ficek, Edmund F., Thomas P. Henderson, and Ross

H. Johnson. *Real Estate Principles and Practices.* Columbus, Ohio: Charles E. Merrill Publishing Company, 1976.

Kratovil, Robert. *Real Estate Law,* 6th ed. Englewood Cliffs, N.J.: Prentice-Hall, Inc., 1974.

Shenkel, William M. *The Real Estate Professional.* Homewood, Ill.: Dow Jones-Irwin, Inc., 1976.

NOTICE TO CUSTOMER
as required by Federal Reserve Regulation "Z"   LOAN NO. _____

will lend to the borrower(s) in this transaction the amount below indicated. Interest computations on this amount will be at the contractual rate of
_____% on the outstanding balance. The **ANNUAL PERCENTAGE RATE** which includes with the contractual rate those costs listed
below as **PREPAID FINANCE CHARGE** is _____% and will begin to accure on _____. Beginning on the
_____ day of _____ 19_____ and due the _____ day of the month thereafter payments for Principal and Finance Charge,
will be due in_____ monthly installments of_____.

A. **AMOUNT OF LOAN** committed in this transaction .... $_____
B. Less **PREPAID FINANCE CHARGE** costs due at time of closing
    1. Loan Discount... $_____
    2. Loan Processing Fee... $_____
    3. Interest Thru .... $_____
    4. Private or F.H.A. Mortgage Insurance.................... $_____
    5. _____ $_____
    6. _____ $_____
    7. _____ $_____
                                        Total **PREPAID FINANCE CHARGE** $_____
C. Equals **AMOUNT FINANCED** in this transaction.. $_____
D. Other costs not included in **FINANCE CHARGE:**   PAID BY CASH   PAID FROM LOAN
                                                                                    PROCEEDS
    1. Title Insurance or Abstract .... $_____ $_____
    2. Opinion on Title .... $_____ $_____
    3. Appraisal... $_____ $_____
    4. Credit Report.. $_____ $_____
    5. Survey.. $_____ $_____
    6. Tax Escrow.. $_____ $_____
    7. Insurance Escrow... $_____ $_____
    8. Hazard Insurance Premium............................... $_____ $_____
    9. Recording Fee... $_____ $_____
    10. _____ $_____ $_____
    11. _____ $_____ $_____
                                Total Charges Paid From Loan Proceeds $_____
E. **NET PROCEEDS**... $_____
F. This Institution's security interest in this transaction is a _____ on property located at_____
    _____ also specifically described in the documents furnished for this loan.
    The documents executed in connection with this transaction cover all after-acquired property and also stand as security for future advances, the
    terms for which are described in the documents.

G. Late payment formula:
        In event of default a late charge of 5% of the Principal and Interest payment will be charged for each installment not received by the
        Association within 15 days after the installment is due.

H. Prepayment formula:
        When amount prepaid equals or exceeds 20% of the original loan, not more than 90 days interest on the amount prepaid may be charged
        beyond the date of payment.

I. Rebate formula:
        None

J. Miscellaneous disclosures:
        This Mortgage also secures the payment of any additional loans up to but not exceeding $5000.00 at the Mortgagee's option.

*K. **FINANCE CHARGE** includes:
    1. Total Prepaid Finance Charge (from B)................................. $_____
    2. Total Interest to be Earned over life of Loan........................ $_____
    3. _____ $_____
    4. _____ $_____
    5. _____ $_____
                                            Total **FINANCE CHARGE** $_____

    TOTAL PAYMENTS on this transaction (Principal and Interest) will be .... $_____

INSURANCE

PROPERTY INSURANCE: Property insurance, if written in connection with this loan, may be obtained by borrower through any person of his choice,
provided however, the creditor reserves the right to refuse, for reasonable cause, to accept an insurer offered by the borrower. If borrower desires property insurance to be obtained from or through the creditor, the cost will be $_____ for the_____ year term of the initial policy.   OTHER
INSURANCE: Credit life, accident, health or loss of income insurance is not required to obtain this loan. No charge is made for such insurance and No
such insurance may be provided unless the borrower signs the appropriate statement below. _____ is available at a cost of
$_____ for the _____ year term of the initial policy.   (TYPE OF INSURANCE)

I desire_____ insurance coverage   I DO NOT desire such insurance coverage.

_____   _____
DATE   SIGNATURE   DATE   SIGNATURE

                        I hereby acknowledge receipt of the disclosures made in this notice.

                                                    _____
                                                    BORROWER   DATE

BY_____   _____
                                                    BORROWER   DATE
* Not required for 1st mortgage purchase loans.

FIG. 11-1—Regulation Z statement.

A. U.S. DEPARTMENT OF HOUSING AND URBAN DEVELOPMENT	B. TYPE OF LOAN
SETTLEMENT STATEMENT	

B. TYPE OF LOAN

1. ☐ FHA   2. ☐ FMHA   3. ☐ CONV. UNINS.

4. ☐ VA   5. ☐ CONV. INS.

6. FILE NUMBER:	7. LOAN NUMBER:

8. MORT. INS. CASE NO.:

C. NOTE: This form is furnished to give you a statement of actual settlement costs. Amounts paid to and by the settlement agent are shown. Items marked "(p.o.c.)" were paid outside the closing; they are shown here for informational purposes and are not included in the totals.

D. NAME OF BORROWER:	E. NAME OF SELLER:	F. NAME OF LENDER:

G. PROPERTY LOCATION:	H. SETTLEMENT AGENT:	I. SETTLEMENT DATE:
	PLACE OF SETTLEMENT:	

J. SUMMARY OF BORROWER'S TRANSACTION:		K. SUMMARY OF SELLER'S TRANSACTION:	
100.	**GROSS AMOUNT DUE FROM BORROWER**	**400.**	**GROSS AMOUNT DUE TO SELLER**
101.	Contract sales price	401.	Contract sales price
102.	Personal property	402.	Personal property
103.	Settlement charges to borrower (line 1400)	403.	
104.		404.	
105.		405.	
Adjustments for items paid by seller in advance		*Adjustments for items paid by seller in advance*	
106.	City/town taxes to	406.	City/town taxes to
107.	County taxes to	407.	County taxes to
108.	Assessments to	408.	Assessments to
109.		409.	
110.		410.	
111.		411.	
112.		412.	
120.	**GROSS AMOUNT DUE FROM BORROWER**	**420.**	**GROSS AMOUNT DUE TO SELLER**
200.	**AMOUNTS PAID BY OR IN BEHALF OF BORROWER**	**500.**	**REDUCTIONS IN AMOUNT DUE TO SELLER**
201.	Deposit or earnest money	501.	Excess deposit (see Instructions)
202.	Principal amount of new loan(s)	502.	Settlement charges to seller (line 1400)
203.	Existing loan(s) taken subject to	503.	Existing loan(s) taken subject to
204.		504.	Payoff of first mortgage loan
205.		505.	Payoff of second mortgage loan
206.		506.	
207.		507.	
208.		508.	
209.		509.	
Adjustments for items unpaid by seller		*Adjustments for items unpaid by seller*	
210.	City/town taxes to	510.	City/town taxes to
211.	County taxes to	511.	County taxes to
212.	Assessments to	512.	Assessments to
213.		513.	
214.		514.	
215.		515.	
216.		516.	
217.		517.	
218.		518.	
219.		519.	
220.	**TOTAL PAID BY/FOR BORROWER**	**520.**	**TOTAL REDUCTION AMOUNT DUE SELLER**
300.	**CASH AT SETTLEMENT FROM OR TO BORROWER**	**600.**	**CASH AT SETTLEMENT TO OR FROM SELLER**
301.	Gross amount due from borrower (line 120)	601.	Gross amount due to seller (line 420)
302.	Less amounts paid by/for borrower (line 220) ( )	602.	Less reduction amount due seller (line 520) ( )
303.	**CASH (☐ FROM) (☐ TO) BORROWER**	**603.**	**CASH (☐ TO) (☐ FROM) SELLER**

HUD 1A REV. 5/76 MID-WEST PRTG. CO.   **LENDER'S COPY**

FIG. 11-2—RESPA Settlement Statement, page 1, lender's copy.

A.	U.S. DEPARTMENT OF HOUSING AND URBAN DEVELOPMENT SETTLEMENT STATEMENT	B. TYPE OF LOAN

B. TYPE OF LOAN

1. ☐ FHA   2. ☐ FMHA   3. ☐ CONV. UNINS.

4. ☐ VA   5. ☐ CONV. INS.

6. FILE NUMBER: 7. LOAN NUMBER:

8. MORT. INS. CASE NO.:

C. NOTE: This form is furnished to give you a statement of actual settlement costs. Amounts paid to and by the settlement agent are shown. Items marked "(p.o.c.)" were paid outside the closing; they are shown here for informational purposes and are not included in the totals.

D. NAME OF BORROWER: E. NAME OF SELLER: F. NAME OF LENDER:

G. PROPERTY LOCATION: H. SETTLEMENT AGENT: I. SETTLEMENT DATE:

PLACE OF SETTLEMENT:

J. SUMMARY OF BORROWER'S TRANSACTION:		K. SUMMARY OF SELLER'S TRANSACTION:
100.	GROSS AMOUNT DUE FROM BORROWER	
101.	Contract sales price	
102.	Personal property	
103.	Settlement charges to borrower (line 1400)	
104.		
105.		
	Adjustments for items paid by seller in advance	
106.	City/town taxes to	
107.	County taxes to	
108.	Assessments to	
109.		
110.		
111.		
112.		
120.	GROSS AMOUNT DUE FROM BORROWER	
200.	AMOUNTS PAID BY OR IN BEHALF OF BORROWER	
201.	Deposit or earnest money	
202.	Principal amount of new loan(s)	
203.	Existing loan(s) taken subject to	
204.		
205.		
206.		
207.		
208.		
209.		
	Adjustments for items unpaid by seller	
210.	City/town taxes to	
211.	County taxes to	
212.	Assessments to	
213.		
214.		
215.		
216.		
217.		
218.		
219.		
220.	TOTAL PAID BY/FOR BORROWER	
300.	CASH AT SETTLEMENT FROM OR TO BORROWER	
301.	Gross amount due from borrower (line 120)	
302.	Less amounts paid by/for borrower (line 220) ( )	
303.	CASH (☐ FROM) (☐ TO) BORROWER	

HUD 1A REV. 5/76 MID-WEST PRTG. CO.

BORROWER'S COPY

FIG. 11-2—RESPA Settlement Statement, page 1, borrower's copy.

A.	**U.S. DEPARTMENT OF HOUSING AND URBAN DEVELOPMENT** **SETTLEMENT STATEMENT**	**B. TYPE OF LOAN**

B. TYPE OF LOAN

1. ☐ FHA   2. ☐ FMHA   3. ☐ CONV. UNINS.

4. ☐ VA   5. ☐ CONV. INS.

6. FILE NUMBER:

7. LOAN NUMBER:

8. MORT. INS. CASE NO.:

C. NOTE: This form is furnished to give you a statement of actual settlement costs. Amounts paid to and by the settlement agent are shown. Items marked "(p.o.c.)" were paid outside the closing; they are shown here for informational purposes and are not included in the totals.

D. NAME OF BORROWER:	E. NAME OF SELLER:	F. NAME OF LENDER:

G. PROPERTY LOCATION:	H. SETTLEMENT AGENT:	I. SETTLEMENT DATE:
	PLACE OF SETTLEMENT:	

J. SUMMARY OF BORROWER'S TRANSACTION:	K. SUMMARY OF SELLER'S TRANSACTION:	
	400.	**GROSS AMOUNT DUE TO SELLER**	
	401.	Contract sales price	
	402.	Personal property	
	403.		
	404.		
	405.		
		Adjustments for items paid by seller in advance	
	406.	City/town taxes to	
	407.	County taxes to	
	408.	Assessments to	
	409.		
	410.		
	411.		
	412.		
	420.	**GROSS AMOUNT DUE TO SELLER**	
	500.	**REDUCTIONS IN AMOUNT DUE TO SELLER**	
	501.	Excess deposit (see Instructions)	
	502.	Settlement charges to seller (line 1400)	
	503.	Existing loan(s) taken subject to	
	504.	Payoff of first mortgage loan	
	505.	Payoff of second mortgage loan	
	506.		
	507.		
	508.		
	509.		
		Adjustments for items unpaid by seller	
	510.	City/town taxes to	
	511.	County taxes to	
	512.	Assessments to	
	513.		
	514.		
	515.		
	516.		
	517.		
	518.		
	519.		
	520.	**TOTAL REDUCTION AMOUNT DUE SELLER**	
	600.	**CASH AT SETTLEMENT TO OR FROM SELLER**	
	601.	Gross amount due to seller (line 420)	
	602.	Less reduction amount due seller (line 520)	( )
	603.	**CASH (☐ TO) (☐ FROM) SELLER**	

HUD 1A REV. 5/76 MID-WEST PRTG. CO.   **SELLER'S COPY**

FIG. 11-3—RESPA Settlement Statement, page 1, seller's copy.

A.	U.S. DEPARTMENT OF HOUSING AND URBAN DEVELOPMENT SETTLEMENT STATEMENT	B. TYPE OF LOAN

B. TYPE OF LOAN

1. ☐ FHA   2. ☐ FMHA   3. ☐ CONV. UNINS.

4. ☐ VA   5. ☐ CONV. INS.

6. FILE NUMBER: 7. LOAN NUMBER:

8. MORT. INS. CASE NO.:

C. NOTE: This form is furnished to give you a statement of actual settlement costs. Amounts paid to and by the settlement agent are shown. Items marked "(p.o.c.)" were paid outside the closing; they are shown here for informational purposes and are not included in the totals.

D. NAME OF BORROWER: E. NAME OF SELLER: F. NAME OF LENDER:

G. PROPERTY LOCATION: H. SETTLEMENT AGENT: I. SETTLEMENT DATE:

PLACE OF SETTLEMENT:

J. SUMMARY OF BORROWER'S TRANSACTION:

100.	GROSS AMOUNT DUE FROM BORROWER	
101.	Contract sales price	
102.	Personal property	
103.	Settlement charges to borrower (line 1400)	
104.		
105.		
	Adjustments for items paid by seller in advance	
106.	City/town taxes	to
107.	County taxes	to
108.	Assessments	to
109.		
110.		
111.		
112.		
120.	GROSS AMOUNT DUE FROM BORROWER	
200.	AMOUNTS PAID BY OR IN BEHALF OF BORROWER	
201.	Deposit or earnest money	
202.	Principal amount of new loan(s)	
203.	Existing loan(s) taken subject to	
204.		
205.		
206.		
207.		
208.		
209.		
	Adjustments for items unpaid by seller	
210.	City/town taxes	to
211.	County taxes	to
212.	Assessments	to
213.		
214.		
215.		
216.		
217.		
218.		
219.		
220.	TOTAL PAID BY/FOR BORROWER	
300.	CASH AT SETTLEMENT FROM OR TO BORROWER	
301.	Gross amount due from borrower (line 120)	
302.	Less amounts paid by/for borrower (line 220)	( )
303.	CASH (☐ FROM) (☐ TO) BORROWER	

K. SUMMARY OF SELLER'S TRANSACTION:

400.	GROSS AMOUNT DUE TO SELLER	
401.	Contract sales price	
402.	Personal property	
403.		
404.		
405.		
	Adjustments for items paid by seller in advance	
406.	City/town taxes	to
407.	County taxes	to
408.	Assessments	to
409.		
410.		
411.		
412.		
420.	GROSS AMOUNT DUE TO SELLER	
500.	REDUCTIONS IN AMOUNT DUE TO SELLER	
501.	Excess deposit (see Instructions)	
502.	Settlement charges to seller (line 1400)	
503.	Existing loan(s) taken subject to	
504.	Payoff of first mortgage loan	
505.	Payoff of second mortgage loan	
506.		
507.		
508.		
509.		
	Adjustments for items unpaid by seller	
510.	City/town taxes	to
511.	County taxes	to
512.	Assessments	to
513.		
514.		
515.		
516.		
517.		
518.		
519.		
520.	TOTAL REDUCTION AMOUNT DUE SELLER	
600.	CASH AT SETTLEMENT TO OR FROM SELLER	
601.	Gross amount due to seller (line 420)	
602.	Less reduction amount due seller (line 520)	( )
603.	CASH (☐ TO) (☐ FROM) SELLER	

HUD 1A REV. 5/76 MID-WEST PRTG. CO.

WORKSHEET—DETACH AND COMPLETE BEFORE TYPING

FIG. 11-4—RESPA Settlement Statement, page 1, worksheet.

U.S. DEPARTMENT OF HOUSING AND URBAN DEVELOPMENT
SETTLEMENT STATEMENT
PAGE 2

L. SETTLEMENT CHARGES		PAID FROM BORROWER'S FUNDS AT SETTLEMENT	PAID FROM SELLER'S FUNDS AT SETTLEMENT
700.	TOTAL SALES/BROKER'S COMMISSION based on price $ @ % =		
	Division of commission (line 700) as follows:		
701.	$ to		
702.	$ to		
703.	Commission paid at Settlement		
704.			
800.	ITEMS PAYABLE IN CONNECTION WITH LOAN		
801.	Loan Origination Fee %		
802.	Loan Discount %		
803.	Appraisal Fee to		
804.	Credit Report to		
805.	Lender's Inspection Fee		
806.	Mortgage Insurance Application Fee to		
807.	Assumption Fee		
808.			
809.			
810.			
811.			
900.	ITEMS REQUIRED BY LENDER TO BE PAID IN ADVANCE		
901.	Interest from to @ $ /day		
902.	Mortgage Insurance Premium for mo. to		
903.	Hazard Insurance Premium for yrs. to		
904.	yrs. to		
905.			
1000.	RESERVES DEPOSITED WITH LENDER FOR		
1001.	Hazard insurance mo. @ $ /mo.		
1002.	Mortgage insurance mo. @ $ /mo.		
1003.	City property taxes mo. @ $ /mo.		
1004.	County property taxes mo. @ $ /mo.		
1005.	Annual assessments mo. @ $ /mo.		
1006.	mo. @ $ /mo.		
1007.	mo. @ $ /mo.		
1008.	mo. @ $ /mo.		
1100.	TITLE CHARGES		
1101.	Settlement or closing fee to		
1102.	Abstract or title search to		
1103.	Title examination to		
1104.	Title insurance binder to		
1105.	Document preparation to		
1106.	Notary fees to		
1107.	Attorney's fees to		
	(includes above items No.:)		
1108.	Title insurance to		
	(includes above items No.:)		
1109.	Lender's coverage $		
1110.	Owner's coverage $		
1111.			
1112.			
1113.			
1200.	GOVERNMENT RECORDING AND TRANSFER CHARGES		
1201.	Recording fees: Deed $; Mortgage $; Releases $		
1202.	City/county tax/stamps: Deed $; Mortgage $		
1203.	State tax/stamps: Deed $; Mortgage $		
1204.			
1205.			
1300.	ADDITIONAL SETTLEMENT CHARGES		
1301.	Survey to		
1302.	Pest inspection to		
1303.			
1304.			
1305.			
1400.	TOTAL SETTLEMENT CHARGES (enter on lines 103 and 502, Sections J and K)		

The Undersigned Acknowledges Receipt of This Settlement Statement and Agrees to the Correctness Thereof.

_____
Buyer

_____
Seller

HUD 1B REV. 5/76 MID-WEST PRTG. CO.   LENDER'S COPY

FIG. 11-5—RESPA Settlement Statement, page 2, lender's copy.

U.S. DEPARTMENT OF HOUSING AND URBAN DEVELOPMENT
SETTLEMENT STATEMENT
PAGE 2

L. SETTLEMENT CHARGES	PAID FROM BORROWER'S FUNDS AT SETTLEMENT
700. **TOTAL SALES/BROKER'S COMMISSION** based on price $ @ % =	
Division of commission (line 700) as follows:	
701. $ to	
702. $ to	
703. Commission paid at Settlement	
704.	
800. **ITEMS PAYABLE IN CONNECTION WITH LOAN**	
801. Loan Origination Fee %	
802. Loan Discount %	
803. Appraisal Fee to	
804. Credit Report to	
805. Lender's Inspection Fee	
806. Mortgage Insurance Application Fee to	
807. Assumption Fee	
808.	
809.	
810.	
811.	
900. **ITEMS REQUIRED BY LENDER TO BE PAID IN ADVANCE**	
901. Interest from to @ $ /day	
902. Mortgage Insurance Premium for mo. to	
903. Hazard Insurance Premium for yrs. to	
904. yrs. to	
905.	
1000. **RESERVES DEPOSITED WITH LENDER FOR**	
1001. Hazard insurance mo. @ $ /mo.	
1002. Mortgage insurance mo. @ $ /mo.	
1003. City property taxes mo. @ $ /mo.	
1004. County property taxes mo. @ $ /mo.	
1005. Annual assessments mo. @ $ /mo.	
1006. mo. @ $ /mo.	
1007. mo. @ $ /mo.	
1008. mo. @ $ /mo.	
1100. **TITLE CHARGES**	
1101. Settlement or closing fee to	
1102. Abstract or title search to	
1103. Title examination to	
1104. Title insurance binder to	
1105. Document preparation to	
1106. Notary fees to	
1107. Attorney's fees to	
(includes above items No.: *)*	
1108. Title insurance to	
(includes above items No.: *)*	
1109. Lender's coverage $	
1110. Owner's coverage $	
1111.	
1112.	
1113.	
1200. **GOVERNMENT RECORDING AND TRANSFER CHARGES**	
1201. Recording fees: Deed $; Mortgage $; Releases $	
1202. City/county tax/stamps: Deed $; Mortgage $	
1203. State tax/stamps: Deed $; Mortgage $	
1204.	
1205.	
1300. **ADDITIONAL SETTLEMENT CHARGES**	
1301. Survey to	
1302. Pest inspection to	
1303.	
1304.	
1305.	
1400. **TOTAL SETTLEMENT CHARGES** *(enter on lines 103 and 502, Sections J and K)*	

The Undersigned Acknowledges Receipt of This Settlement Statement and Agrees to the Correctness Thereof.

_____   _____
Buyer   **Seller**

HUD 1B REV. 5/76 MID-WEST PRTG. CO.   **BORROWER'S COPY**

FIG. 11-6—RESPA Settlement Statement, page 2, borrower's copy.

L. SETTLEMENT CHARGES		PAID FROM SELLER'S FUNDS AT SETTLEMENT
700.	TOTAL SALES/BROKER'S COMMISSION based on price $ @ % =	
	Division of commission (line 700) as follows:	
701.	$ to	
702.	$ to	
703.	Commission paid at Settlement	
704.		
800.	ITEMS PAYABLE IN CONNECTION WITH LOAN	
801.	Loan Origination Fee %	
802.	Loan Discount %	
803.	Appraisal Fee to	
804.	Credit Report to	
805.	Lender's Inspection Fee	
806.	Mortgage Insurance Application Fee to	
807.	Assumption Fee	
808.		
809.		
810.		
811		
900.	ITEMS REQUIRED BY LENDER TO BE PAID IN ADVANCE	
901.	Interest from to @ $ /day	
902.	Mortgage Insurance Premium for mo. to	
903.	Hazard Insurance Premium for yrs. to	
904.	yrs. to	
905.		
1000.	RESERVES DEPOSITED WITH LENDER FOR	
1001.	Hazard insurance mo. @ $ /mo.	
1002.	Mortgage insurance mo. @ $ /mo.	
1003.	City property taxes mo. @ $ /mo.	
1004.	County property taxes mo. @ $ /mo.	
1005.	Annual assessments mo. @ $ /mo.	
1006.	mo. @ $ /mo.	
1007.	mo. @ $ /mo.	
1008.	mo. @ $ /mo.	
1100.	TITLE CHARGES	
1101.	Settlement or closing fee to	
1102.	Abstract or title search to	
1103.	Title examination to	
1104.	Title insurance binder to	
1105.	Document preparation to	
1106.	Notary fees to	
1107.	Attorney's fees to	
	(includes above items No.:)	
1108.	Title insurance to	
	(includes above items No.:)	
1109.	Lender's coverage $	
1110.	Owner's coverage $	
1111.		
1112.		
1113.		
1200.	GOVERNMENT RECORDING AND TRANSFER CHARGES	
1201.	Recording fees: Deed $; Mortgage $; Releases $	
1202.	City/county tax/stamps: Deed $; Mortgage $	
1203.	State tax/stamps: Deed $; Mortgage $	
1204.		
1205.		
1300.	ADDITIONAL SETTLEMENT CHARGES	
1301.	Survey to	
1302.	Pest inspection to	
1303.		
1304.		
1305.		
1400.	TOTAL SETTLEMENT CHARGES (enter on lines 103 and 502, Sections J and K)	

The Undersigned Acknowledges Receipt of This Settlement Statement and Agrees to the Correctness Thereof.

_____   _____
Buyer   Seller

FIG. 11-7—RESPA Settlement Statement, page 2, seller's copy.

U.S. DEPARTMENT OF HOUSING AND URBAN DEVELOPMENT
SETTLEMENT STATEMENT
PAGE 2

L. SETTLEMENT CHARGES		PAID FROM BORROWER'S FUNDS AT SETTLEMENT	PAID FROM SELLER'S FUNDS AT SETTLEMENT
700.	TOTAL SALES/BROKER'S COMMISSION based on price $ @ % =		
	Division of commission (line 700) as follows:		
701.	$ to		
702.	$ to		
703.	Commission paid at Settlement		
704.			
800.	ITEMS PAYABLE IN CONNECTION WITH LOAN		
801.	Loan Origination Fee %		
802.	Loan Discount %		
803.	Appraisal Fee to		
804.	Credit Report to		
805.	Lender's Inspection Fee		
806.	Mortgage Insurance Application Fee to		
807.	Assumption Fee		
808.			
809.			
810.			
811.			
900.	ITEMS REQUIRED BY LENDER TO BE PAID IN ADVANCE		
901.	Interest from to @ $ /day		
902.	Mortgage Insurance Premium for mo. to		
903.	Hazard Insurance Premium for yrs. to		
904.	yrs. to		
905.			
1000.	RESERVES DEPOSITED WITH LENDER FOR		
1001.	Hazard insurance mo. @ $ /mo.		
1002.	Mortgage insurance mo. @ $ /mo.		
1003.	City property taxes mo. @ $ /mo.		
1004.	County property taxes mo. @ $ /mo.		
1005.	Annual assessments mo. @ $ /mo.		
1006.	mo. @ $ /mo.		
1007.	mo. @ $ /mo.		
1008.	mo. @ $ /mo.		
1100.	TITLE CHARGES		
1101.	Settlement or closing fee to		
1102.	Abstract or title search to		
1103.	Title examination to		
1104.	Title insurance binder to		
1105.	Document preparation to		
1106.	Notary fees to		
1107.	Attorney's fees to		
	(includes above items No.:)		
1108.	Title insurance to		
	(includes above items No.:)		
1109.	Lender's coverage $		
1110.	Owner's coverage $		
1111.			
1112.			
1113.			
1200.	GOVERNMENT RECORDING AND TRANSFER CHARGES		
1201.	Recording fees: Deed $; Mortgage $; Releases $		
1202.	City/county tax/stamps: Deed $; Mortgage $		
1203.	State tax/stamps: Deed $; Mortgage $		
1204.			
1205.			
1300.	ADDITIONAL SETTLEMENT CHARGES		
1301.	Survey to		
1302.	Pest inspection to		
1303.			
1304.			
1305.			
1400.	TOTAL SETTLEMENT CHARGES (enter on lines 103 and 502, Sections J and K)		

The Undersigned Acknowledges Receipt of This Settlement Statement and Agrees to the Correctness Thereof.

_____   _____
Buyer   Seller

HUD 1B REV. 5/76 MID-WEST PRTG. CO.

WORKSHEET—DETACH AND COMPLETE BEFORE TYPING

FIG. 11-8—RESPA Settlement Statement, page 2, worksheet.

REVIEW QUESTIONS

1. To purchase property under an FHA loan the purchaser must

   (A) be a United States citizen
   (B) usually certify that he or she will occupy the property
   (C) both of the above
   (D) none of the above

2. A package mortgage is used to

   (A) cover the cost of such items as appliances
   (B) cover the cost of the purchase of the property
   (C) both of the above
   (D) neither of the above

3. A mortgage that is repaid in equal installments containing the principal and the interest is a

   (A) balloon mortgage
   (B) straight term mortgage
   (C) package mortgage
   (D) amortized mortgage

4. To compute the dollar value of a loan discount, each point is equal to

   (A) 1% of the down payment
   (B) 1% of the sales price
   (C) 1% of the amount to be loaned
   (D) 1% of the appraised value

5. Loan discounts for FHA and VA loans are paid by the

   (A) buyer   (C) lender
   (B) seller   (D) mortgagee

6. Regulation Z

   I. controls mortgage interest rates charged
   II. requires disclosure of the interest charges

   (A) I only   (C) both I and II
   (B) II only   (D) neither I nor II

7. A purchase money mortgage

   I. can be given by the purchaser to the seller as partial payment
   II. allows the buyer to obtain title to the property

   (A) I only   (C) both I and II
   (B) II only   (D) neither I nor II

8. The truth-in-lending statutes

   (A) limit the number of discount points that can be paid by the seller
   (B) limit the number of discount points paid by the purchaser
   (C) both A and B
   (D) neither A nor B

9. A construction loan is considered

   (A) a permanent form of financing
   (B) a method of self-financing
   (C) an interim form of financing
   (D) none of the above

10. The primary reason conventional loans are not discounted like FHA loans is that the

    (A) state government regulates the amount of interest charged
    (B) market for conventional loans can adjust because the interest rates are not fixed
    (C) FHA does not allow the mortgage broker to charge discount points
    (D) none of the above

11. Discount points are considered

    (A) rate equalization factors
    (B) police powers
    (C) origination fees
    (D) none of the above

12. An amortized loan is

    (A) repaid within a prescribed term
    (B) repaid on a regular installment basis
    (C) the opposite of a blanket mortgage
    (D) both A and B

13. In making a $15,000 loan, how much will the lender charge the seller if the mortgage is to be discounted 5 points?

    (A) $450   (C) $750
    (B) $500   (D) $600

14. Truth-in-lending statutes require which of the following to be disclosed?

   (A) the finance charge as an annual percentage
   (B) the number, amount, and due date of all payments
   (C) the method of computing unearned finance charges
   (D) all of the above

15. The VA

   (A) guarantees loans   (C) discounts loans
   (B) insures loans   (D) sells loans

16. Which type of loan may contain prepayment penalties?

   (A) an FHA loan
   (B) a VA loan
   (C) a conventional loan
   (D) none of the above

17. MGIC is a private company that

   (A) makes second mortgages
   (B) guarantees senior mortgages
   (C) insures portions of a loan
   (D) none of the above

18. If the interest rate charged on a loan exceeds the legal limits, the lender is in violation of

   (A) Regulation Z
   (B) foreclosure statutes
   (C) the statute of frauds
   (D) usury laws

19. HUD administers which of the following?

   (A) FHA   (C) MICA
   (B) PMI   (D) MGIC

20. If the borrower pays the balance of the loan in advance of the due date, he or she may be subject to

   (A) acceleration penalties
   (B) loan discounts
   (C) prepayment penalties
   (D) none of the above

Chapter 12
Real Estate Appraisal

ONE of the most challenging aspects of the real estate business is the determination of the price or value of the rights to real estate. Inasmuch as the market is relatively disorganized, and there is virtually no standardization of the commodity, it is difficult to estimate an exchange or market value of a property. Other types of markets such as the stock market can more readily determine the value of the commodities exchanged on it. In real estate, buyers and sellers need guidance from experts before setting listing prices or preparing offers. Many real estate professionals involved in the real estate decision-making process also need such advice when making transactions.

Appraising is a specialty in the real estate business requiring professional qualifications. While real estate brokers and salespersons are constantly involved in making decisions regarding value, they usually do not perform on the same level as a professional appraiser. The term *probable sales price* best describes the definition of the valuation activities of a typical broker or salesperson. Use of the full *appraisal process* requires much more than estimating the sales price of the property.

Appraisal specialists include those mentioned earlier in this text. They are usually members of the American Institute of Real Estate Appraisers (AIREA), the Society of Real Estate Appraisers (SREA), or American Society of Appraisers (ASA). By enrolling in educational programs offered by these organizations they are able to gain the training and expertise needed to serve the industry.

Regardless of the reason for the appraisal, it is necessary to follow the steps in the appraisal process which allows the appraiser to consider all social, political, and legal aspects which might affect the income-producing abilities of the property.

REASONS FOR APPRAISALS

All real estate transactions involve determining the value of land and any improvements which may be on it. The need for appraisals can typically be found in the different types of transactions which occur involving real property. For example, appraisals are most likely required for any of the following reasons.

In connection with the transfer of ownership:

Aid prospective buyers in determining an offering price

Aid prospective sellers in determining a selling price

Establish the value of an estate's assets

Establish the value of property being exchanged or merged through some form of reorganization.

In connection with obtaining credit for financial purposes:

Arrive at the value of security offered for a proposed mortgage loan

Provide a sound basis for real estate decision-making for the mortgagee

Establish a basis for insurance and value of the property.

To establish just compensation in condemnation proceedings:

Estimate the value before the act of condemnation

Estimate the value after the act of condemnation.

To establish a basis for taxation:

Estimate applicable depreciation rates on buildings and to value nondepreciable items such as land

Determine gift or inheritance tax values.

REAL ESTATE APPRAISAL DEFINITIONS

The study of real estate is similar to that of a foreign language: Unless you know the terminology or vocabulary, you cannot communicate with others in the business. Appraisal has many definitions which must be mastered before a person can have a basic understanding of the topic.

An Appraisal

Simply defined, an *appraisal* is an estimate or opinion of value. The fundamental purpose of any appraisal is to *estimate* the value of a *particular* property for a *defined* purpose at a *particular* time.

Capitalization

Capitalization is the process of reflecting future income in terms of present value. Part of the capitalization process is the development of a *capitalization rate*. A "cap" rate is a percentage made up of the interest rate (a return on the investment in the land and building) plus the *recapture rate* (a return of the original investment in the building).

A return on the land and the building indicates that the investor expects to earn income on the money invested in the property. Because real estate investment carries higher risks than a savings account at a financial institution or the purchase of a government bond, it is only reasonable that the investor receive a higher rate of return. The risk

rate is calculated by determining the amount of return (in the form of a percent) which is needed to attract an investor to a particular investment. The basic amount of this percentage calculation is typically that of the minimum return of a government bond. To that amount allowances are added to reflect other varied risks involved in the property.

Since buildings depreciate, it is necessary to compensate the owner for the value lost. For this reason, the capitalization rate includes a return of investment or recapture of the building's value. This rate is determined by dividing the *remaining economic life* of the building into 100. For example, a building with a remaining economic life of 20 years has an annual recapture rate of 5% (100 ÷ 20 = 5). The recapture rate and the risk rate are then combined and applied to the property to derive the present value of the future benefits. Sample problems on capitalization have been provided in Chapter 15.

Depreciation

Depreciation is a loss in property value for any reason. *Accelerated depreciation* is a method of reflecting depreciation that enables the owner of an asset to take more of the depreciation during the early years of the asset's life. *Contingent depreciation* is a loss in property value because of expectations of a decline in property services. *Depletion* is the exhaustion of a resource, such as the removal of a mineral deposit. *Economic obsolescence* is a loss in property value caused by events outside the property that unfavorably affect income or income potentials. *Functional obsolescence* is a loss in property value because of a loss in the ability of the physical property to provide services as compared with other alternatives. *Physical depreciation* is a loss in property value due to wearing away or simple deterioration.

Certain types of depreciation are *curable,* that is, the item causing the devaluation may be repaired or replaced for a reasonable cost. The value added by so doing must be greater than the cost. If it is not, the depreciation is considered *incurable.* "Incurable" is the term used to describe the types of depreciation which either cannot be cured or are impractical to cure because of the cost.

Gross Rent Multiplier

The *gross rent multiplier* (GRM) is a factor used in arriving at an estimation of real estate value. The factor is obtained by dividing the known sales prices of comparable properties by the rental income of these properties. It is often the average quotient arrived at from the above division (sales price divided by rental income) of several comparable properties. The *gross* rental income is then multiplied by this factor. The gross rent multiplier is most closely aligned with the *market data approach* to value.

Example:

The resulting multipliers are utilized to arrive at the gross rent multiplier (GRM).

Sales Price	Gross Monthly Rent	Multiplier
$17,500	$175	100
18,900	180	105
17,750	180	99*
18,000	185	97*

(*rounded)

With market data shown above, we might conclude properties in a certain neighborhood are selling for 100 times their gross monthly rent.

If our subject property is renting for $182.50, then $182.50 times 100 equals $18,250.00, the estimated value using the GRM.

Highest and Best Use

The highest and best use, both practical and legal, is that which will produce the greatest net income stream or intrinsic value over a period of time. Every property has a highest and best use as of a single point in time. It is not always possible to calculate the value of the property based on actual economic income. In some instances it is necessary to include the services or benefits the property provides as an increment of "non money" income or intrinsic value. This term is probably one of the most widely used terms in the real estate business. *Consistent use* is basic to this concept. A property in transition from one use to another cannot be valued on the basis of one use for land and another for improvements.

Economic Life

The period over which a property will yield the investor a return of the investment, over and above the economic or gross rent attributable to the land, is termed economic life.

Value

Value can have many meanings. When the term is used in relation to real estate it means that we must examine two factors to gauge its reliability: *utility* and *scarcity*.

To have value in real estate, both factors must be present to some degree. Even though both may be present, an additional consideration must be made. Can the prospective purchaser buy the property with the means available? *Purchasing power* must be considered.

There are many different types of value. The most commonly sought value is *market value*. Other types of value include assessed value, insurable value, loan value, and condemnation value.

Since market value is utilized the most, we shall study it in detail. A basic definition for market value can be found in *Real Estate Appraisal Terminology*, by Byrl N. Boyce, which is:

"The highest price in terms of money which a property will bring in a *competitive and open market* under all conditions requisite to a fair sale, the *buyer and seller,* each *acting prudently, knowledgeably* and assuming the price is not affected by undue stimulus."

Implicit in this definition is the consummation of a sale as of a specified date and the passing of the title from the seller to the buyer under conditions whereby:

1. The buyer and the seller are typically motivated.
2. Both parties are well informed or well advised, and each acts in what is considered his or her own best interests.
3. A reasonable time is allowed for exposure in the open market.
4. Payment is made in cash or its equivalent.
5. Financing, if any, is on terms generally available in the community at the specified date and typical for a property of this type in its locale.
6. The price represents a normal consideration for the properties sold unaffected by special financing amounts and/or terms, services, fees, costs, or credits incurred in the transaction.

Numerous definitions of market value have been devised over the years by professional organizations, governmental bodies, courts, etc. The supreme courts of most states have handed down definitions of market value for use in the lower courts. These definitions are subject to change.

Persons performing appraisal services which may be subject to litigation should seek the exact definition of market value in the jurisdiction in which the services are being performed.

Stated in simpler form, *market value is the price at which a willing seller would sell and a willing buyer would buy, both being informed and knowledgeable and neither being under duress.*

It is of great importance that value, price, and cost not be used interchangeably since they are not always the same. Price and value may, for example, appear to be the same if two similar properties in the same neighborhood are compared. However, if different financing plans are used to purchase each property, the actual prices might vary greatly due to the types of financing used. Usually the only time cost and value are likely to result in a similar value is when the improvements are new and the property is being used for its highest and best use. Otherwise many factors come into play regarding the location of the property and its relation to surroundings which cause value and price to vary.

Principle of Substitution

The basis of this principle can be found in the idea that, when two or more like properties with substantially the same utility become available, the one with the lowest price attracts the greatest demand. In the case of market value, the principle indicates that the informed buyer will not pay more than that paid for comparable properties, nor will the seller sell for less than that paid for comparable properties. It follows that a buyer will not pay more for an existing property than the cost to produce new. Obviously, the principle of substitution holds true through all three approaches to value.

THE APPRAISAL PROCESS

As the topic of appraisal has been discussed through the preceding discussion of terminology, you may have been wondering how the appraiser determines value. Obviously, an orderly method or procedure must be used. Before the appraiser gives his or her estimate or *opinion of value* either orally or in written form the appraisal process is applied. It must be used because it allows the appraiser to consider the property on a step by step basis, gathering all the relevant data required to support the final opinion of value. Such support is needed because appraisal is an art not an exact science, and the appraisal process provides the only logical approach to establishing real estate value. It is because of these efforts that the designated appraiser is held in high esteem by the real estate industry.

Perhaps the most detailed approach to the appraisal process has been developed and refined by the American Institute of Real Estate Appraisers (AIREA). The process as outlined by the Institute has several steps. (See page 152.)

Definition of the Problem

Logically, the first step in the appraisal process is the development of a concise statement of the problem which the appraiser is to consider. This prevents any question regarding what the objective of the appraisal is to be. Five basic factors are considered in this first step. They are as follows:

1. Identification of the real estate to be appraised —This includes both the legal description and the street address of the property.
2. Identification of the property rights—An appraisal is not solely an indication of the physical land and improvements but, more importantly, includes an opinion of the value of the rights which the owners have in the ownership or use of the land and improvements. In any case the rights to be considered are stated at the outset so that the appraiser can adequately identify the value being sought.
3. Date of the value—Value as of a *specific* date must be given. This is essential because of the varying factors which can increase and decrease value.
4. Purpose of the appraisal—A statement must be made as to the purpose or objective of the appraisal, thus allowing the appraiser to define the objective of the report.
5. Definition of value—As we have seen earlier in this chapter, the appraiser can find several different values for a property for different purposes. An exact written *definition of the value* sought should be included in the process at this point.

Preliminary Survey and Appraisal Plan

The preliminary survey and appraisal plan involves a number of items for the appraiser to consider. It is at this stage that such criteria as the data required, sources of such data, time schedule for the report, personnel required to complete the report, and a flow chart showing steps of completion for all elements of the report are defined. It is also at this stage that the appraiser can first calculate the proposed fee for the appraisal report. Obviously, the appraiser will be asked to quote a firm fee in advance of receiving a commitment to perform the assignment. This is usually part of a fee proposal indicating what work steps and schedules will be used in completing the appraisal assignment. The proposal is submitted to the owner of the property who then determines whether the appraiser receives the assignment.

Data Collection and Analysis

The collection of data relating to specific real property should include general data on the economic background of the region, the city, and the neighborhood in which the property is located. Such data will include elements which have a bearing on the value of the property, but which are found outside the property itself. Typical types of information found in the general data section include population characteristics, statistics on employment, and various other factors relating to economic trends as they might affect the subject property. Specific neighborhood data would include such information as zoning controls, utilities available, shopping facilities, schools, and typical land use within the immediate area of the subject property.

The second grouping of data to be collected is concerned with specific economic factors such as population, construction costs, current interest rates, and trends for the future.

Specific data collected for the appraisal can be divided into two areas, data collected on the subject property itself, and data collected on properties comparable to the subject property.

It is in this section that the appraiser includes subject property data regarding the title, the site of the subject property, and the improvements upon the land. The appraiser looks at such title items as type of ownership, identity of ownership, easements, zoning regulations, and any other restrictions upon the use of the property. Data relating to the physical structure would include a complete description of the improvement and analysis of its style, design, and layout, along with information regarding the site such as a description of its size, shape, and topography. The final step in this stage is determining the highest and best use of the site. Obviously the determination of the highest and best use is of critical importance to the determination of the value of the property.

Specific data gathered on comparable properties would include information similar to that gathered for the subject property. However, it would also include data on sales prices of comparable properties or perhaps the income derived from the rental of properties which may be reasonably compared with the subject property. It is essential to note that no two properties are identical, and for that reason the appraiser must determine what adjustments must be made to reflect the differences in the properties and the effect such differences have on the respective market values of the properties.

THE THREE APPROACHES TO VALUE

The appraiser has three approaches to determining the value of a property: *cost, market data,* and *income.* These three approaches combine the use of all definitions given so far.

In the majority of assignments, an appraiser utilizes all three approaches. On occasion he or she may believe the value indication from one approach will be more significant than that from the other two, yet uses all three as a check against each other and to test his or her own judgment. Obviously there are appraisal problems in which they cannot be applied. A value indication for vacant land cannot be obtained through use of the cost approach, nor one for a specialized property such as a municipal garden by the market data approach, nor, but rarely, one for an owner-occupied home by the income approach. The use of all three approaches is pertinent in the solution of most appraisal problems; their application is well established in appraisal technique and held to be part of the fundamental procedure.

Cost Approach

In the cost approach, the appraiser obtains a preliminary indication of value by adding to an estimate of the land's value an estimate of the depreciated reproduction cost of the building and other improvements. This approach is based on the assumption that the *reproduction cost* is the upper limit of value. This also assumes that a newly constructed building would have advantages over the existing building, so the appraiser must also evaluate any disadvantages or deficiencies of the existing building as compared with the new building. The measure of this deficiency is called *depreciation.*

Depreciation may be one or all of three kinds:

1. Deterioration or the physical wearing out of the property

2. Functional obsolescence or lack of desirability in terms of layout, style, and design as compared with that of a new property serving the same function

3. Economic obsolescence relating to a loss of value from causes outside the property itself.

The cost approach consists of five steps:

1. Estimate of the site's value as if vacant

2. Estimate of the current cost of reproducing the existing improvements

3. Estimate of depreciation from all causes

4. Deduction of depreciation from current reproduction costs

5. Addition of the site's value and the depreciated reproduction cost of improvements.

In discussing the cost approach, it is essential to know the difference between *replacement cost* and *reproduction cost*. Reproduction cost is today's cost to produce an exact replica of a property using the identical design and materials. Replacement cost is today's cost of an equally desirable property in which some of the functional obsolescence might possibly be cured. You must understand the distinguishing characteristics of these two basic concepts.

Since the cost approach utilizes the "cost new" estimation of cost less depreciation, it is necessary to be able to calculate the depreciation. While the methods used are too complex to discuss in this introductory chapter, you should be aware that they include market methods, the capitalization method, the straight-line method, the engineering method, and the breakdown method. More information for the utilization of these methods can be found in the texts included in the suggested readings list at the end of the chapter.

Market Data Approach

The market data approach is essential in almost every appraisal of the value of real property. The value estimated by this approach frequently is defined as "the price at which a willing seller would sell and a willing buyer would buy, neither being under abnormal pressure." This definition assumes that both the buyer and seller are fully informed as regards the property and the state of the market for that type of property, and that the property has been exposed in the open market for a reasonable time.

The application of this approach produces an estimate of the value of property by comparing it with similar properties of the same type and class which have been sold recently or are currently being offered for sale in competing areas. The process utilized in determining the degree of comparability between two properties involves judgment as to their similarity with respect to many factors such as location, construction, age and condition, layout, and equipment. The sales prices of those properties deemed most comparable tend to set the range in which the value of the subject property will fall. Further consideration of the comparative data indi-

cates to the appraiser a figure representing the value of the subject property, that is, the probable price at which it could be sold by a willing seller to a willing buyer as of the date of the appraisal.

The data involved in the application of this process concern comparable properties as well as the subject property and varies with the type of property. Elements of comparison, however, are basic and apply regardless of the type of property. They are (1) sales or asking prices of comparable properties, (2) conditions influencing each sale, (3) location of each property, and (4) description of land and improvements of each property.

Income Approach

In using the income approach, the appraiser is concerned with the present worth of the future potential benefits of a property. This is generally measured by the net income which a fully informed person is warranted in assuming the property will produce during its remaining useful life. After comparison with investments of similar type and class, this net income is capitalized into a value estimate.

Selecting the capitalization rate is one of the most important steps in the income approach. A variation of only one-half of 1% can make a difference of many thousands of dollars in the capitalized value of the income. The difference between an annual income of $27,500 capitalized at 5% and at $5\frac{1}{2}\%$ is $50,000.

The work to be done in assembling and processing income data is of four kinds:

1. Obtaining the rent schedules and the percentage of occupancy for the subject property and for comparable properties for the current year and for several years in the past. This information provides gross rental data and shows the trend in rentals and occupancy. These data are then related and adjusted by the comparative method to ascertain the estimate of gross income which the subject property should produce to attract investors in the market.

2. Obtaining expense data such as taxes, insurance, and operating costs being paid by the subject property and by comparable properties. The trend in these expenses is also necessary.

3. Estimating the remaining useful economic life of the building to establish the probable duration of its income.

4. Selecting the appropriate capitalization rate and the applicable technique and method for processing the net income.

USE OF THREE APPROACHES

Since all approaches are not applicable to all properties, it might be helpful to critique each of these approaches.

The cost approach is frequently used where a lack of data prevents the other approaches from being used. It is commonly used for buildings such as post offices, libraries, and schools. The income approach is used for properties for which information such as rent rolls and expense items is readily available. Through the use of capitalization it is possible to determine the amount of risk involved in the real estate investment. It must be used cautiously, however, since it is confronted by many variables.

Perhaps the most commonly used, the market approach is employed when recent information is available on comparable properties ("comps"). While this concept is relatively simple to use and can provide a quick analysis of the data, caution must be exercised because of the potential error introduced by subjective use of the comps.

RECONCILIATION, FINAL ESTIMATE, AND THE APPRAISAL REPORT

The final step in the appraisal process is correlation of the three indications of value derived by the cost, income, and market data approaches. In correlating these three approaches into a final estimate of value, the appraiser takes into account the purpose of the appraisal, the type of property, and the adequacy of the data processed in each of the three approaches. These considerations influence the weight to be given to each approach.

The appraiser does not obtain a final estimate of value by averaging the three individual indications of value arrived at by means of the cost, market data, and income approaches. He or she instead takes the three preliminary value estimates and examines the spread between minimum and maximum figures. The most emphasis is placed on the approach which appears to be the most reliable as an indication of the answer to the specific appraisal problem. This estimate is then tempered in accordance with his or her judgment as to the degree of reliance to be placed on the other two indications of value.

The form of the final report might be a completed standardized form, a one-page letter, or a large volume in a narrative form.

All appraisals must contain the date and purpose for which the appraisal was conducted, the value estimate derived, a description of the property, any qualifying statements affecting the property, and a certificate by the appraiser with his or her signature.

An appraisal report is a word portrayal of the property, the facts concerning the property, and the reasoning by which the appraiser has developed the estimate of value. The best report is the one which, in the fewest number of words, permits the reader to follow intelligently the appraiser's reasoning and to concur with the conclusions reached thereby. As every report is an answer to a question from a client, it should show the facts considered and clearly outline the reasoning employed by the appraiser in arriving at an answer.

THE APPRAISAL PROCESS

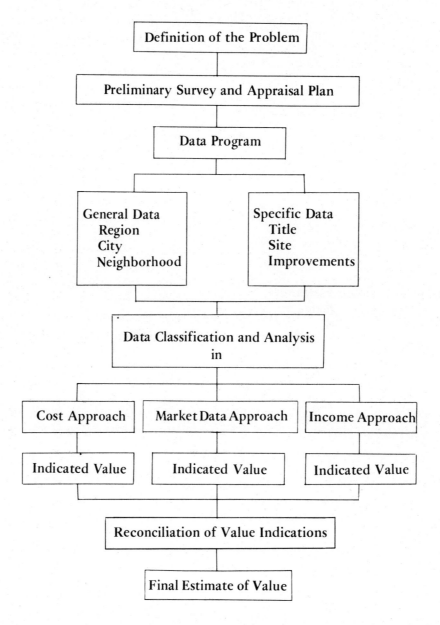

FIG. 12-1—A topical representation of the appraisal process. Reprinted with permission of the American Institute of Real Estate Appraisers.

SUGGESTED READINGS

(See the appropriate chapter in the following books.)

American Institute of Real Estate Appraisers. *The Appraisal of Real Estate,* 6th ed. Chicago: American Institute of Real Estate Appraisers, 1973.

Babcock, Henry A. *Appraisal Principles and Procedures.* Homewood, Ill.: Richard D. Irwin, Inc., 1968.

Boyce, Byrl N. *Real Estate Appraisal Terminology.* Cambridge, Mass.: Ballinger Publishing Company, 1975.

Friedman, Edith J. *Encyclopedia of Real Estate Appraising.* Englewood Cliffs, N.J.: Prentice-Hall, Inc., 1968.

Kahn, Sanders and Frederick Case. *Real Estate Appraisal and Investment,* 2nd ed. New York: The Ronald Press Company, 1977.

Ring, Alfred A. *Valuation of Real Estate,* 2nd ed. Englewood Cliffs, N.J.: Prentice-Hall, Inc., 1967.

Ring, Alfred A. and Jerome Dasso. *Real Estate Principles and Practices,* 8th ed. Englewood Cliffs, N.J.: Prentice-Hall, Inc., 1977.

Robinson, Peter C. *How to Appraise Commercial Properties.* Englewood Cliffs, N.J.: Prentice-Hall, Inc., 1971.

Ventolo, William L., Jr., and Martha R. Williams. *Fundamentals of Real Estate Appraisal.* Chicago: Real Estate Education Company, 1975.

Weimer, Arthur M., Homer Hoyt, and George F. Bloom. *Real Estate,* 7th ed. New York: The Ronald Press Company, 1978.

REVIEW QUESTIONS

1. A capitalization rate includes

   I. a recapture rate for both land and buildings
   II. return on investment in both land and buildings

   (A) I only
   (B) II only
   (C) both I and II
   (D) neither I nor II

2. Depreciation can be attributed to

   (A) economic obsolescence
   (B) functional obsolescence
   (C) physical deterioration
   (D) all of the above

3. If a building has an estimated remaining economic life of 35 years, the appropriate recapture rate will be

   (A) 28.5%
   (B) 33.3%
   (C) 2.86%
   (D) 3.33%

4. Licensees in the real estate industry most commonly use which appraisal approach in their day-to-day business?

   (A) cost
   (B) income
   (C) market
   (D) none of the above

5. The most accurate approach in attempting to appraise an old public library building is

   I. market
   II. income

   (A) I only
   (B) II only
   (C) both I and II
   (D) neither I nor II

6. A real estate appraisal provides the owner of the property with

   I. an estimate of the value of the property
   II. a stated definition of the value estimated

   (A) I only
   (B) II only
   (C) both I and II
   (D) neither I nor II

7. Real estate appraisers are paid

   (A) based on the value determined
   (B) on a commission basis
   (C) on a fee basis by the broker representing the seller
   (D) none of the above

8. Curable types of depreciation include

   I. economic obsolescence
   II. functional obsolescence

   (A) I only
   (B) II only
   (C) both I and II
   (D) neither I nor II

9. Ethically it is permissible for an appraiser to hold

    I.   a disclosed interest in the subject property
    II. an undisclosed interest in the subject property

    (A) I only   (C) both I and II
    (B) II only   (D) neither I nor II

10. An MAI must

    I.   be a member of NAR
    II. only appraise for a financial institution

    (A) I only   (C) both I and II
    (B) II only   (D) neither I nor II

11. A woman owns a building valued at $103,000 using the income method. She desires a 12% return on her investment. What net annual income must be generated by the building to meet this requirement?

    (A) $858,333
    (B) $12,360
    (C) $90,640
    (D) none of the above

12. Using the cost approach, if the site is valued at $10,000 and the improvements have been depreciated 40% and have a remaining value of $60,000, what was the cost of the improvements new?

    (A) $110,000   (C) $150,000
    (B) $100,000   (D) $160,000

13. A property has gross annual income of $8,000 and monthly expenses of $600. It has been valued at $147,000. What was the capitalization rate?

    (A) 6.6%   (C) .54%
    (B) .61%   (D) 5.4%

14. In appraising a special-purpose structure, the most reliable approach to valuation is the

    (A) market data approach
    (B) cost approach
    (C) income approach
    (D) none of the above

15. Economic obsolescence occurs from

    (A) factors within the subject property
    (B) lack of maintenance of the structure
    (C) both A and B
    (D) neither A nor B

16. Capitalization is a process for

    (A) disbursing present income
    (B) converting future income into present value
    (C) both A and B
    (D) neither A nor B

17. The income approach could best be applied to

    (A) a church
    (B) a new single-family residence
    (C) an apartment complex
    (D) two of the above

18. The appraisal process consists of which of the following steps?

    (A) making a preliminary survey and planning the appraisal
    (B) defining the problem and writing the appraisal report
    (C) applying the approaches, correlating the data, and making a final estimate of value
    (D) all of the above

19. Which of the following would yield a 10% capitalization rate?

    (A) gross income of $8,000; sales price of $80,000
    (B) net expenses of $8,000; sales price of $80,000
    (C) net income of $8,000; sales price of $80,000
    (D) gross expenses of $8,000; sales price of $80,000

20. If the established monthly GRM is 105 and a property has a gross income of $6,000 annually and monthly expenses of $200, what is the estimated market value using the GRM method?

    (A) $630,000   (C) $882,000
    (B) $73,500   (D) $52,500

Chapter 13

Contracts

THE basis for all relationships in the brokerage business is found in the law and the requirements it establishes for guidelines. Since almost all real estate dealings originate with an agreement known as a contract, it is essential for real estate salespersons to understand the basic elements of contracts. Furthermore, contracts establish the legal relationship between the parties involved, so each basic element must be understood.

TYPES OF CONTRACTS

There are several types of contracts. Specific rules exist to aid in their identification. Among the types of contracts are the following.

Bilateral

A bilateral contract is a contract in which both parties make promises to each other. Example: A says to B, "I will pay you $10,000 if you will promise to sell me this land." If B agrees, A has promised the payment of $10,000 and B has promised to sell him the land.

Unilateral

A unilateral contract is a contract in which one party gives a promise to another party in exchange for some actual performance by the second party. The promise made by the first party is not legally binding until the actual performance by the second party. Example: A says to B, "I will pay you $100 if you plow this field." If B plows the field, B has both accepted A's offer and performed his or her part of the contract. At this point, A's promise to pay B $100 is legally binding.

Express

An express contract is a contract in which the agreement is stated in words, either oral or written. Example: A says to B, "I will pay you $100 if you promise me to plow this field." B says, "It's a deal."

Implied

An implied contract is a contract in which the agreement between the parties can be inferred from their conduct alone, *without* spoken or written words. Example: A says to B, "I will pay you $100 if you promise me to plow this field." B says nothing, but walks over to the barn, straps on the plow, and begins plowing. The contract has been established.

ESSENTIALS OF A CONTRACT

All the following points must be present for a contract to be valid:

1. *Offer.* An offer must be made.
2. *Acceptance.* There must be acceptance of the offer.
3. *Consideration.* Something of value must be given up to make the contract binding.
4. *Legal capacity.* The parties must be legally competent to enter into contracts.
5. *Validity.* The contract must be free of duress, fraud, undue influence, and mistakes.
6. *Illegality and impossibility.* The purpose of the contract must be legal, and it must be possible to perform.

From your readings, you should be aware that a working knowledge of the requirements listed above is essential. English common law, established prior to the Revolutionary War, has been altered by individual states from time to time, but the same basic principles hold true throughout the United States.

A portion of the common law especially important to the real estate business is the statute of frauds. Its purpose is to prevent various types of contracts from being fraudulently entered into. In real estate, the statute of frauds has a primary impact in the following cases:

1. All contracts for the sale or purchase of real estate must be in writing and signed by the parties involved.
2. Any contract for the lease of real estate for a period of more than 1 year must be in writing and signed by the parties involved to be enforceable.

Certain states go beyond requirements of the statute of frauds by placing additional requirements on the writing of contracts.

Under common law, writing was never necessary for the formation of a contract; and today, in the absence of statutory requirements, an oral contract is as enforceable as a written contract.

A few types of contracts are required by statute almost everywhere to be in writing. Each state has a statute of frauds which dictates generally which types of contracts must be in writing. The purpose of the statute of frauds or any statute that demands that a certain type of contract be in writing is to produce certainty in the obligation and to remove the possibility of proving a nonexistent undertaking by possibly perjured evidence.

These state statutes of frauds are based on the English statute of frauds and are all quite similar in substance, although quite different in phraseology and style. Generally, under the statute of frauds in most states, the following contracts must be in writing:

1. Contracts whereby an executor or administrator of an estate promises to pay a debt or liability of a deceased person from his or her own property
2. Contracts whereby one party promises to pay the debt or liability of another party
3. Contracts where a promise to marry is the bargained-for exchange
4. Contracts that create or transfer any interest in land
5. Contracts for the sale of goods in which the sale exceeds a certain dollar amount
6. Contracts not to be performed within a year from the time they were made.

In order for the written requirement of the statute of frauds to be satisfied, most states require that the written memorandum disclose the following information: (1) the identity of the contracting parties, either by name or description; (2) identification of the subject matter of the contract; and (3) the consideration.

There is room for considerable flexibility as to what constitutes a sufficient memorandum. Generally, the statute of frauds is viewed as a procedural device which renders oral contracts which should have been in writing *unenforceable.* The statute does not prevent the existence of a valid contract, but merely makes written evidence necessary to establish it. In 18 states, the statute of frauds states that the contract is void or invalid unless in writing.

Since the validity of a contract can vary greatly from situation to situation, it is necessary to be aware of several definitions which indicate the status of a contract.

Valid

A valid contract possesses all the required elements of a contract, is for a legal purpose, and legally binds all the parties involved to the agreement.

Void

Any agreement which has no legal status, that is, one which never formed a legal contract and was therefore never binding on the parties, is considered a void contract. For example, an agreement made with a person who has been legally declared incompetent is void from the outset.

Voidable

A voidable contract is a contract in which one party or the other may take action to have the agreement declared void. As described later in the chapter, the parties capable of avoiding the contract change under different circumstances.

BASIC ELEMENTS OF A CONTRACT

In any contract there must be a "meeting of the minds"—or in legal terminology, an offer and acceptance.

Offer

The offer is the initial step in the formation of a contract and is of course an essential element. In the absence of an offer, no contract can result, because the party who is alleged to be the offeror has not defined what responsibility he or she is willing to assume nor what will be accepted in return for the offer. In the normal course of the real estate business, the offer is usually made by the purchaser. That is, he or she offers to purchase for a specified amount and under certain conditions.

The terms of the offer to purchase real estate have become quite stylized over the years, and we accept without question the fact that the purchaser is almost always the offeror. Yet, in the practical operation of the real estate business, we know that the true offeror is the owner of the property who has offered to sell it to anyone who will meet his or her terms. From a legal standpoint, however, we view the owner who has listed property for sale not as an offeror but as one who is soliciting offers from prospective buyers and who has, in a listing contract, merely defined the general range of offers he or she will consider. The practice of considering the buyer the offeror in the real estate business is so well established that the preparation of an offer to sell usually presents a unique and novel problem for both brokers and attorneys.

The offer, to be effective, must be reasonably certain. While the offeror may clearly understand what is meant by his or her offer, this is not the legal standard by which the offer is measured. The law provides an arbitrary standard by which the clarity and certainty of the offeror's terms are measured, the standard of the so-called reasonable person. That is, if the offer is clearly intelligible to a reasonable person, it is sufficiently clear and definite in its terms to satisfy the standards required by contract law. The basic reason for the requirement of reasonable certainty is that, unless it is reasonably certain, any resulting agreement cannot be an agreement at all because of the basic inability to define the terms of the agreement.

The offeror is in complete command of the terms of the offer. At this stage of the negotiating process the offeror is under no obligation of any kind. That is, the offer is a free and voluntary act on the part of the one who makes it, and he or she cannot be compelled by any rule of law to make an offer on terms that will be acceptable to the owner of the property or even an offer that makes any economic sense. The offeror is free to make the offer on any terms or conditions he or she chooses. The offeree, after all, is not under any compulsion to accept the offer and the offeree's remedy in the event that the offer is unacceptable is simply to decline to act upon it.

One of the most important features of this element of control of the offer is that it may be withdrawn at any time before it is acted upon. Once again, it is the free and voluntary act of the offeror, and the offeree is not injured by the withdrawal unless and until the offeree has acted upon it. This rule is true even though the offer, by its terms, specifies that it will be open for a stated period of time. It may be arbitrarily withdrawn until acted upon.

The offer must of course be communicated to the offeree. In the real estate business, this technical requirement is satisfied by the execution of an offer to purchase the property and delivery of it either to the property owner or to the broker who represents the owner, who is the owner's agent. Delivery (or communication) to the agent is the same, legally, as delivery to the principal, the owner. There remains, nevertheless, the technical requirement of communication of the offer to the offeree. Without it, there can be no valid acceptance. The mere fact that one has decided that one is willing to make an offer upon certain terms is not, by itself, enough to constitute an offer to purchase. It must, either directly or indirectly, be communicated to the seller before the seller can act upon it. So far as the real estate business is concerned the important point to be noted is that communication to the seller's agent, the broker or salesperson, is the equivalent of communication to the owner of the property.

Critically important to the formation of the contract to sell real estate is the fact that the offer must be in writing. Since under the statutes of frauds which apply to contracts for the sale of real estate all contracts must be in writing to be enforceable, and because the offeror is in command of the terms of the offer, the offer must be in writing. Without a written offer, the offeree has no way in which he or she can bind the offeror to the terms of the offer. The requirement that the contract be in writing to be enforceable and the degree of control exercised by the offeror demand that the offer be in writing. In the absence of a written offer it is legally almost impossible to prove the existence of an enforceable agreement.

The proper execution of the offer is quite important. When dealing with individuals, it is generally a simple matter to be sure that the offer is properly executed. The signature of the individual on the written offer is sufficient. So far as other legal entities are concerned, however, the matter of the sufficiency of the execution is a completely different matter that goes directly to the validity of the offer. Entities other than individual persons must have clearly established authority to act. It is not enough, for example, that an individual be an officer of a corporation; he or she must be authorized by the corporation to enter into a contract, whether it relates to real estate or any other subject matter. The question of capacity generally is considered below. However, in connection with the offer itself, it should be noted that, to be effective, it must be executed properly, either by a person who is competent or an officer or representative who has authority.

Acceptance

The next essential step in the formation of a contract is the acceptance of the offer. The offer by itself is meaningless unless and until the one to whom the offer is made indicates that it is satisfactory and that he is willing to enter into an agreement under which he will receive the fruits of the offer and will be willing to do what the offeror demands in return. The acceptance of the offer, usually by the seller in the real estate business, is a simple assent to the terms of the offer and an expression of intent to be bound by the terms of the resulting agreement. Legally, it must be just that

and nothing more. Adding to or altering the terms of the offer does not satisfy the definition of the term *acceptance*. The acceptance must be absolute, without any change in the terms of the offer. If not, it is not an acceptance; it is something less and a contract will not result.

The acceptance of the offer, in order to be legally effective, must be unequivocal. That is, it must be absolute, without any exceptions or any additional terms. In terms of the legal effect of the reaction of the offeree there are only two alternatives: The offeree either accepts each and every term of the offer without exception, or the offeree rejects the offer. These are the only two courses of action open to the offeree. As noted earlier, the offeror is in complete command of the offer. It is a voluntary act, and the offeror is under no obligation to proceed on any other basis than the one specified. There is no such thing as a conditional acceptance of an offer. The addition of any terms to the offer in the acceptance destroys the acceptance and by necessary implication rejects the offer. Such a response is, in legal effect, a counteroffer or new offer (discussed below); it cannot operate as an acceptance.

The acceptance of the offer must be communicated to the offeror. That is, positive action must be taken by the offeree to bind the offeror to the terms of the offer. The offeree may not simply decide that he or she accepts the offer; the law requires positive evidence of the decision that is calculated to reach the offeror; it must be communicated. In most cases, the offer will dictate the method by which it must be accepted. For example, the offer might provide that written acceptance must be received by the offeror by a specified time. In such a case, it is the responsibility of the offeree to use whatever means necessary to see that the acceptance is actually delivered to the offeror by the stated time. Nothing less than this will make the acceptance valid.

The typical language encountered in standard offers to purchase real estate is not quite so specific, usually providing simply that the offer must be accepted "on or before" a specified time. If such an offer is mailed to the offeree, then the offeree is entitled to assume that mailing of his or her acceptance by the time specified will result in a binding contract, since the offeror has by implication indicated that the mails are an acceptable agency for communication. If however, as is typically the case, the offer is delivered to the broker as agent for the seller, it is necessary that the acceptance be delivered to the offeror. That is, delivery to the agent (broker) is legally the same as delivery to the principal (seller) and does not constitute the broker as agent for the purchaser. Therefore delivery of the acceptance back to the broker does not constitute delivery to the offeror. It must be delivered by either the offeree (seller) or the agent (broker) to the offeror to be a legally effective acceptance.

The acceptance of the offer must be in writing for the same reasons that the offer must be in writing. The statute of frauds demands a written agreement to be enforceable in court.

Consideration

Consideration is a technical requirement of contract law which is necessary to make the agreement of the parties enforceable. The concept of *consideration* is not only one of the most difficult notions to define in the area of contract law, it is also one of the most difficult to justify. It would seem to be sufficient that the two parties to a contract intend for it to be legally enforceable, without imposing the technical requirement that there be some consideration to make their commitments binding. While the general trend in contract law is to place more emphasis upon the intent of the parties to be bound to keep their promises, it is not safe to conclude that a court would so rule in a given case. Simply defined, consideration is something of value which is committed by each party to a contract. The commitment to pay or to do something of value constitutes consideration and makes the promises of the parties enforceable.

Consideration has long been considered the third major element required before a binding contract can result even though there has been a valid offer and acceptance. The element of consideration is the thing of value which is committed by each party on his side of the agreement without which he cannot hold the other side to his promise. The existence of consideration is so much a part of most real estate contracts that it is seldom necessary to look for it. Assume the typical offer and acceptance for the purchase of real estate.

1. The buyer offers (promises to pay) $10,000 for the seller's property, and
2. The seller accepts and agrees (promises) to convey the property for $10,000.
3. A binding contract results because there is consideration to support each promise—the promise of the other party.

In this example, it should be noted that the buyer does not tender or hand over $10,000 at the time of the offer, nor does the seller tender the property or surrender it to the purchaser. Each one has, however, promised to perform an act of substantial value. Consideration need not be money paid; a promise to perform an act of value to the other side is sufficient. The promise itself is valuable, even though in a given case the question of how valuable may be difficult to answer. Two aspects of consideration are important from a practical standpoint in the real estate business:

1. The value which must be given to constitute legally adequate consideration has no relationship whatsoever to actual value. So long as something of value is given, the requirement is satisfied. In the above example if we were to assume that the fair market value of the property being bargained for is $20,000, the promise to pay $10,000 for it is still adequate consideration to support and permit enforcement of the seller's promise to convey the property. The law of contracts does not require that full or market value be offered to make the contract binding upon the seller. The reverse is also true. That is, if we assume that the property has a fair market value of only $5,000, the promise of the seller to convey it is still adequate to bind the purchaser's offer to pay $10,000 for it. The law does not make the contract for the parties; but when they have made it in good faith, the law enforces it.

2. Earnest money is conspicuous by its absence from the foregoing discussion. The reason is that a typical *earnest money deposit* is not essential to make the contract for the sale of real estate binding upon the parties. It is made binding by the mutual promises of the two parties, and the earnest money deposit adds nothing to its binding nature. The true function of the earnest money deposit is to serve as a source for payment of damages to the seller in the event that the purchaser breaches the contract and does not keep his or her promise.

Legal Capacity

Each party to a contract must have the legal capacity or power to enter into it and to commit himself or herself to the performance of its terms. Technically, this requirement has nothing to do with the actual formation of a contract; however, it is an underlying requirement that cannot safely be ignored in any business transaction. That is, a contract with a person who has no power or capacity to enter into it is not a contract at all. The matter of capacity goes directly to the question of enforceability of the agreement. The law is quite technical in this area; it is designed to protect the incompetent from his or her own improvident acts and to protect a business entity from the unauthorized acts of one of its members. In view of the disastrous consequences of entering into a contract with a person who lacks the power to agree, it is important to be aware of the legal limitations of various persons and organizations.

Contracts entered into by insane persons, minors (sometimes referred to as "infants"), or those intoxicated generally are not considered binding contracts. Contracts entered into by such persons are either void or voidable by the individuals who are classified as above but not by the other party to the contract.

The legal capacity of the parties to enter into a binding contract is an important feature of contract law and one with which the real estate broker and salesperson must be familiar. It is important to recognize the limitations of the parties in the negotiation and execution of the contract of sale. As a general rule, the capacity of the parties required to enter into the contract of sale is the same as that required for the execution of a deed. The requirements for various entities are:

1. Individuals must be of age and must be mentally competent: Minors (those less than 18, generally) may enter into contracts prior to reaching majority but then have an option to avoid them if they choose to do so when they reach majority. This is true for all contracts except those for necessities. While housing might fall into the category of a necessity, the rule is not hard and fast. When the housing falls in the luxury category, the minor may still retain the right to disaffirm or avoid the contract upon coming of age or at any time prior to attaining majority. The safest course is to deal with a minor on transactions involving significant value only through a legally appointed guardian. Recent legislation reducing the age of majority for almost all purposes to 18 should help to minimize the number of problems which arise in this area.

A mentally incompetent person can pose a serious problem in the brokerage business because he or she may be difficult to recognize and because there is no effective way to avoid

the problem except through the exercise of good judgment. There are two possible cases: the person who is actually incompetent at the time of the transaction but has not been adjudged incompetent by any court, and the adjudged incompetent who has been placed under formal guardianship.

The adjudged incompetent has been placed under a guardianship through a court proceeding, and this fact is a matter of public record and therefore a matter which the public is obliged to know. Once the guardianship has been established, the incompetent (the ward) has no capacity to enter into contracts, and there is no effective way to deal with such a person except through the guardian. The incompetent's contracts are absolutely void and cannot be enforced.

The actual but not adjudged incompetent is frequently more difficult to recognize, because such a person may not always exhibit evidence of incompetence. There is a certain natural hesitancy on the part of relatives of incompetents to take the necessary action to have a guardian appointed. The fact that the proceeding is a matter of public record and the stigma associated with incompetence make such a step distasteful to many people. As a result, many incompetents are never adjudged as such. Their contracts may be voidable if they were incompetents at the time the contracts were entered into. They are not void and it takes affirmative action to void them, but it is quite possible that such contracts can be later set aside. Recognizing the incompetent is the most effective way of dealing with the problem. It is not practical to make a detailed investigation of each person dealt with in any business. It is, therefore, necessary to develop and use good judgment in this area.

2. Partnerships may be dealt with through any general partner and in the partnership name. Under the UPA it is not necessary that all partners join in the execution of documents relating to real estate transactions. Each general partner has the authority to bind the firm, and third persons dealing with a partner are entitled to rely on the partner's representations that he or she has such authority. Even if one partner does not in fact have the authority he or she purports to have, this is an internal partnership matter and outsiders are not bound to know that that one partner is exceeding his or her authority.

3. Corporations can only be bound by the acts of

those who have actual authority or those who appear to the general public to have authority by virtue of the office they hold in the corporation. As far as real estate transactions are concerned, the safe course to follow is to obtain a resolution of the board of directors authorizing a specific officer to buy or sell real estate. It is even then necessary to obtain approval of the stockholders in the event that the corporation is the seller and the real estate being sold represents substantially all of its assets. It is recommended that an attorney be consulted when dealing with corporations, because of the limitations on the authority of various officers.

4. Associations which are neither formal partnerships nor corporations do not have a clearly recognized status. The only safe way to deal with them, as far as real estate transactions are concerned, is to treat them as a group of individuals selling individual interests in the property, that is, as though they were tenants in common. Each one of the members of the association (or syndicate, or other designation) must have the capacity to deal with his or her own property. Legal counsel should always be sought.

5. Governmental units are strictly controlled by statutes or ordinances and have no capacity to conduct business of any kind unless they are specifically authorized by the governing statutes to do so. It is very important in dealing with any governmental unit to verify its authority to buy or sell or to enter into a contract to do either. An attorney should always be consulted in such transactions.

6. Court officers such as receivers, commissioners, etc., must have specific court authority to enter into contracts which will be binding upon the property being dealt with. Court officers do not have authority to buy or sell real estate simply because they have been appointed court officers. Formal approval of the court is always essential. Again, an attorney should always be consulted in connection with transactions with court officers to be sure of their authority and that the necessary documentation is preserved as a matter of record to avoid later complications so far as the title to the real estate is concerned.

7. Fiduciaries generally must have specific authority to deal with real estate, and the authority must be in proper form to be made a matter of record if necessary. The term "fiduciaries" as used here includes executors, administrators, trustees, and agents. In considering the question of capacity

to enter into contracts involving real estate, it is important to be aware that none of them have inherent authority and in each case the authority must be verified. An attorney's opinion should always be obtained as to the authority of the fiduciary, since by definition a fiduciary deals with someone else's property.

Common Contract Provisions

In addition to the legal requirements of a contract, most agreements for real estate must contain other basic provisions such as:

1. *Date of agreement.* The date of agreement is of course the date on which the parties entered into the agreement or contract. Some states require this item to be on all contracts for the sale of any interest in land, either under the statute of frauds or some other statute.

2. *Names and signatures of the parties involved.* In most states the statute of frauds requires that the contracting parties be identified and that they sign the contract. In some contract forms for the sale of land, the broker or agent for the buyer and/or seller must also be identified.

3. *Legal description of the property.* A contract for the sale of land should contain a legal description of the property being sold. Such a description should either define the location and give the dimensions of the property to be conveyed in the agreement or should enable the parties to obtain that information.

4. *Consideration.* A contract for the sale of an interest in land must include, under the statute of frauds in nearly all the states, some statement of consideration to be exchanged for that interest.

5. *Terms of payment.* In addition to the consideration to be paid, a contract for the sale of land should describe in detail the terms of payment. The contract should describe how much is being paid in cash and when it is to be paid. If the buyer is taking over an existing mortgage, obtaining his or her own mortgage from a lending institution, or receiving partial financing from the seller, then important items regarding the terms of financing (e.g., acceptable rate of interest, amount to be borrowed, and repayment schedule) should also be detailed in the contract.

6. *Special contingencies.* Any special contingencies, or conditions for the fulfillment of the contract, should of course be written into the

contract. The most common contingency is the ability of the buyer to obtain financing.

7. *Date and place of closing (approximate date).* A contract for the sale of land should include a provision naming the date and place of closing. The date of closing may be simply an approximate date, in order to give the buyer time to obtain financing and inspect the title. The place of closing may be at any convenient place—the office of the mortgagee's attorney, the mortgagee's place of business, the real estate agent's office, or elsewhere.

Validity of Contracts

Every contract must be free from undue influence, duress, fraud, and mistakes of fact or law as outlined below:

Duress. If a contract is entered into by force (threat of personal injury) against the will of one of the parties involved in the contract, the forced party may void the contract at his or her election.

Undue influence. In any case in which one of the parties has taken unfair advantage of the other parties to the contract because of a particular relationship which exists, the contract is voidable by the party who was unjustly treated.

Misrepresentation. Misrepresentation might best be described as an *innocent* misstatement of fact. In other words, one of the parties has indicated something regarding the contract *to be* when in fact *it was not.* The party to whom the misrepresentation was made has the right to treat the contract as voidable. A *deliberate* misstatement of fact is called *fraud.*

Mistakes. Two types of mistakes can occur in the formation of contracts—mistakes of *fact* and mistakes of *law:*

A mistake of *fact* occurs when one or both parties assume something to be a fact which is incorrect and this error is included in their agreement. An erroneous description of real estate in a purchase agreement is an example. Such a mistake can be corrected by the process of reformation (correction) of the contract if it is a minor error; if, however, the error is so substantial (e.g., 10 acres of ground as opposed to 20 acres of ground) that there is no "meeting of the minds," the contract is voidable and can be set aside by one of the parties.

A mistake of *law,* however, occurs when one

party has an erroneous notion of the legal obligations he or she has assumed by entering into the contract. For example, the purchaser of a home might conclude that she is not obligated to complete payment for it if she changes her mind prior to the date of closing. Contract law compels her to keep her promise (or pay damages for breach of contract), since there was no material factual mistake and the buyer is presumed to know the legal consequences of entering into a binding contract. The fact that she did *not* know these legal consequences is immaterial.

Illegality and Impossibility

Even though all of the foregoing conditions are met in conjunction with the formation of a binding contract, we must still consider two important questions involving contract law. The first is the legality of the purpose of the contract, which determines whether or not it is void, either in whole or in part. The second is the matter of impossibility of performance, which determines whether or not the contract is void. Each is discussed separately below.

Illegality of Purpose

Clearly, if a contract requires the performance of a criminal act by one of the parties, it cannot be enforced. Such a contract would be in violation of the law at the outset, and no court would entertain a lawsuit to compel performance by either party. A contract to commit a criminal act, however, is not the only form of illegality which must be considered. A wide variety of other objectives are illegal in the sense that they would violate public policy, would be in restraint of trade, would be injurious to third persons, would violate usury statutes, would constitute gambling contracts, etc.

In the area of real estate transactions a few examples may serve to illustrate the impact of the general contract law rule:

1. A enters into a lease with B for the use of property for the purpose of operating a gambling casino in a state where gambling is illegal. Since the purpose of the lease violates a criminal statute, it is void and cannot be enforced by either party.

2. A deeds real estate to S, his son, on the condition that S never marry. The deed is not void, but the condition violates public policy and the effect of the deed will be an absolute transfer of title and the condition will be disregarded.

The point to be noted in connection with illegality of purpose is that the illegal purpose need not be criminal in nature to make the contract voidable (unenforceable as to the legal condition), but that a contract for a criminal purpose is totally void.

Impossibility of Performance

Occasionally, parties enter into otherwise binding contracts which, for one reason or another, prove to be impossible to perform. The question then arises as to whether there is relief available to the party who promised to do the impossible. The answer hinges upon the definition of "impossible" as it has developed under contract law. There are two possibilities when one party finds it impossible to keep his or her promise:

1. It is impossible for *one party* to keep his promise. For example, A promises to sell a farm to B, but it is impossible for A to do so because he does not own the farm. Is A excused under the doctrine of impossibility? No. It may be impossible for A to deed the farm, but it is not impossible for anyone in the world to deed it to B. A is liable for breach of contract to B. To have the benefit of the defense of impossibility of performance, A would have to prove that *no one* could deed the property.

2. A closely related question is the problem of difficulty or unanticipated expense of performance. Suppose a contractor agrees to dig a basement for a house in an area which he believes to be sand and gravel and has priced the job at $1,000. Upon performing the excavation work, it is found that below the topsoil is pure granite and that the excavation will cost upward of $10,000. Is he relieved from performing his contract? No. Extreme or extraordinary difficulty of performance does not relieve him from his obligation. In this case, clearly the doctrine of impossibility will be of no avail, since it is not *impossible* to perform the contract; it is merely very costly and difficult.

The doctrines of difficulty and impossibility of performance in the real estate area are closely related, and their impact on a given transaction may be dramatic. In the first example, the law could compel A to buy the farm at whatever price he had to pay in order to carry out his promise to deed the farm to B. As an alternative A could be found liable to B for money damages for the difference between the agreed upon purchase price and the price B has to pay for another comparable farm.

Enforcement of Contracts for Real Estate

Generally, the enforcement of contracts is limited to the collection of money damages for any breach of contract which may occur. That is, contracts are enforced by the implied threat of a suit for damages. The parties know, or are presumed by the law to know, that if they fail to keep a promise that is enforceable under contract law principles, the party injured may maintain a lawsuit for the breach and can obtain a judgment entitling that person to recover whatever damages he or she can show have resulted from the breach. While this remedy is always available, our law recognized early that in certain situations an award of money damages is not a really satisfactory remedy and that in certain situations the injured party can only receive real justice by the performance for which he or she bargained. This is the doctrine known as *specific performance*. It is not a usual remedy but is reserved for unique situations in which money damages are clearly insufficient. It is considered an extraordinary remedy, and its availability is quite limited. In most states today, it is limited to contracts for unique chattels (one-of-a-kind art works, for example), situations in which a judgment for money damages would be meaningless (where the defendant is insolvent, for example), and contracts for the purchase of an interest in real estate, on the theory that each piece of real estate is unique and different from any other piece of real estate. The inclusion of real estate as a matter of course in this area is quite significant and is therefore considered in detail below.

The law today still considers each parcel of real estate to be absolutely unique and different from any other parcel of real estate, no matter where it is located. This is true even though the parcel may be a lot in a subdivision in which there are hundreds of other lots with precisely the same dimensions, facing the same street, and alike as two peas in a pod to anyone who might inspect them. In many cases, the buyer of such a lot may in fact be quite easily satisfied with another lot or money damages for the loss of the bargain. The important point is that the buyer does not have to be satisfied legally with anything other than the lot or parcel for which he or she bargained. If the buyer chooses the remedy of specific performance, he or she is favored with a conclusive presumption that nothing else will be satisfactory. The basic difference between a judgment for damages and one for specific performance is as follows.

A judgment for money damages is simply a conclusion of the court that the plaintiff is entitled to so many dollars from the defendant. The court does not in any way compel the defendant to pay the money. This is accomplished by formal *execution* of the judgment under which the sheriff may seize assets and sell them if the defendant fails to pay the judgment. There may be small satisfaction to the plaintiff if no assets are found, and further action to enforce the judgment may be cumbersome and expensive.

A decree of specific performance, however, constitutes an order from the court to the defendant to perform. This is a different matter entirely, because failure to obey is contempt of court and is punishable by severe measures, even including confinement in jail until the defendant does as ordered.

Potential Results of Nonperformance

Every breach of contract entitles the party that was injured to sue for damages. The theory behind *compensatory damages* is to put the injured party in as good a position, so far as money damages can put her, as she would have occupied had the party who breached the contract fully performed. Generally, in a sales contract, the measure of compensatory damages is the difference between the contract price and the market price at the time and place of delivery.

The parties to a contract may stipulate in the contract that a certain sum will be paid by a party who breaches the contract. This stipulation is called a *liquidated damages clause*. Such a stipulation by the parties may be determined in the courts to be a penalty clause and not a liquidated damage clause and therefore be unenforceable as payment for a breach.

Generally, a provision in a contract fixing the amount of damages payable for a breach must meet two requirements for it to be considered an enforceable liquidated damage clause: (1) The harm caused by the breach must be very difficult to estimate accurately; and (2) the amount so fixed must be a reasonable forecast of just compensation for the harm caused by the breach.

In many jurisdictions, when the buyer in a contract of sale has made installment payments and then becomes unable to perform further and therefore breaches the contract, he may have to forfeit the money he has paid to the seller. This forfeiture is often based on a contract provision by which, in the event of default by the buyer, all payments are to be retained by the seller as liquidated damages.

In the real estate field, such a forfeiture of monetary consideration could take place if the contract used in the sale of the property was a long-term land contract as opposed to a mortgage. Long-term land contracts are written so as to allow the seller of the property to cancel the contract, retake possession, and retain all prior payments upon the buyer's default. Some states adhere to the strict view that these contractual provisions ought to be enforced as written. In other states, there has been a trend toward expanding the buyer's rights under long-term land contracts and treating such contracts more like mortgages. (See Chapter 10.)

A party to a contract who has partly performed his or her side of the agreement and is injured by the complete failure of the other party to perform has a remedy available in *rescission* of the contract and restitution of his or her performance. Under this remedy, the injured party may elect to treat his or her duty under the contract as discharged (rescission) and, further, receive damages that pay for part performance and so put him or her back in the position occupied before entering into the contract.

For example, a buyer of goods has paid the full price of an item, or any part of it. She may rescind the contract and recover the payments where the seller has materially failed in performance by failing to deliver on time or delivering the wrong goods.

Or, where a seller of land wrongfully repossesses the land, the buyer may elect to rescind the contract and demand restitution of payments.

Equitable Title

Equitable title is based on the notion that in certain circumstances the courts have the power to enforce specifically an obligation to sell land, and generally do so. The obligation may be created by will, court order, or contract. The equitable title passes, then, when the obligation is created. This obligation is created most commonly by a contract to convey an interest in land. Equitable title passes in this case when the contract is formed.

In a contract to convey an interest in land, equitable title becomes vested in the purchaser of this interest at the time the contract is formed. From the formation of the contract until closing, however, the seller of the interest in land retains the legal title to this interest.

Assignment of Contracts

Most real estate contracts can be assigned. The parties involved assume different names, including:

1. *Assignor.* The assignor is the party who conveys a contractual right which he possesses to an assignee. Example: A and B have a contract by which B owes A $100 for services performed. A assigns his contractual right to the $100 for services performed to C. A is the assignor. C is the assignee.
2. *Assignee.* The assignee is the party who is con-veyed the contractual right by the assignor. See the example above.

Two essential results follow an effective assign-ment. The assignor's right against the debtor is ex-tinguished, and a similar right is created in the assignee. Example: In the above example, after A assigns his contractual right against B to C, A no longer has any claim to the $100 in question and C now has a contractual right against B for $100. B's responsibility remains unchanged, as he still owes $100.

SUGGESTED READINGS

(See the appropriate chapter in the following books.)

Dasso, Jerome, Alfred A. Ring, and Douglas McFall. *Fundamentals of Real Estate.* Englewood Cliffs, N.J.: Prentice-Hall, Inc., 1977.

Kratovil, Robert. *Real Estate Law,* 6th ed. Engle-wood Cliffs, N.J.: Prentice-Hall, Inc., 1974.

Lusk, Harold F. and William B. French. *Law of the Real Estate Business,* 3rd ed. Homewood, Ill.: Richard D. Irwin, Inc., 1975.

Owens, Don. *Complete Guide to Modern Real Estate Transactions.* Englewood Cliffs, N.J.: Pren-tice-Hall, Inc., 1975.

Shenkel, William M. *The Real Estate Professional.* Homewood, Ill.: Dow Jones-Irwin, Inc., 1976.

Weimer, Arthur M., Homer Hoyt, and George F. Bloom. *Real Estate,* 7th ed. New York: The Ronald Press Company, 1978.

REVIEW QUESTIONS

1. An accepted offer to purchase contains the sig-natures of

   I. the buyer
   II. the seller

   (A) I only
   (B) II only
   (C) both I and II
   (D) neither I nor II

2. A contract by a person signed voluntarily while drunk is

   (A) void
   (B) voidable
   (C) valid
   (D) illegal

3. A counteroffer

   I. results in a new contract if accepted
   II. invalidates the original offer

   (A) I only
   (B) II only
   (C) both I and II
   (D) neither I nor II

4. The concept of duress is based on

   (A) deception
   (B) fear

   (C) abuse of power
   (D) the commission of a crime

5. Consideration in a contract is

   (A) not essential
   (B) an exchange of promises
   (C) more than 10% of the purchase price
   (D) all of the above

6. The statute of frauds requires contracts for the sale of real estate to be

   (A) in writing to be enforceable
   (B) in outline form
   (C) reviewed by the county recorder
   (D) all of the above

7. If a purchaser has signed a contract under duress, it is generally

   (A) voidable by the seller
   (B) voidable by the buyer
   (C) valid
   (D) void

8. A contract is generally void if it

    I. was entered into with a minor
    II. requires an illegal act for performance

    (A) I only   (C) both I and II
    (B) II only   (D) neither I nor II

9. A contract involving an exchange of promises between the parties is a

    (A) unitarian contract
    (B) binary contract
    (C) unilateral contract
    (D) bilateral contract

10. Which of the following items does not terminate an offer to sell real estate?

    (A) lapse of reasonable time
    (B) rejection of the offer by the offeree
    (C) death of the sales agent
    (D) a revocation of the offer

11. Once the contract for the sale of real property has been signed, the purchaser has

    (A) legal title to the real estate
    (B) the right to possess the real estate
    (C) nothing until he or she receives the deed
    (D) equitable title in the real estate

12. Which of the following may not be a contract?

    (A) a deed
    (B) an option
    (C) a mortgage
    (D) none of the above

13. An expressed contract can be

    (A) oral   (C) both A and B
    (B) written   (D) neither A nor B

14. A contract may be assigned

    I. unless prohibited in the agreement
    II. to a third party

    (A) I only   (C) both I and II
    (B) II only   (D) neither I nor II

15. The acceptance of an offer must be

    (A) communicated to the offeror
    (B) received by the time specified in the offer
    (C) both A and B
    (D) neither A nor B

16. To execute an offer properly

    I. the signature of the offeror on a written offer is sufficient
    II. an officer of a corporation must be duly authorized to act

    (A) I only   (C) both I and II
    (B) II only   (D) neither I nor II

17. In the case of an offer

    I. the offeror controls the terms of the contract
    II. there may be conditional acceptance by the offeree

    (A) I only   (C) both I and II
    (B) II only   (D) neither I nor II

18. Consideration is

    (A) not required to have a binding contract
    (B) something that makes promises enforceable
    (C) both A and B
    (D) neither A nor B

19. Earnest money deposits

    I. are essential to the contract for the sale of real property
    II. serve as a source of payment of damages to the seller in case of a breach by the buyer

    (A) I only   (C) both I and II
    (B) II only   (D) neither I nor II

20. Under the UPA

    I. all partners must be dealt with in the execution of documents relating to real estate transactions
    II. third parties may rely upon a partner's representation of capacity to contract

    (A) I only   (C) both I and II
    (B) II only   (D) neither I nor II

Chapter 14

The Brokerage Business and Agency Relationships

VOCABULARY

You will find it important to have a complete working knowledge of the following words and concepts found in the text or the glossary.

agreeing and assuming	gross income	quitclaim deed
cash flow	habendum clause	release of liability
consideration	indefeasible	remainder
contingent proposition	insurance of title	reversion
conveyance	IREM	severalty
CPM	joint tenants	special agency
debt service	lessee	special warranty deed
deed	lessor	subject to the mortgage
estate from period to period	listing contract	sublease
estate for years	merchantable title	surety
exclusive agency	net lease	tenancy at sufferance
exclusive right to sell	net operating income	tenancy at will
fiduciary	offer to purchase	tenants by the entirety
fiduciary deed	open listing	tenants in common
general agency	percentage lease	universal agency
general warranty deed	proposition	

BROKERAGE CONTRACTS

EVERY broker or salesperson must have a working knowledge of the legal documents involved in the transfer of property rights. The discussion of the documents which follows is to some degree a review of material covered, yet it adds new dimensions to several of the topics presented earlier. This chapter discusses certain principles relating to contracts and options involved in real estate practice, as well as some fundamental factors concerning deeds and mortgages.

The broker and salesperson will discover that in real estate practice they come in contact with the following types of contracts: agency contracts, propositions, and conditional sales contracts. These different types of instruments will be discussed in this order.

AGENCY RELATIONSHIPS

The most basic contract found in the brokerage business is that established between the principal and the agent. Different levels of responsibility can exist in an agency, depending upon the amount of authorization the agent has from the principal. There are three basic categories: (1) universal agency, (2) general agency, and (3) special agency.

The universal agent is allowed to perform all lawful acts for the principal, the general agent performs specific types of activities, and the special agent performs a specific type of action. The special agent is the most common found in the brokerage business: a seller authorizes an agent to find a purchaser for a specific piece of property. It is important to note that the broker whom the salesperson represents is the agent and the seller is the principal. The salesperson is actually not a party to the agency agreement.

In most states an agency relationship created for the purpose of the sale of a property must be in writing. Termination of the contract can occur through an act of the parties or through operation of law:

Most common (handwritten margin note)

By act of the parties: (1) mutual consent, (2) completion of the contract, (3) expiration of time as found in the contract, (4) revocation of the principal, or (5) refusal by the agent to continue with the contract.

Operation of law: (1) insanity of either party, (2) death of either party, (3) destruction of the object, or (4) bankruptcy of either party.

Fiduciary Relationship

An agency contract creates a relationship in which the agent must exercise much greater caution in his or her actions for the principal than usual. The agent's actions must be reasonable and prudent.

Such a fiduciary relationship also obligates the agent to a high level of loyalty, obedience, and performance of the task contracted for. If the agent does not fulfill these obligations, it is possible that the principal might have just cause for a lawsuit against the agent.

Agent's Compensation

Because of the great number of agency relationships created, many disagreements over when commissions have been earned seem to arise. In general, the agent has earned a commission when a purchaser—ready, willing, and able to meet the terms of the listing—has been brought to the principal. Should the principal fail to complete a sale under such circumstances, the agent would have earned, and thus would be eligible to collect, the commission.

When the actual commission is earned can usually be determined by the language in the agency agreement (listing contract).

TYPES OF LISTING CONTRACTS

There are several types of listing contracts which create the agency relationship:

1. *Open listing.* The principal contacts as many brokers as he or she desires to represent the property but is liable for payment of a commission only to the broker who actually sells the property. No restrictions are placed on the seller's right to sell the property himself without paying a commission to anyone.
2. *Exclusive agency.* Under the terms of an exclusive agency contract, the owner appoints the broker with whom he or she has listed the property as the exclusive agent for procuring a pur-

chaser during the term of the listing. The owner thus becomes obligated to pay a commission to the listing broker if the property is sold during the term of the listing by the broker or any other person. The only exception to such a rule is that an exclusive agency contract does not deprive the owner of his or her right to sell the property to a buyer procured by his or her own efforts, and thus not be liable for a commission to the listing broker.

3. *Exclusive right to sell.* Under this type of listing contract, the owner obligates himself to pay the broker the commission if the property is sold, regardless of who procures the purchaser. This type of contract obviously is most advantageous to the broker and therefore is used most often by the industry. It is also most advantageous to the seller because it motivates the broker to expend time and funds to market the property since the broker is assured a commission even if the owner sells the property.
4. *Multiple listing.* Under a multiple listing agreement, brokers who have procured exclusive right to sell listing contracts from owners cooperate with other broker members of the Multiple Listing Service (MLS) to provide a larger market for their listed properties. The listing broker then shares a previously negotiated portion of the sales commission with the broker who found the purchaser for the property.

Requirements of Valid Listing Contracts

A listing contract, which is the basis of most real estate transactions, is the instrument whereby the owner of real estate lists property for sale with a broker.

The following principles are applicable to listing contracts:

1. Under the statute of frauds, which requires certain agreements to be in writing, the listing contract, being an agreement to pay a real estate commission, must be in writing.
2. The listing contract must be signed by the owner. This again is a requirement of the statute of frauds and usually of the real estate license law. In this connection, it should be signed by *all* the owners in order to be valid and enforceable. For instance, the listing contract involving real estate owned by a husband and wife should be signed by both parties. If four persons own the real estate, as tenants in common, the listing contract should be signed by all four parties.

3. Listings without a specific termination are improper. Thus a listing should be given for a specific or computable period of time, such as "until July 5, 19XX" or "for a period of 90 days from this date."

4. The owner must be given a copy of the listing contract.

Under the usual form listing contract, the broker is entitled to payment of a commission if he or she produces a purchaser ready, willing, and able to pay the purchase price upon the terms stipulated in the listing contract.

THE PROPOSITION (OFFER TO PURCHASE)

The proposition, or the offer to purchase real estate, is the instrument whereby a prospective purchaser offers in writing to purchase real estate upon certain specific terms. Since it is the foundation of the particular real estate transaction, it must be carefully drawn so that there may be a complete agreement between the purchaser and the seller. It must be definite, specific, and certain. It must clearly establish the rights, obligations, and duties of both parties with reference to the sale and purchase. A proposition containing ambiguities may well lead to the failure (fall through) of the transaction.

It should be pointed out that the proposition is simply an offer, until such time as it is accepted without condition by the seller. Since it constitutes a mere offer, it may be withdrawn at any time by the purchaser prior to its acceptance by the seller. The reason for this is that, in the offer, there is no consideration present, which is a requisite element of every enforceable contract.

When, however, the offer has been accepted unconditionally by the seller, the contract ripens into existence. The legal consideration is found in the mutual promises of the parties—the promise of the purchaser to purchase upon specific terms, and the promise of the seller to sell upon these terms. These mutual promises support each other and provide the legal consideration for the contract.

If the seller attaches any conditions to his or her acceptance, such conditional acceptance immediately terminates the offer. The conditional acceptance becomes, in effect, a *counteroffer* by the seller. If this counteroffer is unqualifiedly accepted by the purchaser, then the contract ripens into existence, and there is a "meeting of the minds."

Contents of the Proposition

Legal Description. The proposition, first of all, contains a description of the property to be sold. This description must be so specific and certain as to allow no doubt as to the premises for which the offer is being made.

In the case of residential property, ordinarily a street and number description is sufficient. However, the careful broker or salesperson, in preparing the proposition, uses not only a proper street address, but also an accurate legal description, ordinarily obtainable from the owner's deed or from a local title company.

Farm acreage can generally be adequately described by number of acres and by location as to street, road, and township. Here again, however, careful draftsmanship of the proposition uses a specific legal description by metes and bounds.

A more difficult problem arises when a certain portion of a larger tract of ground is being sold. This problem may readily be solved by obtaining from a surveyor a specific legal description, so that no doubt may arise as to the boundaries of the property being purchased.

A word of warning: Tax duplicate descriptions, which in many cases are inaccurate and incomplete, should never be used in preparing a proposition.

The Terms of Sale. Following the description of the property in question, the specific terms of the sale are set forth in the proposition. Generally speaking, the terms of sale may be grouped into five general categories:

1. *The cash sale.* Drafting terms of the cash sale, free and clear, ordinarily presents no difficulties and is written: "The purchaser hereby agrees to pay for said property the sum of $10,000, upon the following terms: cash."

2. *The sale subject to an existing mortgage.* The proposition may be made subject to the existing mortgage on the premises. The language used is: ". . . upon the following terms: purchaser shall take title to said real estate subject to the existing mortgage upon the same, the balance of the purchase price over and above the balance due upon said mortgage at the date of closing to be paid in cash."

In this type of sale, *subject to an existing mortgage*, we should understand two important considerations. First, the seller is *not* relieved from liability; he still remains liable for his personal obligation on the mortgage note he has signed. Secondly, the purchaser does not assume personal liability on the mortgage. Thus, in the event of foreclosure, the mortgagee may secure a personal judgment against the seller (who signed the mortgage note) but, as far as the purchaser is concerned, no personal judgment may be obtained; only the property may be subjected to sale to satisfy the judgment obtained by the mortgagee. Any deficiency resulting from the sale may be enforced against the seller who signed the mortgage note. No such deficiency may be enforced against the buyer who took title subject to the mortgage and who therefore assumed no personal liability.

3. *Sale subject to assumption of mortgage.* It is important that we understand the difference between a sale subject to an existing mortgage and a sale *subject to the assumption of an existing mortgage.* Where the mortgage is assumed by the purchaser, several consequences result. First, as in the case of the sale subject to an existing mortgage, the seller is *not* relieved from liability; again, the seller remains liable for the personal obligation on the mortgage note the seller has signed. The purchaser, however, assumes personal liability on the mortgage note. Thus, in the event of foreclosure, the mortgagee may take a personal judgment against both the original seller and the purchaser, subject to the sale of the property, and enforce any deficiency resulting from the sale against both parties.

In the assumption situation, the purchaser becomes the principal primarily liable for the debt, and the seller becomes a *surety.* Under the general principles applicable to the law of suretyship, if the principal (the purchaser) defaults in payment, the surety (the seller) may pay the deficiency and then has the right to sue the principal (the purchaser) for the amount so paid.

In drafting a proposition calling for the assumption of a mortgage, the language used is similar to that used for a sale subject to a mortgage, except that a clause is added providing that the purchaser shall "assume and agree to pay the unpaid balance due upon said mortgage at the date of closing." This language is also incorporated in the deed at the closing of the transaction.

Again, we should repeat that, in both situations, the seller who signs the original note and mortgage is *not* relieved from personal liability by reason of the sale of the mortgaged property. His or her personal liability in this regard is terminated only in two ways: (a) by execution of a *release of liability agreement,* entered into by the seller, purchaser, and mortgagee, by virtue of which the seller is fully released and the mortgagee agrees to look solely to the purchaser for payment of the mortgage, or (b) by payment in full.

4. *The sale on conditional sales contract.* The conditional sales contract is effective for use where the purchaser in question does not have a sufficient down payment to complete the purchase of the property by securing adequate mortgage financing. In this type of sale, in addition to the down payment, the purchaser makes stipulated monthly payments, with interest, and legal title remains with the seller until the purchase price is fully paid, at which time the deed of conveyance is executed. In the event of default, the seller is entitled to secure immediate possession and to retain the down payment and all subsequent payments as liquidated damages for the purchaser's default. (See Chapter 10 for recent developments in this area.)

5. *The purchase money mortgage.* A purchase money mortgage is a mortgage taken back by the seller from the purchaser upon the sale of real estate. This situation may arise when the seller is willing to finance the purchaser in an amount over and above the down payment that the purchaser has available. Here again, the terms should be carefully spelled out in the proposition, with particular reference to the amount of the mortgage, the rate of interest, how the interest is computed and payable, the amount of the monthly or installment payments, the grace period, and any provision with reference to prepayment privileges.

The Contingent Proposition. The purchaser may wish to make his or her offer contingent upon the occurrence of a certain event. Generally, these contingencies fall into five categories.

1. *Subject to the purchaser's ability to obtain a conventional mortgage loan.* The purchaser may require conventional mortgage loan financing to supply the funds necessary to complete the purchase price. In this case, such a contingency should be spelled out specifically in the proposition:

This proposition is specifically contingent upon the purchaser's ability to obtain a firm commitment for a conventional first mortgage loan upon said premises in an amount not less than $26,000 with a rate of interest not to exceed 8½% per annum, amortized monthly over a period of not less than 25 years. Should the purchaser fail to obtain such a commitment within a period of 30 days following acceptance of this proposition, then this proposition shall become void, and the earnest money deposit made this date shall be refunded to the purchaser.

2. *Subject to the purchaser's ability to obtain an FHA mortgage loan.* When an FHA loan is needed by the purchaser, similar language may be used. In such cases, the rate of interest need not be stipulated, as it is fixed by law. All other details, however, should be stated in the contingency language, including the number of discount points the seller will pay.

3. *Subject to the purchaser's ability to obtain a VA mortgage loan.* The language of contingency again is similar to that involved in the FHA loan. No rate of interest need be stipulated, as it is fixed by law. In the case of FHA and VA mortgages, more time should be allowed for obtaining the commitment, including the number of discount points the seller will pay.

4. *Subject to the purchaser's ability to sell his or her existing property.* The purchaser may be unable to complete purchase of the property in question unless and until he or she has sold and disposed of currently owned property. In this situation, the contingency should be spelled out so as to include a minimum sale price and a time limit for final consummation of the sale of the purchaser's present property.

5. *Subject to zoning for an intended use.* The purchaser may wish to purchase the property in question only if it can be zoned for an intended use. The proposition therefore must be drafted subject to this contingency. The drafting of this contingency is difficult, as provision must be made for the possibility that the zoning order may be appealed, and final disposition may be delayed over a considerable period of time. Such propositions generally provide that, if an appeal is made, the proposition shall become void.

Rents and Insurance. After the terms of sale and any contingencies are spelled out, the proposition generally makes provisions for the proration of rents, where rental property is involved. Rents are prorated between the seller and the purchaser as of the date of closing.

The proposition also provides for the proration or cancellation, as the case may be, of existing hazard insurance. In case of a proration, the unearned portion of the insurance premium is charged to the purchaser at the time of closing. If the insurance is cancelled, the seller will generally receive a short-rate premium refund directly from the insurance company, which is usually less than a pro rata premium refund.

Taxes. The proposition should provide for the handling of real estate taxes at the time of closing. This may be done by two methods: the installment method and the proration method.

The installment method provides for the purchaser to assume a certain subsequent installment of taxes and all taxes payable thereafter: "The purchaser shall assume all taxes upon said real estate beginning with the installment due and payable in May 19XX, and all installments due and payable thereafter."

The proration method provides for the apportionment of taxes between the seller and the buyer on a calendar-year basis. With this method, the seller pays all taxes assessed for the prior calendar year and remaining unpaid, as well as all taxes assessed for the current calendar year apportioned to the date of sale.

Assessment. The property sold may be subject to assessments for municipal improvements, such as streets, sewers, curbs, etc. The improvements may be in various stages, with the contract let and the work not started, or the work in process, or the work completed. The broker should be thoroughly familiar with the status of any such assessments, and the proposition should specifically state whether payment should be the seller's or purchaser's responsibility.

Abstract of Title and Title Insurance. The proposition contains a clause providing for the furnishing at the seller's expense of an abstract of title showing a merchantable title to the real estate in question. A *merchantable title* is one acceptable to examining attorneys of experience in the particular community. The proposition generally further provides for the securing of a title insurance policy if the title is not merchantable. If the title is neither merchantable nor insurable, the purchaser should be released from the terms of the proposition and his or her earnest money refunded.

Deeds of Conveyance. Provision is made in the proposition for execution by the seller to the purchaser of a deed of conveyance at the closing of the transaction. Usually a general warranty deed is provided for, although a special warranty deed or a quitclaim deed may be indicated. These different types of deeds will be discussed later.

What Personal Property Is Included. The sale of real estate includes all fixtures attached thereto. Generally speaking, a fixture is personal property which has become real property by reason of its adaptability to the real estate and reason of its being permanently affixed to the same. The line of distinction between personal property and fixtures may, however, be a shadowy one. Therefore the proposition should specifically spell out what is included with the property. A careful broker knows what the seller intends to sell and what the buyer intends to buy, and these items should be specifically mentioned in the proposition, in order that there will be no misunderstanding at the date of closing.

Default Clause. The obligations of the purchaser upon default of his or her obligations without a legal excuse should be spelled out in the proposition. Many propositions provide that upon such default the purchaser shall forfeit his or her earnest money deposits as liquidated damages in lieu of all other remedies available to seller. In the absence of such a liquidated damage clause, the purchaser may be liable to respond in actual damages for failure to so perform.

Signature of the Purchaser. The proposition of course should be signed by all the purchasers.

Acceptance by the Seller. As already indicated, the proposition becomes a legal contract when it is accepted without condition by the seller. In this connection, it is of vital importance that *all owners and their respective spouses sign the acceptance.*

The Conditional Sales Contract

In our discussion of propositions, we have already recognized the conditional sales contract as being widely used in the sale of real estate. It is used to purchase real estate on a time or installment basis and is an effective method of making the purchase of real estate available to a buyer who does not have sufficient funds to make the necessary down payment over and above mortgage financing. We now discuss some of the essential features of the conditional sales contract.

The Title. Under the conditional sales contract, the legal title does not pass to the purchaser until the balance of the contract, both principal and interest, has been paid in full, at which time the seller ex-

ecutes and delivers to the purchaser the deed in satisfaction of the contract.

The purchaser, however, becomes vested with an equitable title and for many purposes becomes in effect the owner of the real estate, with certain rights and obligations as outlined in the contract. We shall see that in the event of default, this equitable interest may be lost to the purchaser.

Payments. Most conditional sales contracts provide for an initial payment in cash, and further provide for stipulated monthly payments, with interest on the unpaid balance provided for. The rate of interest is always stipulated, and the computation and payment of interest is handled as outlined in the contract. Frequently, interest is computed in advance, either monthly or semiannually, and is included in the monthly payments. Another method used is to provide for payment of interest in addition to the monthly principal payments called for. Most forms of conditional sales contracts give full prepayment privileges to the purchaser, so that he or she may make additional payments at any time. Any such additional payments of course result in interest savings to the purchaser.

Improvements. With reference to the improvements on real estate, the contract usually provides that the purchaser shall keep such improvements adequately insured and in a proper state of repair. There is generally a provision which requires the purchaser to secure the written consent of the seller before making any additions or improvements or doing any remodeling of the premises.

Assignability. Most conditional sales contracts contain a stipulation that the purchaser has no right to sell or assign the contract without the owner's written assent. This, however, does not prevent sale of the purchaser's interest to a customer who can pay cash, as the purchaser can use the cash proceeds to pay off his or her contract in full, secure a proper deed, and then deed the property to the new purchaser.

Default. Upon default of the purchaser under the conditional sales contract, and upon the continuance of this default after any grace period stipulated in the contract, the owner may bring action to eject the purchaser from the premises and to cancel the contract. In such cases, the purchaser forfeits the down payment and all monthly payments as liquidated damages for his or her default. Such a liquidated damage clause prevents the seller from enforcing any other claims as against the defaulting purchaser. The forfeiture clause will usually be held to be a liquidating damages clause if the amount of payments received by the seller amounts to a small percentage of the total contract price.

Options

Simply speaking, an option is an instrument whereby an owner of real estate, for a valuable consideration, gives and grants to another person the right and privilege for a stipulated period of time to purchase the real estate at a certain price.

In our discussion of propositions, we saw that the proposition, duly accepted, contained mutual promises, a promise of the seller to sell and promise of the purchaser to buy, and that these mutual promises supported each other and provided the legal consideration necessary for the contract. The accepted proposition is therefore what is commonly called a *bilateral contract*.

The option, however, is what we call a *unilateral contract*. This means that it is an instrument under which only one party is bound. This party is the seller, who is obligated to convey the real estate if the purchaser exercises the option and tenders the purchase price. The purchaser is under no obligation to purchase; he or she has the right and the option to do so as desired. For this reason, there are no mutual promises in an option as there are in an accepted proposition. Since there are no such mutual promises, the legal consideration for the option must be found somewhere else. Usually it is found in a cash payment made for the option by the prospective purchaser to the owner.

This payment for the option may be only nominal in nature, or it may be substantial. Where a substantial payment is involved, the option generally provides that such payment shall be credited upon the purchase price if the option is exercised.

If the option is not exercised, the down payment is retained by the owner as payment for the option.

Options of course contain a time limitation for exercise by the purchaser. If not exercised within a given time limit, the option automatically expires.

The option is effective in land assembly operations. For example, a broker who is employed to assemble numerous tracts of land for a manufacturing concern secures options on all such tracts. He does not use the proposition method of purchase, as he might find himself unable to purchase one or more of the tracts and yet be bound to purchase the others.

There is one very important observation to be made about options. Since a possible or probable purchase of land is involved, the option should be just as carefully drawn and as specific in detail as the proposition, with reference to the legal description, terms of sale, rents and insurance, taxes, assessments, abstract of title, deed of conveyance, inclusion of personal property contemplated by the purchaser, etc.

For the reasons already discussed with reference to the acceptance of propositions, options should be signed by all the owners and their respective spouses, in order to be valid and effective. That is, the option itself must be a legally binding contract.

Deeds

The deed of course is the instrument for the conveyance of a title to real estate. In this discussion, we examine several different types of deeds and then examine the structure of the deed of conveyance. This material provides an excellent review of information presented in earlier chapters.

Types of Deeds

The General Warranty Deed. Most propositions call for the execution by the seller of a general warranty deed. As the name indicates, the deed contains several warranties and covenants on the part of the seller. In executing such a deed, the grantor (seller) makes the following warranties:

1. That the grantor is possessed of an *indefeasible fee simple absolute title* to the real estate (a fee simple title is the highest title under the law, involving full and complete rights of ownership, to the exclusion of all others).
2. That there are no encumbrances against the real estate other than those specifically expressed in the deed.
3. That the grantee (purchaser) shall have quiet enjoyment of the real estate *and* that the grantor (seller) will warrant and defend the title to the real estate against any and all claims, from the beginning of time to the execution of the deed of conveyance.

Where there is an unbroken chain of general warranty deeds, each grantor in the chain may be liable to all subsequent grantees for any claim arising prior to the date of conveyance by that particular grantor. Where the chain is broken by the execution of a deed other than a general warranty deed, subsequent grantees may not look for redress to any grantors who may have executed warranty deeds prior to the date when the chain was broken.

The Special Warranty Deed. The *special warranty deed* is a deed of a limited warranty, and the warranty contained therein is limited to any claim arising out of the period of ownership of the grantor executing it. Thus if an owner held title from January 1 to October 31 and was willing to warrant the property for that period, he or she would be executing a special warranty deed with warrants only against any claims arising out of that particular period. The warranty would not extend back to the beginning of time.

The Quitclaim Deed. The quitclaim deed is a deed of release. It conveys without warranty whatever right, claim, title, or interest the grantor may have in the real estate conveyed. If the grantor has a fee simple title, the quitclaim deed will convey the same. If the grantor has no title, nothing will be conveyed by the quitclaim deed.

Quitclaim deeds are generally used to convey lesser interests in real estate, such as life estates or minor interests, and are also widely used to correct prior conveyances which have been improperly executed.

Judicial Deeds. Many titles to real estate are conveyed by judicial deeds, which, as the name implies, are deeds executed pursuant to a court order. Examples of such conveyances are deeds of executors, administrators, guardians, and trustees; sheriff's deeds executed by virtue of foreclosure proceedings; and commissioner's deeds executed in partition proceedings. Such deeds, assuming that the judicial proceedings in the particular case have been legally pursued, are effectual to convey good title to the real estate, but *without* warranties.

Essential Elements of a Deed

The essential parts of a proper deed are: the granting clause, the legal description, the statement of encumbrances, the signature clause, and the acknowledgment. In addition, the deed must usually be duly recorded. These are discussed in order.

The Granting Clause. The granting clause contains the names of the grantor and the language of conveyance; for example, "AB and BB, husband and wife, of Any County, Your State, convey and warrant to CD, of Any County, Your State. . . ."

Many old deed forms also include a *habendum clause* which leading authorities feel is no longer necessary since it adds nothing to the granting clause. (Such a habendum clause normally would begin, "To have and to hold.")

In this connection, we stress again that the marital status of all grantors must be shown, such as "AB and BB, husband and wife," or "AB, an unmarried

adult." We have already outlined the reasons for this in our discussion on the acceptance of propositions.

Note that the granting clause also contains the name of the grantee (purchaser). In the example given above, there is a single grantee. When there is more than one grantee, a question arises as to the type of estate that is taken. These estates may fall into several categories.

The first category is an *estate by the entireties.* This estate exists only between a husband and wife and is created by the execution of a deed to two people who are in fact husband and wife, for example, "to AB and BB, husband and wife." This estate has the following characteristics:

1. *Full right of survivorship.* The surviving spouse succeeds to the full title on the death of one spouse, free of all claims of creditors of the deceased spouse. Any other heirs of the deceased spouse have no interest in the real estate.

2. *Immunity from individual judgments.* A judgment against one spouse only cannot be enforced against the real estate during the joint lives of the husband and wife. Only joint judgments against both spouses may be so enforced.

3. *Nonseverability.* So long as both spouses live, neither can convey said real estate without the consent of the other spouse.

The second category is a *joint tenancy.* A joint tenancy, although recognized under the law, is not favored by the law, and therefore must be spelled out with certainty. It is generally created by using the following language: "to CD and EF, as joint tenants and not as tenants in common." This estate may be created in two or more persons and may also be created in a husband and wife, where the instrument clearly indicates that they are to take "as joint tenants and not as tenants by the entirety." The joint tenancy has the following characteristics:

1. *Full right of survivorship,* as in the case of tenants by the entireties, discussed above.

2. *Nonimmunity from individual judgments.* A judgment against one joint tenant may be enforced against his or her undivided interest in the property, and such interest sold to satisfy the judgment. Such action in effect destroys the joint tenancy, and the purchaser at a judicial sale becomes a tenant in common with the other joint tenant.

3. *Severability.* One joint tenant may destroy the

joint tenancy by conveying his interest to a third party, who becomes a tenant in common with the other joint tenant.

The third category is *tenancy in common*. This type of tenancy is created by a conveyance to two or more persons, with no language indicating that another type of estate is created, for example, "to AB, BC, and CD." In a tenancy in common, there are no rights of survivorship. For example, upon AB's death his interest passes to his heirs by law or to the devisees under his will. It does not pass to BC and CD (unless they are his heirs or devises). In addition, the undivided interest of each tenant in common is subject to individual judgments against him. Also, he may convey his interest to a third person. Here again, a tenancy in common may be created in a husband and wife, as tenants in common and not as tenants by the entirety.

A fourth category is a *life estate with a reversion*. A grantor who owns the fee simple title may convey an estate to another person for and during the natural life of the other person. This creates a life estate and gives the life tenant the use and occupancy and the rents and profits of the real estate during the life of the tenant. However, the grantor who owns the fee has conveyed a lesser estate than she owns, and is thus vested with a reversion, which comes into enjoyment upon the death of the life tenant. Thus, when AB conveys to CD "for and during the period of her natural life," CD has a life estate and AB has a reversion.

A fifth category is a *life estate with a remainder*. By proper conveyance, a grantor may create a life estate in one person, and then provide that, upon the death of that person, another person shall take title. The other person has a remainder interest, that is, the interest remaining after the life estate. Thus, when AB conveys "to CD for and during the period of her natural life, remainder on her death to EF," CD has the life estate and EF has the remainder. Nothing remains to the grantor AB.

The granting clause also contains an expression of the consideration for the conveyance. This can be expressed as "one dollar and other valuable considerations."

The Legal Description. The deed must contain an accurate and specific legal description of the property conveyed, also indicating the county where it is located. We have seen in our discussion of propositions that a street address may suffice for residential properties, but this is not true in the case of a deed, in which an exact legal description

must be used. This is generally obtainable from the abstract of title or a proper survey.

Statement of Encumbrances. Below the legal description, the deed generally contains a statement of existing encumbrances, indicating that the property is conveyed subject to such encumbrances. Following are examples:

1. Subject to the unpaid balance of a mortgage in the original principal sum of $25,000 executed to the Last National Bank of Anytown on April 1, this year, and recorded in Mortgage Book 1, page 1. (If an assumption of the mortgage is involved, the language "which unpaid balance grantee herein assumes and agrees to pay" would be added.)

2. Subject to taxes for this year due and payable in next year and subject to taxes due and payable thereafter.

3. Subject to the unpaid balance of a certain sewer assessment, Municipal Assessment Record 2, page 2, which unpaid balance grantee herein assumes and agrees to pay.

4. Subject to all covenants and restrictions of record.

5. Subject to all easements of record, and subject to all legal highways and rights of way.

Signature Clause. The signature clause in the deed contains the date of execution and the signatures of the grantors. All grantors and the spouses of those who are married must sign exactly as their names appear in the granting clause.

Acknowledgments. Most states require all conveyances to be acknowledged before a public official, such as a notary public, if the individuals desire to record the deed. The grantors appear before such an officer and acknowledge the execution of the conveyance to be their voluntary act and deed. The officer certifies this fact on the instrument, signs it, attaches his or her seal, and states the date of expiration of his or her commission.

The acknowledgment is almost always necessary to entitle the deed to be recorded.

Recording. A properly executed deed is effectual between the parties without recording, but in order to be effectual against all the world, it must be recorded in the proper office and, when so recorded, its existence is known to all the world. For example, if AB conveyed to CD, who failed to record her deed, and later AB conveyed to EF, who recorded his deed, EF's title, assuming that EF had no actual knowledge of the prior deed and paid a valuable consideration in good faith, would be superior to CD's title. CD would be left with a remedy against AB, her original grantor, for fraud.

PROPERTY MANAGEMENT

Another area concerned with contractual agreements in the real estate industry is property management. It involves two types of contracts: the lease and, in most cases, a second contract which establishes a principal and agency relationship.

What Is Property Management?

Property management includes the management of any property occupied by a tenant rather than just the owner. Such properties range from farmlands to the largest high-rise, commercial-residential centers being constructed today. The property manager's job includes leasing and the collection of rents, as well as coordinating the services and maintenance the tenants require.

The leasing and management of real estate for others has become a specialized aspect of the real estate business, and the professional property manager performs an important function quite apart from the brokerage business. The management of real property for others has become important enough that most licensing statutes now require a broker's or salesperson's license of those who are engaged in the management and leasing of property belonging to others. A fine distinction is usually drawn, however, to exempt from the real estate licensing law provisions those who are full-time employees of the owner of a particular apartment or shopping center complex, or corporations, such as oil companies, which own many pieces of real estate used in connection with their primary business. Since the full-time employee of such a property owner is not engaged in offering property management services, for a fee, to the general public, he or she may be exempted from the licensing requirements imposed on others. This appears to be justified on the theory that the full-time property manager is subject to all the normal employer-employee rules, and incompetence can be dealt with by discharge from employment. Presumably, the owner of properties substantial enough to require in-house management is sophisticated enough to make the protection of mandatory licensing procedures unnecessary. So far as the general public is concerned, however, the performance of property management services for a fee is much the same as for brokerage services. Therefore this aspect of the real estate business is considered separately below.

Management of the Property of Others

When one undertakes to perform property management and leasing services for the general public on a fee basis, local real estate licensing laws generally come into play. More importantly, however, so does the law of principal and agent. The property manager, for a fee, is represented to the public as an expert or professional in the field, and the law requires several qualifications and imposes some sanctions on his conduct:

1. Qualifications required of the property manager by the law are quite similar to those required of real estate brokers and other professionals who purport to have the necessary qualifications to represent others. Quite simply, when one purports to be a professional property manager, the law requires that one *be* a professional. That is, the property manager must have a certain level of expertise in the field and failure to have it does not relieve him or her from liability for losses suffered by the owner as a result of incompetent management of the property . The law recognizes this requirement in an appropriate lawsuit charging mismanagement by the professional property manager.

2. More important than the question of competency is the fact that the property manager is an agent of the owner and has therefore assumed the responsibilities of a fiduciary. The fiduciary relationship which exists between the agent and the principal is jealously protected by our legal system, since it is based upon mutual trust and confidence. The agent owes a high duty of loyalty to the principal and may not deal with the principal as a stranger. As a result, strict requirements to account for all funds, to refrain from accepting unrevealed rebates (kickbacks) from suppliers and contractors, and to refrain from making any personal profit from transactions entered into on behalf of the principal are the responsibilities of the property manager. This is not to say that the fee arrangement between the principal (property owner) and the agent (property manager) is not flexible enough to permit incentives and rewards for better than average performance. Quite the contrary—such arrangements are quite common. Nevertheless, the total compensation of the property manager must be made known to the employing property owner.

While the trend in property management is toward specializing in specific types of buildings, the property manager must have certain basic skills to be able to perform the job well. The manager must be familiar with local economic conditions and must have the necessary business connections to be able to provide information to clients as requested.

The professional property manager prepares a budget, reviews it with the owner, and, upon their mutual agreement, must then live with this forecast, managing the property within the budget. The periodic statement of receipts and disbursements is matched against the budget and includes such items as:

Income:
Apartments
Garages—parking
Stores
Offices
Other—such as vending machines, washers, and
   dryers
Gross possible income
Less vacancies and collection losses
Total actual income collected

Expenses:
Maintenance and operating
   Payroll
   Supplies
   Painting and decorating
   Maintenance and repairs including
   plumbing, electric, and carpentry
   services
Total

Utilities
   Electricity
   Water
   Gas
   Heating fuel
Total

Administrative
   Management fees
   Other administrative expense
Total

Taxes and insurance
   Insurance
   Real estate taxes
   Other taxes
Total

Total operating expenses

Net operating income

In addition to the above statement of receipts and disbursements, an operating statement (profit and loss) might be prepared to interpret expenses. This statement is prepared on an accrual rather than a cash basis and may include accrued taxes, depreciation, and amortization of certain expenses.

The manager of course reports to the owner nonoperating expenses such as a mortgage payment, which is called *debt service*. After deduction of all expenses and debt service from the income from all sources, the amount left over for the owner is called *cash flow*.

A successful property manager is one who selects tenants carefully from those who will be able to meet the financial obligation being entered into in a lease. From the collection of rents, the manager must be capable of maintaining proper financial controls and records for reporting to the owner of the property.

Certified Property Manager

The Certified Property Manager (CPM) is a REALTOR® who specializes in property management and is a member of the Institute of Real Estate Management (IREM). IREM, along with other professional real property management authorities, indicates that the following points should be included in management contracts:

1. A complete and accurate description of the property to be managed
2. Definite beginning and ending dates for the duration of the contract
3. A statement of the compensation to the manager and the method to be used for its calculation
4. A listing of the duties the property manager is to perform during the contract, including limitations on authority
5. Types of reports required and the frequency of such reports.

Property management is a complex topic, but it can be broken down into three basic functions the property manager must perform: (1) market the property so as to secure tenants who provide income; (2) maintain financial records for the property indicating what controls have been placed over income and expense items, and (3) provide basic services, such as maintenance and security, for tenants. Above all, it must be remembered that the basic goal of the property manager is to provide the highest possible net return to the property owner while seeing to it that the investment is preserved.

Real Estate Transactions: Parties Involved and Their Actions

THE MAKER OR THE DOER OF THE ACTION	THE ACTION	THE RECIPIENT OF THE ACTION
PRINCIPAL (Owner)	LISTING OF REAL ESTATE (A listing contract)	AGENT (Broker)
OFFEROR (One who originates an offer)	AN OFFER (To sell or to buy or to lease, etc.)	OFFEREE (One to whom an offer is made)
GRANTOR (Owner/Seller transferring ownership)	DEED (Transferring ownership)	GRANTEE (Recipient/purchaser receiving ownership)
VENDOR (Seller)	SALE OF REAL ESTATE (Contract of sale)	VENDEE (Buyer)
OPTIONOR (Owner of property, prospective grantor, or lessor)	AN OPTION (To purchase or lease real estate)	OPTIONEE (Prospective grantee or lessee)
LESSOR (Landlord or Owner)	RENTAL REAL ESTATE (Lease agreement)	LESSEE (Renter or Tenant)
ASSIGNOR (One who makes an assignment)	ASSIGNMENT OF CONTRACT	ASSIGNEE (Recipient of an assignment)
LIENOR (Claimant or party aggrieved)	LIEN (Court judgment, mechanic's lien, unpaid taxes, mortgages, etc.)	LIENEE (Formal Debtor)
MORTGAGOR OR TRUSTOR (Borrower)	LOAN ON REAL ESTATE (Mortgage or deed of trust)	MORTGAGEE OR TRUSTEE (Beneficiary (lender), trustee holding title for tender)
CONDEMNOR (Public Agency)	CONDEMNATION (Exercise of the right of eminent domain)	CONDEMNEE (Property Owner)

FIG. 14-1—Real estate transactions. *The various real estate transactions and parties involved— who originates an action, what the action is, and who receives the action.*

SUGGESTED READINGS

(See the appropriate chapter in the following books.)

Dasso, Jerome, Alfred A. Ring, and Douglas McFall. *Fundamentals of Real Estate.* Englewood Cliffs, N.J.: Prentice-Hall, Inc., 1977.

Hines, Mary Alice. *Principles and Practices of Real Estate.* Homewood, Ill.: Richard D. Irwin, Inc., 1976.

Kratovil, Robert. *Real Estate Law,* 6th ed. Englewood Cliffs, N.J.: Prentice-Hall, Inc., 1974.

Lusk, Harold F. and William B. French. *Law of the Real Estate Business,* 3rd ed. Homewood, Ill.: Richard D. Irwin, Inc., 1975.

O'Donnell, Paul T. and Eugene L. Maleady. *Principles of Real Estate.* Philadelphia, Pa.: W. B. Saunders Company, 1975.

Ring, Alfred A. and Jerome Dasso. *Real Estate Principles and Practices,* 8th ed. Englewood Cliffs, N.J.: Prentice-Hall, Inc., 1977.

Weimer, Arthur M., Homer Hoyt, and George F. Bloom. *Real Estate,* 7th ed. New York: The Ronald Press Company, 1978.

REVIEW QUESTIONS

1. The difference between exclusive right to sell and exclusive agency is

   (A) the agent's promise to pay all promotional expenses
   (B) the principal's reservation of the right to sell his or her own home
   (C) the principal's reservation of the right to pay the agent no commission
   (D) the principal's reservation of the right to pay the agent no commission if the principal should sell the property

2. When an agent has produced a buyer who is ready, willing, and able, the agent has generally

   (A) consummated the sale
   (B) established his or her personal competence
   (C) earned a commission
   (D) accounted to the principal

3. An agency agreement may be terminated by all of the following except

   (A) revocation by the principal
   (B) reciprocity
   (C) renunciation by the agent
   (D) mutual consent

4. Upon the death of a broker his or her listings will always be taken over by

   (A) a salesperson
   (B) a spouse
   (C) a trust company
   (D) none of the above

5. A real estate listing contract is

   (A) a list of all property owned by one person
   (B) a list of all property for purposes of taxation
   (C) the employment of a broker by the owner to sell real property
   (D) none of the above

6. The relationship of a licensed real estate broker to his principal is that of a

   (A) salesperson   (C) superior
   (B) beneficiary   (D) fiduciary

7. A broker may lawfully receive a commission from

   I. a co-broker
   II. the owner

   (A) I only   (C) both I and II
   (B) II only   (D) neither I nor II

8. An authorization to a person to act for and in behalf of another in a real estate transaction is called

   (A) a special agent
   (B) an option
   (C) power of attorney
   (D) an escrow

9. An attorney-in-fact is the holder of

   (A) power of attorney
   (B) a law degree
   (C) a listing
   (D) a decree from a court

10. When the buyer does not have sufficient money for an earnest money deposit,

    I.   the broker may loan him money from his or her escrow account
    II. the broker may take a personal check and hold it without depositing it in an escrow account

(A) I only   (C) both I and II
(B) II only   (D) neither I nor II

11. Once an agreement of sale is signed, the purchaser has

(A) legal title   (C) real title
(B) equitable title   (D) blind title

12. A seller of real estate is also known as a

(A) grantee   (C) vendee
(B) vendor   (D) broker

13. When the contract for sale of real property includes personal property as well, the seller should provide which of the following?

(A) bill of sale
(B) chattel mortgage
(C) estoppel certificate
(D) a registered mortgage

14. An option contract differs from a contract of sale in that the

(A) contract of sale requires consideration
(B) option needs no consideration
(C) option need not be consummated
(D) contract of sale is enforceable by either party to it

15. An option without valid consideration is

(A) valid   (C) revocable
(B) void   (D) enforceable

16. The clause in a deed which sets forth the interests being conveyed is the

(A) habendum clause
(B) testimonium clause
(C) indenture clause
(D) demure clause

17. A legal document which transfers legal possession of real property but does not transfer ownership is a

(A) deed   (C) deposition
(B) mortgage   (D) lease

18. The act of taking private property for public benefit is called

(A) condemnation
(B) eminent domain
(C) police powers
(D) none of the above

19. A deed must be signed by the

    I.   grantor
    II. grantee

(A) I only   (C) both I and II
(B) II only   (D) neither I nor II

20. Which of the following is not necessary for a valid transfer of title to real estate?

    I.   delivery of the deed
    II. recording of the deed

(A) I only   (C) both I and II
(B) II only   (D) neither I nor II

Chapter 15

Real Estate Mathematics

VOCABULARY

You will find it important to have a complete working knowledge of the following words and concepts found in the text or the glossary.

assessed value	debit	liabilities
assets	expense	lien
credit	income	owner's equity
		tax liability

IN this chapter, the student must review the mathematical skills necessary for success in the real estate business and the uniform examinations. The problems used in this section are in a narrative or story format. The student must be able to read the problem and supply the correct answer from his or her interpretation of the story. The problems cover fractions, decimals, percentages, area, volume, perimeter, and the proration methods needed for settlements.

FRACTIONS

A fraction is considered to be a quotient of two numbers. It may not be the quotient of two whole numbers. The top number of a fraction is called the numerator and represents the dividend. The bottom number of the fraction is called the denominator and represents the divisor. Thus $3 \div 4 = 3/4$: where the 3 is the numerator and 4 is the denominator. A fraction of this form, where the numerator is less than the denominator, is called a simple fraction and always has a value less than 1. So that 1/2, 19/32, 52/100, 191/231 are all simple fractions. If the numerator should be larger than the denominator, this is referred to as an improper fraction. Therefore 4/3 is considered an improper fraction, and if the division were completed would result in a mixed number (a whole number plus a simple fraction or 1⅓).

Each fraction should be reduced to the lowest possible terms or converted to a mixed number upon the completion of each problem.

Addition and Subtraction of Fractions

Prior to performing the addition or subtraction of two or more fractions each one must be put in terms common to the other. This is referred to as finding the common denominator. The simplest way to find a common denominator is to multiply the numerator (top) and denominator (bottom) of one fraction by the denominator (bottom) of the other fraction. Then repeat the process on the second fraction, using the denominator from the first.

After the common denominator is found the addition or subtraction may be performed by adding the numerators, and the fraction should be reduced to its lowest terms.

Example—Addition:
$$1/7 + 3/8 = ?$$
$$1/7 \times 8/8 = 8/56$$
$$3/8 \times 7/7 = 21/56$$

Now add the numerators:
$$8/56 + 21/56 = 29/56$$

Example—Subtraction:
$$7/9 - 1/4 = ?$$
$$7/9 \times 4/4 = 28/36$$
$$1/4 \times 9/9 = 9/36$$

Now subtract the numerators:
$$28/36 - 9/36 = 19/36$$

If more than two fractions are to be added, multiply the numerator and denominator of each fraction by the denominators of the other fractions and then sum the numerators over the common denominator.

Example:

1/4 + 3/5 + 7/9 = ?
1/4 × 5/5 × 9/9 = 45/180
3/5 × 4/4 × 9/9 = 108/180
7/9 × 4/4 × 5/5 = 140/180

Now add:

$$\frac{45}{180} + \frac{108}{180} + \frac{140}{180} = \frac{293}{180} \text{ or } 1\frac{113}{180}$$

Multiplication of Fractions

To multiply two or more fractions, place the product of the numerator over the product of the denominator and reduce to the lowest terms.

Example:

3/4 × 2/3 = ?

$$\frac{3 \times 2}{4 \times 3} = \frac{6}{12} = \frac{1}{2}$$

Example:

9/10 × 3/5 × 4/7 = ?

$$\frac{9 \times 3 \times 4}{10 \times 5 \times 7} = \frac{108}{350} = \frac{54}{175}$$

Division of Fractions by Fractions

In the division of fractions, the first fraction is the dividend and the second is the divisor. In order to divide a fraction by a fraction, invert (turn upside down) the divisor and multiply the two numbers as you did in multiplying two fractions.

Example:

5/12 ÷ 2/3 = ?
5/12 × 3/2 = 15/24 = 5/8

Cancelation Between Fractions

Cancelation is the taking out of factors (numbers) common to both numerator and denominator before multiplying or dividing. This is done by comparing the numerator of one fraction to the denominator of another and dividing out the common factor.

Example:

$$\frac{35}{84} \times \frac{21}{25} = \frac{\overset{7}{\cancel{35}}}{\underset{4}{\cancel{84}}} \times \frac{\overset{1}{\cancel{21}}}{\underset{5}{\cancel{25}}}$$

$$= 7/4 \times 1/5 = 7/20$$

The common factors were 5 and 21.

DECIMALS

A decimal is merely the numerator of a fraction following the decimal point. The denominator of the fraction then is 10, 100, 1000, etc. If the numerator is one place to the right of the decimal point, then the denominator of the fraction is 10; if it is two places or two numerals to the right, then the denominator is 100, etc.

Example:

.3 = 3/10 = three tenths
.03 = 3/100 = three hundredths
.003 = 3/1000 = three thousandths

Converting Fractions to Decimals

To change a fraction, simply divide the numerator (top) by the denominator (bottom) and express the answer in decimal form.

Example:

3/5 = 3.00 ÷ 5 = .60

or

$$3/5 = 5\overline{\smash{\big)}\,3.00}^{\,.60}$$

If when dividing the last number a series or a repeating number occurs, round off the third digit. If the third digit is less than 5, drop the number. If it is greater than 5, round off to the next highest number.

Example:

$$1/3 = 3\overline{\smash{\big)}\,1.000}^{\,.333} = .33$$

$$2/3 = 3\overline{\smash{\big)}\,2.000}^{\,.666} = .67$$

Adding or Subtracting Decimals

Place the numbers in the proper columns, paying attention to keeping the decimal points and columns in line, and perform the function.

Example:

$$1.075 + .18 = 1.255 \quad \text{or} \quad 1.075 - .18 = .895$$

Multiplying Decimals

Multiply decimals just as you would whole numbers. Once the product is obtained, begin at the right of the decimal point and count the total number of digits to the right contained in all numbers being multiplied. This will tell you how many digits are to be to the right of the decimal point in the product.

Example:

6.3	(1 digit to right of the decimal point)
× 2.11	(2 digits to right of the decimal point)
13.293	(3 digits to right of the decimal point)

Example:

$$6.7 \times .002 = .0134$$

In this case there were not enough whole numbers to fill the four columns to the right of the decimal point, so a zero was inserted to fill the spot.

Dividing Decimals

It is easiest to divide by moving the decimal point of the divisor to the right until it becomes a whole number. Also, move the decimal point of the dividend the same number of places to the right. Then perform normal division by whole numbers.

Example:

$$5.5 \overline{)31.36} \quad \text{becomes} \quad 550 \overline{)3136.0} = 5.7$$

PERCENTS

Percent indicates that a whole number or quantity has been divided into 100 equal parts, and the percentage represents the number of parts to be used. To convert a percent to a decimal move the decimal point two places to the left. To convert a decimal to a percent move the decimal point two places to the right and add the percent sign (%).

Example:

25% means 25 one-hundredths or 25/100 or .25

Example:

30% = .30
3.5% = .035

PRACTICE PROBLEMS: FRACTIONS, DECIMALS, PERCENTS

Fractions

Add the following fractions:
1. 1/6 + 1/8 =
2. 3/7 + 4/9 =
3. 19/20 + 3/5 =
4. 1/8 + 5/12 =
5. 3/4 + 1/16 =

Subtract the following fractions:
6. 1/6 − 1/8 =
7. 4/7 − 4/9 =
8. 19/20 − 3/5 =
9. 5/12 − 1/8 =
10. 3/4 − 1/16 =

Multiply the following fractions:
11. 1/8 × 1/4 =
12. 1/9 × 11/12 =
13. 3/4 × 7/16 =
14. 4/5 × 8/9 =
15. 5/12 × 1/5 =

Divide the following fractions:
16. 1/8 ÷ 1/4 =
17. 1/9 ÷ 11/12 =
18. 3/4 ÷ 7/6 =
19. 4/5 ÷ 8/9 =
20. 5/12 ÷ 1/5 =

Decimals and Percents

Add the following decimals:
1. .5 + .075 + .125 =
2. .073 + 1.25 + .93 =
3. .82 + .73 + 2.584 =
4. .0016 + 1.043 + .3 =

Subtract the following decimals:
5. 1.25 − .075 =
6. .073 − .0016 =
7. 1.4874 − .896 =
8. 2.043 − 1.0012 =

Multiply the following decimals:

9. .075 × 1.257 =
10. .342 × .0017 =
11. .7589 × 1.2 =
12. .346 × 3.476 =

Divide the following decimals:

13. .34 ÷ .516 =
14. 1.25 ÷ .07 =
15. .78 ÷ .4 =
16. 1.29 ÷ .432 =

Change the following percents to decimals:

17. 75% =
18. 125% =
19. 27.56% =
20. 43.2% =

Change the following decimals to percents:

21. .0025 =
22. .567 =
23. .493 =
24. 3.475 =

GEOMETRIC FORMULAS FOR REAL ESTATE

In many instances the real estate agent deals with flat or plane surfaces of which he or she needs to know the area. Among the most commonly encountered areas are floor space and lot areas. Though these may appear in an infinite variety of shapes, some of the most common are quadrilateral (four-sided), trilateral (three-sided), and circular.

Rectangles

The most common forms of quadrilaterals are known as rectangles. A square is a special form of the rectangle, with all four of its sides equal. Another unique characteristic of all rectangles is that all the interior angles are equal to ·90 degrees. There are other forms of quadrilaterals for which this is not true, such as trapezoids. A third characteristic of all rectangles is that the opposite sides are parallel.

The area of a rectangle may then be found by using the formula $A = lw$, where A = area, l = length or measure of the longer side, and w = width or measure of the shorter side. By multiplying the length (l) times the width (w) the area (A) of a rectangle may be found.

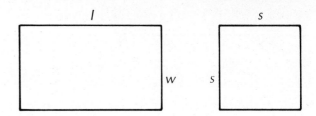

If the area of a rectangle is known and the measure of one side is known, the measure of the remaining side may be determined by dividing the area (A) by the measure of the known side.

Example:

What is the floor space of a building which has a length of 60 feet and a width of 40 feet?

    Solution:

      Area = length × width
      A = lw
      A = 60 feet × 40 feet
      A = 2,400 square feet

    Example:

      A = 2,400 square feet
      l = 60 feet
      w = ?

    Solution:

      We know that A = lw
      Then $\dfrac{A}{l}$ = w
                2,400/60 = 40 feet

Rectangle

60 feet

40 feet

60 feet

?   2,400 square feet

Squares

Since the square is a unique form of the rectangle with all four sides equal in length, only the measure of one side (s) needs to be known to find the area of the square.

Example:

Area = side × side
A   = s × s or A = s²
A   = 20 feet × 20 feet
A   = 400 square feet

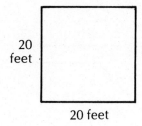

20 feet

20 feet

Triangles

The area of a triangle is equal to one-half the measure of the base times the height (the distance from the base to the apex).

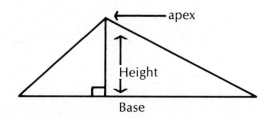

apex

Height

Base

Vertex: A point of joining together.

Height: The distance from the vertex of the two sides adjoining the base along a perpendicular line to the base.

Example:

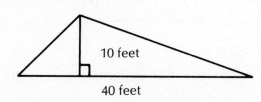

10 feet

40 feet

Area = ½ base × height
A   = ½ bh
A   = ½ (40 feet)(10 feet)
A   = ½ (400)
A   = 200 square feet

Right Triangles

The right triangle is unique in that one of the sides is always perpendicular to the base of the triangle and the area calculation can be made using the existing dimensions.

Another characteristic of the right triangle is that, if the lengths of two sides of the triangle are known, the length of the third side may be found. This is based on the Pythagorean theorem; this theorem states that the square of the length of the hypotenuse of a right triangle is equal to the sum of the squares of the length of the other two sides.

Example:

a = altitude, b = base, c = hypotenuse.

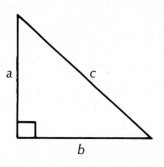

a

c

b

$c^2 = a^2 + b^2$

The length of side $c = \sqrt{a^2 + b^2}$

The length of side $a = \sqrt{c^2 - b^2}$

The length of side $b = \sqrt{c^2 - a^2}$

Example:

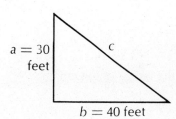

a = 30 feet

c

b = 40 feet

$c^2 = a^2 + b^2$
$c = \sqrt{a^2 + b^2}$
$c = \sqrt{(30)^2 + (40)^2}$
$c = \sqrt{900 + 1600}$
$c = \sqrt{250}$
$c = 50$

Circles

Circumference is equal to the distance around the outside of the circle.

Diameter is the straight-line distance between two opposite points on the circumference, passing through the center.

Radius is the distance from the center of the circle to a point on the circumference. The radius is equal to one-half the diameter of the circle.

Pi (π) is equal to the circumference divided by the diameter. $\pi = 3.1416$

Circumference (C) = $\pi \times$ diameter (D), so that $C = \pi D$.

Diameter (D) = circumference (C) $\div \pi$, so that $D = C \div \pi$.

Radius (r) = diameter (D) $\div$ 2, so that $r = D \div 2$.

Area (A) = $\pi \times$ radius squared (r^2), so that $A = \pi r^2$.

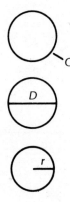

Example:

A circular lot has a diameter of 20 feet.

1. What is the circumference of the lot?
   $C = \pi D$
   $C = 3.1416 \times 20$ feet
   $C = 62.832$ feet

2. What is the radius of the circle?
   $r = D \div 2$
   $r = 20$ feet $\div$ 2
   $r = 10$ feet

3. What is the area of the circle?
   $A = \pi r^2$
   $A = 3.1416\,(10)(10)$
   $A = 314.16$ square feet

Rhomboids

Quadrilateral (four-sided) parallelograms (opposite sides are parallel) have oblique angles, and only the opposite sides are equal in length. (An oblique angle is one that is greater than 90 degrees.) If all four sides are of equal length, then the shape is a rhombus.

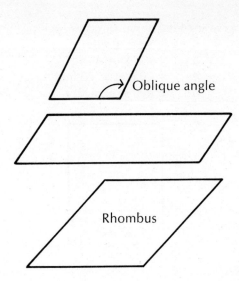

The area of a rhomboid is found by multiplying the length of one of the parallel sides (*s*) by the distance between the parallel sides (*d*).

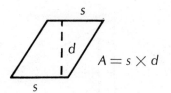

Example:
$A = s \times d$
$A = 25$ feet $\times$ 15 feet
$A = 375$ square feet

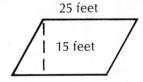

Trapezoid

A quadrilateral that has only two sides that are parallel is called a trapezoid.

Example:
a is parallel to *b*, and *h* = the distance between lines *a* and *b*.

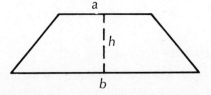

The area of a trapezoid is equal to one-half the sum of the parallel sides $\left[\dfrac{a+b}{2}\right]$ times the distance between them (h).

> *Example:*
>
> $A = \dfrac{a+b}{2} \times h$
>
> $A = \dfrac{30 \text{ feet} + 50 \text{ feet}}{2} \times 25 \text{ feet}$

$A = 40 \text{ feet} \times 25 \text{ feet}$

$A = 1000 \text{ square feet}$

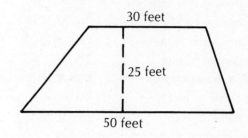

The Area of Odd-Shaped Figures

Quite often the lot a real estate agent is selling does not have a regular shape. If possible, it should be broken down into a series of figures that he or she can find the area of:

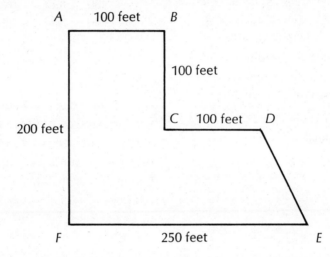

The figure above breaks down into three geometric shapes that are easy to work with:

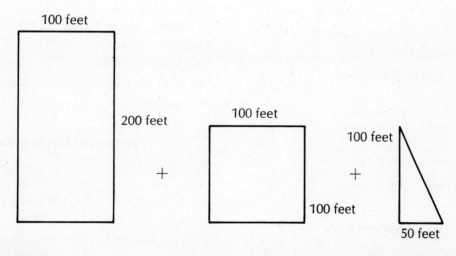

Rectangle	Square	Triangle
$A = lw$	$A = s^2$	$A = \frac{1}{2}bh$
$A = 200' \times 100'$	$A = 100^2$	$A = \frac{1}{2}(50')(100')$
$A = 20{,}000 \text{ square feet}$ +	$A = 10{,}000 \text{ square feet}$ +	$A = 2500 \text{ square feet}$

Total area = 32,500 square feet

...rmulas for the Solution of Math Problems

...length × width	$A = L \times W$
Inte... = principal × rate	$I = P \times R$
Interest = mortgage × rate	$I = M \times R$
Cost = selling price × rate	$C = SP \times R$
Tax = assessment × rate	$T = A \times R$
Percentage = base × rate	$P = B \times R$
Value = income × factor	$V = I \times F$
Income = value × rate	$I = V \times R$

Selling price = rent × gross rent multiplier

$$SP = R \times GRM$$

Net income = gross income — expense

$$NI = GI - E$$

Commission = selling price × rate $C = SP \times R$

Circumference of a circle = 3.1416 × diameter

Diameter of a circle = 0.31831 × circumference

Area of a circle = 3.1416 × square of radius or
.7854 × square of diameter

Area Equivalents

Area	Acres	Metric Area (square kilometers)
Township	23,040	93.312
Section	640	2.592
1/2 Section	320	1.296
1/4 Section	160	.648
1/8 Section	80	.324
1/16 Section	40	.162
1/32 Section	20	.081
1/64 Section	10	.0405

Linear Equivalents

Pole	5.5	yards	5.03	meters
Furlong	220.0	yards	201.168	meters
Perch	5.5	yards	5.03	meters
Broad	22.0	yards	20.12	meters
Hektar	2.47	acres	9,995.72	square meters
Degree	69.167	miles	111.359	kilometers
Minute	1.153	miles	1.856	kilometers
Second	6,087.84	feet	1,856.79	meters

Area Conversion Table

To convert from:	to:	multiply by:
Square inches	Square centimeters	6.452
Square feet	Square meters	0.093
Square yards	Square meters	0.836
Acres	Square meters	4,046.849
Square miles	Square kilometers	2.592

Examples of One Acre Equivalents

10	rods	by	16	rods
8	rods	by	20	rods
5	rods	by	32	rods
4	rods	by	40	rods
5	yards	by	968	yards
20	yards	by	242	yards
10	yards	by	484	yards
40	yards	by	121	yards
220	feet	by	198	feet
110	feet	by	396	feet
60	feet	by	726	feet
60	feet	by	726	feet
120	feet	by	363	feet
300	feet	by	145.2	feet
400	feet	by	108.9	feet

Other Conversions

320 rods = 1 mile

144 square inches = 1 square foot

9 square feet = 1 square yard

272¼ square feet = 1 square rod

30¼ square yards = 1 square rod

7.92 inches = 1 link, 25 links = 1 rod

100 links = 66 feet = 22 yards = 4 rods = 1 chain

10 chains long by 1 broad, or 10 square chains = 1 acre

1 acre = 160 square rods = 4,840 square yards = 43,560 square feet

30¼ square yards = 1 square rod, perch, or pole

40 square rods = 1 rood

4 roods = 1 acre

2.47 acres = 1 hektar

640 acres = 1 square mile = 1 section

36 square miles or 36 sections = 1 township

To Convert Metric to Metric

1 kilometer (km)	=	100 decameters (dm)
	=	1,000 meters (m)
	=	100,000 centimeters (cm)
	=	1,000,000 millimeters (mm)
1 decameter (dm)	=	10 meters (m)
	=	1,000 centimeters (cm)
	=	10,000 millimeters (mm)
1 meter (m)	=	100 centimeters (cm)
	=	1,000 millimeters (mm)
1 centimeter (cm)	=	10 millimeters (mm)

Metric Conversions

To convert from:	to:	multiply by:
Inches	Centimeters	2.54
Feet	Meters	.305
Yards	Meters	.9144
Rods	Meters	5.03
Chains	Meters	20.13
Links	Centimeters	20.04
Miles	Kilometers	1.61
Centimeters	Inches	.394
Meters	Feet	3.28
Meters	Yards	1.09
Meters	Rods	5.995
Meters	Chains	.0497
Centimeters	Links	.0499
Kilometers	Miles	.621

PRACTICE PROBLEMS: PERIMETER, AREA, VOLUME

1. How many acres in a square mile? 640

2. How many square feet in an acre? 43560

3. How many square feet in the property below?

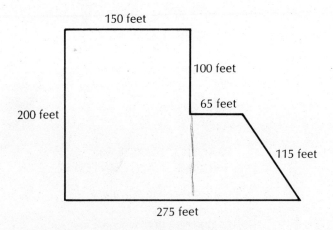

4. What is the price of a lot measuring 373′ × 154′ at a cost of $1,000 per acre?

5. How many acres are contained in a lot 300 feet × 450 feet?

6. If concrete costs $16.50 per cubic yard and labor costs are $.20 a square foot, what would be the cost to build a driveway 28 feet long, 9 feet wide, and 6 inches thick?

7. Building restrictions are such that a 20-foot front yard setback, a 15-foot back yard set-back, and a side yard setback of 15 feet are required. How much area on the lot is build-able if the dimensions are 120′ × 150′?

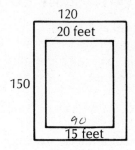

8. Farmer A wants to lease a portion of his farm to Farmer B for cultivation. Farmer B is willing to pay $50 an acre for the tillable land. The area in question has a large pond in the center of it. The outside dimensions are 310 × 240 rods. The pond is circular and has a diameter of 90 rods. How many acres is Farmer B leasing and what is the cost of the lease?

9. How far would a person have to walk to go completely around a circular 1-acre pond with a diameter of 14.28 rods?

10. Compute the cubic content of an industrial warehouse that is 260′ × 340′ and has an average height of 40 feet.

11. A certain lot measures 80′ × 135′ and costs $.63 per square foot. A home is erected on the lot at a cost of $1.85 per cubic foot. The dimensions of the house are 40′ × 60′ × 10′. What is the value of the property?

12. What is the price of a lot measuring 264 feet wide and 660 feet deep at $800 per acre?

13. Compute the proposed cost of the following property:

A	Land	125′ × 100′ @ $ 1/square foot
B	Two-story building	40′ × 60′ @ $25/square foot
C	Full basement	40′ × 60′ @ $ 5/square foot
D	Driveway	10′ × 80′ @ $ 4/square foot
E	Sidewalks	3′ × 70′ @ $ 3/square foot
F	Yard improvements	$5,000

14. A farmer sold a real estate developer three sites of land. Site X had an area twice that of site Y. Site Y was three times larger than site Z. Site Z contained 3 acres. What is the area contained in each site and how many acres does the

farmer have left in the original quarter section of land that he owns?

COMPUTING RATES—SIMPLE CAPITALIZATION

Rate is expressed as a percent. It is usually related to income or value of an investment. Using the simple rate formula we can determine the income, value, or rate of return on a property.

$$Income = rate \times value$$

To find the income to be produced from a property that has a certain value we multiply this value by the desired rate. The income is usually a net figure.

Example:

A man owns a building worth $50,000 and desires a 10% return from his property. What income must the property produce to attain this?

Income = rate × value
Income = 10% × $50,000

Income = .10 × $50,000
Income = $5,000/year to produce the
  desired rate of income

Using the same information, if the man knew his income and his desired rate of return and wanted to find the value of his property, he could do so using the components of the above formula.

Example:
Income = rate × value
Income/rate = value
$5,000/.10 = value

.10 $\overline{\smash{)}\,\$5,000}$ = 1.0 $\overline{\smash{)}\,\$50,000}$
     $50,000 = value

Therefore by dividing the income by the rate we can find the value of the property if it is unknown.
  If the same man knew the value of the same property and knew his net income to be the same, using the same components he could find the rate of return on his property by dividing the income by the known value.

PROFIT AND LOSS

Profit or loss is measured by the sales price against the cost of the property. If the cost is less than the sales price, a profit will be made. If the cost is greater than the sales price, a loss will take place.

$$Profit\ or\ loss = sales\ price - cost$$

Example:
Profit = $10,000 − $8,000
Profit = $2,000

Profit and loss may be expressed as a percent. It is usually based on a percent of the cost.

Example:
Profit of $2,000 and cost of $8,000
$2,000/$8,000 = ¼ = 25% profit

To find the cost divide the sales price by either (1 + profit) or (1 − loss).

Example:
Sales price = $10,000

Profit = 25%

Cost = ?

$$C = \frac{SP}{1 + P}$$
$$= \frac{\$10,000}{1 + .25}$$
$$= \frac{\$10,000}{1.25}$$
$$= \$8,000$$

PRACTICE PROBLEMS:
RATE, INCOME, VALUE, INTEREST

Income = rate × value
Income/value = rate
$5,000/$50,000 = rate
    .10 = rate
Convert to percentage:
Rate = .10 = 10%

1. What is the indicated value of a stream of income on a yield of $600 per month if similar incomes are yielding 8% per annum return on investment?

2. The value of a house at the end of 6 years was estimated to be $7,650. Based on a straight-line depreciation rate of 2½%, what was the original cost of the house?

3. What is the indicated value of a stream of income on a yield of $1,000 per month with an average annual yield of 13%?

4. How long will it take an investor to recapture her initial investment at a rate of 12% per year return of her money?

5. A person has a property which produces a gross income of $325 per month. Monthly expenses average $155. What is the net income per year on the property?

6. A large barn was converted into 10 apartments with the following rentals: four @ $200 per month, three @ $175 per month, and three @ $150 per month. The operating expenses were $10,000, and the debt service was $6,000. What is the yield on the owner's equity if $50,000 is invested in the property? Give both the dollar figure and rate.

7. The monthly interest on a $23,000 loan is $300. What is the annual simple interest rate?

8. What is the quarterly interest payment on a loan of $40,000 with an annual interest rate of 9%?

PRACTICE PROBLEMS: PROFIT AND LOSS

1. A man bought two lots side by side that measured 50 feet (*w*) × 100 feet (*l*) and 100 feet (*w*) × 100 feet (*l*). He paid a total of $4,500 for them. He later divided them into three lots of equal frontage and sold them for $2,000 each. What is the percent of return on his original investment?

2. If a house sold for $35,000 at a loss of 6%, what was the original cost of the house?

3. A person buys a lot for $5,000 and sells it at a 15% profit. What was the sales price?

4. A person buys a property for $43,500 and sells it for $65,000. What was the percent of profit?

5. A woman bought a house for $23,750 and sold it at a $3,400 loss. What was her percent of loss?

COMMISSION

The salesperson's and broker's commissions are generally based on a percentage of the gross sales price of the property.

Example:
Sales price $30,000
Commission fee 6%
$30,000 × .06 = $1,800 commission

PRACTICE PROBLEMS: COMMISSION

1. As a salesperson, you realize that it takes an average of 10 showings to sell a house. You calculate that each showing has an average cost of $20. If you are paid one-half of the 8% commission for selling a $50,000 property, what is your net income on this sale?

2. The commission rate for selling an apartment building is 6% of the first $10,000 and 5% of anything over that. Broker Jones received a commission of $760. What was the sales price of the apartment building?

3. An 80-acre tract was listed for sale at $400 per acre but was sold for $27,500 with the condition that the purchaser pay the broker's commission of 8%. What was the net gain for the purchaser?

4. If you are a salesperson for a $95,000 property, the brokerage fee is 8%, and you will receive 50% of the total fee, what is the dollar amount the brokerage firm will receive from the sale?

5. A broker keeps five-eighths of an 8% commission. The salesperson sold the property for $48,500. How much does the salesperson receive for selling the property?

SETTLEMENT STATEMENT MATH METHODS

Mortgage Balances

1. Beginning principal balance × interest rate = annual interest
2. Annual interest ÷ 12 = monthly interest
3. Constant monthly payment − monthly interest = amount to principal reduction
4. Beginning principal balance − principal reduction = new principal balance

Repeat the process for as many months as needed. For example the process would be repeated 300 times for a 25-year loan.

Example: 25-year loan, 8% interest for $50,000, $475 constant.

1. Beginning principal balance × interest rate = annual interest
$50,000 × .08 = $4,000

2. Annual interest ÷ 12 = monthly interest
   $4,000 ÷ 12 = $333.33

3. Constant monthly payment − monthly interest
   = principal reduction
   $475.00 − $333.33 = $141.67

4. Beginning principal balance − principal reduction = new principal balance
   $50,000.00 − $141.67 = $49,858.33

Interest Prorated

Use the 30-day method for calculations.

1. Compute the annual interest on the mortgage balance by multiplying the rate by the mortgage balance.
2. Divide the annual interest by 12 to obtain the monthly interest.
3. Divide the monthly interest by 30 to obtain the daily interest to the nearest cent.
4. Count the number of days since the last mortgage payment through the closing date.
5. Multiply the number of days by the daily interest figure to obtain the amount being prorated.
6. If the interest is computed in advance, the seller will receive the difference between the prepaid amount of interest and the daily amount used to closing.
7. If the interest is in arrears, the seller will owe for the number of days since the last payment until the closing.

Example: A $10,000.00 mortgage balance after the last payment at 12% interest. There are 15 days between the last payment and the closing.

1. $10,000.00 × .12 = $1,200.00 annual interest
2. $1,200.00/12 = $100.00/month
   $100.00/30 = $3.33/day
   15 days × $3.33 = $49.95

15 days is equal to ½ month. The difference between ½ month's interest of $50.00 and the $49.95 computed daily is due to rounding off.

Taxes—Computed and Prorated

For purposes of your examination, taxes are computed annually from January 1 to December 31. Each month is considered to have 30 days, and a year has 360 days. Taxes are computed by multiplying the rate by the assessed value of the land and improvements.

Example:
(Land) $5,000 + (improvements)
$12,000 = (assessed value) $17,000
Rate = $9.40/$100 of assessed value
Annual taxes = (land + improvements) rate
Annual taxes = ($5,000 + $12,000) $9.40/$100
Annual taxes = $17,000 × $9.40/$100
Annual taxes = $1,598

The rate will be expressed as so many dollars per $100 of assessed value.

To prorate taxes for settlement:

1. Compute the amount of time the seller will possess the property in the year of the settlement through the settlement.
2. Compute the annual taxes.
3. Find the monthly amount of the taxes and multiply the amount by the time of settlement to obtain the prorated amount.
4. If taxes were prepaid, subtract the prorated amount from the prepaid taxes to find how much the seller will receive at the settlement. If taxes are paid in arrears, the seller will be charged the prorated share at the settlement.

Example:
Assessed value of land ($5,000) + improvements ($12,000) = total assessed value = $17,000
Rate $9.40/$100
Annual taxes = $1,598 due December 31

At closing on June 15:
$1,598/12 = $133.17/month
Seller has held property 5½ months
($133.17)(5½) = $732.44 taxes to be prorated

Insurance Prorated (30-day month)

Most insurance is paid in advance either 1 or 3 years. Therefore upon cancelation or assignment of the policy in force the seller desires a refund of the prepaid premiums. This amount represents the unused portion of the seller's premium. In order to compute the unused portion:

1. Compute the time remaining on the policy

Example:	Day	Month	Year
Expiration date	20	8	NY
Date of closing	10	6	TY
Time remaining	10	2	1

2. Multiply the remaining by the rates.

Example: Policy has a premium of $360 per year paid 3 years in advance

Year = $360
Month = $360/12 = $30/month
Daily = $30/30 = $1/day

Time remaining × rate
    = amount to seller

1 year × $360 =	$360
2 months × $30 =	$60
10 days × $1 =	$10
Amount to seller	$430

Rent Prorated

Rent is usually paid in advance. The purchaser is concerned with obtaining his or her share of the rent at the settlement when he or she takes possession of the property.

1. Divide the monthly amount by 30 and round off to the nearest cent to obtain the daily rate.
2. Multiply the daily rate by the number of days the seller has had possession of the property to closing.
3. Subtract this amount from the monthly rent, and the remainder is owed the buyer.

Example: The monthly rent of $180 is paid in advance; the closing is on the 20th of the month. Prorate the rent:

$180/30 = $6/day
20 days seller has possession × $6 = $120
$180 − $120 = $60 to buyer

PRACTICE PROBLEMS: MORTGAGE BALANCES, RENT, TAX, INSURANCE, INTEREST PRORATIONS

Mortgage Balances

1. Balance after last payment, $38,500; interest rate, 8%; constant payment, $328 per month. What is the balance of the mortgage after the next payment?

2. Balance after May 15, $24,250; interest rate, 7%; constant monthly payment, $210. What is the mortgage balance after the July 15 payment?

Rent

3. Mr. David is purchasing a four-unit apartment building. The building contains two one-bedroom apartments renting for $180 per month; one two-bedroom apartment renting for $210 per month; one three-bedroom apartment renting for $270 per month. All rents are due on the first of the month and are current. The closing is to take place on the 20th. Prorate the rents to determine the total amount owed to Mr. David at closing.

Taxes

4. A property is assessed at 40% of its appraised value. The appraised value is $37,500 and the tax rate is $8.27 per $100. Taxes are due January 1 each year in advance. If the sale of the property closed on July 10th, how much would the buyer owe the seller for the prorated taxes at closing?

Insurance

5. A home is covered by a 3-year fire insurance policy which expires July 11, NY. The premium on the policy was $489.00 and has been paid in full. The home was sold and closing was set for September 23, TY. How much money will be credited the seller at closing if the policy is assumed by the purchaser?

Interest

6. The outstanding mortgage balance after the September 1st payment was $38,500. The monthly PI constant is $328. The interest is computed in arrears at 8¾%. What amount would be debited to the seller if settlement takes place September 20th?

Chapter 16

Listing, Offer to Purchase, and Settlement Forms

VOCABULARY

You will find it important to have a complete working knowledge of the following words and concepts found in the text or the glossary.

agent	debit	offer to purchase
bill of sale	deposit	open listing
binder	earnest money	PITI
broker	escrow	principal
chattels	exclusive agency	salesperson
counteroffer	exclusive right to sell	vendee
credit	multiple listing	vendor

THIS chapter and the ones which follow may well be the most important for those students who plan to enter the real estate industry. The object of this chapter is to familiarize you with some of the specific problems and procedures in the brokerage business. Particular attention has been given to the mechanics of completing listing contracts, offers to purchase, and settlement statements. Careful attention should be paid to the details in preparing these documents so you will be very familiar with them in their completed forms when you take your state examination and once you have entered the business.

The student should totally master the forms involved in these transactions for a basic understanding of all facets of the agreements involved in a real property transaction.

The forms used in this and the following chapters are educational forms designed for testing and to point out certain pertinent parts of a transaction. They are not recommended for your daily use in the business. The future real estate salesperson or broker should become acquainted with the particular forms used in a specific area, since they vary in format from firm to firm and city to city.

EXCLUSIVE AUTHORIZATION TO SELL (LISTING)

See form on page 206; tear out of the form also appears at the end of the text.

Section 1

1. *Sales price*—Enter the amount for which the property is listed.
2. *Type home*—Architectural style of the property.
3. *Total bedrooms*—Enter the number of bedrooms.
4. *Total baths*—Enter the number of bathrooms.
5. *Address*—Enter the number and name of street of the property, and the city.
6. *Jurisdiction of*—Enter the county and state where the property is located.
7. *Amount of loan to be assumed*—Enter the loan balance.
8. *As of what date*—The date of the loan balance entered in item 7.
9. *Taxes and insurance included*—Enter "yes" if taxes and insurance are included in the monthly payments, or "no" if they are not.
10. *Years to go*—Enter the number of years remaining in the life of the loan.

11. *Amount payable monthly*—Enter the monthly payment on the loan in item 7 and the interest rate being charged.

12. *Type of loan*—Enter the form of financing of the loan in item 7. For example, FHA or conventional; if not otherwise stated in the story, assume it to be conventional.

13. *Mortgage company*—Enter the name of the mortgagee of the loan in item 7 and the address if available.

14. *2nd mortgage (or 2nd trust)*—Enter the name of the mortgagee and the address, and the amount of the second loan.

15. *Owner's name*—Enter the name(s) of the owners of the property.

16. *Phones (home and business)*—Enter the owner's phone numbers.

17. *Tenant's name*—Enter the name of the person(s) in possession of the property if leased.

18. *Phones (home and business)*—Enter the phone numbers of the tenant(s) if the property is leased.

19. *Possession*—Enter the date the seller will give possession of the property to the buyer and the type of possession to be given.

20. *Date listed*—Enter the date (day, month, year) the listing is taken.

21. *Exclusive for*—Enter the number of days for which the listing contract will be in effect; for example, 90 days.

22. *Date of expiration*—Enter the date upon which the listing expires; for example, a 90-day listing beginning April 3, this year, expires July 3, this year; a 60-day listing beginning July 27, this year, expires September 27, this year.

23. *Listing broker*—If the person taking the listing is a broker, insert his or her name and the company name, or the company name if the listing agent is a salesperson.

24. *Phone*—Enter the telephone number of the listing broker.

25. *Key available at*—Enter the location at which the key may be obtained in order to show the property; for example, "key in office."

26. *Listing salesperson*—If the person taking the listing is a salesperson, enter his or her name.

27. *Home phone*—Enter the telephone number of the listing salesperson.

28. *How to be shown*—Enter specific instructions as to how the property is to be shown; for example, "by appointment with owners only."

Section 2

The items in this section are basically self-explanatory. The information needed to complete the listing form is given in the body of the listing narrative. This information gives the physical description of the property. The student must pay close attention to these items and enter them correctly on the listing agreement, since he or she will later be tested upon the information transferred to the exclusive authorization to sell form without benefit of the narrative.

Section 3

This section includes information to be used for computing the tax for the listed property.

Note: The vertical line marking off the box for Section 3 is for instructional purposes only. The line does not appear on the ETS form used on the RELE.

Land assessment—Enter the dollar amount for which the land has been assessed.

Improvements—Enter the dollar amount for which the improvements to the property have been assessed.

Total assessment—Enter the sum of the land assessment and the improvements.

Tax rate—Enter the given tax rate. This rate is usually expressed as dollars of taxes per $100 of total assessed valuation; for example, $6.72/$100.

Total annual taxes—Enter the product of the total assessment and the tax rate.

Section 4

Enter any information concerning the schools and public transportation facilities that might affect the property; also, any information concerning the shopping areas near the property.

Remarks—Enter any conditions on which the sale is to be contingent or any other vital information not listed elsewhere in the exclusive authorization to sell form.

Section 5

This is the legal section of the form and establishes the contractual agreement between the seller (principal) and the broker (agent).

5-1. *Date*—Enter the date the contract is entered into.

5-2. Enter the name of the real estate firm taking the listing.

REAL ESTATE LISTING CONTRACT (EXCLUSIVE RIGHT TO SELL)

SALES PRICE _____1_____ TYPE HOME _____2_____ TOTAL BEDROOMS __3__ TOTAL BATHS __4__

ADDRESS _____5_____ JURISDICTION OF _____6_____

AMT. OF LOAN TO BE ASSUMED $ __7__ AS OF WHAT DATE __8__ TAXES & INS. INCLUDED __9__ YEARS TO GO __10__ AMOUNT PAYABLE MONTHLY $ __11__ @ __%__ TYPE LOAN __12__

MORTGAGE COMPANY __13__ 2nd MORTGAGE __14__

OWNER'S NAME __15__ PHONES (HOME) __16__ (BUSINESS) __16__

TENANT'S NAME __17__ PHONES (HOME) __18__ (BUSINESS) __18__

POSSESSION __19__ DATE LISTED: __20__ EXCLUSIVE FOR __21__ DATE OF EXPIRATION __22__

LISTING BROKER __23__ PHONE __24__ KEY AVAILABLE AT __25__

LISTING SALESMAN __26__ HOME PHONE __27__ HOW TO BE SHOWN: __28__

Section 1

ENTRANCE FOYER ☐	CENTER HALL ☐	AGE	AIR CONDITIONING ☐	TYPE KITCHEN CABINETS
LIVING ROOM SIZE	FIREPLACE ☐	ROOFING	TOOL HOUSE ☐	TYPE COUNTER TOPS
DINING ROOM SIZE		GARAGE SIZE	PATIO ☐	EAT-IN SIZE KITCHEN ☐
BEDROOM TOTAL: DOWN UP		SIDE DRIVE ☐	CIRCULAR DRIVE ☐	TYPE STOVE ☐
BATHS TOTAL: DOWN UP		PORCH ☐ SIDE ☐ REAR ☐	SCREENED ☐	BUILT-IN OVEN & RANGE ☐
DEN SIZE	FIREPLACE ☐	FENCED YARD	OUTDOOR GRILL ☐	SEPARATE STOVE INCLUDED ☐
FAMILY ROOM SIZE	FIREPLACE ☐	STORM WINDOWS ☐	STORM DOORS ☐	REFRIGERATOR INCLUDED ☐
RECREATION ROOM SIZE	FIREPLACE ☐	CURBS & GUTTERS ☐	SIDEWALKS ☐	DISHWASHER INCLUDED
BASEMENT SIZE		STORM SEWERS ☐	ALLEY ☐	DISPOSAL INCLUDED ☐
NONE ☐ 1/4 ☐ 1/3 ☐ 1/2 ☐ 3/4 ☐ FULL ☐		WATER SUPPLY		DOUBLE SINK ☐ SINGLE SINK ☐
UTILITY ROOM		SEWER ☐	SEPTIC ☐	STAINLESS STEEL ☐ PORCELAIN ☐
TYPE HOT WATER SYSTEM:		TYPE GAS: NATURAL ☐	BOTTLED ☐	WASHER INCLUDED ☐ DRYER INCLUDED ☐
TYPE HEAT		WHY SELLING		LAND ASSESSMENT $
EST. FUEL COST				IMPROVEMENTS $
ATTIC ☐		PROPERTY DESCRIPTION		TOTAL ASSESSMENTS $
PULL DOWN STAIRWAY ☐ REGULAR STAIRWAY ☐ TRAP DOOR ☐				TAX RATE
NAME OF BUILDER		LOT SIZE		TOTAL ANNUAL TAXES $
SQUARE FOOTAGE		LOT NO. BLOCK SECTION		
EXTERIOR OF HOUSE				

Section 2 *Section 3*

NAME OF SCHOOLS: ELEMENTARY _____ JR. HIGH: _____

HIGH: _____ PAROCHIAL: _____

PUBLIC TRANSPORTATION: _____

NEAREST SHOPPING AREA: _____

REMARKS: _____

Section 4

Date: _____5-1_____

In consideration of the services of _____5-2_____ (herein called "Broker") to be rendered to the undersigned (herein called "Owner"), and of the promise of Broker to make reasonable efforts to obtain a Purchaser therefor, Owner hereby lists with Broker the real estate and all improvements thereon which are described above, (all herein called "the property"), and the Owner hereby grants to Broker the exclusive and irrevocable right to sell such property from 12:00 Noon on _____5-3_____, 19 ____ until 12:00 Midnight on _____5-4_____, 19 ____ (herein called "period of time"), for the price of _____5-5_____ Dollars ($ __5-6__) or for such other price and upon such other terms (including exchange) as Owner may subsequently authorize during the period of time.

It is understood by Owner that the above sum or any other price subsequently authorized by Owner shall include a cash fee of _____5-7_____ per cent of such price or other price which shall be payable by Owner to Broker upon consummation by any Purchaser or Purchasers of a valid contract of sale of the property during the period of time and whether or not Broker was a procuring cause of any such contract of sale.

If the property is sold or exchanged by Owner, or by Broker or by any other person to any Purchaser to whom the property was shown by Broker or any representative of Broker within sixty (60) days after the expiration of the period of time mentioned above, Owner agrees to pay to Broker a cash fee which shall be the same percentage of the purchase price as the percentage mentioned above.

Broker is hereby authorized by Owner to place a "For Sale" sign on the property and to remove all signs of other brokers or salesmen during the period of time, and Owner hereby agrees to make the property available to Broker at all reasonable hours for the purpose of showing it to prospective Purchasers.

Owner agrees to convey the property to the Purchaser by deed with the usual covenants of title and free and clear from all encumbrances, tenancies, liens (for taxes or otherwise), but subject to applicable restrictive covenants of record. Owner acknowledges receipt of copy of this agreement.

Section 5

WITNESS the following signature(s) and seal(s):

Date Signed: _____5-8_____ _____5-12_____ (Owner)

Listing Agent _____5-9_____

Address _____5-10_____ Telephone _____5-11_____ (Owner)

5-3.   Enter the date the contract is to begin (day, month, and year).

5-4.   Enter the date the contract is to expire (day, month, and year).

5-5.   Enter the listing price as you would write it on a check.

5-6.   Enter the numerals representing the listing price.

5-7.   Enter the sales fee or broker's commission as a percent.

5-8.   *Date signed*—Enter the date the parties to the contract signed below.

5-9.   *Listing broker*—Enter the name of brokerage firm followed by the agent's name.

5-10. *Address*—Enter the address as given in Section 1, item 5.

5-11. *Telephone*—Enter the telephone number of the seller.

5-12. *Seller*—Enter the name(s) of the seller(s); this is where sellers sign the contract.

Listing—Offer—Settlement Guidelines

1.   TY = this year.
2.   NY = next year.
3.   DAFC = days after final closing.
4.   All calculations in this text are done using a 30-day month. Therefore:
     10 days = ⅓ month; 15 days = ½ month; 20 days = ⅔ month.
5.   Round off all figures to the nearest cent. For ½ cent or more round up; if less than ½ cent, drop.
6.   Your answer may differ by a few cents due to rounding; check the examples to see how figures are rounded off.
7.   Compute math using both hand calculation and your calculator.

OFFER TO PURCHASE AGREEMENT

This is a document used by the purchaser to convey his or her offer to the seller. Upon acceptance by the seller this document then becomes a contractual arrangement setting forth the final details of the transaction and how it is to be executed. The numbers refer to the sample offer to purchase agreement which follows. (Tear-out forms also appear in the back of the book.)

Section 1

This section describes the date the offer is made along with the various parties involved in the offer, including the purchaser, seller, and broker.

1.   Enter the date the offer is taken.
2.   Enter the name(s) of the purchaser(s).
3.   Enter the name(s) of the seller(s).
4.   Enter the brokerage firm name.

Section 2

This section describes the real estate being sold based on the legal description and street addresses.

5.   Enter the county and state.
6.   Enter the legal description.
7.   Enter the number, street, city, and state.

Section 3

This section describes the purchase price and how it is to be paid by the offeror.

8.   Enter the purchase price written as you would write a check. In the parentheses enter the purchase price in numerical form.
9.   Enter the manner in which the purchase price is to be paid; for example, new mortgage at 8¾% for 25 years to be repaid in 300 equal installments of principal and interest for 80% of the purchase price, and the balance in cash.
10. Enter the amount of the earnest money deposit received as you would write a check and in the parentheses enter the numerical amount. *Note:* The earnest money deposit will be a part of the down payment when doing the calculations for the settlement.

Section 4

Paragraph 3 in this section tells how the property is to be conveyed, when possession is to take place, and who is to pay for the deed preparation.

11. Enter the location at which the settlement will take place.
12. Enter the date the settlement is proposed to take place.

Paragraph 5 arranges for the proration of all taxes, interest, and impounded escrow deposits as of the date of settlement.

Paragraph 6 places the risk on the seller for any loss or damage which might occur to the property prior to settlement.

REAL ESTATE SALES CONTRACT (OFFER TO PURCHASE AGREEMENT)

This AGREEMENT made as of _____ 1 _____ , 19_____ ,

among _____ 2 _____ (herein called "Purchaser"),

and _____ 3 _____ (herein called "Seller"),

and _____ 4 _____ (herein called "Broker"),

provides that Purchaser agrees to buy through Broker as agent for Seller, and Seller agrees to sell the following described real estate, and all improvements

thereon, located in the jurisdiction of _____ 5 _____ ,

(all herein called "the property"): _____ 6 _____

_____ , and more commonly known as_____ 7 _____

_____ (street address).

1. The purchase price of the property is _____ 8

Dollars ($ _____ 8 _____), and such purchase price shall be paid as follows:

_____ 9 _____

2. Purchaser has made a deposit of _____ 10 _____ Dollars ($ _____ 10 _____)
with Broker, receipt of which is hereby acknowledged, and such deposit shall be held by Broker in escrow until the date of settlement and then applied
to the purchase price, or returned to Purchaser if the title to the property is not marketable.

3. Seller agrees to convey the property to Purchaser by Deed with the usual covenants of title and free and clear from all monetary encumbrances,
tenancies, liens (for taxes or otherwise), except as may be otherwise provided above, but subject to applicable restrictive covenants of record. Seller further
agrees to deliver possession of the property to Purchaser on the date of settlement and to pay the expense of preparing the deed of conveyance.

4. Settlement shall be made at _____ 11 _____ on or before

_____ 12 _____ , 19_____ , or as soon thereafter as title can be examined and necessary documents prepared, with
allowance of a reasonable time for Seller to correct any defects reported by the title examiner.

5. All taxes, interest, rent, and impound escrow deposits, if any, shall be prorated as of the date of settlement.

6. All risk of loss or damage to the property by fire, windstorm, casualty, or other cause is assumed by Seller until the date of settlement.

7. Purchaser and Seller agree that Broker was the sole procuring cause of this Contract of Purchase, and Seller agrees to pay Broker for services

rendered a cash fee of _____ 13 _____ per cent of the purchase price. If either Purchaser or Seller defaults under such Contract, such defaulting party shall
be liable for the cash fee of Broker and any expenses incurred by the non-defaulting party in connection with this transaction.

Subject to: _____

_____ 14 _____

_____

8. Purchaser represents that an inspection satisfactory to Purchaser has been made of the property, and Purchaser agrees to accept the property
in its present condition except as may be otherwise provided in the description of the property above.

9. This Contract of Purchase constitutes the entire agreement among the parties and may not be modified or changed except by written instrument executed by all of the parties, including Broker.

10. This Contract of Purchase shall be construed, interpreted, and applied according to the law of the jurisdiction of _____ 15 _____ and shall
be binding upon and shall inure to the benefit of the heirs, personal representatives, successors, and assigns of the parties.

All parties to this agreement acknowledge receipt of a certified copy.

WITNESS the following signatures:

_____ 16 _____   _____ 18 _____
             Seller   Purchaser

_____ 16 _____   _____ 18 _____
             Seller   Purchaser

_____ 17 _____
             Broker

Deposit Rec'd $ _____ 19 _____

Personal Check   20   Cash

Cashier's Check   Company Check

Sales Agent: 21

13. Enter the brokerage or sales fee as a number; for example, 6%.
14. Enter any other conditions or remarks pertinent to the sale or on which it may be contingent (inclusion of personal property, separate bill of sale, restatement of financing, possession, etc.).

Section 5

15. Enter the name of your state.
16. Enter the signature(s) of the seller(s).
17. Enter the signature of the broker.
18. Enter the signature(s) of the purchaser(s).
19. Enter the dollar amount of earnest money deposit received.
20. Circle the manner in which the earnest money was conveyed.
21. Enter the signature of the sales agent, broker, or salesperson.

SETTLEMENT (CLOSING) GUIDE

The following guide to the settlement proceedings in a real estate transaction is not a total listing of all items one might encounter. It is designed to cover the general items found in a settlement. The various debits and credits may vary in each individual transaction, since many of the items are negotiable between the seller and purchaser. In solving the problems following this material, one should read the narratives carefully or follow the completed forms in order to determine the actual placement of an individual item. (See forms which follow; additional tear-out forms appear at the back of the book.)

Some simple bookkeeping practices must be followed to complete the settlement statement properly. They are:

1. The term "debit" is defined as something owed. This pertains to both the buyer's and seller's settlement statements.
2. The term "credit" is something that is receivable to both the buyer and the seller.
3. Since a double-entry accounting system is employed, the sum of the buyer's debits must equal the sum of the credits, and likewise with the seller. Do not try to balance the two statements, since they must be treated individually even though they appear on the same form for purposes of the Uniform Test.

The order in which the items appear on the settlement is a matter of choice.

Purchase price—The amount to be paid by the purchaser at settlement for the property is entered as a debit to the buyer. Since it is received by the seller, it is entered as a credit on his or her statement.

Deposit—The earnest money amount paid by the purchaser which is to be used as part of the purchase price should be entered as a credit to the buyer. No entry to the seller.

Sales commission (broker's fee)—The fee charged by the broker for the sale of the property is an expense to the seller and should be debited. No entry to the buyer unless the buyer has agreed to pay the broker a fee to find a property.

New first mortgage (trust)—If the buyer is obtaining a new loan to purchase the property, enter this amount as a credit since it is the means by which he or she is to pay the sales price.

Assumed mortgage (trust)—If the loan of the seller is being assumed by the buyer, enter this amount as a credit to the buyer and a debit to the seller. The amount is being used by the buyer to pay for the property to reduce the amount owed. The seller will use this amount to reduce the cash he or she will receive. In effect, the assumption is a credit for the buyer from the seller against the purchase price.

Pay existing mortgage—The seller pays off the existing loan. This amount is debited to the seller, and the property may be transferred free and clear.

Second mortgage (trust)—If a second loan is required to meet the purchase price by the buyer, enter the amount as a credit. No entry to the seller.

Purchase money mortgage (second trust)—If the seller takes a purchase money mortgage for part of the sales price, enter the amount as a credit to the buyer against the sales price and a debit to the seller against his or her cash receivable.

Land contract—If the seller sells the property under a land contract, enter the amount of the contract as a credit to the purchaser against the sales price and a debit to the seller against the cash to be received.

Taxes in arrears, prorated—If the taxes are not yet due and payable, prorate the annual amount of taxes including the day of settlement. Credit the purchaser and debit the seller.

Taxes in advance, prorated—If the taxes have been paid in advance, prorate the amount including the day of settlement and subtract it from the prepaid amount. The remainder should be debited to the buyer and credited to the seller.

Delinquent taxes—If the taxes are delinquent, this amount should be charged to the seller. No entry to the buyer.

Fire insurance, canceled—Credit the remaining premium balance to the seller.

Fire insurance, new policy—Enter the cost of the new policy as a debit to the purchaser.

Fire insurance, assigned policy—If the seller assigns the existing policy to the purchaser, prorate the premium and enter the remaining amount as a debit to the purchaser and a credit to the seller.

Interest in arrears—If the loan is assumed or paid by the seller and interest is calculated in arrears, prorate to the date of closing the monthly interest and enter it as a debit to the seller. If the loan is assumed, enter the prorated amount as a credit to the buyer.

Interest in advance—If the interest on a loan is computed in advance and the loan is assumed or paid off by the seller, then enter as a credit. If the purchaser is assuming, then enter the prorated amount as a debit.

Interest on new loan—Interest may be charged on a newly originated loan. Enter the amount as a debit to the purchaser.

Rent in advance—Enter the prorated amount as a credit to the purchaser and a debit to the seller.

Rent in arrears—If rent is collected in arrears, enter the prorated amount as a debit to the purchaser and a credit to the seller.

Title insurance, owner's policy—Enter as a debit to the seller.

Title insurance, mortgagee's policy—Enter as a debit to the purchaser.

Deed preparation—Enter as a debit to the seller.

Abstract continuation—Enter as a debit to the seller.

Opinion or examination of the abstract—Enter as a debit to the purchaser.

Appraisal fee—A negotiable item. It may be charged to the seller if requested by the purchaser, or charged to the purchaser if requested by the lending institution.

Attorney fees, purchaser—Debit the purchaser for any additional legal fees charged to him or her.

Attorney fees, seller—Debit the seller for any additional legal fees charged to him or her.

Loan origination fee—Debit the purchaser for the cost of originating the new loan. In the case of an assumption, a loan assumption fee may be charged.

FHA discount points—By law are debited to the seller.

VA discount points—By law are debited to the seller.

Conventional discount points—Negotiable if charged.

Recording, deed—Debit to the purchaser.

Recording, mortgage—Debit to the purchaser.

Escrow balance, assumed—Debit to the purchaser and credit to the seller for the account balance.

Escrow payoff, existing loan—Credit to the seller as an offsetting item to the loan balance.

Survey—May be negotiable but generally charged as a debit to the purchaser.

Prepayment penalty—Debit to the seller for prepaying loan balance.

Conveyance tax—Debit to the seller.

Special assessments—Negotiable.

Settlement fees—Negotiable.

Credit report—Debit to the purchaser.

Photo fee—Debit to the purchaser.

Sale of chattels—If bought by purchaser, debit to the purchaser and credit to the seller. Such items are sold under a separate bill of sale given by the vendor (seller) to the vendee (buyer).

Balance due from the purchaser—The amount owed by the purchaser at settlement after subtracting the credits from his or her debits. Enter as a credit, since it is needed to balance the double-entry system.

Balance due seller—The amount received by the seller at settlement after subtracting the debits from the credits. Enter as a debit if the credits exceed the debits as a balancing item. Enter as a credit if the debits exceed the credits.

SUGGESTED ENTRIES

They will not hold true in every transaction. Entries should be determined by information supplied in the narrative.

SETTLEMENT STATEMENT WORKSHEET

Complete the Settlement Statement Worksheet on the basis of information furnished in the Listing, Offer to Purchase Agreement, and Settlement Problems only. Do not add other items. Use the 30-day method of computation.

	BUYER'S STATEMENT		SELLER'S STATEMENT	
	DEBIT	CREDIT	DEBIT	CREDIT
Purchase Price or Sales Price	XX			XX
Deposit		XX		
Sales Commission (Broker's Fee)			XX	
Financing:				
New 1st Mortgage (Trust)		XX		
Assumed Mortgage (Trust)		XX	XX	
Pay Existing Mortgage (Trust)			XX	
2nd Mortgage (Trust)		XX		
2nd Purchase Money Mortgage		XX	XX	
Land Contract		XX	XX	
Taxes in Arrears – Prorated		XX	XX	
Taxes in Advance – Prorated	XX			XX
Delinquent Taxes			XX	
Fire Insurance – Cancelled				XX
Fire Insurance – New Policy	XX			
Fire Insurance – Assigned Policy	XX			XX
Interest in Arrears		XX	XX	
Interest in Advance	XX			XX
Interest on New Loan	XX			
Rent in Advance		XX	XX	

SETTLEMENT STATEMENT WORKSHEET

Complete the Settlement Statement Worksheet on the basis of information furnished in the Listing, Offer to Purchase Agreement, and Settlement Problems only. Do not add other items. Use the 30-day method of computation.

	BUYER'S STATEMENT		SELLER'S STATEMENT	
	DEBIT	CREDIT	DEBIT	CREDIT
Rent in Arrears	XX			XX
Title Insurance — Owner's			XX	
Title Insurance — Mortgagee's	XX			
Deed Preparation			XX	
Abstract Continuation			XX	
Opinion of Abstract (Examination)	XX			
Appraisal Fee	Negotiable			
Attorney's Fee — Purchaser	XX			
Attorney's Fee — Seller			XX	
Loan Origination Fee	XX			
Loan Discount — Points				
FHA			XX	
VA			XX	
Conventional	Negotiable			
Recording Deed	XX			
Recording Mortgage	XX			
Escrow Balances				
Assumed	XX			
Payoff Existing Loan				XX
Survey	XX			

SETTLEMENT STATEMENT WORKSHEET

Complete the Settlement Statement Worksheet on the basis of information furnished in the Listing, Offer to Purchase Agreement, and Settlement Problems only. Do not add other items. Use the 30-day method of computation.

	BUYER'S STATEMENT		SELLER'S STATEMENT	
	DEBIT	CREDIT	DEBIT	CREDIT
Prepayment Penalty			XX	
Conveyance Tax			XX	
Special Assessments	Negotiable			
Settlement Fee	Negotiable			
Credit Report	XX			
Photo Fee	XX			
Sale of Chattels	XX			XX
Balance Due from Purchaser		XX		
Balance Due Seller			XX	
	XXX	XXX	XXX	XXX

PROBLEM 101

On August 22, this year, you as salesperson for College Real Estate of Anytown, Your State, listed the property owned by Mr. Jack Nickless and his wife, Margaret, at 2785 Nulsen Drive in Anytown. At the time you obtained a 90-day exclusive authorization to sell listing. The house is a frame Cape Cod with three bedrooms downstairs, two full baths, a full basement, and all built-in appliances in the kitchen, except an automatic dishwasher. The recreation room is 14' X 18' with a fireplace. The home was originally constructed in 1955. It has hardwood floors, with carpeting in the 18' X 22' living room, dining room, and all bedrooms. The house has city water and sewers, electricity, and is heated by natural gas. It also has aluminum storm doors and windows and a two-car attached garage. The lot is 120' X 140' on the west side of the street and has a legal description of Lot 18 in the McCary Addition to the City of Anytown, County of Madison, Your State, as recorded in Plat Book 5, page 26.

The Nicklesses have an outstanding mortgage balance as of August 1 of $10,586. The payments are $125 per month, including principal and interest only, and are due the first of each month. The interest rate is 7% paid in advance. The loan is assumable, and the mortgagee is the Anytown Savings and Loan Company. There is a fire and extended-coverage insurance policy that expires April 30, next year, and has been paid in advance at $80 per year. The coverage is for $24,000. The taxes are $8.50/$100, with the property having an assessed value for the land of $1,500 and the improvements of $6,500. The taxes are payable by December 31, this year, and have not yet been paid. The Nicklesses feel they can give possession on or before 10 days after the final closing.

The terms are set at a listing price of $28,500 payable in cash, or cash plus the assumption of the existing mortgage. They will not accept an exchange. They also desire to have the house shown only by appointment between 10 a.m. and 7 p.m., Monday through Saturday. They can be reached for an appointment at 821-5168, and the key will be available at the College Real Estate office. The Nicklesses also agree to the 6% brokerage fee.

The Offer

On September 3, this year, Mr. Charles Vance and his wife, Wilma, are shown the Nickless house. Both Mr. and Mrs. Vance like the house and make an offer of $28,000 that same day. They ask in the offer that the washer and dryer be included in the sales price. The offer is to run until midnight of the next day if it is not accepted prior. The offer is contingent upon the Vances' being able to obtain new financing in the amount of 80% of the purchase price for 25 years at a rate not to exceed 8%. They also tender $1,000 earnest money by check to you and ask that, if accepted, the closing take place at the College Real Estate offices. You immediately submit the offer to the Nicklesses, and they accept the following afternoon.

Settlement

With the terms of the contract being met, closing was set for September 30, this year, at the College Real Estate offices. In addition to the purchase price, deposit, new mortgage and insurance proration, and brokerage fee, the following will be charged at the closing:

Title examination, ½% of the sale price, will be charged to the purchaser. The recording fee for the new mortgage, $25.00, will be charged to the purchaser. The appraisal fee, $40.00, will be charged to the sellers. The mortgagee's title insurance, $75.00, will be charged to the purchaser. The recording fee, $7.50, and the deed preparation fee, $50.00, will be charged to the sellers. The loan origination fee, 1% of the amount financed, will be charged to the purchaser, and the survey fee, $50.00, will be charged to the sellers.

In later problems, you will be asked to use the information provided in the problem narratives to complete the exclusive authorization to sell (listing), the offer to purchase agreement, and the settlement statement. For this problem, however, the forms have been completed as a model for your study.

Nickless

REAL ESTATE LISTING CONTRACT (EXCLUSIVE RIGHT TO SELL)

SALES PRICE $28,500.00   TYPE HOME Cape Cod   TOTAL BEDROOMS 3   TOTAL BATHS 2

ADDRESS 2785 Nulsen Dr., Anytown   JURISDICTION OF Madison County, Your State

AMT. OF LOAN TO BE ASSUMED $ 10,586.00   AS OF WHAT DATE Aug. 1, TY   TAXES & INS. INCLUDED NO   YEARS TO GO ___   AMOUNT PAYABLE MONTHLY $ 125 @ 7 %   TYPE LOAN Conv.

MORTGAGE COMPANY Anytown Savings and Loan Company   2nd TRUST $ N/A

ESTIMATED EXPECTED RENT MONTHLY $ ___   TYPE OF APPRAISAL REQUESTED ___

OWNER'S NAME Jack Nickless and Margaret Nickless (H & W)   PHONES (HOME) 821-5168   (BUSINESS) ___

TENANT'S NAME N/A   PHONES (HOME) ___   (BUSINESS) ___

POSSESSION On or Before 10 DAFC   DATE LISTED: Aug. 22, TY   EXCLUSIVE FOR 90 days   DATE OF EXPIRATION Nov. 22, TY

LISTING BROKER College Real Estate   PHONE ___   KEY AVAILABLE AT College Real Estate

LISTING SALESMAN You as Salesman   HOME PHONE ___   HOW TO BE SHOWN: By Appointment

ENTRANCE FOYER ☐	CENTER HALL ☐	AGE 22	AIR CONDITIONING ☐	TYPE KITCHEN CABINETS
LIVING ROOM SIZE 18 x 22	FIREPLACE ☐	ROOFING	TOOL HOUSE ☐	TYPE COUNTER TOPS
DINING ROOM SIZE		GARAGE SIZE 2-car attached	PATIO ☐	EAT-IN SIZE KITCHEN ☐
BEDROOM TOTAL: 3 DOWN 3 UP		SIDE DRIVE ☐	CIRCULAR DRIVE ☐	BREAKFAST ROOM ☐
BATHS TOTAL: 2 DOWN 2 UP		PORCH ☐ SIDE ☐ REAR ☐	SCREENED ☐	BUILT-IN OVEN & RANGE ☑
DEN SIZE	FIREPLACE ☐	FENCED YARD	OUTDOOR GRILL ☐	SEPARATE STOVE INCLUDED ☐
FAMILY ROOM SIZE	FIREPLACE ☐	STORM WINDOWS ☑	STORM DOORS ☑	REFRIGERATOR INCLUDED ☑
RECREATION ROOM SIZE 14 x 18	FIREPLACE ☑	CURBS & GUTTERS ☐	SIDEWALKS ☐	DISHWASHER INCLUDED no
BASEMENT SIZE Full		STORM SEWERS ☑	ALLEY ☐	DISPOSAL INCLUDED ☑
NONE ☐ 1/4 ☐ 1/3 ☐ 1/2 ☐ 3/4 ☐ FULL ☑		WATER SUPPLY City		DOUBLE SINK ☐ SINGLE SINK ☐
UTILITY ROOM SIZE		SEWER ☑	SEPTIC ☐	STAINLESS STEEL ☐ PORCELAIN ☐
TYPE HOT WATER SYSTEM:		TYPE GAS: NATURAL ☑	BOTTLED ☐	WASHER INCLUDED ☐ DRYER INCLUDED ☐
TYPE HEAT Gas		WHY SELLING		LAND ASSESSMENT $ 1500.00
EST. FUEL COST				IMPROVEMENTS $ 6500.00
ATTIC ☐		PROPERTY DESCRIPTION		TOTAL ASSESSMENT $ 8000.00
PULL DOWN STAIRWAY ☐	REGULAR STAIRWAY ☐ TRAP DOOR ☐			
MAIDS ROOM ☐	TYPE BATH			TAX RATE $8.50/100
LOCATION				TOTAL ANNUAL TAXES $ 680.00
NAME OF BUILDER		LOT SIZE 120 x 140		
SQUARE FOOTAGE		LOT NO. 18		

EXTERIOR OF HOUSE Frame McCary Addition to the city of Anytown in the County of Madison, Your State/Plat Book 5, pg. 26

NAME OF SCHOOLS: ELEMENTARY: ___   JR. HIGH: ___

HIGH: ___   PAROCHIAL: ___

PUBLIC TRANSPORTATION: ___

NEAREST SHOPPING AREA: ___

REMARKS: The property may be shown by appointment only between 10:00 a.m. and 7:00 p.m. Monday through Saturday. The key is available at the College Real Estate Office.

Date: August 22, this year

In consideration of the services of College Real Estate (herein called "Broker") to be rendered to the undersigned (herein called "Owner"), and of the promise of Broker to make reasonable efforts to obtain a Purchaser therefor, Owner hereby lists with Broker the real estate and all improvements thereon which are described above, (all herein called "the property"), and the Owner hereby grants to Broker the exclusive and irrevocable right to sell such property from 12:00 Noon on August 22 , 19 TY until 12:00 Midnight on November 22 , 19 TY (herein called "period of time"), for the price of twenty-eight thousand five hundred Dollars ($ 28,500.00) or for such other price and upon such other terms (including exchange) as Owner may subsequently authorize during the period of time.

It is understood by Owner that the above sum or any other price subsequently authorized by Owner shall include a cash fee of 6 per cent of such price or other price which shall be payable by Owner to Broker upon consummation by any Purchaser or Purchasers of a valid contract of sale of the property during the period of time and whether or not Broker was a procuring cause of any such contract of sale.

If the property is sold or exchanged by Owner, or by Broker or by any other person to any Purchaser to whom the property was shown by Broker or any representative of Broker within sixty (60) days after the expiration of the period of time mentioned above, Owner agrees to pay to Broker a cash fee which shall be the same percentage of the purchase price as the percentage mentioned above.

Broker is hereby authorized by Owner to place a "For Sale" sign on the property and to remove all signs of other brokers or salesmen during the period of time, and Owner hereby agrees to make the property available to Broker at all reasonable hours for the purpose of showing it to prospective Purchasers.

Owner agrees to convey the property to the Purchaser by warranty deed with the usual covenants of title and free and clear from all encumbrances, tenancies, liens (for taxes or otherwise), but subject to applicable restrictive covenants of record. Owner acknowledges receipt of copy of this agreement.

WITNESS the following signature(s) and seal(s):

Date Signed: August 22, this year

Listing Agent You as sales person for College Real Estate

Address 2785 Nulsen Drive   Telephone 821-5168

Jack Nickless (Owner)

Margaret Nickless (Owner)

REAL ESTATE SALES CONTRACT (OFFER TO PURCHASE AGREEMENT)

This AGREEMENT made as of _____ September 3 _____, 19 TY,

among _____ Charles Vance and Wilma Vance (H & W) _____ (herein called "Purchaser"),

and _____ Jack Nickless and Margaret Nickless (H & W) _____ (herein called "Seller"),

and _____ College Real Estate _____ (herein called "Broker"),

provides that Purchaser agrees to buy through Broker as agent for Seller, and Seller agrees to sell the following described real estate, and all improvements thereon, located in the jurisdiction of _____ Madison County, Your State _____,

(all herein called "the property"): _____ Lot 18 McCary Addition to the City of Anytown, County of Madison, Your State as recorded in Plat Book 5, page 26 _____, and more commonly known as 2785 Nulsen Dr., Anytown, Your State _____ (street address).

1. The purchase price of the property is _____ twenty-eight thousand dollars _____ Dollars ($ 28,000.00), and such purchase price shall be paid as follows: 80% of purchase price from new mortgage for 25 years at no more than 8% interest; the remainder in cash at the time of closing.

2. Purchaser has made a deposit of _____ one thousand and no/100———(by check)——— Dollars ($ 1000.00) with Broker, receipt of which is hereby acknowledged, and such deposit shall be held by Broker in escrow until the date of settlement and then applied to the purchase price, or returned to Purchaser if the title to the property is not marketable.

3. Seller agrees to convey the property to Purchaser by Deed with the usual covenants of title and free and clear from all monetary encumbrances, tenancies, liens (for taxes or otherwise), except as may be otherwise provided above, but subject to applicable restrictive covenants of record. Seller further agrees to deliver possession of the property to Purchaser on the date of settlement and to pay the expense of preparing the deed of conveyance.

4. Settlement shall be made at _____ the offices of College Real Estate _____ on or before _____ September 30 _____, 19 TY, or as soon thereafter as title can be examined and necessary documents prepared, with allowance of a reasonable time for Seller to correct any defects reported by the title examiner.

5. All taxes, interest, rent, and impound escrow deposits, if any, shall be prorated as of the date of settlement.

6. All risk of loss or damage to the property by fire, windstorm, casualty, or other cause is assumed by Seller until the date of settlement.

7. Purchaser and Seller agree that Broker was the sole procuring cause of this Contract of Purchase, and Seller agrees to pay Broker for services rendered a cash fee of _____ 6 _____ per cent of the purchase price. If either Purchaser or Seller defaults under such Contract, such defaulting party shall be liable for the cash fee of Broker and any expenses incurred by the non-defaulting party in connection with this transaction.

Subject to: _____ the washer and dryer being included in the sales price _____

8. Purchaser represents that an inspection satisfactory to Purchaser has been made of the property, and Purchaser agrees to accept the property in its present condition except as may be otherwise provided in the description of the property above.

9. This Contract of Purchase constitutes the entire agreement among the parties and may not be modified or changed except by written instrument executed by all of the parties, including Broker.

10. This Contract of Purchase shall be construed, interpreted, and applied according to the law of the jurisdiction of _____ Your State _____ and shall be binding upon and shall inure to the benefit of the heirs, personal representatives, successors, and assigns of the parties.

All parties to this agreement acknowledge receipt of a certified copy.

WITNESS the following signatures and seals:

Jack Nickless (SEAL) Seller

Margaret Nickless (SEAL) Seller

College Real Estate (SEAL) Broker

Charles Vance (SEAL) Purchaser

Wilma Vance (SEAL) Purchaser

Deposit Rec'd $ 1000.00

(Personal Check)   Cash

Cashier's Check   Company Check

Sales Agent: You as salesperson for College Real Estate

PROBLEM 101

SETTLEMENT STATEMENT WORKSHEET

Complete the Settlement Statement Worksheet on the basis of information furnished in the Listing, Offer to Purchase Agreement, and Settlement Problems only. Do not add other items. Use the 30-day method of computation.

	BUYER'S STATEMENT		SELLER'S STATEMENT	
	DEBIT	CREDIT	DEBIT	CREDIT
Sales Price	28,000.00			28,000.00
Brokerage Fee			1,680.00	
New Mortgage		22,400.00		
Nickless Mortgage			10,522.75	
Deposit		1,000.00		
Taxes		510.03	510.03	
Insurance	46.69			46.69
Title Examination	140.00			
Recording New Mortgage	25.00			
Appraisal Fee			40.00	
Mortgage Title Insurance	75.00			
Deed Recording Fee			7.50	
Deed Preparation			50.00	
Loan Origination Fee	224.00			
Survey Fee			50.00	
Balance Due from Buyer		4,600.66		
Balance Due Seller			15,186.41	
	$28,510.69	$28,510.69	$28,046.69	$28,046.69

SUGGESTED READINGS

(See the appropriate chapter in the following books.)

Brown, Robert Kevin. *Essentials of Real Estate.* Englewood Cliffs, N.J.: Prentice-Hall, Inc., 1970.

Lusk, Harold F. and William B. French. *Law of the Real Estate Business,* 3rd ed. Homewood, Ill.: Richard D. Irwin, Inc., 1975.

O'Donnell, Paul T. and Eugene L. Maleady. *Principles of Real Estate.* Philadelphia, Pa.: W. B. Saunders Company, 1975.

Semenow, Robert W. *Selected Cases in Real Estate.* Englewood Cliffs, N.J.: Prentice-Hall, Inc., 1973.

Shenkel, William M. *The Real Estate Professional.* Homewood, Ill.: Dow Jones-Irwin, Inc., 1976.

Ring, Alfred A. and Jerome Dasso. *Real Estate Principles and Practices,* 8th ed. Englewood Cliffs, N.J.: Prentice-Hall, Inc., 1977.

Weimer, Arthur M., Homer Hoyt, and George F. Bloom. *Real Estate,* 7th ed. New York: The Ronald Press Company, 1978.

Calculations

1. *Brokerage fee:*

   $28,000 \times .06 = \$1,680$

2. *New mortgage:*

   $28,000 \times .80 = \$22,400$

3. *Nickless mortgage:*

   $10,586 \times .07 = \$741.02$

   $741.02/12 = \$61.75$

   $125.00 - \$61.75 = \$63.25$

   $10,586.00 - \$63.25 = \$10,522.75$

4. *Taxes:*

   $1,500.00 + \$6,500.00 = \$8,000.00$

   $8,000.00 \times \$8.50/\$100 = \$680.00$

   $680/12 = \$56.67$

   56.67×9 months $= \$510.03$ to purchaser

5. *Title examination:*

   $.005 \times \$28,000 = \$140$

6. *Loan origination fee:*

   $.01 \times \$22,400 = \$224$

7. *Insurance:*

   $80.00/12 = \$6.67/\text{month}$

	Day	Month	Year
Expiration date	30	4	NY
Closing date	30	9	TY
Remaining	0	7	0

   6.67×7 months prepaid $= \$46.69$ to seller

Part III

Testing Your Understanding of Real Estate Concepts

Chapter 17

Final Preparation for Uniform Licensing Examination

AT this point you have completed your studies in preparing for the RELE and should be making final preparations for the licensing examination. This chapter is designed to give the student hints in preparing to take the Uniform Test. Since most students are not in the habit of taking examinations as part of their daily routine, these guidelines should be of help in preparation for the test. The student should be aware of the type of examination he or she is about to take and what the breakdowns are as to emphasis on the subject matter to be tested.

You should note that this is a multiple-choice test with 130 questions. The first 100 questions deal with the uniform aspects of the real estate business, and the remaining 30 questions will be unique to the individual's own state. Students should check with their licensing agency to determine the subject areas covered on this portion of the examination.

THE EXAMINATIONS

Salesperson's Examination

The salesperson's examination contains 130 questions, and the examinee is permitted up to 4½ hours to complete it. The examination is divided into two separate examinations, the Uniform Test and the State Test.

The Uniform Test

The Uniform Test contains 100 multiple-choice questions in the subject areas described below. Approximately 27 questions deal with arithmetic functions. These questions are found throughout the examination and not in a separate arithmetic section.

1. *Real estate contracts (26 questions).* This section examines the general definition of essential elements of a contract and specific contracts used in real estate transactions, including leases, listing agreements, and options. Candidates are required to interpret a completed listing contract

and a completed sales contract (offer to purchase agreement). They are expected to answer questions dealing with the listing and sales contracts solely on the basis of the completed sample instruments. These questions appear at the beginning of the examination. (Samples of these forms appear in Chapter 16.)

2. *Financing (20 questions).* The questions in this section deal with (a) financing instruments (10 questions) and (b) means of financing (10 questions). The topics covered include sources of financing, the FHA, the VA, truth-in-lending, basic definitions of major types of financing instruments, mortgages and their breakdown (including types, loan fees, placement procedures, terms for a loan, etc.), secondary financing, default, and foreclosure.

3. *Real estate ownership (19 questions).* (a) Deeds (6 questions), including the definitions, necessary elements, recording, and acknowledgment. (b) Interests in real property (8 questions), including estates in land, ownership, public powers over private property, and special interests in land. (c) Condominiums (2 questions), including general information about condominiums, rights, duties, and responsibilities of ownership. (d) Federal Fair Housing Act (3 questions), including general knowledge pertaining to the act, policies, and procedures.

4. *Real estate brokerage (20 questions).* The areas tested include: (a) Law of agency (10 questions), including types, rights, and functions of principal and agent. (b) Property management (2 questions), including general scope of the function of the property manager. (c) Settlement procedures (8 questions), including validity of title, settlement charges, proration, and credit.

5. *Real estate valuation (15 questions).* The areas tested include: (a) Appraisal (6 questions), including general knowledge concerning the def-

inition and approaches to value, and the process and terminology of appraisal. (b) Planning and zoning (3 questions), including public control of land use, public planning and zoning, private subdivision, and land development. (c) Property description (3 questions), including types of property descriptions, reading a plat map, and other terms and concepts. (d) Taxes and assessments (3 questions), including real property taxation, special assessments, liens, etc.

The State Test

This test contains 30 questions and requires a knowledge of the specific rules, regulations, and practices unique to each jurisdiction. The examinee should contact the licensing agency to obtain a listing of the specific areas covered in this section.

The Broker's Examination

The test contains 130 questions, and the examinee is permitted up to 4½ hours to complete it. This examination also is divided into two separate tests, the Uniform Test and the State Test.

The Uniform Test

The Uniform Test contains 100 questions. The areas examined are:

1. *Real estate instruments (30 questions).* In this section the examinee must interpret a listing contract and an offer to purchase, and complete a settlement worksheet using the other two documents. Samples of this document are found in Chapter 16.
2. *Basic elements of real estate values, deeds, and contracts (20 questions).* In this section the examinee is questioned about the approaches to value, the appraisal process, the valuation of partial interests, and knowledge and application of appraisal terminology. Also tested are aspects of deeds and contracts including the elements of a deed, types of deeds, passing title, essentials of a contract, and types and uses of contracts.
3. *Leases, property management, and real estate financing (20 questions).* In this section the examinee is questioned concerning tenancies, leases, landlord-tenant relations, and property management. The financing questions deal with types of mortgages (deeds of trust), the FHA, VA-backed loans, and other governmental agencies and acts concerned with real estate financing.
4. *Legal and governmental aspects of real estate (10 questions).* The examinee is questioned con-

cerning the Federal Fair Housing Act, the Truth-in-Lending Act including Regulation Z, interests in real property, the law of agency, the Statute of Frauds, planning, zoning, assessment, and taxation.

5. *Arithmetic functions (20 questions).* In this section the examinee is questioned about arithmetic problems related to real estate.

The State Test

The examinee should follow the same information presented to the salesperson examinee.

Next, students should concern themselves with how the examinations are to be graded, and the minimum score needed on each section to pass the examination, since this varies from state to state. Also of importance is that each question has a value of 1 point; there are 130 questions.

Preparing for the Examinations

To prepare to take the examination, the student should study the necessary materials throughout the preparation period, building and retaining a little more knowledge about the field of real estate with each study session or lesson. It will prove profitable if during the preparation period the student continually practices the skills needed for the examination. Along with acquiring the new knowledge necessary, the student should review and sharpen old skills.

One area of constant review should be mathematics, since this is an area in which many students feel inadequate. Students should review the principles and formulas and, most of all, practice the skills needed to solve the various types of mathematical questions found on the examination.

The area of vocabulary is also of great importance in this type of examination. Students should review the vocabulary lists provided in this book and practice applying the meanings to real estate situations. This type of preparation is long-term in nature. It is not designed for short-term cramming.

If you have prepared yourself methodically throughout your studies for the examination, you should not be faced with the problem of whether or not it is necessary to cram at the last moment. You should have a good grasp of the body of knowledge concerning real estate and how it applies to the examination. However, if you have not prepared adequately over time, there is not a great deal you can do in a short period of time to prepare for an examination such as this that covers such a broad spectrum of skills.

Question Structures

The examinee should be aware that even though the examinations consist of only multiple-choice questions, there are two different forms of the multiple-choice questions which are used. The first form is referred to as the incomplete statement. This is the most familiar format, and is shown in the following example:

Example:

The title to real estate is

(A) assigned
(B) transferred
(C) inherited
(D) all of the above

The answer to this example is (D). By definition a title can be assigned (A), transferred (B), and conveyed (C); therefore, all of the above (D). The student should take caution to read the question and each alternative.

The second form of question used contains two statements or possibilities.

Example:

Essential elements of a valid mortgage include which of the following?

I. the property must be adequately described
II. the mortgagor must have capacity

(A) I only
(B) II only
(C) both I and II
(D) neither I nor II

The examinee must read the statement and both possibilities. Then the examinee must determine whether the first statement or possibility is correct or incorrect and then whether the second statement or possibility is correct or incorrect. The examinee then should look at the four alternatives and decide which one applies. If the examinee believes that *only* statement I is correct then alternative (A) should always be selected. If the examinee believes that *only* statement II is correct then alternative (B) must be selected. If the examinee believes that both statements are true then alternative (C) must be selected. If the examinee believes that neither statement I nor II is correct then alternative (D) must be selected. Since both elements are essential to a valid mortgage, (C) is the correct alternative to be selected.

Guidelines to Better Test Taking

1. Read the question thoroughly and completely and then read all possible choices before choosing the one best answer.

   In a multiple-choice examination such as the RELE, distractors may be of two types. In a problem such as a math question, there may be information that is unnecessary to obtain the solution. In a question based on vocabulary, more than one answer may appear to be correct, but only one is actually the *best* answer. If you are not properly prepared or do not read the entire question, then these types of questions will appear to be tricky or unfair. However, if you know the material, you should not be fooled by these various distractors.

2. Beware of negatives, both in the use of negative prefixes on words or the placement of the word "not." Know the vocabulary so you will not be fooled by the various prefixes and their use.

3. Eliminate the wrong answers from the possible selections. Certain choices will be recognizable immediately as being wrong. This will help you narrow down your possible choices. You can usually eliminate two or even three answers at once if you have read the question carefully and have an understanding of the material pertaining to it. In other questions there may be two answers that are possibly true, but one will be slightly better than the other. At this point your knowledge and reasoning power will help you decide.

4. If you are not sure of an answer, guess at what you feel the correct response should be. On the RELE you are not penalized for guessing; if it is a wrong guess, it will not lower your score any more than if it were left blank.

5. Do not let questions bog you down. If a question takes more than a minute or so, go on to the next question and come back later if you have time. Budget your time proportionately among the questions and sections on the test. Do the questions that are easy for you and get them out of the way quickly; then return to the more difficult questions.

6. When you are unsure of an answer, put a question mark next to the question in the test booklet and return to it when you are reviewing the questions at the end of the examination to see if that is still the response you desire. Some other question may have given you the clue to what the correct response is.

Solving Math Problems

1. Read the problem carefully and decide what is being asked.

2. Reread the problem for the pertinent information given.

3. Decide what principle or principles of math need to be applied to the problem.

4. See how to apply the required principles.

5. Carefully apply each principle and reach a solution.

6. Check your work for errors in both computation and methodology.

7. If you use a calculator, note on the blank pages of the test booklet or in the margins the various calculations made. This will facilitate review and allow you to see where errors are made and which other calculations are affected by such errors.

In summary, you will do your best on the examination if you have adequately prepared prior to the examination, read the questions carefully, think before you answer, and allow time to check your work.

SUGGESTED READING

Bulletin of Information for Applicants, Real Estate Licensing Examinations. Princeton, N.J.: Educational Testing Service, 1977.

Chapter 18

Sample Licensing Examination for Salespersons

Due to security restrictions maintained by ETS, the sample salesperson's examination provided in this chapter is not a licensing examination that has actually been used in any state. It is, however, the same as the salesperson's RELE in format and in the subject areas covered. It focuses on the major areas included in any state's licensing examination for salespersons.

When you enter the examination center for the salesperson's RELE, you will be given an examination booklet and an answer sheet. The examination booklet will include a completed listing contract and a completed sales contract (offer to purchase agreement). The examination proctor will give detailed directions for filling out the answer booklet which is suitable for computer grading.

DIRECTIONS

1. Read the completed listing contract and the completed sales contract (offer to purchase) thoroughly to become familiar with the contents.
2. Answer questions 1 through 15, using the completed forms as you would on the actual licensing examination.
3. Proceed with the remaining questions.
4. The actual examination is a 4½-hour examination. The practice examination does not include the State Test, so you should allow no more than 3½ hours for its completion.

QUESTION BREAKDOWN

1. Questions 1 through 26 cover real estate contracts; of these questions, 1 through 15 refer to the Uniform Examination completed listing contract and completed sales contract (offer to purchase agreement) included in the examination booklet.

2. Questions 27 through 46 cover aspects of real estate financing.

3. Questions 47 through 65 cover real estate ownership.

4. Questions 66 through 85 cover real estate brokerage.

5. Questions 86 through 100 cover real estate valuation.

REAL ESTATE LISTING CONTRACT (EXCLUSIVE RIGHT TO SELL)

SALES PRICE __$82,000.00__   TYPE HOME __Southern Colonial__   TOTAL BEDROOMS __4__   TOTAL BATHS __3__

ADDRESS __19 Westwood Dr., Anytown__   JURISDICTION OF __County of Monroe, Your State__

AMT. OF LOAN   AS OF   TAXES & INS.   YEARS   AMOUNT PAYABLE   TYPE
TO BE ASSUMED $ __66,086.00__   WHAT DATE __Mar. 1, TY__   INCLUDED __yes__ TO GO ____   MONTHLY $__20.98__ @ _8_ % LOAN __Conv.__

MORTGAGE COMPANY __Midwest Federal Savings & Loan__   2nd MORTGAGE ____

OWNER'S NAME __Steven Hughes, Sally Hughes (Brother & Sister)__   PHONES (HOME) __337-9801__   (BUSINESS) ____

TENANT'S NAME ____   PHONES (HOME) ____   (BUSINESS) ____

POSSESSION __Complete 30 DAFC__   DATE LISTED: __March 2, TY__   EXCLUSIVE FOR __90__ DATE OF EXPIRATION __June 2, TY__

LISTING BROKER __Big Red Realty Co.__   PHONE ____   KEY AVAILABLE AT ____

LISTING SALESMAN __You, as salesperson__   HOME PHONE ____   HOW TO BE SHOWN: __by appt. 10 a.m.–7 p.m. M-S__

ENTRANCE FOYER ☐	CENTER HALL ☐	AGE	AIR CONDITIONING ☐	TYPE KITCHEN CABINETS
LIVING ROOM SIZE 24' x 20'	FIREPLACE ☐	ROOFING	TOOL HOUSE ☐	TYPE COUNTER TOPS
DINING ROOM SIZE 20' x 16'		GARAGE SIZE 2-car attached	PATIO ☐	EAT-IN SIZE KITCHEN ☐
BEDROOM TOTAL: 4 DOWN	UP 4	SIDE DRIVE ☐	CIRCULAR DRIVE ☐	TYPE STOVE ☐
BATHS TOTAL: 3 DOWN 1	UP 2	PORCH ☐ SIDE ☐ REAR ☐	SCREENED ☐	BUILT-IN OVEN & RANGE ☑ electric
DEN SIZE	FIREPLACE ☑	FENCED YARD	OUTDOOR GRILL ☐	SEPARATE STOVE INCLUDED ☐
FAMILY ROOM SIZE	FIREPLACE ☐	STORM WINDOWS ☐	STORM DOORS ☐	REFRIGERATOR INCLUDED ☐
RECREATION ROOM SIZE	FIREPLACE ☐	CURBS & GUTTERS ☑	SIDEWALKS ☐	DISHWASHER INCLUDED ✔
BASEMENT SIZE		STORM SEWERS ☐	ALLEY ☐	DISPOSAL INCLUDED ☑
NONE ☐ 1/4 ☐ 1/3 ☐ 1/2 ☐ 3/4 ☐ FULL ☑		WATER SUPPLY City		DOUBLE SINK ☑ SINGLE SINK ☐
UTILITY ROOM		SEWER ☑ City	SEPTIC ☐	STAINLESS STEEL ☑ PORCELAIN ☐
TYPE HOT WATER SYSTEM: Electric		TYPE GAS: NATURAL ☐	BOTTLED ☐	WASHER INCLUDED ☐ DRYER INCLUDED ☐
TYPE HEAT Electric		WHY SELLING		LAND ASSESSMENT $ 7,500
EST. FUEL COST				IMPROVEMENTS $ 20,000
ATTIC ☐		PROPERTY DESCRIPTION		TOTAL ASSESSMENTS $ 27,500
PULL DOWN STAIRWAY ☐ REGULAR STAIRWAY ☐ TRAP DOOR ☐		Recorded in Plat Book 7, Page 24, Lot No. 83, Weatherly Addition to City of Anytown, County of Monroe, Your State		TAX RATE $8.40/$100
NAME OF BUILDER		LOT SIZE 195' x 225'		TOTAL ANNUAL TAXES $2,310.00
SQUARE FOOTAGE		LOT NO. 83 BLOCK	SECTION	
EXTERIOR OF HOUSE				

NAME OF SCHOOLS: ELEMENTARY: ____   JR. HIGH: ____

                     HIGH: ____   PAROCHIAL: ____

PUBLIC TRANSPORTATION: ____

NEAREST SHOPPING AREA: ____

REMARKS: __No FHA or VA; cash or cash and assumption of present mortgage__
              __Owners to keep refrigerator.__

                                                                      Date: __March 2, TY__

In consideration of the services of __Big Red Realty__ (herein called "Broker") to be rendered to the undersigned (herein called 'Owner'), and of the promise of Broker to make reasonable efforts to obtain a Purchaser therefor, Owner hereby lists with Broker the real estate and all improvements thereon which are described above, (all herein called "the property"), and the Owner hereby grants to Broker the exclusive and irrevocable right to sell such property from 12:00 Noon on __March 2__ , 19 __TY__ until 12:00 Midnight on __June 2__ , 19 __TY__ (herein called "period of time"), for the price of __Eighty-two thousand and no/100__ Dollars ($ __82,000.00__) or for such other price and upon such other terms (including exchange) as Owner may subsequently authorize during the period of time.

It is understood by Owner that the above sum or any other price subsequently authorized by Owner shall include a cash fee of __7__ per cent of such price or other price which shall be payable by Owner to Broker upon consummation by any Purchaser or Purchasers of a valid contract of sale of the property during the period of time and whether or not Broker was a procuring cause of any such contract of sale.

If the property is sold or exchanged by Owner, or by Broker or by any other person to any Purchaser to whom the property was shown by Broker or any representative of Broker within sixty (60) days after the expiration of the period of time mentioned above, Owner agrees to pay to Broker a cash fee which shall be the same percentage of the purchase price as the percentage mentioned above.

Broker is hereby authorized by Owner to place a "For Sale" sign on the property and to remove all signs of other brokers or salesmen during the period of time, and Owner hereby agrees to make the property available to Broker at all reasonable hours for the purpose of showing it to prospective Purchasers.

Owner agrees to convey the property to the Purchaser by deed with the usual covenants of title and free and clear from all encumbrances, tenancies, liens (for taxes or otherwise), but subject to applicable restrictive covenants of record. Owner acknowledges receipt of copy of this agreement.

WITNESS the following signature(s) and seal(s):

Date Signed: __March 2, TY__   *Steven Hughes* _____ (Owner)

Listing Agent __Big Red Realty Co., You as Salesperson__

Address __19 Westwood Dr., Anytown__   Telephone __337-9801__   *Sally Hughes* _____ (Owner)

REAL ESTATE SALES CONTRACT (OFFER TO PURCHASE AGREEMENT)

This AGREEMENT made as of _____ March 15 _____ , 19 TY ,

among _____ Calvin Rockwell and Lucy Rockwell (H & W) _____ — (herein called "Purchaser"),

and _____ Steven Hughes and Sally Hughes (Brother & Sister) _____ — (herein called "Seller"),

and _____ Big Red Realty _____ — (herein called "Broker"),

provides that Purchaser agrees to buy through Broker as agent for Seller, and Seller agrees to sell the following described real estate, and all improvements thereon, located in the jurisdiction of County of Monroe, Your State _____ ,

(all herein called "the property"): Lot No. 83, Weatherly Addition to the City of Anytown, County of Monroe, Your State as recorded in Plat Book 7, Page 24. _____ , and more commonly known as 19 Westwood Drive, Anytown, Your State _____ (street address).

1. The purchase price of the property is Eighty Thousand Five Hundred and no/100 _____

Dollars ($ 80,500.00 _____), and such purchase price shall be paid as follows:
Contingent upon a firm commitment for a new loan for 90% of the sales price @ 8¼% for 30 years. The balance to be paid in cash.

2. Purchaser has made a deposit of Two Thousand Five Hundred _____ Dollars ($ 2,500.00 ____) with Broker, receipt of which is hereby acknowledged, and such deposit shall be held by Broker in escrow until the date of settlement and then applied to the purchase price, or returned to Purchaser if the title to the property is not marketable.

3. Seller agrees to convey the property to Purchaser by Deed with the usual covenants of title and free and clear from all monetary encumbrances, tenancies, liens (for taxes or otherwise), except as may be otherwise provided above, but subject to applicable restrictive covenants of record. Seller further agrees to deliver possession of the property to Purchaser on the date of settlement and to pay the expense of preparing the deed of conveyance.

4. Settlement shall be made at _____ on or before
_____ April 20 _____ , 19 TY , or as soon thereafter as title can be examined and necessary documents prepared, with allowance of a reasonable time for Seller to correct any defects reported by the title examiner.

5. All taxes, interest, rent, and impound escrow deposits, if any, shall be prorated as of the date of settlement.

6. All risk of loss or damage to the property by fire, windstorm, casualty, or other cause is assumed by Seller until the date of settlement.

7. Purchaser and Seller agree that Broker was the sole procuring cause of this Contract of Purchase, and Seller agrees to pay Broker for services rendered a cash fee of ____ 7 ____ per cent of the purchase price. If either Purchaser or Seller defaults under such Contract, such defaulting party shall be liable for the cash fee of Broker and any expenses incurred by the non-defaulting party in connection with this transaction.

Subject to: Financing (above para. 1); refrigerator remains with property

8. Purchaser represents that an inspection satisfactory to Purchaser has been made of the property, and Purchaser agrees to accept the property in its present condition except as may be otherwise provided in the description of the property above.

9. This Contract of Purchase constitutes the entire agreement among the parties and may not be modified or changed except by written instrument executed by all of the parties, including Broker.

10. This Contract of Purchase shall be construed, interpreted, and applied according to the law of the jurisdiction of Your State and shall be binding upon and shall inure to the benefit of the heirs, personal representatives, successors, and assigns of the parties.

All parties to this agreement acknowledge receipt of a certified copy.

WITNESS the following signatures and seals:

| *Steven Hughes* | (SEAL) Seller | *Calvin Rockwell* | (SEAL) Purchaser |
| *Sally Hughes* | (SEAL) Seller | *Lucy Rockwell* | (SEAL) Purchaser |

Big Red Realty _____ (SEAL) Broker

Deposit Rec'd $ 2,500.00 _____

Check   (Cashier's)   Cash

Sales Agent: You as salesperson for Big Red Realty

THE SALESPERSON'S EXAMINATION

Choose the one best answer to each question.

1. The exclusive authorization to sell (listing) expires

   (A) March 2, this year
   (B) May 2, this year
   (C) June 2, this year
   (D) July 2, this year

2. The property contains
   I. a 24' X 20' living room with fireplace
   II. two full baths downstairs

   (A) I only
   (B) II only
   (C) both I and II
   (D) neither I nor II

3. If the property sold for the original listed price, how much could the seller expect to receive after deducting only the sales fee?

   (A) $82,000
   (B) $66,260
   (C) $76,260
   (D) none of the above

4. According to the listing contract, possession will be

   (A) complete
   (B) the landlord's
   (C) within 30 days after final closing
   (D) two of the above

5. The lot contains
   I. 43,875 square feet
   II. approximately 1.01 acres

   (A) I only
   (B) II only
   (C) both I and II
   (D) neither I nor II

6. The sellers hold as

   (A) tenants in severalty
   (B) tenants by the entirety
   (C) joint tenants with right of survivorship
   (D) tenants in common

7. The property contains a
   I. full unfinished basement
   II. built-in dishwasher

   (A) I only
   (B) II only
   (C) both I and II
   (D) neither I nor II

8. The annual real property taxes are

   (A) $6,880
   (B) $2,310
   (C) $630
   (D) $1,600

9. The purchasers will take title as

   (A) tenants in severalty
   (B) tenants by the entirety
   (C) joint tenants with right of survivorship
   (D) tenants in common

10. The legal description is by

    (A) government survey
    (B) metes and bounds
    (C) platted subdivision
    (D) none of the above

11. The sales price in the offer is

    (A) $82,000
    (B) $78,500
    (C) $80,500
    (D) none of the above

12. The offer is contingent upon
    I. a new loan for $70,650
    II. the refrigerator remaining

    (A) I only
    (B) II only
    (C) both I and II
    (D) neither I nor II

13. The sales fee is

    (A) $5,740
    (B) $5,795
    (C) $5,635
    (D) none of the above

14. The new loan will be for

    (A) $70,650
    (B) $73,800
    (C) $72,450
    (D) none of the above

15. The offer was accepted

    (A) by the Hughes on March 16, this year
    (B) by the Rockwells on March 18, this year
    (C) by the Hughes on March 18, this year
    (D) none of the above

16. Under an estate for years lease

    (A) there is no specific termination date
    (B) there is no automatic renewal
    (C) both A and B
    (D) neither A nor B

17. An option may be

    (A) oral   (C) both A and B
    (B) assigned   (D) neither A nor B

18. A deed limitation on the use and enjoyment of real property is

    (A) an option   (C) an easement
    (B) a restriction (D) a license

19. A lessee under a typical lease may

    I. mortgage his or her interest in the property
    II. install trade fixtures

    (A) I only   (C) both I and II
    (B) II only   (D) neither I nor II

20. The signing of the deed by the grantor

    (A) automatically passes title to the grantee
    (B) executes the deed
    (C) both A and B
    (D) neither A nor B

21. A profit a pendre is

    (A) less than an estate in land
    (B) inheritable
    (C) assignable
    (D) all of the above

22. If Mr. Martin is forced to sign a contract at gunpoint, he has been subjected to

    (A) undue influence   (C) slander
    (B) libel   (D) duress

23. To be valid, a deed must be

    (A) in writing
    (B) between competent parties
    (C) both A and B
    (D) neither A nor B

24. Ownership of real property may be acquired by

    (A) a will   (C) both A and B
    (B) a deed   (D) neither A nor B

25. To transfer title to personal property, the vendor uses

    (A) a bill of sale
    (B) a deed
    (C) an easement
    (D) none of the above

26. To assign an option is to

    (A) witness the option
    (B) record the option
    (C) formalize the option by putting it in writing
    (D) transfer the rights under the option

27. FHA financing

    I. is administered through HUD
    II. allows the purchaser a second mortgage to meet down payment requirements

    (A) I only   (C) both I and II
    (B) II only   (D) neither I nor II

28. A straight term loan is repaid

    (A) in variable amounts according to the market
    (B) by paying interest only until the final payment
    (C) in equal installments
    (D) none of the above

29. A construction loan is considered

    (A) a junior mortgage
    (B) a permanent form of financing
    (C) a means of financing personal property
    (D) an interim form of financing

30. The amount a lender will loan is generally based on

    (A) the appraised value for loan purposes
    (B) the final sales price
    (C) the listed price
    (D) the appraised value for loan purposes or the sales price, whichever is lower

31. If the loan/value ratio is 85% and the property was appraised for $42,250 and sold for $43,500, how much would the purchaser be allowed to borrow?

    (A) $35,913
    (B) $39,975
    (C) $34,800
    (D) none of the above

32. To be valid, a mortgage must be

    (A) in writing
    (B) between competent parties
    (C) executed by the mortgagor
    (D) all of the above

33. To purchase property with an FHA loan, the purchaser must
    (A) make less than $25,000 per year gross salary
    (B) certify that he or she will occupy the property
    (C) both A and B
    (D) neither A nor B

34. A package mortgage is used to
    (A) buy such personal items as major appliances
    (B) cover construction costs
    (C) both A and B
    (D) neither A nor B

35. MGIC is a private company that
    (A) makes loans
    (B) guarantees loans
    (C) insures loans
    (D) none of the above

36. Regulation Z
    I. controls the mortgage interest rates charged
    II. requires disclosure of the interest charges
    (A) I only   (C) both I and II
    (B) II only   (D) neither I nor II

37. A purchase money mortgage
    I. is given by the buyer to the seller in partial payment of the purchase price
    II. allows the buyer to retain title to the property
    (A) I only   (C) both I and II
    (B) II only   (D) neither I nor II

38. The truth in lending statutes
    (A) limit the number of discount points paid by the seller to 10
    (B) limit the number of discount points paid by the buyer to 1
    (C) both A and B
    (D) neither A nor B

39. A conditional sales contract and a purchase money mortgage are similar in that
    (A) the title is conveyed immediately to the buyer
    (B) a mortgage is required

    (C) the seller assumes no financial risk
    (D) none of the above

40. In making a $15,000 loan, how much would the lender charge the seller at closing if mortgages were being discounted 5 points?
    (A) $450   (C) $500
    (B) $750   (D) $600

41. VA loans are
    (A) guaranteed
    (B) insured
    (C) conventional
    (D) none of the above

42. In considering a borrower's ability to repay a loan, the lender considers
    (A) the amount of the borrower's income
    (B) the stability of the borrower's income
    (C) the debt service of the borrower
    (D) all of the above

43. The advantage(s) to the seller of selling on contract might be
    (A) speed in closing
    (B) quick occupancy
    (C) continued stream of income
    (D) all of the above

44. If the borrower pays the balance of the loan in advance of its due date, he or she may be subject to
    (A) acceleration charges
    (B) prepayment penalties
    (C) loan discounts
    (D) none of the above

45. If the interest rate charged on a loan is in excess of the legal limit, the lender is in violation of the
    (A) truth in lending laws
    (B) Regulation Z requirements
    (C) statute of frauds
    (D) usury laws

46. If the FHA interest rate is fixed at 8¼% and the conventional rate is currently 9½%, how many discount points will be charged at closing to the seller?
    (A) 1¼   (C) 5
    (B) 10   (D) 6

47. The deed which contains the least liability for the grantor is a

    (A) general warranty deed
    (B) special warranty deed
    (C) trustee's deed
    (D) quitclaim deed

48. An easement for a water line is an example of an

    (A) easement appurtenant
    (B) easement in gross
    (C) easement implied
    (D) easement prescribed

49. To protect against an encroachment, the purchaser should obtain

    (A) an appraisal
    (B) an abstract
    (C) title insurance
    (D) a survey

50. A life in estate has a duration of

    (A) any fixed term
    (B) the life of an individual
    (C) no more than 50 years
    (D) none of the above

51. A joint tenancy with the right of survivorship

    I.   conveys an equal interest to the tenants
    II. occurs only if a marriage exists

    (A) I only
    (B) II only
    (C) both I and II
    (D) neither I nor II

52. Which practices may be contrary to the 1968 Federal Fair Housing Law?

    (A) block busting
    (B) racial steering
    (C) sex discrimination
    (D) all of the above

53. Private property taken by the government for public use is acquired under

    (A) escheat
    (B) intestate
    (C) inchoate
    (D) eminent domain

54. Fee simple ownership of land is

    (A) a feudal form of ownership
    (B) a legal life estate
    (C) a leasehold
    (D) none of the above

55. A true easement appurtenant

    (A) is limited by federal statute to 1 year
    (B) runs with the land
    (C) is a personal right of the grantee
    (D) none of the above

56. When a life estate terminates,

    (A) the dower interest of the life tenant's spouse attaches
    (B) fee simple interest vests in the heirs of the life tenant
    (C) the remainderman is entitled to possession
    (D) the property automatically escheats

57. The process used by the government to take private property for public use is

    (A) escheat
    (B) eminent domain
    (C) condemnation
    (D) none of the above

58. If a woman should die intestate and with no heirs with the capacity to inherit her property, the real property will

    (A) be foreclosed and sold at public auction
    (B) be condemned and sold under eminent domain
    (C) escheat to the state
    (D) none of the above

59. If a tree is cut down and later its lumber is used in the construction of a dance floor for a night club,

    I.   it underwent severance
    II. it has become a trade fixture

    (A) I only
    (B) II only
    (C) both I and II
    (D) neither I nor II

60. Under tenancy in common ownership, each owner must

    (A) have an equal interest in the property
    (B) have unity of title
    (C) both A and B
    (D) neither A nor B

61. According to the 1968 Federal Fair Housing Act,

    I.   blockbusting is mandatory in all white neighborhoods

II. racial steering is required to maintain proper balance

(A) I only
(B) II only
(C) both I and II
(D) neither I nor II

62. If a seller should decide to sell only to white Protestants, a salesperson should

(A) take the listing from the seller
(B) place this restriction under "further conditions"
(C) not accept the listing
(D) none of the above

63. The increase in value achieved when two or more pieces of real estate are combined is

(A) escrow
(B) residual
(C) plottage
(D) escheat

64. The 1968 Civil Rights Act, Title VIII, is called

(A) affirmative action
(B) the open housing rule
(C) the Federal Fair Housing Act
(D) none of the above

65. A single property subdivided into several portions with each user owning stock in the corporation that owns the property is

(A) a cooperative
(B) a condominium
(C) an apartment
(D) none of the above

66. Once a contract for the sale of real estate has been signed, the purchaser has

(A) legal title to the real estate
(B) the right to possess the real estate
(C) nothing until he receives an executed deed
(D) equitable title to the property

67. The seller of real estate under a listing contract is the

(A) principal
(B) vendor
(C) agent
(D) both A and B

68. An accepted listing contract contains the signature of

I. the buyer
II. the seller

(A) I only
(B) II only
(C) both I and II
(D) neither I nor II

69. The principal may sell the property through his or her own efforts and still be obligated to pay for the sales fee under

(A) an open listing
(B) an exclusive agency listing
(C) an exclusive right to sell listing
(D) all of the above

70. The counteroffer in real estate

(A) terminates the original offer
(B) if accepted would result in a contract
(C) both A and B
(D) neither A nor B

71. NAR affiliates grant which designation(s)?

(A) MAI
(B) GRI
(C) CPM
(D) all of the above

72. It is usually the duty of the property manager to

I. lease the units and collect the rents
II. supervise the maintenance of the property

(A) I only
(B) II only
(C) both I and II
(D) neither I nor II

73. A commission of $2,375 is received from the sale of a property. The rate is 6½%. What was the gross price of the property?

(A) $39,583.33
(B) $36,538.46
(C) $37,853.43
(D) none of the above

74. A home sold at 91% of the original listing price. The seller received $32,475 gross for the property. What was the original listing price?

(A) $32,475
(B) $34,184
(C) $36,083
(D) $35,687

75. The taxes on a property are $960 per year. The house was assessed at $24,000. What is the tax rate per $100 of assessed value?

(A) $12
(B) $4
(C) $25
(D) none of the above

76. The seller received $21,000.00 after the sales

fee of $1,340.40 was paid. The sales fee was what percent of the sales price?

(A) 5%   (C) 7%
(B) 6%   (D) 8%

22 340.44

77. The sale of a property yielded the seller a loss of 25%. The sales price was $30,000. What was the original cost of the property?

(A) $37,500   (C) $40,000
(B) $22,500   (D) $36,000

78. The bank requires 2 months' interest escrowed in advance. If the loan is for $6,500 at 7½%, how much interest is to be escrowed?

(A) $40.63   (C) $487.50
(B) $81.26   (D) none of the above

79. A home sells for $75,000, the commission rate is 8%, and you as sales agent will receive one-quarter of the commission for listing the property. How much will you receive?

(A) $6,000   (C) $1,500
(B) $4,500   (D) $3,000

80. You purchase a home for $32,500 and desire to sell it at a net profit of 20% and you must also pay a 7% commission. What is the sales price?

(A) $39,000 *2730*   (C) $41,935
(B) $41,275   (D) none of the above

81. If a closing is to take place August 20, this year, and the expiration of the fire insurance policy is November 30, this year, what will be the prorated share at closing if the annual premium is $480.00? *40 mo   1.33 PD*

(A) $120.00   (C) $133.33
(B) $150.00   (D) $123.33

1074.84

82. The taxes on the Jones' property are $8.47/$100. The property has been appraised at $42,300. The assessed value is 30% of the appraised value. The Joneses close the sale of their home on August 10, this year. What is the prorated amount owed by the Joneses if taxes are due and payable December 31, this year?

(A) $1,074.84   (C) $656.85
(B) $3,582.81   (D) $2,189.51

83. A mortgage has an interest rate of 8½% in arrears and a PI constant of $230.70 with an outstanding balance of $19,479.33. The payments are due on the first of each month and the closing takes place on the 20th. What is the prorated amount of interest at the closing?

(A) $91.72   (C) $92.00
(B) $137.98   (D) none of the above

84. The recording system
    I. cures all defects in title
    II. insures title against loss due to third-party claims

(A) I only   (C) both I and II
(B) II only   (D) neither I nor II

85. The summary of the recorded documents pertaining to the title to a property is called

(A) a recorder's digest
(B) a binder for title insurance
(C) an abstract
(D) a settlement statement

86. The three approaches to value in the appraisal process are

(A) cost, market, depreciation
(B) market, cost, income
(C) income, capitalization, comparison
(D) none of the above

87. If you own a building worth $95,000.00 and desire a return of 14%, what net income is needed each month to attain this?

(A) $13,300.00 (C) $9,500.00
(B) $133,000.00 (D) $1,108.33

88. It is the job of the appraiser to

(A) establish value   (C) both A and B
(B) estimate value   (D) neither A nor B

89. A property has a gross annual income of $9,600 and monthly expenses of $700. The purchaser desires a 12% capitalization rate including a 7% return of her money. What is the estimated value of the building?

(A) $80,000   (C) $74,167
(B) $10,000   (D) $85,833

90. Using the cost approach, if the land is valued

at $10,000 and the improvements have been depreciated 40% and have a present value of $60,000, what was the cost of the improvements new?

(A) $110,000 (C) $150,000
(B) $100,000 (D) $160,000

91. Replacement cost is

(A) the cost of reproducing the structure with the same materials and design
(B) the price for which similar properties are selling
(C) the cost of replacing the structure with one of the same utility
(D) none of the above

92. An area is zoned to be residential. A factory is already within this area. The factory

(A) is a preexisting nonconforming use
(B) is required to be torn down
(C) must cease operation
(D) none of the above

93. A township contains how many square miles?

(A) 1 (C) 16
(B) 6 (D) 36

94. The zoning regulations in an area may control the

(A) structure height
(B) structure type
(C) building materials used
(D) all of the above

95. The area of 1 square mile is equal to a

(A) range (C) section
(B) township (D) check

96. The tax levies on real property are considered to be

(A) non valendum
(B) ad valorem
(C) ad hoc
(D) none of the above

97. Depreciation may occur from

I. the loss in value due to any cause
II. incurable functional obsolescence

(A) I only (C) both I and II
(B) II only (D) neither I nor II

98. Functional obsolescence may be

(A) curable (C) both A and B
(B) incurable (D) neither A nor B

99. The market approach to estimating value should be used on

(A) residential property only
(B) residential and income properties
(C) vacant land only
(D) all cases where comparable sales are available

100. A property has a gross monthly rent multiplier of 103. The annual net income from rent was $2,400 with monthly expenses of $90. What is the value of the property?

(A) $358,440 (C) $247,200
(B) $20,600 (D) $29,870

Chapter 19

Sample Licensing Examination for Brokers

DUE to security restrictions maintained by ETS, the sample examination provided in this chapter is not a licensing examination that has actually been used in any state. It is, however, the same as the broker's RELE in format and in the subject areas covered. It focuses on the major areas included in any state's licensing examination for brokers.

When you enter the examination center for the broker's examination, you will be given completed listing and offer to purchase forms and an answer booklet suitable for computer grading. Before the examination starts, the examination proctor will give detailed directions for filling out the examination answer booklet.

DIRECTIONS

1. Study the completed listing and offer to purchase forms carefully.

2. Using the forms and additional settlement information, prepare the settlement worksheet in good form.

3. Answer questions 1 through 30 using the completed forms as you would on the actual license examination.

4. Proceed with the remaining questions.

5. The actual examination, which includes a Uniform Test and State Test, is a 4½ hour examination. The sample examination does not include the State Test, so you should allow no more than 3½ hours for its completion.

BROKER'S SAMPLE EXAMINATION ADDITIONAL SETTLEMENT INFORMATION

Prepare a settlement statement in accordance with the information provided on the Exclusive Authorization to Sell form and the Offer to Purchase Agreement. The closing is set for July 15, this year.

The following additional charges should be considered:

The abstract continuation is $50.00; the preparation of deed is $10.00; and the abstract examination and opinion are $40.00. The loan assumption fee is 1%, and the buyer's recording fees are $22.50.

The insurance has a $150.00 premium and expires August 20, this year. The rental unit of the duplex is currently occupied at a rate of $175.00 per month, which is due in advance on the first of each month. Interest is in arrears. Taxes were due and payable on January 1, this year, and have not yet been paid.

THE BROKER'S EXAMINATION

Choose the one best answer

Real Estate Instruments

1. The listing expires

   (A) May 12, this year
   (B) August 12, this year
   (C) August 12, next year
   (D) none of the above

2. The property contains

   I. a living room 12' × 16' with a fireplace
   II. a full basement

   (A) I only   (C) both I and II
   (B) II only   (D) neither I nor II

3. How much could the seller expect to receive after deduction of the brokerage fee from the listed price?

   (A) $1,800   (C) $27,300
   (B) $28,200   (D) $26,750

4. The possession of rental unit is

   (A) complete
   (B) landlord's
   (C) after 30 days
   (D) none of the above

5. The total square footage of the structure is

   (A) 1200 square feet
   (B) 2400 square feet
   (C) 3600 square feet
   (D) none of the above

REAL ESTATE LISTING CONTRACT (EXCLUSIVE RIGHT TO SELL)

SALES PRICE __$30,000__   TYPE HOME __Duplex__   TOTAL BEDROOMS __2/unit__   TOTAL BATHS __1/unit__

ADDRESS __1900 Main Street, Anytown__   JURISDICTION OF __Delaware County, Your State__

AMT. OF LOAN TO BE ASSUMED $ __23,595.00__   AS OF WHAT DATE __May 1__   TAXES & INS. INCLUDED __no__   YEARS TO GO ____   AMOUNT PAYABLE MONTHLY $__200.00__ @ __7½__ %   TYPE LOAN ____

MORTGAGE COMPANY ____   2nd MORTGAGE ____

OWNER'S NAME __Steven Jennings__   PHONES(HOME) ____ (BUSINESS) ____

TENANT'S NAME ____   PHONES (HOME) ____ (BUSINESS) ____

POSSESSION __Landlord's at closing__   DATE LISTED: __May 12, TY__   EXCLUSIVE FOR __90__   DATE OF EXPIRATION __Aug. 12, TY__

LISTING BROKER __Acme Realty__   PHONE ____ KEY AVAILABLE AT ____

LISTING SALESMAN __You, as salesperson for Acme Realty__   HOME PHONE ____ HOW TO BE SHOWN:

ENTRANCE FOYER ☐	CENTER HALL ☐	AGE FOYER	AIR CONDITIONING ☑	TYPE KITCHEN CABINETS
LIVING ROOM SIZE 12' x 16'	FIREPLACE ☐	ROOFING	TOOL HOUSE ☐	TYPE COUNTER TOPS
DINING ROOM SIZE		GARAGE SIZE	PATIO ☐	EAT-IN SIZE KITCHEN ☑
BEDROOM TOTAL: 2/unitDOWN UP		SIDE DRIVE ☐	CIRCULAR DRIVE ☐	TYPE STOVE ☐
BATHS TOTAL: 1/unit DOWN UP		PORCH ☐ SIDE ☐ REAR ☐	SCREENED ☐	BUILT-IN OVEN & RANGE ☑
DEN SIZE	FIREPLACE ☐	FENCED YARD	OUTDOOR GRILL ☐	SEPARATE STOVE INCLUDED ☐
FAMILY ROOM SIZE	FIREPLACE ☐	STORM WINDOWS ☐	STORM DOORS ☐	REFRIGERATOR INCLUDED ☑
RECREATION ROOM SIZE	FIREPLACE ☐	CURBS & GUTTERS ☐	SIDEWALKS ☐	DISHWASHER INCLUDED ✓
BASEMENT SIZE		STORM SEWERS ☑	ALLEY ☐	DISPOSAL INCLUDED ☐
NONE ☑ 1/4 ☐ 1/3 ☐ 1/2 ☐ 3/4 ☐ FULL ☐		WATER SUPPLY		DOUBLE SINK ☐ SINGLE SINK ☐
UTILITY ROOM ✓		SEWER ☑	SEPTIC ☐	STAINLESS STEEL ☐ PORCELAIN ☐
TYPE HOT WATER SYSTEM: Electric		TYPE GAS: NATURAL ☐	BOTTLED ☐	WASHER INCLUDED ☐ DRYER INCLUDED ☐
TYPE HEAT Electric		WHY SELLING		LAND ASSESSMENT $ 2,000.00
EST. FUEL COST				IMPROVEMENTS $ 6,000.00
ATTIC ☐		PROPERTY DESCRIPTION		TOTAL ASSESSMENTS $8,000.00
PULL DOWN STAIRWAY ☐ REGULAR STAIRWAY ☐ TRAP DOOR ☐		Gilbert's Addition, Anytown, Delaware Co., Your State		TAX RATE $9.50/$100
NAME OF BUILDER		LOT SIZE 75' x 200'		TOTAL ANNUAL TAXES $760.00
SQUARE FOOTAGE 1200/unit		LOT NO. 6 BLOCK SECTION		
EXTERIOR OF HOUSE				

NAME OF SCHOOLS: ELEMENTARY:: ____   JR. HIGH: ____

HIGH: ____   PAROCHIAL: ____

PUBLIC TRANSPORTATION: ____

NEAREST SHOPPING AREA: ____

REMARKS: ____

Date: __May 12, TY__

In consideration of the services of _____ __Acme Realty__ _____ (herein called "Broker") to be rendered to the undersigned (herein called 'Owner"), and of the promise of Broker to make reasonable efforts to obtain a Purchaser therefor, Owner hereby lists with Broker the real estate and all improvements thereon which are described above, (all herein called "the property"), and the Owner hereby grants to Broker the exclusive and irrevocable right to sell such property from 12:00 Noon on __May 12__ , 19 __TY__ until 12:00 Midnight on __Aug. 12__ , 19 __TY__ (herein called "period of time"), for the price of __Thirty thousand and no/100__ Dollars ($__30,000.00__) or for such other price and upon such other terms (including exchange) as Owner may subsequently authorize during the period of time.

It is understood by Owner that the above sum or any other price subsequently authorized by Owner shall include a cash fee of __6__ per cent of such price or other price which shall be payable by Owner to Broker upon consummation by any Purchaser or Purchasers of a valid contract of sale of the property during the period of time and whether or not Broker was a procuring cause of any such contract of sale.

If the property is sold or exchanged by Owner, or by Broker or by any other person to any Purchaser to whom the property was shown by Broker or any representative of Broker within sixty (60) days after the expiration of the period of time mentioned above, Owner agrees to pay to Broker a cash fee which shall be the same percentage of the purchase price as the percentage mentioned above.

Broker is hereby authorized by Owner to place a "For Sale" sign on the property and to remove all signs of other brokers or salesmen during the period of time, and Owner hereby agrees to make the property available to Broker at all reasonable hours for the purpose of showing it to prospective Purchasers.

Owner agrees to convey the property to the Purchaser by deed with the usual covenants of title and free and clear from all encumbrances, tenancies, liens (for taxes or otherwise), but subject to applicable restrictive covenants of record. Owner acknowledges receipt of copy of this agreement.

WITNESS the following signature(s) and seal(s):

Date Signed: __May 12, TY__   *Steven Jennings*   (Owner)

Listing Agent __Acme Realty, You as Salesperson__

Address __1900 Main Street__   Telephone ____   (Owner)

REAL ESTATE SALES CONTRACT (OFFER TO PURCHASE AGREEMENT)

This AGREEMENT made as of _____ June 3 _____ , 19 TY ,

among _____ William F. Jones and Sarah I. Jones (H & W) _____ (herein called "Purchaser"),

and _____ Steven Jennings _____ (herein called "Seller"),

and _____ Acme Realty _____ (herein called "Broker"), provides that Purchaser agrees to buy through Broker as agent for Seller, and Seller agrees to sell the following described real estate, and all improvements thereon, located in the jurisdiction of _____ Anytown, Delaware County, Your State _____ ,

(all herein called "the property"): _____ Lot 6, Gilberts Addition to the City of Anytown, Delaware County, Your State _____ , and more commonly known as _____ 1900 Main Street, _____ Anytown, Your State _____ (street address). _____

1. The purchase price of the property is _____ twenty-nine thousand and no/100 _____

Dollars ($ 29,000.00), and such purchase price shall be paid as follows: _____ cash and assumption of existing mortgage _____

2. Purchaser has made a deposit of _____ two thousand _____ Dollars ($ 2,000.00) with Broker, receipt of which is hereby acknowledged, and such deposit shall be held by Broker in escrow until the date of settlement and then applied to the purchase price, or returned to Purchaser if the title to the property is not marketable.

3. Seller agrees to convey the property to Purchaser by Deed with the usual covenants of title and free and clear from all monetary encumbrances, tenancies, liens (for taxes or otherwise), except as may be otherwise provided above, but subject to applicable restrictive covenants of record. Seller further agrees to deliver possession of the property to Purchaser on the date of settlement and to pay the expense of preparing the deed of conveyance.

4. Settlement shall be made at _____ Acme Realty _____ on or before _____ July 20 _____ , 19 TY , or as soon thereafter as title can be examined and necessary documents prepared, with allowance of a reasonable time for Seller to correct any defects reported by the title examiner.

5. All taxes, interest, rent, and impound escrow deposits, if any, shall be prorated as of the date of settlement.

6. All risk of loss or damage to the property by fire, windstorm, casualty, or other cause is assumed by Seller until the date of settlement.

7. Purchaser and Seller agree that Broker was the sole procuring cause of this Contract of Purchase, and Seller agrees to pay Broker for services rendered a cash fee of _____ 6 _____ per cent of the purchase price. If either Purchaser or Seller defaults under such Contract, such defaulting party shall be liable for the cash fee of Broker and any expenses incurred by the non-defaulting party in connection with this transaction.

Subject to: _____ tenants rights at time of closing; assumption of existing mortgage, prorate fire insurance; $20.00/day liquidated damage. Offer to be open for 8 days. Closing within 5 days after delivery of the abstract but must be on or before July 20. _____

8. Purchaser represents that an inspection satisfactory to Purchaser has been made of the property, and Purchaser agrees to accept the property in its present condition except as may be otherwise provided in the description of the property above.

9. This Contract of Purchase constitutes the entire agreement among the parties and may not be modified or changed except by written instrument executed by all of the parties, including Broker.

10. This Contract of Purchase shall be construed, interpreted, and applied according to the law of the jurisdiction of _____ Your State _____ and shall be binding upon and shall inure to the benefit of the heirs, personal representatives, successors, and assigns of the parties.

All parties to this agreement acknowledge receipt of a certified copy.

WITNESS the following signatures:

_____ *Steven Jennings* _____ Seller _____ *William F Jones* _____ Purchaser

_____ Seller _____ *Sarah I Jones* _____ Purchaser

_____ Acme Realty _____ Broker

Deposit Rec'd $ 2,000.00

(Personal Check)   Cash

Cashier's Check   Company Check

Sales Agent: You, as salesperson for Acme Realty

Brokers Examination Problem

SETTLEMENT STATEMENT WORKSHEET

Complete the Settlement Statement Worksheet on the basis of information furnished in the Listing, Offer to Purchase Agreement, and Settlement Problems only. Do not add other items. Use the 30-day method of computation.

	BUYER'S STATEMENT		SELLER'S STATEMENT	
	DEBIT	CREDIT	DEBIT	CREDIT
SALE PRICE	29,000			29,000
SALE FEE			1740	
DEPOSIT		2000		
MORTGAGE BAL	23,489.61		~~23~~	
INTREST PRORATE				
TAXES	~~460~~			~~460~~
RENT	~~87.50~~	87.50	87.50	
INSURANCE				
DEED PREP				
~~ESCROW~~				
ABSTRACT CONT.	$50			
DEED	$10			
ABSTRACT + OPINION	$40			
ASSUMPTION FEE	$290			
RECORDING FEE	22.50			
BALANCE DUE SELLER				
" " BUYER				

6. The seller holds title

OK (A) in severalty
(B) as a tenant in common
(C) as a joint tenant
(D) as a tenant by the entirety

7. The property has a
   I. breakfast room
   II. dishwasher

   (A) I only
   (B) II only
   (C) both I and II
   (D) neither I nor II

8. The annual taxes are

   (A) $190
   (B) $570
   (C) $760
   (D) none of the above

9. The purchasers will take title

   (A) in severalty
   (B) as tenants in common
   (C) as joint tenants
   (D) none of the above

10. The sales price offered is

    (A) $30,000
    (B) $29,000
    (C) $27,500
    (D) $21,000

11. The legal description is by

    (A) government survey
    (B) metes and bounds
    (C) platted subdivision
    (D) none of the above

12. The offer is contingent upon

    (A) a new loan of $23,950
    (B) assumption of the existing loan
    (C) a land contract for the purchase price
    (D) none of the above

13. Closing is to take place
    I. at Walnut Savings and Loan
    II. 5 days after delivery of the abstract

    (A) I only
    (B) II only
    (C) both I and II
    (D) neither I nor II

14. The sales fee is
    I. 7% of the gross sales price
    II. $2,030

    (A) I only
    (B) II only
    (C) both I and II
    (D) neither I nor II

15. The listing broker is

    (A) you
    (B) Acme Realty
    (C) both A and B
    (D) neither A nor B

16. The tax proration is

    (A) $411.65 credit to the seller
    (B) $411.65 debit to the buyer
    (C) $411.65 debit to the seller
    (D) none of the above

17. The amount of the loan being assumed is

    (A) $29,000.00
    (B) $23,595.00
    (C) $23,542.47
    (D) $23,489.61

18. The settlement will take place

    (A) July 15, this year
    (B) June 10, this year
    (C) May 12, this year
    (D) none of the above

19. The loan assumption fee is

    (A) $290.00
    (B) $235.42
    (C) $234.89
    (D) $236.00

20. The earnest money deposit is

    (A) $2,000
    (B) $1,000
    (C) $6,347
    (D) none of the above

21. The total down payment is

    (A) $5,510.39
    (B) $6,510.39
    (C) $4,510.39
    (D) $3,510.39

22. The insurance proration is

    (A) $12.50
    (B) $13.78
    (C) $14.60
    (D) $15.02

23. The rent prorated is

    (A) $175.00
    (B) $87.50
    (C) $262.50
    (D) none of the above

24. The interest prorated is

    (A) $146.81
    (B) $1761.72
    (C) $73.41
    (D) $70.29

25. The balance due from the buyer is

    (A) $3,249.83
    (B) $3,152.43
    (C) $3,352.43
    (D) $3,209.83

26. The total numbers of buyer's debits and credits are
    - (A) 5 debits, 6 credits
    - (B) 8 debits, 2 credits
    - (C) 6 credits, 5 debits
    - (D) 5 debits, 5 credits

27. The balance due the seller is
    - (A) $3,249.83
    - (B) $3,049.83
    - (C) $3,152.43
    - (D) $3,352.43

28. The total numbers of seller's debits and credits are
    - (A) 6 debits, 5 credits
    - (B) 7 debits, 2 credits
    - (C) 8 debits, 2 credits
    - (D) none of the above

29. The total number of discount points paid at closing is
    - (A) 1
    - (B) 2
    - (C) 3
    - (D) none of the above

30. The financial obligations of the seller assumed by the buyer amount to
    - (A) $23,974.67
    - (B) $24,062.17
    - (C) $24,076.77
    - (D) $24,126.77

Real Estate Values, Deeds, and Contracts

31. For a deed to be valid
    - (A) it must be executed by the grantor
    - (B) it must be executed by the grantee
    - (C) both A and B
    - (D) neither A nor B

32. A contract which creates the debit in a mortgage loan transaction is
    - (A) a deed
    - (B) a mortgage agreement
    - (C) a promissory note
    - (D) a bond

33. The deed form containing the greatest liability to the grantor is a
    - (A) general warranty deed
    - (B) trust deed
    - (C) sheriff's deed
    - (D) quitclaim deed

34. A digest of the history of the recorded documents pertaining to the title to real property is
    - (A) a deed
    - (B) a mortgage
    - (C) an abstract
    - (D) title insurance

35. If a person signs a contract under duress, the contract is
    - (A) void
    - (B) voidable
    - (C) illegal
    - (D) none of the above

36. The usual agency relationship exists between
    - (A) the broker and the sales agent
    - (B) the salesperson and the seller
    - (C) the broker and the seller
    - (D) all of the above

37. A counteroffer in real estate
    - (A) terminates the original offer
    - (B) if accepted would result in a contract
    - (C) both A and B
    - (D) neither A nor B

38. The term "agent" means
    - (A) the grantor of authority to act for another
    - (B) the grantee of authority to act for another
    - (C) the one who conferred authority on another
    - (D) none of the above

39. Which of the following must be in writing?
    I. an option
    II. a lease for less than 1 year
    - (A) I only
    - (B) II only
    - (C) both I and II
    - (D) neither I nor II

40. Capitalization is a process for
    - (A) discounting
    - (B) converting future net income into present value
    - (C) accumulation of assets
    - (D) none of the above

41. Market value and selling price are
    - (A) always equal
    - (B) never equal
    - (C) sometimes equal
    - (D) none of the above

42. Which method is preferred for the appraisal of a church?

    (A) cost   (C) income
    (B) market   (D) capitalization

43. Capitalization principles can be employed in

    (A) the market approach
    (B) the cost approach
    (C) the income approach
    (D) all of the above

44. Depreciation occurs from

    (A) economic obsolescence
    (B) functional obsolescence
    (C) loss in value due to any cause
    (D) all of the above

45. An area was zoned to be residential. A gas station had already been built in the area. The gas station

    (A) is a preexisting nonconforming use
    (B) is required to be torn down
    (C) must cease operation
    (D) none of the above

46. Zoning regulations may regulate

    (A) building height
    (B) building style
    (C) building material
    (D) all of the above

47. If you had $45,000 to invest and you desired a 12% return, what would your net income need to be?

    (A) $5,400 per year   (C) both A and B
    (B) $450 per month   (D) neither A nor B

48. The ownership of real property may be acquired by

    (A) a will   (C) both A and B
    (B) a deed   (D) neither A nor B

49. The deed form which contains no warranties is

    (A) a special warranty deed
    (B) a general warranty deed
    (C) a quitclaim deed
    (D) none of the above

50. Curtesy is an example of

    (A) a legal life estate
    (B) a nonfree hold estate
    (C) an estate at will
    (D) none of the above

Leases, Property Management, and Financing

51. The maximum amount the VA will guarantee on a loan is

    (A) $17,500 or 60% of the purchase price, whichever is less
    (B) 97% of the first $25,000 of the purchase price
    (C) $42,000 total on any size loan
    (D) there is no upper limit

52. The largest source of residential mortgage money is

    (A) commercial banks
    (B) insurance trusts
    (C) savings and loan associations
    (D) mutual savings banks

53. To be valid a mortgage or deed of trust must be

    (A) in writing
    (B) between competent parties
    (C) executed by the parties
    (D) all of the above

54. The mortgage type that includes fixtures and equipment in the loan is a

    (A) blanket mortgage
    (B) purchase money mortgage
    (C) wraparound mortgage
    (D) package mortgage

55. When the FHA insures a loan, the insurance protects the

    (A) buyer   (C) mortgagor
    (B) seller   (D) mortgagee

56. An amortized loan is repaid

    (A) in equal installments
    (B) by paying interest only until the last payment
    (C) in variable amounts according to the market
    (D) none of the above

57. A mortgage taken back by the seller as partial payment for the property is a
    - (A) purchase money mortgage
    - (B) wraparound mortgage
    - (C) straight term mortgage
    - (D) land contract

58. Which of the following is not a usual function of a property manager?
    - (A) appraisal
    - (B) advertising
    - (C) renting
    - (D) maintenance

59. NAR grants which of the following designations?
    - (A) PUD
    - (B) MICA
    - (C) CPM
    - (D) PMI

60. If the property in a foreclosure sale sells for less than the amount of the debt,
    - (A) the mortgagee may levy against the other assets of the mortgagor
    - (B) the mortgagee must be satisfied with what is received
    - (C) the mortgagee may hold another sale for the property
    - (D) none of the above

61. In an FHA loan, if discount points are charged, they are paid by the
    - (A) buyer
    - (B) seller
    - (C) either the buyer or the seller
    - (D) neither the buyer nor the seller

62. The clause in a mortgage (or deed of trust) which allows the lender to advance the due date of the debt is
    - (A) a prepayment clause
    - (B) an acceleration clause
    - (C) a judgment clause
    - (D) a habendum clause

63. Unless restricted by the lease, a lessee may
    I. mortgage his or her interest in the property
    II. sublet the property
    - (A) I only
    - (B) II only
    - (C) both I and II
    - (D) neither I nor II

64. Under a lease, a tenant is
    - (A) liable for any waste he or she might commit on the property
    - (B) liable for all normal wear on the property
    - (C) both A and B
    - (D) neither A nor B

65. An estate for years
    - (A) has a specific termination date
    - (B) is not automatically renewable
    - (C) both A and B
    - (D) neither A nor B

66. The type of loan that has no prepayment penalty and has insurance premiums is
    - (A) FHA
    - (B) VA
    - (C) conventional
    - (D) none of the above

67. In regard to FHA loans, which of the following is true?
    - (A) FHA programs are administered through HUD
    - (B) down payments usually come from the purchaser's assets
    - (C) both A and B
    - (D) neither A nor B

68. A conventional mortgage is
    - (A) not guaranteed by a government agency
    - (B) not made at an interest rate fixed by the federal government
    - (C) both A and B
    - (D) neither A nor B

69. If the interest rate on a loan exceeds the legal limits, the lender has violated
    - (A) deficiency laws
    - (B) usury laws
    - (C) eminent domain laws
    - (D) escheat laws

70. A mortgage that covers two or more pieces of property is called
    I. a wraparound mortgage
    II. a blanket mortgage
    - (A) I only
    - (B) II only
    - (C) both I and II
    - (D) neither I nor II

Legal and Government Aspects

71. Is racial steering contrary to the 1968 Federal Fair Housing Law?

    (A) yes
    (B) no
    (C) usually, but with exceptions
    (D) none of the above

72. Housing discrimination occurs when a person seeking to purchase a home is treated differently because of

    (A) race   (C) sex
    (B) religion   (D) all of the above

73. If a seller desires to sell only to white Protestants, you as broker or salesperson should

    (A) honor the listing
    (B) include that condition in the listing agreement
    (C) not take the listing
    (D) none of the above

74. If a real estate broker has found a buyer who is ready, willing, and able to buy under the terms of the listing and a contract has been consummated, the broker has

    (A) earned his commission
    (B) completed the sale
    (C) violated his or her contract
    (D) none of the above

75. Complaints regarding discrimination in housing may be made directly to

    (A) the courts   (C) both A and B
    (B) HUD   (D) neither A nor B

76. Federal law prohibits

    I. refusal to show listed property to any potential purchaser
    II. stating different contractual terms or prices to different potential purchasers

    (A) I only   (C) both I and II
    (B) II only   (D) neither I nor II

77. Title VIII of the Civil Rights Act of 1968 is also known as

    (A) the affirmative fair housing marketing plan
    (B) the Federal Fair Housing Law
    (C) the open housing rule
    (D) none of the above

78. If a prospect who is a member of a minority group asks to be shown properties in white neighborhoods, the broker

    (A) must oblige and show homes in white neighborhoods
    (B) must ask the neighbors of the listed property if it would be all right
    (C) must never show such properties
    (D) both A and B

79. Of the following items, which would not terminate an offer to sell real estate?

    (A) lapse of reasonable time
    (B) rejection of the offer by the offeree
    (C) death of the sales agent
    (D) a revocation of the offer

80. The statute of frauds requires that contracts for the sale of real estate be

    (A) in writing to be enforceable
    (B) in outline form
    (C) reviewed by the county recorder
    (D) all of the above

Arithmetic Functions

81. If a closing is to take place on September 10, 1977, and the fire insurance policy expires on June 20, 1978, with an annual premium of $360, what is the amount to be prorated?

    (A) $270   (C) $250
    (B) $280   (D) $210

82. The seller received $21,000 after the brokers took their fee of 6%. What was the selling price of the property?

    (A) $21,000   (C) $22,340
    (B) $22,600   (D) $23,430

83. What interest would be escrowed if the bank requires 2 months in advance on a $10,000 loan at 8¾%?

    (A) $875.00   (C) $72.92
    (B) $1,750.00   (D) $145.84

84. A broker received a commission of $2,400 on a sale and his fee was 7%. What was the sales price of the property?

    (A) $38,750.00   (C) $34,285.71
    (B) $40,000.00   (D) $31,233.52

85. Property yielded the seller a profit of 25%. The sales price was negotiated at $50,000. What was the cost of the property originally?

(A) $45,000   (C) $40,500
(B) $37,500   (D) $40,000

86. A house sold at 95% of its original price. The seller's price was $30,000. What was the property's original listing price?

(A) $31,500   (C) $29,500
(B) $32,500   (D) $31,579

87. Taxes on a property are $960 per year. What is the prorated amount from January 1 to settlement on July 20?

(A) $80.00   (C) $453.60
(B) $533.40   (D) $613.60

88. You buy a home for $30,000. You desire a 20% profit when you sell the home and you must pay a 6% brokerage fee. For what price must you sell the home?

(A) $31,800   (C) $36,000
(B) $38,298   (D) $34,350

89. If property is selling at $1,200 per acre, what is the gross sales price of a plot ½ X ¼ mile?

(A) $96,000
(B) $48,000
(C) $103,680
(D) none of the above

90. If you had $90,000 to invest and you desired a 12% return, what would your net income need to be?

(A) $10,800 per year
(B) $900 per month
(C) both A and B
(D) neither A nor B

91. What area is contained in the NW ¼ of the SE ¼ of the NW ¼ of the N ½ of section 12?

(A) 20 acres   (C) 5 acres
(B) 10 acres   (D) 40 acres

92. A township contains how many square miles?

(A) 1   (C) 36
(B) 6   (D) 16

93. If a house has dimensions of 50' X 36' and sells for $24,750, what is the price per square foot?

(A) $12.50   (C) $13.25
(B) $13.75   (D) $13.60

94. If a plot has 348,480 square feet and sells for $700 an acre, what is the selling price?

(A) $5,400   (C) $5,600
(B) $5,200   (D) $6,300

95. A warehouse is 20 feet wide, 24 feet deep, and 18 feet high and is valued at 75¢ a cubic foot. What is the value?

(A) $8,640   (C) $6,500
(B) $7,567   (D) $6,480

96. A salesperson is to receive 40% of the total 6% brokerage fee on a $21,000 sale. What is her share?

(A) $1,260   (C) $504
(B) $405   (D) $630

97. What is the semiannual interest on a loan of $6000 with an annual interest rate of 7%?

(A) $420   (C) $210
(B) $105   (D) none of the above

98. If a person borrowed $8,000 at 9% on January 1, this year, and repaid the debt on August 15, this year, how much interest did he have to pay?

(A) $360   (C) $450
(B) $720   (D) $510

99. The annual interest rate on a loan is 8½%. The first month's interest is $84.25. What is the amount of the loan?

(A) $12,437.83   (C) $11,894.12
(B) $11,498.21   (D) $11,849.21

100. The fee schedule for selling an apartment house is 5% of the first $10,000 and 2½% of any amount over $10,000. As a salesperson you receive 50% of the fee. If you receive $250, what is the sales price?

(A) $10,000   (C) $20,000
(B) $25,000   (D) $12,500

Appendixes

Appendix A

Illustrated Structure

As a real estate salesperson, it is essential that you be familiar with all the basic drawings of a residential property, as well as the basic elements of construction involved in a single-family structure.

The materials which follow include all the basics you need to know to be properly informed in dealing with clients interested in single-family purchases.

The following figures have been provided by courtesy of Paul I. Cripe, Inc., Civil Engineers, Indianapolis, Indiana.

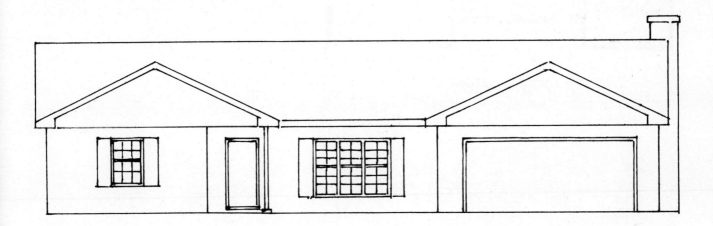

Fig. 1   Illustrated Structure
(The Following Figures, 2 through 6 Generally Relate To The Structure Shown In Front Elevation, Above)

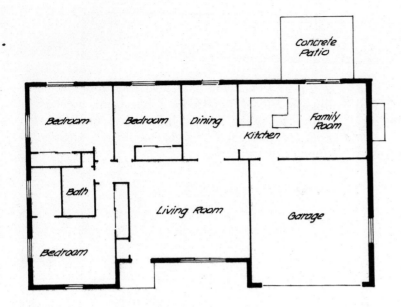

Floor Plan

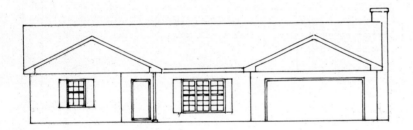

Front Elevation

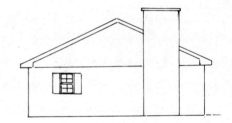

Right Side Elevation

Fig. 2   Several Typical Views Included In A Set Of House Plans

Contour Line

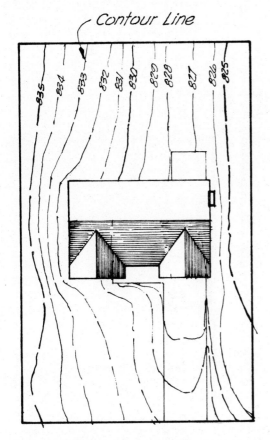

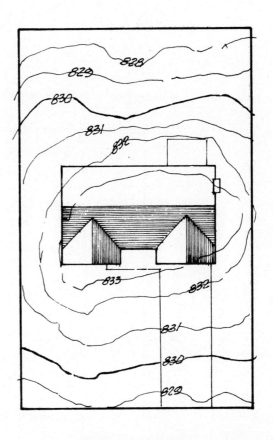

Plan View
Construction on a side sloping lot

Plan View
Construction on top of a slight knoll

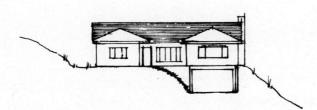

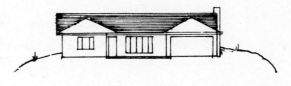

Front Elevation
Construction on a side sloping lot

Front Elevation
Construction on top of a slight knoll

Fig. 3 Topographical Considerations Related To House Construction

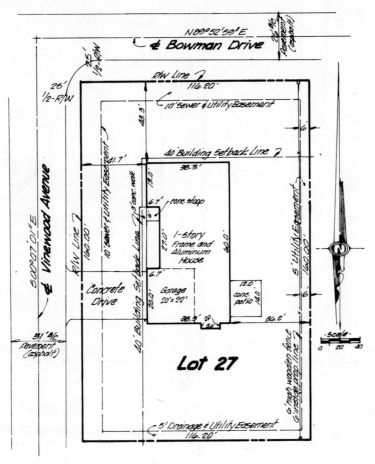

CIVIL ENGINEERING   **PAUL I. CRIPE, INC.**   SUBDIVISION DESIGN
LAND SURVEYING   150 E. MARKET STREET   BUILDING DESIGN
           INDIANAPOLIS, IND. 46204
           636-5411

January 21, 19'

Last Federal Savings and Loan Association
700 North Market Street
Indianapolis, Indiana 46204

Gentlemen:

    I the undersigned, hereby certify that the within plat is true and correct and represents a survey made by me on the 15th day of November, 19__, of real estate described as follows:

    Lot #27 in Willow Creek Addition - Section Five, as per plat thereof recorded October 31, 1977, as Instrument #77-70273 in the Office of the Recorder of Marion County, Indiana.

    Based thereon, I further certify that the building situated on the above described real estate is located within the boundaries of said premises. I have shown on said plat the distances from the sides and front of the building to points on the side lines and front line of the lot. I further certify that the buildings on the adjoining property do not encroach on the lot or real estate in question.

    The property is improved with a one story frame dwelling, located at 5861 Vinewood Avenue, Indianapolis, Indiana.

Fig. 4   Mortgage Survey

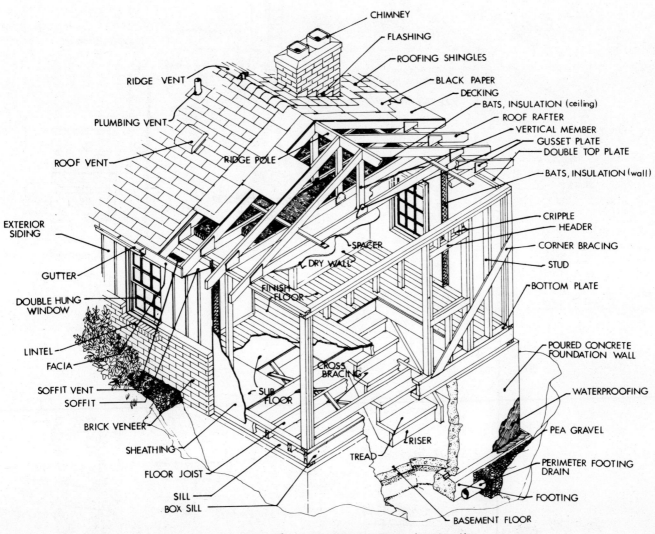

Fig. 5   Wood Frame House Construction
(Isometric View)

CHIMNEY
FLASHING
ROOFING SHINGLES
BLACK PAPER
DECKING
BATS, INSULATION (ceiling)
ROOF RAFTER
VERTICAL MEMBER
GUSSET PLATE
DOUBLE TOP PLATE
BATS, INSULATION (wall)
CRIPPLE
HEADER
CORNER BRACING
STUD
BOTTOM PLATE
POURED CONCRETE FOUNDATION WALL
WATERPROOFING
PEA GRAVEL
PERIMETER FOOTING DRAIN
FOOTING
BASEMENT FLOOR

RIDGE VENT
PLUMBING VENT
ROOF VENT
RIDGE POLE
SPACER
DRY WALL
FINISH FLOOR

EXTERIOR SIDING
GUTTER
DOUBLE HUNG WINDOW
LINTEL
FACIA
SOFFIT VENT
SOFFIT
BRICK VENEER
SHEATHING
FLOOR JOIST
SILL
BOX SILL
SUB FLOOR
CROSS BRACING
RISER
TREAD

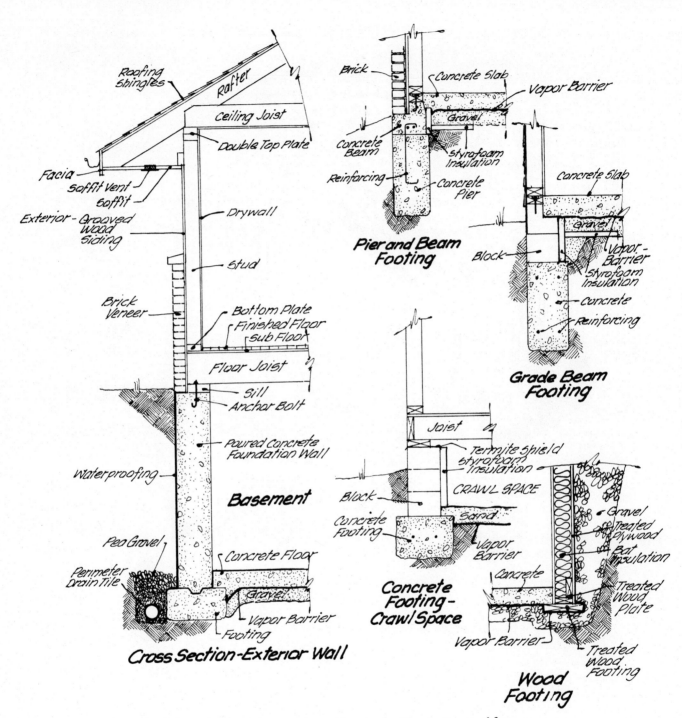

Fig. 6   Wood Frame House Construction
(Detailed Cross Sectional Views)

Fig. 7—Key Construction Details

1. Window Head Frame (Header)
2. Wall Sheathing, Diagonal
3. Verge Board
4. Gutter
5. Window Jamb Trimmer
6. Wall Building Paper
7. Window Sill Frame
8. Cripple Stud
9. Wall Siding
10. Window Shutters
11. Corner Bracing 45°
12. Corner Studs, Double
13. Sole Plate (Bottom Plate)
14. Box Sill
15. Basement Areaway
16. Basement Sash
17. Grade Line
18. Gravel Fill
19. Ridge Board
20. Collar Beam

21. Roof Rafters
22. Interior Partition Plates
23. Interior Studs
24. Cross Bracing
25. Plaster Base, Lath
26. Gable Studs
27. Interior Window Trim
28. Plaster Walls
29. Cross Bridging
30. Second Floor Joists
31. Arch Framing
32. Insulation, Batts
33. Dining Nook
34. Interior Door Trim
35. Plaster Base, Rock Lath
36. Finish Floor
37. Floor Lining Felt
38. Sub-Flooring, Diagonally
39. Sill Plate
40. Termite Shield
41. Girder
42. Plate Anchor Bolt
43. Post
44. Foundation Wall
45. Frame Partition
46. Tarred Felt Joint Cover
47. Drain Tile
48. Footing
49. Flue Liner Tops
50. Chimney Cap
51. Brick Chimney
52. Flashing & Counter Flashing
53. Spaced 1" x 4" decking
      (Wood Shingles)
54. Tight Roof Decking
      (all other coverings)
55. Ceiling Joists
56. Exterior Wall Plates
      (Double)
57. Lookouts
58. Furring Strips
59. Stair Rail & Balusters

60. Stair Landing Newel
61. Finish Flooring Over Felt
      Over Sub-Flooring on
      wood joists
62. Book Shelves
63. Picture Mould
64. Mantel and Trim
65. Damper Control
66. Base Top Mould
67. Ash Dump
68. Baseboards
69. Shoe Mould
70. Hearth
71. Plaster Ceiling
72. Boiler or Furnace
73. Cleanout Door
74. Basement Concrete Floor
75. Fill - Gravel/Stone
76. Roof Cover (Shingles)
77. Roofing Felts
78. Soffit of Cornice
79. Facia of Cornice
80. Vert. Board & Batten Siding
81. Fire Stops
82. Ribbon Plate
83. Stair Wall Partition
84. Stair Rail or Easing
85. Starting Newel
86. Cased Opening Trim
87. Main Stair Treads & Risers
88. Wall Stair Stringer
89. Face Stringer & Moulds
90. Starting Riser & Tread
91. First Floor Joists
92. Basement Stair Rail & Post
93. Basement Stair Horses
94. Basement Stair Treads & Risers
95. Basement Post (lally column)
96. Facia Board
97. Cornice Bed Mould
98. Leader Head or Conductor Head
99. Belt Course

100. Porch Rafter
101. Porch Ceiling Joists
102. Porch Ceiling Soffit
103. Porch Roof Beam
104. Porch Beam Facia
105. Entrance Door Trim
106. Leader, Downspout or Conductor
107. Porch Trellice
108. Porch Column
109. Porch Column Base
110. Concrete Porch Floor
111. Concrete Stoop
112. Entrance Door Sill
113. Stoop Foundation

Appendix B

Answers to Review Questions, Chapters 3-14

Chapter 3: The Real Estate Business

1. C	6. C	11. D	16. D
2. B	7. B	12. A	17. C
3. C	8. D	13. C	18. D
4. A	9. C	14. A	19. D
5. C	10. D	15. D	20. A

Chapter 4: Regulation of the Real Estate Business

1. C	6. B	11. D	16. B
2. C	7. A	12. C	17. B
3. C	8. D	13. A	18. A
4. A	9. C	14. D	19. D
5. B	10. C	15. D	20. D

Chapter 5: Legal Aspects of Real Estate

1. D	6. C	11. A	16. C
2. C	7. B	12. C	17. C
3. C	8. C	13. D	18. A
4. C	9. A	14. B	19. D
5. B	10. D	15. D	20. A

Chapter 6: Ownership of Real Property

1. B	6. A	11. A	16. C
2. C	7. B	12. B	17. D
3. A	8. A	13. B	18. B
4. C	9. C	14. C	19. B
5. B	10. C	15. B	20. C

Chapter 7: Transfer of Real Property

1. A	6. C	11. B	16. A
2. B	7. A	12. B	17. D
3. B	8. D	13. C	18. D
4. C	9. A	14. C	19. A
5. C	10. C	15. D	20. B

Chapter 8: Evidence and Assurance of Title

1. C	6. C	11. C	16. A
2. C	7. C	12. C	17. B
3. C	8. C	13. D	18. B
4. C	9. C	14. B	19. C
5. D	10. B	15. B	20. C

Chapter 9: Landlord and Tenant Relationships

1. D	6. B	11. A	16. A
2. D	7. D	12. D	17. A
3. A	8. C	13. A	18. C
4. D	9. A	14. C	19. B
5. C	10. A	15. D	20. D

Chapter 10: Mo and Land Contrac

1. C	6.
2. D	7. C
3. D	8. C
4. B	9. B
5. B	10. D

Chapter 11: Real Estate Fi

1. D	6. B		16. C
2. C	7. C		17. C
3. D	8. D	13. C	18. D
4. C	9. C	14. D	19. A
5. B	10. B	15. A	20. C

Chapter 12: Real Estate Appraisal

1. B	6. C	11. B	16. B
2. D	7. D	12. B	17. C
3. C	8. B	13. C	18. D
4. C	9. A	14. B	19. C
5. D	10. A	15. D	20. D

Calculations:

11. Value $\times$ rate = income
$103,000 $\times$ .12 = $12,360

12. $60,000/.6 = $100,000

13. Net income/value = rate
($8,000 — $7,200)/$147,000 = rate
$800/$147,000 = .0054 or .54%

19. Net income/value = rate
$8,000/$80,000 = .10 or 10%

20. Gross monthly income $\times$ GRM = value
$6,000/12 $\times$ 105 = value
$500 $\times$ 105 = $52,500

Chapter 13: Contracts

1. C	6. A	11. D	16. C
2. B	7. B	12. D	17. A
3. C	8. B	13. C	18. B
4. B	9. D	14. C	19. B
5. B	10. C	15. C	20. B

Chapter 14: The Brokerage Business and Agency Relationships

1. D	6. D	11. B	16. A
2. C	7. C	12. B	17. D
3. B	8. C	13. A	18. A
4. D	9. A	14. C	19. A
5. C	10. D	15. B	20. B

$1/2 \times 1/4 = 1/8$

Appendix C

Solutions to Math Problems, Chapter 15

PRACTICE PROBLEMS: FRACTIONS, DECIMALS, PERCENTS

Fractions

1. $1/6 + 1/8 = 7/24$
2. $3/7 + 4/9 = 55/63$
3. $19/20 + 3/5 = 31/20$ or $1\ 11/20$
4. $1/8 + 5/12 = 13/24$
5. $3/4 + 1/16 = 13/16$
6. $1/6 - 1/8 = 1/24$
7. $4/7 - 4/9 = 8/63$
8. $19/20 - 3/5 = 7/20$
9. $5/12 - 1/8 = 7/24$
10. $3/4 - 1/16 = 11/16$
11. $1/8 \times 1/4 = 1/32$
12. $1/9 \times 11/12 = 11/108$
13. $3/4 \times 7/16 = 21/64$
14. $4/5 \times 8/9 = 32/45$
15. $5/12 \times 1/5 = 5/60 = 1/12$
16. $1/8 \div 1/4 = 4/8 = 1/2$
17. $1/9 \div 11/12 = 12/99 = 4/33$
18. $3/4 \div 7/6 = 18/28 = 9/14$
19. $4/5 \div 8/9 = 36/40 = 9/10$
20. $5/12 \div 1/5 = 25/12 = 2\ 1/12$

Decimals and Percents

1. $.5 + .075 + .125 = .7$
2. $.073 + 1.25 + .93 = 2.253$
3. $.82 + .73 + 2.584 = 4.134$
4. $.0016 + 1.043 + .3 = 1.3446$
5. $1.25 - .075 = 1.175$
6. $.073 - .0016 = .0714$
7. $1.4874 - .896 = .5914$
8. $2.043 - 1.0012 = 1.0418$
9. $.075 \times 1.257 = .094275$
10. $.342 \times .0017 = .0005814$
11. $.7589 \times 1.2 = .91068$
12. $.346 \times 3.476 = 1.202696$
13. $.34 \div .516 = .65891$
14. $1.25 \div .07 = 17.857$
15. $.78 \div .4 = 1.95$
16. $1.29 \div .432 = 2.9861$
17. $75\% = .75$
18. $125\% = 1.25$
19. $27.56\% = .2756$
20. $43.2\% = .432$
21. $.0025 = .25\%$
22. $.567 = 56.7\%$
23. $.493 = 49.3\%$
24. $3.475 = 347.5\%$

PERIMETER, AREA, VOLUME

1. 640 acres = 1 sq mile

2. 43,560 sq ft = 1 acre

3.

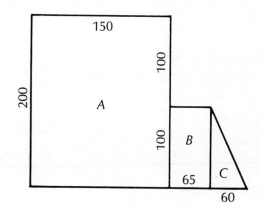

Area $A = (150)(200) = 30,000$
Area $B = (100)(\ 65) = \ \ 6,500$
Area $C = \frac{1}{2}(60)(100) = \ \ 3,000$
Total $\qquad\qquad\qquad$ 39,500 sq ft

4. $A = L \times W$
$A = 373 \times 154$
$A = 57,442$ sq ft

$57,442/43,560 = 1.3187$ acres
$1.3187\ (\$1,000.00) = \$1,318.70$

5. $A = L \times W$
$A = 300 \times 450$
$A = 135,000$ sq ft

1 acre = 43,560 sq ft
$135,000/43,560 = 3.1$ acres

6. Labor costs $= 28 \times 9 \times \$.20 = \$50.40$
Concrete costs $= (28 \times 9 \times .5)/27 \times \$16.50 =$ $\$77.00$

$\$50.40 + \$77.00 = \$127.40$

7. $A = L \times W$
    $L = 150 - (20 + 15) = 115$
    $W = 120 - (15 + 15) = 90$
    $A = 115 \times 90 = 10,350$ sq ft

8. $A = L \times W$
    $A = 310 \times 240$
    $A = 74,400$ sq rods
    $A = 74,400/160$
    $A = 465$ acres

    $A = \pi r^2$
    $A = 3.1416 (45)^2$
    $A = 3.1416 (2025)$
    $A = 6361.74$ sq rods
    $A = 6361.74 \div 160$
    $A = 39.76$ acres

    $\quad 465 \quad$ acres
    $- \quad 39.76$ acres
    $\overline{\quad 425.24 \text{ acres}}$

    $\quad 425.24$
    $\times \quad \$50.00$
    $\overline{\$21,262.00}$

9. $C = \pi d$
    $C = (3.1416)(14.28)$
    $C = 44.86$ rods

10. $V = L \times W \times H$
    $V = 340 \times 260 \times 40$
    $V = 3,536,000$ cu ft

11. $A = L \times W$
    $A = 80 \times 135$
    $A = 10,800$

    Cost = area $\times$ price
    Cost = $10,800 \times \$.63$
    Cost = $\$6,804$

    $V = L \times W \times H$
    $V = 40 \times 60 \times 10$
    $V = 24,000$ cu ft

    Cost = $V \times$ price
    Cost = $24,000 \times \$1.85$
    Cost = $\$44,400$

    $\quad \$44,400$
    $+ \quad 6,804$
    $\overline{\quad \$51,204}$

12. $264 \times 660 \qquad = 174,240$ sq ft
    $174,240 \div 43,560 = 4.0$ acres
    $4 \times \$800 \qquad = \$3,200$

13. Land $\qquad\qquad 125 \times 100 \times \$\ 1 = \$\ 12,500$
    Two-story
    $\quad$ building $\quad 2 \times \ 40 \times \ 60 \times \$25 = \ 120,000$
    Full basement $\quad 40 \times \ 60 \times \$\ 5 = \quad 12,000$
    Driveway $\qquad\ 10 \times \ 80 \times \$\ 4 = \quad\ 3,200$
    Sidewalks $\qquad\ 3 \times \ 70 \times \$\ 3 = \qquad 630$
    Yard improvements $\qquad\qquad\quad = \quad\ 5,000$
    $\overline{\qquad\qquad\qquad\qquad\qquad\qquad \$153,330}$

14. Site Z = 3 acres
    Site Y = 3 acres $\times$ 3 = $\quad$ 9 acres
    Site X = 9 acres $\times$ 2 = 18 acres
    $\overline{\qquad\qquad\qquad\qquad\qquad 30 \text{ acres}}$

    160 acres = one quarter section
    $- \quad 30$
    $\overline{130 \text{ acres remain}}$

PRACTICE PROBLEMS: RATE, INCOME, VALUE, INTEREST

1. Let x = value of stream of income
    $.08x = \$600 \times 12$ months
    $.08x = \$7,200$
    $x = \$7,200/.08$
    $x = \$90,000$

2. $6 \times 2\frac{1}{2}\% = 15\%$ depreciation at the end of 6 years
    x = original value of house
    Original value less depreciation = present value

    $x - (.15x) = \$7,650$
    $\quad .85x = \$7,650$
    $\qquad x = \$7,650/.85$
    $\qquad x = \$9,000$

3. $\quad RP = AY$
    $.13(P) = (\$1,000.00/\text{month})(12)$
    $.13\ P = \$12,000.00$
    $\quad P = \$12,000.00/.13$
    $\quad P = \$92,307.69$

4. $12\% \quad$ = return each year
    $100\% \quad$ = total amount invested
    $100/12 = 8.33$ years

5. Net income per month = $\$325 - \$155 = \$170$
    $\$170 \times 12 = \$2,040$

6. Income = 4 × $200 × 12 months = $ 9,600
               3 × $175 × 12 months = $ 6,300
               3 × $150 × 12 months = $ 5,400
               Gross income   = $21,300
               Less expenses   = 10,000
               Less debt service = 6,000
               Net income   = $ 5,300

$ROI = \$5,300/\$50,000$
$ROI = 10.6\%$

7. $RP = I$
$R(\$23,000) = (\$300 \times 12 \text{ months})$
$R = \$3,600/\$23,000$
$R = 15.7\%$

8. $RP = I$
$.09(\$40,000) = \$3,600$
$\$3,600/4 = \$900$ quarterly payment

PRACTICE PROBLEMS: PROFIT AND LOSS

1. 3 × $2,000 = $6,000 total sale price of 3 lots
$6,000 — original investment = profit
$6,000 — $4,500 = $1,500 profit
ROI = profit/original investment
$ROI = \$1,500/\$4,500$
$ROI = 33\frac{1}{3}\%$

2. Loss = sales price — cost
Cost = sales price/(1 — loss)
Cost = $35,000/(1 — .06)
Cost = $35,000/.94
Cost = $37,234.04

3. Profit = sales price — cost
Sales price = cost + profit
Sales price = $5,000 + .15 ($5,000)
Sales price = $5,000 + $750
Sales price = $5,750

4. Profit = sales price — cost
Profit = $65,000 — $43,500
Profit = $21,500
% Profit = profit/cost
% Profit = $21,500/$43,500
% Profit = .494 = 49.4%

5. Loss = sales price — cost
$3,400 = $20,350 — $23,750
% Loss = $3,400/$23,750
% Loss = .143 or 14.3%

PRACTICE PROBLEMS: COMMISSION

1. Expenses   = 10 showings at $20 each = $200
Commission = ½ (.08) ($50,000) = $2,000
Net income = commission less expenses
Net income = $2,000 — $200 = $1,800

2. x = selling price
$.06(\$10,000) + .05(x - \$10,000) = \$760$
$\$600 + .05x - 500 = \$760$
$.05x = \$660$
$x = \$13,200$

3. Commission = .08($27,500) = $2,200 $32,000
Original offering = 80 acres ×   −27,500
   $400 = $32,000   4,500
Difference in offer and asked price =   − 2,200
   $2,300 $ 2,300

4. $95,000 × .08 = $7,600
$7,600/2 = $3,800

5. $SP \times R = C$
$48,500 × .08 = $3,880
⅜ ($3,880) = $1,455 for the salesperson

PRACTICE PROBLEMS: MORTGAGE BALANCES, RENT, TAX, INSURANCE, INTEREST PRORATIONS

Mortgage Balances

1. $38,500 × .08 = $3,080.00
$3,080.00/12 = $256.67/month
$328.00 — $256.67 = $71.33
$38,500.00 — $71.33 = $38,428.67 after payment

2. $24,250.00 × .07 = $1,697.50
$1,697.50/12 = $141.46/month
$210.00 — $141.46 = $68.54
$24,250.00 — $68.54 = $24,181.46 after June 15 payment

$24,181.46 × .07 = $1,692.70
$1,692.70/12 = $141.06/month
$210.00 — $141.06 = $68.94
$24,181.46 — $68.94 = $24,112.52 after July 15th payment

Rent

3. 30 — 20 = 10 days remaining

1-bedroom (two)
$180/30 days = $6/day
$6 × 10 days remaining = $60

2-bedroom (one)
$210/30 days = $7/day
7 × 10 days remaining = $70

3-bedroom (one)
$270/30 days = $9/day
$9 × 10 days remaining = $90

Total $120 + $70 + $90 = $280 owed Mr. David

Taxes

4. $37,500
   <u>×   .4</u>
   $15,000

   $15,000 × $8.27/$100 = $1,240.50 annual taxes
   $1,240.50/12 = $103.375 or $103.38/month
   $103.38 × 6⅓ months = $654.71 charged to seller
   $1,240.50 − $654.71 = $585.79 charged to buyer

Insurance

		Day	Month	Year
		41	18	77
5.	Expires	1̶1̶	7̶	7̶8̶
	Close	23	9	77
	Remaining	18	9	0

$489/3 = $163/year
$163/12 = $13.58/month
$13.58/30 = $.45/day
18 ($.45) + 9 ($13.58) = $8.10 + $122.22
   = $130.32 to seller

Interest

6. $38,500.00
   <u>×   .0875</u>
   $3,368.75/year

   $3,368.75/12 = $280.73/month
   $280.73/30 = $9.36/day
   $9.36 × 20 days = $187.20

Appendix D

Answers to Sample Salesperson's Examination and Sample Broker's Examination

ANSWERS TO SAMPLE SALESPERSON'S LICENSING EXAMINATION

1. C	21. D	41. A	61. D	81. C
2. D	22. D	42. D	62. C	82. C
3. C	23. C	43. D	63. C	83. C
4. D	24. C	44. B	64. C	84. D
5. C	25. A	45. D	65. A	85. C
6. D	26. D	46. B	66. D	86. B
7. B	27. A	47. D	67. D	87. D
8. B	28. B	48. B	68. B	88. B
9. B	29. D	49. D	69. C	89. B
10. C	30. D	50. B	70. C	90. B
11. C	31. A	51. A	71. D	91. C
12. B	32. D	52. D	72. C	92. A
13. C	33. D	53. D	73. B	93. D
14. C	34. C	54. D	74. D	94. D
15. A	35. C	55. B	75. B	95. C
16. B	36. B	56. C	76. B	96. B
17. B	37. C	57. C	77. C	97. C
18. B	38. D	58. C	78. B	98. C
19. C	39. D	59. C	79. C	99. D
20. B	40. B	60. D	80. C	100. D

Calculations

3. $82,000 × .07 = $5,740
   $82,000 − $5,740 = $76,260

5. 195′ × 225′ = 43,875 sq ft
   43,875 sq ft/43,560 sq ft = 1.01 acres

8. $7,500 + $20,000 = $27,500 assessed value
   $27,500 × $8.40/$100 = $2,310 annual taxes

13. $80,500 × .07 = $5,635

14. $80,500 × .90 = $72,450

31. $42,250 × .85 = $35,913

40. $15,000 × .05 = $750

46. 9½ − 8¼ = 1¼ % difference
    1¼ % = 10 points

73. I/R = value
    $2,375/.065 = $36,538.46

74. I/R = value
    $32,475/.91 = $35,686.81 or $35,687

75. $960/$24,000 = .04 or $4/$100

76. $21,000 + $1,340.40 = $22,340.40
    $1,340.40/$22,340.40 = .06 or 6%

77. 100% − 25% loss = 75%
    $30,000 = 75%
    $30,000/.75 = $40,000 cost new

78. $6,500 × .075 = $487.50
    $487.50/12 = $40.63
    $40.63 × 2 = $81.26

79. $75,000 × .08 = $6,000
    $6,000/4 = $1,500

80. $32,500 × 1.20 = $39,000
    $39,000/.93 = $41,935.48 or $41,935

81.
	Day	Month	Year
Expiration date	30	11	TY
Closing date	20	8	TY
Remaining	10	3	0

3⅓ months × $40 = $133.33

82. $42,300 × .30 = $12,690 assessed value
    $12,690 × $8.47/$100 = $1,074.84/year
    $1,074.84/12 = $89.57/month
    $89.57 × 7⅓ months = $656.85

83. ($19,479.33 × .085)/12 = $137.98/month
    $137.98/30 = $4.60/day
    20 × $4.60 = $92.00

87. $95,000 × .14 = $13,300/year
    $13,300/12 = $1,108.33/month

89. 12 × $700 = $8,400 annual expenses
    $9,600 − $8,400 = $1,200 net income
    $1,200/.12 = $10,000

90. $60,000/.60 = $100,000

100. $2,400 + $1,080 = $3,480 gross income annually
     $3,480/12 = $290/month
     $290 × 103 = $29,870

ANSWERS TO SAMPLE BROKER'S
LICENSING EXAMINATION

1. B	21. A	41. C	61. B	81. B
2. D	22. C	42. A	62. B	82. C
3. B	23. B	43. C	63. C	83. D
4. B	24. C	44. D	64. A	84. C
5. B	25. A	45. A	65. C	85. D
6. A	26. A	46. D	66. A	86. D
7. B	27. C	47. C	67. C	87. B
8. C	28. C	48. C	68. C	88. B
9. D	29. D	49. C	69. B	89. A
10. B	30. A	50. A	70. B	90. C
11. C	31. A	51. A	71. A	91. C
12. B	32. C	52. C	72. D	92. C
13. B	33. A	53. D	73. C	93. B
14. D	34. C	54. D	74. A	94. C
15. B	35. B	55. D	75. C	95. D
16. C	36. D	56. A	76. C	96. C
17. D	37. C	57. A	77. B	97. C
18. A	38. B	58. A	78. A	98. C
19. C	39. A	59. C	79. C	99. C
20. A	40. B	60. A	80. A	100. A

Calculations

3. $30,000 × .06 = $1,800
   $30,000 − $1,800 = $28,200

16. $760/12 = $63.33/month
    $63.33 × 6.5 = $411.65

17. $23,595 × .075 = $1,769.63 annual interest
    $1,769.63/12 = $147.47 monthly interest
    $200 − $147.47 = $52.53 paid on principal in
    May
    $23,595 − $52.53 = $23,542.47, amount of
    loan on June 1
    $23,542.47 × .075 = $1,765.69 annual interest
    $1,765.69/12 = $147.14 monthly interest
    $200 − $147.14 = $52.86 paid on principal in
    June
    $23,542.47 − $52.86 = $23,489.61, amount of
    loan on July 1

19. $23,489.61 × .01 = $234.89 or $234.90

21. $29,000 − $23,489.61 = $5,510.39

22. $150/12 = $12.50/month
    $12.50/30 = $.42/day
    (1 × $12.50) + (5 × $.42) = $12.50 + $2.10
    = $14.60

23. $175 × ½ month = $87.50

24. $23,489.61 × .075 = $1,761.72 annual interest
    $1,761.72/12 = $146.81 monthly interest
    $146.81 × ½ month = $73.41

47. $45,000 × .12 = $5,400 annual income
    $5,400/12 = $450 monthly income

81.

	Day	Month	Year
Expires	20	6	1978
Close	10	9	1977
Remaining	10	9	0

   9⅓ × $30 = $280

82. $21,000/.94 = $22,340.43 = $22,340

83. $10,000 × .0875 = $875
    ($875/12) × 2 = $145.84

84. $2,400/.07 = $34,285.71

85. $50,000/1.25 = $40,000

86. $30,000/.95 = $31,578.95 or $31,579

87. $960/12 = $80/month
    $80/month × 6⅔/months = $533.40

88. 1.2 × $30,000 = $36,000
    $36,000/.94 = $38,297.87 or $38,298

89. ½ mile × ¼ mile = 80 acres
    80 acres × $1,200 = $96,000

90. $90,000 × .12 = $10,800/year
    $10,800/year divided by 12 = $900/month

93. 50′ × 36′ = 1,800 sq ft
    $24,750/1,800 = $13.75/sq ft

94. 348,480/43,560 = 8.0 acres
    8 acres × $700 = $5,600

95. 20′ × 24′ × 18′ = 8,640 cu ft
    8,640 × $.75 = $6,480

96. $21,000 × .06 = $1,260
    $1,260 × .40 = $504

97. $6,000 × .07 = $420
    $420/2 = $210

98. $8,000 × .09 = $720
    $720/12 = $60
    $60 × 7½ months = $450

99. $84.25 × 12 = $1,011/year
    $1,011/.085 = $11,894.12

100. $250 × 2 = $500 total commission
     $10,000 × .05 = $500
     Sales price = $10,000

Solution to Sample Brokers Examination Problem

SETTLEMENT STATEMENT WORKSHEET

Complete the Settlement Statement Worksheet on the basis of information furnished in the Listing, Offer to Purchase Agreement, and Settlement Problems only. Do not add other items. Use the 30-day method of computation.

	BUYER'S STATEMENT		SELLER'S STATEMENT	
	DEBIT	CREDIT	DEBIT	CREDIT
Purchase Price	29,000.00			29,000.00
Deposit		2,000.00		
Loan Balance — Assumed		23,489.61	23,489.61	
Loan Assumption Fee — 1%	234.90			
Interest Prorated		73.41	73.41	
Taxes Prorated — Arrears		411.65	411.65	
Insurance Prorated	14.60			14.60
Sales Fee — Commission 6%			1,740.00	
Abstract Continuation			50.00	
Deed Preparation			10.00	
Abstract Examination & Opinion	40.00			
Recording Fees	22.50			
Rent — Prorated		87.50	87.50	
Balance Due from Buyer		3,249.83		
Balance Due to Seller			3,152.43	
	$29,312.00	$29,312.00	$29,014.60	$29,014.60

Calculations

1. *Loan balance assumed*
   $23,595.00 × .075 = $1,769.63
   May 1
   $1,769.63/12 = $147.47/month
   $200.00 − $147.47 = $52.53
   $23,595.00 − $52.53 = $23,542.47 after June 1 payment

   $23,542.47 × .075 = $1,765.69
   $1,765.69/12 = $147.14/month
   $200.00 − $147.14 = $52.86
   $23,542.47 − $52.86 = $23,489.61 after July 1 payment

2. *Interest in arrears—prorated*
   $23,489.61 × .075 = $1,761.72
   $1,761.72/12 = $146.81/month
   15 days = ½ month
   $146.81/2 = $73.41

3. *Broker's commission*
   $29,000.00 × .06 = $1,740.00

4. *Taxes prorated*
   $8,000.00 × $9.50/$100 = $760/year
   $760.00/12 = $63.33/month
   $63.33 × 6½ months = $411.65

5. *Insurance prorated*
   $150.00/12 = $12.50/month
   $150.00/360 = $.42/day
   1($12.50) + 5($.42) = $14.60

6. *Rent prorated*
   $175.00/month/2 = $87.50
   15 days = ½ month

7. *Loan assumption fee*
   $23,489.61 × .01 = $234.90

Appendix E

Practice Problems for Real Estate Transactions

PROBLEM 102

On the morning of September 26, this year, Mrs. Carolyn Turner, a widow, called Held Real Estate about the possibility of listing her home for sale. You, as salesperson for Held Real Estate, took the call, and the next morning obtained a 90-day exclusive authorization to sell listing on her residence at 1516 Alta Drive in Anytown, Your State, phone 334-3388.

Upon examination of the premises you obtained the following information: The house is a 3-bedroom ranch-style home with a frame exterior. The yard is fenced, and there is a screened porch and patio in the rear. The house was originally built 14 years ago and has a two-car attached garage and a roof composed of asphalt shingles. There are storm windows and doors. The house has the city amenities of curbs, gutters, sidewalks, and storm sewers in the front and access from the rear by means of an alley into the driveway at the side of the house which runs to the garage. It has city water and electricity. The heating system is natural gas forced-air and the house is centrally air-conditioned. There are 1½ baths, a 16' X 18' living room with a fireplace, a 14' X 16' dining room, and a 12' X 12' den with a fireplace. There is no basement, but there is a 6' X 8' utility room where the furnace and a 40-gallon gas water heater are kept along with a washer and dryer. In the kitchen, the cabinets are wood and the counter tops are Formica. The gas stove, built-in oven, and dishwasher are included in the sales price. There is also a stainless-steel double sink with a built-in disposal unit. The attic is unfinished, with a pull-down stairway. The house was custom built by John H. Hammer and contains a total of 2,400 square feet.

The home is located near Anytown High School, Binford Middle School, Public School 101, and St. Peter's Catholic Elementary. It is 5 minutes from the Monroe Shopping Mall, which may also be reached by the city bus line which runs one block north of the property.

The lot is 100' X 120' and legally described as Lot 45 in Lakewood Addition in the City of Anytown, County of Madison, Your State, as recorded in Plat Book 6, page 31. The assessed valuation of the land is $2,000, and of the improvements $7,000. The present tax rate is $7.00/$100, and the taxes for the year are due December 31, this year, and have not yet been paid.

The mortgage is held by Home Federal Savings and Loan Association of Anytown. The monthly payments are $96, including only principal and interest at 6% in arrears. The balance after the September 15th payment was $9,650.

Mrs. Turner has a fire and extended coverage insurance policy in effect for $27,000, which expires June 10, next year. The annual premium is $144 and is prepaid.

After the discussion, a listing price of $27,000 is placed upon the property, and Mrs. Turner feels she can give complete possession within 15 days after the final closing, since she is moving to a condominium in Florida and needs to give notification of when she will be there. She has no desire to exchange properties. The sales fee is set at 7%. Mrs. Turner wishes the property to be shown by appointment only and leaves a key at the Realtor's office.

The Offer

On October 19, this year, Mr. Robert R. David and his wife, Nancy F. David, of 2415 Eastside Drive, Anytown, make an offer through Held Real Estate to Mrs. Turner after you have shown them the house. The offer is for $27,000 contingent on approval for financing under a new deed of trust for at least $24,000 for a period of 20 years in 240 equal installments at an interest rate not to exceed 8½% from a local institution within 30 days after acceptance of their offer. The remainder is to be in cash. They also would like to close on or before November 23, this year, and they say it would be agreeable to close at Mrs. Turner's mortgagee's office. They also ask for $23/day liquidating damages for each day Mrs. Turner might hold over after the 15 days. The Davids desire to purchase the washer and dryer under a separate bill of sale for $400. Upon completion of the offer, the Davids give you a cashier's check for $1,000 as earnest money.

The offer is accepted, as is, the same day, and the parties proceed to fulfill the contract.

Settlement

The closing is set for November 15 and the Davids have been approved for financing. The deed preparation fee to be paid by the seller is $30, and the recording fees to be paid by the purchaser are $31. The loan origination fee is 1%, and the owner's title insurance is ½% of the sales price. The mortgagee's title insurance is $75. The Davids will assume Mrs. Turner's fire insurance policy.

(Forms for an exclusive authorization to sell, an offer to purchase agreement, and a settlement statement are supplied for your use on this problem in the back of this book.)

PROBLEM 103

On September 15, this year, you listed the property owned by Mr. John T. Murphy and his wife, Betty, located at 125 West 3rd Street, Anytown, Your State. You took a 60-day exclusive authorization to sell listing. The structure is a one-story duplex with two identical units. The Murphys occupy one side, while the other is rented for $180/month with 9 months remaining on the lease. The structure was constructed 9 years ago on a cement block foundation and has no basement. It is legally described as Lots 104 and 105 in the City of Anytown, County of Blue, Your State. Each unit consists of a 16' X 18' living room, a 12' X 12' dining room, a kitchen with all built-in appliances including a dishwasher, 1½ baths, and 3 bedrooms. It is carpeted throughout. The exterior is brick with wood trim. Each unit has a gas forced-air heating and air-conditioning unit, a 30-gallon gas water heater, and all city utilities including electricity, water, sewers, and garbage pickup. The tenant is responsible for his own utilities. The lot size is 150' X 200' on the north side of West 3rd Street.

The assessed value of the land is $3,000, and of the improvements $12,000. The current year's tax rate is $9.25/$100, and the taxes were due January 1, this year, but have not yet been paid.

The outstanding mortgage balance after the September 1st payment is $28,500. The monthly payments are $450/month and include principal, interest, taxes, and insurance. The principal and interest constant is $328/month while taxes run $110/month and the insurance is $12/month. The payments are due on the first of each month, and 8% interest is payable in arrears. The mortgage is held by Martin Savings and Loan of Anytown.

The premises are covered by a fire insurance policy for $50,000. The policy was originally issued at a cost of $450 for 3 years paid in advance and expires August 15, next year.

The listing price is set at $52,900, and the sales fee is to be 6%. The Murphys will give possession subject to tenants' rights at the closing. The rent is payable on the first day of each month and is collected in advance. The Murphys will sell the property as is and desire cash or cash assumption of their existing mortgage. They do not desire a trade. They wish to be contacted prior to showing the house at their home phone, 478-5168, and will leave a key at City Realty.

The Offer

On October 3, this year, Mark Jones (single) submits an offer to you for the Murphy property for $50,000. The offer is contingent upon Mr. Jones' finding new financing for 90% of the sales price within 30 days for 30 years in 360 equal installments at an interest rate not to exceed 8¾% and that the Murphys will take back a second mortgage for $2,000 for 5 years at an interest rate of 8¾%. The offer is open for 4 days.

The Murphys counter the offer on that day with a $51,000 sales price and all other terms remaining the same. The counteroffer is to expire October 7. On October 6, Mr. Jones accepts the counteroffer and later is approved for financing.

Mr. Jones has given you a $500 earnest money deposit by personal check. Mr. Jones desires to close no later than November 20, this year.

Settlement

The final closing is set for November 10, this year, at the City Realty offices in Anytown. The taxes, rent, and insurance are to be prorated as of day of closing. The insurance policy is being assumed by the purchaser. The deed preparation fee to be paid by the sellers is $25.00, and the owner's title insurance policy is to be paid by the sellers in the amount of $182.50. The purchaser will pay $75.00 for the mortgagee's title insurance. There is $634 in the seller's escrow. The purchaser's attorney fee is $75.00, and the loan origination fee will be 1% of the loan amount. Recording fees for the buyer are $28.00, and the seller is to pay the $75.00 appraisal fee. The rent is current as of November 1, this year.

(Forms for an exclusive authorization to sell, an offer to purchase agreement, and a settlement statement are supplied for your use on this problem in the back of this book.)

PROBLEM 104

On June 15, this year, you as salesperson for ABC Realty secured a 120-day exclusive authorization to sell listing agreement on a property at 321 Rose Street, Anytown, Your State, owned by Edward

Smith and his wife, Mary. It is a two-bedroom ranch with one bath. The house has a full basement, 25' X 35'. There is a 30-gallon electric water heater and electric baseboard heat. The measurements are 12' X 15' in the living room, and 10' X 12' in the dining room. There are a well and a septic system. The lot is 150' X 200' and legally described as Lot 6, Bloom Addition, Anytown, Brown County, Your State. The house is 22 years old. The roof is composition and was replaced 3 years ago, at which time the owner put in new storm windows and doors. The Smiths paid off their original mortgage 2 years ago and would consider taking a 15-year purchase money mortgage if the buyer would put 30% down at 8% to be repaid in 180 equal installments monthly, including principal and interest only. The land is assessed for $2,000 and the improvements for $5,000, and the tax rate is $8.25/$100. The taxes are due December 31, this year, and have not been prepaid. The Smiths will leave the kitchen appliances including the stove, refrigerator, and portable dishwasher. They will sell the air-conditioner, washer and dryer, and lawnmower separately. The property is listed for $24,500. The commission is set at 6%, and possession will be at closing.

The Offer

On August 1, this year, the Smiths' property is shown by you to Mr. Robert Armstrong and his wife, Betty, who agree to buy it at the listed price. The Armstrongs feel that 30% down is too much for them and instruct you to draw up the contract for 20% down at the 8% interest for 15 years and 180 equal monthly payments including principal and interest. They also wish to have the water system checked and certified by the health authorities at the seller's expense. They will be willing to offer $675 for the air-conditioner, washer, dryer, and lawnmower. Settlement is desired by September 1, this year. A deposit of $500 cash is taken.

Settlement

All the terms in the offer to purchase and listing contract are met, and the settlement is scheduled for September 1, this year.

In addition to the purchase price, deposit, purchase money mortgage, proration of taxes, and sales fee, the following charges will be assessed at closing:

The title examination fee, ½% of the sales price, and the recording fee for the mortgage, $50, are charged to the purchaser. The appraisal fee of $40

and the well examination fee and certification, $35, are charged to the seller.

(Forms for an exclusive authorization to sell, an offer to purchase agreement, and a settlement statement are supplied for your use on this problem in the back of this book.)

PROBLEM 105

On April 15, this year, you, as agent for Big Red Realty, list the home of Otis Brown and his wife, Mary, at 24 Laurel Avenue, Anytown, Your State, for 90 days. It is a 1½-story Cape Cod with a stone exterior. It has a full basement, 30' X 42', a living room with fireplace, 14' X 20'; a dining room, 10' X 12'; two bedrooms and a bathroom on the second floor, and one bedroom and bath on the first floor. The eat-in size kitchen is equipped with a double steel sink, electric stove, and refrigerator which are to be included in the sales price. Also, there is a disposal and dishwasher to be included. The heating and air-conditioning system is electric, and there are storm windows and doors. There is a two-car attached garage with a cement driveway at the side. The roof is slate. The lot is 80' X 110' and described as Lot 8, Block 4, Section 1, Laurel Addition to Anytown, Green County, Your State. The property has an assessed value of land of $2,500 and improvements of $7,000. The tax rate is $8.40/$100, with the taxes due by January 1, next year. The Browns feel they should net $30,080 after your commission of 6%. The present 30-year first trust was placed on the property 6 years ago by the Third State Savings and Loan Association. As of April 1, this year, a $25,920 balance remains with principal and interest payments of $274/month at 8% in arrears. The taxes and insurance are paid by the owners. The Browns will leave a key at Big Red Realty and desire to be called at 334-8311 before the house is shown. It will be available for immediate complete possession at closing.

The Offer

On July 4, this year, you show the Brown house to Mr. Charles Joseph and his wife, Clara. They like the house and make an offer through Big Red Realty for $32,000. The offer is contingent upon the Josephs being able to obtain FHA financing for $30,550 for 25 years at the present FHA rate of interest to be repaid in 300 equal monthly installments. The Josephs also insist on settlement by August 10, this year. The offer is to remain open until tomorrow midnight. The Josephs also specify that the closing be held in the offices of their attorney, Mr. Will Reamington. They give you a $500 personal check as earnest money. The offer is prepared by you and given to the Browns immediately. The Browns accept the offer the same day.

Settlement

The Josephs are approved for financing in the desired amount. The taxes are to be prorated. The Josephs are to provide fire insurance at a cost of $182. The lending institution desires a tax escrow of 2 months' taxes in advance. The loan origination fee is 1%. Title insurance for the mortgagee is $75 charged to the purchaser, and an owner's policy is charged to the seller for $187.50. The appraisal fee is $50 charged to the purchaser; also, a photo fee of $15 and survey fee of $55 are charged to the purchaser. The seller must pay 5 discount points at closing. The closing will take place August 10, this year. The mortgage payments are current.

(Forms for an exclusive authorization to sell, an offer to purchase agreement, and a settlement statement are supplied for your use on this problem in the back of this book.)

PROBLEM 106

On August 1, this year, Harvey L. Jones and his wife, Lois Jones, called you, as a salesperson for Community Realty, to list their property. On August 2, you go to the Joneses' home at 1221 Wayside Drive in Anytown, Your State, to obtain the necessary information.

The Joneses live in a 3-bedroom ranch-style home with 1½ baths. The living room is 14' X 20' and the dining room is 12' X 14'. There is a den with a fireplace. They have a one-car garage and patio in the rear. There is no basement, but there is an 8' X 12' utility room where the washer and dryer are kept. They are to be included in the sales price. The house is all electric and has all city utilities. There are sidewalks, curbs, and gutters. The kitchen has an electric range and oven built in; the sink is double and stainless steel. The disposal, dishwasher, and refrigerator are all included in the listing price. The lot is 150' X 150' and is assessed at $3,000 and the improvements are assessed at $8,000. The tax rate is $7.40/$100. The property is described as Lot 21, Block 9, Section C, the Smallwood Addition to the City of Anytown, County of Madison, Your State. There is an additional 5-acre plot adjoining the rear of the Joneses' lot that they will sell with the house or separately for $10,000.

There is an outstanding mortgage of $10,120 after the August 1 payment is made. The loan was executed 13 years ago for 25 years at 7½% in arrears when the property was new. The loan is assumable. The monthly payments are $175/month including principal and interest only. The mortgage is held by First Federal Loan Company. There is a fire insurance policy with a premium of $270 for 3 years paid in advance that expires May 1, next year. The taxes are due December 31, this year.

Mr. Jones would like to sell his garden tractor under separate bill of sale for $850.

After further discussion you agree on a 90-day listing for $38,500. Your commission will be 6%. The Joneses leave a key at the office and wish to be called at home, 339-6111, before the house is shown. They can give possession at closing.

The Offer

On August 10, Mr. William Dallas and his wife, Nancy, make an offer of $37,750 for the Jones property and $10,000 for the additional acreage. They also include a $750 offer on the tractor. The offer is contingent upon the Dallases finding financing for 80% of the sales price for 30 years in 360 equal installments of principal and interest at 8¾%. Also, they desire to purchase the additional acreage on a land contract at the listed price with 30% down and a contract for 10 years at 8¾%. They will pay cash for the tractor. The offer is to remain open until midnight August 15, this year. You take a $500 deposit by personal check. On August 12, this year, the Joneses accept the offer as is. All parties then move to fulfill it. The settlement is to be before September 1, this year, at Community Realty.

Settlement

The Dallases are approved for financing, and the Joneses have the contract drawn up at a cost of $75.00. There is a loan origination fee of 1%, and 2 discount points are charged the buyer on the new loan. The buyer has additional legal fees of $125.00 for the abstract examination. The abstract cost to the seller is $100.00. There are recording fees to the buyer of $37.50 and to the seller of $12.50. The insurance and taxes are to be assumed and prorated. The closing takes place August 31, this year.

(Forms for an exclusive authorization to sell, an offer to purchase agreement and a settlement statement are supplied for your use on this problem in the back of this book.)

Appendix F

Solutions to Practice Problems for Real Estate Transactions

Calculations—Problem 102

1. *Sales fee:*
    $27,000 \times .07 = $1,890

2. *Taxes:*
Land	$2,000.00
Improvements	7,000.00
Total assessment	$9,000.00

    $9,000.00 \times $7.00/$100.00 = $630.00
    $630.00/12 = $52.50/month
    10½ months \times $52.50 = $551.25

3. *Insurance:*
	Day	Month	Year
Expiration date	10	6	NY
Closing date	15	11	TY
Remaining	25	6	0

    $144.00/12 = $12.00/month
    $144.00/360 = $.40/day
    6($12.00) + 25($.40) = $82.00

4. *Turner trust:*
Beginning balance	$9,650.00
Interest rate	$\times$.06
Annual interest	$579.00

    $579.00/12 = $48.25/month interest
    $96.00 − $48.25 = $47.75 reduction after Oct. 15
    $9,650.00 − $47.75 = $9,602.25 remaining balance

5. *Interest, in arrears:*
    $9,602.25 \times .06 = $576.14
    $576.14/12 = $48.01

6. *Loan origination fee:*
    $24,000 \times .01 = $240.00

7. *Owner's title insurance:*
    $27,000 \times .005 = $135

Calculations—Problem 103

1. *Murphy mortgage:*
    $28,500.00 \times .08 = $2,280.00
    $2,280.00/12 = $190/month
    $328 − $190 = $138

After Oct. 1 payment $28,500 − $138 = $28,362
$28,362.00 \times .08 = $2,268.96
$2,268.96/12 = $189.08
$328.00 − $189.08 = $138.92
After Nov. 1 payment
$28,362.00 − $138.92 = $28,223.08

2. *Jones mortgage:*
    $51,000 \times .90 = $45,900

3. *Interest prorated on Murphy mortgage:*
    $28,223.08 \times .08 = $2,257.85
    $2,257.85/12 = $188.15/month
    $188.15/30 days = $6.27/day
    $6.27 \times 10 days = $62.70

4. *Taxes:*
Land	$ 3,000.00
Improvements	12,000.00
Assessed value	$15,000.00

    $15,000 \times $9.25/$100 = $1,387.50
    $1,387.50/12 = $115.63
    $115.63 \times 10⅓ months = $1,194.80
    or $115.63 \times 10 months = $1,156.30

10 days \times $1,387.50/360 =	38.50
	$1,194.80

5. *Rent:*
    $180/month/30 days = $6/day
    $6 \times 20 days remaining = $120 to buyer

6. *Insurance:*
	Day	Month	Year
Expiration date	15	08	NY
Closing date	10	11	TY
Remaining	5	9	0

    $150.00/12 = $12.50/month
    $150.00/360 days = $.42/day
    5($.42) + 9($12.50) = $114.60

7. *Loan origination fee:*
    $45,900 \times .01 = $459

8. *Brokerage fee:*
    $51,000 \times .06 = $3,060

Calculations—Problem 104

1. *Purchase money mortgage:*
    $24,500 \times .80 = $19,600

2. *Taxes, prorated:*
   (For calculation purposes, all months have 30 days)
   $7,000 \times \$8.25/\$100 = \$577.50$
   $\$577.50/12 = \$48.13/month$
   $\$48.13 \times 8$ months $= \$385.04$

3. *Sales fee:*
   $\$24,500 \times .06 = \$1,470$

4. *Title examination fee:*
   $\$24,500 \times .005 = \$122.50$

Calculations—Problem 105

1. *Sales fee:*
   $\$32,000 \times .06 = \$1,920$

2. *Brown mortgage balance:*
   $\$25,920.00 \times .08 = \$2,073.60$
   After April $\$2,073.60/12 = \$172.80/month$ interest
   $\$274.00 - \$172.80 = \$101.20$ principal
   $\$25,920.00 - \$101.20 = \$25,818.80$ after May payment
   $\$25,818.80 \times .08 = \$2,065.50$
   $\$2,065.50/12 = \$172.13$
   $\$274.00 - \$172.13 = \$101.87$
   $\$25,818.80 - \$101.87 = \$25,716.93$ after June payment
   $\$25,716.93 \times .08 = \$2,057.35$
   $\$2,057.35/12 = \$171.45$
   $\$274.00 - \$171.45 = \$102.55$
   $\$25,716.93 - \$102.55 = \$25,614.38$ after July 1 payment
   $\$25,614.38 \times .08 = \$2,049.15$
   $\$2,049.15/12 = \$170.76$
   $\$274.00 - \$170.16 = \$103.24$
   $\$25,614.38 - \$103.24 = \$25,511.14$ after Aug. 1 payment

3. *Interest, prorated in arrears:*
   $\$25,511.14 \times .08 = \$2,040.89$
   $\$2,040.89/12 = \$170.07$
   $\$170.07/30 = \$5.67$
   $\$5.67 \times 10 = \$56.70$ interest through Aug. 10 closing

4. *Taxes prorated:*

Land	$2,500
Improvements	7,000
Assessed value	$9,500

   $\$9,500 \times \$8.40/\$100 = \$798.00$

$\$798.00/12 = \$66.50/month$ or $\$2.22/day$
$7(\$66.50) + 10(\$2.22) = \$487.70$ owed by seller

5. *Loan origination fee:*
   $\$30,550.00 \times .01 = \$305.50$

6. *Tax escrow:*
   $\$66.50/month \times 2$ months $= \$133.00$

7. *Discount points:*
   1 point $= 1\%$
   $\$30,550.00 \times .05 = \$1,527.50$

Calculations—Problem 106

1. *Jones mortgage interest in arrears:*
   $\$10,120.00 \times .075 = \$759.00$
   $\$759.00/12 = \$63.25/month$
   Seller owes entire month $= \$63.25$

2. *Dallas new mortgage:*
   $\$37,750 \times .80 = \$30,200$

3. *Commission, 6%:*
   $\$37,750 \times .06 = \$2,265$
   $\$10,000 \times .06 = \$600$
   $\$2,265 + \$600 = \$2,865$

4. *Land contract balance:*
   $\$10,000 \times .70 = \$7,000$
   $\$3,000$ down payment by buyer

5. *Taxes prorated, owed in arrears:*

Land	$ 3,000.00
Improvements	8,000.00
Assessed value	$11,000.00

   $\$11,000.00 \times \$7.40/\$100 = \$814.00/year$
   $\$814.00/12 = \$67.83/month$
   $8(\$67.83) = \$542.64$ to be charged to seller

6. *Insurance, prorated:*

	Day	Month	Year
Expiration date	1	5	NY
Closing date	31	8	TY
Remaining	0	8	0

   $\$270.00/3 = \$90.00/year$
   $\$90.00/12 = \$7.50/month$
   8 months remaining on policy
   $8(\$7.50) = \$60.00$

7. *Loan origination fee:*
   $\$30,200 \times .01 = \$302.00$

8. *Discount points:*
   $\$30,200 \times .02 = \$604.00$

PROBLEM 102

REAL ESTATE LISTING CONTRACT (EXCLUSIVE RIGHT TO SELL)

SALES PRICE $27,000.00   TYPE HOME Ranch   TOTAL BEDROOMS 3   TOTAL BATHS 1½

ADDRESS 1516 Alta Drive, Anytown   JURISDICTION OF Madison County, Your State

AMT. OF LOAN TO BE ASSUMED $ 9,650.00   AS OF WHAT DATE Sept. 15, TY   TAXES & INS. INCLUDED no   YEARS TO GO   AMOUNT PAYABLE MONTHLY $ 96.00 @ 6 %   TYPE LOAN Conv.

MORTGAGE COMPANY Home Federal Savings and Loan   2nd MORTGAGE

OWNER'S NAME Carolyn Turner (widow)   PHONES (HOME) 334-3388   (BUSINESS)

TENANT'S NAME N/A   PHONES (HOME)   (BUSINESS)

POSSESSION Complete - 15 DAFC   DATE LISTED: Sept. 27, TY   EXCLUSIVE FOR 90 days   DATE OF EXPIRATION Dec. 27, TY

LISTING BROKER Held Real Estate   PHONE   KEY AVAILABLE AT Held Real Estate

LISTING SALESMAN You, as salesperson for Held Real Estate   HOME PHONE   HOW TO BE SHOWN: by appointment

ENTRANCE FOYER ☐ CENTER HALL ☐	AGE 14 yrs.	AIR CONDITIONING ☑	TYPE KITCHEN CABINETS wood
LIVING ROOM SIZE 16' x 18' FIREPLACE ☑	ROOFING asphalt-shingle	TOOL HOUSE ☐	TYPE COUNTER TOPS Formica
DINING ROOM SIZE 14' x 16'	GARAGE SIZE 2-car attached	PATIO ☑	EAT-IN SIZE KITCHEN ☐
BEDROOM TOTAL: 3 DOWN UP	SIDE DRIVE ☑	CIRCULAR DRIVE ☐	TYPE STOVE ☐
BATHS TOTAL: 1½ DOWN UP	PORCH ☑ SIDE ☐ REAR ☑	SCREENED ☑	BUILT-IN OVEN & RANGE ☑ gas
DEN SIZE 12' x 12' FIREPLACE ☑	FENCED YARD yes	OUTDOOR GRILL ☐	SEPARATE STOVE INCLUDED ☐
FAMILY ROOM SIZE FIREPLACE ☐	STORM WINDOWS ☑	STORM DOORS ☑	REFRIGERATOR INCLUDED ☐
RECREATION ROOM SIZE FIREPLACE ☐	CURBS & GUTTERS ☑	SIDEWALKS ☑	DISHWASHER INCLUDED yes
BASEMENT SIZE	STORM SEWERS ☑	ALLEY ☑	DISPOSAL INCLUDED ☑
NONE ☑ 1/4 ☐ 1/3 ☐ 1/2 ☐ 3/4 ☐ FULL ☐	WATER SUPPLY city		DOUBLE SINK ☐ SINGLE SINK ☐
UTILITY ROOM 6' x 8'	SEWER ☑	SEPTIC ☐	STAINLESS STEEL ☑ PORCELAIN ☐
TYPE HOT WATER SYSTEM: 40 gal. gas	TYPE GAS: NATURAL ☑	BOTTLED ☐	WASHER INCLUDED ☐ DRYER INCLUDED ☐
TYPE HEAT gas, forced air	WHY SELLING		LAND ASSESSMENT $ 2,000.00
EST. FUEL COST	moving to condominium		IMPROVEMENTS $ 7,000.00
ATTIC ☑ Unfinished	PROPERTY DESCRIPTION		TOTAL ASSESSMENTS $ 9,000.00
PULL DOWN STAIRWAY ☑ REGULAR STAIRWAY ☐ TRAP DOOR ☐	Plat Book 6, Page 31		TAX RATE $7.00/$100
NAME OF BUILDER John H. Hammer	LOT SIZE 100' x 120'		TOTAL ANNUAL TAXES $630.00
SQUARE FOOTAGE 2400	LOT NO. 45 BLOCK SECTION		
EXTERIOR OF HOUSE Frame Lakewood Addition in the City of Anytown, County of Madison, Your State			

NAME OF SCHOOLS: ELEMENTARY: P.S. 101   JR. HIGH: Binford Middle School

HIGH: Anytown High School   PAROCHIAL: St. Peter's Catholic, Elementary

PUBLIC TRANSPORTATION: City bus – 1 block

NEAREST SHOPPING AREA: Monroe Mall 5 min.

REMARKS: No exchange

Date: Sept. 27, TY

In consideration of the services of Held Real Estate (herein called "Broker") to be rendered to the undersigned (herein called 'Owner'), and of the promise of Broker to make reasonable efforts to obtain a Purchaser therefor, Owner hereby lists with Broker the real estate and all improvements thereon which are described above, (all herein called "the property"), and the Owner hereby grants to Broker the exclusive and irrevocable right to sell such property from 12:00 Noon on Sept. 27 , 19 TY until 12:00 Midnight on Dec. 27 , 19 TY (herein called "period of time"), for the price of Twenty-seven thousand and no/100 Dollars ($ 27,000.00) or for such other price and upon such other terms (including exchange) as Owner may subsequently authorize during the period of time.

It is understood by Owner that the above sum or any other price subsequently authorized by Owner shall include a cash fee of 7 per cent of such price or other price which shall be payable by Owner to Broker upon consummation by any Purchaser or Purchasers of a valid contract of sale of the property during the period of time and whether or not Broker was a procuring cause of any such contract of sale.

If the property is sold or exchanged by Owner, or by Broker or by any other person to any Purchaser to whom the property was shown by Broker or any representative of Broker within sixty (60) days after the expiration of the period of time mentioned above, Owner agrees to pay to Broker a cash fee which shall be the same percentage of the purchase price as the percentage mentioned above.

Broker is hereby authorized by Owner to place a "For Sale" sign on the property and to remove all signs of other brokers or salesmen during the period of time, and Owner hereby agrees to make the property available to Broker at all reasonable hours for the purpose of showing it to prospective Purchasers.

Owner agrees to convey the property to the Purchaser by deed with the usual covenants of title and free and clear from all encumbrances, tenancies, liens (for taxes or otherwise), but subject to applicable restrictive covenants of record. Owner acknowledges receipt of copy of this agreement.

WITNESS the following signature(s) and seal(s):

Date Signed: Sept. 27, TY   *Carolyn Turner*

(Owner)

Listing Agent Held Real Estate, You as salesperson

Address 1516 Alta Dr.   Telephone 334-3388

(Owner)

REAL ESTATE SALES CONTRACT (OFFER TO PURCHASE AGREEMENT)

This AGREEMENT made as of _____ October 19 _____ , 19 __TY__ ,

among ___ Robert R. David and Nancy F. David (H & W) ___ (herein called "Purchaser"),

and ___ Carolyn Turner (Widow) ___ (herein called "Seller"),

and ___ Held Real Estate ___ (herein called "Broker"),
provides that Purchaser agrees to buy through Broker as agent for Seller, and Seller agrees to sell the following described real estate, and all improvements
thereon, located in the jurisdiction of __Madison County, Your State__ ,

(all herein called "the property"): __Lot 45 in Lakewood Addition in the City of Anytown, County of Madison, Your State, as recorded__
__in Plat Book 6, Page 31.__ , and more commonly known as __1516 Alta Drive,__

__Anytown, Your State__ (street address).

1. The purchase price of the property is __Twenty-seven thousand and no/100__

Dollars ($ __27,000.00__), and such purchase price shall be paid as follows:

___ A new trust for at least $24,000.00 for a period of 20 years in 240 equal installments at an interest rate not to exceed 8½% ___

___ from a local institution within 30 days after acceptance; remainder to be paid in cash. ___

2. Purchaser has made a deposit of __one-thousand and no/100__ Dollars ($ __1000.00__)
with Broker, receipt of which is hereby acknowledged, and such deposit shall be held by Broker in escrow until the date of settlement and then applied
to the purchase price, or returned to Purchaser if the title to the property is not marketable.

3. Seller agrees to convey the property to Purchaser by Deed with the usual covenants of title and free and clear from all monetary encumbrances,
tenancies, liens (for taxes or otherwise), except as may be otherwise provided above, but subject to applicable restrictive covenants of record. Seller further
agrees to deliver possession of the property to Purchaser on the date of settlement and to pay the expense of preparing the deed of conveyance.

4. Settlement shall be made at __Home Federal Savings & Loan of Anytown__ on or before
___ November 23 ___ , 19 __TY__ , or as soon thereafter as title can be examined and necessary documents prepared, with
allowance of a reasonable time for Seller to correct any defects reported by the title examiner.

5. All taxes, interest, rent, and impound escrow deposits, if any, shall be prorated as of the date of settlement.

6. All risk of loss or damage to the property by fire, windstorm, casualty, or other cause is assumed by Seller until the date of settlement.

7. Purchaser and Seller agree that Broker was the sole procuring cause of this Contract of Purchase, and Seller agrees to pay Broker for services
rendered a cash fee of ___ 7 ___ per cent of the purchase price. If either Purchaser or Seller defaults under such Contract, such defaulting party shall
be liable for the cash fee of Broker and any expenses incurred by the non-defaulting party in connection with this transaction.

Subject to: __The purchase of the washer and dryer under a separate bill of sale for $400.00. Liquidating damages of__
__$23/day Possession within 15 days of final closing.__

8. Purchaser represents that an inspection satisfactory to Purchaser has been made of the property, and Purchaser agrees to accept the property
in its present condition except as may be otherwise provided in the description of the property above.

9. This Contract of Purchase constitutes the entire agreement among the parties and may not be modified or changed except by written instrument executed by all of the parties, including Broker.

10. This Contract of Purchase shall be construed, interpreted, and applied according to the law of the jurisdiction of __Your State__ and shall
be binding upon and shall inure to the benefit of the heirs, personal representatives, successors, and assigns of the parties.

All parties to this agreement acknowledge receipt of a certified copy.

WITNESS the following signatures and seals:

Carolyn Turner (SEAL) Seller

Robert R David (SEAL) Purchaser

_____ (SEAL) Seller

Nancy F. David (SEAL) Purchaser

__Held Real Estate__ (SEAL) Broker

Deposit Rec'd $ __1000.00__

(Check) (Cashier's) Cash

Sales Agent __You, as salesman for Held Real Estate__

PROBLEM 102

SETTLEMENT STATEMENT WORKSHEET

Complete the Settlement Statement Worksheet on the basis of information furnished in the Listing, Offer to Purchase Agreement, and Settlement Problems only. Do not add other items. Use the 30-day method of computation.

	BUYER'S STATEMENT		SELLER'S STATEMENT	
	DEBIT	CREDIT	DEBIT	CREDIT
Sales Price	27,000.00			27,000.00
Sales Fee — 7%			1,890.00	
Deposit		1,000.00		
Taxes		551.25	551.25	
Insurance	82.00			82.00
Turner Trust			9,602.25	
Interest			48.01	
David Trust		24,000.00		
Loan Origination Fee	240.00			
Deed Preparation Fee			30.00	
Recording Fees	31.00			
Owner's Title Insurance			135.00	
Mortgagee's Title Insurance	75.00			
Washer & Dryer — Separate Bill of Sale	400.00			400.00
Balance Due from Buyer		2,276.75		
Balance Due to Seller			15,225.49	
	$27,828.00	$27,828.00	$27,482.00	$27,482.00

REAL ESTATE LISTING CONTRACT (EXCLUSIVE RIGHT TO SELL)

SALES PRICE $52,900.00   TYPE HOME Duplex   TOTAL BEDROOMS 3/unit   TOTAL BATHS 1½/unit

ADDRESS 125 West 3rd St., Anytown   JURISDICTION OF Blue County, Your State

AMT. OF LOAN TO BE ASSUMED $ 28,500.00   AS OF WHAT DATE 9/1/TY   TAXES & INS. INCLUDED yes   YEARS TO GO ___   AMOUNT PAYABLE MONTHLY $450.00 @8 %   TYPE LOAN Conv.

MORTGAGE COMPANY Martin Savings and Loan   2nd MORTGAGE

OWNER'S NAME John T. Murphy and Betty Murphy (H & W)   PHONES (HOME) 478-5168   (BUSINESS)

TENANT'S NAME   PHONES (HOME)   (BUSINESS)

POSSESSION Complete/Landlord's   DATE LISTED: Sept. 15, TY   EXCLUSIVE FOR 60 days   DATE OF EXPIRATION Nov. 15, TY

LISTING BROKER City Realty   PHONE   KEY AVAILABLE AT City Realty

LISTING SALESMAN You, as salesperson   HOME PHONE   HOW TO BE SHOWN: By appointment

ENTRANCE FOYER ☐	CENTER HALL ☐	AGE 9 years	AIR CONDITIONING ✔	TYPE KITCHEN CABINETS
LIVING ROOM SIZE 16' x 18'	FIREPLACE ☐	ROOFING	TOOL HOUSE ☐	TYPE COUNTER TOPS
DINING ROOM SIZE 12' x 12'		GARAGE SIZE	PATIO ☐	EAT-IN SIZE KITCHEN ☐
BEDROOM TOTAL: 3/unit DOWN	UP	SIDE DRIVE ☐	CIRCULAR DRIVE ☐	TYPE STOVE ☐
BATHS TOTAL: 1½/unit DOWN	UP	PORCH ☐ SIDE ☐ REAR ☐	SCREENED ☐	BUILT-IN OVEN & RANGE ✔
DEN SIZE	FIREPLACE ☐	FENCED YARD	OUTDOOR GRILL ☐	SEPARATE STOVE INCLUDED ☐
FAMILY ROOM SIZE	FIREPLACE ☐	STORM WINDOWS ☐	STORM DOORS ☐	REFRIGERATOR INCLUDED ✔
RECREATION ROOM SIZE	FIREPLACE ☐	CURBS & GUTTERS ☐	SIDEWALKS ☐	DISHWASHER INCLUDED yes
BASEMENT SIZE		STORM SEWERS ✔	ALLEY ☐	DISPOSAL INCLUDED ☐
NONE ✔ 1/4 ☐ 1/3 ☐ 1/2 ☐ 3/4 ☐ FULL ☐		WATER SUPPLY city		DOUBLE SINK ☐ SINGLE SINK ☐
UTILITY ROOM		SEWER ✔ city	SEPTIC ☐	STAINLESS STEEL ☐ PORCELAIN ☐
TYPE HOT WATER SYSTEM: 30 gal. gas		TYPE GAS: NATURAL ✔	BOTTLED ☐	WASHER INCLUDED ☐ DRYER INCLUDED ☐
TYPE HEAT gas forced air		WHY SELLING		LAND ASSESSMENT $ 3,000.00
EST. FUEL COST				IMPROVEMENTS $ 12,000.00
ATTIC ☐		PROPERTY DESCRIPTION		TOTAL ASSESSMENTS $ 15,000.00
PULL DOWN STAIRWAY ☐	REGULAR STAIRWAY ☐	TRAP DOOR ☐	City of Anytown, County of Blue, Your State	TAX RATE $9.25/$100
NAME OF BUILDER		LOT SIZE 150' x 200'		TOTAL ANNUAL TAXES $ 1387.50
SQUARE FOOTAGE		LOT NO. 104-105 BLOCK	SECTION	
EXTERIOR OF HOUSE Brick with wood trim.				

NAME OF SCHOOLS: ELEMENTARY: ___ JR. HIGH: ___

HIGH: ___ PAROCHIAL: ___

PUBLIC TRANSPORTATION: ___

NEAREST SHOPPING AREA: ___

REMARKS: Garbage pick up, will not accept trade; 9 mos. remaining on lease; $180 rent monthly on rental unit; rental unit possession subject to tenants' rights.

Date: Sept. 15, TY

In consideration of the services of City Realty (herein called "Broker") to be rendered to the undersigned (herein called "Owner"), and of the promise of Broker to make reasonable efforts to obtain a Purchaser therefor, Owner hereby lists with Broker the real estate and all improvements thereon which are described above, (all herein called "the property"), and the Owner hereby grants to Broker the exclusive and irrevocable right to sell such property from 12:00 Noon on Sept. 15, 19 TY until 12:00 Midnight on Nov. 15, 19 TY (herein called "period of time"), for the price of Fifty-two thousand nine hundred and no/100 Dollars ($ 52,900.00) or for such other price and upon such other terms (including exchange) as Owner may subsequently authorize during the period of time.

It is understood by Owner that the above sum or any other price subsequently authorized by Owner shall include a cash fee of 6 per cent of such price or other price which shall be payable by Owner to Broker upon consummation by any Purchaser or Purchasers of a valid contract of sale of the property during the period of time and whether or not Broker was a procuring cause of any such contract of sale.

If the property is sold or exchanged by Owner, or by Broker or by any other person to any Purchaser to whom the property was shown by Broker or any representative of Broker within sixty (60) days after the expiration of the period of time mentioned above, Owner agrees to pay to Broker a cash fee which shall be the same percentage of the purchase price as the percentage mentioned above.

Broker is hereby authorized by Owner to place a "For Sale" sign on the property and to remove all signs of other brokers or salesmen during the period of time, and Owner hereby agrees to make the property available to Broker at all reasonable hours for the purpose of showing it to prospective Purchasers.

Owner agrees to convey the property to the Purchaser by deed with the usual covenants of title and free and clear from all encumbrances, tenancies, liens (for taxes or otherwise), but subject to applicable restrictive covenants of record. Owner acknowledges receipt of copy of this agreement.

WITNESS the following signature(s) and seal(s):

Date Signed: Sept. 15, TY

John T Murphy (Owner)

Listing Agent City Realty, You as salesperson

Address 125 W. 3rd St.   Telephone 478-5168

Betty Murphy (Owner)

REAL ESTATE SALES CONTRACT (OFFER TO PURCHASE AGREEMENT)   PROBLEM 103 (page 260)

This AGREEMENT made as of _____ October 3 _____ , 19 TY ,

among _____ Mark Jones _____ (herein called "Purchaser"),

and _____ John T. Murphy and Betty Murphy (H & W) _____ (herein called "Seller"),

and _____ City Realty _____ (herein called "Broker"),

provides that Purchaser agrees to buy through Broker as agent for Seller, and Seller agrees to sell the following described real estate, and all improvements thereon, located in the jurisdiction of _____ Blue County, Your State _____ ,

(all herein called "the property"): _____ Lots 104 and 105 in the city of Anytown, County of Blue, Your State _____

_____ , and more commonly known as _____ 125 West 3rd Street _____

_____ Anytown, Your State _____ (street address).

1. The purchase price of the property is _____ fifty thousand and no/100 _____

Dollars ($ 50,000.00), and such purchase price shall be paid as follows:

_____ 90% new mortgage for 30 years at 360 equal installments at an interest rate not to exceed 8¾% and a $2000. second _____

_____ mortgage at 8¾% to seller and remainder in cash _____

2. Purchaser has made a deposit of _____ five hundred and no/100 _____ Dollars ($ 500.00) with Broker, receipt of which is hereby acknowledged, and such deposit shall be held by Broker in escrow until the date of settlement and then applied to the purchase price, or returned to Purchaser if the title to the property is not marketable.

3. Seller agrees to convey the property to Purchaser by Deed with the usual covenants of title and free and clear from all monetary encumbrances, tenancies, liens (for taxes or otherwise), except as may be otherwise provided above, but subject to applicable restrictive covenants of record. Seller further agrees to deliver possession of the property to Purchaser on the date of settlement and to pay the expense of preparing the deed of conveyance.

4. Settlement shall be made at _____ City Realty _____ on or before

_____ November 20 _____ , 19 TY , or as soon thereafter as title can be examined and necessary documents prepared, with allowance of a reasonable time for Seller to correct any defects reported by the title examiner.

5. All taxes, interest, rent, and impound escrow deposits, if any, shall be prorated as of the date of settlement.

6. All risk of loss or damage to the property by fire, windstorm, casualty, or other cause is assumed by Seller until the date of settlement.

7. Purchaser and Seller agree that Broker was the sole procuring cause of this Contract of Purchase, and Seller agrees to pay Broker for services rendered a cash fee of _____ 6 _____ per cent of the purchase price. If either Purchaser or Seller defaults under such Contract, such defaulting party shall be liable for the cash fee of Broker and any expenses incurred by the non-defaulting party in connection with this transaction.

Subject to: _____ Financing from paragraph one (above) _____

_____

_____

_____

8. Purchaser represents that an inspection satisfactory to Purchaser has been made of the property, and Purchaser agrees to accept the property in its present condition except as may be otherwise provided in the description of the property above.

9. This Contract of Purchase constitutes the entire agreement among the parties and may not be modified or changed except by written instrument executed by all of the parties, including Broker.

10. This Contract of Purchase shall be construed, interpreted, and applied according to the law of the jurisdiction of _____ Your State _____ and shall be binding upon and shall inure to the benefit of the heirs, personal representatives, successors, and assigns of the parties.

All parties to this agreement acknowledge receipt of a certified copy.

WITNESS the following signatures and seals:

_____ (SEAL) Seller	_Mark Jones_ (SEAL) Purchaser
_____ (SEAL) Seller	_____ (SEAL) Purchaser
City Realty (SEAL) Broker	

Deposit Rec'd $ _____ 500.00 _____

(Check)   Cash

Sales Agent: You, as salesman for City Realty

(Counter) OFFER TO PURCHASE AGREEMENT   PROBLEM 103

This AGREEMENT made as of _____ October 3 _____ , 19 __TY__ ,

among ____ Mark Jones _____ (herein called "Purchaser"),

and ____ John T. Murphy and Betty Murphy (H & W) _____ (herein called "Seller"),

and ____ City Realty _____ (herein called "Broker"),

provides that Purchaser agrees to buy through Broker as agent for Seller, and Seller agrees to sell the following described real estate, and all improvements

thereon, located in the jurisdiction of _____ County of Blue, Your State _____ ,

(all herein called "the property"): __ Lot 104 and 105 in City of Anytown, County of Blue, Your State __

_____ , and more commonly known as __ 125 West 3rd Street __

__ Anytown, Your State _____ (street address).

1. The purchase price of the property is __ fifty-one thousand and no/100 _____

Dollars ($ __51,000.00__), and such purchase price shall be paid as follows:

__ 90% new mortgage for 30 years at 360 equal installments at an interest rate not to exceed 8¾%, and a $2000 second __

__ mortgage at 8¾% to seller for 5 years and remainder in cash __

2. Purchaser has made a deposit of __ five hundred and no/100 _____ Dollars ($ __500.00__)

with Broker, receipt of which is hereby acknowledged, and such deposit shall be held by Broker in escrow until the date of settlement and then applied to the purchase price, or returned to Purchaser if the title to the property is not marketable.

3. Seller agrees to convey the property to Purchaser by Deed with the usual covenants of title and free and clear from all monetary encumbrances, tenancies, liens (for taxes or otherwise), except as may be otherwise provided above, but subject to applicable restrictive covenants of record. Seller further agrees to deliver possession of the property to Purchaser on the date of settlement and to pay the expense of preparing the deed of conveyance.

4. Settlement shall be made at _____ City Realty _____ on or before

__ November 20 _____ , 19 __TY__ , or as soon thereafter as title can be examined and necessary documents prepared, with allowance of a reasonable time for Seller to correct any defects reported by the title examiner.

5. All taxes, interest, rent, and impound escrow deposits, if any, shall be prorated as of the date of settlement.

6. All risk of loss or damage to the property by fire, windstorm, casualty, or other cause is assumed by Seller until the date of settlement.

7. Purchaser and Seller agree that Broker was the sole procuring cause of this Contract of Purchase, and Seller agrees to pay Broker for services

rendered a cash fee of ____ 6 ____ per cent of the purchase price. If either Purchaser or Seller defaults under such Contract, such defaulting party shall be liable for the cash fee of Broker and any expenses incurred by the non-defaulting party in connection with this transaction.

Subject to: _____ Financing from paragraph 1 above; counter offer expires Oct. 7, TY _____

_____

_____

_____

8. Purchaser represents that an inspection satisfactory to Purchaser has been made of the property, and Purchaser agrees to accept the property in its present condition except as may be otherwise provided in the description of the property above.

9. This Contract of Purchase constitutes the entire agreement among the parties and may not be modified or changed except by written instrument executed by all of the parties, including Broker.

10. This Contract of Purchase shall be construed, interpreted, and applied according to the law of the jurisdiction of __ Your State __ and shall be binding upon and shall inure to the benefit of the heirs, personal representatives, successors, and assigns of the parties.

All parties to this agreement acknowledge receipt of a certified copy.

WITNESS the following signatures and seals:

John T. Murphy (SEAL) Seller   _Mark Jones_ (SEAL) Purchaser

Betty Murphy (SEAL) Seller   _____ (SEAL) Purchaser

____ City Realty ____ (SEAL) Broker

Deposit Rec'd $ ____ 500.00 ____

(Check)   Cash

Sales Agent: You as salesman for City Realty

PROBLEM 103 (page 260)

SETTLEMENT STATEMENT WORKSHEET

Complete the Settlement Statement Worksheet on the basis of information furnished in the Listing, Offer to Purchase Agreement, and Settlement Problems only. Do not add other items. Use the 30-day method of computation.

	BUYER'S STATEMENT		SELLER'S STATEMENT	
	DEBIT	CREDIT	DEBIT	CREDIT
Sales Price	51,000.00			51,000.00
Sales Fee — 6%			3,060.00	
Deposit		500.00		
Murphy Mortgage Balance			28,223.08	
Interest Prorated — Murphy			62.70	
New Mortgage — Jones		45,900.00		
Second Mortgage		2,000.00	2,000.00	
Taxes		1,194.80	1,194.80	
Rent		120.00	120.00	
Insurance	114.60			114.60
Deed Preparation			25.00	
Owner's Title Policy			182.50	
Mortgagee's Title Policy	75.00			
Seller's Escrow Balance				634.00
Buyer's Attorney Fee	75.00			
Recording Fee	28.00			
Appraisal Fee			75.00	
Loan Origination Fee 1%	459.00			
Balance Due From Buyer		2,036.80		
Amount Due Seller			16,805.52	
	$51,751.60	$51,751.60	$51,748.60	$51,748.60

REAL ESTATE LISTING CONTRACT (EXCLUSIVE RIGHT TO SELL)

SALES PRICE $24,500.00   TYPE HOME Ranch   TOTAL BEDROOMS 2   TOTAL BATHS 1

ADDRESS 321 Rose Street, Anytown   JURISDICTION OF Brown County, Your State

AMT. OF LOAN   AS OF   TAXES & INS.   YEARS   AMOUNT PAYABLE   TYPE
TO BE ASSUMED $ None   WHAT DATE   INCLUDED   TO GO   MONTHLY $ @   % LOAN

MORTGAGE COMPANY   2nd MORTGAGE

OWNER'S NAME Edward Smith and Mary Smith (H & W)   PHONES (HOME)   (BUSINESS)

TENANT'S NAME   PHONES (HOME)   (BUSINESS)

POSSESSION at closing   DATE LISTED: June 15, TY   EXCLUSIVE FOR 120 days   DATE OF EXPIRATION Oct. 15, TY

LISTING BROKER ABC Realty   PHONE   KEY AVAILABLE AT

LISTING SALESMAN You as salesperson for ABC Realty   HOME PHONE   HOW TO BE SHOWN:

ENTRANCE FOYER ☐	CENTER HALL ☐	AGE 22 yrs.	AIR CONDITIONING ☐	TYPE KITCHEN CABINETS
LIVING ROOM SIZE 12' x 15'	FIREPLACE ☐	ROOFING Composition	TOOL HOUSE ☐	TYPE COUNTER TOPS
DINING ROOM SIZE 10' x 12'		GARAGE SIZE	PATIO ☐	EAT-IN SIZE KITCHEN ☐
BEDROOM TOTAL: 2 DOWN UP		SIDE DRIVE ☐	CIRCULAR DRIVE ☐	TYPE STOVE ☐
BATHS TOTAL: 1 DOWN UP		PORCH ☐ SIDE ☐ REAR ☐	SCREENED ☐	BUILT-IN OVEN & RANGE ☐
DEN SIZE	FIREPLACE ☐	FENCED YARD	OUTDOOR GRILL ☐	SEPARATE STOVE INCLUDED ☑
FAMILY ROOM SIZE	FIREPLACE ☐	STORM WINDOWS ☑	STORM DOORS ☑	REFRIGERATOR INCLUDED ☑
RECREATION ROOM SIZE	FIREPLACE ☐	CURBS & GUTTERS ☐	SIDEWALKS ☐	DISHWASHER INCLUDED portable
BASEMENT SIZE 25' x 35'		STORM SEWERS ☐	ALLEY ☐	DISPOSAL INCLUDED ☐
NONE ☐ 1/4 ☐ 1/3 ☐ 1/2 ☐ 3/4 ☐ FULL ☑		WATER SUPPLY well		DOUBLE SINK ☐ SINGLE SINK ☐
UTILITY ROOM		SEWER ☐	SEPTIC ☑	STAINLESS STEEL ☐ PORCELAIN ☐
TYPE HOT WATER SYSTEM: electric 30 gal.		TYPE GAS: NATURAL ☐	BOTTLED ☐	WASHER INCLUDED ☐ DRYER INCLUDED ☐
TYPE HEAT electric		WHY SELLING		LAND ASSESSMENT $ 2,000.00
EST. FUEL COST				IMPROVEMENTS $ 5,000.00
ATTIC ☐		PROPERTY DESCRIPTION		TOTAL ASSESSMENTS $7,000.00
PULL DOWN REGULAR TRAP STAIRWAY ☐ STAIRWAY ☐ DOOR ☐		Bloom Addition, Anytown, Brown County, Your State		TAX RATE $8.25/$100
NAME OF BUILDER		LOT SIZE 150' x 200'		TOTAL ANNUAL TAXES $ 577.50
SQUARE FOOTAGE		LOT NO. 6 BLOCK SECTION		
EXTERIOR OF HOUSE				

NAME OF SCHOOLS: ELEMENTARY: JR. HIGH:

HIGH: PAROCHIAL:

PUBLIC TRANSPORTATION:

NEAREST SHOPPING AREA:

REMARKS: Will take 15 yr. purchase money mortgage at 8%, 30% downpayment, 180 equal monthly payments including principal and interest only
          Air conditioner, washer, dryer, and lawn mower sold separately.

                              Date: June 15, TY

In consideration of the services of   ABC Realty   (herein called "Broker") to be rendered to the undersigned (herein called "Owner"), and of the promise of Broker to make reasonable efforts to obtain a Purchaser therefor, Owner hereby lists with Broker the real estate and all improvements thereon which are described above, (all herein called "the property"), and the Owner hereby grants to Broker the exclusive and irrevocable right to sell such property from 12:00 Noon on   June 15   , 19 TY   until 12:00 Midnight on   Oct. 15   , 19 TY (herein called "period of time"), for the price of Twenty-four thousand five hundred and no/100   Dollars ($ 24,500.00   ) or for such other price and upon such other terms (including exchange) as Owner may subsequently authorize during the period of time.

It is understood by Owner that the above sum or any other price subsequently authorized by Owner shall include a cash fee of   6   per cent of such price or other price which shall be payable by Owner to Broker upon consummation by any Purchaser or Purchasers of a valid contract of sale of the property during the period of time and whether or not Broker was a procuring cause of any such contract of sale.

If the property is sold or exchanged by Owner, or by Broker or by any other person to any Purchaser to whom the property was shown by Broker or any representative of Broker within sixty (60) days after the expiration of the period of time mentioned above, Owner agrees to pay to Broker a cash fee which shall be the same percentage of the purchase price as the percentage mentioned above.

Broker is hereby authorized by Owner to place a "For Sale" sign on the property and to remove all signs of other brokers or salesmen during the period of time, and Owner hereby agrees to make the property available to Broker at all reasonable hours for the purpose of showing it to prospective Purchasers.

Owner agrees to convey the property to the Purchaser by deed with the usual covenants of title and free and clear from all encumbrances, tenancies, liens (for taxes or otherwise), but subject to applicable restrictive covenants of record. Owner acknowledges receipt of copy of this agreement.

WITNESS the following signature(s) and seal(s):

Date Signed: June 15, TY

Edward Smith
                              (Owner)

Listing Agent   ABC Realty, you as salesperson

Address   321 Rose St.   Telephone

Mary Smith
                              (Owner)

REAL ESTATE SALES CONTRACT (OFFER TO PURCHASE AGREEMENT)

This AGREEMENT made as of _____ August 1 _____ , 19 TY ,

among _____ Robert Armstrong and Betty Armstrong (H & W) _____ (herein called "Purchaser"),

and _____ Edward Smith and Mary Smith (H & W) _____ (herein called "Seller"),

and _____ ABC Realty _____ (herein called "Broker"),

provides that Purchaser agrees to buy through Broker as agent for Seller, and Seller agrees to sell the following described real estate, and all improvements thereon, located in the jurisdiction of _____ Brown County, Your State _____ ,

(all herein called "the property"): Lot 6, Bloom Addition, Anytown, Brown County, Your State

_____ , and more commonly known as ___ 321 Rose Street ___

Anytown, Your State _____ (street address).

1. The purchase price of the property is twenty-four thousand five hundred and no/100

Dollars ($ 24,500.00), and such purchase price shall be paid as follows:

15 yr purchase money mortgage at 8%, 180 equal monthly installments including principal and interest only

with 20% of purchase as down payment

2. Purchaser has made a deposit of five hundred and no/100 Dollars ($ 500.00) with Broker, receipt of which is hereby acknowledged, and such deposit shall be held by Broker in escrow until the date of settlement and then applied to the purchase price, or returned to Purchaser if the title to the property is not marketable.

3. Seller agrees to convey the property to Purchaser by Deed with the usual covenants of title and free and clear from all monetary encumbrances, tenancies, liens (for taxes or otherwise), except as may be otherwise provided above, but subject to applicable restrictive covenants of record. Seller further agrees to deliver possession of the property to Purchaser on the date of settlement and to pay the expense of preparing the deed of conveyance.

4. Settlement shall be made at _____ ABC Realty _____ on or before

September 1 _____ , 19 TY , or as soon thereafter as title can be examined and necessary documents prepared, with allowance of a reasonable time for Seller to correct any defects reported by the title examiner.

5. All taxes, interest, rent, and impound escrow deposits, if any, shall be prorated as of the date of settlement.

6. All risk of loss or damage to the property by fire, windstorm, casualty, or other cause is assumed by Seller until the date of settlement.

7. Purchaser and Seller agree that Broker was the sole procuring cause of this Contract of Purchase, and Seller agrees to pay Broker for services rendered a cash fee of ___ 6 ___ per cent of the purchase price. If either Purchaser or Seller defaults under such Contract, such defaulting party shall be liable for the cash fee of Broker and any expenses incurred by the non-defaulting party in connection with this transaction.

Subject to: ___ Inspection and certification of well by health officials, at sellers expense; air conditioner, washer, dryer, and lawn mower sold separately for $675.00

8. Purchaser represents that an inspection satisfactory to Purchaser has been made of the property, and Purchaser agrees to accept the property in its present condition except as may be otherwise provided in the description of the property above.

9. This Contract of Purchase constitutes the entire agreement among the parties and may not be modified or changed except by written instrument executed by all of the parties, including Broker.

10. This Contract of Purchase shall be construed, interpreted, and applied according to the law of the jurisdiction of ___ Your State ___ and shall be binding upon and shall inure to the benefit of the heirs, personal representatives, successors, and assigns of the parties.

All parties to this agreement acknowledge receipt of a certified copy.

WITNESS the following signatures and seals:

Edward Smith (SEAL) Seller

Mary Smith (SEAL) Seller

ABC Realty _____ (SEAL) Broker

Robert Armstrong (SEAL) Purchaser

Betty Armstrong (SEAL) Purchaser

Deposit Rec'd $ 500.00

Check ___ (Cash)

Sales Agent: You as salesman for ABC Realty

PROBLEM 104

SETTLEMENT STATEMENT WORKSHEET

Complete the Settlement Statement Worksheet on the basis of information furnished in the Listing, Offer to Purchase Agreement, and Settlement Problems only. Do not add other items. Use the 30-day method of computation.

	BUYER'S STATEMENT		SELLER'S STATEMENT	
	DEBIT	CREDIT	DEBIT	CREDIT
Purchase Price	24,500.00			24,500.00
Deposit		500.00		
Purchase Money Mortgage		19,600.00	19,600.00	
Taxes – Prorated		385.04	385.04	
Sales Fee – 6%			1,470.00	
Title Examination	122.50			
Recording Fee – Mortgage	50.00			
Appraisal Fee			40.00	
Well Examination & Certifica.			35.00	
Washer, Dryer, A/C, Lawnmower	675.00			675.00
Balance Due From Purchaser		4,862.46		
Balance Due Seller			3,644.96	
	$25,347.50	$25,347.50	$25,175.00	$25,175.00

PROBLEM 105

REAL ESTATE LISTING CONTRACT (EXCLUSIVE RIGHT TO SELL)

SALES PRICE __$32,000.00__ TYPE HOME __Cape Cod__ TOTAL BEDROOMS __3__ TOTAL BATHS __2__

ADDRESS __24 Laurel Avenue, Anytown__ JURISDICTION OF __Green County, Your State__

AMT. OF LOAN TO BE ASSUMED $ __25,920.00__ AS OF WHAT DATE __Apr. 1, TY__ TAXES & INS. INCLUDED __ YEARS TO GO __24__ AMOUNT PAYABLE MONTHLY $__274.00__ @ __8__ % TYPE LOAN __Conv.__

MORTGAGE COMPANY __Third State Savings and Loan Assoc.__ 2nd MORTGAGE __

OWNER'S NAME __Otis Brown and Mary Brown (H & W)__ PHONES (HOME) __334-8311__ (BUSINESS) __

TENANT'S NAME __ PHONES (HOME) __ (BUSINESS) __

POSSESSION __Complete at closing__ DATE LISTED: __Apr. 15, TY__ EXCLUSIVE FOR __90 days__ DATE OF EXPIRATION __July 15, TY__

LISTING BROKER __Big Red Realty__ PHONE __ KEY AVAILABLE AT __Big Red Realty__

LISTING SALESMAN __You, as salesperson for Big Red Realty__ HOME PHONE __ HOW TO BE SHOWN: __By appointment__

ENTRANCE FOYER ☐	CENTER HALL ☐	AGE 6	AIR CONDITIONING ☑	TYPE KITCHEN CABINETS
LIVING ROOM SIZE 14' x 20'	FIREPLACE ☑	ROOFING Slate	TOOL HOUSE ☐	TYPE COUNTER TOPS
DINING ROOM SIZE 10' x 12'		GARAGE SIZE 2-car attached	PATIO ☐	EAT-IN SIZE KITCHEN ☑
BEDROOM TOTAL: 3 DOWN 1 UP 2		SIDE DRIVE ☑	CIRCULAR DRIVE ☐	TYPE STOVE ☐
BATHS TOTAL: 2 DOWN 1 UP 1		PORCH ☐ SIDE ☐ REAR ☐	SCREENED ☐	BUILT-IN OVEN & RANGE ☐
DEN SIZE	FIREPLACE ☐	FENCED YARD	OUTDOOR GRILL ☐	SEPARATE STOVE INCLUDED ☑ electric
FAMILY ROOM SIZE	FIREPLACE ☐	STORM WINDOWS ☑	STORM DOORS ☑	REFRIGERATOR INCLUDED ☑
RECREATION ROOM SIZE	FIREPLACE ☐	CURBS & GUTTERS ☐	SIDEWALKS ☐	DISHWASHER INCLUDED ✓
BASEMENT SIZE 30' x 42'		STORM SEWERS ☐	ALLEY ☐	DISPOSAL INCLUDED ☑
NONE ☐ 1/4 ☐ 1/3 ☐ 1/2 ☐ 3/4 ☐ FULL ☑		WATER SUPPLY		DOUBLE SINK ☑ SINGLE SINK ☐
UTILITY ROOM		SEWER ☐	SEPTIC ☐	STAINLESS STEEL ☑ PORCELAIN ☐
TYPE HOT WATER SYSTEM: electric		TYPE GAS: NATURAL ☐	BOTTLED ☐	WASHER INCLUDED ☐ DRYER INCLUDED ☐
TYPE HEAT electric		WHY SELLING		LAND ASSESSMENT $ 2,500.00
EST. FUEL COST				IMPROVEMENTS $ 7,000.00
ATTIC ☐		PROPERTY DESCRIPTION		TOTAL ASSESSMENTS $ 9,500.00
PULL DOWN STAIRWAY ☐ REGULAR STAIRWAY ☐ TRAP DOOR ☐		Laurel Addition to Anytown, Green County, Your State		TAX RATE $8.40/$100
NAME OF BUILDER		LOT SIZE 80' x 110'		TOTAL ANNUAL TAXES $ 798.00
SQUARE FOOTAGE		LOT NO. 8 BLOCK 4 SECTION 1		
EXTERIOR OF HOUSE Stone				

NAME OF SCHOOLS: ELEMENTARY: __ JR. HIGH: __

HIGH: __ PAROCHIAL: __

PUBLIC TRANSPORTATION: __

NEAREST SHOPPING AREA: __

REMARKS: __

Date: __Apr. 15, TY__

In consideration of the services of __Big Red Realty__ (herein called "Broker") to be rendered to the undersigned (herein called "Owner"), and of the promise of Broker to make reasonable efforts to obtain a Purchaser therefor, Owner hereby lists with Broker the real estate and all improvements thereon which are described above, (all herein called "the property"), and the Owner hereby grants to Broker the exclusive and irrevocable right to sell such property from 12:00 Noon on __Apr. 15__, 19 __TY__ until 12:00 Midnight on __July 15__, 19 __TY__ (herein called "period of time"), for the price of __Thirty-two thousand and no/100__ Dollars ($__32,000.00__) or for such other price and upon such other terms (including exchange) as Owner may subsequently authorize during the period of time.

It is understood by Owner that the above sum or any other price subsequently authorized by Owner shall include a cash fee of __6__ per cent of such price or other price which shall be payable by Owner to Broker upon consummation by any Purchaser or Purchasers of a valid contract of sale of the property during the period of time and whether or not Broker was a procuring cause of any such contract of sale.

If the property is sold or exchanged by Owner, or by Broker or by any other person to any Purchaser to whom the property was shown by Broker or any representative of Broker within sixty (60) days after the expiration of the period of time mentioned above, Owner agrees to pay to Broker a cash fee which shall be the same percentage of the purchase price as the percentage mentioned above.

Broker is hereby authorized by Owner to place a "For Sale" sign on the property and to remove all signs of other brokers or salesmen during the period of time, and Owner hereby agrees to make the property available to Broker at all reasonable hours for the purpose of showing it to prospective Purchasers.

Owner agrees to convey the property to the Purchaser by deed with the usual covenants of title and free and clear from all encumbrances, tenancies, liens (for taxes or otherwise), but subject to applicable restrictive covenants of record. Owner acknowledges receipt of copy of this agreement.

WITNESS the following signature(s) and seal(s):

Date Signed: __Apr. 15, TY__ __Otis Brown__ (Owner)

Listing Agent __Big Red Realty, you as salesperson__

Address __24 Laurel Ave.__ Telephone __334-8311__ __Mary Brown__ (Owner)

REAL ESTATE SALES CONTRACT (OFFER TO PURCHASE AGREEMENT)

This AGREEMENT made as of _____ July 4 _____, 19 TY ,

among _____ Charles Joseph and Clara Joseph (H & W) _____ (herein called "Purchaser"),

and _____ Otis Brown and Mary Brown (H & W) _____ (herein called "Seller"),

and _____ Big Red Realty _____ (herein called "Broker"),

provides that Purchaser agrees to buy through Broker as agent for Seller, and Seller agrees to sell the following described real estate, and all improvements thereon, located in the jurisdiction of _____ Green County, Your State _____ ,

(all herein called "the property"): Lot 8, Block 4, Section 1, Laurel Addition, Anytown, Green County, Your State _____ , and more commonly known as _24 Laurel Avenue_

_____ Anytown, Your State _____ (street address).

1. The purchase price of the property is _thirty-two thousand and no/100_

Dollars ($ 32,000.00), and such purchase price shall be paid as follows:

F.H.A. financing for 25 yrs at present rate of interest in the amount of $30,550.00 paid in 300 equal installments of principal and interest. The remainder in cash.

2. Purchaser has made a deposit of _five hundred and no/100_ Dollars ($ 500.00) with Broker, receipt of which is hereby acknowledged, and such deposit shall be held by Broker in escrow until the date of settlement and then applied to the purchase price, or returned to Purchaser if the title to the property is not marketable.

3. Seller agrees to convey the property to Purchaser by Deed with the usual covenants of title and free and clear from all monetary encumbrances, tenancies, liens (for taxes or otherwise), except as may be otherwise provided above, but subject to applicable restrictive covenants of record. Seller further agrees to deliver possession of the property to Purchaser on the date of settlement and to pay the expense of preparing the deed of conveyance.

4. Settlement shall be made at _____ Law offices of Will Reamington _____ on or before _____ August 10 _____, 19 TY , or as soon thereafter as title can be examined and necessary documents prepared, with allowance of a reasonable time for Seller to correct any defects reported by the title examiner.

5. All taxes, interest, rent, and impound escrow deposits, if any, shall be prorated as of the date of settlement.

6. All risk of loss or damage to the property by fire, windstorm, casualty, or other cause is assumed by Seller until the date of settlement.

7. Purchaser and Seller agree that Broker was the sole procuring cause of this Contract of Purchase, and Seller agrees to pay Broker for services rendered a cash fee of ____6____ per cent of the purchase price. If either Purchaser or Seller defaults under such Contract, such defaulting party shall be liable for the cash fee of Broker and any expenses incurred by the non-defaulting party in connection with this transaction.

Subject to: _____

_____

_____

_____

8. Purchaser represents that an inspection satisfactory to Purchaser has been made of the property, and Purchaser agrees to accept the property in its present condition except as may be otherwise provided in the description of the property above.

9. This Contract of Purchase constitutes the entire agreement among the parties and may not be modified or changed except by written instrument executed by all of the parties, including Broker.

10. This Contract of Purchase shall be construed, interpreted, and applied according to the law of the jurisdiction of _Your State_ and shall be binding upon and shall inure to the benefit of the heirs, personal representatives, successors, and assigns of the parties.

All parties to this agreement acknowledge receipt of a certified copy.

WITNESS the following signatures and seals:

Otis Brown (SEAL) Seller		*Charles Joseph* (SEAL) Purchaser
Mary Brown (SEAL) Seller		*Clara Joseph* (SEAL) Purchaser
Big Red Realty (SEAL) Broker		

Deposit Rec'd $ 500.00

(Check)   Cash

Sales Agent   You as salesman for Big Red Realty

PROBLEM 105

SETTLEMENT STATEMENT WORKSHEET

Complete the Settlement Statement Worksheet on the basis of information furnished in the Listing, Offer to Purchase Agreement, and Settlement Problems only. Do not add other items. Use the 30-day method of computation.

	BUYER'S STATEMENT		SELLER'S STATEMENT	
	DEBIT	CREDIT	DEBIT	CREDIT
Sales Price	32,000.00			32,000.00
Deposit		500.00		
Sales Fee — 6%			1,920.00	
Brown Mortgage Balance			25,511.14	
Interest Prorated—In Arrears			56.70	
Josephs Mortgage		30,550.00		
Taxes — Prorated		487.70	487.70	
Loan Origination Fee — 1%	305.50			
Fire Insurance	182.00			
Title Insurance — Owner's			187.50	
Title Insurance — Mortgagee	75.00			
Tax Escrow — 2 months	133.00			
Appraisal Fee — F.H.A.	50.00			
Photo Fee	15.00			
Survey Fee	55.00			
Discount Points — 5 points			1,527.50	
Balance Due From Buyer		1,277.80		
Balance Due to Seller			2,309.46	
	$32,815.50	$32,815.50	$32,000.00	$32,000.00

REAL ESTATE LISTING CONTRACT (EXCLUSIVE RIGHT TO SELL)

SALES PRICE __$38,500.00__ TYPE HOME __Ranch__ TOTAL BEDROOMS __3__ TOTAL BATHS __1½__

ADDRESS __1221 Wayside Drive, Anytown__ JURISDICTION OF __Madison County, Your State__

AMT. OF LOAN TO BE ASSUMED $ __10,120.00__ AS OF WHAT DATE __Aug. 1, TY__ TAXES & INS. INCLUDED _____ YEARS TO GO __12__ AMOUNT PAYABLE MONTHLY $__175__ @ __7½__% TYPE LOAN _____

MORTGAGE COMPANY __First Federal Loan Company__ 2nd MORTGAGE _____

OWNER'S NAME __Harvey L. Jones and Lois Jones (H & W)__ PHONES (HOME) __339-6111__ (BUSINESS) _____

TENANT'S NAME _____ PHONES (HOME) _____ (BUSINESS) _____

POSSESSION __Complete at closing__ DATE LISTED: __Aug. 2, TY__ EXCLUSIVE FOR __90 days__ DATE OF EXPIRATION __Nov. 2, TY__

LISTING BROKER __Community Realty__ PHONE _____ KEY AVAILABLE AT __Community Realty__

LISTING SALESMAN __You, as salesperson for Community Realty__ HOME PHONE _____ HOW TO BE SHOWN: __By appointment__

ENTRANCE FOYER ☐	CENTER HALL ☐	AGE 13	AIR CONDITIONING ☐	TYPE KITCHEN CABINETS
LIVING ROOM SIZE 14' x 20'	FIREPLACE ☐	ROOFING	TOOL HOUSE ☐	TYPE COUNTER TOPS
DINING ROOM SIZE 12' x 14'		GARAGE SIZE 1 car	PATIO ☑	EAT-IN SIZE KITCHEN ☐
BEDROOM TOTAL: 3 DOWN UP		SIDE DRIVE ☐	CIRCULAR DRIVE ☐	TYPE STOVE ☐
BATHS TOTAL: 1½ DOWN UP		PORCH ☐ SIDE ☐ REAR ☐	SCREENED ☐	BUILT-IN OVEN & RANGE ☑
DEN SIZE	FIREPLACE ☑	FENCED YARD	OUTDOOR GRILL ☐	SEPARATE STOVE INCLUDED ☐
FAMILY ROOM SIZE	FIREPLACE ☐	STORM WINDOWS ☐	STORM DOORS ☐	REFRIGERATOR INCLUDED ☑
RECREATION ROOM SIZE	FIREPLACE ☐	CURBS & GUTTERS ☑	SIDEWALKS ☑	DISHWASHER INCLUDED ☑
BASEMENT SIZE		STORM SEWERS ☑	ALLEY ☐	DISPOSAL INCLUDED ☑
NONE ☑ 1/4 ☐ 1/3 ☐ 1/2 ☐ 3/4 ☐ FULL ☐		WATER SUPPLY city		DOUBLE SINK ☑ SINGLE SINK ☐
UTILITY ROOM 8' x 12'		SEWER ☑	SEPTIC ☐	STAINLESS STEEL ☑ PORCELAIN ☐
TYPE HOT WATER SYSTEM: electric		TYPE GAS: NATURAL ☐	BOTTLED ☐	WASHER INCLUDED ☑ DRYER INCLUDED ☑
TYPE HEAT electric		WHY SELLING		LAND ASSESSMENT $ 3,000.00
EST. FUEL COST				IMPROVEMENTS $ 8,000.00
ATTIC ☐		PROPERTY DESCRIPTION		TOTAL ASSESSMENTS $ 11,000.00
PULL DOWN STAIRWAY ☐ REGULAR STAIRWAY ☐ TRAP DOOR ☐		Smallwood Addition, City of Anytown, County of Madison, Your State		TAX RATE $7.40/$100
NAME OF BUILDER		LOT SIZE 150' x 150'		TOTAL ANNUAL TAXES $ 814.00
SQUARE FOOTAGE		LOT NO. 21 BLOCK 9 SECTION C		
EXTERIOR OF HOUSE				

NAME OF SCHOOLS: ELEMENTARY: _____ JR. HIGH: _____

HIGH: _____ PAROCHIAL: _____

PUBLIC TRANSPORTATION: _____

NEAREST SHOPPING AREA: _____

REMARKS: __Additional five (5) acres for sale at $10,000.00. Garden tractor for sale under separate bill of sale for $850.00.__

Date: __Aug. 2, TY__

In consideration of the services of __Community Realty__ (herein called "Broker") to be rendered to the undersigned (herein called "Owner"), and of the promise of Broker to make reasonable efforts to obtain a Purchaser therefor, Owner hereby lists with Broker the real estate and all improvements thereon which are described above, (all herein called "the property"), and the Owner hereby grants to Broker the exclusive and irrevocable right to sell such property from 12:00 Noon on __Aug. 2__, 19__TY__ until 12:00 Midnight on __Nov. 2__, 19__TY__ (herein called "period of time"), for the price of __Thirty-eight thousand five hundred and no/100__ Dollars ($__38,500.00__) or for such other price and upon such other terms (including exchange) as Owner may subsequently authorize during the period of time.

It is understood by Owner that the above sum or any other price subsequently authorized by Owner shall include a cash fee of ____6____ per cent of such price or other price which shall be payable by Owner to Broker upon consummation by any Purchaser or Purchasers of a valid contract of sale of the property during the period of time and whether or not Broker was a procuring cause of any such contract of sale.

If the property is sold or exchanged by Owner, or by Broker or by any other person to any Purchaser to whom the property was shown by Broker or any representative of Broker within sixty (60) days after the expiration of the period of time mentioned above, Owner agrees to pay to Broker a cash fee which shall be the same percentage of the purchase price as the percentage mentioned above.

Broker is hereby authorized by Owner to place a "For Sale" sign on the property and to remove all signs of other brokers or salesmen during the period of time, and Owner hereby agrees to make the property available to Broker at all reasonable hours for the purpose of showing it to prospective Purchasers.

Owner agrees to convey the property to the Purchaser by deed with the usual covenants of title and free and clear from all encumbrances, tenancies, liens (for taxes or otherwise), but subject to applicable restrictive covenants of record. Owner acknowledges receipt of copy of this agreement.

WITNESS the following signature(s) and seal(s):

Date Signed: __Aug. 2, TY__ _Harvey L. Jones_ (Owner)

Listing Agent __Community Realty, You as Salesperson__

Address __1221 Wayside Dr.__ Telephone __339-6111__ _Lois Jones_ (Owner)

PROBLEM 106

REAL ESTATE SALES CONTRACT (OFFER TO PURCHASE AGREEMENT)

This AGREEMENT made as of _____ August 10 _____ , 19 TY ,

among _____ William Dallas and Nancy Dallas (H&W) _____ (herein called "Purchaser"),

and _____ Harvey Jones and Lois Jones (H&W) _____ (herein called "Seller"),

and _____ Community Realty _____ (herein called "Broker"),
provides that Purchaser agrees to buy through Broker as agent for Seller, and Seller agrees to sell the following described real estate, and all improvements
thereon, located in the jurisdiction of _____ Madison County, Your State _____ ,

(all herein called "the property"): __ Lot 21, Block 9, Section C of Smallwood Addition to the City of Anytown, __

County of Madison, Your State _____ , and more commonly known as __ 1221 Wayside Drive __

Anytown, Your State _____ (street address).

1. The purchase price of the property is __ thirty-seven thousand seven hundred fifty and no/100 __

Dollars ($ 37,750.00), and such purchase price shall be paid as follows:
80% conventional new mortgage for 30 years in 360 equal installments of principal and interest only at 8¾%

2. Purchaser has made a deposit of __ five hundred and no/100 __ Dollars ($ 500.00)
with Broker, receipt of which is hereby acknowledged, and such deposit shall be held by Broker in escrow until the date of settlement and then applied
to the purchase price, or returned to Purchaser if the title to the property is not marketable.

3. Seller agrees to convey the property to Purchaser by Deed with the usual covenants of title and free and clear from all monetary encumbrances,
tenancies, liens (for taxes or otherwise), except as may be otherwise provided above, but subject to applicable restrictive covenants of record. Seller further
agrees to deliver possession of the property to Purchaser on the date of settlement and to pay the expense of preparing the deed of conveyance.

4. Settlement shall be made at _____ Community Realty _____ on or before
_____ September 1 _____ , 19 TY , or as soon thereafter as title can be examined and necessary documents prepared, with
allowance of a reasonable time for Seller to correct any defects reported by the title examiner.

5. All taxes, interest, rent, and impound escrow deposits, if any, shall be prorated as of the date of settlement.

6. All risk of loss or damage to the property by fire, windstorm, casualty, or other cause is assumed by Seller until the date of settlement.

7. Purchaser and Seller agree that Broker was the sole procuring cause of this Contract of Purchase, and Seller agrees to pay Broker for services
rendered a cash fee of _____ 6 _____ per cent of the purchase price. If either Purchaser or Seller defaults under such Contract, such defaulting party shall
be liable for the cash fee of Broker and any expenses incurred by the non-defaulting party in connection with this transaction.

Subject to: _____ Purchase of the additional 5 acres land contract at listed price with 30% down and a contract for 10 years _____
_____ at 8¾%. Will pay $750 in cash for the tractor. Offer open until midnight August 15, this year. _____

8. Purchaser represents that an inspection satisfactory to Purchaser has been made of the property, and Purchaser agrees to accept the property
in its present condition except as may be otherwise provided in the description of the property above.

9. This Contract of Purchase constitutes the entire agreement among the parties and may not be modified or changed except by written instrument executed by all of the parties, including Broker.

10. This Contract of Purchase shall be construed, interpreted, and applied according to the law of the jurisdiction of __ Your State __ and shall
be binding upon and shall inure to the benefit of the heirs, personal representatives, successors, and assigns of the parties.

All parties to this agreement acknowledge receipt of a certified copy.

WITNESS the following signatures and seals:

Harvey L. Jones (SEAL) Seller	*William Dallas* (SEAL) Purchaser
Lois Jones (SEAL) Seller	*Nancy Dallas* (SEAL) Purchaser
Community Realty (SEAL) Broker	

Deposit Rec'd $ 500.00

(Check)   Cash

Sales Agent   You as salesman for Community Realty

PROBLEM 106

SETTLEMENT STATEMENT WORKSHEET

Complete the Settlement Statement Worksheet on the basis of information furnished in the Listing, Offer to Purchase Agreement, and Settlement Problems only. Do not add other items. Use the 30-day method of computation.

	BUYER'S STATEMENT		SELLER'S STATEMENT	
	DEBIT	**CREDIT**	**DEBIT**	**CREDIT**
Purchase Price	37,750.00			37,750.00
Deposit		500.00		
Jones Mortgage Balance			10,120.00	
Interest Prorated			63.25	
Dallas New Mortgage		30,200.00		
Commission – 6%			2,865.00	
Additional acreage	10,000.00			10,000.00
Land Contract Balance		7,000.00	7,000.00	
Taxes Prorated		542.64	542.64	
Insurance Prorated	60.00			60.00
Loan Origination Fee 1%	302.00			
Discount Points – 2 points	604.00			
Sellers and Buyers Fees	125.00		75.00	
Abstract			100.00	
Recording Fees	37.50		12.50	
Garden Tractor – Separate Bill of sale	750.00			750.00
Balance Due from Buyer		11,385.86		
Balance Due to Seller			27,781.61	
	$49,628.50	$49,628.50	$48,560.00	$48,560.00

Appendix G

Glossary of Real Estate Terms

Abandonment: The voluntary surrender, relinquishment, disclaimer, or cession of property or rights.

Abatement: Termination; end.

Abatement of nuisance: Termination of a nuisance.

Abrogate: To repeal; to make void; to annul.

Absolute fee simple: Complete ownership and control without condition or limitation.

Abstract of judgment: A summation of the essentials of a court judgment.

Abstract of title: A summary of the conveyances, transfers, and other facts relied on as evidence of title, together with all such facts appearing on record which may impair the validity. It should contain a brief but complete history of the title.

Accelerated depreciation: A method of depreciation used in the computation of income taxes, which speeds up the write-off of the value of the property at a rate greater than normal depreciation.

Acceleration clause: A clause giving the lender the right to call all sums owed him immediately due and payable upon the occurrence of a specified event, such as default, sale, etc.

Acceptance: Acceptance is determined by the seller's or his agent's agreement to the terms of the agreement of sale; approval of the negotiation on the part of the agent.

Access right: The right of an owner to have ingress and egress to and from his or her real property.

Accessibility: Ease or difficulty of approach to real property, either via public land or by private property maintained for public use.

Accession: In its legal meaning, generally used to signify the acquisition of property by incorporation or union with other property.

Accretion: The act of growing; usually applied to the gradual and imperceptible accumulation of land through natural causes, as out of the sea or a river.

Accrued depreciation: The difference between the cost of replacement at the date of the original appraisal and the present appraised value.

Acknowledgment: A formal declaration of one's signing of an instrument before a duly authorized public official.

Acknowledgment of a deed: A form of authenticating instruments conveying property or otherwise conferring rights. It is a public declaration by the grantor that the act evidenced by the instrument is his or her act or deed.

Acquisition: Making property one's own; obtaining the ownership of or an interest in property.

Acre: A unit of land measure equal to 43,560 square feet.

Actual age: The number of years a structure has actually existed.

Ad valorem tax: A tax according to a fixed percentage of value.

Adjacent: Usually used to designate property which is in the neighborhood of other property but which does not actually touch such property; sometimes used to mean touching or contiguous, e.g., immediately adjacent.

Adjoining: Touching or contiguous, as distinguished from lying near or adjacent.

Administration: The management of a business, activity, or resource.

Administration of real estate resources: The efficient utilization of real estate resources to achieve desired results.

Administrator: A person to whom letters of administration, that is, authority to administer the estate of a deceased person who died intestate, have been granted by the proper court.

Administrator's deed: A deed used to convey the property of one who has died intestate (leaving no will).

Advance: In regard to a construction loan, a periodic transfer of funds from the lender to the borrower during the construction process.

Advance fee: A fee paid in advance of service rendered in the sale of property or in obtaining a loan.

Advancement: A gift from a parent to a child in anticipation of the share the child will eventually inherit from the parent's estate, which is intended to be deducted therefrom.

Adverse possession: The occupation of land under circumstances which indicate that such occupation started and has continued under an insistence of right on the part of the occupant.

Advertising real estate: The act of informing the public in order to produce action regarding real estate; public announcements to aid in the sale of real property.

Affiant: Any person who has made an affidavit.

Affidavit: A statement or declaration reduced to writing and sworn to or affirmed before a public official who has authority to administer an oath or affirmation.

Affirm: To confirm or verify.

Affirmation: The confirmation of a former judgment or court order; the confirmation by a principal of an agent's acts.

Affirmative action program: A detailed plan used to overcome the causes and effects of discriminatory policies in the hiring, employment and/or training of minority group members; the program also investigates complaints made to HUD concerning housing.

After-acquired property: Property acquired after a particular date or event, e.g., the execution of a mortgage to property not yet owned.

Agency: The relationship between principal and agent, arising from a contract wherein the agent is employed by the principal to perform certain acts dealing with third parties.

Agent: One who represents another, who is known as the principal.

Agreement: A coming together of minds; in contract law, a meeting of the minds.

Agreement of sale: A written agreement whereby the purchaser agrees to buy specific real estate and the seller agrees to sell upon specific terms and conditions set forth in the contract.

Air rights: Rights in real property to use the space above the surface of the land.

AIREA: See American Institute of Real Estate Appraisers.

Alienation: The voluntary act or acts by which one person transfers his or her own property to another. There can be involuntary alienation as in the event of unpaid taxes, bankruptcy, etc.

Allodial land: Land held in absolute independence, without being subject to any rent, service, or acknowledgment to a superior; opposed to "feud."

Allodial system: A system of free individual ownership of real property under which ownership may be complete except for government-held rights.

Alluvion: Soil deposited by natural accretion, i.e., an increase of earth on a shore or river bank.

Amenities, amenity return: Satisfactions received through using rights in real property and not in monetary form.

American Bankers' Association (ABA): A trade association of commercial bankers.

American Institute of Real Estate Appraisers (AIREA): A trade association of real estate appraisers, which conducts educational programs, publishes materials, and promotes research on real estate appraisal. Confers MAI (Member, Appraisal Institute) and RM (Residential Member).

American Society of Appraisers (ASA): The national professional and trade association for appraisers and their firms.

American Society of Real Estate Counselors (ASREC): A national professional and trade association of developers, consultants, and experienced advisors on all real estate matters. Confers CRE (Counselor on Real Estate).

Amortization: The process of paying an obligation through a series of payments over time. Generally the payments are made in equal amounts, including principal and interest, and at uniform time intervals.

Amortized mortgage: A mortgage in which repayment is made according to a plan requiring the payment of certain amounts at specified times so that all the debt is repaid at the end of the term.

Annuity: An amount of money or its equivalent which represents one of a series of periodic payments.

Apportionment: The division of rights or liabilities among several persons entitled to them or liable for them in accordance with their respective interests.

Appraisal: An opinion or estimate of value of property. Also refers to the report setting forth the estimate and conclusion of value.

Appraisal inventory: A compilation of all separate items comprising property included in an appraisal report and valued by the appraiser.

Appraisal report: A report of the appraised value, together with pertinent information concerning the property appraised and the evidence and analysis leading to the reported value estimate.

Appraiser: One who is in the business of making appraisals on the basis of a fee or salary in conjunction with some compensated employment.

Appreciation: An increased value in property.

Appurtenance: Property that is an accessory to other property to which it is annexed.

Arterial highway: A major route into a prime traffic area.

Artisan's lien: A lien given under common law to one skilled in some kind of mechanical craft or art for the reasonable charges for his or her work.

ASREC: See American Society of Real Estate Counselors.

Assemblage: The act of bringing together two individuals or things to form a new whole; specifically, the cost of assembling parcels of land under a single ownership. See plottage.

Assessed valuation: The process by which a value is placed upon property by a public official or officials as a basis for taxation.

Assessed value: The value placed on property for the purpose of taxation.

Assessment: A levy or tax imposed on real estate for improvements or taxes.

Assessor: An official whose responsibility is to determine assessed values for taxation.

Assets: Property of any kind under ownership

Assignee: A person to whom an assignment is made; a successor in interest to the rights of a party to a contract.

Assignment: A transfer or setting over of property, or some right or interest therein, from one person to another. In its ordinary application, the word is limited to the transfer of choses in action, e.g., the assignment of a contract.

Assignor: A person who makes an assignment of interest in a contract.

Assumption agreement: The undertaking of a debt or obligation of another by contract.

Assumption of a mortgage: The undertaking of a mortgage, by the buyer, which is currently held against the real estate the buyer is purchasing.

Attachment: Taking property into the legal custody of an officer by virtue of the directions contained in a writ of attachment; a seizure under a writ of a debtor's property.

Attachment of property: A writ issued in the course of a lawsuit, directing the sheriff or law officer to attach the property of the defendant to satisfy the demands of the plaintiff.

Attest: To affirm a statement or document to be genuine or accurate.

Attestation: The act of witnessing the execution of a paper and subscribing the name of the witness in testimony of such fact.

Attorney in fact: One who is authorized to perform certain acts for another under a power of attorney.

Auction: A public sale of property to the highest bidder.

Authentication: Such official attestation of a written instrument as will render it legally admissible as evidence in a law court.

Avulsion: The removal of land from one owner to another when a stream, etc., suddenly changes its course.

Axial growth: City growth which moves out along main transportation routes, taking the form of fingerlike extensions.

Backfill: The replacement of excavated earth against a structure or to fill a hole.

Balloon mortgage payment: A large payment during the term of a mortgage, often at the end.

Balustrade: A supporting column for a handrail.

Bargain and sale deed: A deed which conveys the land described but does so without any warranties.

Barter: The exchange of goods or commodities for other goods or commodities.

Base and meridian: Imaginary lines used by surveyors as a reference to find and describe land location. (Base lines run east and west, meridian lines run north and south.)

Base line: A part of the rectangular survey system; a parallel which serves as a reference for other parallels.

Base molding: Molding used at the top of a baseboard.

Base shoe: Molding used at the junction of a baseboard and the floor; more commonly known as a carpet strip.

Baseboard heating: A system of heating in which the radiators or convectors are located in or on the wall, replacing the baseboard itself.

Basic employment, urban growth employment: Employment in establishments that receive their income from outside the community.

Basic income: Income received from outside the community.

Batten: Narrow strips of wood or metal used to cover joints; may be used for a decorative effect.

Beam: A horizontal load-supporting member.

Bedroom community: A suburban community in which a large number of a major city's workers reside.

Beltline highway: A limited-access highway which surrounds a city.

Bench mark: Permanent markers placed by surveyors at important points, upon which local surveys are based.

Beneficiary: A person having the enjoyment of property of which a trustee, executor, etc., has the legal possession; the person to whom a policy of insurance is payable.

Benefit-cost ratio: A measure of social benefits to dollar cost.

Bequeath: Commonly used to denote a testamentary gift; synonymous with "to devise."

Bequest: That which is given according to the terms of a will.

Betterment: A property improvement which increases the property value.

Bilateral contract: A contract under which two parties exchange promises for the performance of certain acts; for example, Mr. A promises to buy Mr. B's house, and Mr. B promises to sell it to Mr. A.

Bill of sale: A written instrument which evidences the transfer of title to personal property from seller to buyer.

Binder: A preliminary agreement in writing as evidence of good faith by the offerer; the memorandum of an agreement for insurance, intended to give temporary protection pending investigation of the risk and issuance of a formal policy. See title insurance.

Blacktop: Asphalt paving.

Blanket mortgage: A mortgage that has two or more properties pledged or conveyed as security for a debt.

Blight: Decay, as in the case of a neighborhood.

Blockbusting: The illegal practice of introducing a nonconforming user or use into a neighborhood for the purpose of causing an abnormally high turnover of property ownership in the area.

Board foot: A unit of measurement for lumber; 144 cubic inches; 1 foot wide, 1 foot long, 1 inch thick.

Bona fide: Good faith.

Bona fide purchaser: A purchaser who, for a valuable consideration paid in the belief that the vendor had a right to sell, purchases a particular property.

Bond: An instrument used as evidence of a debt; also a guarantee of performance.

Borough: A land division of a city having its own charter.

Bracing: Lumber nailed at an angle in order to provide rigidity.

Breach: The breaking or violation of a law, right, or duty, either by commission or omission; failure to meet a contractual obligation.

Breakeven point: The amount of income needed to just meet the total amount of expenses for a project.

Breezeway: A covered passage, open on two sides, connecting a house with a garage or other parts of the house.

Bridging: Small wood or metal pieces used to brace floor joists.

Broker: An agent who negotiates for the sale, leasing, management, or financing of a property or of property rights on a commission basis.

Brokerage: The business of a broker; the selling of products or assets of others.

BTU: British thermal unit; the amount of heat required to raise the temperature of 1 pound of water 1°F.

Budget mortgage: A type of amortizing mortgage which includes in the monthly payments of principal and interest other costs such as taxes and fire insurance; referred to as a PITI monthly payment.

Builder: One who improves land by erecting structures.

Building codes: Government regulations specifying minimum construction standards.

Building line: A setback line; a line set by law or deed restriction a certain distance from a street in front of which an owner cannot build.

Building paper: A heavy, waterproof paper used as sheathing in wall or roof construction.

Building permit: Authorization by a local government for the erection, alteration, or remodeling of improvements within its jurisdiction.

Building restrictions: Limitations on the use of property established by legislation or by covenants or limitations in deeds.

Built-in: Such features built as part of the house, e.g., cabinets, etc.

Bundle of rights theory: The definition of ownership based on the concept of combining all possible interests in land into a whole.

Business-government relations: The framework of laws, codes, regulations, and contracts between business and government within which business operates.

Business risk: Anticipation of losses caused by internal operating inefficiencies and external factors.

Buyer's market: A market characterized by many available properties and few potential users demanding them at prevailing prices.

Buying, assuming, and agreeing to pay: Undertaking and promising to pay the seller's personal liability for a debt at the time of purchase.

Buying subject to: Phrase meaning no personal liability is assumed in regard to a mortgage debt which exists against real estate at the time of purchase.

By-laws: In reference to condominiums, the day-to-day rules and regulations for operation of the project. They usually appear as an appendix to the master deed and are recorded. Generally, self-imposed rules adopted by a corporation or other group.

California ranch house: A one-story house having a style similar to that of a ranch.

Cape Cod architecture: A style featuring a steeply sloped gable roof, dormer windows for second-story rooms, windows with shutters, a square chimney, and usually having Early American decor.

Capital asset: Any asset of a permanent nature used for the production of income (land, buildings, machinery, equipment, etc.).

Capital gain: Income that results from the sale of an asset and not from the usual course of business. (Capital gains are taxed at a lower rate than ordinary income.)

Capital recapture: The manner in which the investment in a property is to be returned to investors; normally stated as a rate or dollar amount per unit of time.

Capitalism: An economic system based on the principles of ownership of private property, equality, and personal rights.

Capitalization: The process of reflecting future income in present value; capitalization in perpetuity is capitalization without a time limit.

Capitalization rate: A percentage made up of the interest rate (return on the investment) plus the recapture rate (return of the original investment).

Carport: A roof over part of a driveway, usually extending from the side of a house.

Carrying charges: Charges for holding property, such as tax expense on idle property or property under construction.

Casement windows: Windows with frames of wood or metal which swing outward.

Cash flow: The net income from a property before depreciation and other noncash expenses.

Caveat emptor: Let the buyer beware. The maxim expresses the general idea that the buyer purchases at his or her peril, and that no warranties, either express or implied, are made by the seller.

CCIM: Certified Commercial and Investment Member. A designation conferred by RNMI.

Central business district: The downtown shopping and office area of a city.

Central city: The downtown area of a city; also, a city that is the center of a geographic trade area for which it performs certain market and service functions.

Certificate of no defense: An instrument executed by the mortgagor, upon the sale of the mortgage, to the assignee as to the validity of the full mortgage debt. See estoppel certificate.

Certificate of sale: A document issued to the highest bidder at a foreclosure sale to indicate ownership.

Certificate of title: A certificate issued by a person who has examined the record of title of real estate as to the state of the title of such real estate.

Certificates of beneficial interest: The ownership shares in a trust or mutual fund.

Certified residential broker (CRB): Designation granted by NIREB.

Certiorari: An appellate proceeding for reexamination of the action of an inferior tribunal, or an auxiliary process to enable the appellate court to obtain further information in a pending cause.

Cestui que use: One who has the right to receive the profits and benefits of the lands or tenements, the legal title and possession of which are held by another person as trustee.

Chain measures: A series of 100 interconnected wire links each of which is 1 foot in length. A chain 66 feet in length, composed of interconnected wire links each of which is 7.92 inches long. (10 square chains of land equal 1 acre.)

Chain of title: Successive conveyances, or other forms of alienation, affecting a particular parcel of land, arranged consecutively, from the government or original source of title down to the present holder.

Chancellor: The name given in some states to the judge of a court of chancery (equity).

Chancery: A court of equity; the system of jurisdiction administered in courts of equity.

Change: The appraisal principle which describes existence in three states: integration, equilibrium, and degeneration; holds that it is the future not the past which is of prime importance in estimating value.

Chattel mortgage: A mortgage of personal property to secure a debt. See security interest.

Chattel personal: An object of movable personal property.

Chattel real: An item usually considered personal property which is annexed to or attached to real estate.

Chattels: Items of personal property.

Chose in action: A right of action for recovery of a debt.

Circuit breaker: The electrical instrument which automatically breaks an electric circuit when an overload occurs.

Circulating fireplace: A type of fireplace which is built around a metal form, containing air ducts to distribute heat by convection.

Civil action: Any lawsuit between private parties.

Clapboard: The boards used for siding, which are usually thicker at one edge.

Clear title: A title free of any encumbrances or defects.

Close: A parcel of land, enclosed by a fence, hedge, or visual enclosure; in surveying it has several meanings and could easily be confused with "closing." Close also refers to completing a transaction; when real estate formally changes ownership.

Closing: The transaction at which the title to real estate is transferred pursuant to a contract of sale.

Closing costs: The costs of the settlement in the transfer of property ownership, such as recording fees, attorney fees, title insurance premium, etc.

Closing statement: A listing of the debits and credits of the buyer and seller in a real estate transaction for the final financial settlement of the transaction.

Cloud on the title: An outstanding claim or condition which affects the title to property and which cannot be removed without a quitclaim deed or court action.

Cluster housing: A housing arrangement in which units are placed close together to allow for large recreational or common areas.

Code of ethics: The standards adopted by NAR and the various real estate boards for the business conduct of members.

Codicil: Some addition to or amendment of one's last will and testament.

Cognovit clause: The borrower confesses judgment or gives written authority to the lender to secure a judgment that can be attached to the borrower's property as a lien; a waiver of any defense to the claim.

Cognovit note: A note which authorizes a confession of judgment and admission of the validity of a claim for money.

Collar beam: The beam that joins together the pairs of opposite roof rafters above the attic floor.

Collateral: Anything of value that a borrower pledges as security.

Collateral security: An additional obligation to guarantee performance of a contract.

Collusion: A secret combination, conspiracy, or concert of action between two or more persons for fraudulent or deceitful purposes.

Colonial architecture: The traditional design, usually using the characteristics of New England homes; usually two-story houses with balanced openings along the main facade, windows constructed with small panes, shutters and dormer windows on the third floor, with attention to small detail.

Color of title: A writing upon the face of a document professing to pass title but which does not, either through want of title in the grantor or a defective mode of conveyance; that which appears to be good title, but as a matter of fact, is not good title.

Combed plywood: A grooved building plywood used mainly for interior finish.

Combination door: A permanent door that employs a screen panel for summer and glass panel for winter.

Commercial acre: The remnant of an acre of newly subdivided land after the land devoted to streets, sidewalks, etc., has been deducted.

Commercial banks: National or state chartered banks which operate on a basis of stock ownership. The dividends are distributed to the shareholders. The depositors have no share in the management.

Commercial paper: Bills of exchange or other debt instruments used in place of money.

Commercial properties: Properties intended for use in business areas.

Commingle: To mix, as to deposit a client's funds in the broker's personal account.

Commission: An agent's compensation for the performance of his duties; in real estate, a percentage of the selling price of property or percentage of rentals.

Commitment: For a mortgage, a statement by the lender of the conditions and terms under which he or she will lend. A conditional commitment is a statement that mortgage funds will be provided if certain conditions are met which permit an owner or developer to begin construction. A firm commitment is a written notification that a financial institution will lend money and on what terms it will do so.

Common law: Rules developed by usage; judge-made law.

Common property: Land considered to be public property; also, a legal term denoting an incorporeal hereditament consisting of a right of one person in the land of another.

Common wall: The wall which serves two dwellings simultaneously.

Community Associations Institute (CAI): A national association of homeowners' associations.

Community property: In certain states, the property owned by the "community" or marriage of husband and wife; property owned by the marriage and not in shares.

Compaction: The act of compressing soil added as fill to a lot so that it will bear the weight of buildings without the danger of their settling, tilting, or cracking.

Comparables: Properties of like nature which might be compared to one another through careful study, thereby allowing a value to be determined for one of them.

Competence: Under the law of evidence, being of such form as to be admissible in court for use as evidence.

Competent: Legally qualified and mentally capable to transact business.

Complainant: The party who instigates a legal action.

Compound interest: The interest paid on the original principal and on the accrued interest from the time it became due.

Concentric circle hypothesis: Transportation is assumed to be the central force in community growth. Therefore the land values are highest where mobility is greatest.

Concentric circles: Ring growth around the nucleus of an urban area.

Conclusive evidence: Incontrovertible evidence.

Condemnation: The process by which property of a private owner is taken for public use without the owner's consent but with the owner's awareness and with payment of just compensation.

Condition: A future and uncertain event upon the happening of which is made to depend the existence of an obligation, or that which subordinates the existence of liability under a contract to a certain future event.

Conditional fee: See fee simple conditional.

Conditional sale: A term most frequently applied to a sale wherein the seller reserves the title to the goods, though the possession is delivered to the buyer, until the purchase price is paid in full.

Conditional sales contract: A contract for the sale of property specifying that delivery is to be made to the buyer with the title to remain vested in the seller until the conditions of the contract have been fulfilled.

Conditional vendee: The buyer under a conditional sales contract.

Conditional vendor: The seller under a conditional sales contract.

Condominium: The individual ownership of a single unit in a multiunit structure, together with an interest in the common land areas and the underlying ground.

Condominium conversion: A process by which rental units are turned into individually owned units.

Conduit: A metal pipe through which electrical wiring is installed.

Confession of judgment: An entry of judgment upon the debtor's voluntary admission without defense in a legal proceeding. See cognovit note.

Confirmation: The ratification of a transaction known to be voidable.

Confirmation of sale: A court approval of the sale of property by an executor, administrator, guardian, or conservator of an estate.

Confiscation: The seizure of property without compensation.

Conformity: The blending of the use of real estate and improvements upon it with the surroundings so as to appear harmonious.

Consequential damage: The impairment of value which arises as an indirect result of an act.

Conservation: The process of saving resources or of using them in such a way that they will not be depleted.

Consideration: Anything of value given or given up by both parties to a contract and necessary to the enforcement of the contract.

Constant: The percentage of the unpaid balance of a loan which is represented by the sum of the principal and interest payments for the following year, which is needed to fully amortize the loan.

Constant payment: A regular, periodic payment which does not fluctuate in amount and which includes both interest and amortization.

Constant-payment mortgage: A loan reduction plan whereby the borrower pays a fixed amount each month, part to be applied to repayment of the principal and the remainder to payment of interest.

Construction loan: A loan to finance the improvement of real estate, generally short-term or interim financing pending completion of improvements.

Constructive eviction: Inability of a tenant to retain possession by reason of a condition making occupancy hazardous or unfit for its intended use.

Constructive notice: Notice rendered by the public records.

Constructive trustee: One who is a trustee by operation of law resulting from unlawful possession of property of another.

Consultant: An advisor on matters who receives a fee for his or her services and advice.

Consumer goods: Goods used or purchased primarily for personal, family, or household purposes.

Contemporary architecture: Modern design, as differentiated from the traditional; functional design.

Contiguous: Adjacent; touching or adjoining.

Contingencies: Possible future events which are uncertain.

Contingent fees: Payment to be made upon future occurrences, conclusions, or results of services to be performed.

Contract: A written or oral agreement to perform or not to perform certain obligations.

Contract for deed: See conditional sales contract.

Contract rent: Rent stipulated in a lease agreement.

Contractor: One who has the responsibility for and supervises the improvement of land.

Contribution: A payment by each, or by any, of several having a common interest or liability of his or her share in the loss suffered, or in the money necessarily paid by one of the parties in behalf of the others; holds that maximum real property values are achieved when the improvements on the site produce the highest return commensurate with the investment.

Control data: The means of using the transactions of real properties to adjust the market data utilized in the comparative approach to valuation. Such control data is necessary in order to segregate certain influences which have caused changes in real estate values, either generally or specifically.

Convenience factor: The commonly recognized and easily understood quality offering advantages and values to a particular parcel of real property over that of other properties.

Conventional home: A home that is constructed totally at the site. It is the opposite of a factory-built or mobile home.

Conventional loan: A mortgage loan made by a financial institution, conforming to its own standards, modified within legal bounds by mutual consent of the parties involved, and without insurance or guarantee by the FHA or VA.

Conventional mortgage: A mortgage that is not insured by a public agency.

Conversion: A change in the use of real estate by altering improvements but without destroying them; legally, the unlawful taking of possession of the property of another.

Conversion value: Value created by converting from one state or use to another.

Conveyance: In its common use, refers to a written instrument transferring the title to land or some interest therein from one person to another. Transfer of title or ownership to real estate from one party to another.

Cooperative: Ownership form in which a single property is subdivided into several use portions, with each user owning stock in the corporation that owns the property and occupying a portion of it.

Cooperative apartment: An apartment complex owned by a corporation or a trust, in which each owner purchases stock to the value of his or her apartment and is given a proprietary lease.

Cooperative ownership: Usually a form of apartment ownership in which an occupant acquires ownership by purchasing shares in a corporation. The cooperative property is owned in severalty. The cooperative plan is permitted to place extensive restraints on the alienation of the units as well as their use and improvements.

Co-ownership: Ownership of the same property by two or more persons.

Corner influence: The effect of street intersections upon the adjoining property.

Corner influence table: A statistical table which attempts to reflect the additional value accorded a lot with a corner location.

Corporation: A group of different persons or parties established and treated by law as an individual or unit with rights and liabilities, or both, distinct from those of the persons composing it. A corporation is a creature of law with certain powers and duties of a natural person. Created by law, it may continue for any length of time the law prescribes.

Corporeal rights: Possessory rights in real property.

Correction deed: A written instrument which corrects an error in a recorded deed.

Correction line: The line every 24 miles that runs due north and south from the base line in order to compensate for the narrowing of the earth in the rectangular method of survey.

Cost: That which must be given up to obtain property. The replacement cost is the cost of replacing real estate improvements with an alternative of like utility. Reproduction cost is the cost of replacing real estate improvements with an exact replica.

Cost approach to value: Valuation reached by estimating the cost of providing a substitute for that which is being valued. Depreciation must be deducted in making the valuation.

Cost of capital: The amount that must be paid to attract money into an investment project.

Cost of reproduction: The normal cost of duplication of a property.

Counselor: One who assists clients with advice regarding use and management of assets.

Counterflashing: Flashing used on chimneys at the roof line to cover the shingle flashing and to prevent moisture from entering.

County: A civil division of a territory organized for political and judicial purposes.

Covenant: Used in contracts as synonymous with promise; in deeds, it may be a positive or negative undertaking by one or both parties.

Covenant for further assurance: An undertaking, in the form of a covenant, on the part of the vendor of real estate to perform such further acts for the purpose of perfecting the purchaser's title as the latter may reasonably require.

CPM: Certified property manager; a member of IREM of NAREB.

CRB (certified residential broker): A designation conferred by RNMI.

CRE (counselor on real estate): A designation conferred by ASREC.

Credit: The power of an individual to secure money, or obtain goods on time, in consequence of the favorable opinion held by the community, or by the particular lender, as to his or her solvency and reliability; a debt considered from the creditor's standpoint, or that which is to be incoming or due to one.

Crossroad development: Pattern of city growth characterized by fingerlike extensions moving out along the main transportation routes.

Cubical content: The actual space within the outer surfaces of outside walls and contained between the outer surfaces of the roof and the finished surface of the lowest basement or cellar floor; the actual space that lies within the interior dimensions of a structure.

Cul-de-sac: A deadend street with a widened, circular area at the end to enable a car to make a U-turn.

Curable depreciation: Any deficiency that can be cured.

Curable penalty: Element of depreciation whose cost of repair or correction is offset by the increase in value of the property caused by the repair or correction. Incurable penalty occurs when the cost of repair adds less than its cost to the property's value.

Current assets: Liquid assets such as cash, accounts receivable, and merchandise inventories.

Current liabilities: Short-term debts, generally debts due within 1 year's time.

Curtesy: The right a husband has in a wife's real estate at her death.

Custodian: One who is responsible for the care of something entrusted to him or her; e.g., a custodian of a public building.

Custom-built house: A house sold before construction begins and built to the owner's specifications.

Cyclical fluctuation: Variations around a trend in activity that recur from time to time; fluctuations remaining after removal of trend and seasonal factors that recur regularly.

Damages: Indemnity to the person who suffers a loss or harm from an injury; a sum recoverable as amends from a wrong; an adequate compensation for the loss suffered or the injury sustained.

Data assembly: Gathering, analyzing, and classifying data pertaining to a subject property.

Data plant: A collection of information about real properties maintained usually by an appraiser, mortgage lender, and the like.

Datum: The horizontal plane from which heights and depths are measured.

De facto: In fact or in reality.

Dealer-builder: A builder who constructs structures from prefabricated components, usually as the local representative of a prefabricated house manufacturer.

Debit: The amount charged as due or owing.

Debt: Something which must be repaid or a duty owed, such as a loan.

Debt capital: Money borrowed for a particular business purpose.

Debt service: Annual amount to be paid by a debtor to retire an obligation to repay borrowed money.

Debt service coverage: The requirement that earnings be a percentage or dollar sum higher than debt service.

Debtor: The party who owes money to another.

Decedent: A deceased person.

Decentralization: Dispersion from a center point or figure.

Deciduous trees: Trees which do not keep their leaves through the autumn and winter.

Decree: The final determination of the rights of the parties to a suit.

Decree of foreclosure: The decree by a court for the sale of property to pay an obligation found to be due and owing.

Dedication: An offer of land to some public use, made by an owner and accepted for such use by or on behalf of the public.

Deed: An instrument conveying title to real property.

Deed covenants: The warranties made by a seller of property to protect the buyer against items such as liens, encumbrances, or title defects.

Deed money escrow: An agreement where money is retained by a third party to be delivered to a seller of real estate upon the receipt of the deed to the property sold.

Deed restrictions: Limitations placed upon the use of real property in the deed to that property.

Deed of trust: An instrument in use in many states, taking the place and serving the uses of a common-law mortgage, by which the legal title to real property is placed in one or more trustees to secure the repayment of a sum of money or the performance of other conditions.

Default: Failure to fulfill a duty or to discharge an obligation.

Defeasance clause: The clause in a mortgage that permits the mortgagor to redeem his or her property upon the payment of the obligations to the mortgagee.

Defective title: A title which would be impaired were an outstanding claim proved to be valid.

Defects in title: Imperfections that cast a reasonable doubt on the marketability of title.

Defendant: A party sued in a legal action.

Deferred maintenance: An existing but unfulfilled need for repairs and rehabilitation.

Deferred payments: Money payments which are to be made at some date in the future.

Deficiency judgment: A judgment for that part of a secured debt that was not liquidated by the proceeds from the sale of foreclosed real property.

Delegation of authority: A transfer of authority by one person to another.

Delinquency: A financial obligation which is in default, such as an overdue loan.

Delivery: The transfer from one person to another of an item, or a right or interest therein, which means more than physical transfer of possession. However, in the popular sense, in the case of a contract or lease or the like, it implies a transfer of the actual contract or document to the possession of the other party.

Demand: The amount of a good or service which will be bought at various prices (and under varying conditions).

Demand note: A note which is payable on demand of the holder.

Demise: The transfer of interest or conveyance of an estate primarily by lease.

Demographic: Pertaining to population structure.

Demographic characteristics: Political, social, and economic characteristics of a population of people.

Density: The number of units present per unit of area such as dwellings per acre or persons per square mile.

Deposit, earnest money: A sum of money or other consideration tendered in conjunction with an offer to purchase rights in real property as evidence of good faith.

Depositary: The party receiving a deposit. The obligation on the part of the depositary to keep the item with reasonable care and, upon request, restore it to the depositor, or otherwise deliver it, according to the original agreement.

Depreciation: Loss in property value. Accelerated depreciation is a method of reflecting depreciation that enables the owner of an asset to take more of the depreciation during the early years of the asset's life. Contingent depreciation is a loss in property value because of expectations of a decline in property services. Depletion is the exhaustion of a resource such as the removal of a mineral deposit. Economic obsolescence is a loss in property value from events outside the property that unfavorably affect income or income potential. Functional obsolescence is a loss in property value because of a loss in the ability of the physical property to provide services as compared with alternatives. Physical depreciation is a loss in property value due to wearing away or deterioration.

Depreciation, accrued: The actual amount of depreciation existing in a property at a given date.

Depreciation allowance: The amounts to be claimed or allowed for depreciation.

Depreciation base: Cost of an asset that is to be depreciated.

Depreciation methods: The methods used to measure decreases in the value of an improvement through depreciation. In appraising, the methods generally used are annuity, sinking fund, and straight-line. In accounting, it relates to various methods by which capital impairment is computed. In addition to the three methods used in appraising, accountants also use declining balance (and variations thereof), weighted rate, and accelerated.

Depreciation rate: The periodic amount or percentage at which the usefulness of a property is used up, especially the percentage at which amounts are computed to be set aside as an accrual for future depreciation.

Depreciation, straight line: An accounting term showing the reduction of the cost or other basis of property, less estimated salvage value, in equal amounts over the estimated useful life of the property.

Depreciation, sum of the years' digits: Annual depreciation computed by applying changing fractions to the cost or other basis of property reduced by estimated salvage. The numerators of the fraction change each year to the estimated remaining useful life of the asset, and the constant denominator is the sum of all the years' digits corresponding to the estimated useful life of the asset. For example, the fraction for the first year's depreciation on a 5-year asset is 5/15. The 5 is the estimated useful life remaining, and 15 is computed by adding together each year's remaining useful life, i.e., $5 + 4 + 3 + 2 + 1 = 15$.

Depth table: A technique for real estate appraisal using statistical tables based on the theory that added depth increases the value of land.

Descent: The process by which the property of a decedent passes to his or her legal heirs.

Desist and refrain order: An order issued by a real estate commissioner to stop an action in violation of the real estate law.

Deterioration: A worsening of the condition of a property.

Determinable fee: An estate which may last forever is a "fee," but if it may end on the happening of a merely possible event, it is a "determinable," or "qualified fee."

Developer: One who prepares land for income production, the making of improvements, and the sale of completed properties.

Devise: A testamentary disposition of land or realty. Leaving real property through a will.

Devisee: The person to whom lands or other real property are devised or given by will.

Direct reduction mortgage: A mortgage which is to be repaid by periodic fixed amounts plus interest on the unpaid balance.

Directional growth: The direction in which the residential sections of a city are destined to expand.

Disability: The lack of legal capacity to perform an act.

Disaffirm: To repudiate; to revoke a consent once given; to disclaim the intention of being bound by an antecedent transaction.

Discharge: The release or performance of a contract or other obligation.

Discount rate: The correlation between dollars transmitted from a lender to a borrower and dollars that must be repaid by the borrower. If a lender advances $960 and the borrower must repay $1,000, the discount rate is

$$\frac{\$40}{\$1,000} = 4\%.$$

Discounting: A means of converting any cash flow into present value at a selected rate of return; based upon the premise that one would pay less than $1 today for the right to receive $1 at a future date.

Discretion: Power or privilege of a fiduciary to act unhampered by legal restrictions or limitations on his normal authority.

Disintermediation: An outflow of funds from savings institutions by investors to reinvest their monies elsewhere where the rates of return are expected to be higher.

Disposable income: The income left to a household after taxes.

Disposable field: A drainage area, not close to the water supply, where refuse from the septic tank is dispersed, being drained into the ground through tile and gravel filtration.

Dispossess: To put one out of possession of real estate.

Distress: The act of distraining; assuming possession of a tenant's chattels by a landlord in order to satisfy, in whole or in part, a claim for rent in arrears. Another common word for this is "distrain."

Distributee: One who receives part of the property of a person who dies intestate.

Distribution: The division and transfer of the property of a decedent.

District: A city area with a land use different from that of adjacent areas, e.g., commercial, industrial, or residential.

Documentary evidence: Evidence supplied by written instruments such as contracts, deeds, etc.

Documentary stamp: The revenue stamp issued for payment of a tax on documents such as deeds.

Documents: Written records; in real estate, contracts, deeds, leases, mortgages, etc.

Domicile: A place where a person lives or has his home; in a strict legal sense, the place where he has his true, fixed, permanent home and principal establishment, and to which place he has, whenever he is absent, the intention of returning.

Dominant tenement or estate: That to which a servitude or easement is due, or for the benefit of which it exists. For example, land which includes the right to the use of a right of way over other land.

Donee: A person who receives a gift.

Donor: The one who makes a gift to another.

Double, duplex: Two dwelling units under one roof. A double usually denotes two dwellings side by side, and a duplex, one dwelling above the other.

Doubling up: The occupation of a dwelling unit by two or more families.

Dower: The legal rights a widow possesses to her deceased husband's real estate.

Down payment: Initial partial payment of the total selling price.

Downzoning: A public action by which the local government reduces the allowable density for subsequent development (e.g., fewer housing units, fewer stores, etc.) or allowable use from a high to low use (e.g., multifamily to single-family).

Drainage: The running off of water from the surface of land.

Duress: Unlawful pressure placed upon a person to coerce him to perform some act against his will.

Dutch Colonial: The style of architecture that features a gambrel roof, exterior walls of masonry or wood, and porches at the side; especially adapted to flat sites and difficult to fit into a steep slope.

Earnest money: Money paid to evidence good faith when an offer of purchase is submitted to a property owner by a prospective purchaser.

Easement: The right which ownership of one parcel of land has to use or control the use of another parcel of land owned by another; such rights and obligations run with the land itself and are not mere personal rights of an individual.

Easement appurtenant: An easement which runs with the land and is transferred to another in the conveyance of the title.

Easement in gross: An easement which does not run with the land and therefore is not transferred through the conveyance of the title.

"Easy" money: A financial situation that occurs when lenders have an abundance of funds available for lending. The terms of the loans are favorable to borrowers.

Eaves: The lower part of a roof that protrudes over the wall.

Economic base: The major economic support of a community.

Economic base analysis: A technique for analyzing the major economic supports of a community; analysis as a means of predicting population, income, or other variables having an effect on real estate value or land utilization.

Economic goods: Goods that have scarcity and utility; goods that provide desired services but are not in sufficient abundance to be free.

Economic life: The period over which a property will yield the investor a return on the investment, over and above the economic or ground rent due to land.

Economic obsolescence: Lessened desirability or useful life arising from economic forces, such as changes in optimum land use, legislative enactments which restrict or impair property rights, and changes in supply-demand relationships. Loss in the use and value of property arising from the factors of economic obsolescence is to be distinguished from loss in value from physical deterioration and functional obsolescence.

Economic rent: The base rent payable for the right of occupancy of vacant land.

Economics: Allocation of scarce resources.

Economy: The efficient use of resources with an eye to productivity.

Effective age: A statement regarding the amount of depreciation that has occurred on a property. The amount is stated in terms of the number of years that would ordinarily be associated with the degree of depreciation.

Effective demand: Desire for property backed by the ability to purchase.

Effective gross revenue: A method to determine income less allowance for vacancies, contingencies, and sometimes collection losses, but before deductions for any operating expenses.

Egress: A way out; exit; an outlet.

Ejectment: Legal action brought to regain possession of property.

Elasticity: Ability of the supply of real estate to respond to price increases over a short period of time.

Emancipate (a child): To release a child from parental control for purposes of legal capacity or competency.

Embezzlement: A statutory offense consisting of the fraudulent conversion of another's personal property by one to whom it has been entrusted, with the intention of depriving the owner thereof, the gist of the offense being usually the violation of relations of fiduciary character.

Emblements: Crops growing on the property which require annual care and usually are the possession of the tenant.

Eminent domain: The right of the government to take private property for public use, with just compensation.

Enabling act: A state statute used to provide a legal base for zoning codes or other local governmental action.

Encroachment: An improvement which intrudes upon property adjacent to that on which it was meant to be constructed.

Encumbrance: A claim against a property.

English architecture: The design using the characteristics of Elizabethan, Tudor Cotswold, and other English styles; frequently large stone houses with slate shingles on gabled roofs, mullioned casement windows, and wainscotted interiors. Exposed timbers constitute the structural frame of authentic Elizabethan houses, although in modern adaptations the half-timbering is purely decorative. Between the half-timbers there usually is plaster, although in the original types the spaces were filled with brick nogging.

Entrepreneur: One who organizes, manages, and assumes responsibility for a business.

Equality of economic opportunity: A state of affairs in which all people have equal chances for the same jobs at equal pay, regardless of race, creed, color, or sex.

Equitable title: The right that exists in equity to obtain absolute ownership to property when title is held in another's name. Also, an interest in land that may not amount to fee simple ownership, but is such that a court will take notice of the rights of the holder of such interest.

Equity: Justice. Also, in finance, the value of the interest of an owner of property exclusive of the encumbrances on that property.

Equity funds: Capital invested to gain a residual ownership interest in property.

Equity interest: The amount of the value or total combined worth of a property minus any debts outstanding against it. The amount of the interest may be established through: (1) cash originally put into the property (down payment), (2) the amortization of any debt against the property, (3) any appreciation in the value of the property.

Equity participation: That percentage of the income or other return on the investment required by a lender in excess of the normal interest received for financing a real estate project.

Equity of redemption: The right to redeem property during the foreclosure period.

Erosion: The wearing away of the ground surface.

Escalator clause: A clause in a contract providing for the upward or downward adjustment of specific terms to cover certain contingencies, e.g., right to increase interest rates on a loan under specified conditions.

Escheat: The reversion of private property to the state.

Escrow: The arrangement for the handling of instruments or money not to be delivered until specified conditions are met.

Escrow holder: The third party who receives a deed or item from a grantor to be held until the performance of a condition by the grantee or until the occurrence of a contingency, then to be delivered to the grantee.

Estate (several types): The degree of interest a person has in land with respect to the nature of the right, its duration, or its relation to the rights of others. Estate in expectancy is a classification of estates by time of enjoyment when possession will be at some future time. An estate in possession is a classification of estates by time of enjoyment when possession is present. Estate in severalty is the ownership in a single individual; a classification of estates by number of owners where the number is one. A freehold estate is a nonleasehold estate such as a fee simple estate, fee tail estate, or life estate. Fee simple estates are the most complete form of estate ownership; the "totality of rights" in real property. A fee tail estate is an estate or a limited estate in which transfer of the property is restricted in that the property must pass to the descendants of the owner. Originally used to insure the passing of land in a direct ancestral line. A life estate is an estate that has a duration of the life of an individual.

Estate for years: A leasehold interest in lands by virtue of a contract for the possession for a specified period of time.

Estate of inheritance: An estate which may be passed on to heirs. All freehold estates are estates of inheritance, except estates for life.

Estate at will: The occupation of lands and tenements by a tenant for an unspecified period terminable by one or both parties.

Estate in reversion: The remnant of an estate left in the grantor, to commence in possession after the termination of some lesser estate granted by him or her to another.

Estoppel: A legal doctrine under which one is precluded and forbidden to deny his own act or deed.

Estoppel certificate: The certificate which shows the unpaid principal of a mortgage and the interest thereon, if the principal or interest notes are not produced or if the seller asserts that the amount due under the mortgage which the purchaser is to assume is less than shown on record.

Et al.: And others.

Et ux.: And wife.

Ethics: The moral principles, such as those owed by a member of a profession or craft to the public, to clients, and to professional associates.

Eviction: The ouster from possession of real property of one in possession under a valid lease.

Eviction notice: A notice to a tenant to vacate premises because of nonpayment of rent or other violation of the lease agreement.

Evidence: That which tends to prove or disprove any matter in question, or to influence the belief respecting it.

Ex officio: By virtue of the office; without any other warrant or appointment than that resulting from the holding of a particular office.

Ex parte: One side only, or done in behalf of only one person.

Exception: An objection; a reservation; a contradiction.

Excess rent: The monetary difference between contract rent and economic rent.

Exchange: The process of trading an equity in a piece of property for the equity in another piece of property.

Exchange brokerage: The process of bringing two parties together in transactions involving trading of properties.

Exchangor: The broker or salesperson who accomplishes the exchange.

Exclusive agency listing: A listing contract providing that the agent shall receive a commission if the property is sold as a result of the efforts of that agent or any other agent, but not as a result of the efforts of the principal; the contract further provides that the agent will receive a commission if a buyer is secured under the terms of the contract.

Exclusive listing: The contract to market property as an agent, according to the terms of which the agent is given the exclusive right to sell the property or is made the exclusive agent for its sale. The term is also applied to the property which is listed.

Exclusive right to sell listing: A contract between owner and agent giving agent the right to collect a commission if the property is sold by anyone during the term of the agreement.

Exculpatory clause: A clause often included in leases that clears or relieves the landlord of liability for personal injury to tenants as well as for property damages.

Execute: To complete; to perform.

Execution: The act of performing the final judgment or decree of a court; the formal action, usually signing, taken to complete a legal document and make it binding.

Executor: The person who is designated in a will as one who is to administer the estate of the testator.

Executor's deed: A deed given by an executor of the estate.

Exempt: To release, discharge, waive, relieve from liability.

Existing mortgage: The debt contract in which the seller of real estate is the mortgagor, which is to be assumed by the purchaser.

Exoneration (in suretyship): The right which a surety has, on payment of the principal debtor's obligation, to look to the principal debtor for reimbursement.

Expansible house: A home created for future additions.

Expansion joint: A bituminous fiber strip used to separate units of concrete to prevent cracking because of expansion as a result of temperature changes.

Express contract: One expressed in words, either written or oral.

Expropriation: The act or process whereby private property is acquired for public use, or the rights therein modified by a sovereignty or any entity vested with the necessary legal authority; e.g., where property is taken under eminent domain.

Extended coverage endorsement: An addition to a fire insurance policy which extends the coverage to include losses caused by windstorm, hail, explosion, riot, aircraft, vehicle, and smoke damage.

Extensive margin: Extra benefits derived from adding increasing amounts of land to a productive state.

Extinguishment: The destruction or cancellation of a right, power, contract, or estate.

Extra use: Use (or activity) level in excess of a real or normal level of use.

Facade: The front or face of a building.

Factor: A commercial agent who sells goods consigned to him, for a principal, but uses his own name.

Fair value: Reasonable value, consistent with all known facts, at which the purchaser is willing to pay the price and the seller is willing to sell at the price.

Fannie Mae: Federal National Mortgage Association.

Farm and Land Institute: Brings together specialists in the sale, development, planning, management, and sydication of land to establish professional standards through educational programs for members. Confers AFLM (Accredited Farm and Land Member).

Feasibility survey: The analysis of the cost/benefit ratio of an economic endeavor prior to its undertaking.

Fed: Federal Reserve Board.

Federal Deposit Insurance Corporation: Federal agency that insures deposits at commercial banks and savings banks.

Federal Home Loan Bank: A district bank of the Federal Home Loan Bank System that lends only to member financial institutions such as savings and loan associations.

Federal Home Loan Bank Board: The administrative agency that charters federal savings and loan associations and exercises regulatory authority over members of the Federal Home Loan Bank System.

Federal Home Loan Bank System: The network of Federal Home Loan Banks and member financial institutions.

Federal Housing Administration (FHA): A federal agency that insures mortgage loans.

Federal National Mortgage Association: Federal agency that buys and sells FHA-insured and VA-guaranteed mortgage loans. Popularly known as "Fannie Mae."

Federal savings and loan association: A savings and loan association with a federal charter issued by the Federal Home Loan Bank Board. A federally chartered savings and loan association is in contrast to a state-chartered savings and loan association.

Federal Savings and Loan Insurance Corporation: Federal agency which insures savers' accounts at savings and loan associations.

Fee: An estate of inheritance in real property; compensation for a particular act.

Fee simple: In modern estates, the terms "fee" and "fee simple" are substantially synonymous. The term "fee" is of Old English derivation.

Fee simple absolute: An estate in real property by which the owner has the greatest power over the title which it is possible to have; an absolute estate. It expressly establishes the title of real property in the owner, without any limitation or end. He or she may dispose of it by sale, trade, or will, as desired.

Fee simple conditional: A fee that may terminate upon the occurrence of a specific event, the time of which is uncertain and/or the event itself may or may not ever occur.

Fee simple determinable: See fee simple conditional.

Fee simple limited: See fee simple conditional.

Fee tail: A freehold estate of inheritance limited so as to descend to a particular class of heirs of the person to whom it is granted.

Felony: A crime graver than those termed "misdemeanor"; the word is defined by several of the statutes and codes of the United States and includes crimes punishable by death or imprisonment in a penitentiary or state prison.

Feudal system: A political and social system which prevailed throughout Europe during the eleventh, twelfth, and thirteenth centuries under which ownership of land was vested in the monarch and subjects had only privileges of its use as opposed to private or allodial ownership.

Feudal tenure: See feudal system.

Feuds: Grants of land.

FHA: See Federal Housing Administration.

FHLMC: Federal Home Loan Mortgage Corporation.

Fidelity bond: A bond posted as security for the discharge of an obligation of personal services.

Fiduciary: One who holds title to property for the benefit of another; or one who holds a position of trust and confidence.

Filtering: Upward mobility of people of one income group into homes that have recently dropped in price and that were previously occupied by persons in the next higher income group.

Filtering down: In housing, the process of passing the use of real estate to successively lower-income groups as the real estate produces less income.

Financial institutions: Organizations that deal in money or claims to money and serve the function of channeling money from those who wish to lend to those who wish to borrow. Such organizations include commercial banks, savings and loan associations, savings banks, and insurance companies.

Financial intermediary: A financial institution which acts as an intermediary between savers and borrowers by selling its own obligations for money and, in turn, lending the accumulated funds to borrowers. This type of institution includes savings associations, mutual savings banks, life insurance companies, credit unions, and investment companies.

Financial risk: Possibility of losses created by the amount of and legal provisions concerning borrowed funds.

Finish floor: Strips that are applied over wood joists, deadening felt, and diagonal subflooring before finish floor is installed; finish floor is the final covering on the subflooring; wood, linoleum, cork, tile, or carpet.

Fire stop: A solid, tight closure of a concealed space, built to prevent the spread of fire and smoke through such a space.

Firm commitment: A commitment assumed by the FHA to insure a mortgage of a specified mortgagor; an unqualified promise to make a loan under specified conditions.

First mortgage: The mortgage which prevails as a lien over all other mortgages.

Fiscal controls: Efforts to control the level of economic activity by manipulation of the amount of federal tax and spending programs and the amount of surplus or deficit.

Fixity of location: The characteristic which subjects real estate to the influence of its surroundings and prevents it from escaping such influence.

Fixture: A chattel permanently attached to real estate, and becoming accessory to it, and part and parcel of it.

Flashing: Sheet metal or other material used to protect a building from water seepage.

FLI: See Farm and Land Institute.

Floor load: The weight-supporting capabilities of a floor, measured in pounds per square foot; the weight, stated in pounds per square foot, which may be safely placed upon the floor of a building if it is uniformly distributed.

Flow of funds: An accounting method (used primarily by the Federal Reserve) to describe the sources and uses of the nation's funds in a given period of time.

FNMA: Federal National Mortgage Association, the secondary market agency for FHA and VA loans.

Footing: The base of a foundation wall or column.

Forced sale: The act of selling property under compulsion as to time; frequently the result of legal proceedings ordering the sale.

Forced sale value: The price realized at the forced sale.

Foreclosure: The legal process by which a mortgagee, after default by the mortgagor, forces sale of the property mortgaged in order to recover his or her loan.

Forfeiture: Deprivation or destruction of a right in consequence of the nonperformance of some obligation or condition.

Forgery: The legal offense of imitating or counterfeiting documents or signatures in an effort to deceive.

Forthwith: At once; promptly.

Foundation: The supporting portion of a structure below the first floor construction, including the footings.

Foundation wall: The masonry wall below ground which supports the building.

Franchise: A specific privilege conferred by government or contractually by a business firm.

Fraud: Intentional deception or trickery used to gain an unfair advantage over another.

Freehold: An estate in real property with no measurable length of time or termination date.

French architecture: Any of several styles originating in France; very common in smaller houses and the perfectly balanced, rectangular formal house with a steep roof, hipped at the ends, its plaster walls one story high, with dormer windows provided for second-floor rooms. The French farmhouse style is informal, of stone, painted brick, or plaster, sometimes with half-timbering used as an accent. Norman French architecture is large in scale, usually distinguished by a round tower.

Front foot: A measure (1 foot in length) of the width of lots taken along their frontage upon a street.

Front foot cost: Cost of a piece of real estate expressed in terms of front foot units.

Frostline: The depth to which frost will penetrate the soil. Footings should be placed below this depth to prevent movement.

Full face rate of interest: Rate of interest stated in the debt.

Functional obsolescence: Defects in the plan or design of a structure that detract from its marketability and value.

Functional plan: The special arrangement of real estate improvements as it relates to property services.

Functional utility: The total of a property's attractiveness and usefulness.

Funds: Cash or any other resource having value which may be sold in order to buy some other asset.

Furring: The strips of wood or metal applied behind a wall or other surface to even it, to form an air space, or to give the wall an appearance of greater thickness.

Gable roof: A steeply pitched roof with sloping sides.

Gambrel roof: A curb roof having a flatter upper slope and a steep lower slope.

General Assembly: State Senate and House of Representatives.

General mortgage bond: A document representing an obligation secured by a mortgage.

General warranty: A provision that guarantees the quality of title to property conveyed and undertakes to defend that title and to pay damages if the title is defective.

GI loan: A mortgage loan granted veterans, which is guaranteed by the VA subject to their restrictions.

Gift deed: A deed given without consideration.

Ginnie Mae: Government National Mortgage Association (GNMA).

Girder: A large beam used to support smaller beams, joists, and partitions.

GNP: Gross national product.

Good faith: An honest intention to abstain from taking conscious advantage of another.

Governmental survey: The process adopted in 1785, also known as the rectangular survey, used for describing land and establishing boundaries. It is used to describe both large and small tracts of land in legal descriptions.

Grade: The ground level taken at the foundation.

Grading: The process of plowing and raking a lot to give it a desired contour and drainage.

Graduated lease: A lease that provides for a variable rental rate, often based upon future determination; sometimes rent is based upon the result of periodical appraisals; used largely in long-term leases.

Graduate Realtors Institute (GRI): Educational program for REALTORS® sponsored by NAR. Awards GRI (Graduate, Realtors Institute).

Grand jury: A group of persons who inquire as to the commission of offenses, hearing evidence only against the accused, and in proper cases return indictments or accusations against such accused.

Grant: A transfer of real property by a written instrument. A private grant is the transfer of real property from one person to another. A public grant is a government transfer of ownership of real property to a private party.

Grantee: One who receives a transfer of real property by deed.

Grantor: One who transfers real property by deed.

GRI: Graduate Realtors Institute, and that program's designation.

Grid: A chart used for the purpose of rating the borrower risk, property, and neighborhood.

Gridiron pattern: A layout of streets that resembles a gridiron; a system of subdivision with blocks of uniform length and width and streets that intersect at right angles.

GRM: Gross rent multiplier.

Gross earnings: The total revenue from operations, before deduction of the expenses incurred in gaining such revenues.

Gross income: The total income from property before any expenses are deducted.

Gross income multiplier: A technique for estimating real estate value based on some factor (multiplier) times the gross income derived from the property in the past. See gross rent multiplier.

Gross lease: A lease of property under the terms of which the lessor is to assume all property charges regularly incurred as the result of property ownership, e.g., taxes, maintenance, etc.

Gross national product: The total value of all goods and services produced in the economy in any given period; also, the accounting method used to list the major income and expenditure (product) accounts of the nation.

Gross profits: Total profits computed before the deduction of general expenses.

Gross rent multiplier: A factor used in arriving at an estimate of real estate value. The factor is obtained by dividing known sales prices of comparable properties by the rental income of those properties. It is usually the average quotient arrived at from the above division (sales price by rental income) of several comparable properties. The gross rental income of a particular property is then multiplied by this factor.

Gross revenue: Total revenue from all sources before subtraction of expenses incurred in gaining such revenue.

Gross sales: The total amount of sales as shown by invoices, before deducting returns, allowances, etc.

Ground lease: A lease for the use of the land only.

Ground rent: The earnings of improved property proportionally credited to earnings of the ground itself after allowance is made for earnings of improvements; often called "economic rent."

Guaranteed mortgage: A mortgage in which a party other than the borrower assures payment in the event of default by a mortgagor, e.g., VA-guaranteed mortgages.

Guaranteed sale: The written commitment by a broker that within a specified period of time he or she will, in absence of a sale, purchase a given piece of property at a specified sum.

Guide meridian: A correction line which runs due north and south to compensate for the narrowing of the earth. Used in rectangular survey.

Habendum: The second part of a deed following that part which names the grantee. It describes the estate conveyed and to what use.

Habendum clause: The "have and to hold" clause which defines or limits the quantity of the estate granted in the premises of the deed. Not essential today per leading authorities unless the estate being granted is a limited one.

Haec verba: In the exact words.

Half-timbering: A means of construction of house walls with the timber frame exposed, the space between timbers being filled with masonry or plaster on laths; also simulated half-timbering, with boards applied on plaster walls as decoration.

Header: One beam which is placed perpendicular to joists and to which joists are nailed in framing for a chimney, stairway, or other opening.

Height density: A zoning regulation designed to control the use or occupancy within a certain area by designating the maximum height of the structures.

Heirs: Persons appointed by law to succeed to the real estate of a decedent, in case of intestacy.

Hereditaments: A larger and more comprehensive word than either "land" or "tenements," and meaning anything capable of being inherited, whether it be corporeal, incorporeal, real, personal, or mixed.

High-rise apartment building: An indefinite term used to describe the modern elevator apartment building.

Highest and best use: The utilization of real property to its greatest economic advantage; the use that provides the highest land value; the use of land that provides a net income stream to the land that when capitalized provides the highest land value.

Hip roof: A pitched roof that features sloping sides and ends.

Holdover tenant: A person who remains in possession of leased property after expiration of the leased term.

Holographic will: A will written entirely by the testator with his own hand.

Homeowners Loan Corporation: A federal agency that refinanced mortgages in default in the early 1930s.

Homestead: A dwelling with its land and buildings; a dwelling with its land and buildings protected by a homestead law.

Homestead exemption: The interest of the head of a family in his or her owned residence that is exempt from the claims of creditors.

Horizontal Property Act: The laws enacted by the various states, which permit creation of the condominium form of real property ownership.

Housing stock: The total inventory of dwelling units. This includes forms both owned and rented.

Housing starts: Newly constructed housing units. This includes both single-family and multifamily domiciles.

HUD (Housing and Urban Development): A federal department created in 1965 to solve the complex housing problems of the American city by utilization of the vast resources of the federal government in coordination with the various state and local governments. Administrations under HUD include FNMA, FHA, Public Housing, Urban Renewal, and Community Facilities.

Hundred percent location: A city retail business location which is considered the best for attracting business.

Hypothecate: To pledge something without delivering possession of it to the pledgee.

Hypothesis of median location: A theory stating that there is the tendency for businesses and other entities to locate at their lowest time and cost point.

Identity of interest: The system whereby the builder and sponsor of a housing project subsidized by the government have ownership interests in each other.

Implied: Contained in substance or essence or by fair inference but not actually expressed; deductible by inference or implication.

Implied contract: One implied by the acts and/or conduct of the parties involved.

Improper improvement: Out-of-place improvement; improvement which does not conform to the best use of the site.

Improved value: The difference between the income-producing ability of a property and the amount required to pay a return on the investment in the property.

Improvement: That which is erected or constructed upon land to release the income-earning potential of the land; buildings or appurtenances on land. An overimprovement is an improvement of real estate in excess of that justifiable to release the earning power of land. An underimprovement is an improvement insufficient to release the earning power of the land.

Improvements to land: Publicly owned additions such as curbs, sidewalks, street lighting system, and sewers, constructed so as to permit the development of privately owned land for utilization. (As opposed to improvements on land, which are usually privately owned.)

In personam: Against the person. Applied to actions in which the court is to impose upon the defendant a personal obligation to obey the order, judgment, or decree.

Incentive: Payment or reward for taking a certain action, usually in excess of fixed compensation and based upon better performance than required by agreement.

Inchoate dower: A wife's interest in the real estate of her husband during his life, which may become a right of dower upon his death.

Income: A stream of financial benefits generally measured in terms of money as of a certain time; a flow of service. It is the origin of value.

Income method: A method of appraising real property basing the value of the property upon the net amount of income produced by it.

Income/price ratio: Net income compared to the selling price of the property.

Income property: A property in which the income is generated by means of commercial rentals or in which the returns attributable to the real estate can be so segregated as to permit direct estimation. The income may come from several sources; e.g., commercial rents, business profits attributable to real estate other than rents, etc.

Incompetent: One who is mentally incapable; any person who, though not insane, is not considered legally competent enough to properly manage and take care of self or property and therefore could easily be taken advantage of by designing persons.

Incorporeal rights: Nonpossessory rights in real estate.

Increment: An increase. Used in reference to the increases in land values that accompany population growth and increasing wealth in the community.

Incremental income tax: The additional income tax caused by a given investment.

Incurable depreciation: A defect which cannot be removed or which it is impractical to remove. A defect in the "bone structure" of a building. It is measured by age-life tables or life expectancy.

Indenture: Any contract by which two or more parties enter into reciprocal obligations.

Independent contractor: A self-employed person, or one employed by another who has no right of control over the employee except as to final results.

Indirect lighting: Light that is reflected from the ceiling or other object external to the source.

Industrial districts: Areas in which the primary or major improvements to land are in the nature of factory, warehouse, or related property.

Industrial park: An area in which the land is developed specifically for use for industrial purposes.

Industrial property: In a broad sense, all the tangible and intangible assets pertinent to the conducting of an enterprise for the manufacturing, processing, and assembling of finished products from raw or fabricated materials. Also, in a limited sense, the land, fixed improvements, machinery, and all equipment (fixed or movable) comprising the facilities devoted to such enterprise.

Infant: A person not of full age; a minor lacking legal capacity to enter into contracts other than for necessities.

Infiltration: Displacement by persons of a lower economic status.

Inflation: An economic circumstance that occurs when real purchasing is decreased as a result of rate price increases being greater than the advances in productivity.

Infrastructure: The network of public facilities located within the community (e.g., roads, schools, sewers, parks, utilities, etc.).

Ingress: A place or means of entering; entrance.

Inheritance: An estate in lands or tenements or other things so great that it is infinite and therefore inheritable; an estate of inheritance is the maximum degree of ownership recognized.

Injunction: An order of the court to restrain one or more parties to a suit or proceeding from performing an act which is deemed unjust in regard to the rights of some other party in the suit or proceeding or compelling positive action.

Input-output analysis: A technique for analysis of an economy through description of the production and purchases of specific sectors of the economy.

Installment contract: An agreement providing for the payment of a specified amount in periodic installments by the buyer as a condition precedent to the performance by the seller.

Installment note: A note which provides that payments of a certain sum be paid periodically on the dates specified in the instrument.

Institute of Real Estate Management (IREM): National organization to professionalize members who are involved in all elements of property management through standards of practice, ethical considerations, and educational programs. Confers CPM (Certified Property Manager), AMO (Accredited Management Organization), ARM (Accredited Resident Manager).

Institutional advertising: Advertising intended to popularize a particular company as opposed to the promotion of its products or services.

Institutional lender: A mortgagee who is a bank, insurance company, pension fund, savings and loan association, etc.

Instrument: Any formal legal document, such as a contract, deed, or grant.

Insulation: A heat-retarding material applied in outside walls, top-floor ceilings, or roofs to prevent the passage of heat or cold into or out of the house.

Insurable interest: An ownership interest which an insurer will recognize as a property right, the loss of which will result in true loss of money value to the insured party.

Insurable value: The value at which an insurer will recognize any loss.

Insurance coverage: The total amount of insurance carried.

Insurance rate: The ratio of the insurance premium to the total amount of insurance carried thereby—usually expressed in dollars per $100 or per $1,000—sometimes in percent.

Insurance risk: A general or relative term denoting the hazard involved in the insuring of property. The premium or cost of insurance is determined by the relative risk or hazard considered to be involved.

Insured mortgage: A mortgage in which a party other than the borrower, in return for the payment of a premium, assures payment in the event of default by a mortgagor, e.g., FHA-insured mortgages, PMI (private mortgage insurance).

Intangible assets: The elements of property in an enterprise that are represented in the established organization—doing business, good will, and other rights incident to the enterprise—as distinguished from the physical items comprising the plant facilities and working capital.

Intangible value: An asset's worth which is not immediately available in dollars but which may be of significant value. An example of this is good will.

Intensive margin: Extra benefits derived from adding increasing amounts of labor and capital to land.

Interchange: A system of underpasses and overpasses for routing traffic on and off highways without interfering with through traffic and for linking two or more highways.

Interest rate: The percentage of a sum of money charged for its use.

Interest rate risk: The risk of loss due to changes in the interest rate. Earnings, or the value of a property, may be affected as a result of changes in prevailing interest rates in the money market. When interest rates go up or down, properties are generally capitalized at higher or lower rates.

Interim financing: A temporary or short-term loan secured by a mortgage, which is generally paid off from the proceeds of permanent financing. See construction loan.

Internal rate of return: The predetermined earning rate requirement for a project; usually established by comparison with other return opportunities available to the investor.

International Real Estate Federation, American Chapter: Promotes understanding of real estate among those involved in the real estate business throughout the world.

Interpret: To construe; to seek out the meaning of language; legally, to determine the intent of an agreement between parties.

Interurbia: A contiguous urban development larger than a city or metropolitan area.

Intestate: A person who has died without leaving a valid will disposing of his or her property and estate.

Inventory: A detailed list of articles, giving the code number, quantity, and value of each; a formal list of the property of a person or estate; a complete listing of stock on hand made each year by a business.

Inversely related cost: Cost that declines as volume of activity to which it relates increases.

Investment: Monies placed in a property with the expectation of producing a profit, assuming a reasonable degree of safety and ultimate recovery of principal; especially permanent use, as opposed to speculation.

Investment calculation: Estimation of value for a particular investor or user.

Investment property: The property which is within itself a business enterprise consisting of all tangible and intangible assets considered integral with the property, assembled and developed as a single unit of utility for lease or rental (in whole or in part) to others for profit.

Involuntary lien: A lien imposed against property without consent of an owner, e.g., taxes, special assessments, and federal income tax.

IREF: See International Real Estate Federation.

IREM: See Institute of Real Estate Management.

Irrevocable: Incapable of being revoked, modified, withdrawn, or changed.

Irrigation districts: Quasi-political districts created under special laws to provide for water services to property owners in the district, an operation governed to a great extent by law.

Italian architecture: A style which varies from a completely balanced design to an informal composition with formal treatment and openings. Typical details include completely framed window openings, circular heads over exterior openings, high windows and doors, and S-shaped red tile on the roof.

Jamb: The side post or lining of a doorway, window, or other such opening.

Joint: The space between the adjacent surfaces of two components connected by nails, glue, cement, or mortar.

Joint and several: A duty against two or more, which may be enforced against all jointly or against each individually.

Joint note: A note signed by two or more persons who share equal liability for repayment.

Joint tenancy: Joint ownership with right of survivorship. All joint tenants have equal rights in the property with the right to automatic succession to title of the whole upon the death of one tenant.

Joint venture: An arrangement under which two or more individuals or businesses participate in a single project as partners.

Joist: One of the series of parallel beams to which the boards of a floor and ceiling laths are fixed and which in turn are supported by larger beams, girders, or bearing walls.

Judgment: The final verdict of a court of competent jurisdiction on a matter presented to it. Money judgments provide for the payment of claims presented to the court.

Judgment creditor: The person who has received a decree or judgment of the court against his debtor for money due him for any cause.

Judgment debtor: The person against whom a judgment has been issued by the court for monies owed.

Judgment lien: The statutory lien upon the real and personal property of a judgment debtor, which is created by the judgment itself.

Judicial notice: The doctrine that a court will, of its own knowledge, assume certain facts to be true without the production of evidence in support of them. It is said that the court takes judicial notice of such facts because they are common knowledge.

Judicial sale: A court action which serves to enforce the judgment lien; the property is sold under judicial process to pay the debt.

Junior lien: A lien granted after the granting of an earlier lien on a different debt against the same property.

Junior mortgage: A mortgage having claim ranking below that of another mortgage which preceded it in time.

Jurat: The clause written at the foot of an affidavit stating when, where, and before whom such affidavit was sworn.

Jurisdiction: A political subdivision with power to govern its own affairs; in law, the power of a court to try specific suits.

Key lot: A lot in such a position that one side is adjacent to the rear of other lots. It is considered to be the least desirable of the lots in a subdivision.

Kiln-dried lumber: Lumber that was dried in a large ovenlike chamber for a period of time dependent upon its thickness and grade. This reduces the moisture content.

Knob-and-tube wiring: A method of wiring whereby the wires are attached to the house frame with porcelain knob insulators and porcelain tubes. Not used very frequently any more.

Laches: The established doctrine of equity under which, apart from any question of statutory limitation, courts will discourage delay and sloth in the enforcements of rights and will decline to try suits not brought within a reasonable time.

Land: In a physical sense, the earth's surface; in a legal sense, ground and everything annexed to it, whether by nature or by humans.

Land contract: A written agreement by which real estate is sold to a buyer who pays a portion of the purchase price when the contract is signed and completes payment in installments made over a specified period of years, with the title remaining with the seller until the total purchase price or a stipulated portion of the purchase price is paid.

Land economics: That branch of economics which deals with utilization of land resources in the attainment of objectives set by society.

Land grant: A gift of government land to a university, public utility, or railroad, or for a purpose that would be in the best interest and benefit of the general public; also, the original granting of land from the public sector to the private sector commonly used in the early history of the United States.

Land improvements: Physical alterations in, or construction of a more-or-less permanent nature attached to or appurtenant to, land, of such character as to increase its utility and/or value.

Land planning: The designing of land area uses, road networks, and layout for utilities to achieve efficient utilization of real estate resources.

Land trust certificate: An instrument used in financing larger real estate transactions. The investor receives a trust certificate as evidence of his or her share in the trust which is used as the investment vehicle.

Landlord: The owner of real estate which is leased to others.

Landmarks: A monument or erection set up on the boundary line of two adjoining parcels to fix such boundary.

Landscaping: The utilization of a lawn and plantings to improve the appearance of a lot.

Latent defects: Physical weaknesses or construction defects not noticeable after a reasonable inspection of the property.

Lateral and subjacent support: The right to have land supported by the adjoining land or the soil beneath by the owner of the adjoining property who excavates to the boundary line between the two properties.

Law: In a legal sense, an established rule or standard of conduct or action that is enforceable by government. A license law is a law that regulates the practices of real estate brokers and salespersons. Real estate law is the body of laws relating to real estate; generally evolved from the English common law but now including regulations such as zoning, building codes, etc.

Layout: The design or floor plans for the arranging of rooms in an apartment or an office.

Lease: A transfer of possession and the right to use property to a tenant for a stipulated period, during which the tenant pays rent to the owner; the contract containing the terms and conditions of such an agreement. A graded or step-up lease is a lease with a rental payment that increases over specified periods of time. A ground lease is a lease for vacant land upon which the tenant may erect improvements. An index lease is a lease in which the rental payment varies in accordance with variation in an agreed upon index of prices or costs. A lease with option to purchase is a lease in which the lessee has the right to purchase the real property for a stipulated price at or within a stipulated time. A leasehold is an estate held under lease. A net lease is a lease in which the tenant pays certain agreed upon property expenses such as taxes or maintenance. A percentage lease is a lease in which the rental is based upon a percentage of the lessee's sales income. A tax participation clause (in a lease) is an agreement in a lease whereby the lessee agrees to pay all or a stated portion of any increase in real estate taxes.

Lease-purchase agreement: An arrangement whereby a portion of the rent is applied toward a down payment. Upon payment of the down payment the tenant, using borrowed funds, purchases the property and becomes the owner outright rather than a mere lessee.

Leased fee: A property held in fee whereby a lease conveys the right of use and occupancy to others. A property which has the right to receive ground rentals over a period of time, and consisting of the further right of ultimate repossession at the termination of the lease.

Leasehold: An estate in real property that transfers possession to the tenant for a fixed period of time.

Leasehold policy: A form of title insurance taken out by the lessee in order to protect his or her interest in the property. It is commonly used in insuring commercial property because of the value of the fixtures and equipment which are added.

Legal capacity: One's capability, power, or fitness to enter into a contractual agreement as determined by law.

Legal description: A means of identifying the exact boundaries of land by metes and bounds, by a plat, or by township and range survey system. Metes refer to measures; bounds refer to direction. Metes and bounds descriptions are means of describing land by measurement and direction from a known point or marker on land. A plat is a recorded map of land that identifies a parcel by a number or other designation in a subdivision. A township and range survey system is a system of legal description of land with a township as the basic unit of measurement. A base line is a parallel that serves as a reference for other parallels. Meridians are the north-south lines of survey, 6 miles apart. Parallels are the east-west lines of survey, 6 miles apart. A principal meridian is a meridian that serves as a reference for other meridians. A range is a north-south row of townships; the 6-mile strip of land between meridians. A section is a 1-mile square in a township. A tier is an east-west row of townships; the 6-mile strip of land between parallels. A township is a 6-mile square of land bounded by parallels and meridians and composed of 36 sections.

Legal rate of interest: The maximum rate of interest that may be charged in accordance with state law.

Legality of object: An essential element of every contract is that it be for a legal purpose. If not so, the contract is automatically void.

Lessee: The party who possesses the right to possession of real estate for a limited time under a lease. The lessee is commonly referred to as the tenant.

Lessor: The landlord under a lease; one who conveyed a right or estate in realty to another under a lease.

Leverage: A financial method applied with the anticipation that the property acquired will increase in return so that the investor will realize a profit not only on his or her own investment but also on the borrowed funds, with the borrowed funds being predominant.

Levy: A seizure of property to satisfy a judgment; the imposition of a tax.

LHA: Local Housing Authority.

Liability: Any debt or obligation; an obligation or duty that must be performed.

License: A personal privilege to perform some act or series of acts upon the land of another without possessing any estate therein; a permit or authorization to do what, without a license, would be unlawful.

License year: The period of time for which a license retains its validity. Usually specified in the licensing act, it generally differs from a calendar year.

Licensee: A person to whom a license is granted.

Lien: A charge or claim upon property which encumbers it until the obligation is satisfied.

Lien theory: The state law providing a lender a lien against real estate as collateral for a loan. This is less protective to lenders than title theory.

Lien theory of mortgage: The mortgage theory under which title to mortgaged property vests in the borrower, with the lender having a lien against the real estate.

Life estate: An estate in land held during the term of a certain person's life. The estate terminates upon the death of the holder. The estate may be held by more than one person. The balance of the estate resides in the remainderman who will succeed to the title upon termination of the life estate.

Limited-access highway: A highway designed for the constant flow of traffic. The entrance and exit opportunities have been predetermined and set at specific intervals.

Limited partnership: A partnership in which some partners make only specified contributions and in return have only limited liabilities.

Lintel: The horizontal board over a door or window that supports the load.

Liquidated damages: The amount agreed upon as payment for a breach of contract by the parties themselves and in advance.

Liquidity: Measurement of the ability one has to sell his or her property quickly.

Lis pendens: A pending suit. The doctrine of lis pendens creates a lien against the property of a defendant in a lawsuit pending its final resolution.

Listing contract: A written agreement or contract between a principal and an agent providing that the agent will receive a commission for finding a buyer who is ready, willing, and able to purchase a particular property under terms specified in the agreement. A multiple listing is a listing that, in addition to employing the agent, provides for the services of other agents who have agreed among themselves that they will cooperate in finding a purchaser for the property. An open listing contract provides that the agent shall receive a commission if the property is sold as a result of the efforts of that agent or if the agent produces a buyer under the terms of the contract before the property is sold.

Litigation: A contest in a court of justice for the purpose of enforcing a right; a lawsuit.

Load-bearing wall: An integral part of the house, which helps support the floors or roof and is relatively permanent in structure.

Load center: The electrical distribution center for the structure, either the main center or a branch center. The center is equipped with circuit breaks instead of a main switch and fuse box.

Loan fee: The service charge made by the lender for the granting of a loan in addition to required interest.

Loan maturity: The life of the loan. The amount of time the loan will remain in existence until the debt is retired. A 20-year loan has a maturity of 20 years.

Loan value: The basic value which determines amount a lending institution will lend on a property.

Loan/value ratio: The amount of mortgage debt and the market or appraisal value of the property for debt purposes, usually expressed as a percentage. For example, an 80% loan/value ratio on a $100,000 property means a mortgage of up to $80,000 may be obtained. The greater the loan/value ratio, the greater the financial leverage available to the purchaser.

Local Housing Authority (LHA): The local body whose major concern is public housing.

Localization of income: Income production at fixed locations; e.g., from real estate, which has a fixed and unique location.

Location: Position of land and improvements in relation to other land and improvements and to local or general economic activity.

Location quotient: An analytic technique using proportionality comparisons, for example, the comparison of the percentage of an activity in a city with the percentage of the same activity in the nation.

Locked-in period: A period of time during which the borrower of a mortgage may not repay any of the principal. This is written into the contract.

Lot: A specific plot of land.

Louver: An opening filled with a series of horizontal slats set at an angle to permit ventilation without admitting rain, sunlight, or vision.

MAI: A designation for a person who is a member of the American Institute of Appraisers, a group associated with NAR.

Maintenance: The keeping up or the expenditures necessary to keep a property in condition to perform the services for which it is designed.

Maintenance reserve: The sum of money allotted to cover the costs of maintenance.

Majority age: The age at which an individual is capable of entering into a binding contract; sometimes referred to as "legal age" or "adulthood."

Malfeasance: The performance of an act that is unlawful or wholly wrong.

Management contract: An agreement used to define the rights and duties of the contracting parties. It enumerates in detail the method of payment and the rates of compensation of the agent for renting of space and maintaining another's property.

Management process: A set of guidelines for action, for the implementation of decisions; an orderly means for the accomplishment of objectives.

Mandatory: Containing a command; imperative.

Map: A representation of some feature on the earth's surface such as physical features or boundary lines, and the like.

Margin of security: The dollar differential between the amount of the mortgage loan(s) and the appraised value of a property.

Marginal land: Land which has returns that barely meet the costs of operation.

Marginal revenue: An additional amount of revenue resulting from a given business decision.

Marginal satisfaction: An alteration in the level of satisfaction derived from the occurrence of a given event.

Marginal utility: The worth of one additional unit of a good or a service that is produced.

Market: A set of arrangements for bringing buyers and sellers together through the price mechanism. A buyer's market is a market in which buyers can fulfill their desires at lower prices and on more advantageous terms than those prevailing earlier. It is a market characterized by many properties available and few potential users demanding them at prevailing prices. A capital market is comprised of the activities of all lenders and borrowers of equity and long-term debt funds. A money market is a market for borrowed funds, generally short-term. A seller's market is a market in which potential sellers can sell at prices higher than those prevailing in an immediately preceding period. It is a market characterized by very few properties available and a large number of users and potential users demanding them at prevailing prices.

Market analysis: An estimate of value developed for the purpose of arriving at a selling or marketing price.

Market comparison (market approach): The approach to real property appraisal which compares a certain property to equivalent properties which have sold recently to develop a value.

Market indicators: Sign posts or indexes of market activity.

Market price: The price paid for an object regardless of external influences.

Market rent: The amount charged for rent; established by pricing the rent at a level near that of similar properties in the market area.

Market value: The price property would command in the market.

Marketable title: Such a title as is free from reasonable doubt in law and in fact; one which can be readily sold or mortgaged to a reasonably prudent purchaser or mortgagee.

Marketing function: The determination of how land will be put to use after the limits are set by zoning and other restrictions both public and private.

Marketing myopia: A Failure to match the needs with the people who have needs.

Master deed: The title document used in condominium projects, which creates both the fee units and the common interests involved in the projects.

Master switch: An electrical wall switch which controls several fixtures or outlets in a room.

Maximum rent: The greatest amount of rent that may be charged as set down in a rent regulation or order.

Mechanic's lien: A claim created by law for the purpose of securing a priority of payment of the price or value of work performed and materials furnished in erecting or repairing a building or other structure, and as such it attaches to the land as well as to the buildings erected thereon. It is enforceable by foreclosure proceedings.

Megalopolis: An urban area of great size.

Merger: In real estate law, the doctrine that a lesser interest is absorbed by a greater estate when both are owned by the same person. E.g., when a tenant buys the fee simple, the leasehold is absorbed into the fee and he is then the owner and no longer a tenant.

Meridians: The imaginary north-south lines that intersect base lines to form a point of origin for the measurement of land.

Messuage: The residence and all the adjacent buildings and the land around it.

Metes and bounds: The boundary lines of land, with their terminal points and angles.

MGIC: Mortgage Guarantee Insurance Corporation.

Microeconomics: The science of economic functions from the viewpoint of the individual firm or decision maker.

Mill: In taxes, equals one-tenth of 1 cent; a measure used to state the property tax rate; a tax rate of 1 mill on the dollar is the same as a rate of one-tenth of 1% of the assessed value of the property.

Misdemeanor: A criminal offense of lesser grade than that of a felony and usually punishable only by fine.

Misrepresentation: Transmitting an untruth from one person to another via words or other conduct. Presenting something not in accordance with the facts.

Mission architecture: The architectural style employing the characteristics of early California missions, generally Spanish in style.

Mistake of fact: Errors which do not state the true conditions of the contract. If curable, these errors of fact do not generally void the contract.

Mistake of law: Occurs when a party to a contract having full knowledge of the facts comes to an erroneous conclusion as to their legal effect. The party may not void the contract under a mistake of law based on the erroneous conclusion.

Mobile home: A manufactured standardized home which is entirely constructed in a factory and then transported to the site. It is the opposite of a conventionally built home.

Model house: A house used for exhibition in order to sell other houses.

Modern architecture: The architectural style that employs the principles of contemporary, functional design, intended to combine esthetic quality and utility in a home.

Modern English architecture: An architectural design consisting of many elements of the Elizabethan and Tudor styles, but called modern because it is of more recent vintage. Prominent characteristics are the rough plaster or stucco exterior, the steep roof slopes with variegated and graduated slate or red tile, and having no cornices or eaves.

Modernization: A process involving the restoration of a structure to its maximum attractiveness and productivity without altering any of its property functions.

Modular construction: Prefabrication in three dimensions; i.e., entire rooms of houses or apartments are built in the factory and shipped to their eventual location where very little on-site labor is required.

Modular planning: The designing of structures using a designated minimum dimension of length and width such as 4 feet.

Moisture barrier: A material used to stop or slow down the flow of moisture into walls.

Monetary controls: Efforts by the Federal Reserve to influence the level of economic activity by regulating the availability of money and the rate of interest.

Monopoly: An economic condition attained when one party controls the entire market.

Monuments: Visible marks or indications left on natural or other objects indicating the lines and boundaries of a survey.

Moral turpitude: Conduct contrary to the social duty owed by one person to another, criminal in nature.

Moratorium: A temporary suspension, often by statute, of enforcement of the liability for a financial obligation.

Mortgage (several types): The pledge of real property to secure a debt; the conveyance of real property as security for a debt; the instrument that is evidence of the pledge or conveyance. A mortgage bond is evidence of debt secured by a mortgage in favor of individual parties as a group, usually with the mortgage held by a third party in trust for the mortgage bond creditors. A mortgage broker is an agent who, for a commission, brings a mortgagor and mortgagee together. A mortgage company is a firm that, for a fee, brings mortgagor and mortgagee together or that acquires mortgages for the purpose of resale. An open-end mortgage is a mortgage with provisions for future advances to the borrower without the necessity of writing a new mortgage. A package mortgage is a mortgage in which the collateral is not limited to real property but includes personal property in the nature of household equipment. A purchase money mortgage is a mortgage that is given in part payment of the purchase price as security for repayment of funds. Subject to mortgage means the grantee takes title but is not responsible for the mortgage beyond the value of his or her equity in the property.

Mortgage bank correspondents: The various mortgage bankers who serve as agents of lenders for the purpose of placing and servicing mortgage loans in a local community.

Mortgage brokerage: The business of bringing together the lender and borrower, with additional services such as aiding in the closing of a loan.

Mortgage commitment: A notice in writing from the lending institution promising the mortgage loan in the future and also specifying the terms and conditions of the loan.

Mortgage company: The private corporation whose principal function is to originate and service mortgage loans sold to financial institutions.

Mortgage constant: The percentage of an original loan balance represented by a constant annual mortgage payment required to retire the debt on schedule.

Mortgage correspondent: A representative of a lender of money on the security of real property; a representative of a potential mortgagee.

Mortgage guaranty insurance: The insurance issued against financial loss. It is available to mortgage lenders from MGIC, a private company organized in 1956, and others who have since entered the field.

Mortgage insurance premium: The amount the borrower pays for the insurance on a loan by the FHA.

Mortgagee: The creditor or lender under a mortgage.

Mortgagor: The debtor or borrower under a mortgage.

Motivation research: Analysis of consumers in an attempt to determine why prospective buyers react as they do to products or services or to advertisements used in attempting to sell them.

Mud entrance: A vestibule or small room designed for entrance from a play yard or alley.

Multifamily structure: A dwelling for (usually) five or more household units.

Multiple exchange: Three or more principals involved in the exchanging of various pieces of property.

Multiple listing: A cooperative listing arrangement whereby listings are taken and distributed to the other brokers so that they will have an opportunity to sell the property.

Multiple nuclei: A theory of urban growth emphasizing separate nuclei and differentiated districts occurring in clusters.

Mutual savings bank: A financial institution in which the depositors are the owners. Mutual savings banks are a primary source of home mortgage funds.

Mutual water company: A water company created by or for water users in a specific area with the object of securing an ample water supply at a more reasonable rate; stock is issued to users.

NAR: National Association of Realtors®.

National Association of Real Estate License Law Officials (NARELLO): An association composed of real estate commissioners and other officers and officials charged with the responsibility of enforcing the license laws of the various states, provinces, etc.

National Savings and Loan League: The national professional and trade association for individual savings and loan associations.

Necessaries: An economic term referring to the essentials required for existence, such as food and shelter.

Negative fraud: The act of not disclosing to the buyer a material fact, thereby inducing him to enter into a contractual situation causing him damage or loss.

Net income: That amount of money which remains after expenses are subtracted from income, also termed "profit."

Net lease: An arrangement between the lessee and lessor whereby the lessee pays the charges against the property and the lessor nets the rental payments received.

Net listing: A listing stating the minimum amount the *seller* will accept.

Net worth: The value remaining after all debts and obligations are removed.

Nominal interest rate: The rate of interest in the contract.

Nonbearing wall: A wall used as a divider and not to carry any load.

Nonresident: One who does not reside within the state or is not from that particular state.

Nonzoning: Not placing any restriction on the use of the land via regulations, etc.

Note: An acknowledgment and promise to pay a debt. It must be in writing and signed.

Novation: The substitution of a new obligation for an old one, e.g., where parties to an agreement accept a new debtor in the place of an old one.

Nuisance: Conduct or activity which results in actual physical interference with another person's reasonable use or enjoyment of his or her property for any lawful purpose.

Obligee: One to whom a debt is owed.

Obligor: One who is bound by debt.

Obsolescence: Loss in property value because of the existence of a less costly alternative that provides comparable or more desirable property services.

Occupancy: Physical possession.

Offer: To present a set of terms intended to result in a contract subject to another's acceptance. This is not a contract until accepted by the other party.

Offeree: The one who receives an offer, such as when the owner of property for sale receives an offer from a potential buyer based on certain terms subject to the seller's acceptance.

Offeror: The one making the offer.

OILSR: Office of Interstate Land Sales Regulation.

Oligopoly: Control of a market by a limited number of participants.

Open-end clause: A clause in a mortgage which provides a method of advancing additional funds against a note after partial payment. To meet new obligations the debt can be quickly restored to its original amount.

Open-end mortgage: A mortgage given to secure future loans made from time to time, usually back up to the original balance after partial repayment has been made.

Open house: A house that is available for inspection by potential purchasers without appointments.

Open listing: An authorization given by a property owner to a real estate agent wherein said agent is given the nonexclusive right to secure a purchaser; open listings may be given to any number of agents without liability to compensate any except the one who first secures a buyer ready, willing, and able to meet the terms of the listing, or secures the acceptance by the seller of a satisfactory offer. The seller retains the right to sell directly without payment of any commission.

Operating expense: Generally any expense occurring periodically which is necessary to produce net income before depreciation.

Operating expense ratio: The relationship between operating expenses and project gross income.

Operating profit: Profit arising from the regular operation of a firm engaged in performing physical services (public utilities, etc.), excluding income from other sources and expenses other than those of direct operation.

Opinion of title: Legal opinion stating that title to the property is clear and merchantable or pointing out defects which must be cured.

Option (to purchase real estate): The right to purchase property at a stipulated price and under stipulated terms within a period of time; the instrument that is evidence of such a right.

Optionee: The one who receives an option, such as the potential purchaser of real estate.

Optionor: The one who gives the option, such as the owner of the real estate.

Oral contract: A verbal agreement; one which is not placed in writing.

Ordinance: A public regulation (usually local laws).

Orientation: The position of a structure on a site and its general relationship to its surroundings.

Original cost: The initial cost; the amount paid to build on or acquire the property.

Outdoor living: Referring to the use of porches, patios, terraces, lawns, gardens, and rooms opening into the yard, or which have extensive glass areas which tend to "bring in the outdoors."

Overall interest rate: The rate that includes interest on the land, interest on the building, and a recapture of capital.

Overbuilding: The building of more structures of a particular type than can be absorbed by the market at prevailing prices.

Overhang: The part of the roof extending beyond the walls, used to shade buildings and cover walks.

Owner's policy: A title insurance policy taken out to protect the owner's interest in the real estate.

Ownership of real property: The holding of rights or interests in real estate.

Package mortgage: A form of mortgage used with new residential sales. Included in the debt is the cost of certain mechanical or electrical equipment. Interest, principal, and equipment are all paid for by means of one equal monthly payment.

Panel heating: A means of radiant heating, with pipes or ducts built into walls, floor, or ceiling, which serve as heating panels.

Panic selling: The illegal practice of inducing fear among property owners in a particular neighborhood that an abnormally high turnover might occur as the result of the introduction of a nonconforming use or user into the area.

Parapet: A low protective wall or barrier built around the edge of a balcony, roof, bridge, or the like.

Parcel of real estate: A particular piece of land and its improvements.

Parity: Equality; often used to refer to an equivalence between farmers' current purchasing power and their purchasing power at a selected base period, maintained by government support of commodity prices.

Parking lot: A parcel of real estate used for the storage of automobiles. Usually about 300 square feet per auto is required for parking space and aisles.

Parol evidence: Oral or verbal evidence.

Parquet floor: Hardwood flooring laid in squares or patterns instead of being laid in strips.

Partially amortized mortgage: A combination of an amortized mortgage and a term mortgage (straight term mortgage).

Participation loan: A mortgage loan made by one lender with other lenders purchasing interests in the loan.

Participation mortgage: A loan in which the lender receives debt repayment plus a share of the profits from ownership.

Partition: A division of real or personal property among co-owners of real estate through a legal proceeding brought for that purpose.

Partition action: Court proceedings in which co-owners seek to divide the property into individual shares.

Partition proceedings: A legal procedure by which an estate held by tenants in common is divided and title in severalty to a designated portion given to each of the previous tenants in common.

Partnership: A contractual union of two or more parties who share in risks and profits of a business venture.

Party wall: A wall built partly on the land of one owner and partly on the land of another, for the common benefit of both, on supporting timbers used in the construction of contiguous buildings.

Pass-through securities program: A GNMA mortgage-backed security program wherein the principal and interest on the mortgages purchased by the investors are passed through to them as they are collected.

Patent: A conveyance from the federal government to a private buyer.

Payback period: Period of time necessary for the cash flow from a project to equal the amount of money invested.

Pennsylvania farmhouse: An architectural style that employs a Colonial residential type of design with stone walls, sometimes pargeted with plaster and whitewashed, characteristically informal.

Per capita: By the head; according to the number of individuals.

Percentage lease: A lease under which the lessee pays rent according to the amount of business he or she does, usually a percentage of the gross from the business. There is usually a provision for a minimum rent payment.

Performance bond: A bond used to guarantee the specific completion of an endeavor in accordance with a contract, such as that supplied by a contractor guaranteeing the completion of a building or a road.

Perimeter heating: Any system in which the heat registers are located along the outside dimensions of a room, especially under the windows.

Periodic tenancy: A tenancy that continues for successive periods (such as month to month) and continues until terminated by notice of one of the parties.

Permanent loan: Long-term financing through a mortgage loan or deed of trust.

Perpetual easement: An easement without a time limit.

Perpetuity: Without limitation as to time; theoretically, forever.

Personal property: The exclusive right to exercise control over personalty; all property objects other than real estate.

Personalty: All property other than realty; chattels.

Physical depreciation: Physical deterioration inherent in the property, which impairs its use.

Pier: A column of masonry, used to support other structural members.

Pitch: The incline of a roof.

PITI: Stands for principal, interest, taxes, insurance when they are all included in one mortgage payment.

Plaintiff: The party who originates an action at law.

Planned unit development: A design for an area which provides for intensive use of land often through a combination of private and common areas with arrangements for sharing responsibilities for the common areas. Typically, zoning boards consider the entire development and allow its arrangements to be substituted for traditional subdivisions. An example is a residential cluster development.

Planning: The process of formulating a program in advance to achieve desired results. Long-range planning is planning for a period of years in the future. This type of planning is used as a framework for shorter-range planning.

Plat, plat map: A map that shows boundary lines of parcels of real estate, usually of an area that has been subdivided into a number of lots.

Plat book: A book containing a series of plat maps.

Plat book designation: The location of the recorded subdivision of a tract of land. It has a distinguishing name or number so that it can be readily located in the public records.

Plenum: The chamber in a warm-air furnace where the air is heated and from which the ducts carry the warm air to the registers.

Plottage: The extent to which value is increased when two or more lots are combined in a single ownership or use.

Plottage increment: The appreciation in unit value attained by joining smaller ownerships into a large single ownership.

Plottage value: Increased value to land created by joining small parcels into large tracts.

Plywood: Laminated wood made up in several layers; several thicknesses of wood glued together with the grain at different angles for strength.

PMI: Private mortgage insurance.

Points: A charge assessed by a lending institution to increase the yield of a mortgage loan so that it is competitive with other investments. Sometimes the loan origination fee is referred to in terms of points.

Police power: The right of the state to enact laws and enforce them for the order, safety, health, morals, and general welfare of the public.

Portico: A roof supported by columns. It may be part of a building or by itself.

Power of attorney: A written authorization to an agent to perform specified acts on behalf of his principal.

Prefabricated house: A house with components that are pre-built and sometimes partly assembled prior to delivery to the building site.

Prefabrication: The process of manufacturing component parts of a structure in a factory for later assembly on-site.

Prepayment penalty: The penalty levied on the mortgagor or trustor for early payment of the obligation.

Prepayment privilege: A mortgage contract clause permitting the borrower to pay loan payments in advance of their due date.

Prepayment yield: The sum that may be realized by paying a debt prior to the date due.

Prerogative: A sovereign power.

Prescription: The name given to a mode of acquiring property rights in land of another by continuous use, without claiming ownership.

Present value: The value today, computed by measuring all future benefits of an investment and converting those benefits into terms of today's dollars.

Price: The amount of money at which property is offered for sale or is exchanged for at a sale; value in terms of money.

Price level: A relative position on the scale of prices as determined by a comparison of prices (of labor, materials, capital, etc.) at one time with prices at other times.

Prima facie: Presumptive evidence of fact which is legally sufficient to establish that fact unless rebutted by evidence to the contrary.

Principal: One who has another act for him; one who is represented by an agent; also, the amount of a debt.

Principal meridian: Part of the rectangular method of survey. It is a meridian which serves as a reference for the other meridians.

Priority: When two persons have similar rights in respect to the same subject matter, but one is entitled to exercise his right to the exclusion of the other, he is said to have priority.

Private sector: The portion of the economy which produces goods and services consumed, in contrast to the portion containing governmental bodies.

Probate: A word originally meaning merely "relating to the proofs of wills," in American law it is now a general name or term used to include all matters over which probate courts have jurisdiction, which in many states are the estates of deceased persons and of persons under guardianship as well as trusts and trustees.

Profit a prendre: A right to take part of the soil or produce of the land of another.

Promisee: One to whom a promise is made.

Promissory note: A written promise by one person to pay a certain sum of money to another individual at some future specified time. In real property financing, it serves as evidence of a debt for which a mortgage on the property is held as security.

Property: The exclusive right to exercise control over an economic good.

Property brief: A folder that presents pertinent information about a property.

Property management: The operation of real property, including the leasing of space, collection of rents, selection of tenants, and the repair and renovation of the buildings and grounds.

Property manager: An agent for the owner of real estate in all matters pertaining to the operation of the property or properties which are under his or her direction, who is paid a commission for his or her services.

Property owners association: An organization with the purpose of administering private regulations affecting residential land uses.

Property services: The benefits accruing from the use of property.

Proposition: An offer to do something; in real estate, an offer to purchase.

Proprietorship: A business run by its owner as an individual rather than as a corporation.

Proration: The allocation of costs or revenues due between the buyer and the seller of real property.

Proration of taxes: The division of taxes equally or proportionately in accordance with time of use.

Prospectus: A printed document describing the characteristics of a specific property.

Public domain: That land to which title is held by the federal government.

Public housing: Housing owned by a governmental body.

Public Housing Administration: A unit of the HUD, which administers legislation providing for loans and subsidies to local housing authorities to encourage the development of low-rental dwelling units.

Public property: A property, the title to which is vested in the community.

Public sector: That portion of the economy which is most affected by governmental bodies and which contains governmental bodies themselves.

Public trustee: The public official in each county whose office has been created by law and to whom title to real property is conveyed by trust deed to protect the interests of beneficiaries.

Punitive damages: The fine assessed to the wrongdoer in excess of damages actually suffered.

Purchase and lease back: A method whereby an investor becomes the actual owner of property through purchase for cash from the original owner-occupant, who continues to occupy and use the property under a long-term lease from the new owner.

Purchase money mortgage: A mortgage given concurrently with a conveyance of land, by the vendee to the vendor, on the same land, to secure the unpaid balance of the purchase price.

Purchase on contract: The purchase of property on installments with title remaining with the seller.

Purchasing power risk: Risk that the value of an investment will decline as a result of inflation (decline in the purchasing power of the dollar).

Purpose of appraisal: To estimate the dollar value of the future utility of a parcel of real property for a specific purpose.

Qualities of value: Scarcity, desire, ability to buy, and utility.

Quantity survey: A means of determining building replacement cost in which all elements of labor, materials, and overhead are priced and totaled to obtain the building cost.

Quarter round: A molding that presents a profile of a quarter-circle.

Quasi: Corresponding to, or similar to; having a limited legal status.

Quasi-contract: An obligation similar to a contract, which is implied by law.

Quiet enjoyment: The right of an owner to use property without interference by others.

Quiet title suit: Legal action to remove a defect, cloud, or questionable claim against the title to property.

Quitclaim deed: A deed conveying only the right, title, and interest of the grantor in the property described, as distinguished from a deed which guarantees that actual ownership is being transferred.

Racial steering: The unlawful practice of influencing a minority person's housing choice.

Radiant heat: A form of heating which transmits hot water or air through ducts embedded in the walls, ceiling, or floors; panel heating.

Radiator: A configuration of metal tubes, usually cast iron, heated by steam or hot water from the boiler. Heat is transferred to the objects in a room by radiation, and to the air by convection.

Rafters: The sloping wood components of a roof.

Ranch style: A one-story home design, usually with a rambling plan and without a basement.

Range: A part of the rectangular system of survey; a north-south row of townships; the 6-mile strip of land between meridians.

Ratification: The approval or adoption of an act performed on behalf of a person without previous authorization.

Real estate: Land with or without buildings or improvements.

Real estate broker: An agent who negotiates the sale of real property or real property services for a preset commission that is contingent on success.

Real estate business: A form of business that deals in rights to land and improvements.

Real estate developing: Preparing land for use, constructing buildings and other improvements, and making the completed properties available for use.

Real estate financing: The channeling of monies into the production and use of real estate; facilitating the production and use of real estate through borrowed or equity funds.

Real estate investment corporation: A corporation that sells its securities to the public and has a special interest in real estate or is a builder or developer of real estate.

Real estate investment trust: A trust designed in a form similar to that of an investment or mutual fund for the purpose of allowing investors to channel funds into the real estate investment market. Special federal law permits pooled investments in real estate and mortgages without exposure to corporate income taxes.

Real estate market function: The process of placing real properties and their services into the hands of consumers.

Real estate marketing: The process of putting real properties and their services into the hands of consumers. Brokerage and property management are the two main subdivisions of real estate marketing.

Real estate operator: Any individual engaged in the real estate business acting for himself rather than as an agent.

Real estate salesperson: Any person who for a compensation or valuable consideration has contracted with a real estate broker to sell or offer to sell or negotiate the sale or exchange of real estate, or to lease, rent, or offer for rent any real estate, or to negotiate leases thereof, or of the improvement thereon, as a whole or partial vocation.

Real Estate Securities and Syndication Institute (RESSI): Provides educational opportunities in the field of marketing securities and syndication of real estate.

Real estate syndicate: A partnership formed for participation in a real estate venture. Partners may be limited or unlimited in their liability.

Real estate tax: A money charge levied upon real property for support of local government and for public services.

Real property: The exclusive right to exercise control over real estate.

REALTOR®: A broker who is affiliated with a local real estate board that is a member of NAR.

Realtors National Marketing Institute (RNMI): Provides educational programs for REALTORS® in the area of commercial and investment properties, residential sales, and real estate office administration. Confers CRB (Certified Residential Broker), CCIM (Certified Commercial and Investment Member).

Realty: Land and all fixtures permanently attached to it.

Reappraisal lease: A lease having a clause calling for the periodic reevaluation of rents.

Recapture: A provision for predicting the return of investment. It may be accomplished by inclusion in the capitalization rate in the income approach to valuation.

Recapture rate: The rate of interest necessary to provide for the return of the initial investment. Not to be confused with interest rate, which is the rate of interest on an investment.

Receiver: One appointed by the courts to take control and possession of property pending litigation and some final order by the court.

Receiver clause: A clause in the mortgage to prevent dissipation of the value of the asset that secures a loan. This clause provides for the orderly appointment of a receiver to take over residential property abandoned by the mortgagor. The receiver rents, manages, and thus conserves the value of the property.

Reciprocity: The mutual exchange of privileges between groups or states. In the case of real estate it is the automatic recognition of the license of one state in another. Many states do not have reciprocity agreements.

Reconstructed operating statement: Operating revenue and expense figures put into a standard format which permits comparisons with similar properties.

Recording: The process of entering or recording a copy of certain legal instruments or documents, such as a deed, in a government office provided for this purpose, thus making a public record of the document for the protection of all concerned and giving constructive notice to the public at large.

Recording acts, registry laws: Laws providing for the recording of instruments affecting title as a matter of public record to preserve such evidence and give notice of their existence and content; laws providing that the recording of an instrument informs all who deal in real property of the transaction and that, unless the instrument is recorded, a prospective purchaser without actual notice of its existence is protected against it.

Recourse: The right to a claim against a prior owner of a property or note.

Rectangular survey: The government system of land description, noted for greater accuracy; it is adaptable to the measurement of extensive territory.

Redemption: The regaining of title to real property after a foreclosure sale. An equity of redemption is the interest of the mortgagor in real property prior to foreclosure. A statutory right of redemption is the right under law of the mortgagor to redeem title to real property before a foreclosure sale for a limited period of time.

Redevelopment: The process of clearance and reconstruction of blighted areas.

Red-lining: The refusal to lend money within a specific area for various reasons. This practice is now illegal.

Refinancing: The negotiation of a new mortgage loan to replace and pay off the unpaid balances of existing mortgages.

Reformation: An action to correct an error in a deed or other document.

Regime: A listing of the system of rules or regulations affecting the owners of a condominium project.

Regional analysis: A process applied to real estate, pertaining mainly to local economies and the surrounding area; for other purposes, the area of a "region" may be defined more broadly.

Registrar of deeds, recorder: The government officer in charge of a land records office.

Registration: Recording; inserting in an official register.

Regression: The appraisal principle that maintains that the value of high-quality properties will be adversely affected by the presence of low-quality properties.

Regulation Z: Regulations regarding credit disclosure issued by the Board of Governors of the Federal Reserve System to aid in implementation of the Truth-in-Lending Act.

Regulations: A set of rules for controlling activities or procedures. Coercive regulations are regulations which provide penalties for noncompliance. An inducive regulation is a regulation which provides incentive for compliance.

Rehabilitate: The process of removing blight by repairing and renovating rather than by destroying improvements.

Release: The giving up of a right or claim by the person in whom it exists to the person against whom it might have been enforced.

Release clause: The stipulation that, upon payment of a specific amount of money to the holder of a trust deed or mortgage, the lien of the instrument as to a specific described lot or area shall be removed, e.g., from the blanket lien on the whole area involved.

Remainder: The right of a person to an estate in land that matures at the end of another estate; a classification of estates by time of enjoyment. A contingent remainder is an interest that will become a remainder only if some condition is fulfilled.

Remainderman: One who is entitled to the remainder of the estate after a particular estate carved out of it has expired.

Remodel: To make physical alterations other than keeping the property in repair.

Renewal: The process of redevelopment or rehabilitation in urban areas; often used in relation to rebuilding or restoration of blighted areas.

Rent: The return on land or real property; the price paid for the use of real property belonging to another.

Rent controls: The legal regulation of the maximum rental payment for the use of real property.

Rent multiplier: A number used to estimate value by multiplying it by the rent. A rent multiplier may be either a gross rent multiplier or a net rent multiplier. See gross rent multiplier.

Rent schedule: A plan to estimate the rents to be paid; also, records kept of rentals actually paid in a specific period.

Rental value: The value for a stated period of the right to use and occupy property; the amount a prospective tenant is warranted in paying for a stated period of time, e.g., a month, a year, etc., for the right to use and occupy real property under certain prescribed or assumed conditions.

Replace: To restore to a former plan or condition.

Replacement cost: The estimated cost of building a substantially similar structure as of a certain time utilizing modern materials at present costs and having equal utility.

Replacement reserves: Funds allotted for replacement of building components, equipment, etc.

Replevin: An action to regain possession of goods.

Representation: The principle upon which the issue of a deceased person takes or inherits the share of an estate his or her immediate ancestor would have taken or inherited if living.

Reproduction cost: The cost to duplicate at current prices an asset as closely as possible as of a certain time not knowing for corrective measures.

Rescission: The annulment or abrogation of a contract and the placing of the parties to it in the positions they were in before the contract was entered into.

Research and development: The process of creating new products or new methods.

Reservation: A clause in a deed or other instrument of conveyance by which the grantor reserves some estate, interest, or profit in the real estate conveyed.

Reserve fund: For multifamily properties, an amount budgeted from income to replace short-lived items such as furniture and equipment; the distinctive feature of a budget mortgage loan on residential property; the monthly payments on such a loan including certain sums which are impounded or reserved to pay taxes and insurance when due; a mortgagee's escrow account.

Reserves: Portions of earnings allotted to take care of possible losses in the conduct of business; listed on the balance sheet as a liability item.

Residence: The property in which one actually lives as his or her home.

Residual: That which remains; an appraisal technique to estimate the amount of net annual income derived from property; that which is left after deduction; the remainder of the income.

Residual techniques: Allocation of a portion of income to part of an asset, with the remainder (or residual) flowing automatically to the rest of the asset. Also, the allocation of part of the income to cover debt payments with the balance accruing to the equity being built up in the property.

Residuary: Pertaining to the residue.

RESPA (Real Estate Settlement Procedures Act): A federal act passed in 1975 to force disclosure of all aspects of financing to potential borrowers.

RESSI: See Real Estate Securities and Syndication Institute.

Restriction: The term as used in relation to real property means the owner of real property is restrained or prohibited from doing certain things relating to the property, or using the property for certain purposes. For instance, the requirement in a deed that a lot may be used for the construction of not more than a single-family dwelling costing not less than $10,000 is termed a restriction. Also, a legislative ordinance affecting all properties in a given area, requiring that improvements on property shall not be constructed any closer to the street curb than 25 feet is a restriction by operation of law.

Restrictive covenant: A clause in a deed in which there is an agreement between the seller and the purchaser in regard to certain restraints as to the use of the property, and which is binding on all subsequent owners.

Return on investment: The percentage correlation between the price an investor pays and the stream of income dollars he or she obtains from the investment.

Revenue stamps: Stamps issued by the state government, which must be purchased and affixed in the amounts provided by law to documents or instruments representing original issues, sales and transfers of deeds of conveyance, stocks, and bonds; these stamps are evidence that transfer taxes have been paid.

Reversion: A right to future possession retained by an owner at the time of transfer of some limited interest in real property.

Reversion value: The estimated value of a reversion as of a given date determined actuarially.

Reversionary right: The right of a person to receive possession and use of property upon the termination or defeat of an existing limited estate carrying the rights of possession and use and vested in another person.

Reversioner: A person who is entitled to a reversion.

Reverter: That portion of an estate which returns or goes back to an owner (or reverts) or his or her heirs after the end or termination of an estate such as a leasehold or a life estate.

Revocation: A withdrawal; a recall; a repudiation; the taking back of a power or authority that has been previously conferred, such as the revoking of a license; the withdrawal of an offer prior to its acceptance.

Ridge: A horizontal line at the joining of the top edges of two sloping roof surfaces. The rafters for both slopes are nailed at the ridge.

Ridge board: A board placed on its edge at the ridge of the roof so as to support the upper ends of the rafters; also called a roof tree, ridge piece, ridge plate, or ridge pole.

Right of occupancy: The privilege to occupy and use property for a specified period of time under the terms of some contract such as a lease or other formal agreement.

Right of survivorship: The distinguishing feature of any joint tenancy. It is the automatic succession to the interest of a deceased joint owner.

Right of way: A grant serving as an easement upon land, whereby the owner by agreement gives to another the right of passage over his or her land to construct a roadway, or use as a roadway, a specific part of his or her land, or the right to construct through and over his or her land, telephone, telegraph, or electric power lines; or the right to place underground water mains, gas mains, or sewer mains.

Riparian: Belonging or relating to the banks of a river, stream, waterway, etc.

Riparian grant: The transmittal of riparian rights.

Riparian lease: The document defining the terms, conditions, and date of expiration of the rights to use lands lying between the high water mark and the low water mark.

Riparian owner: One who owns land adjoining a watercourse.

Riparian rights: The rights of a landowner to water on, under, or immediately adjacent to his or her land and its uses.

Riser: An upright board at the rear of each step of a stairway. In heating, a riser is a duct slanted upward to carry hot air from the furnace to the room above.

Risk: The degree of danger of future loss of capital or income.

Risk rating: The method by which various risks are evaluated, usually employing grids to develop precise and relative figures for the purpose of determining the overall soundness of a loan.

RNMI: See Realtors National Marketing Institute.

Rod: The unit of linear measure equal to a length of 5½ yards.

Roman brick: A form of thin brick with slimmer proportions than the standard building brick.

Row houses: A series of individual houses having identical architectural features and the presence of a common wall between two units.

Rules of thumb: The cost indicators sometimes used to assist in estimating the value of a property. Examples are price per front foot, gross rent multiplier, price per square foot, cost per room, and cost per apartment unit. These are usually guidelines or averages based on experience in the same vicinity.

Running with the land: A covenant is said to run with the land when either the liability to perform it or the right to take advantage of it passes to the subsequent grantees of that land.

Safe rate: The rate of interest on government bonds, utility bonds, or bank savings.

Sale-lease back: A plan that allows for the simultaneous transfer of ownership and execution of the lease—the grantor becomes the lessee and the grantee the lessor.

Sales contract: The contract by which the buyer and the seller agree to terms of a sale of property.

Sales expenses: Costs incurred in the sale of real property. Broker's commissions, advertising costs, and costs incurred in the preparation of the property for sale are examples of common expenses.

Sales kit: A file of information concerning the properties a broker has for sale.

Salvage value: The estimated worth of an item after it is fully depreciated.

Sanborn insurance maps: A series of maps showing locations of individual structures in many cities; developed for underwriting insurance.

Sandwich lease: A leasehold interest which is present between the primary lease and the operating lease. In subleasing property, when the holder of a sublease in turn sublets to another, his or her position is that of being sandwiched between the original lessee and the second sublessee.

Sash: Wood or metal frames containing one or more window panes.

Satisfaction: The written acknowledgment of the release of a mortgage or trust deed lien on the records upon payment of the secured debt.

Savings bank: A type of bank which receives savings in the form of the deposits in mortgages and other securities allowed by law. These banks, with the exception of a few in New Hampshire, are mutual institutions and are governed by self-perpetuating boards of trustees.

Savings and loan association: A state or federally chartered thrift institution that specializes in making residential mortgages.

Scarcity: The amount of limitation of real estate facilities in relation to their demand.

Scribing: The fitting of woodwork to an irregular surface.

Seal: A particular sign, made to attest in the most formal manner, the execution of an instrument.

Seasonal fluctuations: Variations in economic activity that recur at about the same time each year.

Seasoned mortgage: A mortgage in which periodic payments have been made for a long period of time and the borrower's payment pattern is well established.

Second mortgage: A mortgage made by a home buyer to generate enough capital for the down payment required under the first mortgage. (FHA does not permit this on loans it insures for first mortgages.) Such mortgages are also used to secure borrowings for home improvements or other related purposes.

Secondary financing: The loan secured by a second trust deed or a mortgage on real property.

Secret interest: Interest hidden or concealed from third-party knowledge.

Section (of land): A portion of land 1 mile square containing 640 acres, into which the public lands of the United States were originally divided; one thirty-sixth part of a township.

Section 8: A federal program for leasing housing to lower-income families; sponsored through HUD.

Sector hypothesis: A theory stating that sectors of land use arise whereby the highest-priced homes are in the most attractive locations, medium-priced homes follow traffic arteries, and lower-priced homes are near places of employment.

Sector theory: A theory of city growth that considers the city as a circle with wedge-shaped sectors pointing into the center of the urban area.

Sectors: Wedge-shaped areas pointing to the center of the urban area; a recognized pattern of urban growth and development.

Secured party: The party having a security interest in property owned by the debtor. Thus the pledgee, the conditional seller, or the mortgagee are all now referred to as secured parties.

Security: Something of value deposited to make certain the fulfillment of an obligation or the payment of a debt.

Security agreement: The agreement created between the secured party and the debtor that creates the security interest.

Security deposits: The funds placed as collateral by a tenant so that the leased property may be restored to its original condition if need be at the termination of the lease.

Security interest: The interest of the creditor in the property of the debtor in all types of credit transactions. It thus replaces such terms as chattel mortgage, pledge, trust receipt, chattel trust, equipment trust, conditional sale, and inventory lien.

Seed money: The money needed to begin a project, such as the funds needed for acquiring or controlling a site, obtaining zoning, making feasibility studies, etc.

Seised: Possessed of an estate in fee.

Seisin: In the legal sense, possession of premises with the intention of asserting a claim to a freehold estate therein; practically, the same as ownership.

Self-liquidating mortgage: A mortgage which, by means of constant periodic payments, will be fully paid off at the end of its term.

Self-regulating: A system of controls over the conduct of a group, all of whom voluntarily submit to such rules, e.g., the code of ethics adopted by NAR.

Seller's market: An economic market in which sellers can sell at prices higher than those prevailing in an immediately preceding period; a market in which a limited number of properties is available and there is a large number of users and potential users demanding them at prevailing prices.

Senior mortgage: The mortgage having a claim preferential to that of another mortgage.

Separate property: Property owned by a husband or wife which is not jointly owned property; property acquired by either spouse prior to the marriage or by gift or devise after the marriage.

Septic tank: An underground receptacle in which sewage from the house is reduced to liquid by bacterial action and then drained off.

Service property: A property devoted to or available for utilization for a special purpose, but which has no independent marketability in the generally recognized acceptance of the term, such as a church property, a public museum, or a school.

Servicing: The collection of payments on a mortgage. Servicing by the lender also consists of operational procedures covering accounting, bookkeeping, insurance, tax record, loan payment follow-up, delinquent loan follow-up, and loan analysis.

Servient tenement: Property subject to an easement which benefits another property, called the "dominant tenement."

Setback: The distance from curb or other established line, within which no buildings may be erected.

Setback ordinance: An ordinance prohibiting the erection of a building or structure in the area between the curb and the setback line.

Set-off: A counterclaim or cross-demand charged by a defendant against the claim of a plaintiff in an action seeking money damages.

Settlement: The process at the closing of a sale of real estate negotiated by a real estate broker whereby the broker accounts to his or her principal for the earnest money deposit and deducts commission and advances by use of a form of settlement statement.

Severalty: Ownership by a person in his or her own right.

Severalty ownership: Owned by only one person; sole ownership.

Severance damage: The reduction in value caused by separation. Commonly, the damage resulting from the taking of a fraction of the whole property, reflected in a lowered utility and value in the land remaining and brought about by reason of the fractional taking.

Shake: A hand-split shingle, usually edge-grained.

Sheathing: The structural covering, usually consisting of boards, plywood, or wallboards, placed over exterior studding or rafters of a house.

Shed roof: A single-pitch roof that slopes from front to back or back to front.

Sheriff's deed: A deed executed by the sheriff pursuant to a court order in connection with the sale of property to satisfy a judgment.

Sheriff's sale: A sale of property, conducted by a sheriff, or sheriff's deputy, by virtue of his or her authority as an officer pursuant to a court ordered sale.

Shopping center: A planned area for shopping, usually in an outlying location. Typically, stores are surrounded by a parking area. A mall-type shopping center is a shopping center in which the stores face inward toward an enclosed walkway rather than fronting on the parking lot, so that the shoppers can stay inside one building while they visit various stores.

Sill: The lowest part of the frame of a house, resting on the foundation and supporting the uprights of the frame. The board or metal forming the bottom side of an opening, as a door sill, window sill, etc.

Simple interest: The interest computed on the original principal alone.

Simulation: The use of a controlled environment in which to test the effects of a decision.

Single-family home: A dwelling designed for occupancy by one household only.

Sinking fund: A fund set aside from the income of a property which, with accrued interest, will pay for replacement of the improvements as they wear out.

SIR: See Society of Industrial Realtors.

Site: A parcel of real estate that is suitable for improvement.

Siting: The placement and orientation of a house in reference to its lot.

Situs: Location.

Skylease: A long-term lease on the space above a parcel of real estate; the upper stories of a building to be erected by the tenant.

Slander of title: A false and malicious statement, oral or written, made in disparagement of a person's title to real property, causing him special damage.

Slum area: A heavily populated area marked by blight, squalor, or wretched living conditions.

Slum clearance: The removal of blighted improvements by destruction of the improvements.

Society of Industrial Realtors (SIR): Provides educational opportunities to REALTORS® working with industrial property transactions. Confers SIR designation.

Society of Real Estate Appraisers (SREA): A trade association of residential real estate appraisers. Awards SRA, SREA, and SRPA designations.

Social class: A group of people of common social and economic characteristics.

Social overhead capital: The investments by the government for public betterments such as bridges, roads, schools, and parks.

Soil pipe: The pipe which conveys waste from the house to the main sewer line.

Soil pipe and soil stack: The house sewer transporting waste from the house, and the vertical pipe ending in a vent in the roof, which transports vapors from the plumbing system.

Sole or sole plate: The piece, usually a 2 x 4, on which wall and partition studs rest.

Southern Colonial: An architectural design that combines both Georgian and New England Colonial, usually characterized by the use of two-story columns forming a porch across the long facade or at the side of the house.

Sovereign consumer: The theory that the consumer is the decision maker who determines what goods and services are to be provided within the society.

Span: A measure of the distance between structural supports such as walls, columns, piers, beams, girders, and trusses.

Special assessment: A legal charge against real estate levied by a public authority to fund the cost of public improvements such as street lights, sidewalks, street improvements, etc.

Special warranty: A covenant of warranty in a deed, by which the grantor guarantees the title against the claims of persons claiming "by, through, or under" the grantor only.

Special warranty deed: A guarantee only against the acts of the grantor herself and all persons claiming by, through, or under the grantor.

Specific performance: The requirement that a party must perform as agreed under a contract, in contrast to compensation or damages in lieu of performance; the arrangement whereby courts may force either party to a real estate contract to carry out an agreement exactly in accordance with its terms.

Specification: As used in the law relating to patents and machinery, and in building contracts, a particular or detailed statement of the various elements required to define the end product and to which it is to conform.

Specimen tree: A tree of special interest because of its shape or species, placed in a position of prominence in the yard; often a silver spruce, weeping birch, magnolia, or other unique ornamental tree.

Split rate interest: The interest rate paid on property when the rate determined for the buildings differs from the rate determined for the land.

Spot zoning: The allowance of a nonconforming use in an area zoned for a specific purpose.

Spouse: One's wife or husband.

Square-foot method: A means of estimating construction, reproduction, or replacement costs of a building by multiplying the square-foot floor area by the appropriate square-foot construction cost figure.

Squatters rights: The rights to occupancy of land created through long and undisturbed use but with no legal title or arrangement.

SRA: Senior Residential Appraiser.

SREA: Senior Real Estate Analyst.

SRPA: Senior Real Property Appraiser.

Stability of income: The constant annual net income reasonably anticipated over the entire economic life of the property.

Stagflation: An economic condition in which there is no economic growth (stagnation) or rapid or large price increases (inflation).

Stand-by commitment: An agreement by the lender to make funds available at a future date upon specified terms.

Standard depth: The depth chosen as normal, usually the one most common in the neighborhood.

Standard metropolitan area: Defined by the Bureau of Census as a county, or a group of contiguous counties, containing a city of 50,000 population or more.

Standing mortgage: A mortgage that provides for interest payments only, with the entire principal falling due in one payment at maturity of the mortgage.

State association: The association of real estate boards that copes with matters which vitally affect the business of its members within its own state.

State vet's loan: A loan made at 4% interest to eligible war veterans upon security of real property located in any state for the acquisition of homes and farms. The program is administered by the State Department of Veterans' Affairs.

Statement of consideration: Statement in a deed or other sales contract that confirms the fact that the purchaser actually gave something of value for the property.

Status: Standing, state, or condition.

Statute: A particular law enacted and established by the legislative department of the government.

Statute of Frauds: Legislation providing that all agreements affecting title to real estate must be in writing to be enforceable.

Statute of limitations: A statute barring all right of action after a certain period of time from the time when a cause of action first arises.

Statutory lien: A lien granted to a party by the operation of a statute, e.g., the lien of real estate taxes.

Statutory redemption period: The time allowed to a delinquent borrower to cure his deficiencies before his property is taken permanently from him.

Statutory warranty deed: A warranty deed form outlined by state statutes.

Step-up lease: A lease that permits increasing rentals at specified times during the lease period.

Straight-line capital recapture: The amount of dollar investment recovery in each year that is constant throughout the life of the investment.

Straight-line depreciation: See depreciation, straight line.

Straight-term mortgage: A mortgage in which repayment of the principal is in one lump sum at maturity.

Strict foreclosure: The action taken by a court which, after determination that sufficient time has elapsed for a mortgagor to pay a mortgage past due, terminates all right and interest of the mortgagor in the real property. A forced sale of the property is then ordered for the benefit of the creditors secured by the mortgage.

String, stringer: A timber or other support for cross-members. In stairs, the support on which the stair treads rest.

Studs, studding: The vertical supporting timbers in walls and partitions.

Subcontractor: A contractor employed by a general contractor. A subcontractor usually is concerned only with one particular part of the improvement of real estate, such as plumbing, masonry, carpentry, and the like.

Subdividing: Division of a large parcel of land into smaller parcels.

Subdivision: An area of land divided into parcels or lots generally of a size suitable for residential use.

Subject to and agreeing to pay: The purchaser takes title to the real estate and is also obligated to pay the debt along with the original maker of the note.

Subject to mortgage: The purchaser takes title to the property but is not obligated to pay the mortgage. If foreclosure occurs, the purchaser loses his equity and the original mortgagor is responsible for the debt.

Subjective value: A value created in the mind. It is the amount people will pay regardless of cost. In appraising, it is used in the income and market data approaches.

Sublease: One executed by the lessee of an estate to a third person, conveying the same estate for a shorter term than that for which the lessee holds it.

Subordinate: To make subject to, junior to, or inferior to, usually with respect to security.

Subordination clause: The clause in a junior or a second lien which permits retention of priority for prior liens. A subordination clause may also be used in a first deed of trust, permitting it to be subordinated to subsequent liens, for example, the liens of construction loans.

Subrogation: The substitution of one person in the place of another with reference to a lawful claim, demand, or right by virtue of having paid a claim under an insurance contract.

Subsidized housing: Housing for low- and moderate-income families in which rentals are paid in part by the government or in which the government pays a portion of the developer's loan interest costs so that he or she can charge lower rentals.

Subsidy (two types): In real estate, a grant by government that eases the financial burden of holding, using, or improving real property. A direct subsidy is a subsidy which is of direct, visible benefit to the recipient, such as a cash grant. An indirect subsidy is a subsidy whose benefit is felt indirectly, such as tariffs or farm price supports which may affect the land values in a particular area.

Suburb: A development of real estate in areas peripheral to the central area of a city.

Succession: The legal act or right of acquiring property by descent; succeeding to an asset by will or inheritance.

Sufficient description: The real estate which is to be conveyed by the deed can be identified; will stand up in court.

Sui juris: Having legal ability to handle one's own affairs; not under any legal disability.

Summation: An appraisal method for determining an interest rate; an indicated value derived by estimating the reproduction cost, subtracting depreciation, and adding the value of the land; one method of the cost approach.

Summons: A writ directed to the sheriff or other proper officer which requires him to notify the person named in the writ that an action has been brought against him and that he is required to appear, on a day named, and answer the complaint in such action.

Sump pump: An automatic electric pump installed in a basement for the purpose of emptying the sump, a pit serving as a drain for basement water accumulations.

Supermarket: A 20,000- to 40,000- square-foot grocery store that is often free-standing.

Supersession costs: Costs incurred in scrapping existing improvements in order to make possible new land uses.

Supply: Amount available for sale.

Supply and demand, law of: A theory that price or value varies directly, depending upon the quantity of units available and quantity of units desired or demanded by the buying public.

Surcharge: An additional charge added to the usual charge.

Surety: One who undertakes to pay money or to perform any other act in the event that his or her principal fails to do so.

Surplus productivity: An appraisal theory whereby net income remains after the costs of labor, coordination, and capital have been paid. This appraisal tends to fix the value of the land.

Surrender: The process of cancellation of a lease by mutual consent of lessor and lessee.

Survey: The process by which a parcel of land is measured and its boundaries ascertained.

Survivorship: See joint tenancy.

Sustained-yield management: Selective harvesting of slow-growing crops such as trees to provide for a relatively stable yield every year rather than periodic large yields at irregular times.

Swing loan: A short-term loan enabling the purchaser of a new property to purchase that property before having been paid for the equity from the property he or she is presently selling.

Sweat equity: Labor or services put into improving real property to gain possession and title in lieu of money.

Syndicate: A group of individuals, corporations, or trusts who pool money to undertake economic endeavors. The syndicate can assume the structure of a corporation, a trust, a partnership, a tenancy in common, or any other legal ownership form.

Syndication: The process of combining persons or firms to accomplish a joint venture which is of mutual interest.

Tacking: The adding together of successive periods of adverse possession of persons in privity with each other in order to create one continuous adverse possession for the time required by statute to establish title.

Tandem plan: A secondary mortgage market arrangement whereby GNMA purchases certain original mortgages for resale to FNMA or other investors.

Tangible property: Property that, by its nature, may be perceived by the senses. In general, the land, its fixed improvement, furnishings, merchandise, cash, etc.

Tax: A charge or burden, usually monetary in nature, levied upon persons or property for public purposes; a forced contribution of wealth to aid in meeting the public needs of a government.

Tax abatement: The amount of decrease or deduction of a tax improperly levied.

Tax base: The sum of the taxable property values which determines the financial capability of the government to raise funds through taxation.

Tax deed: A deed given upon a sale of lands made for the nonpayment of taxes.

Tax lien: A claim against property arising out of nonpayment of taxes; the claim may be sold by the taxing authority.

Tax penalty: The amount to be paid due to nonpayment of the taxes. Usually expressed as a percent of the unpaid balance.

Tax roll: The list describing the persons and properties subject to a particular tax.

Tax sale: A sale of land for unpaid taxes.

Tax sale certificate: A certificate given to the purchaser of land at a tax sale which transfers the lien but not the title to the purchaser.

Tax shelter: An investment motivated primarily to obtain an income tax deduction to apply against taxable income earned from other sources.

Tax title: The title transferred through a tax sale.

Taxable value: The value upon which the taxes are computed when tax rates have been determined.

Taxation (several types): The right of government to payment for the support of activities in which it engages. A double tax in real estate is the taxation of the property as an asset and the taxation of the property income the owner receives. Estate taxation is the tax imposed by government on property passed by will or descent. A personal property tax is a tax imposed upon owners of personal property. A real property tax is a tax imposed upon the owners of real property.

Taxing district: The geographical area over which a taxing authority levies taxes.

Taxpayer: One who pays a tax.

Tenancy: An interest in real property; the right to possession and use of real property.

Tenancy at sufferance: The wrongful holding over by a tenant whose lease has terminated.

Tenancy at will: Holding possession of premises by permission of the owner or landlord, but without a fixed term.

Tenancy by entirety: An estate held by a husband and wife, in which both are viewed as one person under common law, which thus provides for ownership by the marriage itself and not by the two parties in shares.

Tenancy in common: A holding in one property by two or more parties with interests accruing under different titles, or accruing under the same title but at different periods, or conferred by words of limitation stating that each grantee shall hold a distinct share which need not be equal.

Tenant: One who has the temporary use and occupation of real property owned by another.

Tenant per autre vie: One who holds lands for the period of another's life.

Tenant selection: A process used by property managers to choose rental prospects.

Tenement: Everything of permanent nature, such as land and buildings, which may be owned; in a more restrictive sense, a house or dwelling.

Tentative map: A map of the subdivision submitted to a local planning commission for study and approval.

Tenure: In accordance with the American concept of real estate ownership, this means that all right and title in and to the land rest with the owner.

Tenure in land: The conditions under which an individual holds an estate in lands.

Termites: Antlike insects which feed on wood.

Termite shield: A shield of noncorrodible metal located on top of the foundation wall or around pipes to prevent the entrance of termites.

Term mortgage: A specific type of mortgage loan having a stipulated duration, normally under 5 years, on which only interest is paid. At the expiration of the term the entire principal is paid.

Terms: The conditions spelled out in an arrangement or agreement such as a mortgage or a contract.

Testament: A will.

Testamentary: After death; e.g., a devise of real estate by a will is a testamentary transfer because the will is not operative until after death.

Testator: The person who makes or has made a will.

Time-interval maps: A series of maps that show land use or some other feature as of different dates.

Title (several types): Proof or evidence of ownership or ownership rights. A search of title is a study of the history of the title to a property. A title by descent is a title acquired by the laws of succession; title acquired by an heir in the absence of a will. A title by devise is a title received through a will.

Title company: A corporation whose primary function is to insure titles to real property.

Title guarantee policy: The title insurance provided by the owner in lieu of an abstract of title.

Title insurance: Insurance that a title is clear or clear except for defects noted; a policy of insurance that indemnifies the insured for loss occasioned by unknown defects of recorded title.

Title report: A report, prepared prior to the issuance of title insurance, which states the condition of the title.

Title search: The process of checking the public records and legal proceedings to disclose the current state of a real property's ownership.

Title theory: A state statute allowing lenders or lending institutions to secure the title to property as collateral for a loan.

Title theory of mortgage: The mortgage arrangement whereby title to mortgaged real property vests in the lender.

Topographical map: A map that shows the slope and contour of land; a map of the physical features of a parcel of real estate or an area of land.

Topography: The contour and slope of land and such things as gullies, streams, knolls, and ravines.

Torrens certificate: A document issued by the registrar, in accordance with the Torrens law, which identifies the party who holds the title to property.

Torrens system: A system of land title registration in which the state insures the quality of title against certain defects.

Tort: A private or civil wrong or injury.

Township: A territorial subdivision in the quadrangular survey method 6 miles long, 6 miles wide, and containing 36 sections, each 1 mile square.

Trade area: The geographical area from which purchasers of particular goods and services are ordinarily drawn.

Trade association: A voluntary organization of individuals or firms in a common area of economic activity; the organization has for its purpose the promotion of certain aspects of that common area of activity.

Trade fixtures: Articles of personal property which have been annexed to the freehold and which are necessary to the carrying on of a trade and which may be removed.

Trade-in: A method of guaranteeing an owner a minimum amount of cash on sale of his present property to permit him to purchase another. If the property is not sold within a specified time at the listed price, the broker agrees to arrange financing to purchase the property at an agreed upon discount.

Trades: Used synonymously with "exchange." A transaction in which owners convey the rights in a particular property for rights in another.

Traditional design: The home styling incorporating the ideas of the past, reminiscent of Cape Cod, Colonial, Georgian, and similar architectures.

Transcript: A written record of a proceeding which may have been verbal, such as a record of testimony in a trial.

Transfer book: A book in which all transfers of real estate within the county are kept. Such books are kept by the county recorder and, usually, the auditor.

Transfer tax: The tax required by state law to be paid when real estate is sold.

Transition: Change.

Traverse rod: An instrument for hanging draperies or window curtains on a rod fitted with slides, pulleys, and cords, by means of which draperies may be drawn.

Treads: The horizontal boards forming the stairway.

Trend: A prevailing tendency of behavior of some observable phenomenon, such as economic activity, over a long period of time despite intermittent fluctuations.

Trespass: Any unauthorized entry on another's property; any person who makes such an entry is a trespasser.

Trim: Finish materials such as moldings applied around openings or at the floor and ceiling such as baseboards, cornices, or picture moldings.

Trust: A fiduciary relationship in which an independent party (trustee) holds legal title to property for the beneficiaries of the trust who hold the equitable title during the life of the trust. The trustee may not deal with the property as his own but must deal with it in the best interests of the beneficiaries.

Trust account: A bank account held separate from a broker's personal funds, in which a broker is required by state law to deposit all monies collected for clients. (Also see "escrow account.")

Trust indenture: A document showing the trust agreement.

Trust res: Any property which is the subject of a trust.

Trustee: One who holds legal title to trust assets for the benefit of those holding equitable title. See trust.

Trustor: The one who conveys title of his property to the trustee to be held as security until he has performed his obligation to a lender under the terms of a deed of trust, or for other purposes, such as management.

Truth in Lending Act (TIL): That portion of Public Law 90-231 (the Consumer Credit Protection Act) which requires that the borrower be informed of true credit costs being charged.

Turnkey: A form of housing for low-income families that was originally built by private sponsors to be sold to local housing authorities.

Ultra vires: Beyond the power. Applied to the acts of a corporation beyond the powers granted in its charter.

Unbalanced improvement: An improvement which does not serve the highest best use for the site on which it is placed.

Underimprovement: An improvement which does not serve the highest best use for the site on which it is placed by reason of being smaller in size or less in cost than a building which would bring the site to its highest and best use.

Undisclosed principal: One of the parties to a transaction who is unidentified. This might occur when a broker is instructed to keep the identity of his client a secret.

Undivided interest: Fractional ownership but without physical division into shares.

Undue influence: Taking any fraudulent advantage of another's weakness of mind, distress, or necessity.

Unearned increment: An increase in the value of real estate as a result of no effort on the part of the owner; often due to an increase in population.

Unenforceable contract: One that is a good contract but for some reason cannot be enforced under the law, e.g., an unwritten contract for the sale of real estate which is unenforceable because of the Statute of Frauds.

Uniform Commercial Code: Applicable after January 1, 1965, it establishes a unified and comprehensive scheme for the regulation of security transactions in personal property, superseding the existing statutes on chattel mortgages, conditional sales, trust receipts, assignment of accounts receivable, and others in this field.

Unilateral contract: A contract under which one party promises to do something upon the completed act of another.

Unimproved: As relating to land, vacant, returned to nature, or lacking in essential appurtenant improvements required to serve a useful purpose.

United States governmental survey system: A means of describing or locating real property by reference to the governmental survey; often referred to as the rectangular survey.

United States Savings and Loan League: A trade association of savings and loan associations.

Unities of title: The particular characteristic of an estate held by several in joint tenancy and which contains the unities of interest, title, time, and possession; i.e., all joint tenants have one and the same interest accruing through the same conveyance commencing at one time and held by each through an undivided possession of the whole property.

Unit-in-place costs: A means of estimating building replacement cost in which quantities of materials are costed on an in-place rather than purchased basis and summarized to obtain a building cost.

Urban plan: The community facilities that enable the community to function as a unit, e.g., the system of streets, sewers, water mains, parks, playgrounds, and the like.

Urban property: City property; densely settled property.

Urban renewal: The controlled method of redevelopment within urban areas. Although often used to refer to Title I and other public projects, it also encompasses private redevelopment efforts.

Urban renewal area: A slum area; a blighted, deteriorated, or deteriorating area; an open land area which is approved by HUD as necessary for an urban renewal project.

Urban renewal project: The term applied to the specific activities undertaken by a local public agency in an urban renewal area to prevent and eliminate slum and blight. The activities may involve slum clearance and redevelopment, rehabilitation, or conservation, or a combination thereof.

Urban size rachet: The theory that, once a town reaches a certain size, it will continue to grow of its own accord.

Urban sprawl: Expansion of a municipality over a large geographical area.

Usage: Uniform practice or course of conduct followed in certain businesses or professions or some procedure or phase thereof.

Use: A beneficial interest in land under a trust.

Use density: The number of buildings having a specific use per unit of area; sometimes calculated by a percentage of land coverage or density of coverage.

Use districts: Areas in a city which have land uses that differ from adjacent land uses, e.g., commercial, industrial, and residential.

Use map: Map of the municipal area showing important types of land uses.

User of real estate: One who has the use of property rights, whether it be through ownership, lease, easement, or license.

Usury: The practice of lending money at a rate of interest above the legal rate. This is an illegal practice.

Utility: Ability of real estate to provide useful services; usefulness of real property.

VA: Veterans' Administration of the federal government.

VA-guaranteed mortgage: Veteran's mortgage guaranteed by the VA for an amount not in excess of VA's appraised value of the property.

VA loan: A loan guaranteed by the VA.

Valid: Having force, or binding force; legally sufficient, authorized by law, or incapable of being set aside.

Valley: The internal angle formed as a result of the junction between the two sloping sides of a roof.

Valuation: Estimated worth or price; the act of valuing a property by appraisal.

Value analysis: Estimation of the present worth of the future benefits to be derived from a property investment.

Value calculation: The estimation of the value to be recognized by buyers, sellers, lenders, and renters in the marketplace.

Value figure: A figure used to determine how much capital to invest in the property under consideration.

Value for a purpose: The theory that in real estate emphasis must be placed on different value factors depending upon the purpose of the valuation; the use for which the property is being considered.

Value in exchange: The price an investment asset is predicted to bring based upon comparable market transactions.

Value in use: The price an investor would pay based upon his or her personal opinion of the investment asset's merit.

Value of property: The usefulness of the property relative to its scarcity.

Variance: The authorization to improve or develop a particular property in a manner not authorized by the zoning ordinance; generally granted by a Board of Zoning Appeals.

Vendee: A purchaser of property. The word is more commonly applied to a purchaser of real property.

Vendor: A person who sells property to a vendee. The word is more commonly applied to a seller of real estate.

Vendor's lien: A lien implied to belong to a vendor for the unpaid purchase price of property, when he has not taken any other lien or security beyond the personal obligation of the purchaser.

Veneer: Thin sheets of wood of excellent quality glued over wood of lesser quality.

Vent: A pipe installed to provide a flow of air to or from a drainage system or to provide for the circulation of air within such a system to protect trap seals from siphonage and back-pressure.

Venue: Locality; also, the heading of a legal document showing the state and county to which it refers. Legally, the appropriate forum for filing a lawsuit.

Verbal: By word of mouth; spoken; oral; parol.

Verification: A confirmation of correctness, truth, or authenticity by affidavit, oath, or deposition.

Verified: Confirmed or substantiated by an oath.

Vested: Placed in possession and control; given or committed to another.

Veterans' Administration: An agency of the federal government that, among other activities, guarantees loans made to veterans.

Void: That which is entirely null. A void act is one which is not binding on either party and which is not susceptible of ratification.

Voidable: Capable of being made void; not utterly null and void; hence may be either voided or confirmed.

Voluntary lien: A lien placed on property with the consent of, or as a result of, the voluntary act of the owner.

Wainscotting: Wood lining of an interior wall; also the lower part of a wall when finished differently from the upper wall.

Waiver: The intentional relinquishment of a known right. It is a voluntary act and implies an election by the party to dispense with something of value or to forego some advantage or right.

Wall: A bearing wall is one that supports any vertical load in addition to its own weight. A cavity wall is a thin, non-load-bearing wall supported by the structure. A foundation wall is below or partly below ground, providing support for the exterior or other structural parts of the building. A masonry wall is a bearing or non-bearing wall of hollow or solid masonry units.

Warrant: To guarantee or promise that a certain fact or state of facts, in relation to the subject matter of a transaction, is or shall be as it is represented to be.

Warranted value: A term often erroneously used in place of "warranted price."

Warranty deed: One which contains a general guarantee of the quality of title being conveyed.

Waste: An abuse or destructive use of property by one in rightful possession.

Water rights: An aggregate right consisting of the rights to a water supply; guarantee of access to nearby body of water.

Water softener: A mechanical device for treating hard water by circulating it through a chemical solution.

Water table: Distance from surface of ground to a depth where natural groundwater can be found.

Waterpower rights: A property containing the rights to the use of water as a source of power, developed or undeveloped.

WCR: See Women's Council of Realtors.

Will: A written instrument executed with the formalities of law, whereby a person makes a disposition of property to take effect after death.

Will-cut cruise: The estimated volume of lumber that can be sawed from the timber in a given area. It is obtained by deducting from the stand cruise an allowance for breakage and other waste. (To cruise is to inspect land to determine possible lumber yield.)

Without recourse: An endorser without recourse specially declines to assume any responsibility to subsequent holders for payment of a debt instrument which is transferred by endorsement.

Women's Council of Realtors: Provides educational programs and publications for women REALTORS® whose primary interest is in residential brokerage.

Words of conveyance: The statement that follows the statement of consideration in a deed to show the intent on the part of the grantor to transfer the property.

Working capital: Properly, the readily convertible capital required in a business to allow the regular functioning of operations free from financial embarrassment. In accounting, the excess of current assets less the current liabilities as of any date.

Working drawing: A sketch of a part or a whole structure, drawn to scale and in such detail as to dimensions and instructions as is needed to guide the work on a construction job.

Wraparound loan: A form of junior mortgage which incorporates the full amount of the loan desired with a higher repayment to retire the existing debt. It is used when it is not feasible or desirable to retire the first mortgage.

Writ of execution: An order to carry out the judgment or decree of a court.

X-bracing: Cross-bracing of a partition or floor joist.

Yield: Income of a property—the ratio of the annual net income from the property to the cost or market value of the property.

Zone: The area described by the proper authorities for a specific use, subject to certain restrictions or restraints.

Zoning: Governmental regulation of land use; regulation by local government under police powers of such matters as height, bulk, and use of buildings and use of land. The enabling act is a state statute necessary to provide a legal base for zoning codes. Snob zoning is zoning regulations that require large lots, etc., as a method of excluding those in low-income groups.

Zoning map: A map showing the various sections of the community and the division of the sections into zones of permitted land uses under the zoning ordinance.

Zoning ordinance: The use of police powers by the governing body to regulate and control the use of real estate for the health, morals, safety, and welfare of the general public.

Index

REAL ESTATE LISTING CONTRACT (EXCLUSIVE RIGHT TO SELL)

SALES PRICE _____ TYPE HOME _____ TOTAL BEDROOMS _____ TOTAL BATHS _____

ADDRESS _____ JURISDICTION OF _____

AMT. OF LOAN TO BE ASSUMED $ _____ AS OF WHAT DATE _____ TAXES & INS. INCLUDED _____ YEARS TO GO _____ AMOUNT PAYABLE MONTHLY $ _____ @ ___ % TYPE LOAN _____

MORTGAGE COMPANY _____ 2nd MORTGAGE _____

OWNER'S NAME _____ PHONES (HOME) _____ (BUSINESS) _____

TENANT'S NAME _____ PHONES (HOME) _____ (BUSINESS) _____

POSSESSION _____ DATE LISTED: _____ EXCLUSIVE FOR _____ DATE OF EXPIRATION _____

LISTING BROKER _____ PHONE _____ KEY AVAILABLE AT _____

LISTING SALESMAN _____ HOME PHONE _____ HOW TO BE SHOWN: _____

ENTRANCE FOYER ☐	CENTER HALL ☐	AGE	AIR CONDITIONING ☐	TYPE KITCHEN CABINETS
LIVING ROOM SIZE	FIREPLACE ☐	ROOFING	TOOL HOUSE ☐	TYPE COUNTER TOPS
DINING ROOM SIZE		GARAGE SIZE	PATIO ☐	EAT-IN SIZE KITCHEN ☐
BEDROOM TOTAL: DOWN UP		SIDE DRIVE ☐	CIRCULAR DRIVE ☐	TYPE STOVE ☐
BATHS TOTAL: DOWN UP		PORCH ☐ SIDE ☐ REAR ☐	SCREENED ☐	BUILT-IN OVEN & RANGE ☐
DEN SIZE	FIREPLACE ☐	FENCED YARD	OUTDOOR GRILL ☐	SEPARATE STOVE INCLUDED ☐
FAMILY ROOM SIZE	FIREPLACE ☐	STORM WINDOWS ☐	STORM DOORS ☐	REFRIGERATOR INCLUDED ☐
RECREATION ROOM SIZE	FIREPLACE ☐	CURBS & GUTTERS ☐	SIDEWALKS ☐	DISHWASHER INCLUDED
BASEMENT SIZE		STORM SEWERS ☐	ALLEY ☐	DISPOSAL INCLUDED ☐
NONE ☐ 1/4 ☐ 1/3 ☐ 1/2 ☐ 3/4 ☐ FULL ☐		WATER SUPPLY		DOUBLE SINK ☐ SINGLE SINK ☐
UTILITY ROOM		SEWER ☐	SEPTIC ☐	STAINLESS STEEL ☐ PORCELAIN ☐
TYPE HOT WATER SYSTEM:		TYPE GAS: NATURAL ☐	BOTTLED ☐	WASHER INCLUDED ☐ DRYER INCLUDED ☐
TYPE HEAT		WHY SELLING		LAND ASSESSMENT $
EST. FUEL COST				IMPROVEMENTS $
ATTIC		PROPERTY DESCRIPTION		TOTAL ASSESSMENTS $
PULL DOWN STAIRWAY ☐ REGULAR STAIRWAY ☐ TRAP DOOR ☐				TAX RATE
NAME OF BUILDER		LOT SIZE		TOTAL ANNUAL TAXES $
SQUARE FOOTAGE		LOT NO. BLOCK SECTION		
EXTERIOR OF HOUSE				

NAME OF SCHOOLS: ELEMENTARY: _____ JR. HIGH: _____

HIGH: _____ PAROCHIAL: _____

PUBLIC TRANSPORTATION: _____

NEAREST SHOPPING AREA: _____

REMARKS: _____

_____

_____

Date: _____

Date Signed: _____

_____ (Owner)

Listing Agent _____

Address _____ Telephone _____

_____ (Owner)

REAL ESTATE SALES CONTRACT (OFFER TO PURCHASE AGREEMENT)

This AGREEMENT made as of _____ , 19_____ ,

among _____ (herein called "Purchaser"),

and _____ (herein called "Seller"),

and _____ (herein called "Broker"),

provides that Purchaser agrees to buy through Broker as agent for Seller, and Seller agrees to sell the following described real estate, and all improvements

thereon, located in the jurisdiction of _____ ,

(all herein called "the property"): _____

_____ , and more commonly known as _____

_____ (street address).

1. The purchase price of the property is _____

Dollars ($ _____), and such purchase price shall be paid as follows:

_____

2. Purchaser has made a deposit of _____ Dollars ($ _____)
with Broker, receipt of which is hereby acknowledged, and such deposit shall be held by Broker in escrow until the date of settlement and then applied
to the purchase price, or returned to Purchaser if the title to the property is not marketable.

3. Seller agrees to convey the property to Purchaser by Deed with the usual covenants of title and free and clear from all monetary encumbrances,
tenancies, liens (for taxes or otherwise), except as may be otherwise provided above, but subject to applicable restrictive covenants of record. Seller further
agrees to deliver possession of the property to Purchaser on the date of settlement and to pay the expense of preparing the deed of conveyance.

4. Settlement shall be made at _____ on or before

_____ , 19_____ , or as soon thereafter as title can be examined and necessary documents prepared, with
allowance of a reasonable time for Seller to correct any defects reported by the title examiner.

5. All taxes, interest, rent, and impound escrow deposits, if any, shall be prorated as of the date of settlement.

6. All risk of loss or damage to the property by fire, windstorm, casualty, or other cause is assumed by Seller until the date of settlement.

7. Purchaser and Seller agree that Broker was the sole procuring cause of this Contract of Purchase, and Seller agrees to pay Broker for services

rendered a cash fee of _____ per cent of the purchase price. If either Purchaser or Seller defaults under such Contract, such defaulting party shall
be liable for the cash fee of Broker and any expenses incurred by the non-defaulting party in connection with this transaction.

Subject to: _____

_____

_____

_____

8. Purchaser represents that an inspection satisfactory to Purchaser has been made of the property, and Purchaser agrees to accept the property
in its present condition except as may be otherwise provided in the description of the property above.

9. This Contract of Purchase constitutes the entire agreement among the parties and may not be modified or changed except by written instrument executed by all of the parties, including Broker.

10. This Contract of Purchase shall be construed, interpreted, and applied according to the law of the jurisdiction of _____ and shall
be binding upon and shall inure to the benefit of the heirs, personal representatives, successors, and assigns of the parties.

All parties to this agreement acknowledge receipt of a certified copy.

WITNESS the following signatures:

_____   _____
Seller   Purchaser

_____   _____
Seller   Purchaser

_____
Broker

Deposit Rec'd $ _____

Personal Check   Cash

Cashier's Check   Company Check

Sales Agent:

REAL ESTATE LISTING CONTRACT (EXCLUSIVE RIGHT TO SELL)

SALES PRICE _____ TYPE HOME _____ TOTAL BEDROOMS _____ TOTAL BATHS _____

ADDRESS _____ JURISDICTION OF _____

AMT. OF LOAN
TO BE ASSUMED $ _____   AS OF
WHAT DATE _____   TAXES & INS.
INCLUDED _____   YEARS
TO GO _____   AMOUNT PAYABLE
MONTHLY $_____ @ ___%   TYPE
LOAN_____

MORTGAGE COMPANY _____ 2nd MORTGAGE _____

OWNER'S NAME _____ PHONES(HOME) _____ (BUSINESS) _____

TENANT'S NAME _____ PHONES (HOME) _____ (BUSINESS) _____

POSSESSION _____ DATE LISTED: _____ EXCLUSIVE FOR_____ DATE OF EXPIRATION _____

LISTING BROKER _____ PHONE _____ KEY AVAILABLE AT _____

LISTING SALESMAN _____ HOME PHONE _____ HOW TO BE SHOWN: _____

ENTRANCE FOYER ☐	CENTER HALL ☐	AGE	AIR CONDITIONING ☐	TYPE KITCHEN CABINETS
LIVING ROOM SIZE	FIREPLACE ☐	ROOFING	TOOL HOUSE ☐	TYPE COUNTER TOPS
DINING ROOM SIZE		GARAGE SIZE	PATIO ☐	EAT-IN SIZE KITCHEN ☐
BEDROOM TOTAL: DOWN UP		SIDE DRIVE ☐	CIRCULAR DRIVE ☐	TYPE STOVE ☐
BATHS TOTAL: DOWN UP		PORCH ☐ SIDE ☐ REAR ☐	SCREENED ☐	BUILT-IN OVEN & RANGE ☐
DEN SIZE	FIREPLACE ☐	FENCED YARD ☐	OUTDOOR GRILL ☐	SEPARATE STOVE INCLUDED ☐
FAMILY ROOM SIZE	FIREPLACE ☐	STORM WINDOWS ☐	STORM DOORS ☐	REFRIGERATOR INCLUDED ☐
RECREATION ROOM SIZE	FIREPLACE ☐	CURBS & GUTTERS ☐	SIDEWALKS ☐	DISHWASHER INCLUDED ☐
BASEMENT SIZE		STORM SEWERS ☐	ALLEY ☐	DISPOSAL INCLUDED ☐
NONE ☐ 1/4 ☐ 1/3 ☐ 1/2 ☐ 3/4 ☐ FULL ☐		WATER SUPPLY		DOUBLE SINK ☐ SINGLE SINK ☐
UTILITY ROOM		SEWER ☐	SEPTIC ☐	STAINLESS STEEL ☐ PORCELAIN ☐
TYPE HOT WATER SYSTEM:		TYPE GAS: NATURAL ☐	BOTTLED ☐	WASHER INCLUDED ☐ DRYER INCLUDED ☐
TYPE HEAT		WHY SELLING		LAND ASSESSMENT $
EST. FUEL COST				IMPROVEMENTS $
ATTIC		PROPERTY DESCRIPTION		TOTAL ASSESSMENTS $
PULL DOWN STAIRWAY ☐ REGULAR STAIRWAY ☐ TRAP DOOR ☐				TAX RATE
NAME OF BUILDER		LOT SIZE		TOTAL ANNUAL TAXES $
SQUARE FOOTAGE		LOT NO. BLOCK SECTION		
EXTERIOR OF HOUSE				

NAME OF SCHOOLS: ELEMENTARY: _____ JR. HIGH: _____

HIGH: _____ PAROCHIAL: _____

PUBLIC TRANSPORTATION: _____

NEAREST SHOPPING AREA: _____

REMARKS: _____

_____

_____

Date: _____

In consideration of the services of _____ (herein called "Broker") to be rendered to the undersigned (herein called "Owner"), and of the promise of Broker to make reasonable efforts to obtain a Purchaser therefor, Owner hereby lists with Broker the real estate and all improvements thereon which are described above, (all herein called "the property"), and the Owner hereby grants to Broker the exclusive and irrevocable right to sell such property from 12:00 Noon on _____ , 19_____ until 12:00 Midnight on _____ , 19_____ (herein called "period of time"), for the price of _____ Dollars ($_____) or for such other price and upon such other terms (including exchange) as Owner may subsequently authorize during the period of time.

It is understood by Owner that the above sum or any other price subsequently authorized by Owner shall include a cash fee of _____ per cent of such price or other price which shall be payable by Owner to Broker upon consummation by any Purchaser or Purchasers of a valid contract of sale of the property during the period of time and whether or not Broker was a procuring cause of any such contract of sale.

If the property is sold or exchanged by Owner, or by Broker or by any other person to any Purchaser to whom the property was shown by Broker or any representative of Broker within sixty (60) days after the expiration of the period of time mentioned above, Owner agrees to pay to Broker a cash fee which shall be the same percentage of the purchase price as the percentage mentioned above.

Broker is hereby authorized by Owner to place a "For Sale" sign on the property and to remove all signs of other brokers or salesmen during the period of time, and Owner hereby agrees to make the property available to Broker at all reasonable hours for the purpose of showing it to prospective Purchasers.

Owner agrees to convey the property to the Purchaser by deed with the usual covenants of title and free and clear from all encumbrances, tenancies, liens (for taxes or otherwise), but subject to applicable restrictive covenants of record. Owner acknowledges receipt of copy of this agreement.

WITNESS the following signature(s) and seal(s):

Date Signed: _____   _____

(Owner)

Listing Agent _____

Address _____ Telephone _____   _____

(Owner)

REAL ESTATE SALES CONTRACT (OFFER TO PURCHASE AGREEMENT)

This AGREEMENT made as of _____ , 19_____ ,

among _____ (herein called "Purchaser"),

and _____ (herein called "Seller"),

and _____ (herein called "Broker"),

provides that Purchaser agrees to buy through Broker as agent for Seller, and Seller agrees to sell the following described real estate, and all improvements

thereon, located in the jurisdiction of _____ ,

(all herein called "the property"): _____

_____ , and more commonly known as _____

_____ (street address).

1. The purchase price of the property is _____

Dollars ($ _____), and such purchase price shall be paid as follows:

_____

2. Purchaser has made a deposit of _____ Dollars ($ _____)
with Broker, receipt of which is hereby acknowledged, and such deposit shall be held by Broker in escrow until the date of settlement and then applied
to the purchase price, or returned to Purchaser if the title to the property is not marketable.

3. Seller agrees to convey the property to Purchaser by Deed with the usual covenants of title and free and clear from all monetary encumbrances,
tenancies, liens (for taxes or otherwise), except as may be otherwise provided above, but subject to applicable restrictive covenants of record. Seller further
agrees to deliver possession of the property to Purchaser on the date of settlement and to pay the expense of preparing the deed of conveyance.

4. Settlement shall be made at _____ on or before

_____ , 19_____ , or as soon thereafter as title can be examined and necessary documents prepared, with
allowance of a reasonable time for Seller to correct any defects reported by the title examiner.

5. All taxes, interest, rent, and impound escrow deposits, if any, shall be prorated as of the date of settlement.

6. All risk of loss or damage to the property by fire, windstorm, casualty, or other cause is assumed by Seller until the date of settlement.

7. Purchaser and Seller agree that Broker was the sole procuring cause of this Contract of Purchase, and Seller agrees to pay Broker for services

rendered a cash fee of _____ per cent of the purchase price. If either Purchaser or Seller defaults under such Contract, such defaulting party shall
be liable for the cash fee of Broker and any expenses incurred by the non-defaulting party in connection with this transaction.

Subject to: _____

_____

_____

_____

8. Purchaser represents that an inspection satisfactory to Purchaser has been made of the property, and Purchaser agrees to accept the property
in its present condition except as may be otherwise provided in the description of the property above.

9. This Contract of Purchase constitutes the entire agreement among the parties and may not be modified or changed except by written instrument executed by all of the parties, including Broker.

10. This Contract of Purchase shall be construed, interpreted, and applied according to the law of the jurisdiction of _____ and shall
be binding upon and shall inure to the benefit of the heirs, personal representatives, successors, and assigns of the parties.

All parties to this agreement acknowledge receipt of a certified copy.

WITNESS the following signatures:

_____   _____
                          Seller   Purchaser

_____   _____
                          Seller   Purchaser

_____
                          Broker

Deposit Rec'd $ _____

Personal Check   Cash

Cashier's Check   Company Check

Sales Agent:

REAL ESTATE LISTING CONTRACT (EXCLUSIVE RIGHT TO SELL)

SALES PRICE _____ TYPE HOME _____ TOTAL BEDROOMS _____ TOTAL BATHS _____

ADDRESS _____ JURISDICTION OF _____

AMT. OF LOAN
TO BE ASSUMED $ _____ AS OF WHAT DATE _____ TAXES & INS. INCLUDED _____ YEARS TO GO _____ AMOUNT PAYABLE MONTHLY $ _____ @ ___% TYPE LOAN _____

MORTGAGE COMPANY _____ 2nd MORTGAGE _____

OWNER'S NAME _____ PHONES(HOME) _____ (BUSINESS) _____

TENANT'S NAME _____ PHONES (HOME) _____ (BUSINESS) _____

POSSESSION _____ DATE LISTED: _____ EXCLUSIVE FOR _____ DATE OF EXPIRATION _____

LISTING BROKER _____ PHONE _____ KEY AVAILABLE AT _____

LISTING SALESMAN _____ HOME PHONE _____ HOW TO BE SHOWN: _____

ENTRANCE FOYER ☐	CENTER HALL ☐	AGE	AIR CONDITIONING ☐	TYPE KITCHEN CABINETS
LIVING ROOM SIZE	FIREPLACE ☐	ROOFING	TOOL HOUSE ☐	TYPE COUNTER TOPS
DINING ROOM SIZE		GARAGE SIZE	PATIO ☐	EAT-IN SIZE KITCHEN ☐
BEDROOM TOTAL: DOWN UP		SIDE DRIVE ☐	CIRCULAR DRIVE ☐	TYPE STOVE ☐
BATHS TOTAL: DOWN UP		PORCH ☐ SIDE ☐ REAR ☐	SCREENED ☐	BUILT-IN OVEN & RANGE ☐
DEN SIZE	FIREPLACE ☐	FENCED YARD	OUTDOOR GRILL ☐	SEPARATE STOVE INCLUDED ☐
FAMILY ROOM SIZE	FIREPLACE ☐	STORM WINDOWS ☐	STORM DOORS ☐	REFRIGERATOR INCLUDED ☐
RECREATION ROOM SIZE	FIREPLACE ☐	CURBS & GUTTERS ☐	SIDEWALKS ☐	DISHWASHER INCLUDED
BASEMENT SIZE		STORM SEWERS ☐	ALLEY ☐	DISPOSAL INCLUDED ☐
NONE ☐ 1/4 ☐ 1/3 ☐ 1/2 ☐ 3/4 ☐ FULL ☐		WATER SUPPLY		DOUBLE SINK ☐ SINGLE SINK ☐
UTILITY ROOM		SEWER ☐	SEPTIC ☐	STAINLESS STEEL ☐ PORCELAIN ☐
TYPE HOT WATER SYSTEM:		TYPE GAS: NATURAL ☐	BOTTLED ☐	WASHER INCLUDED ☐ DRYER INCLUDED ☐
TYPE HEAT		WHY SELLING		LAND ASSESSMENT $
EST. FUEL COST				IMPROVEMENTS $
ATTIC		PROPERTY DESCRIPTION		TOTAL ASSESSMENTS $
PULL DOWN STAIRWAY ☐ REGULAR STAIRWAY ☐ TRAP DOOR ☐				TAX RATE
NAME OF BUILDER		LOT SIZE		TOTAL ANNUAL TAXES $
SQUARE FOOTAGE		LOT NO. BLOCK SECTION		
EXTERIOR OF HOUSE				

NAME OF SCHOOLS: ELEMENTARY: _____ JR. HIGH: _____

HIGH: _____ PAROCHIAL: _____

PUBLIC TRANSPORTATION: _____

NEAREST SHOPPING AREA: _____

REMARKS: _____

_____

_____

Date: _____

In consideration of the services of _____ (herein called "Broker") to be rendered to the undersigned (herein called 'Owner"), and of the promise of Broker to make reasonable efforts to obtain a Purchaser therefor, Owner hereby lists with Broker the real estate and all improvements thereon which are described above, (all herein called "the property"), and the Owner hereby grants to Broker the exclusive and irrevocable right to sell such property from 12:00 Noon on _____ , 19_____ until 12:00 Midnight on _____ , 19_____ (herein called "period of time"), for the price of _____ Dollars ($ _____) or for such other price and upon such other terms (including exchange) as Owner may subsequently authorize during the period of time.

It is understood by Owner that the above sum or any other price subsequently authorized by Owner shall include a cash fee of _____ per cent of such price or other price which shall be payable by Owner to Broker upon consummation by any Purchaser or Purchasers of a valid contract of sale of the property during the period of time and whether or not Broker was a procuring cause of any such contract of sale.

If the property is sold or exchanged by Owner, or by Broker or by any other person to any Purchaser to whom the property was shown by Broker or any representative of Broker within sixty (60) days after the expiration of the period of time mentioned above, Owner agrees to pay to Broker a cash fee which shall be the same percentage of the purchase price as the percentage mentioned above.

Broker is hereby authorized by Owner to place a "For Sale" sign on the property and to remove all signs of other brokers or salesmen during the period of time, and Owner hereby agrees to make the property available to Broker at all reasonable hours for the purpose of showing it to prospective Purchasers.

Owner agrees to convey the property to the Purchaser by deed with the usual covenants of title and free and clear from all encumbrances, tenancies, liens (for taxes or otherwise), but subject to applicable restrictive covenants of record. Owner acknowledges receipt of copy of this agreement.

WITNESS the following signature(s) and seal(s):

Date Signed: _____

_____ (Owner)

Listing Agent _____

Address _____ Telephone _____

_____ (Owner)

REAL ESTATE SALES CONTRACT (OFFER TO PURCHASE AGREEMENT)

This AGREEMENT made as of _____ , 19_____ ,

among _____ (herein called "Purchaser"),

and _____ (herein called "Seller"),

and _____ (herein called "Broker"),

provides that Purchaser agrees to buy through Broker as agent for Seller, and Seller agrees to sell the following described real estate, and all improvements

thereon, located in the jurisdiction of _____ ,

(all herein called "the property"): _____

_____ , and more commonly known as _____

_____ (street address).

1. The purchase price of the property is _____

Dollars ($ _____), and such purchase price shall be paid as follows:

_____

2. Purchaser has made a deposit of _____ Dollars ($ _____)
with Broker, receipt of which is hereby acknowledged, and such deposit shall be held by Broker in escrow until the date of settlement and then applied
to the purchase price, or returned to Purchaser if the title to the property is not marketable.

3. Seller agrees to convey the property to Purchaser by Deed with the usual covenants of title and free and clear from all monetary encumbrances,
tenancies, liens (for taxes or otherwise), except as may be otherwise provided above, but subject to applicable restrictive covenants of record. Seller further
agrees to deliver possession of the property to Purchaser on the date of settlement and to pay the expense of preparing the deed of conveyance.

4. Settlement shall be made at _____ on or before

_____ , 19_____ , or as soon thereafter as title can be examined and necessary documents prepared, with
allowance of a reasonable time for Seller to correct any defects reported by the title examiner.

5. All taxes, interest, rent, and impound escrow deposits, if any, shall be prorated as of the date of settlement.

6. All risk of loss or damage to the property by fire, windstorm, casualty, or other cause is assumed by Seller until the date of settlement.

7. Purchaser and Seller agree that Broker was the sole procuring cause of this Contract of Purchase, and Seller agrees to pay Broker for services

rendered a cash fee of _____ per cent of the purchase price. If either Purchaser or Seller defaults under such Contract, such defaulting party shall
be liable for the cash fee of Broker and any expenses incurred by the non-defaulting party in connection with this transaction.

Subject to: _____

_____

_____

_____

8. Purchaser represents that an inspection satisfactory to Purchaser has been made of the property, and Purchaser agrees to accept the property
in its present condition except as may be otherwise provided in the description of the property above.

9. This Contract of Purchase constitutes the entire agreement among the parties and may not be modified or changed except by written instrument executed by all of the parties, including Broker.

10. This Contract of Purchase shall be construed, interpreted, and applied according to the law of the jurisdiction of _____ and shall
be binding upon and shall inure to the benefit of the heirs, personal representatives, successors, and assigns of the parties.

All parties to this agreement acknowledge receipt of a certified copy.

WITNESS the following signatures:

_____   Seller   _____   Purchaser

_____   Seller   _____   Purchaser

_____   Broker

Deposit Rec'd $ _____

Personal Check   Cash

Cashier's Check   Company Check

Sales Agent: _____

REAL ESTATE LISTING CONTRACT (EXCLUSIVE RIGHT TO SELL)

SALES PRICE _____ TYPE HOME _____ TOTAL BEDROOMS _____ TOTAL BATHS _____

ADDRESS_____ JURISDICTION OF_____

AMT. OF LOAN   AS OF   TAXES & INS.   YEARS   AMOUNT PAYABLE   TYPE
TO BE ASSUMED $ _____ WHAT DATE _____ INCLUDED _____ TO GO _____ MONTHLY $_____ @ ___% LOAN_____

MORTGAGE COMPANY_____ 2nd MORTGAGE _____

OWNER'S NAME _____ PHONES(HOME) _____ (BUSINESS)_____

TENANT'S NAME _____ PHONES (HOME) _____ (BUSINESS)_____

POSSESSION _____ DATE LISTED:_____ EXCLUSIVE FOR_____ DATE OF EXPIRATION _____

LISTING BROKER _____ PHONE _____ KEY AVAILABLE AT _____

LISTING SALESMAN _____ HOME PHONE_____ HOW TO BE SHOWN:_____

ENTRANCE FOYER ☐	CENTER HALL ☐	AGE	AIR CONDITIONING ☐	TYPE KITCHEN CABINETS
LIVING ROOM SIZE	FIREPLACE ☐	ROOFING	TOOL HOUSE ☐	TYPE COUNTER TOPS
DINING ROOM SIZE		GARAGE SIZE	PATIO ☐	EAT-IN SIZE KITCHEN ☐
BEDROOM TOTAL: DOWN UP		SIDE DRIVE ☐	CIRCULAR DRIVE ☐	TYPE STOVE ☐
BATHS TOTAL: DOWN UP		PORCH ☐ SIDE ☐ REAR ☐	SCREENED ☐	BUILT-IN OVEN & RANGE ☐
DEN SIZE	FIREPLACE ☐	FENCED YARD	OUTDOOR GRILL ☐	SEPARATE STOVE INCLUDED ☐
FAMILY ROOM SIZE	FIREPLACE ☐	STORM WINDOWS ☐	STORM DOORS ☐	REFRIGERATOR INCLUDED ☐
RECREATION ROOM SIZE	FIREPLACE ☐	CURBS & GUTTERS ☐	SIDEWALKS ☐	DISHWASHER INCLUDED
BASEMENT SIZE		STORM SEWERS ☐	ALLEY ☐	DISPOSAL INCLUDED ☐
NONE ☐ 1/4 ☐ 1/3 ☐ 1/2 ☐ 3/4 ☐ FULL ☐		WATER SUPPLY		DOUBLE SINK ☐ SINGLE SINK ☐
UTILITY ROOM		SEWER ☐	SEPTIC ☐	STAINLESS STEEL ☐ PORCELAIN ☐
TYPE HOT WATER SYSTEM:		TYPE GAS: NATURAL ☐	BOTTLED ☐	WASHER INCLUDED ☐ DRYER INCLUDED☐
TYPE HEAT		WHY SELLING		LAND ASSESSMENT $
EST. FUEL COST				IMPROVEMENTS $
ATTIC		PROPERTY DESCRIPTION		TOTAL ASSESSMENTS $
PULL DOWN STAIRWAY ☐ REGULAR STAIRWAY ☐ TRAP DOOR ☐				TAX RATE
NAME OF BUILDER		LOT SIZE		TOTAL ANNUAL TAXES $
SQUARE FOOTAGE		LOT NO. BLOCK	SECTION	
EXTERIOR OF HOUSE				

NAME OF SCHOOLS: ELEMENTARY:_____ JR. HIGH: _____

                 HIGH:_____ PAROCHIAL: _____

PUBLIC TRANSPORTATION: _____

NEAREST SHOPPING AREA: _____

REMARKS: _____

_____

_____

_____

Date: _____

In consideration of the services of _____ (herein called "Broker") to be rendered to the undersigned (herein called 'Owner"), and of the promise of Broker to make reasonable efforts to obtain a Purchaser therefor, Owner hereby lists with Broker the real estate and all improvements thereon which are described above, (all herein called "the property"), and the Owner hereby grants to Broker the exclusive and irrevocable right to sell such property from 12:00 Noon on _____ , 19_____ until 12:00 Midnight on _____ , 19_____ (herein called "period of time"), for the price of _____ Dollars ($_____) or for such other price and upon such other terms (including exchange) as Owner may subsequently authorize during the period of time.

It is understood by Owner that the above sum or any other price subsequently authorized by Owner shall include a cash fee of _____ per cent of such price or other price which shall be payable by Owner to Broker upon consummation by any Purchaser or Purchasers of a valid contract of sale of the property during the period of time and whether or not Broker was a procuring cause of any such contract of sale.

If the property is sold or exchanged by Owner, or by Broker or by any other person to any Purchaser to whom the property was shown by Broker or any representative of Broker within sixty (60) days after the expiration of the period of time mentioned above, Owner agrees to pay to Broker a cash fee which shall be the same percentage of the purchase price as the percentage mentioned above.

Broker is hereby authorized by Owner to place a "For Sale" sign on the property and to remove all signs of other brokers or salesmen during the period of time, and Owner hereby agrees to make the property available to Broker at all reasonable hours for the purpose of showing it to prospective Purchasers.

Owner agrees to convey the property to the Purchaser by deed with the usual covenants of title and free and clear from all encumbrances, tenancies, liens (for taxes or otherwise), but subject to applicable restrictive covenants of record. Owner acknowledges receipt of copy of this agreement.

WITNESS the following signature(s) and seal(s):

Date Signed: _____   _____
                                                                                          (Owner)

Listing Agent_____

Address _____ Telephone _____   _____
                                                                                          (Owner)

REAL ESTATE SALES CONTRACT (OFFER TO PURCHASE AGREEMENT)

This AGREEMENT made as of _____ , 19_____ ,

among _____ (herein called "Purchaser"),

and _____ (herein called "Seller"),

and _____ (herein called "Broker"),
provides that Purchaser agrees to buy through Broker as agent for Seller, and Seller agrees to sell the following described real estate, and all improvements

thereon, located in the jurisdiction of _____ ,

(all herein called "the property"): _____

_____ , and more commonly known as _____

_____ (street address).

1.   The purchase price of the property is _____

Dollars ($ _____), and such purchase price shall be paid as follows:

_____

2.   Purchaser has made a deposit of _____ Dollars ($ _____)
with Broker, receipt of which is hereby acknowledged, and such deposit shall be held by Broker in escrow until the date of settlement and then applied
to the purchase price, or returned to Purchaser if the title to the property is not marketable.

3.   Seller agrees to convey the property to Purchaser by Deed with the usual covenants of title and free and clear from all monetary encumbrances,
tenancies, liens (for taxes or otherwise), except as may be otherwise provided above, but subject to applicable restrictive covenants of record. Seller further
agrees to deliver possession of the property to Purchaser on the date of settlement and to pay the expense of preparing the deed of conveyance.

4.   Settlement shall be made at _____ on or before

_____ , 19_____ , or as soon thereafter as title can be examined and necessary documents prepared, with
allowance of a reasonable time for Seller to correct any defects reported by the title examiner.

5.   All taxes, interest, rent, and impound escrow deposits, if any, shall be prorated as of the date of settlement.

6.   All risk of loss or damage to the property by fire, windstorm, casualty, or other cause is assumed by Seller until the date of settlement.

7.   Purchaser and Seller agree that Broker was the sole procuring cause of this Contract of Purchase, and Seller agrees to pay Broker for services

rendered a cash fee of _____ per cent of the purchase price. If either Purchaser or Seller defaults under such Contract, such defaulting party shall
be liable for the cash fee of Broker and any expenses incurred by the non-defaulting party in connection with this transaction.

Subject to: _____

_____

_____

_____

8.   Purchaser represents that an inspection satisfactory to Purchaser has been made of the property, and Purchaser agrees to accept the property
in its present condition except as may be otherwise provided in the description of the property above.

9.   This Contract of Purchase constitutes the entire agreement among the parties and may not be modified or changed except by written instrument executed by all of the parties, including Broker.

10.   This Contract of Purchase shall be construed, interpreted, and applied according to the law of the jurisdiction of _____ and shall
be binding upon and shall inure to the benefit of the heirs, personal representatives, successors, and assigns of the parties.

All parties to this agreement acknowledge receipt of a certified copy.

WITNESS the following signatures:

_____   _____
                              Seller   Purchaser

_____   _____
                              Seller   Purchaser

_____
                              Broker

Deposit Rec'd $ _____

Personal Check   Cash

Cashier's Check   Company Check

Sales Agent:

REAL ESTATE LISTING CONTRACT (EXCLUSIVE RIGHT TO SELL)

SALES PRICE _____ TYPE HOME _____ TOTAL BEDROOMS _____ TOTAL BATHS _____

ADDRESS_____ JURISDICTION OF _____

AMT. OF LOAN   AS OF   TAXES & INS.   YEARS   AMOUNT PAYABLE   TYPE
TO BE ASSUMED $_____ WHAT DATE _____ INCLUDED _____ TO GO _____ MONTHLY $_____ @ ___% LOAN_____

MORTGAGE COMPANY_____ 2nd MORTGAGE _____

OWNER'S NAME _____ PHONES(HOME) _____ (BUSINESS)_____

TENANT'S NAME _____ PHONES (HOME) _____ (BUSINESS)_____

POSSESSION _____ DATE LISTED:_____ EXCLUSIVE FOR_____ DATE OF EXPIRATION _____

LISTING BROKER _____ PHONE _____ KEY AVAILABLE AT _____

LISTING SALESMAN _____ HOME PHONE_____ HOW TO BE SHOWN:_____

ENTRANCE FOYER ☐	CENTER HALL ☐	AGE	AIR CONDITIONING ☐	TYPE KITCHEN CABINETS
LIVING ROOM SIZE	FIREPLACE ☐	ROOFING	TOOL HOUSE ☐	TYPE COUNTER TOPS
DINING ROOM SIZE		GARAGE SIZE	PATIO ☐	EAT-IN SIZE KITCHEN ☐
BEDROOM TOTAL: DOWN UP		SIDE DRIVE ☐	CIRCULAR DRIVE ☐	TYPE STOVE ☐
BATHS TOTAL: DOWN UP		PORCH ☐ SIDE ☐ REAR ☐	SCREENED ☐	BUILT-IN OVEN & RANGE ☐
DEN SIZE	FIREPLACE ☐	FENCED YARD	OUTDOOR GRILL ☐	SEPARATE STOVE INCLUDED ☐
FAMILY ROOM SIZE	FIREPLACE ☐	STORM WINDOWS ☐	STORM DOORS ☐	REFRIGERATOR INCLUDED ☐
RECREATION ROOM SIZE	FIREPLACE ☐	CURBS & GUTTERS ☐	SIDEWALKS ☐	DISHWASHER INCLUDED
BASEMENT SIZE		STORM SEWERS ☐	ALLEY ☐	DISPOSAL INCLUDED ☐
NONE ☐ 1/4 ☐ 1/3 ☐ 1/2 ☐ 3/4 ☐ FULL ☐		WATER SUPPLY		DOUBLE SINK ☐ SINGLE SINK ☐
UTILITY ROOM		SEWER ☐	SEPTIC ☐	STAINLESS STEEL ☐ PORCELAIN ☐
TYPE HOT WATER SYSTEM:		TYPE GAS: NATURAL ☐	BOTTLED ☐	WASHER INCLUDED ☐ DRYER INCLUDED ☐
TYPE HEAT		WHY SELLING		LAND ASSESSMENT $
EST. FUEL COST				IMPROVEMENTS $
ATTIC		PROPERTY DESCRIPTION		TOTAL ASSESSMENTS $
PULL DOWN STAIRWAY ☐ REGULAR STAIRWAY ☐ TRAP DOOR ☐				TAX RATE
NAME OF BUILDER		LOT SIZE		TOTAL ANNUAL TAXES $
SQUARE FOOTAGE		LOT NO. BLOCK SECTION		
EXTERIOR OF HOUSE				

NAME OF SCHOOLS: ELEMENTARY:_____ JR. HIGH: _____

HIGH:_____ PAROCHIAL: _____

PUBLIC TRANSPORTATION: _____

NEAREST SHOPPING AREA: _____

REMARKS: _____

_____

Date: _____

In consideration of the services of _____ (herein called "Broker") to be rendered to the undersigned (herein called 'Owner"), and of the promise of Broker to make reasonable efforts to obtain a Purchaser therefor, Owner hereby lists with Broker the real estate and all improvements thereon which are described above, (all herein called "the property"), and the Owner hereby grants to Broker the exclusive and irrevocable right to sell such property from 12:00 Noon on _____ , 19_____ until 12:00 Midnight on _____ , 19_____ (herein called "period of time"), for the price of _____ Dollars ($_____) or for such other price and upon such other terms (including exchange) as Owner may subsequently authorize during the period of time.

It is understood by Owner that the above sum or any other price subsequently authorized by Owner shall include a cash fee of _____ per cent of such price or other price which shall be payable by Owner to Broker upon consummation by any Purchaser or Purchasers of a valid contract of sale of the property during the period of time and whether or not Broker was a procuring cause of any such contract of sale.

If the property is sold or exchanged by Owner, or by Broker or by any other person to any Purchaser to whom the property was shown by Broker or any representative of Broker within sixty (60) days after the expiration of the period of time mentioned above, Owner agrees to pay to Broker a cash fee which shall be the same percentage of the purchase price as the percentage mentioned above.

Broker is hereby authorized by Owner to place a "For Sale" sign on the property and to remove all signs of other brokers or salesmen during the period of time, and Owner hereby agrees to make the property available to Broker at all reasonable hours for the purpose of showing it to prospective Purchasers.

Owner agrees to convey the property to the Purchaser by deed with the usual covenants of title and free and clear from all encumbrances, tenancies, liens (for taxes or otherwise), but subject to applicable restrictive covenants of record. Owner acknowledges receipt of copy of this agreement.

WITNESS the following signature(s) and seal(s):

Date Signed: _____ _____

(Owner)

Listing Agent_____

Address _____ Telephone _____ _____

(Owner)

REAL ESTATE SALES CONTRACT (OFFER TO PURCHASE AGREEMENT)

This AGREEMENT made as of _____ , 19_____ ,

among _____ (herein called "Purchaser"),

and _____ (herein called "Seller"),

and _____ (herein called "Broker"),

provides that Purchaser agrees to buy through Broker as agent for Seller, and Seller agrees to sell the following described real estate, and all improvements

thereon, located in the jurisdiction of _____ ,

(all herein called "the property"): _____

_____ , and more commonly known as _____

_____ (street address).

1. The purchase price of the property is _____

Dollars ($ _____), and such purchase price shall be paid as follows:

_____

2. Purchaser has made a deposit of _____ Dollars ($ _____)

with Broker, receipt of which is hereby acknowledged, and such deposit shall be held by Broker in escrow until the date of settlement and then applied
to the purchase price, or returned to Purchaser if the title to the property is not marketable.

3. Seller agrees to convey the property to Purchaser by Deed with the usual covenants of title and free and clear from all monetary encumbrances,
tenancies, liens (for taxes or otherwise), except as may be otherwise provided above, but subject to applicable restrictive covenants of record. Seller further
agrees to deliver possession of the property to Purchaser on the date of settlement and to pay the expense of preparing the deed of conveyance.

4. Settlement shall be made at _____ on or before

_____ , 19_____ , or as soon thereafter as title can be examined and necessary documents prepared, with
allowance of a reasonable time for Seller to correct any defects reported by the title examiner.

5. All taxes, interest, rent, and impound escrow deposits, if any, shall be prorated as of the date of settlement.

6. All risk of loss or damage to the property by fire, windstorm, casualty, or other cause is assumed by Seller until the date of settlement.

7. Purchaser and Seller agree that Broker was the sole procuring cause of this Contract of Purchase, and Seller agrees to pay Broker for services

rendered a cash fee of _____ per cent of the purchase price. If either Purchaser or Seller defaults under such Contract, such defaulting party shall
be liable for the cash fee of Broker and any expenses incurred by the non-defaulting party in connection with this transaction.

Subject to: _____

_____

_____

_____

8. Purchaser represents that an inspection satisfactory to Purchaser has been made of the property, and Purchaser agrees to accept the property
in its present condition except as may be otherwise provided in the description of the property above.

9. This Contract of Purchase constitutes the entire agreement among the parties and may not be modified or changed except by written instrument executed by all of the parties, including Broker.

10. This Contract of Purchase shall be construed, interpreted, and applied according to the law of the jurisdiction of _____ and shall
be binding upon and shall inure to the benefit of the heirs, personal representatives, successors, and assigns of the parties.

All parties to this agreement acknowledge receipt of a certified copy.

WITNESS the following signatures:

_____ Seller   _____ Purchaser

_____ Seller   _____ Purchaser

_____ Broker

Deposit Rec'd $ _____

Personal Check   Cash

Cashier's Check   Company Check

Sales Agent:

REAL ESTATE LISTING CONTRACT (EXCLUSIVE RIGHT TO SELL)

SALES PRICE _____ TYPE HOME _____ TOTAL BEDROOMS _____ TOTAL BATHS _____

ADDRESS _____ JURISDICTION OF _____

AMT. OF LOAN
TO BE ASSUMED $ _____ AS OF WHAT DATE _____ TAXES & INS. INCLUDED _____ YEARS TO GO _____ AMOUNT PAYABLE MONTHLY $ _____ @ ___% TYPE LOAN _____

MORTGAGE COMPANY _____ 2nd MORTGAGE _____

OWNER'S NAME _____ PHONES(HOME) _____ (BUSINESS) _____

TENANT'S NAME _____ PHONES (HOME) _____ (BUSINESS) _____

POSSESSION _____ DATE LISTED: _____ EXCLUSIVE FOR _____ DATE OF EXPIRATION _____

LISTING BROKER _____ PHONE _____ KEY AVAILABLE AT _____

LISTING SALESMAN _____ HOME PHONE _____ HOW TO BE SHOWN: _____

ENTRANCE FOYER ☐	CENTER HALL ☐	AGE	AIR CONDITIONING ☐	TYPE KITCHEN CABINETS
LIVING ROOM SIZE	FIREPLACE ☐	ROOFING	TOOL HOUSE ☐	TYPE COUNTER TOPS
DINING ROOM SIZE		GARAGE SIZE	PATIO ☐	EAT-IN SIZE KITCHEN ☐
BEDROOM TOTAL: DOWN UP		SIDE DRIVE ☐	CIRCULAR DRIVE ☐	TYPE STOVE ☐
BATHS TOTAL: DOWN UP		PORCH ☐ SIDE ☐ REAR ☐	SCREENED ☐	BUILT-IN OVEN & RANGE ☐
DEN SIZE	FIREPLACE ☐	FENCED YARD	OUTDOOR GRILL ☐	SEPARATE STOVE INCLUDED ☐
FAMILY ROOM SIZE	FIREPLACE ☐	STORM WINDOWS ☐	STORM DOORS ☐	REFRIGERATOR INCLUDED ☐
RECREATION ROOM SIZE	FIREPLACE ☐	CURBS & GUTTERS ☐	SIDEWALKS ☐	DISHWASHER INCLUDED
BASEMENT SIZE		STORM SEWERS ☐	ALLEY ☐	DISPOSAL INCLUDED ☐
NONE ☐ 1/4 ☐ 1/3 ☐ 1/2 ☐ 3/4 ☐ FULL ☐		WATER SUPPLY		DOUBLE SINK ☐ SINGLE SINK ☐
UTILITY ROOM		SEWER ☐	SEPTIC ☐	STAINLESS STEEL ☐ PORCELAIN ☐
TYPE HOT WATER SYSTEM:		TYPE GAS: NATURAL ☐	BOTTLED ☐	WASHER INCLUDED ☐ DRYER INCLUDED ☐
TYPE HEAT		WHY SELLING		LAND ASSESSMENT $
EST. FUEL COST				IMPROVEMENTS $
ATTIC		PROPERTY DESCRIPTION		TOTAL ASSESSMENTS $
PULL DOWN STAIRWAY ☐ REGULAR STAIRWAY ☐ TRAP DOOR ☐				TAX RATE
NAME OF BUILDER		LOT SIZE		TOTAL ANNUAL TAXES $
SQUARE FOOTAGE		LOT NO. BLOCK SECTION		
EXTERIOR OF HOUSE				

NAME OF SCHOOLS: ELEMENTARY: _____ JR. HIGH: _____

HIGH: _____ PAROCHIAL: _____

PUBLIC TRANSPORTATION: _____

NEAREST SHOPPING AREA: _____

REMARKS: _____
_____
_____
_____

Date: _____

In consideration of the services of _____ (herein called "Broker") to be rendered to the undersigned (herein called 'Owner"), and of the promise of Broker to make reasonable efforts to obtain a Purchaser therefor, Owner hereby lists with Broker the real estate and all improvements thereon which are described above, (all herein called "the property"), and the Owner hereby grants to Broker the exclusive and irrevocable right to sell such property from 12:00 Noon on _____ , 19_____ until 12:00 Midnight on _____ , 19_____ (herein called "period of time"), for the price of _____ Dollars ($_____) or for such other price and upon such other terms (including exchange) as Owner may subsequently authorize during the period of time.

It is understood by Owner that the above sum or any other price subsequently authorized by Owner shall include a cash fee of _____ per cent of such price or other price which shall be payable by Owner to Broker upon consummation by any Purchaser or Purchasers of a valid contract of sale of the property during the period of time and whether or not Broker was a procuring cause of any such contract of sale.

If the property is sold or exchanged by Owner, or by Broker or by any other person to any Purchaser to whom the property was shown by Broker or any representative of Broker within sixty (60) days after the expiration of the period of time mentioned above, Owner agrees to pay to Broker a cash fee which shall be the same percentage of the purchase price as the percentage mentioned above.

Broker is hereby authorized by Owner to place a "For Sale" sign on the property and to remove all signs of other brokers or salesmen during the period of time, and Owner hereby agrees to make the property available to Broker at all reasonable hours for the purpose of showing it to prospective Purchasers.

Owner agrees to convey the property to the Purchaser by deed with the usual covenants of title and free and clear from all encumbrances, tenancies, liens (for taxes or otherwise), but subject to applicable restrictive covenants of record. Owner acknowledges receipt of copy of this agreement.

WITNESS the following signature(s) and seal(s):

Date Signed: _____ _____
(Owner)

Listing Agent _____

Address _____ Telephone _____ _____
(Owner)

REAL ESTATE SALES CONTRACT (OFFER TO PURCHASE AGREEMENT)

This AGREEMENT made as of _____ , 19_____ ,

among _____ (herein called "Purchaser"),

and _____ (herein called "Seller"),

and _____ (herein called "Broker"),

provides that Purchaser agrees to buy through Broker as agent for Seller, and Seller agrees to sell the following described real estate, and all improvements

thereon, located in the jurisdiction of _____ ,

(all herein called "the property"): _____

_____ , and more commonly known as _____

_____ (street address).

1. The purchase price of the property is _____

Dollars ($ _____), and such purchase price shall be paid as follows:

_____

2. Purchaser has made a deposit of _____ Dollars ($ _____)
with Broker, receipt of which is hereby acknowledged, and such deposit shall be held by Broker in escrow until the date of settlement and then applied
to the purchase price, or returned to Purchaser if the title to the property is not marketable.

3. Seller agrees to convey the property to Purchaser by Deed with the usual covenants of title and free and clear from all monetary encumbrances,
tenancies, liens (for taxes or otherwise), except as may be otherwise provided above, but subject to applicable restrictive covenants of record. Seller further
agrees to deliver possession of the property to Purchaser on the date of settlement and to pay the expense of preparing the deed of conveyance.

4. Settlement shall be made at _____ on or before

_____ , 19_____ , or as soon thereafter as title can be examined and necessary documents prepared, with
allowance of a reasonable time for Seller to correct any defects reported by the title examiner.

5. All taxes, interest, rent, and impound escrow deposits, if any, shall be prorated as of the date of settlement.

6. All risk of loss or damage to the property by fire, windstorm, casualty, or other cause is assumed by Seller until the date of settlement.

7. Purchaser and Seller agree that Broker was the sole procuring cause of this Contract of Purchase, and Seller agrees to pay Broker for services

rendered a cash fee of _____ per cent of the purchase price. If either Purchaser or Seller defaults under such Contract, such defaulting party shall
be liable for the cash fee of Broker and any expenses incurred by the non-defaulting party in connection with this transaction.

Subject to: _____

_____

_____

8. Purchaser represents that an inspection satisfactory to Purchaser has been made of the property, and Purchaser agrees to accept the property
in its present condition except as may be otherwise provided in the description of the property above.

9. This Contract of Purchase constitutes the entire agreement among the parties and may not be modified or changed except by written instrument executed by all of the parties, including Broker.

10. This Contract of Purchase shall be construed, interpreted, and applied according to the law of the jurisdiction of _____ and shall
be binding upon and shall inure to the benefit of the heirs, personal representatives, successors, and assigns of the parties.

All parties to this agreement acknowledge receipt of a certified copy.

WITNESS the following signatures:

_____   _____
                         Seller   Purchaser

_____   _____
                         Seller   Purchaser

_____
                         Broker

Deposit Rec'd $ _____

Personal Check   Cash

Cashier's Check   Company Check

Sales Agent:

SETTLEMENT STATEMENT WORKSHEET

Complete the *Settlement Statement Worksheet* on the basis of the information given in the test book, even if that information in some respects differs from current real estate practice in your area. For example, clerk fee, notary fees, fee for drawing the deed, transfer fees, credit reports, conveyance tax, etc., are purposely not given and not to be used in the *Settlement Statement Worksheet.* Use 30-day method of computation.

SETTLEMENT DATE:	BUYER'S STATEMENT		SELLER'S STATEMENT	
	DEBIT	CREDIT	DEBIT	CREDIT

SETTLEMENT STATEMENT WORKSHEET

Complete the *Settlement Statement Worksheet* on the basis of the information given in the test book, even if that information in some respects differs from current real estate practice in your area. For example, clerk fee, notary fees, fee for drawing the deed, transfer fees, credit reports, conveyance tax, etc., are purposely not given and not to be used in the *Settlement Statement Worksheet.* Use 30-day method of computation.

SETTLEMENT DATE:	BUYER'S STATEMENT		SELLER'S STATEMENT	
	DEBIT	CREDIT	DEBIT	CREDIT

SETTLEMENT STATEMENT WORKSHEET

Complete the *Settlement Statement Worksheet* on the basis of the information given in the test book, even if that information in some respects differs from current real estate practice in your area. For example, clerk fee, notary fees, fee for drawing the deed, transfer fees, credit reports, conveyance tax, etc., are purposely not given and not to be used in the *Settlement Statement Worksheet.* Use 30-day method of computation.

SETTLEMENT DATE:	BUYER'S STATEMENT		SELLER'S STATEMENT	
	DEBIT	CREDIT	DEBIT	CREDIT

SETTLEMENT STATEMENT WORKSHEET

Complete the *Settlement Statement Worksheet* on the basis of the information given in the test book, even if that information in some respects differs from current real estate practice in your area. For example, clerk fee, notary fees, fee for drawing the deed, transfer fees, credit reports, conveyance tax, etc., are purposely not given and not to be used in the *Settlement Statement Worksheet*. Use 30-day method of computation.

SETTLEMENT DATE:	BUYER'S STATEMENT		SELLER'S STATEMENT	
	DEBIT	CREDIT	DEBIT	CREDIT